P9-CFS-426

BLUE GUIDE

SICILY

Ellen Grady

Somerset Books • London
WW Norton • New York

Blue Guide Sicily
Seventh edition

Published by Blue Guides Limited, a Somerset Books Company
49–51 Causton St, London SW1P 4AT
www.blueguides.com
'Blue Guide' is a registered trademark

Text © Ellen Grady 2006
The right of Ellen Grady to be identified as author of this work has been asserted by her in
accordance with the Copyright Designs and Patents Act, 1988.

All rights reserved. No part of this publication may be reproduced or used in any form or by any
means—photographic, electronic or mechanical, including photocopying, recording, taping or
information storage and retrieval systems—without permission of the publisher.

ISBN 1–905131–12–7

A CIP catalogue record of this book is available from the British Library.

Published in the United States of America by
WW Norton and Company, Inc.
500 Fifth Avenue, New York, NY 10110
USA ISBN 0-393-32889-9

The author and the publisher have made reasonable efforts to ensure the accuracy of all the
information in Blue Guide Sicily; however, they can accept no responsibility for any loss, injury or
inconvenience sustained by any traveller as a result of information
or advice contained in the guide.

Cover photographs: Top: Mosaic (1148) of Christ Pantocrator in the apse
of the duomo at Cefalù (photo: Giacomo Mazza)
Bottom: The theatre at Segesta (photo: Giacomo Mazza)
Spine: Detail from the crown of the Madonna (1653) in the
Museo Alessi, Enna (photo: Charles Godfrey-Faussett)
Title page: Detail of a terracotta altar (early 5th century BC),
in the Museo Archeologico Regionale at Gela
Photo: courtesy of Maria Costanza Lentini

All other acknowledgements, photo credits and copyright information are given
on p. 544, which forms part of this copyright page.

CONTENTS

MAPS & PLANS

PRACTICAL INFORMATION

FOOD & DRINK

EARLY HISTORY

by Charles Freeman

Sicily is at the crossroads of the Mediterranean. The Italian mainland is very close, separated by the narrow Straits of Messina, while the coast of North Africa is only some 250 kilometres away, a day's sailing in good conditions. Anyone passing across the Mediterranean would be likely to make landfall in Sicily and this gave it immense strategic value. The island's fertility also attracted settlement, with the result that periods of prosperity were interspersed with violent conflict over resources. Sicily today is a palimpsest of earlier civilizations, their remains jostling alongside each other against the backdrop of the island's natural beauty.

There are traces of human settlement from the Palaeolithic age (35,000–9000 BC), with the Upper Palaeolithic (18,000–9000) especially rich in sites. These show a population able to exploit a variety of habitats along with the development of burial rituals, decorative artefacts, mostly in stone, and cave art. The art is concentrated in a group of caves at Levanzo and around Monte Pellegrino in the northwest of the island, with the focus mainly on animals, predominantly horses, oxen and deer. In the Mesolithic period (9000–6000 BC) there is more exploitation of the sea with the result that some communities become settled on the coast. However, it was red deer which were the main source of food and hides: their bones make up 70 per cent of remains on some sites. Settled agriculture appears in Sicily c. 6000–5500 BC and appears to have been an imported change. The remains of corn, sheep, and goats are found for the first time in this period. Pottery, known as Sentinello ware, from a Neolithic site near Syracuse, has impressed or incised decoration and from about 5500 is painted, copying styles from Italy. A particularly important trade, until about 2500, was in obsidian from the Aeolian island of Lipari, a volcanic rock which can be easily cut and shaped into stone tools.

The first extensive contact with the wider Mediterranean comes in the Mycenaean age (1600–1150 BC). The Mycenaean strongholds were in the Greek Peloponnese and their chieftains were aggressive traders, whose presence in Sicily reached its height in about 1400 BC. This is the first time that Sicily can be placed within a far-flung trading complex, with evidence of routes which stretched as far east as Rhodes and Cyprus. A harbour site such as *Thapsos*, near modern Syracuse, certainly grew prosperous on trade. Mycenaean civilization disintegrated after 1200, and Sicily, like many other parts of the Mediterranean, retreated into isolation. The island's primary contact for the next three centuries was with Italy.

Sicans, Sicels, Ausonians and Elymians

Greek historians provide some details of the inhabitants of Sicily before the 8th century. Thucydides, writing in the 5th century BC, talked of a native people of Sicily known as the Sicans who were pushed into the southern and western parts of Sicily by newcomers from Italy, the Sicels (hence *Sicilia*) who settled in the eastern part of the island. Thucydides gives a date for the 'invasion' of some three centuries before the first Greek settlement (i.e. about 1050), but other Greek sources suggest it was much earlier, well before the Trojan War, so perhaps 1300–1250. There is some archaeological and linguistic evidence to support the arrival of newcomers from Italy in the 13th century BC, with another group known as the Ausonians, named after their mythical founder Auson, arriving from central Italy perhaps in the 11th century. A third people, the Elymians, whom Thucydides tells us were refugees from Troy, are recorded as having settled in the west of Sicily.

Phoenicians and Greeks

In the 8th century Mediterranean trade began to revive. The Phoenicians, the biblical Canaanites, from the ancient cities of the Levantine coast, are normally seen as the pioneers, probing into the western Mediterranean in search of metals with which to pay their overlords, the Assyrians. They gave confidence to the Greeks who began following the same routes. Naxos was the first Sicilian landfall for those aiming to sail round the toe of Italy from the east and it was here that settlers from Chalcis in Euboea established a base in 734. A small fertile valley gave them the means to settle and the native population appears to have been dispersed. This became the usual practice as a mass of other Greek migrants followed the Chalcidians. The Corinthians settled the best harbour of the coast, Syracuse, the very next year while Euboeans who had earlier settled at Cumae on the west coast of Italy, then took over the harbour at *Zancle* (later Messina) to protect their route to Italy. So quite quickly the better harbours were taken and settlements founded. Excavations at Megara Hyblaea show how temples and an *agora* (a market place) on a native Greek model. were planned into the early settlement. With the best sites on the east coast taken, Greeks moved along the southern coast of Sicily to found Gela (688) and *Acragas* (Agrigento; 580).The Sicel communities were broken up, their populations dispersed or absorbed. The Greek colonisation of Sicily was so successful that grain was soon being exported back to Greece and across to Italy and Africa. Pottery from Athens, Sparta and Corinth is found on Sicilian sites and coinage appears quite early, in the last half of the 6th century. Settlements develop into cities with large temples and other public buildings. They send competitors to the Olympic games and, with plenty of fertile pasture for horses, are especially successful in chariot racing.

Yet there was trouble brewing. The Phoenicians had established their own settlements, on the coast of north Africa, notably Carthage, and in Spain, which was rich in metal resources, and it was inevitable that there would be settlements on Sicily itself. At first these were no more than staging posts concentrated in the west. The most successful Phoenician site was *Motya*, a small island off the west coast (*see p. 149*). It was close to Carthage, defensible (with a perimeter wall 2500m round) and enjoyed good relationships with the native Elymian population. The earliest occupation dates from the late 8th century but by the 7th century there is evidence of industrial activity, in iron and dyes and the population may have reached 15,800 in the 6th century. It was now that the Persian empire absorbed the Phoenician cities of the Levant and gradually the western settlements developed their own independent empire under the control of Carthage.

The Carthaginians

Conflict between Carthaginians and Greeks was perhaps inevitable. The first clashes were over sites outside Sicily as the Carthaginians tried to exclude outsiders from the western Mediterranean. In 514, a Spartan, Doreius, attempted to challenge Carthage's growing power by making a Greek settlement within Carthaginian territory in Sicily, but he was driven out. The Greek cities began mobilising themselves in resistance. It became increasingly common for strong leaders, so-called tyrants, to emerge as rulers of the Greeks. One such was Gelon of Gela (491–477) who decided to make Syracuse his capital by transferring half his own city's population there. In 480 he had a spectacular victory over the Carthaginians at Himera, which led to them being subdued for the next 70 years. In 453, the Greeks then faced another threat, from the Hellenised Sicel, Ducetius. His Sicel League defeated several Greek cities until he was overcome in 451.

In 431 a major war broke out between Athens and Sparta, the Peloponnesian War. One of Sparta's allies, Corinth, still had close ties with its colony Syracuse and the wealth of Sicily made it an important prize. The Athenians saw their chance to exploit local tensions by supporting the city of Segesta against Syracuse and sent a major expedition to take the island. It turned into one of the greatest military disasters in history. Syracuse called on Spartan military expertise and Corinthian naval support and destroyed the Athenian fleet. The historian Thucydides has left a harrowing account of the debacle with the few Athenian survivors being herded off to work in Syracuse's stone quarries. However, while Athens never regained the initiative in Greece (the city surrendered to the Spartans in 404), Syracuse was also weakened. The Carthaginians saw their chance of taking revenge for Himera and in 405 moved from their western enclave to capture Acragas and Gela. It was this crisis which saw the emergence of Syracuse's most successful tyrant, Dionysius I (*see box on p. 359*).

On Dionysius' death, his son Dionysius II became the new ruler of Syracuse. He was a failure. Despite a visit from the Athenian philosopher Plato to school him in the art of good government, the empire collapsed into anarchy. The smaller Greek cities broke away under their own tyrants, who fought among themselves as well as against the Carthaginians. Things became so desperate that the Syracusans sent back to their mother city Corinth to ask for a tyrant to restore order. The man sent was Timoleon. He deposed Dionysius in 344, but then had to face a siege of Syracuse by a resurgent Carthaginian empire. Only an outbreak of plague saved the city from capture. Timoleon finally defeated the Carthaginians at the Crimissus River in 341. He regained control of the smaller Greek cities, and brought about a shortlived but significant period of prosperity. On his death, however, anarchy returned as different groups fought each other for power over Greek Sicily. This was the pattern for the next 70 years. A war leader would emerge, have a few years of success and then be killed or lose control. So one Agathocles came to power as 'general with full powers' of Syracuse in 319 and took on the Carthaginians in a campaign which included a foolhardy expedition to Africa itself but which ended in his defeat both there and in Sicily. He was forced to sue for peace and was assassinated in 289. One of his few achievements had been to marry a stepdaughter of the new Greek ruler of Egypt, Ptolemy I and by doing so, bring Sicily into the wider Hellenistic world (the term 'Hellenistic' being given to the period following the death of Alexander the Great in 323). From now on Sicilian tyrants tended to ape their colleagues in the eastern Mediterranean by taking the trappings of kingship, including a cult of the ruler, courts and a royal family. The most influential legacy of Agathocles was largely unexpected. His mercenary force from Italy, the so-called Mamertines ('sons of the war god Mars' in their native language), exploited the anarchy after his death to seize the city of *Messana* (later Messina), the former Greek city of Zancle, and use it as a base for plundering northeastern Italy. A new tyrant of Syracuse, Hieron II, who like Agathocles presented himself as royalty, defeated them in 265, whereupon the Mamertines called on the Carthaginians for help. The Carthaginians did send a small garrison but the next year the Mamertines went further and appealed to Italy's most successful military power, the city of Rome. It was to be a decision which would change history.

The Romans

The Romans decided to launch an expedition to Sicily. The threat of Roman incursion brought the Carthaginians and Hieron into alliance against them. The Romans defeated the united forces, whereupon Hieron sought an alliance with Rome. It was granted and Hieron became one of the most successful of the Sicilian tyrant-kings. By supplying the Roman armies with grain, he was able to keep his kingdom and status intact, and this in fact became a time of great prosperity for Greek Sicily. Hieron was able to stand by and watch the protracted and debilitating war which Rome waged against the Carthaginians (the First Punic War 264–241 BC).

One of Rome's first successes in Sicily was the capture of Acragas, which had been held by a Carthaginian garrison. However, it became clear that Rome—then without a navy—could never defeat Carthage unless it acquired one. There are few better examples of Rome's resilience than the story of how she became a naval power and despite many setbacks and some major defeats, finally crushed the Carthaginians in a naval victory off the Egadi islands in 241. Carthaginian control of western Sicily, which had lasted many centuries, was brought to an end. The Carthaginians were still not finally defeated, however. In 218 a brilliant leader emerged: Hannibal. Seeking revenge on Rome, he invaded Italy from Spain. Then, in 215, Hieron II of Syracuse died. Syracuse was still an independent state: not wanting to fall under Roman control, she appealed to Carthage for support. Realising how crucially important it would be to regain Sicily as a base for supplies, Hannibal granted it, and sent troops. The Roman counter-attack was swift, and they captured Syracuse in 212 (their victory retarded by the brilliant defence techniques masterminded by the great scientist Archimedes). The Roman general Marcellus freighted such rich booty back in triumph to Rome that Roman conservatives talked of the corruption of their city by the decadence of the Greek East.

Sicily, 'the nurse at whose breast the Roman people is fed' as Cicero was to put it, proved to be vital to Rome for a steady supply of grain to the growing city and the Roman armies. Also an important strategic base, it was Rome's first overseas province and was ruled through a *praetor*, an elected magistrate with military powers. Hieron had instituted a tax in grain and it was comparatively easy for the Romans to divert this to themselves. Sicily would prove to be a well-behaved province: administration was light and cities were given a high degree of independence. By the 2nd century BC there was once again great prosperity on the island. Though the old hilltop cities went into decline, it was because their inhabitants were moving down to take advantage of the new security and opportunities for grain production on lower land. Estates grew large and slaves were brought in *en masse* from Rome's new conquests in the East. Their treatment by the new owners appears to have been brutal, however, and in 135–132 and 104–100, there were major slave revolts (*see box on p. 264*) which took hard fighting to suppress. Oppression of a very different kind came at the hands of corrupt governors, the most notorious of whom was Verres (73–71; *see box on p. 199*). Archaeology suggests that nonetheless the underlying prosperity of the province continued without interruption.

The island could not escape the civil wars which tore the empire apart in the second half of the 1st century BC. When Julius Caesar confronted the ageing general Pompey in Italy in 49, he won over Sicily by promising the Sicilians 'Latin rights', privileges which in earlier times had been given to favoured cities (and which gave access to full Roman citizenship). In the short term it worked (Pompey was defeated in 48) but after Caesar's own assassination in 44, the son of Pompey, Sextus, seized Sicily and withheld the grain supply from Rome. The Sicilians unwisely collaborated with him and when Caesar's great-nephew, Octavian, retook the island, he dealt ruthlessly with any city which did not immediately surrender. The entire population of one, *Tauromenium* (Taormina), was deported and others lost their Latin rights. Octavian (known, from 27 BC, as Augustus, and the first Roman emperor) established several colonies of former Roman soldiers in the province, to enforce better control, and took large tracts of land as imperial estates.

By now the Roman empire was at its furthest extent and the role of Sicily as a source of grain was diminished as Egypt and the North African provinces became major suppliers. A 1st-century AD mosaic of corn-growing provinces in Ostia, the port of the city of Rome, shows symbols of Sicily alongside those of Egypt, Africa and Spain. No legions needed to be stationed on the island and there is only one isolated reference to banditry in the 260s. Mount Etna and Syracuse have occasional mentions as tourist attractions. Sicilians seem to have played little part in imperial administrations, but the archaeological evidence is of general prosperity: well endowed towns with theatres, baths and aqueducts. One source even lists two Sicilian towns, Catania and Syracuse, as thirteenth and fourteenth in a list of celebrated cities of the empire, while the villa at Piazza Armerina shows just how sophisticated life was for the elite in the 4th century.

So life continued until the Western empire began to disintegrate in the 5th century. In 429, the Vandals under their leader Gaiseric took North Africa and began raiding the prosperous coastal towns of Sicily. In 486 he was finally able to take control of the whole island, which he sold eight years later to Odoacer, ruler of Italy following the deposition of the last Western emperor. In 535, a counter-attack by the Eastern, now Byzantine, empire, under its general Belisarius, ended with Sicily becoming part of the empire itself. By now Sicily was heavily Christianised, and papal estates had succeeded the older imperial ones. More letters survive from Pope Gregory the Great (590–604) about his Sicilian estates than about all the others put together.

When Sicily was captured for Byzantium by Belisarius, Syracuse became the main city on the island, even becoming capital of the Byzantine Empire for a brief period in the 7th century. The Byzantines introduced the manufacture of silk, by planting mulberries on the hills behind Messina, particularly subject to the *maestrale* wind from the north-west, cold and salty, which deposits a fine layer of salt on the leaves of the trees: the resulting thread of silk, after the silk-worms have eaten the salty leaves, is stronger.

The Arabs

The island's economy, however, based only on silk and wheat, was ailing, and the population was dramatically decreasing, due to poor farming methods and bouts of famine. When the Arabs landed at Mazara del Vallo in AD 827, called in by the Byzantine governor Euphemius, they were fulfilling a long-held dream. Within 50 years they had taken over governance of the whole island, and were to prove far-sighted and intelligent rulers. They brought with them skilled craftsmen, both Jewish and Muslim. Jewish Berbers from Morocco settled in Syracuse, where they became acclaimed weavers. In Piazza Armerina and Messina their goldsmiths became renowned in the art of making wire from gold mixed with a little copper, which was exported for making filigree jewellery. Arab farmers revolutionised agriculture by introducing terracing, irrigation and water-storage tanks. They planted new crops, ranging from rice, cotton, sugar-cane, pistachios, pomegranates, apricots, peaches and citrus, to indigo, roses and jasmine for the perfume industry, and groves of mulberry trees to feed the silk-worms and intensify production. The island was divided into three administrative districts: Val Demone, Val di Mazara and Val di Noto, each governed by a *cadi*, who reported to an *emir* in Palermo. Numerous settlers came from North Africa and Spain to swell the population, and by the 10th century Sicily was one of the most prosperous countries in Europe, and Palermo was one of the great centres of scholarship and art, surpassed only by Constantinople, and rivalling Cordoba and Cairo for the number of mosques, gardens and fountains. The Arabs called this country *Balad es-Siqilliah*, 'Land of the Sicels'.

The Normans

The Normans probably set their sights on Sicily around 1035, but they too had to wait for the right moment, and theirs too would prove to be an extremely long-drawn-out conquest. The Normans' greatest weapon were their mercenary troops, the most respected and feared in Europe. Their moment came in 1060, when the *cadi* Ibn at-Thumnah of Catania fell foul of Ibn al-Hawwas of Agrigento. He summoned the armies of Robert Guiscard and Roger Hauteville to fight for him; they won that battle, the *cadi* was killed, and the Normans hung onto their spoils. Not only this; they kept fighting. In the same year Roger took Messina; by 1091 the whole island was under his control. Despite their ruthlessness in battle, the Normans proved willing to adapt to the Arab,

Jewish, Greek and Latin traditions which already existed on the island, and different religions and customs were respected. The first Sicilian Parliament met at Mazara del Vallo in 1097. Count Roger was never crowned king, although he is usually known as Roger I of Sicily. In 1099 Pope Urban II named him Great-Count of Calabria and Sicily, and apostolic legate. This prerogative was to prove of fundamental importance for the future of Sicily, because it meant that the ruler had the right to name the bishops in his territory—in practice, total power. When his son Roger II was crowned in 1130, he was probably the wealthiest ruler in Europe, and his court in Palermo the most opulent. Meanwhile Messina flourished as a supply base for the Crusaders.

Norman domination, with its architecture showing a strongly oriental influence, has left many magnificent buildings, of which the churches are its most celebrated achievement today. The interiors of Cefalù and Monreale cathedrals and of the Cappella Palatina in Palermo all have exquisite mosaic decoration.

The Swabians, Angevins, Aragonese and Bourbons
The Norman dynasty did not last long; in 1194 the crown was claimed by Emperor Henry VI of Swabia in the name of his wife Constance (daughter of Roger II), and the last of the Hautevilles were put to death. Henry died young and was succeeded in 1198 by his baby son Frederick II of Hohenstaufen, a great king ('*stupor mundi*' or 'wonder of the world') whose reign was marked by a prolonged struggle with the Papacy. His court in Palermo, drawing on Islamic, Jewish and Christian cultures, was famous for its splendour and learning. Unlike his predecessors, Frederick did not endow monasteries or build cathedrals; he devoted his building energies to creating a line of fortifications running from Germany to southern Italy and Sicily. Castles dominated the cities in this area and fortresses were erected at strategic points inland. The Swabian line ended with the beheading of Conradin in 1268.

Charles of Anjou, brother of Louis IX of France, had the backing of the (French) pope, and was invested with the crown of Sicily and Naples, thus beginning the hated Angevin rule. The famous revolt of 1282, known as the Sicilian Vespers (*see p. 73*), brought an end to that unhappy period, and the Sicilians called Peter of Aragon to be their king. Renowned for his sense of justice and good government, he agreed on condition that after his death Sicily and Aragon would be ruled as separate kingdoms. This did not come to pass, and in the course of time Sicily lost her independence and became a province of Aragon and then of Spain, to be ruled by a series of viceroys for the Spanish and then the Bourbon kings. One of these kings, Alfonso the Generous, founded the University of Catania in 1434, the first in Sicily. Rebellions, famine, unrest and epidemics mark the 15th century, and in 1492 when Muslims and Jews were expelled from Spain's dominions by Ferdinand and Isabella, they were expelled from Sicily too (a quarter of all Jews in the Italian peninsula lived in Sicily).

Architecture and painting in the early 15th century were much influenced by Catalan masters, as can be seen from the south porch of the cathedral and at Palazzo Abatellis in Palermo. Matteo Carnelivari was the most important architect working in Palermo at this time. The Renaissance sculptor Francesco Laurana came to work in Palermo in the middle of the 15th century. Another influential sculptor in the second half of the same century was Domenico Gagini (*see p. 423*); his style was continued into the following century by his son Antonello and his vast progeny. If the dramatic 15th-century fresco of the *Triumph of Death* (now in the Regional Gallery; *see p. 46*) is by a Sicilian master, it is the most important Sicilian painting of this period. The most famous artist of the late 15th century is a painter who forged his reputation outside his native home: Antonello da Messina, whose introduction of the technique of oil painting, which he probably learned in the Netherlands, dramatically altered the history of western art.

Counter-Reformation and Baroque

Because of its position on the Straits, Messina was in closer contact with the mainland than other towns in Sicily, and during the 16th century artists from Florence and Rome often travelled there, attracted by its political and social importance. Sculptors were particularly welcome, as civic administrations endeavoured to beautify their towns with flamboyant 'urban furniture'. When Giovanni Angelo Montorsoli arrived from Florence in 1547, he introduced Tuscan Mannerism with his Orion fountain (*see p. 444*), a work which proved immensely influential. This was the period of the Counter-Reformation, when lavish churches and convents were being erected all over the island in response to the Protestant threat. It was also an age of increased insecurity, as Turkish pirates continually harried ships and coasts. The brilliant victory of the Christians over the Muslims of Mohammed Ali at Lepanto in 1571 did little to solve this particular problem; and in the interior of the island brigands and bandits were making life difficult for farmers and travellers.

From the mid-17th to the end of the 18th centuries numerous splendid Baroque churches were erected in Palermo, many of them by the local architect Giacomo Amato, and the interiors were lavishly decorated with coloured marble, mosaic inlay and stuccoes. Giacomo Serpotta was a great master of this art, while Pietro Novelli of Monreale was the most outstanding of 17th-century Sicilian painters. But it is in eastern Sicily where we find the finest examples of Baroque. The eruption of Mount Etna in 1669, followed by the earthquake of 1693, meant that first Catania, and then most of the other towns, had to be completely rebuilt. Beauty emerged defiantly from tragedy. Architects, sculptors, master-masons, stucco-moulders, wood-carvers and painters were suddenly in great demand, and their art flourished.

In 1713, after the Treaty of Utrecht which concluded the War of the Spanish Succession, Spanish rule in Sicily ended. The island was assigned first to Savoy, then to Austria, and finally to the Bourbons of Naples, who would hold it until 1860.

Revolution and Unification

After Napoleon failed to invade Sicily in 1806, the British took control for a short time, and established a constitution (though it never received sufficient backing to be effective). Disaffection with the Bourbons, whose inept rule left so many Sicilians impoverished and disenfranchised, led to revolution in 1848. Though the rebels were savagely crushed, the revolutionary spirit refused to die, and in 1860 Garibaldi led an attack against the Bourbons which paved the way for Italian Unification. Unification worked better for the north of Italy than for Sicily, who found the rule of the Piedmontese statesman Camillo Cavour unsympathetic, and felt that northern Italian cities were being favoured over southern. What is certain is that the economic position of Sicily remained a long way behind that of the rest of Italy. With the collapse of the sulphur industry and the phylloxera blight which destroyed the vineyards, almost a million and a half Sicilians chose to emigrate, to the Americas and to Australia, between 1895 and 1910.

The twentieth century

Despite economic hardship, the early 20th century was the golden age of Art Nouveau. The inspired work of Ernesto Basile and Francesco Fichera made this style fashionable throughout Sicily, and as a centre of Art Nouveau architecture, Palermo is surpassed in Italy only by Turin and Milan. After the disastrous earthquake which hit Messina in December 1908, the economy of the whole island suffered. Rebuilding was by no means complete when the Second World War broke out. The geographical position of Sicily meant that the Allies chose the island for their first important attack on Hitler in Europe, in 1943. In 1944 civil war broke out on the island, with many islanders calling for independence. The statute for autonomous government was approved by Rome in 1946 and the first modern Sicilian parliament was elected in 1947. No economic miracle has been performed however, and even now thousands of Sicilians are still forced to emigrate in search of work.

THE MAFIA

The origins of the Mafia go back to the use of local agents by the land-owning aristocracy in the 18th and 19th centuries. Anyone and everyone was 'invited' to make regular 'offerings', or provide gratuitous services, to these agents, not only in order to avoid dire consequences, but also to be sure of protection. It became an ingrained custom, called *mafia* only after the Unification of Italy in 1860, using a Piedmontese word; on the island it has always been known as *Cosa Nostra*: 'our thing'. After the Second World War, thanks to collusion between politics and the Mafia, the phenomenon got much worse. Giovanni Falcone, the magistrate who investigated the Mafia and was assassinated in 1992, estimated that there were more than 5,000 'men of honour' in Sicily, chosen after a rigorous selection process. He saw these men as true professionals of crime, who obeyed strict rules. Through the rigid 'protection' system, they have controlled Sicilian business transactions for many years. In 1993 the arrest of Totò Riina, the acknowledged *capo dei capi*, after more than 20 years 'in hiding' in Palermo, closely followed by the capture of Nitto Santapaola outside Catania, local boss in that city since 1982, was greeted, with some scepticism, as a step in the right direction.

FURTHER READING

Art and architecture

Blunt, Anthony, *Sicilian Baroque* (1968). Borsook, Eve, *Messages in Mosaic* (1998). Demus, Otto, *The Mosaics of Norman Sicily* (1987). Garstang, Donald, *Giacomo Serpotta and the Stuccatori of Palermo, 1560–1790* (1984). Guido, Margaret, *Sicily: an archaeological guide* (1967). Leighton, Robert, *Sicily before History: an archaeological survey from the Palaeolithic to the Iron Age* (2002). Sitwell, Sacheverell, *Southern Baroque Revisited* (1967). Tobringer, Stephen, *The Genesis of Noto, an eighteenth-century Sicilian city* (1982).

History

Ahmad, Aziz, *A History of Islamic Sicily* (1975). Falcone, Giovanni, *Men of Honour; the truth about the Mafia* (1992). Finley, M.I., Mack Smith, Denis, and Duggan, Christopher, *History of Sicily* (1987). Hibbert, Christopher, *Garibaldi and his Enemies* (1987). Matthew, Donald, *The Norman Kingdom of Sicily* (1992). Norwich, John Julius, *The Normans in the South* (1967) and *The Kingdom in the Sun* (1970), published in 1 volume as *The Normans in Sicily* (1992). Runciman, Stephen, *The Sicilian Vespers* (1992). Stille, Alexander, *Excellent Cadavers* (1996). History of the Mafia. Trevelyan, Raleigh, *Princes under the Volcano* (2002). English wine merchants in the Belle Epoque.

General

Amman, Peter, *Landscapes of Sicily* (2001), walking guides. Cronin, Vincent, *The Golden Honeycomb* (1954), travel and art guide. Dolci, Danilo, *Poverty in Sicily* (1966 translation) and *Sicilian Lives* (1981 translation), social essays. Lewis, Norman, *In Sicily* (2001). Lewis, Norman, *The Honoured Society* (1984). Lewis, Norman, *The March of the Longshadows* (1987), novel. Maggio, Theresa, *Mattanza: Love and Death in the Sea of Sicily* (2000), autobiography. Maraini, Dacia, *The Silent Duchess* (1998), novel. Maraini, Dacia, *Bagheria* (1993), 1940s childhood memoir. Maxwell, G., *God Protect me from my Friends* (1956); *The Ten Pains of Death* (1959), autobiographical. Price, Gillian, *Walking in Sicily* (2000). Simeti, Mary Taylor, *On Persephone's Island* (2001), autobiographical. Robb, Peter, *Midnight in Sicily* (1999), a chilling and factual account of the Mafia.

Sicilian food

Carluccio, Antonio, *Southern Italian Feast* (1998). Grammatico, Maria and Simeti, Maria Taylor, *Bitter Almonds* (1994). Harris, Valentina, *Southern Italian Cooking* (1994). Pomar, Anna, *La Cucina Tradizionale Siciliana* (1994). Tasca Lanza, Anna, *The Flavors of Sicily* (1997). Tasca Lanza, Anna, *Heart of Sicily: Recipes and Reminiscences of Regaleali* (1993). Simeti, Mary Taylor, *Sicilian Food* (1999). Simeti, Mary Taylor, *Pomp and Sustenance* (1998). Tornabene, Wanda & Giovanna, and Evans, Michele, *Gangivecchio's Sicilian Kitchen* (2001).

THE PROVINCE OF PALERMO

Palermo and its province occupy the northwestern part of the island, geologically the oldest part of Sicily, with sharp, spectacular mountains of Dolomitic limestone, fertile valleys and a beautiful coastline. The province contains many small towns, some of great historical importance such as Piana degli Albanesi, Castelbuono, Caccamo (the site of Sicily's largest castle), and Cefalù, while others are noted for their architecture. The great 18th-century villas of Bagheria are world-famous.

PALERMO

The city of Palermo, capital of the province and of the Sicilian region as a whole, stands on a bay on the north coast at the foot of Mt Pellegrino, a headland described by Goethe as the loveliest he had seen. It has a superb climate. One of the largest and most important cities in the world during the early Middle Ages, some of the great Arab-Norman buildings erected between the 9th and 12th centuries still stand, as well as numerous delightful Baroque churches and oratories of more recent date. During the 18th century, Palermo was the largest town in Italy after Naples. The Museo Archeologico Regionale Salinas and the Galleria Regionale della Sicilia each contain outstanding collections.

Palermo was originally bounded by two rivers, the Kemonia and the Papireto, and occupied an elliptical area centering on the present cathedral. The main street (now the western half of the Corso Vittorio Emanuele) was known as the *Cassaro Vecchio*, a name derived from *castrum* or the Arabic *kasr* (meaning castle). The Saracen citadel, called *Halisa*, the Elect (now Kalsa), stood south of the harbour, in an area thought to have been occupied also by *Neapolis*, another fortified area which was created in the Roman era nearer the port.

By the mid-16th century the rivers had silted up and the harbour was reduced to its existing proportions. From this time onward the plan of Palermo would hinge on two main thoroughfares: the Cassaro, extended to the east in 1565 and prolonged to the sea in 1581, and the Via Maqueda (laid out c. 1600), running roughly parallel with the coast. These bisect one another at the Quattro Canti. In the 19th and 20th centuries the city expanded northwards, from Piazza Verdi along the Viale della Libertà.

In present-day Palermo very few street names are written up on street corners, even though they all have an official name on the maps. This is in the process of being rectified, and in the Jewish Quarter (Giudecca) of the historic centre, roughly corresponding to the area just south of Sant'Agostino, you will notice that the street signs are written in Italian, Arabic and Hebrew, underlining the cosmopolitan character of old Palermo.

HISTORY OF PALERMO

Traces of Palaeolithic settlements have been found in grottoes on Monte Pellegrino. The great fertility of the Conca d'Oro, the plain behind the bay, has supported the inhabitants of Palermo throughout her history. *Panormus*, a Phoenician colony of the 8th–6th century BC, was never a Greek city, despite its Greek name signifying 'all harbour'. It became, instead, an important Carthaginian centre, hotly disputed during the First Punic War, and not finally acquired by Rome until 254 BC. It became a *municipium*, and after 20 BC, a flourishing *colonia*. After the invasions of the Vandals and Ostrogoths it was reconquered for the Byzantine emperors in 535 and remained in their possession until 831, when the Saracens captured it after a prolonged resistance.

Under Muslim rule it was made capital of an emirate (and named *al Medina*) rivalling Cordoba and Cairo in oriental splendour, as 'the city of 1,000 mosques'; the luxuriant gardens and fountains of the city enchanted travellers. It became an important trading post and cosmopolitan centre which showed tolerance towards Christians and Jews.

Taken by Count Roger de Hauteville in 1072, it again reached a high state of prosperity under his son King Roger II (1130–54), and became the centre of trade between Europe and Asia. Under the brilliant reign of Emperor Frederick II of Hohenstaufen (1198–1250; *see p. 14*), the city became famous throughout Europe for its learning and magnificence.

The famous rebellion of the Sicilian Vespers put an end to the misrule of Charles of Anjou in 1282. During the long period of Spanish domination, which became increasingly tyrannical, the city gradually declined. By the Treaty of Utrecht (1713) Sicily was allotted to Vittorio Amedeo of Savoy, who was, however, forced to exchange it for Sardinia (1718) in favour of the Neapolitan Bourbons. Under their rule the island fared little better, though Ferdinand IV established his court at Palermo in 1799 during the French occupation of Naples. The island was granted a temporary constitution in 1811 while under British protection. The city rebelled against misgovernment in 1820 (when Sir Richard Church was relieved of his governorship), 1848, and in April 1860. On 27th May 1860 Garibaldi and the 'Thousand' made a triumphant entry into the city.

Much of the centre of Palermo was badly damaged during air raids during the Second World War. After the war the Mafia took over, and much illegal building took place in the Conca d'Oro. In the 1960s and 1970s it was apparently the most neglected city in Italy, when a vast number of houses in the historical centre were in danger of collapse, and the population there dwindled to some 35,000 (from 125,000 in 1951), representing a mere five per cent of the total population of the municipality. In 1997 an enlightened city government finally approved a detailed plan to restore the old city centre which is now improving considerably.

QUATTRO CANTI & VICINITY

The centre of the city is marked by the monumental crossroads known as the **Quattro Canti**. Laid out in 1608–20 by Giulio Lasso at the central intersection of the four main streets (now Corso Vittorio Emanuele and Via Maqueda). It was named Piazza Vigliena after the Duke of Vigliena, Spanish viceroy in 1611, and is often called *Teatro del Sole* or Theatre of the Sun, because during the course of a day the sun illuminates each of the four corners in turn. The decorative façades bear fountains with statues of the four seasons, four Spanish kings of Sicily, and the four patron saints of Palermo (Cristina, Ninfa, Oliva and Agata). Now a confined and congested road junction, it is still used as a meeting-place by the locals. On Corso Vittorio Emanuele, the Porta Nuova can be seen to the southwest and the sea beyond Porta Felice to the northeast. From Via Maqueda, there is a vista of the hills surrounding the Conca d'Oro.

A few steps along Via Maqueda to the southeast, Piazza Pretoria is almost entirely occupied by a High Renaissance fountain, recently restored (*see box below*). It was designed by the Florentine Francesco Camilliani (1554–55), a disciple of the sculptor Baccio Bandinelli, Michelangelo's rival, and later assembled and enlarged here by Camilliani's son Camillo (*see p. 449*) and also Michelangelo Naccherino (1573).

FONTANA DELLA VERGOGNA

The rivalry between Palermo and Messina, both of which through the centuries have struggled to emerge as the foremost city on the island, can be read in the history of this fountain. Messina was the first to supply its citizens with water from a nearby river by means of a modern aqueduct in 1547. A beautiful fountain, designed by a follower of Michelangelo, was commissioned in celebration of the event and situated beside the cathedral (*see p. 28*). The Senate of Palermo, loath to be outdone, then purchased the enormous fountain which had originally been designed by Camilliani for the gardens of the Tuscan villa of Pietro di Toledo, father-in-law by his daughter Eleonora to Cosimo de' Medici. Vasari was a great admirer of the fountain, which introduced the High Renaissance Mannerist style to Palermo. Occupying almost the whole of the piazza, the great basin is decorated with some 50 statues of monsters, harpies, sirens and tritons. Also copied from Messina was the idea of representing the four rivers, in this case the Oreto, Papireto, Kemonia and Gabriele. Instead of Orion, the figure on the summit was made to represent the Genius of Palermo (*see p. 24 below*). Unfortunately for the city government, the nude and semi-clad white Carrara marble sculptures from Florence did not win the full approval of the pious citizens of Palermo, who dubbed the new arrival the *Fontana della Vergogna*, or Fountain of Shame.

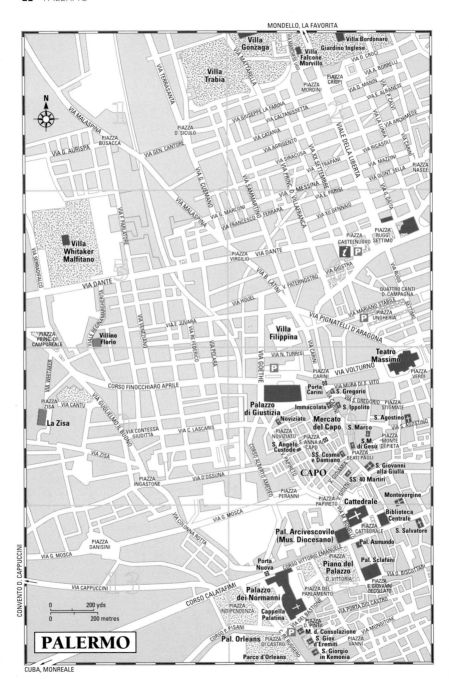

MONDELLO, LA FAVORITA

N

Villa
Gonzaga

Villa Bordonaro

Villa
Falcone
Morvillo

Giardino Inglese

VIA MARCHESE UGO

VIA D. CROCI

Villa
Trabia

VIA MATARELLA

VIA A. BORRELLI

PIAZZA
CAISPI

VIA D. MANIN

VIA P. CALVI

VIA E. ALBANESE

PIAZZA
MORDINI

VIA TERRASANTA

VIA MALASPINA

VIA G. AURISPA

PIAZZA
BUSACCA

PIAZZA
D. SICULO

VIA GIUSEPPE LA FARINA

VIA GEN. CANTORE

VIA CALTANISSETTA

VIALE DELLA LIBERTÀ

VIA LA UMIA

VIA ARCHIMEDE

VIA CARINI

VIA CATANIA

VIA AGRIGENTO

VIA RICASOLI

VIA G. CUSMANO

VIA SIRACUSA

VIA XX SETTEMBRE

VIA MAZZINI

PIAZZA
NASCE

VIA PRINC. DI MESSINA

VIA QUINT. SELLA

VIA MALASPINA

VIA G. MARCONI

VIA D. VILLABIANCA

VIA E. PARISI

VIA G. DAITA

VIA F. PARLATORE

VIA SAMMARTINO

VIA FRANCESCO FERRARA

VIA XII GENNAIO

Villa
Whitaker
Malfitano

VIA SERRADIFALCO

VIALE REGINA MARGHERITA

PIAZZA
CASTELNUOVO

PIAZZA
RUGG
SETTIMO

VIA DANTE

PIAZZA
VIRGILIO

VIA DANTE

VIA B. LATINI

V. PATERNOSTRO

VIA GIOSTRA

VIA RUGG

QUATTRO CANTI
D. CAMPAGNA

VIA HOUEL

PIAZZA
PRINC. DI
CAMPOREALE

VIA WHITAKER

VIA VENEZIANO

VIA F. JUVARA

VIA RE FEDERICO

Villino
Florio

VIA MARIANO STABILE

PIAZZA
UNGHERIA

VIA PIGNATELLI D'ARAGONA

SETTIMO

Villa
Filippina

VIA POLARA

VIA GOETHE

VIA N. TURRISI

VIA CARINI

Teatro
Massimo

PIAZZA
VERDI

CORSO FINOCCHIARO APRILE

PIAZZA
ZISA

VIA CANTU

VIA GUGLIELMO IL BUONO

VIA CONTESSA
GIUDITTA

VIA C. LASCARIS

PIAZZA
CARINI

VIA VOLTURNO

Porta
Carini

VIA MURA DIS. VITO

S. Gregorio

VIA S. GREGORIO

PIAZZA
STIGMATE

La Zisa

VIA ZISA

Palazzo
di Giustizia

Immacolata

S. Ippolito

S. Agostino

VIA S. AGOSTINO

Noviziato

Mercato
del Capo

S. Marco

PIAZZA
INGASTONE

VIA D'OSSUNA

PIAZZA
NOVIZIATO

S. Angelo
Custode

PIAZZA
S. ANNA AL
CAPO

S.M.
di Gesù

PIAZZA
MONTE
DI PIETÀ

SS. Cosma
e Damiano

PIAZZA
BEATI PAOLI

S. Giovanni
alla Giulla

CAPO

SS. 40 Martiri

PIAZZA
PERANNI

PIAZZA
PAPIRETO

Montevergine

VIA G. MOSCA

VIA COLONNA ROTTA

Cattedrale

Biblioteca
Centrale

CONVENTO D. CAPPUCCINI

PIAZZA
DANISINI

VIA G. MOSCA

Pal. Arcivescovile
(Mus. Diocesano)

PIAZZA
CATTEDRALE

S. Salvatore

Pal. Asmundo

Porta
Nuova

CORSO VITTORIO EMANUELE

PIAZZA
D. VITTORIA

Pal. Sclafani

VIA PORTA DI CASTRO

VIA D. BISCOTTARI

VIA CAPPUCCINI

Piano del
Palazzo

S. Giovanni
DECOLLATO

VIA CALATAFIMI

Palazzo
dei Normanni

PIAZZA DEL
PARLAMENTO

VIA DEL BASTIONE

0   200 yds
0   200 metres

CORSO CALATAFIMI

PIAZZA
INDIPENDENZA

Cappella
Palatina

PIAZZA
D. PINTA

M. d. Consolazione

VIA MONGITORE

PALERMO

CORSO P. PISANI

Pal. Orleans

PIAZZA
DI CASTRO

S. Giov.
d'Eremiti

PIAZZA
VANNI

Parco d'Orleans

S. Giorgio
in Kemonia

CUBA, MONREALE

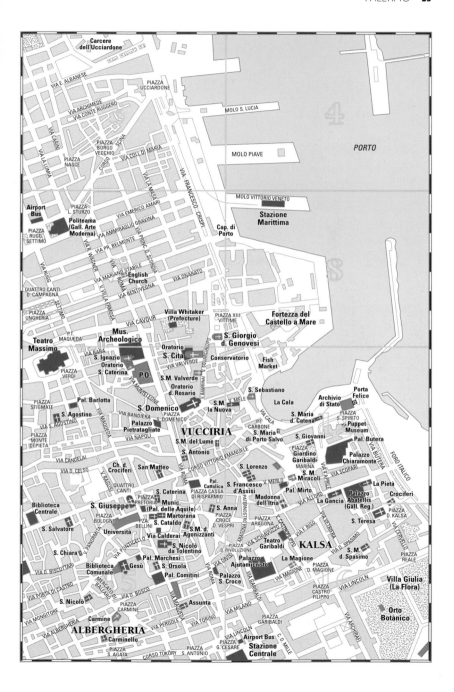

Palazzo delle Aquile

Map p. 23, 11.
Palazzo delle Aquile, named after the eagles which decorate its exterior, but some-times also referred to as Palazzo Pretorio, is the town hall. It was built in 1470, enlarged in the 16th century , and over-restored in 1874. The façade is surmounted by a 17th-century statue of St Rosalia. Visitors are admitted without formality when it is not in use. This was formerly the seat of the Senate which governed the city from the 14th century until 1816, senators being elected from the local aristocracy.

In the atrium is a Baroque portal by Paolo Amato and a Roman funerary monument with statues of a husband and wife. At the foot of the 19th-century staircase stands part of a 16th-century fountain of the *Genius of Palermo*, one of a number of allegor-ical statues in the city with the figure of a king, personifying Civic Rule, entangled in a serpent, representing Wisdom, sometimes with a dog at his feet, for Loyalty, or a lion, for Strength, and an eagle on his shoulder, representing the Empire. On the first floor, the assembly room, which has a 16th-century painted wooden ceiling, is cov-ered with numerous inscriptions relating to events which have taken place there. The other rooms, including that of the mayor, were decorated by Giuseppe Damiani Almeyda (also responsible for the Teatro Garibaldi, *see p. 52*) in 1870 and contain mementoes of Garibaldi and Napoleon.

Another side of the piazza is closed by the flank and dome of the church of **Santa Caterina** (1566–96). The interior, especially the choir, is an elaborate example of Sicilian Baroque, with striking effects of early 18th-century sculptural decoration and marble veneering. In the right transept is a marble statue of *St Catherine* by Antonello Gagini (1534). The frescoes in the cupola are by Vito D'Anna (1751).

San Giuseppe dei Teatini

Map p. 23, 15. *Open Mon–Sat 7.30–12 & 5.30–8; Sun & holidays by prior arrangement 8.30–1 & 6–8.*
Across Via Maqueda is the side of the church of San Giuseppe dei Teatini. The upper church, built by Giacomo Besio of Genoa (1612–45), was the scene of two popular assemblies called by Giuseppe d'Alessi during the revolt of 1647 against the Spanish governors. In the lavish Baroque interior, in addition to the 14 monolithic columns in the nave, eight colossal columns of grey marble support the well-proportioned central dome. The frescoes of the nave roof are copies of the originals by Filippo Tancredi; those in the dome are by Borremans; the stuccoes are outstandingly good. The two large angels holding the stoups on either side of the entrance are by Marabitti. In the fourth chapel of the south aisle, with handsome marble decoration, is a statue of the *Madonna* by the Gagini school, while in the south transept, beneath the altarpiece of *St Andrew of Avellino* by Sebastiano Conca, is a charming frieze of child musicians, and the altar has a bas-relief of a *Madonna amidst Angels*, both by Federico Siragusa (1800). In the choir vault are fine reliefs, with full-length figures, by Procopio Serpotta. In the chapels flank-ing the choir are (right) a Crucifix by Fra' Umile da Petralia (*see p. 287*) and (left) reliefs by Filippo Pennino, and an 18th-century statue of St Joseph. In the north transept,

above an altar of marble mosaic (probably late 17th century), is a painting of St Cajetan (Gaetano) by Pietro Novelli. St Cajetan (1480–1547) founded the Theatine congregation in response to a perceived lack of the monastic spirit in ministers of the clergy.

Next to the church is the former convent of the Teatini di San Giuseppe, now occupied by the university (the building was modified in the 19th century). The small Geological Museum founded here in the early 19th century by the Theatine Giorgio Gemmellaro is now at no. 131 Corso Tuköry (Map p. 23, 15): the **Museo Geologico** (*open Mon–Fri 9–1*), houses a collection of fossils, local rocks, and a woman's skeleton, known as *Thea*, from the Upper Palaeolithic era.

Holy water stoup held by an angel carved in stucco by Ignazio Marabitti in San Giuseppe dei Teatini.

La Martorana

Map p. 23, 15. *Open 8–1 & 3.30–5.30; Sun and holidays 8.30–1.*

Adjoining Piazza Pretoria is **Piazza Bellini** where the majestic columned campanile of La Martorana stands next to the three little red domes of San Cataldo, raised above part of the east wall of the Roman city and surrounded by a few trees; it is fitting that these two beautiful churches, founded by two of Norman Sicily's greatest statesmen, should survive together in the centre of the city.

La Martorana or Santa Maria dell'Ammiraglio, was founded c. 1146 by George of Antioch, a Syrian of the Greek Orthodox faith who became admiral under Roger II. It was presented in 1433 to a convent founded in the 12th century by Eloisa Martorana, wife of Goffredo de Martorana. The Sicilian Parliament met here after the Sicilian Vespers. Since 1935 it has shared cathedral status with San Demetrio in Piana degli Albanesi, a small town of Albanian origin in the province, and officiates services according to the Greek Orthodox rite. Outside, the Norman structure survives on the north and south sides, although a Baroque façade was inserted in 1588 on the north side when the Norman narthex was demolished and the atrium covered.

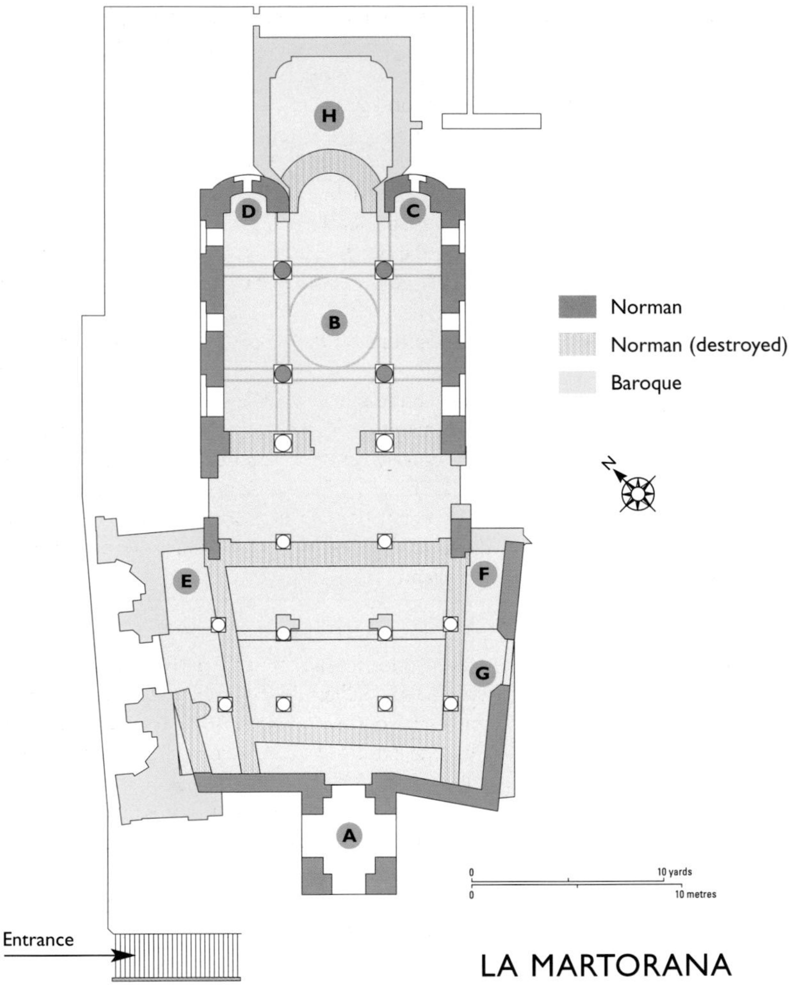

H
D
C
B
Norman
Norman (destroyed)
Baroque
N
E
F
G
A
0
10 yards
0
10 metres
Entrance
LA MARTORANA

The interior

The present entrance **A** is beneath the splendid 12th-century campanile which survived the alterations (only its red dome is missing). Inside, the central Greek-cross plan of the tiny original church can still be detected, despite the Baroque alterations at the west end and the prolongation of the chancel in 1683. The walls at the west end are heavily decorated with Baroque marble and frescoes which at first overpower the original mosaic decoration which remains on and around the central

cupola. The **mosaics**, probably by Greek craftsmen from Constantinople, date from the first half of the 12th century: Christ and the four Archangels are depicted in the dome **B** and, in Arabic lettering, a quotation from a Byzantine hymn; around the drum are Prophets and the Evangelists; on the triumphal arch, the *Annunciation*; in the south apse **C** St Anne, in the north apse **D**, St Joachim; and in the side vaults, four Evangelists, the *Nativity* and the *Dormition of the Virgin*. The balustrades in front of the apses and the mosaic floor are also Norman.

At the west end are two further original mosaic panels (restored; set in Baroque frames) from the destroyed portico: on the north side **E**, *George of Antioch at the Feet of the Virgin*, and, on the south side **F**, *Roger Crowned by Christ*. This is a rare portrait of Roger II of Sicily. Also here are frescoes by Borremans (1717). In the embrasure of the south portal **G** is a 12th-century carved wooden door. Above the main altar **H** is a fine panel painting of the *Ascension* (1533) by Vincenzo da Pavia. It was painted shortly after Vincenzo is supposed to have returned from Rome to Sicily with Polidoro da Caravaggio. In Rome both painters were strongly influenced by Raphael.

Southeast of the church some arches survive of the cloister of the 12th-century Casa Martorana, the Benedictine convent founded by Eloisa Martorana. The convent has disappeared, but the marzipan fruits which used to be made by the nuns here are immortalized by the name *frutti di martorana* (*see. p. 511*), and are still produced by numerous confectioners all over the island.

San Cataldo

In the courtyard, opposite the campanile, is the church of San Cataldo (*open 9.30–12.30*). It was founded by Maio of Bari, William I's chancellor, and because of his early death in 1160 the interior was never decorated. After 1787 it served as a post office and was restored in 1885. The fine exterior has blind arcading round the windows and crenellations at the top of the wall. Three small red domes with little windows rise in the centre. The simple plan of the interior has three aisles ending in apses and three domes high up above the central aisle. The beautiful old capitals are all different. The original mosaic floor and lattice windows survive.

Also facing the square is a small theatre, originally designed for operettas and recently restored, the **Teatro Bellini** (*T: 091 7434311 and 091 74434312, www.teatrobellini.it*).

CORSO VITTORIO EMANUELE TO THE CATHEDRAL

The busy Corso Vittorio Emanuele, the main street of the city, was once called the *Cassaro Vecchio* (from the Arabic *kasr* meaning castle) because it led from the port to the royal castle. On the left-hand side after Quattro Canti (heading southwest away from the port) it passes **Piazza Bologni**, with a statue of Charles V by Scipione Li Volsi (1630), the sculptor from Nicosia who lived in Tusa and whose work bears comparison with the Gagini and Serpotta. The statue is the butt of local jokes about the meaning of the emperor's outstretched hand, suggesting for example that he is indicating the height of the city's tide of litter.

From the far end of the piazza, beside **Palazzo Ugo delle Favare** with its attractive balconies (accommodation available, *see p. 117*), a detour down the interesting old **Via Panormita** on the right takes in the Piazzetta Speciale where the Palazzo Speciale has an 18th-century staircase in its pretty courtyard, and there is a small café. Further on is Piazza Santa Chiara where the church, with a splendid interior, is often used for concerts. Numerous immigrants from Senegal have settled in this part of the city. Via dei Biscottari continues (with a view left down Via Benfratelli to the 14th-century tower of San Nicolò), and passes under a massive arch to emerge in Piazza San Giovanni Decollato beside the impressive **Palazzo Sclafani**, built by Matteo Sclafani in 1330. Part of the original façade has attractive lava decoration around the windows. The fine 14th-century portal has sculptures by Bonaiuto da Pisa. Opposite is the ruined church of San Giovanni Decollato, with a huge Morton Bay fig tree growing through its façade.

Facing Piazza Bologni, across the corso, is the façade of **Palazzo Riso-Belmonte** (1784), the grandest of all the buildings in the city by the pre-eminent Neoclassical architect Giuseppe Venanzio Marvuglia. Further west along the corso is the church of **San Salvatore** (*open 9.30–12.30; closed Tues*), built in 1682 by Paolo Amato. Bombed during the Second World War, the oval interior has been well restored.

On the opposite side of the corso the narrow and decrepit Via Montevergini leads to the church of **Montevergini** (*open 8.30–8*) with a fine façade by Andrea Palma and a little campanile with an onion-shaped dome decorated with early 18th-century tiles, beside an 18th-century loggia for the nuns. After deconsecration in 1866 it became a school for artisans, then the seat of the Fascist party, and was later used (until 1955) as a law court. The trial of Gaspare Pisciotta, who murdered his brother-in-law, the famous bandit Salvatore Giuliano, took place here. In the interior there are some vault frescoes by Borremans, and a Neoclassical sanctuary decorated by Emanuele Cordona with frescoes by Giuseppe Velasco (1750–1827), who was also responsible for the tapestry room at Palazzo Mirto (*see p. 43*).

Further along the corso (no. 429) is the prestigious library, **Biblioteca Centrale della Regione Siciliana** (*open Mon–Fri 8.30–6.30; Sat 8.30–1*), which occupies the former Jesuit college, and is entered by the portal of the adjacent church of Santa Maria della Grotta. It owns over 500,000 volumes and many ancient manuscripts (particularly of the 15th and 16th centuries). Just beyond is Piazza della Cattedrale, with the elaborate flank of the cathedral on the other side of a garden enclosed by a balustrade bearing statues of saints.

The cathedral

Map p. 22, 14. *Open 8–5.30; www.cattedrale.palermo.it*
The cathedral, dedicated to the Assumption of the Virgin, is a building of many styles not too skilfully blended, but remains a striking edifice with golden-coloured stone and sharp contrasts of light and shade. The present church, on the site of an older basilica which did duty as a mosque in the 9th century, was founded in 1185 by Gualtiero Offamiglio (Walter of the Mill), an Englishman who was Archbishop of

The south porch of Palermo cathedral.

Palermo and tutor to the young William II. With unlimited funds at his disposal, Walter intended it to be a political statement of the extent of his power in the Kingdom of Sicily. He didn't live long enough to see it finished though, dying in 1191. His brother Bartolomeo briefly succeeded him, before being sent into exile.

The exterior

Work on the fabric continued for many centuries and in the 15th century much of the exterior acquired a Catalan-Gothic style. The incongruous dome was added by Ferdinando Fuga in 1781–1801. The façade, turned towards the southwest on Via Matteo Bonello, is a fine example of local Gothic craftsmanship (13th–14th centuries). The doorway dates from 1352. Two powerful Gothic arches span the road to a Norman tower transformed into the campanile in the 19th century. The east end, with three intricately decorated apses and two towers matching those at the west end, is almost entirely original 12th-century work. The usual entrance is from the garden with its statue of St Rosalia through the great south porch, a splendid Catalan-Gothic work by Antonio Gambara (1426). In the tympanum there is a delicate relief of the *Redeemer between the Archangel Gabriel and Mary*. Beneath is a frieze of saints in polychrome relief. The remarkable painted intarsia decoration above the three arches, which probably dates from 1296, was discovered during recent restoration work. It represents the Tree of Life in a complicated geometric composition showing Islamic influence. The twelve roundels are decorated with a great variety of symbolic animals

PALERMO CATHEDRAL

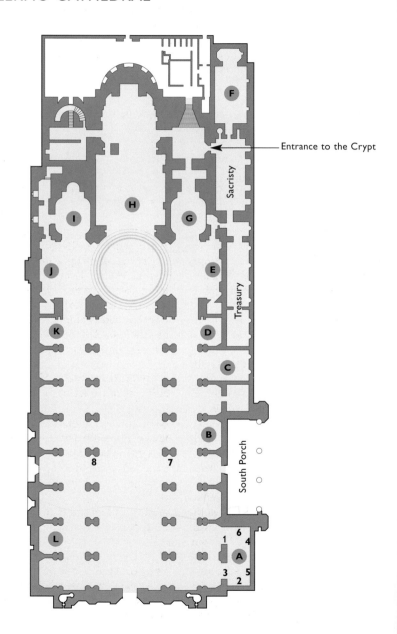

Entrance to the Crypt

Sacristy

Treasury

South Porch

(including fish, cockerels, serpents, crabs, mice, camels, lions, wolves, bears, peacocks, dragons, doves and owls), as well as fruit and flowers and human figures. Intended to be read from left to right, the last roundel seems to represent the sun with the head of Christ in the centre. Beneath the porch, the column on the left, probably preserved from the earlier mosque, is inscribed with a passage from the Koran. The fine wooden doors are by Francesco Miranda (1432).

The interior
The interior is relatively plain, restoration work in the 18th century having removed the majority of the decorative works of art.

A The first two chapels of the south aisle enclose six **royal tombs**. On the left in front is the porphyry sarcophagus (**1**) of **Frederick II of Hohenstaufen** (d. 1250), emperor of Germany and king of Sicily. Frederick's dearly loved first wife, **Constance of Aragon** (d. 1222), lies in the white Roman sarcophagus against the west wall (**2**), with a frieze showing a lion hunt. The tomb on the right (**3**) is of **Henry VI** (d. 1197), emperor of Germany, son of Frederick Barbarossa, and father of Frederick II of Hohenstaufen. Behind, beneath mosaic canopies, are the tombs of the first king of Sicily, **Roger II** (d. 1154; **4**), who was crowned in this cathedral in 1130, and his daughter **Constance de Hauteville** (d. 1198; **5**). Brought out of a convent at the unlikely age of 32 in order to marry Henry, 11 years her junior, she gave birth to her son Frederick eight years later, in the main square of Jesi, to dispel rumours that she was too old to become a mother. The later Aragonese royalties buried here are, on the left (**6**), **Duke William of Athens** (d. 1338), son of Frederick II of Aragon, and (in Frederick II's sarcophagus) **Peter II** (d. 1342), king of Sicily. The smooth porphyry sarcophagi are almost certainly Imperial Roman in

workmanship, because the quarries of this type of stone were already exhausted in the Middle Ages. It is not known how they came to be here in Palermo.

In the nave are statues of saints from a high altar backing (25m) by Antonello Gagini and his family, who worked on it for over 64 years. Known as the Tribuna, this masterpiece was dismantled arbitrarily in the 18th century. Now models of the work, and some fragments of it, are on view in the Diocesan Museum. The canopied stoup (**7**) is of 1557.

B In the fourth chapel of the south aisle is an altarpiece by Pietro Novelli.

C In the sixth chapel are reliquary urns of saints of Palermo, and, used as an altar frontal, the tomb slab of St Cosmas, a Sicilian bishop martyred in 1160.

D The seventh chapel has a fine marble altar (1713).

E In the south transept there is an altarpiece by Giuseppe Velasco and, above the altar, a bas-relief of the *Dormition of the Virgin* by Antonello Gagini (1535).

The **treasury** (*open Mon–Sat 9–5.30; groups only on Sun and holidays*) contains the extraordinary crown of Constance of Aragon (first wife of Frederick II), made by local craftsmen c. 1210, in fine gold filigree set with precious gems, and found in her tomb in the 18th century. Also displayed here are the contents of some of the other royal tombs, 18th- and 19th-century copes, chalices and altar frontals. Beyond the treasury is the sacristy which has two fine portals by Vincenzo Gagini (1568), and the entrance to the Crypt.

F The inner sacristy (usually closed) has a *Madonna* by Antonello Gagini (1503).

The crown (c. 1210) of Queen Constance.

In the **Crypt** are preserved 23 tombs, many of them Roman sarcophagi (all of them numbered and labelled in Italian). The tomb (no. 12) of Archbishop Giovanni Paternò (d. 1511) has a very fine effigy by Antonello Gagini, whose patron he was, resting on a Greek sarcophagus. The tomb (no. 16) of the founder of the cathedral, Archbishop Walter (d. 1190), has a beautiful red, green and gold mosaic border. No. 7 is a large Roman sarcophagus with a scene of the coronation of a poet with the nine muses and Apollo. The tomb of Frederick of Antioch (d. 1305), no. 9, has a Gothic effigy of the warrior semi-recumbent, with his helmet at his feet and sword by his side.

G In the **Cappella di Santa Rosalia** to the right of the choir is a 17th-century silver coffer containing the relics of St Rosalia (*see p. 72*); the reliefs on the walls are 19th century.

H The choir stalls date from 1466. The meridian line on the floor, 22m long, was made by Father Giuseppe Piazzi in 1801. The light coming through the tiny hole in the dome on the right at midday, indicates the zodiac sign for the time of year. The left end of the choir has a *Resurrection of Christ* on the altar, high reliefs, and (in niches), statues of the apostles, all fragments of Antonello Gagini's high altar.

I The chapel on this side houses a large domed **ciborium** in lapis lazuli (1663), and the funerary monument of Bishop Sanseverino (1793).

J In the north transept, at the foot of an early 14th-century wooden Crucifix donated by Manfredi Chiaramonte, are marble statues of mourners by Gaspare Serpotta and Gaspare Guercio. On the altar are fine reliefs with scenes of the *Passion* by Fazio and Vincenzo Gagini.

K In the seventh chapel of the north aisle, there is a statue of the *Madonna* by Francesco Laurana and his school. In the nave (**8**) is a **stoup** attributed to Domenico Gagini, damaged but of fine workmanship.

L The second chapel of the north aisle has an *Assumption* and three reliefs by the Gagini, also once part of the high altar.

Museo Diocesano

Map p. 22, 14. *Open Tues–Sun 9.30–1.30; Sat 10–6; closed Mon. www.diocesipa.it)*
Across the busy Via Matteo Bonello, the **Palazzo Arcivescovile** (Archbishop's Palace), with a portal of 1460 which survived the 18th-century rebuilding, houses the **Museo Diocesano**. Here a large and important collection of marble and mosaic fragments from the cathedral and other churches destroyed during the Second World War, together with splendid paintings dating from the 11th–18th century, are in the process of being restored and displayed to the best advantage.

On the ground floor are 15th-century frescoes, a 12th-century mosaic from the cathedral and a *Madonna della Perla* (1171), egg tempera on board. Vincenzo da Pavia's *San Cono l'Eremita* and *Sant' Antonio Abate* (1550) can also be seen. In the basement level the museum's superb collection of sculpture is displayed, with several examples of the works of the Gagini, as well as works in stucco. On the ground floor again, in the north wing of the palace, 16th- and 17th-century paintings chart the movement from Mannerism to *Caravaggismo*, with one room entirely dedicated to works by Pietro Novelli (*see p. 81*).

On the other side of Via Bonello is the **Loggia dell'Incoronazione**, erected in the 16th–17th centuries using earlier columns and capitals. It takes its name from the tradition that the kings used to show themselves to the people here after their coronation. Behind is the Cappella dell'Incoronata, a Norman building partly destroyed in 1860.

Close to the cathedral, at no. 3 Via Pietro Novelli, is **Palazzo Asmundo** (*open 9.30–2, closed Sun & holidays; www.palazzoasmundo.it*). Built in 1615, it contains beautifully frescoed salons (by Gioacchino Martorana, 1764) that give an insight into the lives of the Sicilian nobility. The collections include paintings, wooden trousseau chests, French and Neapolitan porcelain, majolica tiles and a unique set of census bricks inscribed with details of the donor, they were walled into churches, convents, institutions.

Villa Bonanno

Piazza Vittoria, or Piano del Palazzo, is occupied by Villa Bonanno, a public garden thick with palm trees. At the centre of the old city and in front of the Palazzo dei Normanni, the piazza has been used throughout Palermo's history for public celebrations. Partially protected by a roof are some remains of three **Roman houses** (*open 9–7; Sun and holidays 9–1.30*), the only buildings of this period so far found in the city, one a substantial villa with mosaics including the *Hunt of Alexander*, possibly from an original cartoon by Philoxenos of Eritrea, a Greek painter of the 4th century BC. It is

comparable with work in the Fauno house in Pompeii. Building A is of a later date, probably 2nd century BC. The garden adjoins Piazza del Parlamento with a monument to Philip V of Bourbon, at the foot of the Palazzo dei Normanni. Spanning the corso is the **Porta Nuova**, a triumphal gateway with a conical top celebrating Charles V's Tunisian victory (1535).

PALAZZO DEI NORMANNI & CAPPELLA PALATINA

Map p. 22, 14. *Open Mon–Sat 8.30–12 & 2–5; Sun and holidays 8.30–12.*
Palazzo dei Normanni, or Palazzo Reale, stands in the highest part of the old city. It was built by the Arabs, enlarged by the Normans, and later restored by the Spaniards who added the principal façade. It has always been the palace of the rulers of the island, and here the splendid courts of Roger II and Frederick II held sway over much of Europe. Since 1947 it has been the seat of the Regional Assembly. The long façade (1616) hides the apse of the Cappella Palatina (Palatine Chapel). At the right end is the massive **Torre Pisana**, part of the Norman palace, which houses the **Museo della Specola** (*entrance from no. 1 Piazza del Parlamento, guided visits only from Mon–Fri at 9.30 & 11, closed Aug*), with the instruments used by Father Giuseppe Piazzi, the first director of the astronomical observatory founded here in 1786, including his famous **Ramsden circle**, 1.5m in diameter, by means of which he discovered the first asteroid, Ceres, in 1801. The view over Palermo from the tower is exceptional.

Visiting the palace

The entrance to the palace for visitors is at the back; this is reached by steps down from the left side of the piazza to the very busy and noisy Via del Bastione, which skirts the great wall of the palace around to the right. From the bastions a ramp leads up to the back entrance. Here a monumental staircase (**A**; 1735) leads up to a loggia overlooking the fine courtyard (**B**; 1600). Set into the wall of the loggia is a pillar with an inscription in Greek, Latin and Arabic, relating to a water clock built for Roger II in 1142, probably in Fez, Morocco **C**.

Cappella Palatina

Open Mon–Fri 9–11.45 & 3–4; Sat, Sun and holidays 9–12; closed Easter Mon, 25 Apr, 1 May, 26 Dec and for weddings.
Beneath the portico of seven columns with modern mosaics, is the side entrance to the Cappella Palatina, a jewel of Arab-Norman art built by Roger II c. 1132–40. The interior is famous for its wonderful **mosaics**, one of the finest works of art of its kind in the world. The mosaics were commissioned by Roger II to follow a carefully planned design intended to celebrate his monarchy, and the subjects seem to have been chosen with particular reference to the Holy Spirit and the theology of light. The

Early 12th-century mosaic of Christ Pantocrator surrounded by the four Archangels, in the cupola of the Cappella Palatina of the Palazzo dei Normanni.

earliest and finest mosaics are in the east part of the chapel and are thought to have been the work of Byzantine Greeks (c. 1140–50). Here the splendour of the mosaics is increased by the use of silver as well as gold tesserae.

The light changes constantly so the chapel should, if possible, be visited at different times of the day. A small aisled basilica in form, with a raised choir and a cupola above the central bay, it demonstrates the perfection of this style of architecture. Every detail of the decoration is exquisite. The ten antique columns of the nave are made from granite and cipollino marble; the ceiling (undergoing restoration) is a splendid Saracenic work in carved and painted cedar wood from Lebanon, with rich and varied designs. The ambo and paschal candlestick **D** are good examples of the richest Norman marble decoration. The figure wearing a crown at the foot of the candlestick is one of the few portraits of Roger in existence. He looks like Mr Punch, supporting the seated Christ. The pavement and lower part of the walls are made of white marble inlaid with red, green and gold patterns, each different, combining in a delightful harmony of colour and design with the glittering mosaics on a gold ground above.

In the cupola of the sanctuary **E** is *Christ Surrounded by Angels and Archangels*; on the drum, David, Solomon, Zachariah and St John the Baptist; on the pendentives, the Evangelists. On the triumphal arch, an *Annunciation* is depicted. Above the south apse **F** is a *Nativity*; on the upper part of the south wall, *Joseph's Dream* and the *Flight into Egypt*; on the nave arch, *Presentation in the Temple*; in the middle of the south wall, *Baptism*, *Transfiguration*, and the *Raising of Lazarus*; and on the lower part of the south wall, *Entry into Jerusalem*. On the lower part of the north wall, *Five Bishops of the Greek Church* (among the best preserved mosaic figures in the building), and, on the arch, *three female saints*. Above the north apse **G**, are a *Madonna and Child and St John the Baptist*. In the main apse **H** is the solemn, stern *Christ Pantocrator*, above a late 18th-century mosaic of the *Virgin*.

The mosaics in the nave were probably the last to be carried out (c. 1150–71); they illustrate the book of Genesis in two tiers of scenes between the clerestory windows and in the spandrels of the arches. The cycle begins in the upper tier of the right wall nearest to the sanctuary, showing the first seven days of the *Creation* up to the *Creation of Eve*. The sequence continues in the upper tier of the left wall (beginning at the entrance end) with the *Fall* up to the *Building of the Ark*, striking in its similarity to a Viking longship. The lower tier of the right wall (from the apse end) illustrates the *Flood* up to the *Hospitality of Lot*, and continues in the lower tier of the left wall (entrance end) with the *Destruction of Sodom* and continues up to *Jacob's Dream* and his *Wrestling with the Angel*, which is the last scene in the sequence (nearest to the sanctuary).

In the aisles are scenes from the lives of Sts Peter and Paul, also executed after the mosaics in the apse part of the church, possibly by local artists. The sequence begins at the apse end of the right aisle with *Saul leaving Jerusalem for Damascus* and the last scene in this aisle shows *St Peter's Escape from Prison*. The cycle continues at the entrance end of the left aisle with *Sts Peter and John Healing the Lame Man at the Temple Gate*, and the last scene in this aisle, nearest to the sanctuary, shows the *Fall of Simon Magus*.

PALAZZO DEI NORMANNI & CAPPELLA PALATINA

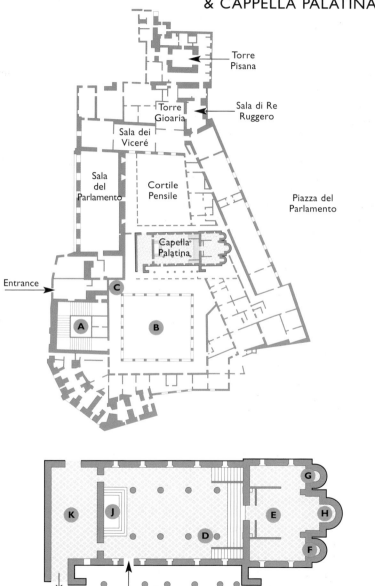

Torre Pisana

Torre Gioaria

Sala di Re Ruggero

Sala dei Viceré

Sala del Parlamento

Cortile Pensile

Piazza del Parlamento

Capella Palatina

Entrance

C

A

B

G

J

K

E

H

D

F

Entrance

Exit

Above the recomposed Norman throne on a dais at the entrance end ⓙ is a 15th-century mosaic of *Christ Enthroned Between Sts Peter and Paul*. The original narthex ⓚ, now the baptistery with a mosaic font, has two beautifully carved mosaic doorways with bronze doors. The sacristy and treasury are usually closed.

Royal Apartments of the palace

The staircase leads up to the top floor of the palace and the former Royal Apartments, largely decorated in the 19th century. The Sala dei Viceré has a series of portraits of viceroys from 1754 to 1837. The Torre Gioaria (from the Arabic *al johara*, the pearl, meaning the centre of the building), or Tower of the Winds (for its built-in air conditioning), preserves part of the Norman building, with four columns. The most interesting room is the so-called **Sala di Re Ruggero** (King Roger's room) with delightful mosaics dating from 1140, including centaurs, birds, palm trees, lions and leopards. In the vault are heraldic beasts. The lower parts of the walls with marble and mosaic decoration, and the floor all survive intact, and there is a beautiful table from Naples, made of a slice of fossilized wood. The Sala da Ballo (ballroom) has a fine view over the piazza to the sea.

Other parts of the palace are not usually shown when in use (ask at the ticket office), including the Sala del Parlamento, or Sala d'Ercole, decorated by Giuseppe Velasco, where the Regional Assembly meets. The vaulted armoury, treasure-chamber and dungeons survive from the Norman period.

The palace environs

Across Corso Re Ruggero is **Palazzo d'Orléans**, now the seat of the president of the Sicilian Region. This was the residence of the exiled Louis Philippe d'Orléans (1773–1850), eldest son of the Duke d'Orléans and the last King of France, at the time of his marriage in 1809 to Marie Amélie, daughter of Ferdinand IV, the Spanish King of the Two Sicilies. Their son Ferdinand Philippe (1810–42) was born here in the following year. The gardens were laid out in 1797 (*open Mon–Fri 9–1 & 3–6; Sat, Sun and holidays 9–1*).

In Piazza della Pinta is the little Oratorio della Compagnia della Madonna della Consolazione (San Mercurio). The stucco decoration in the interior has recently been attributed, as an early work, to Giacomo Serpotta. Via dei Benedettini leads from here to the church of San Giovanni degli Eremiti.

San Giovanni degli Eremiti

Map p. 22, 14. *Open Mon–Sat 9–7, Sun and holidays 9–1.*

The church of San Giovanni degli Eremiti, symbol of the city, is perhaps the most romantic building of Norman Palermo, thanks to its small, carefully tended and luxuriant garden. It was built by Roger II in 1132–48, and has now been deconsecrated. Paths lead up through the beautiful groves, with splendid palm trees, cactus and flowering jasmine, overshadowed by five charming red domes, the tallest one crowning the campanile of the little church. In the bare interior the nave is surmounted by two domes divided by an arch (pierced by a window). At the east end are three apses and three smaller domes, the one on the left part of the campanile.

To the right is an older structure, probably a mosque, consisting of a rectangular hall with cross vaulting and once divided by a row of pillars. Adjoining this (seen from the right of the entrance to the church) is a portico of five arches, whose inner wall is now the right wall of the church, and an open courtyard. The little cloister of the late 13th century has twin columns bearing pointed arches which surround a delightfully peaceful part of the garden.

THE ALBERGHERIA DISTRICT

The Gesù

Map p. 23, 14. *Open 7–11.30 & 5–6.30; Sun and holidays 7–12.30.*

From the Quattro Canti, Via Maqueda leads south past the church of San Giuseppe to Via del Ponticello, which branches off to the right. On the left is Piazza dei Santissimi 40 Martiri. Here the sturdy tower (with a Catalan window) of the 15th-century Palazzo Marchesi forms the base of the campanile of the Gesù church. The palace garden is sometimes open.

Via del Ponticello continues to the church of Gesù, or the church of Casa Professa, the first church to be erected in Sicily by the Jesuits (1564–1633). The splendid interior was beautifully decorated in the 17th and 18th centuries with colourful inlaid marble and sculptures (especially good in the nave chapels, 1665–91; the lovely 18th-century Andronico organ is out of order, although fortunately intact). The entrance wall inside has very fine 18th-century sculptural decoration. In the right aisle, the second chapel has paintings of two saints by Pietro Novelli, and the fourth chapel has a statue of the Madonna by the Gagini school. The presbytery also has remarkably good marble decoration.

Beside the church is the fine Baroque atrium of the Casa Professa, now partly occupied by the town library, **Biblioteca Comunale** (*open Mon–Fri 9–12; Tues, Wed, Thur also 3–6*), founded in 1760. It has over 250,000 volumes, and more than 1,000 incunabula and manuscripts.

Around Piazza Ballarò

Via Casa Professa continues straight on to Piazza Ballarò, the noisy, colourful daily market known since the Arab period as the *Mercato di Ballarò* (from the Arabic *suq al bahlara*), when fruit and vegetables were brought into town through the nearby Porta Sant'Agata. This is part of the Quartiere dell'Albergheria, one of the poorest districts in the city, which was devastated by bombing in 1943. Beyond, the church tower of San Nicolò can be seen, once part of the 14th-century town fortifications.

Via Ballarò continues left through the market to Piazza del Carmine, with more stalls, above which towers the fantastic dome of the church of the **Carmine Maggiore** (*open 8.30–1.30, no visits during Mass*) with its telamones and colourful majolica tiles (1681). The interior contains altars in the transepts by Giuseppe and Giacomo Serpotta

(1683–84); paintings (in the sanctuary) by Tommaso de Vigilia (late 15th century); a statue of *St Catherine* by Antonello Gagini; and a *Madonna* by the Gagini school. The famous organ, built for this church in 1856 by Salvatore Briulotta, has been electrified and has lost its magnificent tone.

In **Via delle Mosche**, behind the church, was born Giuseppe Balsamo in 1743. Under the assumed title of Count Cagliostro, he travelled all over Europe professing skills as a physician and an alchemist until he was sentenced to life imprisonment for freemasonry by the Inquisition six years before he died in 1795. His story fascinated Goethe, who visited his family when he was in Palermo in 1787.

Via Musco and Via Mugnosi lead to the church of the **Carminello** (*open 9–5; Sat 9–1, closed Sun and holidays*), built in 1605 and decorated with stuccoes at the end of the 17th century and the beginning of the 18th. Those on the entrance wall have recently been attributed to Procopio Serpotta, son of Giacomo and the only one of his children to inherit his father's skill.

The straight Via del Bosco leads away from the market back towards Via Maqueda, past some fine palaces. On the corner of Via Maqueda (at no. 100) is **Palazzo Comitini** (*open Mon–Fri 9.30–1.30; Sat and Sun by prior arrangement*) by Nicolò Palma (1771), seat of the province of Palermo. The 18th-century Rococo interior has fine frescoed ceilings, Murano chandeliers and decorative mirrors.

On the opposite side of Via Maqueda (to the right) is the long façade (mid-18th century) of Palazzo Santa Croce. Just beyond is the **Assunta** (*open 9–12 & 4–6.30; Sat and Sun 9–12*), a convent-church built in 1625–28 through the generosity of the Moncada family. The small interior is glowing white, richly decorated in the 18th century with stuccoes by a Giacomo Serpotta (the high altar and angels) at the very height of his skill. The vault frescoes are by Filippo Tancredi, the altarpieces by Borremans. The inlaid marble floor dates from 1638.

Returning towards the Quattro Canti Via Maqueda passes, next to Palazzo Comitini (Map p. 23. 15), the church of **Sant'Orsola** (*open 9–1*), built in 1662. The interior was redecorated in the late 18th century. The two last chapels on either side of the nave contain stuccoes by Giacomo Serpotta (1692), and (in the left chapel) an altarpiece of *St Jerome* by Zoppo di Gangi (*see p. 102*). A fine painting of the *Madonna and Child* (as *Salvator Mundi*) by Pietro Novelli is kept in the sacristy.

Further on, on the opposite side of the road, is the church of **San Nicolò da Tolentino** (*open Tues–Sat 9–12 & 4–7; Sun and holidays 8.30–12*), in the centre of a district where Jews lived freely from the 9th century onwards. However, Ferdinand of Spain expelled them from the city in 1492 and the synagogue here was destroyed, on the site of which the building of the church was begun in 1609. The two altarpieces in the transepts are by Pietro Novelli. The convent houses the city archives.

Just beyond, **Via dei Calderai**, the picturesque 'street of the tinkers', diverges right from Via Roma. It leads to Via Giovanni da Procida where the church of **Santa Maria degli Agonizzanti** is situated (*open 9–5; Sat, Sun and holidays mornings only*), rebuilt in 1784. The polychrome marble high altar has reliefs by Ignazio Marabitti.

East from the Quattro Canti, Corso Vittorio Emanuele leads towards the sea. A short way along on the left is the fine Baroque church of **San Matteo** (*open Tues–Sat 9–1; Sun and holidays 10–11; closed Mon*). It was begun in 1633 by Mariano Smiriglio, and contains lovely stucco work by Giacomo Serpotta and frescoes by Vito D'Anna (1754). Just beyond, the corso intersects with Via Roma, one of the main thorough-fares of the city running north from the station.

EAST OF QUATTRO CANTI

San Francesco d'Assisi

Map p. 23, 12. *Open 7–12 & 4–6.30.*

Beyond Via Roma, the narrow Via Paternostro (with numerous shops selling and repair-ing luggage) curves right towards the attractive piazza in front of the 13th-century church of San Francesco d'Assisi. The façade has a beautiful portal with three designs of zig-zag ornamentation (1302) and a lovely rose window (*pictured overleaf*).

The church was damaged by an earthquake in 1823 and again during air raids in 1943, after which it was restored (with lights for most of the chapels). The Franciscan nave of 1255–77 is flanked by beautiful chapels added in the 14th–15th centuries. Eight statues by Giacomo Serpotta (1723) decorate the inside portal and nave. Above the door is a fine sculpted arch of 1465. In the second chapel in the south aisle there is an altar-piece of *St George and the Dragon* in high relief and carved roundels by Antonello Gagini (1526); in the third chapel there is a *Madonna* attributed to Antonio Gagini flanked by 15th-century statues of saints. The Gothic fourth chapel contains a beautiful 15th-cen-tury *Madonna* by a Catalan sculptor and the sarcophagus of Elisabetta Omodei (1498) attributed to Domenico Gagini. Beyond the side door and another Gothic chapel is the sixth chapel with three bas-reliefs by Ignazio Marabitti (including the altar frontal). The seventh chapel has interesting 14th-century lava decoration on the arches.

The chapel to the right of the sanctuary has a fine polychrome marble intarsia deco-ration (17th–18th century; carefully restored after war damage). The eight figures of Sicilian saints are by Giovanni Battista Ragusa (1717). The altarpiece of the *Immacolata* in mosaic is to a design by Vito D'Anna and below is an elaborate marble altar frontal. The sanctuary has fine 16th-century carved and inlaid choir stalls. The chapel to the left of the sanctuary has intricate marble decoration and an 18th-century wooden statue of St Francis.

In the north aisle the eighth chapel once had a bust of St John in polychrome terra-cotta, attributed to Antonello Gagini. It has been replaced by a cast (the original is in the Museo Diocesano, *see p. 33*). The four statuettes of the Virtues are attributed to Pietro da Bonitate, 15th-century collaborator with Francesco Laurana.

By the door into the sacristy there is a tomb effigy of the young warrior Antonio Speciale attributed to Domenico Gagini (1477) with a touching inscription above it. The fifth chapel has a 14th-century portal with zig-zag ornamentation and remains of early frescoes. The arch of the fourth chapel, the **Cappella Mastrantonio**, is a superb piece by Francesco Laurana and Pietro da Bonitate (1468), the earliest important Renaissance work in Sicily. On the left wall of the chapel, the *Madonna and Saints* has been attributed

to Vincenzo da Pavia. In the second chapel a highly venerated silver statue of the *Immaculate Virgin* (1647) is hidden by a curtain, and the remains of a fresco of St Francis is on the left wall. In the first chapel (light on the right), with a fine 16th-century portal, is a *Madonna and Child with St John*, by Domenico Gagini (with a beautiful base), and a relief of the Madonna.

To the left of the church is the **Oratorio di San Lorenzo**, entrance at no. 5 Via Immacolatella (*open Mon–Fri 9–12*). The interior, designed by Giacomo Amato, is decorated with stuccoes illustrating the *Lives of St Lawrence and St Francis*, perhaps the masterpiece of Giacomo Serpotta (1699–1707). Ten symbolic statues, eight vivacious little reliefs, and the *Martyrdom of St Lawrence* situated above the door, the whole encircled by a throng of joyous cherubs, make up a well-balanced and animated composition. The modelling of the male figures above the windows is especially skilful.

The *Nativity*, by Caravaggio (1609; his last known work), which was stolen from the altar in 1969, has never been recovered.

In Via Paternostro, opposite San Francesco, is the **Antica Focacceria di San Francesco**, a snack bar founded in 1834, with a charming old-fashioned interior. Palazzo Cattolica nearby (no. 48) has a double courtyard by Giacomo Amato (c. 1720).

Palazzo Mirto

Map p. 23, 12. *Open 9–7; Sun and holidays 9–1.*
Via Merlo leads out of the piazza to the right of the façade of San Francesco. At no. 2 an 18th-century gateway leads into Palazzo Mirto . The main façade on Via Lungarini, with a double row of balconies, dates from 1793. The residence of the Lanza-Filangeri family since the early 17th century, it was donated by them, together with its contents, to the region of Sicily in 1982. The well-kept interior is interesting as a typical example of a princely residence in Palermo, with 18th- and 19th-century decorations, including a little 'Chinese' room with a leather floor. The contents include furniture (mostly 18th and 19th century), Capodimonte porcelain and Murano glass. On the ground floor, near the delightful stables (1812), the funerary stele of Giambattista and Elisabetta Mellerio (c. 1820) by Antonio Canova are displayed, purchased by the region of Sicily in 1978 to prevent them being exported.

Beyond, opposite Palazzo Rostagno is the Renaissance church of Santa Maria dei Miracoli of 1547 (*open Mon–Fri 9–5; Sat 9–1; Sun and holidays closed*), with a gracefully elegant, very simple interior. The church was once on the harbour front, and its loggia was used by merchants (now a small theatre, the Teatro Libero).

Piazza Marina and La Cala

Map p. 23, 12.
Santa Maria dei Miracoli overlooks Piazza Marina, once a shallow inlet of the sea. Here 16th-century Aragonese weddings and victories were celebrated by jousting. Later, in the proximity of two prisons (the Vicaria and that of the Inquisition), public execu-

West front of the church of San Francesco d'Assisi.

tions were held here: condemned prisoners were burnt alive, or hung, drawn and quartered. The centre is occupied by the Giardino Garibaldi, with fine palms and enormous Morton Bay figs, *Ficus magnoloides*.

At the seaward end of Piazza Marina is Palazzo Chiaramonte, known as **Lo Steri** (i.e. *hosterium*, or fortified palace), which was occupied by the law courts from 1799 until 1972. The building was restored in 1984 by the University to serve as Rectorate (sometimes open for concerts or exhibitions). Begun in 1307 by the Chiaramonte family, it became the palace of the Spanish viceroys. From 1605–1782 it was the seat of the Inquisition; the graffiti which survive on the prison walls provide a fascinating historical record of the persecutions. The exterior, though deprived of its battlements, retains several of its original windows. Inside are two rooms with wooden ceilings painted by Simone da Corleone and Cecco di Naro (1377–80), in Moorish style.

Beyond the last side of the square is **La Cala**, a shallow basin recently cleaned up and dragged (2005; the most amazing wrecks were found on the seabed, some of which will be restored) for use as a yachting harbour. It is all that remains of the Phoenician port which once extended far into the old town. There are three churches here. On the corner by the corso is the church of **San Giovanni dei Napoletani** (1526–1617). The harmonious interior has a magnificent 17th-century organ by Raffaele La Valle, with its choir-loft decorated with 15 panels, perhaps the work of Vincenzo da Pavia, and a *St John the Baptist* by Zoppo di Gangi.

On the other side of the corso is the late 15th-century church of **Santa Maria della Catena** (*open Mon–Fri 9–12*), probably the work of Matteo Carnelivari (1502–34). Its name *catena* (chain) probably comes from the chain that used to close the old port: it stretched from this bank across the harbour to Castello a Mare. There is also a legend that three innocent people were condemned in 1391 and as custom demanded, were sent to spend the night in this church in prayer; as they prayed their chains dropped from them and they were spared.

A flight of steps leads up to the three-arched porch, which, with its two corner-pilasters, provides an ingenious combination of Gothic and Renaissance styles. The delicate carving of the three doorways is attributed to Vincenzo Gagini. The elegant interior has been beautifully restored. In the first south aisle chapel, under a 16th-century canopy, is a lovely 14th-century fresco of the *Madonna and Child*, discovered in the 1980s. The four statues are by the Gagini school. In the second chapel is a late 15th-century relief of the *Madonna and Child with Angels* from the church of San Nicolò alla Calza. In a chapel with a 16th-century relief are frescoes by Olivio Sozzi (*see p. 321*). The sanctuary is particularly beautiful with elaborate Gothic decoration and double columns.

In the corner of the piazza is the outstanding **Fontana del Garraffo** (Paolo Amato, 1698), a sumptuous piece of Baroque street furnishing surrounded by a little garden. The slender little figure on the top represents *Abundance Chasing Away the Hydra Monster*.

The lower end of the corso, the Cassaro Morto, was virtually destroyed in 1943; the Fontana del Cavallo Marino, with a seahorse by Ignazio Marabitti, is now surrounded by palm trees. The reconstructed Porta Felice (1582–1637) has no arch between the two monumental pillars to allow the tall *vara* (or 'float') of St Rosalia to pass through it on her feast day. The long 17th-century façade of Palazzo Butera stands above the terraced **Mura delle Cattive**, or 'Wall of the Bad Women' (*open 10–7*). The name may refer to a time when women caught in adultery were exposed to public ridicule. Alternatively, it may refer to the widows who, for reasons of decorum, could not take their *passeggiata* with other ladies along the Foro Italico, so they passed the time here in malicious gossip. The busy, broad Foro Italico which runs outside the walls offers a splendid view of Monte Pellegrino, and a large public garden has recently been created on the seafront.

Museo Internazionale delle Marionette Antonio Pasqualino

Map p. 23, 12. *Open Mon–Fri 9–1 & 4–7. www.museomarionettepalermo.it*
At no. 5 Piazza Niscemi is the Museo Internazionale delle Marionette Antonio Pasqualino (International Marionette Museum) founded in 1975. There is a delightful collection of puppets from Sicily and Naples, as well as from Africa, the New Hebrides, Vietnam, Korea, Burma, China, and India (particularly Rajasthan), shadow puppets from Malaysia, Cambodia, and Java and Professor Jingles' Punch and Judy theatre from England, all beautifully displayed.

OPRA DEI PUPI

Sicily has long been famous for its puppet theatres, known as the *opra dei pupi*. In the 19th century, at the height of their popularity, the most important puppet theatres on the island were in Palermo, Trapani, Sortino, Syracuse, Caltagirone, Acireale and Catania. In the 1960s, puppet theatres languished and many closed down, but recently there has been a revival of this traditional entertainment. The puppets, which vary in size from Palermo (small, with jointed knees) to Catania (large, even 30kg, stiff legs), are made of wood, with shiny armour. The puppeteer, who stands on a wooden platform just above the stage, manoeuvres them by using quite heavy iron bars. However cumbersome they may look offstage, they immediately come to life when brought into the scene, and swagger into position with great panache. The plays focus on chivalric episodes in the lives of the paladins of Charlemagne's court, portrayed through the various heroic deeds of Orlando, Rinaldo, Astolfo and others who challenge the Saracens. The key moment in every play is the battle, enacted in the traditional style, with much foot stamping, blood spurting, heads rolling, corpses piling up on both sides of the stage (Christians on one side, Muslims on the other), even the occasional dragon or wizard putting in an appearance. Garibaldi is also a source of inspiration for the *pupari*, as is King Arthur of the Round Table. The Sicilian puppet theatre has been declared a Masterpiece of Intangible Heritage by UNESCO.

Santa Maria della Pietà

Map p. 23, 12. *Open Mon–Sat 8–1 & 4–7.*

Via Butera continues (past a plaque on a wing of Palazzo Butera recording Goethe's stay here in an inn on this site in 1787) to the church of Santa Maria della Pietà, with a splendid Baroque façade by Giacomo Amato (1678–84). The interior is a particularly striking example of local Baroque architecture. The delightful vestibule has stuccoes by Procopio Serpotta and frescoes by Borremans: it supports a splendid nuns' choir. Four choir-screens in gilded wood decorate the nave. The fresco in the vault is by Antonino Grano (1708). The first south altar has a painting of Dominican saints by Antonio and Francesco Manno, and the second, a *Madonna of the Rosary* by Olivio Sozzi. The high altar has a tabernacle in lapis lazuli. The third north altar has a *Pietà* (in the beautiful original frame) by Vincenzo da Pavia and the second, *St Dominic* by Olivio Sozzi.

Galleria Regionale della Sicilia

Map p. 23, 12. *Open 9–1 & 2.30–7; Mon, Sat, Sun and holidays 9–1.*

At no. 4 Via Alloro is Palazzo Abatellis, designed in 1488–95 by Matteo Carnelivari for Francesco Abatellis, appointed 'master-pilot' (or admiral) of Sicily by the

Spaniards, in a style combining elements of the Renaissance with late Catalan-Gothic. Much altered internally during its occupation by Dominican nuns from 1526 until 1943, when it was damaged by bombs, the palace was freely restored in 1954 as the home of the Galleria Regionale della Sicilia. This is a superb collection of Sicilian sculpture and paintings, well documented and beautifully arranged.

Ground floor

A doorway of original design leads out to the courtyard. The ground floor is devoted principally to sculpture.

Room 2: The former chapel is dominated by a famous large fresco of the *Triumph of Death*, detached from Palazzo Sclafani. Dating from c. 1449 it is of uncertain attribution, thought by some scholars to be a Sicilian work and by others to be by Pisanello or his school. Death is portrayed as an archer on a spectral horse, killing the contented and successful (right) with his arrows, while the unhappy, sick and aged (left), among whom are the painter and a pupil, pray in vain for release. The painting has provided inspiration for several artists, among whom Pablo Picasso (*Guernica*).

Room 3: A corridor containing Saracenic ceramics, including a magnificent **majolica vase** of Hispano-Moresque type (13th–14th century), thought to come from Malaga, leads to three rooms devoted to late 15th- and early 16th-century sculpture.

Room 4: Works by Francesco Laurana, principally a bust of **Eleonora of Aragon** (1475), his masterpiece. The works of Laurana were 'rediscovered' in the 19th-century, when his concentration on austere geometrical forms in his aristocratic sculptural portraits was recognised as a distinctive and highly individual new departure. Eleonora, daughter of Ferdinand I, King of Naples, married Ercole d'Este Duke of Ferrara, gave him three children, and presided over a particularly rich period in that city's history.

Rooms 5: Devoted to the Gagini (*see p. 423*); particularly notable are a marble statuette of the *Madonna and Child,* the *Tabernacle of the Ansalone*, the *Madonna of the Good Rest* (1528), and the head of a young boy, all by Antonello Gagini.

Room 6: Contains architectural fragments.

First floor

The first floor is reached by a staircase from the courtyard. It contains the **Picture Gallery** (pinacoteca), with its authoritative series of Sicilian paintings, including 13th–14th-century works, still in the Byzantine manner, and later works showing the influence of various schools (Umbrian, Sienese, Catalan, and Flemish).

Detail from *The Triumph of Death* (c. 1449).

The *Virgin Annunciate* (c. 1474–77) by Antonello da Messina.

Room 7: Contains the *Raising of Lazarus* and *Christ in Limbo*, two small paintings, perhaps Venetian, of the 13th century; a painted 13th-century Crucifix; and other early works.

Room 8: Paintings of the late 14th and early 15th centuries.

Room 9: Early 15th-century Sicilian paintings, including several *Coronations of the Virgin* by the same unknown master, and works by the 'Master of the Trapani Polyptych'.

Room 10: A precious collection of works by Antonello da Messina, including the stunning painting universally considered to be his masterpiece, the **Virgin Annunciate**, and *Sts Gregory, Augustine and Jerome*.

Room 11: Late 15th-century paintings and frescoes by Tommaso de Vigilia and a Crucifix by Pietro Ruzzolone and works by Riccardo Quartararo, notably *Sts Peter and Paul* (1494) and *Coronation of the Virgin*.

Room 12: The upper half of the chapel overlooks the *Triumph of Death* (*see above*) and contains 16th-century works including Andrea da Salerno's *Sts John the Baptist and John the Evangelist* and a copy (1538) of Raphael's *Spasimo* (*see p. 51*)

Room 13: A number of 16th-century works, most notably, by Mabuse, the **Malvagna Triptych** (after 1511) of the *Virgin and Child between Sts Catherine and Barbara* (on the outside, *Adam and Eve*), a painting of extraordinary detail.

Room 14: Paintings by the Tuscan school of the 16th century.

Room 15: 15th–16th-century Flemish paintings: an *Annunciation*, in the style of the Master of Flémalle; works of the 16th-century Antwerp and Bruges schools.

Room 16: Works by Vincenzo da Pavia: *Deposition*, *St Conrad the Hermit* and two scenes from the life of the Virgin. Also Giuseppe Cesari's *Andromeda*; Pietro Novelli's *Communion of St Mary of Egypt* and *Madonna in Glory* (1637); Van Dyck (copy), *Madonna*, his early masterpiece; Leandro Bassano, *Portrait of a Man*.

Antonello da Messina (c. 1430–79)

Antonello da Messina, born around 1430 in Messina, was one of the masters of the Italian Renaissance and the greatest southern Italian painter. Antonello made a number of journeys from Sicily including several to Naples, where he studied with Colantonio, and to Venice (in 1475, four years before his death). His work shows the influence of the Flemish school, particularly Jan van Eyck, in its attention to detail and particular sense of light. He was one of the earliest Italian painters to perfect the technique of painting in oil, and he had an important influence on Giovanni Bellini. His son, Jacobello, and his nephew Antonello de Saliba, were also painters.

La Gancia

Map p. 23, 12. *Open Mon–Sat 9.30–12 & 3–6; Sun and holidays 10–12.30.*
Next to Palazzo Abatellis (at no. 27) is the 15th-century church of La Gancia, or Santa
Maria degli Angeli, entered by the side door. The fine exterior dates from the 15th
century. In the interior (lights in each chapel) the wooden ceiling and 17th-century
organ (no longer in use) date from the transformation begun in 1672. In the second
chapel of the south aisle are Antonello Crescenzio, *Madonna with Sts Catherine and
Agatha* (signed and dated 1528), Pietro Novelli (attributed), *Holy Family*; in the fourth
chapel: Antonello Gagini (attributed), seated *Madonna* (the head of the Christ Child
is modern); fifth and sixth chapels, inlaid marble panels with scenes of the *Flight into
Egypt*: outside is a pulpit made up of fragments of sculpture by the Gagini. The chapel
to the right of the choir has fine marble decoration and stuccoes by Giacomo Serpotta.
On the choir-piers are two delicately carved *Annunciations* attributed to Antonello
Gagini. In the chapel to the left of the choir are more stuccoes by Serpotta, and a
Marriage of the Virgin by Vincenzo da Pavia. North transept: on the wall (high up), *St
Francis* by Zoppo di Gangi. North aisle: in the sixth chapel are two fine reliefs (one of
the *Descent into Limbo*) by Antonello Gagini; in the third chapel, Pietro Novelli's *St
Peter of Alcantara*, and in the second, Vincenzo da Pavia's *Nativity*.

The adjoining convent is famous in the annals of the revolution of 4th April 1860
against Neapolitan rule. The convent bell gave the signal to the insurgents; Francesco
Riso, their leader, was mortally wounded, 13 were captured and shot while two hid
for five days in the vaults of the church, before escaping through the *Buca della
Salvezza*, a hole in the wall next to Palazzo Abatellis.

Via Alloro, a narrow medieval street with some aristocratic palaces, only now
recovering from Second World War bombing, continues back from the church of La
Gancia towards the centre of the city. On the right is the church of the **Madonna
dell'Itria dei Cocchieri** (*open 8.30–3.30; Sat 9–1; Sun and holidays closed*), once the
seat of the confraternity of coachmen. Built in 1596, it has a crypt with 18th-century
frescoes.

THE KALSA DISTRICT

From the seaward end of Via Alloro, Via Torremuzza leads past the church of the
Crociferi or San Mattia, by Giacomo Amato. Further on is the façade (1686–1706) of
the church of **Santa Teresa alla Kalsa** (*open 8–11 & 4.30–6; closed Thur morning*), also
by Amato, and one of his best works. In the interior, the first south chapel contains
Giovanni Odazzi's *Holy Family* (1720); and the second has Ignazio Marabitti's marble
Crucifixion (1780–81). The high altarpiece is by Gaspare Serenario (1746) and the two
statues of female saints in the sanctuary are by Giacomo Serpotta. The second north
altarpiece is by Guglielmo Borremans (1722) and the first is by Sebastiano Conca.

The church faces Piazza della Kalsa (from the Arabic *al halisa*, meaning the elect). This
was one of the oldest parts of the city, fortified by the Arabs in 938. The stately 17th-
century **Oratorio dei Bianchi**, incorporating the church of Victory, built over one of the

gates of the Kalsa citadel, has been restored and is now used as an exhibition venue. The Quartiere della Kalsa is a very poor district, badly damaged by bombs in the Second World War and now under repair.

La Flora and the Botanical Gardens

Map p. 23, 16. *Open Mon–Fri 9–5; Apr–Oct also Sat, Sun and holidays 9–1; closed 25 Dec, 1 Jan, 1 May and 15 Aug; entrance through side gate.*

Via Niccolò Cervello ends at Viale Lincoln across which is the entrance to **Villa Giulia** (*open 8–8*) or La Flora, a delightful garden laid out in 1777, with beautiful trees (the tallest in Palermo) and flowers, much admired by Goethe in 1787. In the centre are four niches in the Pompeian style, and a sundial fountain; towards the sea is another statue of the *Genius of Palermo*, by Marabitti. The **Botanical Garden**, adjoining the Villa, is remarkable for its subtropical vegetation, and one of the loveliest in Europe. The entrance pavilion was built in Greek-Doric style in 1789 by Léon Dufourny; Venanzio Marvuglia worked on the decoration and added the side wings. The garden was laid out by Filippo Parlatore, the important Italian botanist who was born in Palermo. It was opened to the public in 1795. It has ficus trees, bamboo, date palms, lotus trees and many other plants from all over the world. The circular water-lily pond dates from 1796.

Santa Maria dello Spasimo

Map p. 23, 16. *Open 9–11.45.*

From beside the church of Santa Teresa, Via Santa Teresa and Via dello Spasimo lead away from the sea through the Kalsa district to the former church and convent of Santa Maria dello Spasimo, beautifully restored as a cultural centre for exhibitions, concerts and theatre performances. Founded in 1509, the church and convent were never completed, as the area was taken over by the Spanish viceroy in a general plan of strengthening the city's defences. In 1573 the convent was sold to the Senate and the church was used as a theatre after 1582, and again at the end of the 17th century. Part of the convent became an isolation hospital for plague victims in 1624, and in the 19th and 20th centuries it was used as a general hospital. Over the centuries the buildings have been adapted as warehouses, a deposit for the snow brought down from the mountains for making ice creams, and as storage for the débris after the bombardments of the Second World War. After the hospital was finally closed in 1986 a remarkable restoration programme began in 1988.

Beyond the 16th-century cloister is the church (roofless except for the beautiful Gothic apse vault), which has been made safe, leaving a few trees growing in the nave. In 1516 Raphael was commissioned to paint for this church an altarpiece of *Jesus Falling Beneath the Cross*. It came to be known as *Lo Spasimo di Sicilia*; a copy (1538) by Antonello Crescenzio can be seen in the Galleria Regionale. After an adventurous journey, during which, according to Vasari, the painting was lost at sea in a shipwreck, but subsequently discovered on the shore near Genoa, it was finally installed here in 1520. The Spanish viceroy presented it to Philip IV of Spain in 1661 and it is now in the Prado in Madrid. Several copies were made of the painting, and some experts believe that the original may now be in the Prefecture of Catania. The original frame by Antonello Gagini is to be re-installed here, having been found recently in a villa garden in Bagheria and restored by the Fondo per l'Ambiente Italiano. Beyond the church is a little public garden on the bastions, and another chapel used for exhibitions.

Piazza Magione

Map p. 23, 16.

Just beyond Lo Spasimo is Piazza Magione. In the centre, between two agaves, is a small memorial plaque to Giovanni Falcone, who was born in this district in 1939. It was set up by the city of Palermo in 1995, 'in gratitude and admiration' for this courageous magistrate who was assassinated by the Mafia in 1992. At the beginning of Via Castrofilippo is the little **Teatro Garibaldi**, built in 1861, and visited by Garibaldi himself in 1862. Also on this side of the piazza is the fine Norman apse of the church of **La Magione** (*open 9.30–6.30*), which stands in majestic isolation, painstakingly restored after the Second World War bombing devastated the neighbourhood. It was founded for the Cistercians by Matteo d'Aiello before 1151 as the Chiesa della Trinità, but transferred to the Teutonic knights in 1193 by Emperor Henry VI as their mansion, from which it takes its name. It is a precious example of Arab-Norman architecture. The interesting façade has three handsome and very unusual doorways. The beautiful tall interior has a fine apse decorated with twelve small columns. Above the 14th-century stone altar hangs a painted Crucifix. The contents include statues of Christ and also the *Madonna and Child* by the Gagini school, a 15th-century marble triptych, and a tabernacle of 1528. The custodian will show you the charming little Cistercian cloister of c. 1190 around a garden (*open daily except Sun and holidays 9.30–6.30*); one walk with twin columns and carved capitals has survived. A room off the cloister contains a detached 15th-century fresco of the *Crucifixion* with its sinopia. Outside is a delightful garden and a monumental 17th-century gateway on Via Magione.

Via Magione leads to Via Garibaldi, a dilapidated street with some handsome palaces and opulent balconies. Here is **Palazzo Ajutamicristo**, built by Matteo Carnelivari in 1490, with Catalan-Gothic elements (*the courtyard is entered from no. 23; accommodation is available here, see p. 114, and visits can be arranged for small groups by previous arrangement, T: 091 6161894, www.palazzoajutamicristo.com*). Charles V was entertained here on his return from Tunis in 1535. Via Garibaldi, and its continuation south, Corso dei Mille, mark the route followed by Garibaldi on his entry into the city. At the end is **Piazza della Rivoluzione**, the scene of the outbreak of the rebellion of 1848, inspired by Giuseppe La Masa, and mercilessly crushed by the Bourbon troops; even today people use the expression *un quarantotto*, a forty-eight, to mean a total disaster. A fountain here depicts the *Genius of Palermo*. Near the 16th-century Palazzo Scavuzzo is the church of San Carlo (1643–48) with an elliptical interior.

The west end of Piazza Aragona just north of here leads into **Piazza della Croce dei Vespri**, where the graves of many French victims of the Sicilian Vespers were marked in 1737 by a cross. Two sides of the piazza are occupied by the fine 18th-century Palazzo Valguarnera-Ganci, still owned by the family. Visconti used the sumptuous Salone degli

Specchi as the setting for the scene of the great ball in his film *The Leopard*, based on the novel by Giuseppe Tomasi di Lampedusa (*see p. 217*). Nearby is the church of **Sant'Anna** (undergoing restoration) with a fine Baroque façade begun in 1726 by Giovanni Biagio Amico, with sculptures by Giacomo Pennino and Ignazio Marabitti, on designs by Giacomo Serpotta. The interior dates from 1606–36, with frescoes in the south transept by Filippo Tancredi. The enormous, long-abandoned convent next door now houses the **Galleria di Arte Moderna E. Restivo** (*open Tues–Sat 9–8; Sun and holidays 9–1; closed Mon. T: 091 6090308.*) founded in 1910, with 19th- and 20th-century works, mostly by artists from Sicily and southern Italy.

SAN DOMENICO & MUSEO ARCHEOLOGICO

Close to the Quattro Canti, left off Corso Vittorio Emanuele, Via Roma heads north passing (right) the church of **Sant'Antonio di Padova**, which occupies the highest point of the eastern part of the old city. The 14th-century campanile was lowered in height at the end of the 16th century, and the church reconstructed after the earthquake of 1823 in the medieval style of the original. Inside there is a splendid gold-and-blue painting of the *Immaculate Conception*, by Pietro Novelli.

Steps lead down beside the church into the maze of small streets around Piazza Caracciolo and Piazza Garraffello, the scene of a busy daily market known as the **Vucciria**, one of the most colourful sights in the city. All kinds of produce is sold on the streets here, including fish. In Piazza Garraffello is **Palazzo Lo Mazzarino**, where the father of the famous Cardinal Mazarin was born in 1576. The market extends along Via dei Cassari passing the 18th-century church of Santa Maria del Lume, designed by Salvatore Marvuglia. From Piazza Garraffello Via Materassai leads to Piazza San Giacomo La Marina and the 16th-century church of **Santa Maria la Nuova** (*open Mon–Sat 9–12 & 5–6.30*) with a Catalan-Gothic porch (the upper storey was added in the 19th century in neo-Gothic style). The fine interior contains stuccoes in the presbytery and 18th-century paintings.

Close by, towards the sea, you can see the well-sited late Renaissance façade of **San Sebastiano**. Inside are 18th-century polychrome marble altars, stuccoes by Giacomo Serpotta (1692) and 18th-century frescoes. Via Meli leads away from the sea back up towards Via Roma and Piazza San Domenico, in the middle of which rises the **Colonna dell'Immacolata** by Giovanni d'Amico (1724–27), crowned by a *Madonna*.

San Domenico

Map p. 23, 11. *Open Mon–Sun 9–11.30; Sat and Sun also 5–7; cloister by prior request.*
The large church of San Domenico, rebuilt in 1640, has an imposing façade of 1726 in grey and golden brown. Since the middle of the last century the church has served as a burial place for illustrious Sicilians. In the third chapel of the south aisle is a very fine statue of St Joseph by Antonio Gagini. The sixth chapel has a painting of St Vincent Ferrer by Giuseppe Velasquez (1787). The beautiful altarpiece of St Dominic in the south transept is by Filippo Paladini, and on the left wall there is a monument to

Giovanni Ramondetta by Giacomo Serpotta and Gerardo Scudo (1691). In the chapel to the right of the sanctuary is a fine bas-relief of St Catherine attributed to Antonello Gagini, a Neoclassical monument by Benedetto de Lisi (1864), a small *Pietà* in high relief by Antonello Gagini and a pretty little stoup. One of the organs dates from 1781; beneath the one on the right is a small Turrisi Colonna funerary monument, with a female figure by Antonio Canova.

The sanctuary has 18th-century choir stalls. The chapel to the left of the sanctuary has Gaginesque reliefs and the tomb of **Ruggero Settimo** (1778–1863), who convened the Sicilian parliament in this church in 1848. On either side of the altarpiece by Vincenzo da Pavia in the north transept, are funerary monuments by Ignazio Marabitti.

A bust of the painter Pietro Novelli (1608–47, *see p. 81*), is in the north aisle. In the fourth chapel is an altarpiece of *St Raimondo*, using his cloak as a sail, attributed to Filippo Paladini, while in the third chapel is a statue of St Catherine by Antonello Gagini (1527), with reliefs on the base, and on the right, a statue of St Barbara by his school. The second chapel has a terracotta statue of St Catherine of Siena, and the first an altarpiece by Andrea Carreca da Trapani. The fragmentary 14th-century cloister, which was part of the first church built on this site by the Dominicans, can only be visited by booking first.

Next to the church is a small museum dedicated to the Unification of Italy, the **Museo del Risorgimento** (*T: 091 582774, www.storiapatria.it*), with documents and memorabilia relating to this dramatic period of the history of Palermo.

Behind the church, in an area often called La Loggia because at its centre was the loggia of the merchants and bankers of Genoa, there are still many jewellery shops. In Via Bambinai is the **Oratorio del Rosario di San Domenico** (*open Mon–Sat 9–12.30, Sun and holidays closed; www.campodivolo.it/tesori*). The interior is dominated by the masterful, blue-and-red altarpiece by van Dyck, representing the *Virgin of the Rosary with St Dominic and the Patronesses of Palermo*. The artist painted it in Genoa in 1628, having left Palermo because of the plague. The wall paintings of the *Mysteries* are by Novelli (who was particularly influenced by van Dyck), Lo Verde, Stomer, Luca Giordano and Borremans. Giacomo Serpotta's graceful stuccoes (1720) display amazing skill. Statues of elegant society ladies represent various allegorical virtues. The black and white ceramic floor is also well preserved.

Santa Maria di Valverde

Open 9–12.30; closed Sun and holidays.
In the handsome Piazza Cavalieri di Malta, the church of Santa Maria di Valverde was built in 1635 by Mariano Smiriglio. It has a grey marble side portal, and a campanile rebuilt in 1723. The sumptuous Baroque interior (1694–1716), decorated with polychrome inlaid marble, was designed by Paolo Amato and Andrea Palma. On the high altar is an 18th-century wooden statue of the *Madonna of the Rosary* and a fine canvas of the *Madonna of Carmel*. The Virgin and Child are pictured holding the sacred scapula of

The *Madonna of Carmel* (1642) by Pietro Novelli in the church of Santa Maria di Valverde.

the Carmelite Order; to the left, St Theresa of Avila is about to receive from a cherub the emblematic burning arrow of her calling. Painted for this church by Pietro Novelli in 1642, the picture has recently been returned here from the Diocesan Museum. The vault fresco and those on the walls of the choir are by Antonio Grano, while the large one over the choir is by Olivio Sozzi (1750). The church has four highly elaborate altars, of which the most important is that of St Lucy (*see box, p. 349*), for whom there was a strong cult in Palermo. The lovely 15th-century statue of the saint, by an anonymous sculptor, has been replaced here, after being thought lost for more than a century. Dignified and solemn, the saint is wearing a blue dress.

Santa Cita and San Giorgio dei Genovesi

Map p. 23, 11. *Open 9–1.30; closed Sun and holidays. Entry by ticket only, available from the Oratorio del Rosario di Santa Cita.*
Via Bambinai continues as Via Squarcialupo, the large church on the left being Santa Cita or Santa Zita rebuilt in 1586–1603, and badly bombed in 1943. It was built in the early 14th century by a merchant from Lucca (hence the dedication to the 13th-century St Zita, long-suffering patroness of domestic servants, who hailed from there) together with a hospital for Tuscan merchants. In the 16th century the Dominican Fathers, who had acquired the church, allowed wealthy families to bury their dead here, thus ensuring a congruous income for their convent, and permitting the creation of the lavish funerary chapels. The interior contains fine but damaged sculptures by Antonello Gagini (1517–27). In the apse behind the altar is a marble tabernacle surrounded by a magnificent arch, both superbly carved. The splendid altarpiece is a panel painting by Filippo Paladini of *St Agnes of Montepulciano* (1603).

In the second chapel to the left of the choir is the sarcophagus of Antonio Scirotta, also by Gagini; and more sculptures by the same artist are in the second chapel (Platamone) to the right of the choir. The Chapel of the Rosary has refined polychrome marble decoration (1696–1722) and sculpted reliefs by Gioacchino Vitaliano. The crypt under the chapel of the Lanza family is now open to the public; it has an altarpiece of inlaid marble, and a sculpture by Giorgio da Milano.

Adjoining the left side of the church is the **Oratorio del Rosario di Santa Cita** (*usually entered from Via Valverde, opening times the same as above*), reconstructed in the early 17th century, approached through a little garden and loggia. The stucco decoration of the exquisite interior is one of Giacomo Serpotta's masterpieces: between 1685 and 1688 he worked on the nave and in 1717 on the apse. The name Serpotta was a popular generic name meaning snake or lizard; the sculptor often included either reptile in his works as a trademark. A native of Palermo, Giacomo was the son of the sculptor Gaspare Serpotta. He is widely credited with bringing the art of moulding stucco to a pitch worthy of the great stone carvers and ushering in the Rococo. On the entrance wall there is an elaborate representation of the Battle of Lepanto, which commemorates the victory over the Turks in which the Christian fleet was protected by the Madonna of the Rosary (the confraternity of the Rosary had been founded just before the battle in 1571). On the two side walls are New Testament scenes in high relief representing the 15

Mysteries of the Rosary between numerous seated allegorical statues. The decorative frames and stucco drapes are supported by hundreds of mischievous cherubs, for which Serpotta used the street urchins of Palermo as models. The altarpiece of the *Madonna of the Rosary* (1702) is by Carlo Maratta. The ebony benches with mother-of-pearl inlay are of 1702, while the beautiful inlaid marble floor is decorated with eight-pointed stars, symbol of the Madonna.

Nearly opposite Santa Cita is the fine 14th-century doorway of the Conservatorio di Musica. Close by is the isolated 15th-century church of **San Giorgio dei Genovesi** (*open 9–12.30; closed Sun and holidays; entry with ticket from Oratorio del Rosario di Santa Cita*), restructured for the Genoese merchants by Giorgio di Faccio in 1576–91, and intended to be an indication of their wealth and influence (at the time they were the most powerful

One of Serpotta's stucco cherubs (1685–88) modelled from life on a street urchin.

bankers and merchants in Sicily and the Kingdom of Naples). It has a sturdy, Renaissance façade with a newly restored portal; the single-nave interior with two side aisles is also in the purest Renaissance style. Marble tomb-slabs (17th and 18th centuries) cover the floor of the nave. Also the paintings, by Luca Giordano (*Madonna del Rosario*), Bernardo Castello, Filippo Paladini (*St Luke paints the Madonna*) and Palma Giovane (*Martyrdom of St George* and *Baptism of Christ*), have been cleaned and restored before being returned to this church for which they were painted (for many years they were kept in the Palazzo Abatellis gallery).

Beyond lies **Piazza delle Tredici Vittime**, where an obelisk commemorates 13 republicans shot by the Bourbons on 14th April 1860. A huge steel stele, 30m high, was set up here in 1989 to commemorate victims of the struggle against the Mafia. A fence protects recent excavations of 10th-century Arab buildings, and part of the Norman fortifications of the city (restored in the 16th century). To the southeast lies the Cala. Across the busy Via Francesco Crispi are remains of the fortress of **Castello a Mare** (*open Mon–Sat 9–7,*

Sun 9–2), used in the 12th century as a prison, and from the 13th century onwards as a barracks. It was partially restored in 1988–91. Nearby there are remains of an Arab tower.

In Via Cavour, on the other side of Piazza XIII Vittime, is **Villa Whitaker** (1885; now used by the Prefecture), surrounded by a garden. This was one of two properties in Palermo owned by the Whitaker brothers (*see p. 67*).

In front of Piazza San Domenico (*see above*), across Via Roma, the narrow Via Monteleone leads up behind the remarkable Art Deco post office (1933) to (no. 50) the **Oratorio di Santa Caterina d'Alessandria**. The oratory has been owned by the Knights of the Holy Sepulchre of Jerusalem since 1946 (*open Thur only 12–2.45*). The interior has fine stuccoes by Serpotta's son, Procopio (1719–26). It also contains two paintings by Zoppo di Gangi (*see p. 102*), and a *Madonna and Child* by Vincenzo da Pavia above a bench inlaid with ivory and mother-of-pearl. The polychrome marble floor dates from 1730.

Sant' Ignazio all'Olivella

Map p. 23, 11. *Open 9–10 & 5–6; Sat, Sun and holidays 9.30–12.30; call first to make sure T: 091 586867.*

The church of Sant'Ignazio all'Olivella, begun in 1598, has a fine 17th-century façade. The beautiful interior has a barrel vault designed by Venanzio Marvuglia (1772) with frescoes by Antonio Manno (1790). In the first chapel of the south aisle is Filippo Paladini's *St Mary of Egypt*; the second chapel has beautiful 17th-century inlaid marble decorations. In the south transept is an altarpiece by Filippo Paladini (*see p. 261*). The painting over the main altar of the *Trinity* is by Sebastiano Conca (*see p. 298*), and in the sanctuary are two statues by Ignazio Marabitti. In the left transept is an interesting altarpiece, of unusual design, of the *Martyrdom of St Ignatius* by Filippo Paladini (1613).

In the north aisle, the fifth chapel was sumptuously decorated in 1622 and has an altarpiece of *St Philip Neri* by Sebastiano Conca (1740) and two statues by Giovanni Battista Ragusa. The third chapel is also elaborately decorated with polychrome marble and semi-precious stones and an altar frontal in relief. The small fresco in the vault of the *Pietà* is by Pietro Novelli. In the first chapel the altarpiece of the *Archangel Gabriel* is also by Pietro Novelli.

In the Piazza is the façade, by Filippo Pennino, of the **Oratorio di Sant'Ignazio Olivella** or of San Filippo Neri (*open Mon–Sat 9–10 & 5–6; Sun and holidays 9.30–12, call first to make sure, number as above*). It has an interesting Neoclassical interior of 1769 by Venanzio Marvuglia. An early work by Palermo's most accomplished late 18th-century architect, in a relatively unadventurous style, it is decorated with splendid columns and capitals by Filippo Pennino. In the presbytery there is an elaborate sculpture with angels and cherubs by Ignazio Marabitti.

The narrow **Via Bara all'Olivella**, in front of the museum and the church of Sant' Ignazio, is one of the liveliest streets in Palermo, with craft shops, cafés, traditional restaurants and a puppet theatre. It leads to Piazza Verdi and the Teatro Massimo, from where Via Maqueda leads back to the Quattro Canti.

Museo Archeologico Regionale Salinas

Map p. 23, 7. *Open Mon 8.30–1, Tues–Sat 8.30–6.45, Sun and holidays 9–1.30.*
Adjoining the church is the former monastery, now the seat of the Museo
Archeologico Regionale Salinas, one of the finest museums in Italy, illustrating the history of western Sicily from prehistoric times to the Roman era. The museum was
founded in the early 19th century by the university. During that time it acquired various material, including the important Casuccini collection, the most representative
display of Etruscan antiquities outside Tuscany. Undergoing restoration, it also houses finds from excavations in the western part of the island, notably those of Selinunte.

Ground floor

In the centre of the small cloister (**1**) is a triton from a 16th-century fountain. Off this
cloister (right) **Room 2** is used for exhibitions.

Rooms 3 and **4:** Contain Egyptian and
Punic sculpture, including two
Phoenician sarcophagi of the 5th century
BC found near Palermo, and the *Pietra di
Palermo*, a black diorite slab whose
hieroglyphic inscription records the
delivery of 40 shiploads of cedarwood to
Pharaoh Snefru (c. 2700 BC), and which
has proved invaluable in dating ancient
Egyptian history; three pieces from the

same slab are in the museums of
London, Cairo and Berlin.

Room 5: The large cloister has a papyrus
pool in the centre. In the arcades (**a**) are
Roman fragments: in niches: *Zeus
Enthroned* (**b**) from Solunto, derived from
a Greek type of the 4th century BC, and a
colossal statue of *Emperor Claudius* (**c**), in
a similar pose. Here also is an interesting

MUSEO ARCHEOLOGICO
(GROUND FLOOR)

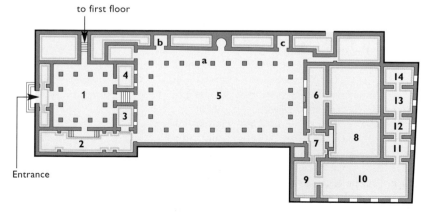

funerary stele with three portrait busts (40–30 BC).

Room 6: Greek inscriptions, the majority from Selinunte.

Room 7: Stelae from Selinunte, and a dedicatory inscription to Apollo from Temple G.

Room 8: Fragments of Temple C; part of the entablature has been assembled.

Room 9: A splendid cornice of lion-head water spouts from the Doric Temple of Victory at Himera (5th century BC), discovered by Pirro Marconi in 1929–30.

Room 10: Famous **metopes of Selinunte**, the most important treasures of the museum. These sculpted panels once decorated the friezes of the temples at Selinunte, and they show the development in the skill of the local sculptors from the early 6th to the end of the 5th centuries BC. On either side of the entrance are three delicate female heads and fragmentary reliefs from Temple E. Beneath the windows are six small Archaic metopes, sculptured in low relief, from an early 6th-century temple, perhaps destroyed by the people of Selinunte themselves to repair their citadel, in the time of Dionysius the Elder (397–392 BC). They represent scenes with Demeter and Persephone (one with a quadriga), three deities, a winged sphinx, the *Rape of Europa*, and *Hercules and the Cretan Bull*. Facing the windows is a reconstruction, incorporating original fragments, of a frieze and cornice with three triglyphs and three stunning Archaic metopes from Temple C (early 6th century), representing the four-horse chariot of Apollo; Perseus, protected by Athena, beheading the Gorgon; and Heracles punishing the Cercopes, the bandits who had attempted to steal his weapons. Also on this wall are parts of two metopes from Temple F, with scenes from the *gigantomachia* (5th century BC). Opposite the entrance, four splendid Classical metopes from Temple E (early 5th century) show Heracles Fighting an Amazon, the Wedding of Zeus and Hera, the Punishment of Actaeon, who is attacked by dogs in the presence of Artemis, and Athena overcoming a Titan.

Rooms 11–14: The Casuccini collection of Etruscan antiquities from Chiusi. Particularly interesting are the urns and tombs in high relief, a number of panels with delicately carved bas-reliefs (many with traces of painting), and a magnificent **oinochoe** of bucchero ware (6th century BC) portraying the story of Perseus and Medusa, perhaps the finest vase of its kind in existence.

First floor
The first floor is reached from the small cloister.

North gallery (Rooms 1 and **2**): Greek and Roman finds from sites in western Sicily, arranged topographically. Selinunte, Lilybaeum, Randazzo, the Aeolian Islands and Marsala are especially well represented. Between the

MUSEO ARCHEOLOGICO
(FIRST FLOOR)

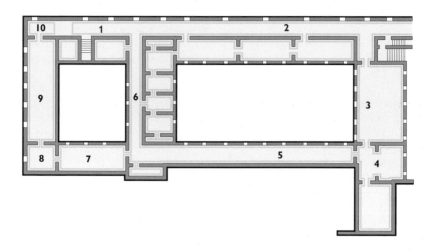

cases, containing vases, terracottas, and bronzes, are sepulchral stelae from Marsala painted with portraits of the deceased, and sections of lead water-pipes, showing junction points and stop-cocks from the Cornelian aqueduct at Termini Imerese.

Room 3: Terracotta figures, mainly from Gela, Himera, and Palazzolo Acreide.

Room 4: More terracottas and a 5th-century kylix fished from the sea off Termini Imerese.

South gallery (Room 5): Contains some of the 12,000 terracotta votive figures found in the sanctuary of Demeter at Selinunte, which can be seen to demonstrate chronology through the evolution of their design.

West gallery (Room 6): Contains some of the more important recent finds from sites in Palermo (fine vases).

Room 7: Large Roman bronzes. The famous **ram** is a superb sculpture dating from the 3rd century BC, probably modelled on an original by Lysippus (or even the work of Lysippus himself) and formerly one of a pair. Up until 1448 they were on the front of the Castello Maniace in Syracuse; in the 18th century they were admired by Jean Houel and Goethe in the Royal Palace in Palermo. The second ram was destroyed in 1848 by a cannon shot. The very fine *Hercules Fighting a Stag* is a Roman copy of a 3rd-century BC original. It decorated a fountain at Pompeii, and was donated to the museum by Francesco I of Bourbon, as his personal inauguration gift.

Room 8: Devoted to **Greek sculpture**: in the centre is a *Satyr Filling a Drinking Cup*, a Roman copy from Torre del Greco of a Praxitelean original. Further items displayed here are a portrait of Aristotle, a Roman copy of an original of c. 330 BC, beautiful 5th-century reliefs and stelae, and a fragment of the frieze of the Parthenon.

Room 9: Roman sculpture: reliefs of vestal virgins, and *Mithras Killing the Bull,* a 2nd-century sarcophagus. On the floor a mosaic pavement (3rd century AD).

Room 10: Roman fragments on the landing at the head of the stairs. Nearby is a small chapel (*usually closed*), which is part of the 17th-century convent.

Second floor: This floor surrounds the Large Cloister. It contains a superb collection of Greek vases. At the top of the stairs to the right is the short gallery with proto-Corinthian pottery of the 7th century BC.

Long gallery: The long gallery has a splendid series of Attic black-figure vases (580–460 BC). Among the lekythoi with figures on a white ground is one (second central case) showing the *Sacrifice of Iphigenea*, signed by Douris. In the fifth central case is a red-figure stamnos with Hercules and the Hydra (480–460 BC).

In the room at the end (right) **red-figure vases** are displayed, including a hydra with the *Judgement of Paris*, and a bell-shaped krater with dionysiac scenes. Another room displays mosaic floors (1st century BC–4th century AD), mostly from Piazza Vittoria in Palermo.

The **wall-paintings** here include five from the 1st century BC from Solunto and a fragment (1st century AD) from Pompeii. The room at the end of the next long corridor contains Italiot vases (4th–3rd century BC), many with reliefs and traces of painting from Puglia, Campania and Sicily. The last long gallery contains the collection of prehistoric and Early Bronze Age material which comes mainly from northwest Sicily. Here are displayed casts of the fine incised drawings (late Palaeolithic) of **masked figures and animals** from Cave B at Addaura on Monte Pellegrino (*see p. 72*). Nearby are the bones of elephants, rhinoceros and hippopotami found in Via Villafranca, Palermo.

SANT'AGOSTINO & THE CAPO DISTRICT

From the Quattro Canti, Via Maqueda runs gradually uphill to the north, passing a large bombed site where the remains of the 14th-century church of Santa Croce and a few neighbouring buildings were demolished in 1981. Plans for the Quartiere del Capo, an important district in the centre of the city, owned by the Church, are uncertain. On its far side is Via Sant'Agostino, home to the **Mercato del Capo**, a businesslike street market for cloth, clothes and household goods, full of life and not unlike the souks in Damascus or Cairo.

Sant'Agostino

Map p. 22, 10. *Open Mon–Sat 7–12 & 4–6; Sun and holidays 7–12.*
Beyond the market, on the right, hidden by traders' stalls, is the church of Sant'Agostino. The unusual tall side portal (restored) is attributed to Domenico Gagini. The beautiful façade, on Via Maestri dell'Acqua, has a late 13th-century portal decorated with lava mosaic and a 14th-century rose window.

The interior, consisting of a single massive nave, was decorated with gilded stuccoes by Giacomo Serpotta and assistants from 1711, with numerous cherubs, statues and lunettes over the side altars. The first altar on the right has a panel painting by Simon de Worbrecht (16th century) of *Blessed William of Aquitaine*; the second altar, a 17th-century *Flight into Egypt*; the fourth altar, by Antonio Grano (17th century), *St Nicholas of Tolentino*; beyond the passage of the right entrance is the chapel of the Madonna del Soccorso, with a bas-relief of the *Eternal Father*. Left of the high altar is the chapel of the Crucifix, with a precious 17th-century reliquary. The fourth altar on the left hand side has a painting by Giuseppe Salerno (Zoppo di Gangi) of *St Thomas of Villanova* and stories from his life. To the left of the second altar is a monument to Francesco Medici, with his bust (1774; surmounted by a cockerel) by Ignazio Marabitti. The 16th-century cloister, with tall pulvins above its capitals, surrounds a little garden. The fine Gothic entrance to the chapterhouse was exposed here in 1962 and restored.

The Mercato del Capo and around

Via Sant'Agostino then widens and continues uphill to the next crossroads at the centre of the Mercato del Capo, the heart of the maze of narrow streets making up the Capo district. Via Porta Carini, with stalls selling fish, fruit and vegetables, leads to **Sant'Ippolito Martire** (1583), with a façade of 1728. A chapel off the south aisle contains numerous ex-votos, and in the north aisle is a damaged 14th-century Byzantine fresco of the Madonna. The 18th-century paintings include the high altarpiece of the *Martyrdom of St Hippolytus* by Gaspare Serenario.

Opposite is the church of the **Immacolata Concezione** (*open 9–12*) built in 1612. The interior, one of the most beautiful in the city, was elaborately decorated during the 17th century with paintings, sculptures, singing galleries, inlaid marble altars, and a sumptuous organ. On the gilded stucco ceiling is a fresco by Olivio Sozzi.

At the end of the street is the Porta Carini, the only one of the three gateways to have survived at the northern limit of the old city, although even this was reconstructed in 1782.

From the crossroads of the Mercato del Capo, Via Cappuccinella continues through the food market and Piazza Sant'Anna al Capo in a very rundown area of the city. In Via Quattro Coronati (right) is the little church of the Quattro Coronati built in 1674. At the next crossroads, Via Matteo Bonello and Via del Noviziato lead right to the church of the **Noviziato dei Gesuiti**, in the area behind the law courts. Built in 1591, the interior preserves some fine 18th-century stuccoes and inlaid marble decoration, as well as an effigy of *St Stanislaus* by Giacomo Pennino (1725).

In the other direction, Via Matteo Bonello leads to the picturesque church of **Sant'Angelo Custode** (on the corner of Via dei Carrettieri), preceded by an outside stair. It dates from the early 18th century. To the west is the wide and busy Via Papireto across which is **Piazza Peranni**, where Palermo's famous flea market, the Mercato delle Pulci, is held.

Via Carrettieri returns down to the Mercato del Capo in Via Beati Paoli, which leads right to **Piazza Beati Paoli**, named after a much-feared secret society which operated in this area in the 17th century. The church of Santi Cosma e Damiano was built after the plague of 1575 and that of Santa Maria di Gesù was founded in 1660 (it contains a large 18th-century vault fresco). Via Beati Paoli continues past the church of San Giovanni alla Guilla, rebuilt in 1669 and badly damaged in World War II. On the right Vicolo Tortorici leads into Piazza Santi 40 Martiri with the church of **Santi Quaranta Martiri alla Guilla** (*open 9–5; Sat 9–1*), founded by some Pisan nobles in 1605 and rebuilt in 1725. It contains splendid frescoes by Guglielmo Borremans. The word *guilla* is derived from the Arabic *wadi*, or river, meaning the church was built on the banks of the river Papireto.

THE NINETEENTH-CENTURY CITY

At the north end of Via Maqueda is **Piazza Verdi**, laid out at the end of the 19th century, now one of the more central squares in the city. It is dominated by the opera house, **Teatro Massimo** (*open Tues–Sun 10–3.30; no visits during rehearsals; www.teatro-massimo.it*), by Giovanni Battista and his son Ernesto Basile from 1875–97, a huge Corinthian-style structure. Among the historic late 19th-century opera theatres in Europe, its stage is exceeded in size only by that of the Paris Opéra and the Vienna opera house. It was inaugurated in 1897 with Verdi's *Falstaff*. In the piazza in front of the theatre are two decorative little kiosks which used to be the ticket offices, also designed by Basile. The most famous architect in Palermo in the period before the First World War, Basile was particularly influenced by the Arab-Norman architecture of the city in developing his style.

From the piazza, Via Maqueda continues north by Via Ruggero Settimo, a street named after the much-loved patriot Ruggero Settimo, president of a short-lived independent Sicily in 1848, proclaimed in defiance of the Bourbons. The road is lined with clothes shops as far as the enormous double Piazza Ruggero Settimo and Piazza Castelnuovo, home to the **Politeama Garibaldi**. This 'Pompeian' structure (completed in 1874, by Giuseppe Damiani Almeyda) is crowned by a bronze quadriga by Mario Rutelli and is now used mostly for concerts, although originally designed to accommodate the circus.

Via Dante leads west out of Piazza Castelnuovo. Once very fashionable, there are several delightful Art Nouveau houses along its length, and it ends by the parks of Villa Serradifalco and Villa Whitaker Malfitano (*see below*). At no. 53 is a charming house, **Palazzo Ziino** (*open Tues–Sun 9.30–7.30*), used mainly for exhibitions, but there is an interesting cast gallery on the first floor, the only one in Sicily.

To the east, in Via Roma, is the **Grande Albergo e delle Palme** (formerly Palazzo Ingham). Richard Wagner stayed here in 1882 with his family and completed *Parsifal*. The building was modified in 1907 by Ernesto Basile. Viale della Libertà, a wide avenue laid out in 1860, with trees and attractive Art Nouveau houses, leads north. Beyond the two squares Mordini and Crispi, the road narrows. On the left it passes a statue of Garibaldi in a garden recently renamed after the magistrate Giovanni Falcone and his wife Francesca Morvillo, both assassinated by the Mafia in 1992.

Opposite is the larger **Giardino Inglese**, a delightful 19th-century public garden. It is bordered on the far side by Via Generale Dalla Chiesa which commemorates General Carlo Alberto Dalla Chiesa, prefect of the province and a *carabiniere*, who was assassinated by the Mafia here in 1982 (plaque), along with his wife and chauffeur, after just five months in office.

Further east towards the sea is the **Ucciardone**, built as a prison by the Bourbons in 1837–60, and now a maximum security jail, near the modern port of Palermo. At no. 134 Via Cristoforo Colombo is the **Museo del Mare** (*open 9.30–12.30, closed Mon*), a very interesting collection of objects relating to the sea, from fishing to shipbuilding—there are historical photos, model ships, cannons and an exhibition on lighthouses.

On the other side of Viale Libertà is **Villa Trabia**, seat of the Lanza di Trabia family, an elegant 18th-century building (now used as local government offices), with beautiful gardens open to the public (*open 8–6, entrance from Via Salinas*).

Across Via Notarbartolo, Viale della Libertà passes (left; no. 52) the head office of the Banco di Sicilia with the **Museo Archeologico della Fondazione Mormino** (*open Mon–Fri 9–1 & 3–5; Sat morning only; closed Sun, holidays and Aug, www.aesnet.it/fondasicilia*), which contains archaeological material from excavations financed by the Bank: a precious collection of Greek vases; Sicilian pottery dating from 15th–19th centuries; prints, maps and watercolours; and numismatic and philatelic collections (that representing the Kingdom of the Two Sicilies is unique in the world).

Viale della Libertà ends in the circular **Piazza Vittorio Veneto**, with its marble Nike monument to freedom. From here Via d'Artigliera (right) leads shortly to Piazza dei Leoni at the south entrance (c 4km from the Quattro Canti) to La Favorita.

THE WESTERN OUTSKIRTS

La Zisa

Map p. 22, 9. Open 9–6.30. Bus no. 124 from Via Mariano Stabile
The palace of La Zisa, now home to the **Museo d'Arte Islamica**, takes its name from the Arabic *al aziz* meaning magnificent. It is the most important secular monument of Arab-Norman architecture to survive in Sicily, and is purely Islamic in inspiration.

The fine exterior has a symmetrical design, although the double-light windows on the upper floors were all destroyed in the 17th century by the Sandoval, who set up their coat-of-arms on the façade and altered the portico. In King William's day the sandstone was faced with plaster decorated in a red and white design. The small pond outside, formerly part of the gardens, collected the water from the fountain in the ground floor hall, which was fed by a nearby Roman aqueduct. A damaged inscription in Kufic letters at the top of the east façade has not yet been deciphered.

HISTORY OF LA ZISA

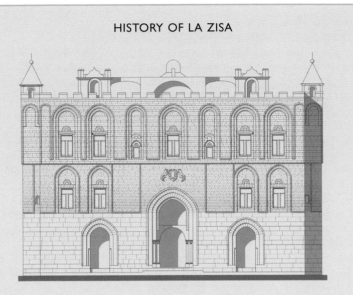

La Zisa was one of a group of palaces built by the Norman kings in their private park of Genoard (used as a hunting reserve) on the outskirts of Palermo. It was begun by William I c. 1164–65 and completed by his son. The palace is known to have been used by Frederick II, but it was already in disrepair in the late 13th century. It was fortified by the Chiaramonti in the 14th century. By the 16th century it was in a ruined state and was drastically reconstructed by the Spanish Sandoval family who owned it from 1635 to 1806. It was expropriated by the Sicilian government in 1955, but then abandoned until part of the upper floors collapsed in 1971. After years of neglect, a remarkable restoration programme was begun in 1974 and it was finally opened to the public in 1990. The structure had to be consolidated throughout, but the astonishing architecture has been preserved. As a finishing touch, the magnificent gardens have recently been imaginatively re-created, with lily ponds, fountains and walks.

The interior

The beautiful interior of the palace is on three floors. The exceptionally thick outer walls (1.9 metres on the ground floor), the original small windows and a system of air vents (also found in ancient Egyptian buildings) kept the palace protected from the extremes of hot and cold. The rooms were all vaulted: the square rooms with cross vaults and the oblong rooms with barrel vaults. Amphorae were used in the construction of the vaults to take the weight of the foundations of the floors above. Some of the vaults have had to be reconstructed in reinforced concrete. The pavements (very few of the original ones remain) were in tiles laid in a herring-bone pattern, except for the ground floor hall which was in marble. The miniature stalactite vaults (known as *mouqarnas*) which decorate niches in some of the rooms and the recesses of many of the windows are borrowed from Arab architectural styles.

On the ground floor are explanatory plans and a display illustrating the history of the building. A model in plexiglass shows the parts where it had to be reconstructed and where iron girders have been inserted to reinforce the building. The small rooms here were originally service rooms or rooms used by court dignitaries. The splendid central hall, used for entertainments, has niches with stalactite vaults. Around the walls runs a mosaic frieze which expands into three ornamental circles in the central recess.

The Norman mosaics (which recall those in King Roger's Room in the Royal Palace; *see p. 38*), show Byzantine, Islamic, and even Frankish influences. A fountain gushed from the opening surmounted by the imperial eagle in mosaic and flowed down a runnel towards the entrance to be collected in the fish pond outside. A majolica floor survives here and the faded frescoes were added in the 17th century. The little columns have beautiful capitals. On the inner side of the entrance arch is a damaged 12th-century inscription in large stucco letters.

Two symmetrical staircases led up to the first floor (replaced by modern iron stairways). Here the living rooms are connected by a corridor along the west front. Numerous fine vaults survive, and a series of air vents (*see above*). Egyptian Muslim objects, including metalwork, ceramics, and wooden lattice work, which served as windows, are displayed in some of the rooms, as well as amphorae found in the vaulting. On the top floor is a remarkable central hall with columns and water channels which was originally an open atrium surrounded by loggias, used in the summer. The small rooms on either side were probably a harem.

Around La Zisa

To the north of the Zisa, in Via dei Normanni, is the church of Gesù, Maria e Santo Stefano which incorporates a Norman chapel built at the same time as the palace. Nearby, at no. 4 Via Gili, is an auditorium and exhibition centre, known as the **Cantieri Culturali della Zisa**. In Piazza Zisa is the 17th-century church of the Annunziata, with Sandoval family funerary monuments.

Villa Whitaker Malfitano

Map p. 22, 5. Open 9–1, closed Sun and holidays, guided visits only; last tickets 12.30.
From the Zisa, Via Whitaker and Via Serradifalco lead north to Villa Whitaker Malfitano at no. 167 Via Dante. Built for Joseph (Pip) and Tina Whitaker by Ignazio Greco in 1887, the house became the centre of English society in Palermo at the

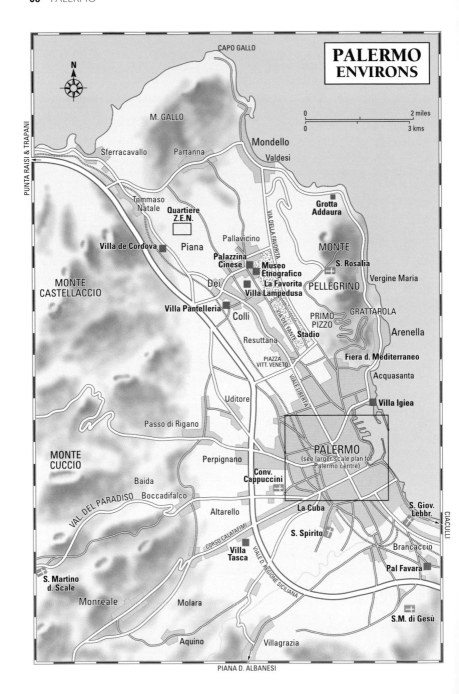

PALERMO ENVIRONS

beginning of the 20th century. The Whitakers were visited by Edward VII in 1907 and by George V and Queen Mary in 1925. Pip Whitaker, descendant of the famous Marsala wine merchants, was owner and excavator of Mozia and the house was left by his daughter on her death in 1971 to the Joseph Whitaker Foundation. The furnishings, Sicilian, French and English, are superb. It is surrounded by a magnificent park (nearly 7ha) of rare trees and plants collected by the owners, an orangery and an orchid nursery.

To the south of Villa Whitaker, at no. 38 Viale Regina Margherita, is the **Villino Florio** (*open 9–1*), one of Ernesto Basile's best works (1889), perfect Art Nouveau in style down to the smallest detail, and furnished by Ducrot. It has been lovingly restored after a fire in 1962, and is now open daily.

Convento dei Cappucini

Marked on the map opposite. *Open 9–12 & 3–5.30. Bus no. 327 runs from Piazza Indipendenza.*

South of La Zisa, at no. 1 Via Cappuccini, is the **Convento dei Cappuccini**, famous for its catacombs. Here, the bodies of priests and friars, aristocrats and wealthy citizens—adults as well as children—were dried by the Capuchins, dressed in their best finery, and hung up along the macabre underground passages in full view; this continued until 1881. There are still more than 6,000 bodies here, including that of a little girl who died nearly a hundred years ago, and was illegally mummified by a friar who died immediately afterwards, taking the secret of her perfect conservation to his tomb.

Outside Porta Nuova, **Corso Calatafimi** begins, which leads to Monreale. On the left is a huge charitable institute built in 1735–38 by Casimiro Agretta; the church façade (1772–76) is by Marvuglia. On the corner is a fountain of 1630, the only one to survive of the many which used to line the road. Opposite is the vast **Albergo dei Poveri**, an intimidating building (1746–72) by Orazio Furetto, built as the Poor House, recently restored and now used for important exhibitions.

La Cuba and the Punic necropolis

Marked on the map opposite. *Open 9–7; Sun and holidays 9–1. Bus no. 389 runs from Piazza Indipendenza.*

Beyond the Albergo dei Poveri are a series of barracks including (on the left, c. 1 km from Porta Nuova) the **Caserma Tuköry** (no. 100) where excavations since 1989 have revealed part of a huge Punic necropolis, with tombs dating from the 6th century BC. Here, separated from the barracks by a wall with a charming modern mural, is the entrance to La Cuba, a Norman palace built by William II (1180) in imitation of the Zisa. The name Cuba comes from the Arabic *kubbeh*, meaning dome. A copy of the Arabic inscription at the top of the outer wall and a model of the Cuba are displayed in a restored stable block. The building is now roofless and a few trees grow inside the walls. In one part are remains of a hall with miniature stalactite vaults, delicate reliefs, and a small cupola decorated with stuccoes. It was once surrounded by water, today replaced by a little garden.

Still further along Corso Calatafimi, opposite a department store and behind no. 575, a short road leads right to the remains of the now derelict 17th-century Villa Di Napoli. Here is the entrance to the delightful old-fashioned citrus grove complete with traditional irrigation methods, which still surrounds the **Cubula**, a little pavilion with its characteristic red dome, built by William I. Once surrounded by a fishpond, it is the only survivor of the many which used to decorate his private park in this area.

THE NORTHERN OUTSKIRTS & MONTE PELLEGRINO

La Favorita

Map p. 68.

La Favorita's extensive area of woods and gardens lies at the foot of Monte Pellegrino. The public park (nearly 3km long), is crossed by a one-way road system, and contains a hippodrome and other sports facilities. The city Stadium (right) and the Istituto Agrario (left) border the west side of the park on Viale del Fante. Just beyond Piazza Niscemi is the main entrance, Porta dei Leoni (c. 7km from the Quattro Canti), to the formal **Parco della Favorita**, an estate bought by Ferdinand of Bourbon in 1799, and laid out by him according to the taste of the times. The Palazzina Cinese (*no admission*), a charming Chinese-style building by Venanzio Marvuglia, was occupied by King Ferdinand and Queen Maria Carolina in 1799–1802 during their enforced exile from Naples under Napoleon. The collection of English prints was a gift from Nelson, when the king declared him Duke of Bronte here in October 1799. The **Museo Etnografico Siciliano Pitrè** (*open 8.30–8; closed Fri and mid-week holidays*) next door, was founded in 1909 by Giuseppe Pitrè. The museum has a wonderful collection illustrating Sicilian life through its customs, costumes, popular arts (such as painted carts and ex-votos), musical instruments, implements and typical everyday objects.

Piana dei Colli

Map p. 68.

The 18th-century summer villas built by the Palermitan nobility to escape the heat of the city between Monte Pellegrino and Monte Castellaccio are notable for their opulent design (often with elaborate outside staircases). In the 20th century many of them were demolished or left to decay, although some are now being preserved.

In Piazza Niscemi is the 18th-century Villa Niscemi (*park open daily 9–sunset, phone to book visit of villa, Sun and holidays 9–1, T: 091 740 4828*). Across Via Duca degli Abruzzi is the small early 18th-century Villa Spina which also has its own park. Nearby is **Villa Lampedusa**, built in 1770 and now used for concerts and exhibitions. This was bought by the Prince of Lampedusa, Giulio Tomasi c. 1845, and described in *The Leopard* by his great-grandson Giuseppe Tomasi.

At Acquasanta, on the coast, reached by Via Imperatore Federico from the south entrance of the Favorita, is the **Villa Igiea**, now a 5-star hotel in a large park. A remarkable Art Nouveau building, it was built as a sanatorium by the Florio at the end of the 19th century and transformed into a hotel in 1900 by Ernesto Basile.

Mondello

Map p. 68.

From the north end of the Parco della Favorita, a road runs through the suburb of Pallavicino and beneath the western slope of Mt Pellegrino, finally reaching the shore and the numerous villas of Mondello. One of the most noted bathing resorts in Sicily, a sandy beach extends for 2km from Monte Pellegrino to Monte Gallo. The opulent Art Nouveau-style restaurant, the Charleston (1910), which overhangs the water, was originally the bathing establishment from which society ladies could discreetly lower themselves into the sea. A garden city was laid out here by an Italo-Belgian society in 1892–1910. There are hundreds of little beach cabins which block the view, and devour much of the narrow beach, but Mondello still has plenty of devoted patrons. At the north end is the old fishing village of Mondello with a medieval tower. To the south is Valdesi, from where Lungomare Cristoforo Colombo returns towards the centre of Palermo following the rocky coast at the foot of Monte Pellegrino. Inland from Mondello is Partanna where the beautiful Villa Partanna survives from 1722–28. Above the promontory, Capo Gallo (527m) rises vertically from the sea (now a nature reserve).

THE FLORIO FAMILY

If Palermo in the 1890s was a capital city of the Belle Epoque, and if Mondello was the most fashionable bathing resort in the world, credit is certainly due to the Florio family . In 1893, when Ignazio married Donna Franca Jacona di San Giuliano, the most beautiful and fascinating woman in Sicily, he owned the Egadi Islands with the tuna fisheries, the Marsala wine company, and a fleet of 99 merchant ships. In 1906 his nephew Vincenzo launched the Targa Florio, a gruelling motor-race on the hair-raising roads of the Madonie Mountains, which still takes place today (for veteran cars only, T: 091 522090, www.targaflorio.tv and www.girodisicilia.com). Donna Franca's home in Palermo was a magnet for poets, artists, royalty and heads of state, while her Cartier jewellery was envied by Queen Mary. Although not untouched by personal tragedy, the Florios glittered on the social horizon of Palermo until well into the 1920s.

Monte Pellegrino

Between the Mondello road and the sea is Monte Pellegrino (606m), described by Goethe as the most beautiful headland in the world: it rises sharply on all sides except the south. The rock, in places covered with trees and cacti, has a remarkable golden colour. Almost certainly the ancient *Heirkte*, the headland was occupied by Hamilcar Barca in the First Punic War and defended for three years (247–244 BC) against the Romans. The Arabs called it *Gebel Grin*, hence the modern name Pellegrino. In the Addaura Caves (*closed due to rock falls*) on the northern slopes prehistoric rock carvings were discovered in 1952. The incised human and animal figures date from the Upper Palaeolithic period: they include an exceptionally interesting scene of uncertain significance with 17 human figures, some with animal masks, who appear to be carrying out a cruel ritual or dance. Plaster casts of the carvings can be seen in the Museo Archeologico Regionale (*see p. 62*).

The most direct approach to Mt Pellegrino from Palermo is from Piazza Generale Cascino, near the fair and exhibition ground (Fiera del Mediterraneo). From here Via Pietro Bonanno ascends to the Santuario di Santa Rosalia , crossing and recrossing the shorter footpath used by people making the annual pilgrimage on 3rd–4th September. A flight of steps zig-zags up the Scala Vecchia (17th century) between the Primo Pizzo (344m; left) and the Pizzo Grattarola (276m). The terrace of the rosy-pink Castello Utveggio (built as a hotel in 1932) provides the best view of Palermo.

Santuario di Santa Rosalia

A small group of buildings marks the Santuario di Santa Rosalia, at 428m, a cavern converted into a chapel in 1625 (*open 7–12.30 & 2.30–8*). It contains a statue of the saint by Gregorio Tedeschi, and a bas-relief of her coronation, by Nunzio La Mattina. The water trickling down the walls is held to be miraculous and is carefully captured by Futuristic-looking metal conduits. The outer part of the cave is filled with an extraordinary variety of ex-votos.

Rosalia, daughter of Duke Sinibald and niece of William II, lived here as a hermit until her death in 1166. She is supposed to have appeared to a hunter on Monte Pellegrino in 1624 to show him the cave where her remains were, since she had never received a Christian burial. When found, her relics were carried in procession through Palermo and a terrible plague, then raging in the town, miraculously ceased. She was declared patron saint of Palermo and the annual procession in her honour (14th–15th July), with a tall and elaborate float drawn through the streets by oxen, became a famous spectacle.

A steep road on the farther side of the adjoining convent climbs up to the summit, from which there is a wonderful view extending from the Aeolian Islands to Etna. Another road from the sanctuary leads to a colossal 19th-century statue by Benedetto de Lisi of St Rosalia, high on the cliff edge.

THE SOUTHERN DISTRICTS

Santo Spirito

Map p. 68. *Open 8–12; 15–20mins' walk from the station. Bus 108.*

From the station Corso Tukõry leads west to Porta Sant'Agata (follow the signs for *Policlinico/Ospedale*). Here Via del Vespro forks left; beyond the Policlinico and just across the railway are the flower stalls and stonemasons' yards outside the cemetery of Sant' Orsola, in the midst of which is the church of Santo Spirito or dei Vespri. This fine Norman church (1173–78) was founded by Gualtiero Offamiglio (Walter of the Mill), Archbishop of Palermo. It has a pretty exterior with arches and bands of volcanic stone and lattice-work windows. The interior has a restored painted wooden ceiling and a painted wooden 15th-century Crucifix.

THE SICILIAN VESPERS

On 31st March 1282 at the hour of vespers, a French soldier offended a young Sicilian bride in front of this church: her husband retaliated by strangling the soldier and the crowd immediately showed their sympathy by killing the other French soldiers present. Their action sparked off a rebellion in the city against the Angevin overlords and by the next morning some 2,000 Frenchmen had been killed. The revolt spread to the rest of the island and in the following centuries the famous 'Sicilian Vespers' came to symbolize the pride of the Sicilians and their struggle for independence from foreign rule. The revolt also had important consequences on the course of European history, as from this time onwards the political power of Charles of Anjou, who had the support of the Papacy, dwindled and he lost his ambition to create an Empire.

San Giovanni dei Lebbrosi and Ciaculli

From Porta Garibaldi near the station, Corso dei Mille leads south to the Oreto; this ancient thoroughfare was used by Garibaldi and his men on their entrance to the city. Just across the river is the **Ponte dell'Ammiraglio**, a fine bridge built by George of Antioch in 1113, and extremely well preserved. Since the river has been diverted it is now surrounded by a derelict garden and busy roads. Here the first skirmish between the Garibaldini and the Bourbon troops took place on 27th May 1860.

A short way beyond is Piazza Scaffa. On the left of the corso, hidden behind crumbling edifices (and now approached from no. 38 Via Salvatore Cappello), is **San Giovanni dei Lebbrosi** (*open Mon–Sat 9.30–11 & 4–5; closed Sun and holidays*), one of the oldest Norman churches in Sicily. Traditionally thought to have been founded by Roger I in 1072, it was more probably erected at the time of Roger II when a leper hospital was built here.

From Piazza Scaffa, Via Brancaccio leads south through the unattractive suburb of Brancaccio. Via Conte Federico continues to the **Castello del Maredolce** (or Favara), which is now in ruins and almost totally engulfed by apartment blocks. The palazzo, once surrounded on three sides by an artificial lake, was built by Emir Jafar in 997–1019, and was later used by the Norman kings and Frederick II. A chapel was built here by Roger II.

To the south, across the motorway, is the ruined 18th-century church of San Ciro near which the Grotta dei Giganti yielded finds of fossil bones. A road leads from here to the suburb of **Ciaculli**, where a huge estate once owned by the Mafia boss Michele Greco, is now farmed by a group of young people. Greco, known as *il Papa* (the Pope), was found guilty of some 100 murders and died in prison. The vegetation and landscape of the park is typical of the Conca d'Oro which once surrounded Palermo.

AROUND PALERMO

MONREALE

On the slopes of the mountain behind Palermo, overlooking the Conca d'Oro, Monreale is the site of one of the most superb churches in the world and certainly the most important Norman building in Sicily, with wonderful mosaics.

The duomo
Open 8–6. Treasury and terrace 9.30–12 & 3.30–5.30.

MONREALE DUOMO: WEST FRONT

Monreale grew up around William II's great church. Begun c. 1174, and already near to completion by 1182, it was one of the architectural wonders of the Middle Ages. In Piazza Vittorio Emanuele, with its Triton fountain by Mario Rutelli, is the usual entrance to the duomo, dedicated to the Madonna and called Santa Maria la Nuova, alluding to a new archbishopric created in her honour. It was the last and most beautiful of the Norman churches built in Sicily, as much for political as for religious motives, an immensely impressive structure high on the hill above Palermo.

THE CONSTRUCTION OF THE DUOMO

William II needed to create a new archbishopric and ensure the sympathy of its new incumbent in order to counterbalance the power of his former tutor, the English archbishop of Palermo, Walter of the Mill, who was supported by the Papacy. By handing over the cathedral to the Cluniac Benedictines, the king made a clever move: the abbot was automatically an archbishop in rank and his appointment needed no further approval, either from the Pope or from the clerics in Sicily, and the French monks had no sympathy for Walter, or for the Vatican. The King justified the enormous expenditure by telling of a dream he had while sleeping under a carob tree during a hunting expedition. The Madonna told him to dig under the tree and use the treasure he would find there to build her a great church. It is estimated that the mosaics were made with 2200kg of pure gold. Hundreds of the finest craftsmen from Constantinople were employed at great expense to expedite the work. The monolithic granite columns of the church came from a pagan temple or temples, the stone being northern European in origin, and some of them have been sawn in half, perhaps to complete a set from a number of damaged columns. The slender marble columns in the cloisters are believed by some scholars to have been brought here by the Benedictine monks from the sunken Roman city of *Baia*, near Naples. There they may once have formed the portico of a villa: some, especially on the east side, show traces of having spent years under the sea, the marble bored in places by a mussel, *Lithophaga mytiloides*. Baia, being subject to a volcanic phenomenon which causes the area to rise and sink alternately, may have been easily accessible at that time. The columns with their capitals do not fit the arches they support (*pictured on p. 80*), perhaps a last-minute adaptation made by the architects, to allow for their use.

The exterior
The façade, facing the adjoining Piazza Guglielmo, flanked by two square towers (one incomplete) and approached by an 18th-century porch, has a fine portal with a beautiful bronze door signed by Bonanno da Pisa (1186). The splendid apses, decorated with interlacing arches of limestone and lava, can be seen from Via del Arcivescovado. The entrance is beneath the portico along the north side built in 1547–69 by Gian

William II receiving the crown of Sicily from Christ, in the duomo of Monreale.

Domenico and Fazio Gagini, complete with benches. Here the portal has a mosaic frieze and a fine bronze door by Barisano da Trani (1179).

The interior

The interior (102m by 40m; *see plan opposite*), remarkably simple in design but glittering with golden and coloured mosaics covering a surface of over 6,400 square metres, gives an immediate impression of majesty and splendour. Similar in concept to the Cappella Palatina, the design is carried out on a much greater scale. Beyond the rectangular crossing, surmounted by a high lantern, with shallow transepts, is a deep presbytery with three apses, recalling the plan of Cluniac abbey churches. The stilted arches in the nave are carried on 18 slender columns with composite capitals, of Roman origin, all of granite except the first on the south side, which is of cipollino marble, representing the archbishop. The ceiling of the nave was restored after a fire in 1811, and then restored again in the 1980s when the 19th-century timber proved to be full of termites; that of the choir bears the stamp of Arab workmanship.

The magnificent series of mosaics tell in pictures the Old and New Testaments (coin-operated lights are essential to see the exquisite details; binoculars are useful). It is not known whether only Greek, or local craftsmen trained by Byzantine artists, were involved in this remarkable project, and the exact date of its completion, thought to be around 1182, is uncertain. The large scenes chosen to illustrate the theme of Christ's Ascension and the Assumption of the Virgin fit an overall scheme designed to celebrate the Norman monarchy and to emphasize its affinity with Jerusalem. Under the rich decoration of the upper walls runs an elegant marble and mosaic dado in Arab style.

Above the arcade in the nave the Genesis cycle in a double tier begins, starting on the upper tier at the eastern end of the south side with the *Creation* and continuing round the western wall and along the northern side to end (on the lower tier) with *Jacob's Dream* and *Jacob wrestling with the Angel*. In the crossing and transepts the story of Christ is illustrated from the Nativity to the Passion. The piers in the transept are covered on all sides with tiers of saints.

The aisle scenes show the Ministry of Christ. On either side of the presbytery are scenes from the lives of Sts Peter and Paul, whose figures are represented in the side apses. In the main apse is the mighty half-length figure of *Christ Pantocrator*, looking rather like an oriental pasha (which is undoubtedly what the craftsmen had in mind) with a solemn and rather severe expression on his face. Below is the enthroned *Madonna with Angels and Apostles*, and lower still, on either side of the east window, figures of saints including Thomas Becket, made within ten years of his martyrdom; Henry II of England was William II's father-in-law. Above the original royal throne (left) *William II Receives the Crown from Christ*; above the episcopal throne (right) *William Offers the Cathedral to the Virgin*. The floor of marble mosaic dates in its present form from 1559, but that of the transepts is the original 12th-century one.

The transept to the right of the choir contains the porphyry sarcophagus of William I (**1**; d. 1166) and that of William II (**2**; d. 1190) in white marble (1575). Here is the

MONREALE DUOMO

Treasury

Choir School

2

4

3

1

Capella del
Crocifisso

Capella San
Benedetto

Cloister

Dormitory

Entrance
North Door

Stairs up
to roof

Fountain

Entrance to
Cloister

New Convent

N

Cappella di San Benedetto (1569), with a relief of the saint by Marabitti (1760). To the left of the choir are the tombs (**3**) of Margaret, Roger and Henry, the wife and sons of William I, and an inscription (**4**) recording the resting-place (1270) of the body of St Louis when on its way back from Tunis; his heart remains buried here.

The treasury
The **treasury** (*admission fee*), which contains precious reliquaries, is entered through the splendid 17th-century Baroque **Cappella del Crocifisso**, by whose entrance is a marble tabernacle by the Gagini school. In the southwestern corner of the nave is the

Decorated column and carved capital in the Chiostro dei Benedettini.

entrance (*admission fee*) to the roof which provides wide views of the Conca d'Oro and the coast. Stairs (180 steps) and walkways lead across the roof above the cloisters and round the apses of the cathedral.

The cloisters

On the south side of the church are the lovely cloisters, the **Chiostro dei Benedettini** (*open Mon–Sat 9–7; Sun and holidays 9–1*) a masterpiece of 12th-century art, with Arab-Norman arches borne by 228 twin columns, with carved Romanesque capitals, of which very few are alike. Many of the columns are also decorated with mosaics or reliefs. They are the work of five master craftsmen, each of whom made some of the capitals, assisted by several apprentices, but only one capital is signed. A prolific confusion prevails of birds, animals, monsters, plants and people, representing religious scenes, mythology, Christian symbolism, and even the sacrifice of a bull to Mithras. The monks grew fruit trees in the enclosure (or *hortus conclusus*): trees symbolizing Paradise—palms, olives, figs and pomegranates. In the southwest corner, a stylized palm tree in a little enclosure of its own forms a charming fountain, used by the monks to wash their hands before entering the refectory; the symbolism of the various elements here alludes to the rite of baptism.

The town

A cool and shady public garden, called **Belvedere**, with lovely trees and views, is entered on the right of the façade of the new convent (1747), now a school. The restored 18th-century town hall occupies part of the Norman royal palace (remnants of which can be seen from behind). In the council chamber is a *Madonna with Two Saints* (in terracotta), attributed to Antonello Gagini (1528), and an *Adoration of the Shepherds*, by Matthias Stomer (17th century). Behind is Via Arcivescovado, from which the magnificent exterior of the east end of the cathedral can be seen. The choir school here incorporates some arches and windows of the Norman palace.

The little town also possesses some fine Baroque churches. The **Chiesa del Monte** in Via Umberto contains stuccoes by Serpotta and his school, and the *Madonna of the Constellation*, by Orazio Ferraro (1612). Higher up, on the left, is the **Collegiata**, with large 18th-century paintings in the nave by Marco Benefial, and an exquisite wood and tortoiseshell *Crucifixion* by Omodei (16th century; on the high altar). On the external wall of the apse is an outstanding panel of majolica tiles, showing the Crucifixion with Monreale in the background; it is probably the work of Giuseppe Mariani (early 18th century).

In Piazza Vaglica is the 18th-century Collegio di Maria close to the church of the Santissima Trinità, with a very elegant interior, and, in Via Venero, the church of **San Castrense**, the patron saint of Monreale, a pretty 18th-century building with stuccoes by the school of Serpotta and an altarpiece by the 17th-century Florentine sculptor Antonio Novelli (1602). High above Monreale is the 19th-century church of Madonna delle Croci, with a fine view.

SAN MARTINO DELLE SCALE

The road between Monreale and San Martino delle Scale ascends to Portella San Martino. Here a path climbs up through a pinewood to (c. 20mins) the **Castellaccio** (766m; *temporarily closed*), the southwestern summit of Monte Cuccio and a splendid viewpoint. The castle was a fortified monastery built by William II as a hospice for the convent of Monreale. It then passed to the Benedictines. Towards the end of the 18th century it was abandoned and fell into ruin until in 1899 it was purchased by the Club Alpino Siciliano. San Martino delle Scale (500m) is a hill resort in pinewoods. The huge Benedictine abbey of **San Martino** (*open 9–12 & 4–6; Sun and holidays 9.30–11.30 & 5–6.30*), possibly founded by St Gregory the Great, was rebuilt after 1347 by Archbishop Emanuele Spinola and the Benedictine Angelo Sisinio, and enlarged c. 1762 by Venanzio Marvuglia. It is now occupied by a college. The church, dating from 1561–95 (with part of the 14th-century masonry in the north wall) contains carved choir stalls (1591–97) by Benvenuto Tortelli da Brescia. *St Benedict* and the *Madonna with Sts Benedict and Scholastica* are both by Pietro Novelli (1603–1647). One of Sicily's finest painters, born in Monreale and court painter to Philip IV of Spain, Pietro Novelli was profoundly influenced by van Dyck's visit to Palermo (1622–24) and through Zoppi di Gangi also by Raphael. His chiaroscuro was perfected in Naples under Jusepe de Ribera. He often appears in his own paintings, recognisable by his fashionable beard and moustache. Six altarpieces here are by Zoppo di Gangi; and there is also a portrait of St Martin by Filippo Paladini. The sacristy contains vestments of the 16th–18th centuries and paintings attributed to

Annibale Carracci and Guercino, and a fine reliquary.

The carved doorway into the convent dates from the 15th century, and nearby is a stoup dated 1396. In the convent, at the foot of the splendid grand staircase (1786) by Marvuglia, is a group of *St Martin and the Beggar*, by Marabitti. A statue of St Benedict, by Benedetto Pompillion, stands in the graceful monastic cloister (1612; altered and enlarged in the 18th cenutry). The Oreto fountain is by Marabitti (1784). The refectory ceiling (*Daniel in the Lions' Den*) was frescoed by Pietro Novelli.

Convento di Baida

Baida is an isolated hamlet backed by a crescent of hills that rise in Monte Cuccio to 1050m. The Convento di Baida (*for admission ring at no. 41 Via del Convento*) was built in 1377–88 by Benedictine monks, expelled by Manfredi Chiaramonte from the Castellaccio, on the site of a 10th-century Arab village (*baidha*, white). The foundation was already in decline in 1499 when Giovanni Paternò took it over as a summer residence for the archbishops of Palermo; in 1595 it passed to the Observantine order. The church, its original Gothic façade pierced by a portal of 1507, has a fine 14th-century apse, and a statue, by Antonello Gagini, of St John the Baptist; traces of the 14th-century cloister remain.

BAGHERIA & THE RUINS OF SOLUNTO

Bagheria is a country town famous for its 18th-century **Baroque villas** set amidst lemon groves and vineyards. It was the birthplace of the artist Renato Guttuso (1912–87), and also of the Oscar-winning film-maker Giuseppe Tornatore, writer and director of *Cinema Paradiso* (1989). Suffocated by uncontrolled building in the last 40 years, which has encroached on the gardens and parks of the villas, the town now hardly lives up to the old Sicilian proverb: '*Baaria, sciuri ppi la via*', ('in Bagheria the flowers grow on the streets'). Many of the villas are neglected. Only two of them, Villa Cattolica and Villa Palagonia, are now usually open to visitors. The gardens of Villa San Cataldo are open on Sundays.

The conspicuous Villa Cattolica, a fine building of c. 1737, houses the **Galleria Comunale di Arte Moderna e Contemporanea** (*open 9.30–7; closed Mon*), which has a large collection of paintings by Renato Guttuso and other contemporary artists. Guttuso's bright blue marble tomb by Giacomo Manzù is in the garden. Near the villa, beyond a railway crossing (right), is the start of the long Corso Butera,which passes the fine Palazzo Inguaggiato attributed to Andrea Giganti (1770), before reaching the piazza in front of the 18th-century Chiesa Madre (*open 7.30–12 & 4.30–8*); the frescoes were carried out by Guttuso in 1923. Villa Butera is visible at the far end of the corso, built in 1658 by Giuseppe Branciforte (façade of 1769).

In front of the Chiesa Madre is the beginning of Corso Umberto which ends at Piazza Garibaldi beside (left) a garden gate (guarded by two monsters) of **Villa Palagonia** (*open 9–12.30 & 3.30–5.30*). The garden, and vestibule and hall on the first floor are open. The fine building was erected in 1705 by Francesco Gravina, Prince of Palagonia (and his architect Tommaso Maria Napoli). His eccentric grandson Ferdinando Gravina Alliata lived in rooms decorated in a bizarre fashion, including the hall with its ceiling covered with mirrors set at strange angles (now very damaged) and its walls encased in marble with busts of ladies and gentlemen. The oval vestibule has frescoes of *Four Labours of Hercules*. The villa is famous for the grotesque statues of monsters, dwarfs, and strange animals set up on the garden wall by Ferdinando (their effect now sadly diminished by the houses which have been built just outside the wall). At the time these carved figures were not to everyone's taste; when Goethe visited the villa in 1787 he was appalled by them.

Opposite is the entrance gate to the avenue which leads up to Villa Valguarnera (not visible from here; *closed to the public*). Built by Tommaso Napoli c. 1713–37, this is the most handsome of the Bagheria villas. The statues above the parapet are by Marabitti.

At no. 12 Via Cherubini is a modern art museum, **Museo Osservatorio dell'Arte Contemporanea in Sicilia** (*open Tues–Sat 5–8.30; closed Sun, Mon and holidays; www.museum-bagheria.it*) dedicated to Sicilian artists including Guttuso and Caruso. Off Via IV Novembre is Villa Trabia (mid-18th century), perhaps by Nicolò Palma, with a façade of 1890. It is surrounded by a neglected park. Near the railway station is the early 18th-century **Villa Cutò**, which is sometimes shown by appointment on guided tours (*T: 091 905438*), and a little further on is **Villa San Cataldo**, which received a neo-Gothic facelift in the early 19th century. The gardens can be visited (*Sat and Sun 9.30–6*), and the little church in the grounds is open for Mass on Sundays.

The frescoed salons of the 18th-century **Villa Aragona Cutò**, just outside town on the Via Consolare, now house a poignant museum dedicated to toys and wax figures, the **Museo del Giocattolo e delle Cere** (*open 9–1 & 3.30–6.30, Sat Sun &PH mornings only, closed Mon*), including a remarkably complete collection of French clockwork figures, made in the 19th century by the Gaultier brothers.

Solunto

Open 9–6; Sun and holidays 9–1.
The solitary ruins of Solunto are in a beautiful position on the slopes of Monte Catalfano (374m) overlooking the sea, and close to Santa Flavia. The archaeological site and museum are open daily. The ancient town of *Solus* is thought to have replaced a Phoenician settlement in the vicinity of the same name (perhaps at Cozzo Cannita where traces of walls have been found), which was destroyed in 397 BC by Dionysius of Syracuse. Solus was built in the 4th century BC on an interesting grid plan similar to the urban layout of some Hellenistic sites in Asia Minor. It fell to the Romans, who named it *Soluntum*, in 254 BC and had been abandoned by the beginning of the 3rd century AD. It was discovered in 1825 and much of the site still remains to be excavated.

The entrance is through a small museum displaying plans of the site alongside Hellenistic capitals, statues, and architectural fragments. A Roman road, beside terraces of prickly pear, mounts the side of the hill past Via delle Terme (with the remains of baths) and curves round to the right into the wide Via dell'Agora. This, the main street, traverses the town to the cliff edge overlooking the sea; it is crossed at regular intervals by side streets with considerable remains of houses on the hillside above. Beyond Via Ciauri and Via Perez is the stepped Via Cavallaro on which are some of the columns and the architrave of the so-called *gymnasium* (restored in 1866), in fact a large private house. This short stretch of Via dell'Agora is also beautifully paved in brick.

The next stepped road, Via Ippodamo da Mileto, links the main hill to another small hill towards the sea. Here on the slope of the hill above is the so-called Casa di Leda on three levels: above four small shops on Via dell'Agora, is an oblong cistern and courtyard with a fountain off which are rooms with mosaic and tiled floors and traces of red wall-paintings. Further up Via Ippodamo da Mileto stand the remains of other interesting houses.

Back on Via dell'Agora, beyond a large sanctuary (on the corner of Via Salinas), the road widens out into the large agora with brick paving in front of nine rectangular exedrae along the back wall, thought to have been used as shelters for the public. On the hillside above are traces of the theatre and a small bouleuterion probably used for council meetings. The hillside higher up may have been the site of the acropolis. Via dell'Agora next passes a huge public cistern, still filled with water, part of a complex system of storage tanks (many vestiges of which are still visible), made necessary by the lack of spring water in the area.

On the edge of the cliff, looking towards Cape Zafferano, in Via Bagnera is a small Roman villa with mosaics and wall-paintings. The view along the coast towards Cefalù, of the Aeolian Islands and Etna, is magnificent. In the foreground are the medieval castle of Solanto and the bay of Fondachello with the villas of Casteldaccia amid luxuriant vegetation on the slopes behind.

At the foot of Mount Catalfano a few lemon groves survive but the area is becoming increasingly developed with up-market holiday homes, as can be seen especially around the fishing village of **Porticello**. A thriving fish market still opens here very early in the morning.

Capo Zafferano is an isolated crag of dolomitic limestone, of great geological interest. On the cape grow dwarf palms and (flowering in the spring) wild orchids.

THE EAST OF THE PROVINCE

TERMINI IMERESE

Termini Imerese is built on the slopes of a hill and divided into an upper and lower town. Much new building has taken place here in the last few decades, to accommodate people working in the nearby industrial area. There is now also a commercial port. *Thermae Himerenses* received its name from the two neighbouring Greek cities of Thermae and Himera. After the sack of Himera in 408 BC by the Carthaginians, the inhabitants of the destroyed city were resettled in Thermae. In 307 BC it was ruled by Agathocles (361–289 BC), a native of the town and the most ferocious of the Greek tyrants of Syracuse. Its most prosperous period followed the Roman conquest. The thermal mineral waters were praised by Pindar. Outside the town are conspicuous remains of a Roman aqueduct built in the 2nd century AD to bring water to the town from a spring 7km away. In the upper town there is a spacious main square, with an old-fashioned men's club. From the belvedere behind the duomo there is a fine view of the coast and the modern port.

Exploring Termini Imerese

The 17th-century **duomo** (*open 9–12 & 3.30–8.30; closed Fri*) has a façade dating from 1912. The four statues of saints are copies of the originals, now removed inside. Beneath the tower (right) is a fragment of a Roman cornice. The interior, with huge columns and capitals, contains sculptures by Giuliano Mancino and Bartolomeo Berrettaro (followers of the Gaginis), including a statue of the Madonna, bas-reliefs, and the four statues of saints (1504–06) from the façade. The chapel also has two 17th-century funerary monuments. In the sanctuary is a Crucifix, painted on both sides, by Pietro Ruzzolone (1484). In the chapel to the left of the choir are reliefs by Marabitti and Federico Siragusa. In the fourth chapel of the south aisle is a marble oval relief of the *Our Lady of the Bridge*, by Ignazio Marabitti.

The **Palazzo Comunale** (town hall), was also built in the 17th century and is approached by an outside staircase. Just out of the piazza, in Via Marco Tullio Cicerone, is the **Museo Civico** (*open Tues–Sat 9–1 & 4–6.30; Sun and holidays 9–1*), founded in 1873. On the ground floor are prehistoric finds from Termini; vases from Himera; coins; Roman capitals, sculptures, inscriptions, architectural fragments, and glass. The last room contains Arab-Norman material and a Renaissance doorway. On the first floor is a chapel frescoed in the 15th century by Nicolò da Pettineo, paintings (16th–19th century) and a natural history collection. It is thought that the prestigious *mesomphalos phiale*, the solid gold libation bowl found in 1980 at Caltavuturo, will be housed here.

In Via Mazzini, which leads out of Piazza Duomo, are the church of **Santa Croce al Monte** containing 16th- and 17th-century Sicilian paintings, and Santa Maria della Misericordia (1600), with a beautiful triptych (*Madonna with Sts John and Michael*), ascribed to Gaspare da Pesaro (1453). Viale Iannelli leads west from Piazza Duomo to the 14th-century church of **Santa Caterina**, with 15th-century frescoes illustrating the life of the saint, probably by the local artists Nicolò and Giacomo Graffeo; they have recently been beautifully restored.

In Villa Palmeri, the **public gardens** laid out in 1845, are remains of a Roman public building, known as the Curia, dating from the 2nd century AD. From the gardens Via dell'Anfiteatro leads to the sparse ruins of the Roman amphitheatre (1st century AD).

From behind the duomo there is a good view down to the pretty blue tiled dome of the church of the **Annunziata**. A road winds down from here to the lower town and, on the site of the Roman baths, the **Grand Hotel delle Terme**, begun in 1890 on a design by Giuseppe Damiani Almeyda). The thermal waters (43°C) still in use here provide natural steam baths and bathing pools.

CACCAMO

Caccamo is a little town of ancient origins in a fine position above olive groves in the hills. There is a tradition that the Carthaginians took refuge here after their defeat at Himera in 480 BC, after their general Hamilcar had committed suicide by throwing himself on the funeral pyre of his dead soldiers, and most of his army had been taken prisoner. The castle was one of the major Norman strongholds on the island, and, never captured, it remained the residence of the dukes of Caccamo until the 20th century.

Exploring Caccamo

The impressive 12th-century castle (*open 9–12.15 & 1–6, T: 091 810 3248 to book visit*), the largest in Sicily, stands at the entrance to the town. Here in 1160 Matthew Bonellus organized a revolt of the barons against William I (the Bad); after the failure of the rebellion, Bonellus was captured and taken to Palermo, where he was hamstrung, blinded and imprisoned. The castle was enlarged by the Chiaramonte in the 14th century, and was sold to the region of Sicily in 1963 by the De Spuches family (*see p. 325*). It is now used for conferences and exhibitions. The main tower of the castle was 70 metres high but toppled in an earthquake in the 19th century. The empty interior has been heavily restored.

From the main road (Corso Umberto) steps and narrow streets lead down to Piazza Duomo, an attractive and unusual square on two levels, with a fine view over the valley. Above the raised terrace, with a balustrade decorated with four statues of the town's patron saints, is the 17th-century **Monte di Pietà** (the palace is now used for exhibitions) flanked by the façades of two churches. On the left is the Oratorio del Santissimo Sacramento, while that on the right is dedicated to the Souls in Purgatory. It contains charming gilded stuccoes in the sanctuary and the custodian will show the crypt below, also beautifully decorated with stuccoes, containing the crumbling, fully clothed skeletons of past inhabitants.

The duomo

The duomo (*ring if locked*) has a fine 17th-century façade. Founded in 1090, it was altered in 1477 and 1614. There is a lovely relief (1660) of St George above the door by Gaspare Guercio. The tall campanile was built above a 14th-century tower of the castle.

In the interior St George (the patron saint) features in a number of fine works of art. In the right aisle is a 15th-century triptych with St George and a charming processional statue of the saint with his dragon. In the south transept the architrave of the door into the sacristy has delicate carvings of the Madonna and Child with Angels and Sts Peter and Paul attributed to Francesco Laurana. The roundels of the *Annunciation* and relief of the *Madonna and Child* are by the Gagini school. The rich treasury and sacristy are also shown on request. They contain 16th–19th-century church silver, a precious collection of vestments and Flemish paintings. In the chapel to the right of the sanctuary is a statue of the *Madonna and Child* by the Gagini school. By the main altar is an unusual font (1466) with four large heads, perhaps representing Matthew, Mark, Luke and John. In the sanctuary are two polychrome wooden statues: *St John the Baptist* by Antonino Siragusa (1532) and *St Lucy* (16th century). An exquisite silver processional statuette of St Rosalia is also kept here. On the main altar are three very fine alabaster carvings (16th–18th century).

In the north transept are two painted terracotta sculptures: a *Madonna and Child* by the Gagini school and a *Pietà* group by the early 15th-century Sienese school. The altar here has 16th- and 17th-century reliquary busts and an early 18th-century Neoclassical carved and gilded altar frontal. In the left aisle an altar decorated with inlaid marble has a 14th-century painted Crucifix, and the first altarpiece of the *Miracle of St Isidore* is a stunning painting by Matthias Stomer. A sedan chair and armour belonging to the De Spuches family are also kept in this aisle.

There are good views of the castle from the old streets behind the duomo. In the other direction Via Cartagine leads to the deconsecrated church of San Francesco and, beyond, the church of Santissima Annunziata, its Baroque façade flanked by two earlier towers. Inside is a carved 16th-century organ case, and the sanctuary has stuccoes by the Serpotta school. The church of **San Benedetto alla Badia** (1615) was attached to a former Benedictine convent. The charming interior has a splendid majolica tiled floor in the nave and choir, once attributed to Nicolò Sarzana, but now thought to date from before 1701. There are also fine wrought-iron grilles. The two graceful female figures in stucco on either side of the sanctuary are by the school of Serpotta.

Santa Maria degli Angeli (1497; *ring at the convent*) has a fine relief of the *Madonna and Child* over the door. Inside its original wooden trussed ceiling is preserved (with 15th-century paintings of Dominican saints) and a statue of the Madonna by Antonello Gagini.

ALIA & ROCCAPALUMBA

Some 30km southeast of Caccamo, **Alia** is a remote town founded by the Arabs, surrounded by spectacular hills and wheat-fields. Later, under Spanish rule, it became the seat of the Santa Croce barons, who built their palace next to the church of Madonna delle Grazie (1639). At the moment the economy is depressed and it is suffering from depopulation.

Well-kept and picturesque nevertheless, Alia has two museums: a small ethno-anthropological collection housed in the Biblioteca Comunale, the public library (*open Mon–Sat 9–1*), and the **Museo Antropologico** at the Cimitero Vecchio (*T: Municipio 091 8210913 office hours to request visit, at least a day before*) dedicated to research carried out in 1995 of a mass grave containing nearly 400 people killed by cholera during the 1837 epidemic. Study of the skeletons has revealed much information about the inhabitants of this area during a period of intense poverty, their appearance, and their afflictions.

Not far from the town (4km), in a dramatic isolated sandstone outcrop, is a group of caves called **Grotte di Gurfa**, entirely carved out by hand during ancient times, and successively used as dwellings. The caves include a mysterious tholos, 16m high.

Scholars date the complex to the Copper Age, about 5,000 years ago, when it would have been either a sanctuary to a divinity, or a burial site, perhaps that of King Minos of Crete. An inscription in Phoenician has recently been discovered close to the entrance of one of the caves. There are some similarities with the hypogeum of Hal Saflieni in Malta and with the Treasury of Atreus at Mycenae.

Roccapalumba

The town of Roccapalumba, on the opposite side of the River Torto to Alia, is known as the *paese delle stelle*, the village of the stars, because the clear air and low light interference allow good observations of the stars at all times of the year. It was founded in 1630 by the Ansalone family at the foot of an enormous, isolated rock—the Rock of the Doves—which is the meaning of the name. The settlement must be much older, because the sanctuary church of the **Madonna della Luce**, partly built into the rock, is one of the oldest Norman churches of the territory, dating back to the 11th century. The prodigious image of the Madonna inside the church is said to have appeared suddenly to protect some travellers assailed by bandits as they were going through the pass. At the end of Via Umberto is an 18th-century public fountain for washing clothes, and the **Specola Pizzo Sauro**, a telescope which can be used on request (*T: 091 8215523*).

HIMERA

Near a large industrial area, including a power station and an important Fiat factory, which occupies the low coastal plain east of Termini Imerese, is the site of *Himera*, close to the Buonfornello exit of the motorway and on the bank of the Fiume Grande (or Imera Settentrionale), but very poorly signposted. On the right of the road, just across the busy railway line are the remains of a temple. Above the road is a conspicuous modern museum, below the site of the ancient city.

The site

Open 9–6; Sun and holidays 9–1.
On the right of the main road are the ruins of a **Doric temple**, peripteral and hexastyle, probably built around 470 BC. This is the only building which remains here of a sanctuary probably dedicated to Athena, on the banks of the River Himera. It is still known as the Temple of Victory, although some scholars no longer believe it was built to celebrate the victory over the Carthaginians. In any case it seems to have been burnt and destroyed by the Carthaginians in 409 BC.

Only the basement and lower part of the columns and part of the cella walls survive. It measured 22 x 55m and had 14 columns at the sides and six in front. The cella had a pronaos and opisthodomos in antis. In the Middle Ages the site was built over and it was only rediscovered in 1823 and excavated by Pirro Marconi in 1929–30, when the splendid lion-head water-spouts from the cornice were taken to the Museo Archeologico in Palermo.

Off the main road, just beyond, a byroad (left; signposted) leads up to the museum and the areas of the city excavated since 1963. The **museum** (*open 9–6, Sun and holidays 9–1*) is a striking modern building, and there are good plans and descriptions of the site. The first section displays finds from the temples in the sacred area on the hilltop, including a votive deposit with fragments of metopes. The second section has material from the city and necropoleis, including ceramics, architectural fragments and votive statues. There is also a section devoted to finds from recent excavations in the surrounding territory, including Cefalù and Caltavuturo.

Just above the museum are excavations of part of the city. Steps continue up to a plateau on the edge of the hill overlooking the plain towards the sea. Here is the **Area Sacra** with a temenos enclosing the bases of an altar and four temples (7th–5th centuries BC). There are also traces of houses here. The view extends along the coast as far as Solunto. In the other direction you can see the village of Gratteri, nestling in the Madonie Mountains.

HISTORY OF HIMERA

This was a colony of *Zancle* (now Messina), founded in 648 BC near the mouth of the River Himera and at the head of the valley which provided access to the interior of the island. It was the westernmost Greek colony on the north coast of Sicily, and the birthplace of the lyric poet Stesichorus (born c. 630 BC). In Plato's *Phaedrus* the story is told of the poet being struck blind for slandering Helen, only to have his sight restored after writing a recantation. It was also the scene of the famous defeat of the Carthaginians by the Greeks in 480 BC which along with victory over the Persians at Salamis prepared the way for what we now call the Golden Age of Pericles: approximately half a century, corresponding largely to the time when Pericles was in command, when the relatively peaceful situation allowed the Athenians to attain great heights in the fields of art, culture, philosophy and democracy. Gelon's victory at Himera was thanks to the fact that he had formed a coalition with other leaders on the island, an idea probably inspired by the Spartan leader Leonidas—his last stand (a few months before) at Thermopylae against the Persians, when he was killed with all his men, was the result of his largely unsuccessful efforts to persuade the Greeks that alliance against a common foe is a sure way to success. Hamilcar had burned his boats on arrival at Himera, he was so certain of victory; when he lost the day, he threw himself on the funeral pyre of his warriors, committing honourable suicide; it was the Carthaginians' first decisive and unexpected defeat in the Mediterranean. The survivors were either taken prisoner or took refuge where Caccamo now stands. The Carthaginians later returned under Hannibal, nephew of Hamilcar, in 409 BC, and took their revenge, crucifying 300 of the strongest men to vindicate Hamilcar, and utterly destroying the city. The inhabitants who survived the battle fled to *Thermae* (now Termini Imerese).

CEFALÙ

Cefalù, with its stunning Norman cathedral and ruins of an ancient acropolis on the rock above the city, is a very picturesque small town with a lovely beach. The old town is still medieval in character, with many enticing shops, restaurants and cafés along its well-kept cobbled streets.

HISTORY OF CEFALÙ

Founded at the end of the 5th or early 4th century BC, the name *Kephaloidion* comes from the head-like shape of the rock which towers above the town. In 307 BC the town was taken by Agathocles of Syracuse. In 857 it was conquered by the Arabs. In 1131 Roger II rebuilt the town, and constructed the magnificent cathedral which became head of a powerful bishopric. In the 1920s the necromancer Aleister Crowley lived near Cefalù, transforming a cottage into the Temple of Thelema ('Do as thou wilt, shall be thy creed'), and scandalizing the locals to the point where he was arrested, found guilty of immoral behaviour, and expelled from Italy.

Exploring Cefalù

At the beginning of Corso Ruggero, the main street of the town, on the right, is the sandstone façade of Maria Santissima della Catena (1780; *closed*) preceded by a high portico with three statues. On the right of the façade are a few large blocks from the old walls (late 5th century BC) on the site of Porta Terra, the main entrance to the old town. The corso continues past (right) Vicolo dei Saraceni (signposted for the *Tempio di Diana*) beyond which begins a path up to the acropolis, and then runs slightly downhill. On the left is the **Osterio Magno**, once King Roger's palace and now used for exhibitions, with a fine 13th-century triple window high up on its façade and (in Via Amendola) windows decorated with black lava.

On the left are a series of nine picturesque, straight, parallel streets which lead downhill to Corso Vittorio Emanuele, with a view of the sea beyond. They possibly reflect the grid plan of the ancient city. The corso continues past the tall, plain façade of the 16th-century church of the Annunziata. To the right opens the little piazza in front of the 15th-century church of the Purgatorio (or Santo Stefano Protomartire), Inside is the tomb of Baron Mandralisca (*see p. 93 below*).

The duomo

Open 8–12 & 3.30–5.30; no shorts or bare shoulders.
Further along the corso on the right, the piazza planted with palm trees leads up to the splendid Duomo. The setting is dramatic, with the formidable rock rising immediately behind it and the small town at its feet. Begun by Roger II in 1131, and intended as his burial place, it was still unfinished at the time of his death in 1154. His suc-

CEFALÙ DUOMO: WEST FRONT

cessors lost interest in the project and it was not consecrated until 1267; Frederick II of Hohenstaufen even removed the royal porphyry tombs—officially for safety—and took them to Palermo, but to carry out this scandalous act he waited until the bishop was away on a mission in the East. Excavations during restoration work have revealed Roman remains on this site. The church is preceded by a raised terrace, part of the original Norman design, surrounded by a balustrade with statues. The soaring façade is flanked by two massive towers with fine windows. Above the narthex built by Ambrogio da Como in 1471 is a double row of blind arcades. The beautiful exterior of the south side and transept are visible from Via Passafiume.

The interior

The basilican interior has 16 ancient columns with Roman capitals, probably from the Temple of Diana (*see p. 94 below*), supporting Arab-Norman arches. The open timber roof of the nave bears traces of painting (1263). The contemporary stained-glass windows high up in the nave are the work of the Palermo artist Michele Canzoneri and were installed in 1985–90. The work is still unfinished; the windows will eventually number 72 and represent episodes from the Old and New Testaments. The crossing is approached through an arch borne by huge columns. In the sanctuary is a 15th-century painted Crucifix attributed to Tommaso de Vigilia.

The presbytery is decorated with exquisite mosaics—the best preserved and the earliest of their kind in Sicily—on a background of dusky gold, symbolic of divinity. They were carried out for Roger II in a careful decorative scheme, reflecting Byzantine models, but much more free and spontaneous than anything seen before from those workshops. The king probably intended them to line the whole interior of the building. It is thought that they are the work of Greek craftsmen, summoned from Constantinople by Roger himself. In the apse is the splendid colossal figure of Christ Pantocrator holding an open book with the Greek and Latin biblical text from John 8:12 ('I am the Light of the World: he that followeth me shall not walk in darkness'). His compassionate expression is that of a trusted friend, wiser and more experienced than ourselves: the wayward locks of hair falling over His forehead add to the humanity of the portrayal. Many believe this to be the finest portrait of Christ in existence, and it has been noted that it is the very close in resemblance to the image on the Shroud (*Sindone*), which is kept in Turin.

On the curved apse wall below are three tiers of figures: the *Virgin in Prayer Between the Four Archangels* (dressed as Byzantine dignitaries; holding loaves of bread symbolizing Salvation), and the Apostles in the two lower registers, quite informal in their stance, as if we had suddenly interrupted their conversation. In the vault of the presbytery are angels and seraphim and on the walls below are (left) prophets, deacon martyrs, and Latin bishop saints, and (right) prophets, warrior saints, and Greek patriarchs and theologians. An inscription beneath the window states that the mosaics of the apse were completed in 1148. The soft folds of the robes, the gentle expressions, the marvellous texture and subtle colour of the angels' wings, are certainly the work of very accomplished artists.

The south aisle and transepts were stripped of their Baroque decoration in the 1970s, in order to restore the building to its Norman aspect, as far as possible. The world-famous 16th-century organs have been lost without trace. Such drastic intervention has been the subject of much heated discussion, but the achieved effect of light and space is breathtaking. In the chapel to the right of the sanctuary is a statue of the *Madonna* by Antonello Gagini. On the left pilaster of the sanctuary, high up in a niche, is a statue of the annunciatory angel. In the Neoclassical chapel to the left of the sanctuary is an elaborate 18th-century silver altar.

From the north aisle is the entrance to the beautiful little cloister which shows the remains of three galleries of twin columns with carved capitals (including Noah's Ark and the Trinacria symbol; *see p. 204*) supporting pointed Arab-Norman arches.

Piazza Duomo

In Piazza Duomo is Palazzo Maria, with medieval traces, and the 17th-century Oratorio del Santissimo Sacramento beside the Neoclassical Palazzo Legambi.

Opposite is Palazzo Vescovile (1793), next to the 17th-century seminary with a hanging garden. Opposite the duomo is the former monastery of Santa Caterina, extensively restored as the town hall a few years ago by the architect Gae Aulenti (who designed the new Musée d'Orsay in Paris).

Museo Mandralisca

Open 9–7; until midnight in summer; www.museomandralisca.com
From Piazza Duomo, Via Mandralisca leads down to the Museo Mandralisca. The palace cellars, containing huge terracotta jars for storing oil, can be seen from the road. Enrico Pirajno, Baron Mandralisca (1809–64) once lived here and he left his remarkable collection to the city as a museum (now run by a private foundation). The Baron was a member of the first Italian parliament and he took a special interest in archaeology (participating in excavations on Lipari and an area near Cefalù) and natural history. He also endowed a local school.

On the ground floor is a mosaic from Cefalù (1st century BC). On the first floor are a famous vase from Lipari showing a vendor of tuna fish (4th century BC); a numismatic collection dating from the Greek period up to the 19th century, with about 400 pieces, particularly notable for its coins from Lipari, Cefalù and Syracuse; and a collection of paintings. In Room 3 is the famous *Portrait of a Man* by Antonello da Messina (c. 1465–72), the jewel of the collection and one of the most striking portraits of the Italian Renaissance. Mandralisca apparently bought this small painting from a pharmacy in Lipari, where he discovered it in use as part of a cupboard door. The sitter, with his mischievous smile, has never been identified. The influence of the Flemish school of painting is evident in this exquisite work, here displayed to great advantage. Also displayed here is a sarcophagus in the form of an Ionic temple which dates from the 2nd century BC Other rooms hold Mandralisca's remarkable collection of some 20,000 shells and also archaeological material, including Italiot vases from Lipari (320–300 BC), and a well-preserved kylix.

The second floor contains more archaeological finds, and miscellaneous objects including a 19th-century dinner service, arms, reliquaries, paintings (*Madonna and Child* attributed to Antonello da Saliba), and an ornithological collection. Mandralisca's important library, which has been expanded, is also accessible.

The port and the Rocca

Corso Ruggero continues down to end at Via Porpora, which leads right to a restored square tower in a gap between the houses. Outside the tiny postern gate a fine stretch of the megalithic walls (5th century BC) built onto the rock can be seen. In the other direction Via Carlo Ortolani di Bordonaro leads past (right) Piazza Francesco Crispi with the church of the Madonna del Cammino. Modern steps lead up to a 17th-century bastion (Capo Marchiafava) where a 14th-century fountain has been placed (good view). Via Ortolani continues down towards the sea and ends beside a terrace overlooking the little port, with picturesque old houses on the seafront.

From here Via Vittorio Emanuele leads back past the church of the Badiola

View of Cefalù and its duomo from the Rocca.

(12th–17th centuries), next to its convent (the old portal survives on the corner of Via Porto Salvo). Opposite is the 16th-century Porta Pescara with a lovely Gothic arch through which the sea can be seen. It is now used to display fishermen's tackle and nets. Beyond, the Discesa Fiume, with wide steps curving down past a few trees, leads to the **Lavatoio**, a picturesque medieval wash-house, where a spring of slightly salty water was converted into a laundry by the Arabs and was still in daily use until quite recently.

From Corso Ruggero and Vicolo dei Saraceni steps and a path lead up (in c. 1 hour) to the Rocca, the summit (278m) of which commands a wonderful view. According to legend, the rock is the head of the shepherd Daphnis. He so loved the nymph Nomia that he promised to be faithful to her, on pain of being blinded. Chimaera then enticed him into the woods, gave him wine and seduced him. Nomia accordingly blinded him, and Hermes, on the orders of Hera, to whom Nomia was dear, turned him into stone. His bitter tears at his folly are said to form the spring that supplies the Lavatoio. On the top of the Rocca is the so-called **Temple of Diana**, with walls made out of huge polygonal blocks and a carved architrave over the entrance. It was probably a sacred edifice built in the 5th–4th century BC over an earlier cistern. Stretches of castellated walls can also be seen here as well as numerous cisterns and ovens, but only vague traces remain of the original castle.

THE MADONIE MOUNTAINS

The Madonie Mountains lie between the Imera Settentrionale to the west and the Pollina river to the east. The Pizzo Carbonara (1979m) is the second highest mountain on the island (after Etna). The area of some 40,000 hectares is protected as a nature reserve known as the *Parco Naturale Regionale delle Madonie*. The vegetation in the upland plains and mountains includes beech, enormous holly trees some 14m high and centuries old, manna ash (manna is still extracted from the bark in the Pollina and Castelbuono area), chestnuts, oaks, poplars, ilexes, cork trees and ancient olives. A rare species of fir, *Abies nebrodensis*, only found here, distinguished by the terminal twigs on the branches which form a neat cross, was saved from extinction in 1969. Apart from these extensive woods the landscape has spectacular rock formations, pastureland where sheep and cattle are grazed, and small hill towns of great interest. For more information on the flora and fauna of the Madonie, visit the museum in Castelbuono.

Gibilmanna

The sanctuary of Gibilmanna is in a beautiful position looking towards the sea, on the slopes of the Pizzo Sant'Angelo (1081m), with woods of olives, cork oaks, pines and chestnuts. The name is derived from the Arabic *gebel*, meaning mountain; and manna, which was extracted from the manna ash trees in the locality, and used for medicinal purposes. There was a sanctuary here founded by the Benedictines in the 6th century; in 1535 it became a **Capuchin convent**, and it is still a famous centre of pilgrimage on Sicily. The sanctuary (*open 8–1 & 3–7*), rebuilt in the 17th century, has been altered many times and its external appearance dates from the 20th century. The interior preserves an 18th-century Baroque altar, a fresco of the Madonna and a Crucifix from an earlier church. The wooden tabernacle on the main altar is by Pietro Bencivinni (1700).

The **Museum of the Franciscan Presence in Sicily** (*open 10.30–12.30 & 3.30–6.30*) preserves works of art from convents and churches in this area of the island. These include 16th–18th-century paintings, church vestments, statuettes (in wax and wood), ex-votos, a rare early 18th-century wooden organ with cane pipes, and an ethnographical collection illustrating monastic life. It is also possible to visit the catacombs. An astronomical observatory (1952) stands on the nearby Cozzo Timpa Rossa (1006m).

Grattieri

A little hill town facing west, Grattieri provides a fine distant view along the coast. The churches (*often closed*) are the 19th-century **Nuova Matrice**, containing four thorns from the Crown of Jesus and a fragment of the True Cross, and the **Matrice Vecchia**, dedicated to the Archangel Michael, built in the 14th century. It has a separate bell-tower with seven bronze bells, one of them dated 1390. Beautiful crochet work is still made here by the women.

Isnello

Isnello is a pleasant little town built along a long rock which gives the town its name, the Rocca dell'Asinello, with the ruins of the castle at one end. The Chiesa Madre has 16th-century frescoes by Antonino Ferraro, 17th-century stuccoes by Giuseppe Li Volsi, and a carved wooden choir and organ loft dating from the early 17th century. A marble ciborium is attributed to Domenico Gagini (1492). The *Deposition* is by Giuseppe Salerno Zoppo di Gangi (*see p. 102*). The little church of **San Michele** has an important painted wooden ceiling, a wooden Crucifix by Fra' Umile da Petralia (*see p. 287*), a painting of *Martyrs* by Giuseppe Salerno Zoppo di Gangi, and a 15th-century fresco of St Leonard. The church of the Rosario (*closed*) contains a painting of the *Madonna of the Rosary* attributed to the Flemish school. The church of the **Annunziata** contains a *Nativity* by Giuseppe Salerno Zoppo di Gangi.

Steps lead up from the piazza by the Chiesa Madre to the church of **Santa Maria Maggiore** (key at no. 4 Via Purgatorio) near the ruins of the castle, and beneath a rock called the Grotta Grande. It has a pretty bell tower. The charming interior has a decorative organ loft over the entrance, and a late 15th- or early 16th-century Crucifix, unusual in its iconography and painted on both sides, hangs from the centre of the nave ceiling. Above the main altar is a *Madonna and Child* of the Gagini school (1547). There is also a charming little statue of the Madonna as a baby, lovingly preserved in a glass case. The quality of the lace, crochet, embroidery and filet here is renowned.

Collesano

The spectacular little medieval town of Collesano has several interesting churches including the duomo (Santa Maria la Nuova) which contains a painted Crucifix of 1555, a fine carved tabernacle of 1489 by Donatello Gagini, and a *Madonna with Angels* by Giuseppe Salerno. The frescoes (1624) are the work of Gaspare Vazano, also known as Zoppo di Gangi. In Santa Maria la Vecchia (1140) is a statue of the *Madonna* by Antonello Gagini. At no. 3 Via Roma is the **Museo Targa Florio** (*open Apr–Oct 9.30–12.30 & 4–7, Nov–Mar 9.30–12.30 & 3–6, closed Mon*), dedicated to the oldest motor race in the world. The pottery made in Collesano is unusual and interesting, both for the shapes of the vases and the colours.

CASTELBUONO

An ancient town of warm rose-coloured stone and mellow old brick, whose rooftops are animated by jackdaws and swifts, Castelbuono basks at the foot of its spectacular castle, in a fold of hills covered with forests of manna ash and chestnuts. Of Byzantine origins, it became the seat of the Ventimiglia princes of Geraci in the 14th century, and the medieval structure of the centre is still intact.

Exploring Castelbuono

The main road leads up past a 16th-century fountain with bas-reliefs and a statue of Venus to Piazza Margherita, with another 16th-century fountain. Here the **Matrice**

Vecchia of 1350 is preceded by a loggia. It contains a marble ciborium attributed to Giorgio da Milano (late 15th century), a huge polyptych on the high altar attributed to Pietro Ruzzolone, and statues and frescoes of the 16th century. The crypt has frescoes of the *Passion of Christ*. Also in the piazza is a building owned by the Ventimiglia family in the 14th–16th century and used as a prison from the 18th century up to 1965. Exhibitions are now held here and it has a local tourist office.

The ancient street continues uphill past the town hall to the castle (*open 9–1 & 3–7*) built by the Ventimiglia family in 1316, and exceptionally well restored. The castle is said to have both a ghost, that of Queen Constance Chiaramonte (14th century), whose footsteps can be heard running through the rooms on the first Tuesday of every month, and a secret passage which unites the castle to the mausoleum of the Ventimiglias. Off the courtyard is the **Chapel of St Anne** (c. 1683) with white stuccoed cherubs on a gold ground by the school of Serpotta. The skull of the saint is preserved here in a 16th-century silver urn, and the chapel possesses a treasury. The castle also houses the Civic Art Gallery (contemporary artists) and a small museum of country life and the extraction of manna. Behind the castle the terrace has a view of the Madonie and the little hill town of Geraci Siculo.

From the Matrice Vecchia a road (signposted) leads up to a piazza with palm trees and a memorial surrounded by cannon used in the First World War. Here is the **Matrice Nuova**, begun at the beginning of the 17th century (and rebuilt in 1830). It contains a painted Crucifix attributed to Pietro Ruzzolone, stucco altars, and a 16th-century triptych. Another road leads up from the right of the Matrice Nuova to the church of **San Francesco**, which has a pretty white and gold interior decorated in the 18th century, with an organ and monks' choir above the entrance. It also has decorative chandeliers and charming little confessionals dating from 1910. Off the right side of the sanctuary, entered through a lovely late 15th-century doorway carved by the school of Laurana, is a pretty octagonal chapel with twisted columns. Here are the tombs of the Ventimiglia family, including one dated 1543 and one 1687, and somewhere, apparently, the secret passage to the castle. The two 15th-century frescoes were detached from the Franciscan convent. The attractive 18th-century cloister (*under repair; delayed by new archaeological discoveries*) of the convent is entered between two marble columns left of the church façade.

At no. 52 Via Roma the former convent of Santa Venera now houses the **Museo Minà Palumbo** (*open 9–1 & 3–7; summer 4–8*). It is named after the naturalist Francesco Minà Palumbo, a native of Castelbuono. His collections, which he carefully catalogued, provide a fascinating documentation of the Madonie. The exhibits include fossils, a botanical and natural history section, minerals, archaeological finds (including prehistoric material), examples of glass produced here from the late 16th to the end of the 18th centuries, and examples of paper produced in the town between 1822 and 1846. There is also an interesting display illustrating the extraction of manna (used for medicinal purposes as a mild laxative, especially for babies, and also as a sweetener in cakes) from the trunks of manna ash trees in the area. Castelbuono and Pollina are the only places in the world where manna is still produced.

Spring meadows in the Madonie.

THE SOUTHERN MADONIE

Sclafani Bagni

A small remote fortress-village on a precipitous crag with superb views, Sclafani Bagni was a fortress from 734 BC, during the Greek colonization. The name derives from *Esculapiifanum*, that is Temple of Asclepius, a place of healing, which stood by a thermal spring. The medieval town gate bears the coat of arms of the Sclafani (Matteo Sclafani, count of the town in 1330, constructed its defences). Higher up the Chiesa Madre or Santa Maria Assunta (*open Mon, Wed, Fri 2–6*) contains a splendid sarcophagus, in white Greek marble, with Bacchic scenes, two statues (the *Madonna* and *St Peter*) by the school of Gagini, an organ by La Valle (1615), and a processional statue of the *Ecce Homo*, made of papier-mâché, the work of Fra' Umile da Petralia. Above, steps lead up to the scant remains of the Norman castle, with an excellent view.

In the lower part of the town is the church of San Giacomo on the edge of the hillside, with charming stuccoes in the interior in very poor condition. The church of San Filippo contains a worn but pretty tiled floor, a 17th-century wooden processional Crucifix in a tabernacle, and two curious statues of waxed canvas (1901), much venerated locally.

Polizzi Generosa

Beautifully positioned at the head of the Imera valley, Polizzi Generosa is a delightful little town which received its name 'Generosa' from Frederick II in 1234. It once boasted 76 churches within its walls, and many of them now belong to local confraternities (who have the keys). From the small **Piazza Umberto**, where all the main roads converge, Via Cardinale Rampolla leads up to the Chiesa Madre with a charming 16th-century porch and two very worn statues of St Peter and St Paul. A Gothic portal has been exposed beside the Renaissance doorway. The church has unfortunately been closed for many years. In the right aisle is a painting of the *Madonna of the Rosary* by Giuseppe Salerno Zoppo di Gangi (*see p. 102*). At the end of the aisle, a chapel on the right (closed by a grille) contains some particularly fine sculptures, including the sarcophagus of Beato Gandolfo da Binasco (recomposed) by Domenico Gagini; reliefs by the Berrettaro family, and a fragment of the *Last Supper* by Domenico Gagini and his workshop. In the sanctuary, but very high up, is a precious large triptych representing the *Madonna Enthroned Amidst Angels* and recently attributed to Rogier Van der Weyden (early 16th century) and is one of the loveliest paintings in Sicily. The picture, painted on Flemish oak, and still in its original frame, shows the Madonna with Sts Catherine and Barbara, all wearing rich scarlet silk gowns, accompanied by angel musicians.

Beside the Chiesa Madre is San Gandolfo la Povera (1622) with a high altarpiece of *St Gandulph* by Giuseppe Salerno Zoppo di Gangi. The road continues up to the church of San Francesco, founded in 1303, now used as an auditorium. On the left is **Piazza Castello** with the ruins of the so-called castle of Queen Blanche of Navarre (11th century). In the walled garden of Baron Casalpietro, two fir trees belonging to the endemic species *Abies nebrodensis* survive; there are only 27 of them left in the world. A little museum of the Madonie, **Museo Ambientalistico Madonita—MAM** (*open 9–1, www.mam.pa.it*) in the piazza illustrates the local natural history.

Below San Francesco is the church of San Nicolò de Franchis (*locked*) founded in 1167 by Peter of Toulouse, with a bell-cote. Nearby is Santa Margherita (or the Badia Vecchia), a 15th-century church. It has delicate white and gold stucco decoration. The barrel vault and sanctuary have 19th-century pictorial decorations, including a copy of Leonardo's *Last Supper*.

Another road from Piazza Umberto leads up to the remains of the circular **Torre di Leo**, named after a family who purchased it in 1240, next to the church of San Pancrazio dei Greci, which contains a painting by a Zoppo di Gangi. From the terrace there is an impressive view of the mountains.

The main street of the little town, Corso Garibaldi, also starts in Piazza Umberto. It leads past the centrally-planned church of San Girolamo by Angelo Italia. Next to it is the former **Collegio dei Gesuiti** (*open 10–1; Sat, Sun also 4–7; Mon closed*), a large building now occupied by the town hall and civic library. The fine interior courtyard has loggias on two levels and a single balcony on the top storey. In the morning visitors are allowed up to the top storey where an open balcony has a fine view over the roofs of the town (and the ruined church of the Commenda below).

The corso continues past a flight of steps (right) which lead up to the large **Palazzo Carpinello** with a long, low façade, and ends at a terrace known as the belvedere which has a magnificent view: the motorway from Palermo to Catania is reduced to a winding stream in the distant valley below, while to the east rise the Madonie Mountains. The ancient church of **Santa Maria Lo Piano**, seat of the Teutonic

Knights, contains 17th-century paintings. Via Malatacca leads down from the corso towards Sant'Antonio Abate, which has a red Islamic dome crowning its bell tower (once a minaret) and also contains a painting by a Zoppo di Gangi. One-storey Arab houses can be seen in this quarter.

PETRALIA SOTTANA & SOPRANA

Petralia Sottana sits on a hillside enclosed by the mountains. The attractive Corso Paolo Agliata passes Santa Maria della Fontana (16th–17th century) and the 18th-century church of San Francesco before reaching Piazza Umberto (with a view of the Imera valley). The Chiesa Madre, which has a lovely bell-tower, was rebuilt in the 17th century. It contains a fine sculpted altarpiece of 1501, and a 17th-century statue of the *Madonna and Child*. Above the town, on the road for Petralia Soprana, is the church and convent of the Santissima Trinità with a marble altarpiece by Gian Domenico Gagini (1542). The women here still weave the brightly coloured rag rugs called *pezzane* or *frazzate*.

Petralia Soprana

Occupying a beautiful position on a hillside (1147m) above pinewoods, Petralia Soprana is one of the most interesting and well preserved little towns in the interior of the island, and the highest in the province. *Petra* was important in the Roman era, and in 1062 it passed into the hands of Count Roger. During the 19th and early 20th centuries rock-salt mines were in operation here, one of which is still in use. The exteriors of the attractive old stone houses have not been covered with plaster as in numerous other Sicilian towns.

In the central **Piazza del Popolo** is a large war memorial, and the neo-Gothic Town Hall (1896). Via Generale Medici leads up past (left) the fine façade of San Giovanni Evangelista (1770; *closed*) to Piazza Fra Umile with a bust commemorating Fra' Umile da Petralia (fl. 1588–1639), the sculptor, famous for his Crucifixes which adorn many churches in Sicily, who was born here (*see p. 287*). On the right is the 18th-century Oratorio delle Anime del Purgatorio with a very worn portal. Further up is Piazza dei Quattro Cannoli with a pretty 18th-century fountain and palace.

Beyond on the right a wide flight of steps leads down to the **duomo**, consecrated in 1497, which has a delightful 18th-century portico. At one end is a squat tower and at the other is the 15th-century campanile with a two-light window in which two quaint statues of St Peter and St Paul have been placed. The gilded and white stucco decoration in the interior was carried out in 1859. On the north side the first altar has a fine painted statue of the Madonna and Child, and the fourth altar a marble statue of the Madonna. The fifth has a high relief of the *Pietà* with symbols of the Passion. In the chapel to the left of the sanctuary is an 18th-century gilded wooden altarpiece. The realistic Crucifix in the sanctuary is the first work of Fra' Umile da Petralia (c. 1624). The polychrome statues of St Peter and St Paul are by the Neapolitan sculptor Gaetano Franzese (1764), and the large painting of their martyrdom is by Vincenzo Riolo. On the fifth south aisle altar is a beautiful *Deposition*, attributed since its recent

View of the town of Gangi.

restoration to Pietro Novelli or the school of Ribera. Above the duomo is the 18th-century domed circular church of San Salvatore (*closed*), which was built on the site of a Norman church. It contains 17th–18th-century statues.

From the other side of Piazza del Popolo Via Loreto leads uphill past a pretty court-yard, several handsome palaces, and the 16th-century church of San Michele. The street ends in the piazza (paved with cobblestones) in front of the attractive façade of **Santa Maria di Loreto**. The façade of 1750 is by two local sculptors named Serpotta and the two little spires on either side are decorated with coloured stones. It is preceded by a wrought-iron gate of 1881. The beautiful interior has a carved high altar-piece attributed to Gian Domenico Gagini (with a *Madonna* attributed to Giacomo Mancini). It also contains paintings by Vincenzo Riolo, 18th–19th-century statues, and a fine sacristy of 1783. On the right a lane (Via Belvedere) leads out under an arch to a terrace beside the apse of the church, with an excellent view which extends as far as Etna on a clear day.

On the edge of the hill, below Corso Umberto, is the church of San Teodoro, founded by Count Roger and rebuilt in 1759. An interesting sarcophagus decorated with animal carvings was discovered here in 1991.

Gangi

East of the Petralias, a few kilometres east of the boundary of the Madonie park, Gangi is a large town stacked up on a ridge at just over a thousand metres in the middle of mountainous countryside. The town's medieval origins can still be appreciated in the street plan. At the top of the hill is the Palazzo Bongiorno, now the Town Hall, formerly the seat of the wealthiest family in the region, decorated with 18th-century frescoes by Gaspare Fumagali. The town was the birthplace of Giuseppe Salerno, known as Zoppo di Gangi (the Cripple of Gangi), whose *Last Judgement* hangs in the church of San Nicolo, and also of his colleague Gaspare Vazano, also known as the Zoppo di Gangi (*see box below*). Attached to the castle is a Renaissance chapel attributed to the Gagini family (early 16th century).

ZOPPO DI GANGI

The two painters that went under the name Zoppo di Gangi or 'Cripple of Gangi' were Giuseppe Salerno (1570–1632) and Gaspare Vazano (1555–1630). Known to have been friends and colleagues, their working relationship remains obscure. It is possible that each was prepared to adopt the same 'trademark', common practice among decorators at the time. Gaspare Vazano, the senior of the pair, is less widely known and seems to have preferred working with frescoes. The majority of works attributed to Zoppo di Gangi were undertaken by Giuseppe Salerno, the younger and arguably

Detail from Giuseppe Salerno's *Last Judgement*, whose iconography borrows heavily from Michelangelo.

more talented of the two. His work demonstrates the influence of Raphael and also, very markedly, and typically for the time, that of Spanish art. His masterpiece, the *Last Judgement*, adorns the church of San Nicolo di Bari in Gangi. Closely based on Michelangelo's work of the same name in the Sistine Chapel, the painting even includes a possible likeness of Salerno in St Bartholomew's flayed skin. Such direct quotation of the master's work in Rome would have lent authority to the painting, and this kind of direct borrowing was not unusual in the 17th century. Works by both Zoppos can be seen in many of the small towns and villages in the area, especially in Isnello and Polizzi Generosa.

THE WEST OF THE PROVINCE

Piana degli Albanesi

In Piana degli Albanesi, the most interesting of the 15th-century Albanian colonies in Sicily, the inhabitants still use their native tongue, are Catholics of the Byzantine-Greek rite, and wear traditional costume for weddings and important festivals. Garibaldi planned the tactics that led to the capture of Palermo from here. Piana is known for its excellent bread, cheeses and huge *cannoli di ricotta*.

In the handsome main street, Via Giorgio Kastriota, is the cathedral of **San Demetrio** of 1498 (*usually open 10–12.30*). On the west wall is a 19th-century painting of *St Nicholas* by Andrea d'Antoni (a pupil of the Neoclassicist early 19th-century painter Giuseppe Patania). On the north wall of the church is a small Byzantine *Madonna and Child*. The statues are attributed to Nicolò Bagnasco, and the damaged apse frescoes are by Pietro Novelli. The iconostasis was decorated with paintings in 1975.

The main street leads uphill to the piazza beside the church of the Madonna Odigitria (1607), on a design by Pietro Novelli. Just out of the square is the church of **San Giorgio**, the oldest church in the town, built in 1495. On the right side is a mosaic by the local artist Tanina Cuccia (1984) and a painting of *St Philip Neri* by Giuseppe Patania. The iconostasis has 20th-century paintings. On the left side is a fresco of St Anthony Abbot by Antonio Novelli and a charming equestrian statue of St George, fully armed. Other churches of interest include San Vito (18th century, with statues) and Santissima Annunziata (1624; with a fresco by Pietro Novelli).

At the lower end of the main street, a stable block (no. 207) has been converted into a library, cultural centre and the delightful **Ethnographical Museum** (*open 9–1 & 3–7; closed Mon*), which has traditional costumes and 18th-century jewellery worn by the women of Piana on display.

A few kilometres south of the town is **Portella della Ginestra**, where there is a memorial to the peasants massacred here while celebrating a traditional May Day festival in 1947. Eleven people were killed and 59 wounded by outlaws led by Salvatore Giuliano from Montelepre. This was later understood as an attempt by right-wing activists, in collusion with the Mafia, to combat Communism and advocate independence for the island (both the right wing and the separatists had just lost votes in the local elections).

Southeast of the town is the **Lago di Piana degli Albanesi**, a reservoir formed in 1923 by an impressive dam between Monte Kumeta (1200m) and Monte Maganoce (900m) across the Belice river, now a nature reserve (*Oasi di Piana degli Albanesi, c/o Cooperativa Palma Nana, T: 091 6254667 and 335 8439580*), a good place to observe migrating duck.

Monte Jato

West of Piana, **San Giuseppe Jato** is fast becoming one of the more interesting destinations for curious and adventurous visitors. Excavations on Monte Jato carried out over the past 25 years by the University of Zürich have unearthed remains of the ancient city of *Jetae* (the Roman *Iaitas*), which flourished from the 4th century BC until it was destroyed by Frederick II in the 13th century. The area now has 21 marked trails, of various levels of difficulty, for trekkers and ramblers, using for the most part ancient and medieval paths and bridle tracks, which had all but disappeared from sight and from memory. The trails offer unforgettable glimpses of historic remains, wildlife, and the lovely countryside of the area. Descriptions of the walks and maps are available from the Azienda Provinciale Turismo office in Palermo and from the local tourist offices.

Outside the nearby village of **San Cipirello**, where in Via Roma there is a small museum (*open 9–1; closed Sun and holidays*) dedicated to the site and displaying unusual statues found at the theatre there, a road leads up through lovely countryside to the site on top of the hill. The best-preserved remains date from the Hellenistic period. From the entrance gate it is a walk of about 20mins to the top of the hill with the theatre (late 4th century BC, reconstructed in the 1st century AD), which could seat 4,000, a Temple of Aphrodite (c. 550 BC), and a large villa on two floors with a peristyle and 25 rooms. The agora has also been partially uncovered. There are splendid views from this isolated spot.

Partinico, Borgetto and Montelepre

Partinico is an agricultural town associated with the name of Danilo Dolci (1924–1997), a philanthropist from Trieste who dedicated his life to opposing the Mafia using non-violent methods. In Piazza Duomo is a fountain of 1716. The Biblioteca Comunale (town library) nearby has a museum (*open Mon–Fri 9–12.30 & 4–6.30*) with finds from Monte Jato and Rocca d'Entella, and a local ethnographical collection, with an oil press and wine cellars. From the duomo, Corso dei Mille leads past a Neoclassical bandstand (1875) to the 17th-century church of San Leonardo with works by the school of Novelli. Opposite is the church of the Carmine (1634).

Not far from Partinico is **Borgetto**, a small farming community where the women are famous for their very particular home-made macaroni. In the hill town of **Montelepre**, the bandit Salvatore Giuliano reigned over a large part of the province, with the support of the Mafia, for seven years before he was murdered here in 1950 by his brother-in-law, Gaspare Pisciotta, at the age of 27. His body was shown to the press in a courtyard in Castelvetrano with the story that he had been tracked down and killed there by the Carabinieri. He remained a mythical figure in the imagination of many Sicilians until 1960, when his connection with the Mafia and local police was revealed, as well as his part in the massacre of peasants at Portella della Ginestra. A remarkable film by Francesco Rosi, *Salvatore Giuliano* (1961), tells his true story; he has also been played by Christopher Lambert in the film *The Sicilian*.

Carini and Terrasini

A lovely town that gives its name to the gulf here, Carini has interesting stalactite caverns in the outskirts, and a fine 16th-century castle (*open 9–1 & 4–8, closed Mon; ask at Tourist Office T: 091 8611339*). The castle is remembered for the tragic story of the

Baronissa di Carini, who in 1563 was murdered by her own father when he believed she had a lover. Called *Iccara* by the Greeks, it was the city of the legendary beauty Laide, thought to be the loveliest woman in the world, and carried off to Athens by General Nikias as a trophy of war in the late 5th century BC.

Beyond the airport at Punta Raisi and Mt Pecoraro is the lovely **Gulf of Castellammare**, which stretches away to Capo San Vito, the mountains behind providing a striking backdrop. It is a popular area for holiday homes, but the countryside is still beautiful, with olive and citrus groves. **Terrasini** is now a holiday resort, with a particularly good civic museum (*open 9–1 & 3.30–7.30*), with a natural history section, an archaeological display consisting of objects found on dives around shipwrecks, and a fine collection of hand-painted Sicilian carts.

THE SOUTH OF THE PROVINCE

Belmonte Mezzagno to Ficuzza

Between Bagheria and Piana degli Albanesi, Belmonte Mezzagno was founded in 1752 and has a scenographic church built in 1776. The valley of the ancient River Eleutheros below is densely inhabited, but some persimmon plantations survive. Above the plain is the ruined castle of **Misilmeri**. It takes its name from the Arab *Menzil el Emir* (dwelling of the Emir). Here in 1068 Count Roger de Hauteville defeated the Saracens, paving the way for Norman domination of Sicily. The castle of **Marineo** (*open Tues–Sun 9–1 & 3–7*), at the foot of an oddly shaped rock, was reconstructed in 1559 by Matteo Carnelivari.

Further south, **Ficuzza** is a village dominated by the Palazzina Reale, a handsome building in sandstone with numerous chimneys and two clocks, now used by the Azienda Forestale. It was built by Venanzio Marvuglia in 1803 as a hunting-lodge for the Bourbons, whose huge estate surrounded the lodge. Behind it extends the **Bosco della Ficuzza**, now a nature reserve, a splendid forest of oak, chestnut and ilex, which is the most extensive and interesting wooded area of its kind left on the island, noted for its fine trees, plants and wildlife. Although once much more extensive, it still covers some 4,000 hectares. Several rough roads and paths run through the woods, although much of it is fenced off for protection. Above the woods rises the **Rocca Busambra** (1613m), a mountain wall of calcareous rock which dominates the plain for many kilometres around. Above the sheer rock face, its summit provides pastureland. Numerous birds nest here, including the golden eagle. The **Gorgo del Drago**, the source of the River Frattina, is a green oasis, with yellow and red rocks.

Cefalà Diana to Castronuovo di Sicilia

To the east, the town of Cefalà Diana has a remarkable bathhouse, the **Bagni di Cefalà** (*open Tues–Sun 9–1; Sat & Sun also 4–7; closed Mon*), which dates back to the 10th–11th centuries and is considered the most interesting Arab building to survive on the island. The baths have a splendid barrel vault and a pretty arch with two capitals and columns at one end. The water used to bubble up here at 38 °C, but since 1989 the spring has been dry, and the baths, in use up until a few years ago, have lost much of their character since their recent restoration. The Kufic inscription on a frieze of tufa ('Of our lord prince the Emir two admirable baths') which runs around the top of the outside wall has virtually disappeared. The 13th-century castle is very prominent on a rocky outcrop to the south (*open Fri 4–7; Sat and Sun 9–1 & 4–7*).

Ciminna, further east, has a number of interesting churches including the Chiesa Madre with 17th-century stuccoes by Scipione and Francesco Li Volsi and a painting of *St John the Baptist* by the architect Paolo Amato (1634–1714), who was born here. The village was famously used as a location in Visconti's film *The Leopard* (1963).

The little hill town of **Mezzojuso** has Arab origins. Settled by Albanians in the 15th century, several of its churches still have services according to the Greek rite. A monastery here has a restoration laboratory for antique books.

Vicari, above the fertile valley of the San Leonardo river, has a wonderfully romantic ruined castle, probably Saracen, with views of extraordinary beauty. Count Roger wintered here after the battles of 1077.

Lercara Friddi, founded in 1605, with its attractive crumbling 18th-century churches, was once important for its sulphur mines. When the sulphur economy collapsed at the end of the 19th century, a thousand families emigrated to Venezuela and the USA, practically depopulating the town. In his compilation of Sicilian reflections *Words are Stones*, the writer Carlo Levi describes the mines and their working conditions here during a strike in 1951.

On the southern border of the province, on a hill overlooking the River Platani, is **Castronuovo di Sicilia**, once a town of strategic importance, now in decline. Much reforestation has been taking place here in the last few years; the inhabitants are farmers and raise milk cows: the cheese made here has superb flavour, as does the bread. Many of the churches contain 18th-century stuccoes by Antonio da Messina, and the 15th-century Chiesa Madre has works by the Gagini family..

Some way further to the east at **Regaleali** is the famous wine estate of the Tasca d'Almerita family on the southern border of the province (best reached from Vallelunga in the province of Caltanissetta). The cellars are open to the public (*open 10–11.30 & 3–6*) and wine and local produce can be purchased (*www.tascadalmerita.it*).

Prizzi to Contessa Entellina and Monte Adranone

To the west, the medieval town of **Prizzi** stands near the lake formed by damming the River Sosio, beneath curious outcrops of rock. Excavations on the Montagna dei Cavalli in the vicinity have revealed 4th–3rd century BC remains, possibly the ancient city of *Hippana*, destroyed by the Romans during the First Punic War. The most interesting finds can be seen in the Museo Civico in Corso Umberto (*open 9–1; closed Mon*).

The little town of **Palazzo Adriano** is a late 15th-century Albanian colony, with its main monuments in Piazza Umberto; it became famous throughout the world when Giuseppe Tornatore used it as a set for his Oscar-winning film *Cinema Paradiso* (1989).

Bisacquino, with stunning mountain views, was once an Arab citadel, then a medieval fortress town. 'Moth-soft Besacquino [sic]' wrote Lawrence Durrell in his *Sicilian Carousel*, an apt description of this gentle place where time stands still. The inhabitants know all about the passage of time: church clocks were still made here until recently. There is a **Museo dell'Orologio da Torre**, a museum of tower clocks, in Via Roma (*ask at the Tourist Office for admission*). The bell-tower of the Chiesa Matrice is unique in Sicily because of its triangular shape. The film director Frank Capra (1897–1991), who won six Oscars, was born in Bisacquino.

At the church (built 1676–1757), attributed to Luigi Vanvitelli, of the outlying Olivetan abbey of **Santa Maria del Bosco** is a terracotta of the Della Robbia school, two large cloisters (one of the 16th century), and a fresco of the *Miracle of the Loaves* (in the refectory).

Contessa Entellina is a charming mountain village that takes its first name from the Countess Caterina Cardona di Chiusa (who gave asylum to Albanian refugees in 1450) and its surname from *Entella* (a town of the Elymians which lies to the north-west on a high, isolated rock). On the extensive plateau, excavations of the ancient city, ravaged in the past by *tombaroli* (clandestine diggers), are in progress. So far the fortifications, part of the medieval fortress, and a building of 4th–3rd century BC have been identified. The necropoleis lay at the foot of the hill. The archaeological area is always open; the museum is at no. 1 Via I Maggio (*open 9–12 & 4–7*).

At **Monte Adranone** (1000m), on the provincial border with Agrigento, excavations of the ancient city of *Adranon* were begun in 1968. This was an indigenous settlement occupied by a Greek colony in the 6th century BC, probably founded by Selinunte. It was destroyed at the end of the 5th century by Carthage. The Carthaginian settlement was conquered by Rome in 263 BC and the site abandoned. Beside the small antiquarium is part of an Iron Age necropolis including the so-called **Tomba della Regina** with an interesting entrance. Tombs of the 5th and 4th centuries BC have also been found here. Other remains include walls and the south gate, a sanctuary, and part of the acropolis to the northeast.

Corleone

Corleone is a picturesque town of Arab origin nestled in the hillside, now surrounded by anonymous modern buildings. In recent years it has been notorious for its powerful Mafia gang, whose boss Totò Riina ruled *Cosa Nostra* for many years until his arrest in 1993, after more than 20 years 'in hiding' in Palermo.

A Lombard colony was established here by Frederick II in 1237. Traces of its importance as a medieval town can be seen in the old centre which preserves some fine palace doorways in its narrow streets. The **Chiesa Madre** (*if closed, ring at the inconspicuous north door approached from the road on the left of the outside steps through a gate*) contains some interesting wooden statues (16th–17th centuries), wooden choir-stalls by Giovanni Battista Li Volsi, and paintings (on the transept altars) by Fra' Felice da Sambuca, and (first north aisle chapel) Tommaso de Vigilia (*Adoration of the Magi*).

The public gardens, laid out in 1820, are well kept and there is an archaeological collection in **Palazzo Provenzano** (*open 9–1 & 3.30–7.30; Sun 9–1*).

THE ISLAND OF USTICA

Ustica, with some 1,400 inhabitants, lies a little over 50km off the coast northwest of Palermo, a small fertile island (just over 8.6 square kilometres), all that remains of an ancient volcano more than a million years old. The colours of Ustica are memorable; Gramsci, the prominent Italian communist who was held here as a political prisoner, remembered the 'impressive rainbows, and the extraordinary colours of the sea and the sky'. Ustica's highest hills rise to c. 240m above sea-level. The island was once covered with trees but few woods remain, the landscape now dotted with cultivated wheatfields, vineyards, almond groves and orchards, with hedges of prickly pear. Capers and lentils are also produced on the island. Ustica has interesting migratory birdlife, including peregrine falcons, kestrels, storks, herons, razorbills and cormorants. The rocky shoreline has numerous grottoes; it is particularly remarkable for its numerous fish—*cernia* (grouper) abound, as well as hake, red mullet, prawns, shrimps, lobsters and (in spring) swordfish—and for its seabed, hosting a great variety of seaweed, including the rare *laminaria*. In 1986 the first marine reserve in the Mediterranean was established around the island's coast, bringing renewed prosperity to the island. The reserve has now been extended to include the whole island. There is no source of water on Ustica apart from some of the caves, such as the Blue Grotto, but there is now a desalinization plant. Baseball and softball are very popular on the island, and teams from Ustica are often in the top division. The pleasant little village above the port of Cala Santa Maria is well kept, and only crowded in the summer months. One road encircles the island, and mule tracks, ideal for trekking, wind through the interior.

HISTORY OF USTICA

The name Ustica, from the Latin *ustum* (burnt), is derived from the colour of its black volcanic rock. Excavations have proved that it was inhabited in prehistoric times and in the Roman era. The Greeks called it *Osteodes*, (the place of bones), in reference to the 6,000 mercenaries abandoned here by the Carthaginians when they rebelled after a pay dispute, at the time of the wars with Syracuse. Attacks of Barbary pirates defeated all attempts to colonize it in the Middle Ages. It remained deserted for many centuries until in 1762 it was repopulated from the Aeolian Islands and Naples by the Bourbons because of its strategic location on the trade route between Naples and Palermo. At the time three towers were constructed to defend the island.

The island was used as a place of exile and as a prison until 1961: Carlo and Nello Rosselli and Antonio Gramsci were held here as political prisoners under the Fascist regime. In September 1943 Italian and British officers met in secret on the island to discuss details of Italy's change of sides.

EXPLORING USTICA

The little village above the port of Cala Santa Maria was laid out on geometric lines by the Bourbons in the 18th century. A road winds up to the piazza (also reached by steps from the port). To the right of the church Via Calvaria leads uphill to the Via Crucis where on the left a path continues up to the **Rocca della Falconiera**, a defensive tower, now used for exhibitions (the fort is also reached by car along a narrow road paved with pebbles). The tower is on the site of a 3rd-century BC settlement, also inhabited in Roman times. It has been excavated on three levels; the most conspicuous remains include a staircase and some 30 cisterns used to collect the rainwater, and a number of tombs.

There are fine views above the lighthouse which marks the eastern tip of the island and the rocky point known as the **Punta Omo Morto**, a nesting-place for numerous birds. To the southwest of the lighthouse a necropolis of the 5th–6th centuries AD has been identified.

On the other side of the village the **Torre Santa Maria**, another Bourbon tower, once used as a prison, has been restored and is now the archaeological museum. The finds from the island, including Bronze Age objects from the village at Faraglioni (*see below*) and underwater finds, are well displayed. Near the tower are remains of a 16th-century Benedictine convent and interesting old houses known as the *centro storico*, with stables, built around courtyards, some of them carefully restored as homes by the local inhabitants.

On the northern tip of the island, at **Faraglioni**, excavations begun in 1989 unearthed a large prehistoric village (14th–13th centuries BC), probably settled from the Aeolian Islands, with some 300 houses built in stone. The defensive walls are among the best fortifications of this period to have been discovered in Italy. The site is not yet open to visitors.

On the west coast, between Cala Sidoti and Caletta is the central zone of the *Riserva Naturale Marina* (*T: 091 6043111*), a protected area marked by red buoys where fishing is prohibited and boats have to keep offshore. Swimming is allowed only at the extreme northern and southern ends of the reserve (limited access). The aquarium here has a fine display of Mediterranean sea plants and fish.

Above the bay is the Bourbon **Torre dello Spalmatore** with fine vaulted rooms, owned by the marine reserve. There are plans to use it as a museum and cultural centre. Just to the south is the lighthouse at Punta Cavazzi which will become a scientific laboratory for marine research. A buoy in the sea here marks an underwater archaeological itinerary for skin-divers where a number of finds from various wrecks have been left *in situ* (*www.archeologiaviva.com*).

Ustica is much visited by skin-divers and the marine reserve collaborates with the fishermen who live on the island to arrange boat trips for visitors. Ustica is now considered to be a world centre for diving and underwater observation. Several organisations organise underwater tours and the island is particularly rich in hidden caves and slopes (*see practical information, p. 125*).

PRACTICAL INFORMATION

GETTING AROUND PALERMO

• **To and from the airport:** Falcone Borsellino Airport is at Punta Raisi, 32km west of Palermo, T: 091 7020111. Coach services run c. every 30mins to the Politeama (Via Emerico Amari) and the central railway station. Hourly *Trinacria Express* fast train connection to the central station (4.45am–9.40pm from Palermo and from 5.40am–5 past midnight from the airport), or the Metro. Taxis are expensive.

• **By car** Parking is difficult in the centre of Palermo. Pay car parks (with parking attendant) are near Piazza Castelnuovo, the station and Via Stabile. Elsewhere there are blue-line areas, for which tickets are purchased at tobacconists or newsagents and then displayed inside the windscreen. If you want to stay longer, you can leave two or three tickets at once. If your car is illegally parked and towed away, telephone the city police (*Vigili Urbani*), T: 091 6954111, or ask a taxi driver to help.

• **By public transport**
City buses tend to be overcrowded, infrequent and very slow because of the traffic. Tickets must be purchased at tobacconists or newsagents and stamped at automatic machines on board. There are two excellent mini-bus circular services, both of which penetrate some of the narrower streets and pass many of the city's most important monuments.

Mini-buses
Linea Gialla (yellow): railway station—Corso dei Mille—Orto Botanico—Kalsa—Via Alloro (Regional Art Gallery in Palazzo Abatellis) —Via Maqueda—Ballarò—Corso Tuköry—Santo Spirito—Via Oreto—railway station.

Linea Rossa (red): Via Alloro (Regional Art Gallery in Palazzo Abatellis) —Quattro Canti—Cassaro (Corso Vittorio Emanuele) — Cathedral—Via Papireto—Via Sant'Agostino—Via Maqueda—Vucciria—Cala—Piazza Marina—Via Alloro (Palazzo Abatellis).

GETTING AROUND THE PROVINCE

• **By bus:** Daily services from Via Balsamo (near the railway station): AST (T: 091 6208111) to Ragusa, Bagheria and Solunto; Cuffaro (T: 091 6161510) to Agrigento; SAIS-Interbus (T: 091 6166028 & 091 6171141, www.saisautolinee.it), c. every hour to Catania (via the motorway in 2hrs 40mins), Enna (in c. 2hrs); also to Cefalù, Piazza Armerina, Messina, Termini Imerese and many mainland destinations; Scoppio (T: 083 6801578 & 083 801005), daily service to/from Otranto; Segesta (T: 091 6169039, 091 346376 & 0923 981120, www.segesta.it) to Trapani, Alcamo, Marsala and Castelvetrano.
Buses 309 and 389 from Piazza Indipendenza in Palermo (frequent service in 20–30mins) to Monreale.
Randazzo (T: 091 8148235) runs from Palermo and Termini Imerese to Caccamo.
Prestia e Comandè (T: 091 586351), Sicilbus (T: 091 346376) and AST (T: 091 6208111) run several times a day

from Palermo Via Balsamo and Piazza Stazione to Piana degli Albanesi, Partinico, Montelepre, San Giuseppe Iato and San Cipirello.

From Cefalù buses run by SAIS (T: 091 6166028) leave from the railway station for the towns and villages of the Madonie Mountains.

• **By rail:** Palermo Centrale for all state railway services (T: 091 6165914) to Agrigento, Messina, Trapani, Catania, Caltanissetta and Enna. Bagheria and S. Flavia–Solunto, Termini Imerese, and Cefalù are on the main Palermo–Messina line. The nearest station to Alia is Roccapalumba (5km from both towns).

• **By boat:** Car ferries and hydrofoils to Ustica run by Siremar (120 Via Crispi, Palermo, T: 091 336631, 091 8449002) and SNAV (T: 091 8449077). Ustica Lines also runs a hydrofoil from Terrasini during the summer. Consult www.bookingitalia.it for up-to-date information on times and prices.

BOAT TRIPS

Aeolian Islands

Trips to the **Aeolian Islands** are run by SMIV Sicilia Cruises every day in summer from **Cefalù**, T: 0921 420601. Hydrofoil services run to the Aeolian Islands (June–Sept). Information from the APT. Giuseppe will take you fishing with him, T: 0921 420683, 0921 420339 or 380 5142939; also try **Pesca Turismo**, T: 338 2309141, www.cefalu-turismo.it.

Ustica

Giannuzzo, T: 091 8449371.
Ustica Mare, T: 091 8449270.
Local fishermen organise 2-hour trips

(in summer) around the island 4–6 times a day. The trip includes visits to the grottoes and swimming time. Tickets from the marine reserve's Centro Accoglienza. The glass-bottomed boat belonging to the marine reserve also takes small groups of 20 around the coast (4 times a day). The trip lasts about an hour and a half.

Salvatore Militello, T: 091 8449002, has a glass-bottomed trimaran for excursions, also by night.

SCUBA DIVING

Ustica

Underwater tours can be organised by **Barracuda**, Contrada Spalmatore, *T: 091 8449132*; **Diving Center**, 4 Via Vittorio Emanuele, *T: 091 8449533*; and **Profondo Blu**, Via Cristoforo Colombo, *T: 091 8449609*)

INFORMATION OFFICES

Palermo APT Palermo: 35 Piazza Castelnuovo, T: 091 6058111 & 091 583847, www.palermotourism.com, www.aapit.pa.it, www.comune.palermo.it; for information on the whole province. Subsidiary offices at the railway station (T: 091 6165914) and airport (T: 091 591698).

Tourist agencies in Palermo
Agenzia Sole Blu Sicilia: 10 Via Mariano Stabile, T: 091 323064 & 091 6122735, soleblusicilia@tin.it. Assistance in finding accommodation, organizing excursions, hiring cars, yachts or motorcycles, finding guides or interpreters, and suggesting itineraries.

Legambiente: Onlus Palermo Futura, 27 Via Malaspina, T: 091 321527, open

Mon–Thur 5.30–7.30; for information on nature reserves.
Lega Italiana Protezione Uccelli: 7 Via Houel, T: 091 323804, for information on birdwatching in the region.
Musei di Charme: consult www.museidicharme.it for information on many of Palermo's smaller museums.
Qanat: it is now possible to explore the underground network of the Arab aqueduct. Book your visit with **Sottosopra** Compagno di Viaggio, 375 via Maqueda, T: 091 580433; they supply the gear.
WWF: 98 Via Albanese, T: 091 333468 and 091 583040, information on parks and reserves.
Offices in the province
Alia 75 Via Vittorio Emanuele, T: 091 8210913; Municipio, 1 Via Regina Elena, T: 091 8210911, www.comunedialia.it
Bagheria Centro Informazioni Turistiche: Corso Umberto, T: 091 909020; can also arrange guided tours, www.comune.bagheria.pa.it
Caccamo Palazzo Monte di Pietà, Piazza Duomo, T: 091 8103248, open Mon–Sat 9–1. **Sicilia & dintorni**, 8 Via del Castello, T: 091 225035, www.siciliaedintorni.it.
Castelbuono Pro Loco: 57 Corso Umberto, T: 0921 673467, www.comune.castelbuono.pa.it
Cefalù 77 Corso Ruggero (corner Via Amendola), T: 0921 421050, www.cefalu-tour.pa.it; 113 Corso Ruggero, T: 0921 923327.
Gangi Pro Loco: 4 Cortile Ospedale, T: 0921 689781, www.comune.gangi.pa.it
Madonie Mountains Ente Parco delle Madonie, 16 Corso Agliata, T: 0921 684011, www.parcodellemadonie.it, www.madonie.it
Monreale Piazza Vittorio Emanuele, T:

091 6409589, www.monreale.net
Petralia Soprana Pro Loco: 8 Via Sopra Convento, T: 0921 640746.
Piana degli Albanesi Municipio, Via Matteotti, T: 091 8574144; www.comunepianadeglialbanesi.it, www.pianaalbanesi.it
Polizzi Generosa Pro Loco: 18 Via Mistretta, T: 0921 649509.
Termini Imerese T: 091 8128253, www.comune.termini-imerese.pa.it, www.prolocotermini.it
Ustica Marine Reserve Visitors' Centre (Centro Accoglienza): Piazza Umberto, T: 091 8449456, www.laboratoriomarino ustica.it; Comune di Ustica, T: 091 8449237, www.comune.ustica.pa.it, www.ustica.net; Pro Loco: Piazza Vito Longo, T: 091 8449190, www.ustica.info, www.isola-ustica.com, www.usticavacanze.it

HOTELS

Palermo
€€€ **Villa Igiea**. A remarkable Art Nouveau building on the sea at Acquasanta, 3km north of the city in a large park. Built as a sanatorium by Donna Franca Florio, it was transformed into a luxury hotel by Ernesto Basile in 1900. The dining room (Sala Basile) is a masterpiece, with walls painted by Bergler, and matching furniture. Tennis courts and pool. 43 Salita Belmonte, T: 091 6312111, www.amthotels.com
€€€ **Excelsior Palace**. A delightful Belle Epoque atmosphere, central position, excellent service and good restaurant. 3 Via Marchese Ugo, T: 091 6256176.
€€€ **Grand Hotel et des Palmes**. Richard Wagner's favourite, this was for-

merly Palazzo Ingham, transformed into a hotel in 1874. Good restaurant, where you will rub shoulders with Italian politicians. 398 Via Roma, T: 091 6028111, www.amthotels.it

€€ **Ai Cavalieri**. Small, discreet hotel in central position, very elegant rooms and patio, no restaurant. 2 Via Sant'Oliva, T: 091 583282.

€€ **Centrale Palace**. A prestigious 19th-century hotel; rooftop terrace, lovely rooms (quieter at the back away from the Via Maqueda, with wonderful views from the top floor), good rooftop restaurant. 327 Corso Vittorio Emanuele, T: 091 336666, www.centralepalacehotel.it

€€ **Grande Albergo Sole**. Newly overhauled, historic hotel where many of the famous have stayed. Very central but not easy if you are driving. 291 Corso Vittorio Emanuele, T: 091 6041111, www.ghshotels.it

€€ **Jolly Hotel del Foro Italico**. Lovely hotel on the seafront close to the Villa Giulia park. Excellent restaurant; pool; free use of bicycles. 22 Foro Italico, T: 091 6165090, www.jollyhotels.it

€€ **Politeama Palace**. Modern hotel in city centre, opposite Politeama Theatre. Comfortable rooms, obliging service, good restaurant. 15 Piazza Ruggero Settimo, T: 091 322777, www.hotelpoliteama.it

€€ **Principe di Villafranca**. Small, refined hotel, central position in the new city; good restaurant, cosy library and lounge with open fireplace, garage and fitness centre. Elegant bedrooms. 4 Via Turrisi Colonna, T: 091 6118523, www.principedivillafranca.it

€€ **Vecchio Borgo**. In a very old district of Palermo, near a colourful daily food market. 1–7 Via Quintino Sella, T: 091

6111446, www.classicahotels.com

€€ **Amarcord**. Tiny new hotel, good value for money, central. 139 Via Mariano Stabile, T: 091 6115144, www.amarcordhotel.it

€€ **Gallery House**. Central, very comfortable little hotel, no restaurant, internet in all rooms.136 Via Mariano Stabile, T: 091 6124758, www.hotelgalleryhouse.com

€€ **Letizia**. Friendly little hotel close to San Francesco and the Vucciria; bright rooms, lots of stairs. 30 Via Bottai, T: 091 589110, www.hotelletizia.com

€ **Ariston**. Centrally situated, small hotel with clean, comfortable rooms and good management. 139 Via Mariano Stabile, T: 091 332434, www.aristonpalermo.it

€ **Joli**. Charming little hotel, central position.11 Via Michele Amari (Piazza Florio), T: 091 6111765/6, www.hoteljoli.com

€ **Posta**. Historic hotel in centre, opposite post office, much used in the past by actors and singers on *tournée*, nice rooms and good service, run by the same family for over 80 years. Garage available. 77 Via Gagini, T: 091 587338, www.hotelpostapalermo.it

€ **Villa Archirafi**. Comfortable hotel with garden, close to Villa Giulia and the Botanical Gardens; impeccable service. 30 Via Abramo Lincoln, T: 091 6168827, villaarchirafi@libero.it

€ **Orientale**. Quite a find, this little family-run hotel occupies part of the huge 18th-century palace built for Prince Alessandro Filangieri di Cutò, and has been a hotel since 1890. Quaint, large rooms, some with smart new bathrooms and air conditioning. No restaurant. 26 Via Maqueda, T: 091 6165727, www.albergoorientale.191.it

Bagheria

€ **Da Franco il Conte**. Friendly, modern establishment with an excellent restaurant and garage, Count Franco is quite a personality. 29/31 Via Vallone de Spuches, Bagheria, T: 091 966815, www.dafrancoilconte.it

Caccamo

€ **La Spiga d'Oro**. Small, simple hotel, in town centre, with restaurant. 78 Via Margherita, T: 091 8148968.

Caltavuturo

€ **Crocco d'Oro**. A very simple inn, with restaurant, in the heart of the town. 75 Via Garibaldi, T: 0921 540657.

Castelbuono

€ **Milocca**, Contrada piano Castagna, T: 0921 671944. Above the town in the woods; pool, excellent restaurant, bowls. The hotel organizes trekking or horseriding in the Madonie park.

Cefalù

€€ **Baia del Capitano**. Nice hotel surrounded by olive trees, out of town but with access to the beach, comfortable rooms with sea view. Contrada Mazzaforno, T: 0921 420003, www.baiadelcapitano.it

€€ **Le Calette**. Elegant hotel on a tiny bay out of town, also apartments to rent. Windsurfing, snorkelling and horse-riding available. 12 Via Cavallaro, T: 0921 424144, www.lecalette.it

€ **Pink**. Incredible colour, comfortable hotel just out of town overlooking Kaldura bay; snorkelling, sailing, pool, hospitable management. Località Kaldura, T: 0921 422275.

Isnello

€€ **Piano Torre Park**. Recently restored 18th-century castle about 15km from Isnello. Restaurant, pool,

tennis and plenty of activities for guests. Località Torre Montaspro, T: 0921 662671.

Mondello

€€ **Addaura**. On the beach, with water sports, pool, garden and good restaurant; comfortable rooms. 4452 Lungomare Cristoforo Colombo, T: 091 6842222, www.addaura.it

€€ **Conchiglia d'Oro**. Just right for families, a quiet hotel with pool. 9 Viale Cloe, T: 091 450032.

€€ **Villa Esperia**. Attractive Art Nouveau building in central position, close to the beach; garden and restaurant, vegetarian meals on request. 53 Via Margherita di Savoia, T: 4 091 6840717, www.hotelvillaesperia.it

Monreale

€€ **Carrubbella Park**. Comfortable hotel with restaurant. 233 Via Umberto, T: 091 6402188.

Montelepre

€€ **Il Castello di Giuliano**. Smart hotel on the outskirts of town. The restaurant is particularly good, so are the local wines. 1 Via Magistrato Pietro Merra, T: 091 8941006.

Petralia Sottana

€ **Madonie**. Charming old hotel in the town centre. Good restaurant. 81 Corso Agliata, T: 091 641106.

Roccapalumba

€ **La Rocca**. Simple hotel close to village centre, children welcome, restaurant serving vegetarian food on request, car park. 8 Via Case Vecchie, T: 091 8215219.

Termini Imerese

€€€ **Grand Hotel delle Terme**, 2 Piazza Terme, T: 091 8113557. Comfortable; in a good position for touring the area; spa, gym and excellent restaurant, in a lovely Art Nouveau building.

Ustica

€€ **Grotta Azzurra**. Very comfortable; built over the Grotta Azzurra, with garden and pool; panoramic views. Contrada San Ferlicchio, T: 091 8449048, www.framonhotels.com

€€ **Clelia**. Welcoming, clean little hotel with good restaurant. 29 Via Sindaco, T: 091 8449039, www.hotelclelia.it

€€ **Punta Spalmatore**. In one of the most beautiful parts of the island, accommodation is in a series of little bungalows surrounded by a garden, for a comfortable holiday; there are many sports facilities and a fitness centre. Good restaurant. Località Spalmatore, T: 091 8449388, www.octotravel.it

€ **Albergo Giulia**. Simple, family-run establishment where you can be sure of a pleasant stay; excellent restaurant. 16 Via San Francesco, T: 091 8449007.

€ **Ariston**. Elegant; small; central position with good restaurant called Da Umberto. Can help arrange dives and excursions. 5 Via della Vittoria, T: 091 8449042.

BED & BREAKFAST

Palermo

€€€ **Palazzo Ajutamicristo**. This sumptuous 15th-century palazzo has a lovely courtyard brimming with palms and banana trees. Watercolour painting courses can be organized. 23 Via Garibaldi, T: 091 6161894, www.palazzo-ajutamicristo.com

€€€ **Palazzo Conte Federico**. An ancient palazzo owned by a descendant of Frederick of Hohenstaufen. English, French and German spoken. 4 Via dei Biscottari (cathedral), T: 091 6511881, www.contefederico.com

€€ **Casa Mendola**. A fascinating old Palermo house with lots of atmosphere. 58 Via Garibaldi, T: 091 6166981.

€€ **Il Laboratorio**. For something quite different, the charming house of a young artist, overlooking Porta Felice. 1 Via Butera, T: 091 327651.

€ **Ai Cartari**. Converted paper-factory near San Francesco church, English and French spoken, very friendly owners. 62 Via Alessandro Paternostro, T: 091 6116372, www.aicartari.com

€ **Casa Pojero**. Beautiful rooms in an ideal position; cooking facilities available, tiny bathrooms, without stairs. English, German and Spanish spoken. 106 Via Emerico Amari (Politeama), T: 091 332416 & 338 4346502, giacco.pojero@libero.it

Cefalù

€ **Ale Robi**. In the old quarter, close to the bastions. 17 Via Porpora, T: 0921 424020, www.alerobi.it

€ **Ma & Mi**. Comfortable rooms, hillside position, car park. 97 Strada provinciale Cefalù-Gibilmanna, T: 0921 424964, www.maemi.it

€€ **Masseria Abazia**. Beautifully restored old farmhouse in the hills behind Cefalù amidst a large olive grove. Guests can use the kitchen, bicycles for hire, horse-riding. French and English spoken. T: 091 6167839, abaziafloris@hotmail.com

Castelbuono

€ **Guarnera**. Charming old country house with a farm next door, which supplies the ingredients for breakfast. Guests can use the kitchen; dinner on request; garden and small pool. French spoken. Contrada Gargi di Cenere, T:

0921 428431, www.gargidicenere.it

Collesano

€ Casale Drinzi. Very welcoming place, English spoken. Contrada Casale Drinzi (500m from Collesano), T: 0921 664027, www.casaledrinzi.it

Mondello

€ Il Banano. Nineteenth-century villa with garden, close to beach and main square; airport transfer at small extra cost, English and Spanish spoken. 3 Via Stesicoro, T: 091 455926, www.ilbanano.com

FARMHOUSE ACCOMMODATION

Alia

€€ Villa Dafne. Ancient wheat farm a short distance from the town; sheep and olives; guests can help on the farm. Excursions are organized on horseback or mountain bike. Cookery lessons on request. Excellent traditional local dishes and good local wines. Contrada Cozzo di Cicero, T: 091 8219174.

Bosco della Ficuzza

€ L'Antica Stazione. What was once the railway station is now a delightful place to stay, just right for naturalists and hikers. Foxes even come into the restaurant. Frazione Ficuzza, T: 091 8460000, www.anticastazione.it

Castelbuono

€€€ Relais Santa Anastasia. Lovely restored Benedictine monastery, now an award-winning wine farm with luxurious rooms, pool, horse-riding. Contrada Santa Anastasia, T: 0921 671959, www.abbaziasantanastasia.it

€€€ Villa Levante. A beautiful castle (open Apr–Oct) with sweeping views over the valley. Self-catering apartments in the corner towers. Restaurant within walking distance at Castelbuono. Activities include trekking and mountain biking. Contrada Vignicella, T: 335 6394574.

€€ Masseria Rocca di Gonato. Remote 12th-century Basilian monastery, rather heavily restored. Good base for botanists (orchids) and bird watchers. The farm raises cattle, sheep, goats, donkeys and horses. Restaurant is crowded at weekends with locals. Contrada Rocca di Gonato, T: 0921 672616, www.roccadigonato.it

Collesano

€ Arione. In a lovely part of the Madonie park, this farm raises thoroughbred horses and sheep and produces olive oil. The food is particularly good; everything is home made, including the bread and the pasta. Contrada Pozzetti, T: 0921 427703, www.agriturismoarione.it

Gangi

€€ Gangivecchio. Beautiful converted monastery. The farm produces award-winning olive oil and runs highly recommended courses in Sicilian cookery for guests. Contrada Gangi Vecchio, T: 0921 644804.

Partinico

€ Arabesque. A few hundred yards from the sea at Balestrate, near Partinico. Citrus fruit and olives are grown and thoroughbred Arab horses are raised. Pool and many activities are on offer. Contrada Manostalla, Balestrate, T: 091 8787755, www.agriturismoarabesque.com

€ Fattoria Manostalla. A lovely old farm in an excellent position. Cattle and sheep are raised, and there are vineyards producing Bianco d'Alcamo. Cookery courses, delta-planing, trekking and mountain biking. Località Manostalla, Villa Chiarelli, Balestrate, T: 091 8787033, www.villachiarelli.it

Petralia Sottana
€ **Monaco di Mezzo**. Ancient farm in lovely countryside, in the Madonie park; organic food; pool; horse-riding, tennis. Contrada Monaco di Mezzo, T: 0934 673710, www.monacodimezzo.com

Piana degli Albanesi
€ **Masseria Rossella**. Eighteenth-century country villa with frescoed ceilings and private chapel, pleasant climate; close to the Ficuzza woods and the Rocca Busambra. Località Rossella, T: 091 8460012, www.masseria-rossella.com

Polizzi Generosa
€ **Santa Venera**. Farm produces hazelnuts and wine; pool; good restaurant specializing in *sfoglio*, the local cheese pie. Contrada Santa Venera, T: 0921 649421, www.santavenera.com

Pollina
€ **Tenuta Luogo Marchese**. Between Pollina and Castelbuono, a lovely farm and equestrian centre, horse-riding lessons, good restaurant, excursions organized in Madonie park. SS 286 km 4700, Contrada Luogo Marchese, T: 0921 420601, www.tenutaluogomarchese.it

San Giuseppe Jato
€€ **Casale del Principe**. In the peaceful countryside near San Giuseppe Jato, a 17th-century monastery transformed into a farm now offers accommodation for visitors, who can help with the farm activities (harvesting grapes and olives, etc). Children especially welcome. Contrada Dammusi, SS 121 Palermo–Agrigento, exit San Giuseppe Jato, T: 091 8579910, www.casaledelprincipe.it

San Mauro Castelverde
€€ **Flugy Ravetto**. Historic farmhouse with very comfortable accommodation, surrounded by ancient olive groves, belonging to one of the oldest aristocratic families of Sicily. Impeccable hospitality, excellent food. Trekking, pool, children's play area. Contrada Ogliastro, T: 0921 675121, www.aziendeflugyravetto.com

Ustica
€ **Hibiscus**. Charming farm offering self-catering accommodation in little cottages, there is a restaurant ten minutes' walk away; the farm produces wine and lentils. French and English spoken. Località Tramontana, T: 091 8449543, www.usticaholidays.com/agriturismo

ROOMS, VILLAS & APARTMENTS TO RENT

Palermo
€€ **Palazzo Marchesi Ugo delle Favare**. Offers an independent self-catering apartment in this medieval palace, a stone's throw from the cathedral. 10 Piazza Bologni, T: 347 8871869.
€€€ **Villa Camastra-Tasca**. A gorgeous house on the fringe of the city, visited by Goethe, Wagner, and half the kings and queens of Europe, surrounded by one of the loveliest gardens in Sicily, with a pool. The villa can take 10 people, plus another four in the cottage in the garden. Cook, butler and chauffeur are included. 399 Via Regione Siciliana, T: 091 6574304, www.luxuryretreats.com

Bagheria
€€ **Villa San Marco**. One of the oldest (16th century), most spectacular, and authentically aristocratic of the Bagheria villas, offers well-appointed self-catering apartments, each with its own veranda

and enormous, mysterious, inviting Sicilian garden. Use of pool June–Sept; air conditioning and heating. 1km from station; English French spoken. T: 091 903817.

RESTAURANTS

Palermo

€€€€ **Il Ristorantino**. Refined little restaurant where Pippo Anastasio takes great care of his guests. Many surprising starters and main-course dishes, followed by unusual desserts. Exceptional wine list. Closed Mon. 19 Piazza De Gasperi (Favorita), T: 091 512861.

✓ €€€€ **Osteria dei Vespri**. Right under the palace where Visconti filmed the ballroom scenes of *The Leopard*, a tavern where you can sample the exciting fusions of Sicilian and Parma cuisine. Extensive wine list including most Sicilian and Italian wines. Closed Sun. 6 Piazza Croce dei Vespri, T: 091 6171631.

€€ **Santandrea**. In a small square close to the church of San Domenico. Delightful restaurant with a special atmosphere; delicious food (exceptional ravioli) and extensive wine list. Closed Tues, Sun in summer. 4 Piazza Sant'Andrea, T: 091 334999.

€€ **Capricci di Sicilia**. Takes pride in presenting the very best cuisine of Palermo, served with only the best Sicilian wines. Closed Mon. 8 Piazza Sturzo (Via Istituto Pignatelli), T: 091 327777.

€€ **Cucina Papoff**. Nice peaceful atmosphere, attentive service, traditional Sicilian cuisine and wines. Closed Sat lunchtime and Sun. 32 Via La Lumia, T: 091 586460.

€€ **Dal Pompiere**. Eating here is great fun; the food is simple and satisfying. Right in the centre of the 'arts and crafts' area of the city. Closed Sun. 107 Via Bara all'Olivella, T: 091 325282.

€€ **Gagini**. A simple, friendly trattoria near the Cala. Closed Mon. 35–37 Via Cassari, T: 091 321518.

€€ **Maestro del brood**. One of the oldest restaurants in town, famous for beef stew with saffron—still excellent, but nowadays people flock here for the imaginative seafood dishes too. Desserts are nothing special, choose fruit. Efficient service. Closed Tues and every evening except Fri & Sat in winter, opens only for lunch in summer, and closes Sun. 7 Via Pannieri (Vucciria), T: 091 329523.

€€ **Piccolo Ristorante Napoli**. This delightful trattoria is a lunchtime venue for Palermitans 'in the know' (open for dinner only Fri & Sat); certainly worth a journey for those who appreciate perfectly cooked fish. Try the spaghetti in fish broth! Good list of Sicilian wines. Closed Sun & Aug. 4 Piazza Mulini a Vento (Politeama), T: 091 320431.

€€ **Stella** (Hotel Patria). Charming trattoria, very popular with the locals. Meals are served in the cool courtyard. The antipasti are good, so are the grilled meats. Closed Sun & Mon lunchtime in summer; Mon & Sun evening in winter. 104 Via Alloro, T: 091 6161136.

€€ **Trattoria Biondo**. Charming, intimate atmosphere, so better for dinner than lunch. The list of Sicilian wines is superb; impeccable cuisine. Closed Wed. 15 Via Carducci (Politeama), T: 091 583662.

€€ **Trattoria Lo Sparviero**. Very good Sicilian food, reasonable prices.

Marvellous grilled vegetables, the best in Palermo; also pizza. 23 Via Sperlinga, T: 091 331163.

€€ **Via dello Spasimo**. Right in front of the Spasimo, delightfully innovative cuisine, good wine list. Closed Sun, open evenings only. 42 Via dello Spasimo, T: 091 6161989.

€ **Le Tre Sorelle**. Historic trattoria (opened in 1888), still offers simple traditional Palermo food, such as *pasta con le sarde* (macaroni with sardines and wild fennel), or *macco di fave* (broad bean soup), using fresh ingredients from the Capo market close by. Closed Sun. Sicilian wines. 110 Via Volturno, T: 091 585960.

€ **Ru fila ri pasta**. Booking advisable at this immensely popular restaurant where the utmost simplicity is the keyword; Palermitan dishes; no cream and no frozen foods are used. Closed Mon. 16–18 Via Salinas, T: 091 7303059.

€ **Tonnara Florio**. A delightfully informal restaurant in an old tuna fishery, offering a constantly changing menu and many kinds of pizza; very popular with Palermitans and visiting celebrities—certainly a place for rubbing shoulders. 4 Discesa Tonnara, T: 091 6376511.

Bagheria

€€€ **Porta del Pepe**. very refined restaurant in the old centre, panoramic terrace. Closed Mon. 5 Via Greco (Piazza Sepolcro), T: 091 900562.

€€ **Don Ciccio**. A popular, reasonably-priced restaurant, run by the same family for generations, with appetizing local dishes; very good cook. Closed Wed and Sun, Aug. 87 Viale del Cavaliere, T: 091 932442.

Caccamo

€€ **La Castellana**. Restaurant in the old grain stores of the castle. Inexpensive set menu and good pizza in the evening. Superb pasta: try *farfalle al limone* (with lemon) or *penne al finocchietto* (with wild fennel); Sicilian wines. 4 Piazza del Monumento, T: 091 8148667.

Castelbuono

€€€ **Nangalarruni**. Renowned in this part of the world, people come a long way to feast on wild fungi, delicious grills, home-made desserts, accompanied by the best wines. Closed Wed. 5 Via Alberghi delle Confraternite, T: 0921 671428.

€ **La Tavernetta**. Excellent local dishes and a wide selection of Sicilian and Italian wines. 7 Via Garibaldi, T: 328 5790642.

Cefalù

€€€ **La Brace**. An elegant restaurant; Dutch-owned, with a vaguely exotic atmosphere. Delicious fish, very good Sicilian winelist. Closed Mon and lunchtime Tues. 10 Via XXV Novembre, T: 0921 423570.

€€€ **Ostaria del Duomo**. Carefully prepared Sicilian food, good wine list. Near cathedral. Closed Mon in winter. 5 Via Seminario, T: 0921 421838.

€€€ **Taverna del Presidente**. Refined restaurant on the seafront, perfect for romantic candlelit dinners, or for an indulgent lunch after a swim. If you don't like fish, the meat dishes are very good too. Sicilian wines. 163 lungomare Giardina, T: 0921 921359. Closed Tues.

€€ **Al Gabbiano**. Traditionally known for its good seafood dishes, also pizza. Closed Mon in winter. 17 Lungomare Giardina, T: 0921 421495.

€ **Il Covo del Pirata**. Delicious sandwiches and salads; lunch only (becomes a music club in the evenings). 59 Via

Vittorio Emanuele (next to the Lavatoio).

Mondello

€€€ **Bye Bye Blues**. Fish dishes a speciality, but the vegetable antipasti are magnificent, too. Superb desserts. Good wine list. Closed Tues. 23 Via del Garofalo, T: 091 6841415.

€€€ **Charleston**. Opulent Art Nouveau establishment jutting out over the sea, very expensive, good cuisine and wines of Sicily, with suitably professional service. Closed Wed. Viale Regina Elena, T: 091 450171.

€€ **Bocca di Bacco**. Historic restaurant (1865) in front of the harbour. Local dishes and some very special recipes; good wine list. 26 Via Torre, T: 091 6840127.

€€ **Sariddu**. Worth a visit for the delicious seafood antipasto; in summer, try watermelon with port for dessert. 48 Piazza Mondello, T: 091 451922.

Monreale

€€ **Bricco and Bracco**. A restaurant for carnivores. No pasta, everything is based on meat, including some unusual cuts and local specialities, all expertly cooked and served. Red wines only, from the best Sicilian vineyards. Closed Mon. 13 Via Benedetto D'Acquisto. T: 091 6417773

€€ **La Botte 1962**. Out of town, on the road to San Martino, this well-known tavern is unfortunately closed from mid-June–mid-September. Very picturesque, excellent local fare is served, accompanied by a good wine list; cheerful open fire in winter. 20 Contrada Lentizzi, SS 186 km 10, T: 091 414051.

€ **Taverna del Pavone**. A short distance from the cathedral, tiny trattoria which serves good pasta, and delicious home-made almond parfait with hot chocolate sauce. Closed Mon. 18 Vicolo Pensato, T: 091 6406209.

Piana degli Albanesi

€€ **Le Due Giare**. Simple and satisfying local dishes. Good wine list. Closed Tues. 26 Viale VIII Marzo, T: 091 8575589.

Polizzi Generosa

€€ **'U Bagghiu**. Traditional mountain fare. 3 Via Gagliardo, T: 0921 49546.

Porticello (Santa Flavia)

Santa Flavia, between Palermo and Bagheria, is just the place to stop for lunch.

€€€ **La Muciara**. Owner Nello 'El Greco' is Roman, his basic ingredients are the fish, pasta and vegetables of Sicily. Superb simple dishes, overlooking the port. 103 Via Roma, T: 091 957868. Closed Mon.

San Cipirello

€ **Apud Iatum**. Fantastic antipasti and appetizing pasta dishes. Closed Mon. 49 Via Trento, T: 091 8576188.

San Giuseppe Jato

€€ **Da Totò**. Also has rooms. Home-made tagliatelle, delicious desserts. Closed Fri evening. 251 Via Vittorio Emanuele, T: 091 8573344.

Sant'Elia (Santa Flavia)

€€ **Le Nasse**. Like Porticello, Sant'Elia is a charming little fishing port. Simple restaurant, excellent seafood dishes, exclusively Sicilian wines. 30 Via dei Cantieri, T: 349 1714237. Closed Wed.

Sferracavallo

Palermitans often go to the village of Sferracavallo when they want to spend an evening eating seafood. There are lots of inexpensive restaurants here, which serve a series of seafood dishes, usually for a fixed price. One of the best, offering an experience of life Palermo-style, is

Temptation, in the main square, T: 091 6911104.
Ustica
€€ **Baia del Sole**. Delicious stuffed baked squid, and pasta with capers, aubergines, shrimps, basil and tomato. Contrada Spalmatore (they will provide transport to/from restaurant if you call them first), T: 091 8449175.
€€ **Giulia**. Booking essential. The restaurant is small and very famous. Chef Pina specializes in *cernia* (grouper), either marinated in lemon, or cooked with breadcrumbs, tomato, olive oil, lemon and garlic. 16 Via San Francesco, T: 091 8449039.
€€ **Mario**. Spaghetti with sea urchins and other superb pasta dishes, including one made with cuttle-fish ink. 21 Piazza Umberto, T: 091 8449505.

PIZZERIE, SNACK BARS & SANDWICHES

Palermo
Antica Focacceria di San Francesco. Sample traditional Palermitan snacks and sandwiches: bread with *panelle* (chick-pea fritters), *meusa* (grilled beef spleen), *purpu* (boiled octopus), *stigghiole* (stuffed intestines of kid or lamb, seasoned and wound around a cane and grilled). Closed Tues. 58 Via Alessandro Paternostro, T: 091 320264.
Antica Trattoria del Monsù. This little restaurant is famous for the delicious, authentic pizza, baked in a stone oven, even at lunchtime. 41 Via Volturno, T: 091 327774.
Bar Mazzara. Simple delicious food, cooked in front of you, and the best *cotoletta palermitana* (breaded grilled steak) of the city. Tomasi di Lampedusa wrote *The Leopard* here. Great sweets too (the

restaurant is over the pastry shop). Open lunchtime only. 15 Via Generale Magliocco.
Focacceria Basile. The best *arancini* (rice balls). 76 Via Bara dell'Olivella (Opera House).
I Cuochini. This snack bar opened more than 100 years ago. Traditional delights. 68 Via Ruggero Settimo.
Minà. A good choice for robust sandwiches. 28 Via Pannieri (Vucciria).
Renna Self-Service. Fresh, simple food in a clean, tidy setting. Very inexpensive. 29/A Via Principe di Granatelli, T: 091 580661.
Sciuscià. Authentic Neapolitan pizza. Closed Tues, open evenings only. 212 Via Dante, T: 091 6822700.
Trappitu. An old olive press, where imaginative fare and pizza are served on a terrace overlooking the sea. 96 Via Bordonaro, T: 0921 921972.
Mondello
Antica Friggitoria Raia. Very good *panelle*, with chick-pea flour, and other traditional snacks. 26 Piazza Mondello.

CAFÉS, ICE CREAM & PASTRY SHOPS

Palermo
Aluia. One of the best pastry shops for local specialities. Via Mazzini, corner 27 Via Libertà.
Antico Caffè Spinnato. Voted Italy's finest coffee bar for 2005. 111 via Principe di Belmonte.
Bar Alba. Worth a trip for its famous ice cream and pastries, but closed Mon. 7 Piazza Don Bosco (Stadium).
Golden. Popular place for Sicilian breakfast. 38 Piazzale de Gasperi (Stadium).
Il Rintocco. Charming coffee house. Unusual coffee, herb teas and hot choco-

late. Closes early at 8pm. 14 Via Orologio.

Liberty. Along this street there are many elegant cafés, but this is the place to come for the best ice cream. 100 Via Principe di Belmonte.

Malavoglia. Tiny little café serving good tea and hot chocolate, tucked away in a very old part of town. 5 Piazzetta Speciale (behind Piazza Bologni).

Massaro. Superb breakfast pastries, perhaps the best in town. 24 Via Basile (University).

Nino Matranga. Prepares his own invention, *cremolosa*, a kind of creamy, squashy sorbet, in 32 flavours, now world-famous. Kiosk at 1 Piazza Gentili (at crossroad between Via Libertà and Via Notarbartolo).

Pasticceria Ruvolo. Comfortable tea room serving the very best cakes and pastries. 121 Via Bara all'Olivella.

Ristoro del Massimo. Tiny coffee bar not far from the Teatro Massimo. Many snacks and sandwiches; inviting *spumoni* (fluffy ice cream) and the best espresso in Palermo. 364 Via Maqueda.

San Michele. Coffee bar, also very good ice cream still prepared as it was in the 19th century. 67 Via Nunzio Morello.

Caffè Vannucci. Old-fashioned tea room. 197 Corso Vittorio Emanuele.

Bagheria

Bar Ester. Famous for ice cream and *cannoli di ricotta*. 113 Via Palagonia, T: 091 931427.

Cerda

Gelateria Cappadonia. Antonio Cappadonia is well known for his skill in making ice cream, and his courage in proposing new flavours—manna, for example, or in spring, artichoke sorbet. 153 Via Roma. Closed Mon except Aug.

Cefalù

Antica Porta Terra. Exceptional ice cream or Sicilian breakfast. 6 Piazza Garibaldi.

Castelbuono

Fiasconaro. The Fiasconaro brothers produce nougat, liquors and a very particular cake called *mannetto*, a light textured sponge cake iced with manna, which served warm, is the ideal accompaniment for tea or hot chocolate. It keeps for weeks, so you can take it home! 10 Piazza Margherita, www.fiasconaro.com

Antica Gelateria del Corso. Another sweet unique to Castelbuono is *testa di turco*, a kind of blancmange with a layer of flaky pastry in the middle, sprinkled with chocolate and cinnamon. Antonio also makes marvellous almond cakes, ice cream, and chocolate-covered roasted almonds. All of these Castelbuono confections are made by hand. 46 Corso Umberto.

Piana degli Albanesi

Kalinikta. The place to come for the celebrated *cassate di ricotta*, but they make delicious ice cream and granita too. 163 Corso Kastriota, T: 091 8571116.

Roccapalumba

Ribaudo. Perfect breakfast pastries and home-made ice cream. 20 Via Umberto.

Ustica

Bar Centrale. A great meeting point, especially in the early morning and a good source of information about the island. Superb old-fashioned ice cream, unusual flavours including cinnamon, jasmine flower, rum baba, blood orange; the lemon flavour, prepared with local fruit, is not to be missed. 8 Piazza Umberto.

BARS

Palermo

Birimbao. Delightful Art Nouveau villa and garden; jazz; sometimes live music. 85 Via dei Leoni (Favorita).

I Grilli Giù. Fashionable cocktail bar which serves delightful Middle Eastern style snacks. 9 Piazza Valverde (S. Domenico).

Kursaal Kalhesa. Wine and coffee bar. Wonderful atmosphere, often live music, an open fire in winter, foreign language newspapers; opens 8.30pm. 21/A Foro Umberto.

Mi Manda Picone. Near church of San Francesco. Welcoming little bar; vast choice of wines, delicious freshly cooked snacks. Open from 6.30pm. 59 Via Alessandro Paternostro, T: 091 6160660.

LOCAL SPECIALITIES

Palermo

De Simone. One of the best-known names in **Sicilian pottery**, at once recognizable for the naive design and distinctive colours: orangey-red, turquoise blue and lemon yellow. There are two stores—698 Via Lanza di Scalea and 13/B Via Daita. **Il Laboratorio Italiano**, 42 Via Principe di Villafranca, is another good address for Sicilian pottery.

Domus Artis, at 6 Via Nino Basile (behind Casa Professa), is where Luigi Arini still makes exquisite **religious articles** using wax, silver and coral, as established by a Vatican ruling in 1566 which indicated the materials, colours and symbolism that artists and craftsmen could use. **Nunzio La Venuta**, makes rocking horses and other toys in wood and papier-mâché, and also small

paintings at 13 Via IV Aprile.

Scimone, 18 Via Miceli, sells good **confectionery**, ask for *dita d'apostolo* (Apostle's finger biscuits).

There are **silversmiths** at **Piazza Meli** (Cala), **coppersmiths** near **Ponte dell'Ammiraglio**, and **tinkers** in Via Calderai. At **Via Bara all'Olivella** (Opera House) no. 38, **Antonio Cuticchio** makes **puppets** for his brother Mimmo, famous *puparu*, who has his theatres close by (at nos 54 & 95; he will show you them free of charge, Tues–Sat 9.30–1 & 4–7.30, afternoon only on Sun).

Alia

Bar Centrale, at 32 Via Garibaldi, has *scattate*, biscuits made of almonds and cinnamon, unique to Alia.

Cefalù

Anchovies, in olive oil with capers or chillies, are prepared by the fishermen of Cefalù. Try **Antica Lavorazione Pesce Azzurro Cefalù**, Contrada Presidiana, T: 0921 424333; or Ankora Delicius, Contrada Piana Marsala.

Monreale

As might be expected, there is an excellent school for **mosaics** in the town where young people learn the art. Examples can be purchased in Piazza Guglielmo II. **Pottery** is also attractive; here they specialize in applying glazed fruits and flowers to earthenware vases.

Polizzi Generosa

The speciality of the local pastry cooks is a pie made with fresh cheese, chocolate and cinnamon, called *sfoglio*.

MARKETS

Palermo

The street markets of Palermo are justly

famous, and should not be missed even by the most hurried visitor. The stalls are set up in the morning around 8 and stay open all day until around 7.30. The biggest are: **Vucciria** (Piazza Caracciolo), for produce (especially fish); **Ballarò** (Piazza Ballarò), for produce and household goods; **Capo** (Via Sant'Agostino), for clothes, cloth and shoes; **Papireto** (Piazza Peranni), for antiques and bric-à-brac, usually called *Mercato delle Pulci*, flea market. **Lattarini** (Piazza Borsa, Via Roma), the name derives from *suq al attarin*, perfume market, but nowadays they sell cloth, ropes, knitting yarn, underwear, boots and army surplus gear. Another food market opens in the afternoon and evening in **Corso Scinà**. A weekly antique market is held on Sun morning in Piazza Marina

FESTIVALS & EVENTS

Palermo *Fistinu di Santa Rosalia*, with celebrations including theatre performances, concerts, fireworks and a street procession with the statue of St Rosalie on a huge cart drawn by oxen, 10–15 July. **Pilgrimage** (with a torchlight procession) to the shrine of St Rosalie on Monte Pellegrino, 3–4 Sept.
Bisacquino Procession which slowly weaves its way through the streets, singing the Passion of Christ in Sicilian. The ceremony ends when one of the young men of the town is symbolically crucified. Good Friday.
Castelbuono *Arruccata di li Ventimiglia* (a historical pageant), in Aug.
Cefalù An evening procession of fishing boats, lit up with lanterns, goes from the harbour to Point Kalura and back for the Madonna della Luce, 14 Aug.
Collesano *Festa della Casazza*, when the life of Christ is re-enacted, Easter. *Paliu du Pipìu*, a turkey race where people bet on the results, 1–3 Aug.
Gibilmanna Pilgrimage on 1st Sunday in Sept.
Gratteri Feast of the patron St James, 8–9 Sept. On the first Thursday after Corpus Domini (June) a very ancient ceremony takes place, with much beating of drums, going back to the time when the young men used to go hunting wolves on that day.
Isnello Feast of the patron St Nicholas, 5–7 Sept. Broad bean and boiled potato feast, 29 June. Pancake feast, 1 May.
Mezzojuso *Il Mastro di Campo*, when the town inhabitants enact the story of a queen who had a love affair with her farmer. Cannons are fired, biscuits are thrown into the crowd, Garibaldi's soldiers intervene, then the actors offer wine and barbecued sausages to everybody. Last Sun before Lent, T: 091 8203657.
Piana degli Albanesi Celebrations are very special here. Women wear gorgeous traditional dress, ancient Albanian hymns are sung in the cathedral, there are readings from the Gospel in seven languages, then a colourful procession takes place, and the traditional red eggs are distributed. Easter Sunday (and Good Friday)
Polizzi Generosa Feast of St Gandulph, 3rd Sun in Sept. Hazelnut fair, Aug. Festivities when a huge bonfire is lit in front of the ruined church of La Commenda, 26 Dec.
Prizzi *Il Ballo dei Diavoli*, or Dance of the Devils. In the morning, Death,

dressed in yellow and the Devils dressed in red and wearing heavy tin masks, race through the streets trying to capture souls to send to Hell (the nearby inn). In the afternoon the Madonna meets her Son Jesus, and they and the angels, who fight with swords, defeat the devils and Good triumphs over Evil once again. Easter Sun, www.comune.prizzi.pa.it.
Sclafani Bagni Procession of the *Ecce Homo*, last Sun in June.

Terrasini '*A festa di li Schietti* is probably of pagan origin and means 'the feast of the Bachelors'. A young man who wants to prove his strength has to lift an orange tree weighing about 50kg with one hand then parade it around the town on his shoulders until he reaches the home of the girl he admires, when the orange tree is raised again. If she is suitably impressed with his strength, she may decide to marry him. Easter Sat & Sun, www.terrasini.org.

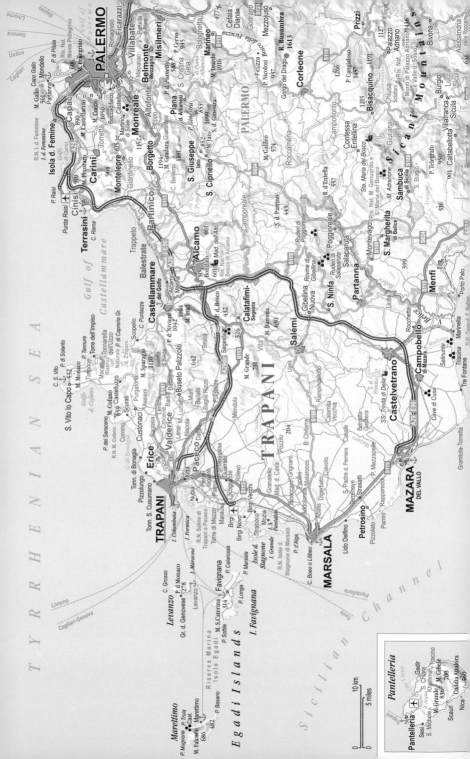

THE PROVINCE OF TRAPANI

Trapani, the most important city on the west coast of the island, is the capital of a province where the wide, open landscapes, full of light reflected off the sea, are picked out in white, straggling, flat-roofed villages. Of all the island's provinces, it is the most North African in atmosphere. The ancient industry of extracting salt from seawater evaporated in the salt pans is still an important part of the local economy and produces a quality of salt that matches the best in the world. Other local products include excellent olive oil, pickled olives and fine DOC wines, including the various Marsalas, the famous *Bianco d'Alcamo,* and those from the island of Pantelleria, close to Tunisia. The province contains almost half the vineyards in Sicily.

TRAPANI

The city of Trapani lies below the headland of Mount Erice, with the Egadi Islands usually visible offshore. The old quarter occupies a scimitar-shaped promontory between the open sea to the north and the port and salt marshes to the south, although from inland the town is approached through extensive modern suburbs laid out on a regular chessboard pattern. The elegant shops in the pedestrianised old town exude an air of opulence, the corso lined with interesting monumental buildings. The collection of decorative arts in the Pepoli Museum is one of the best on the island, particularly famous for its works in coral.

HISTORY OF TRAPANI

Drepana or *Drepanon*, meaning 'scythe' (legend has it that the promontory was dropped by Demeter distracted in her search for Persephone), was the earliest recorded settlement here, once the port for Eryx (modern Erice). It was raised to the status of a Phoenician city when Hamilcar Barca transferred part of the population of Eryx here in 260 BC. It was captured for the Romans by Catulus in 241 BC. It acquired strategic importance as the maritime crossroads between Tunis, Anjou and Aragon in the 13th century. King Theodore of Navarre died of typhoid here contracted near Tunis (1270), and here on the 'Scoglio del Malconsiglio', a rock at the extreme end of the cape, John of Procida is supposed to have plotted the Sicilian Vespers with his confederates. Edward I of England, who landed at Trapani on his return from the Crusades in 1272, received the news of his accession to the throne here. The city was specially favoured by Peter of Aragon, who landed at Trapani as the saviour of Sicily in 1282, and by Charles V.

EXPLORING TRAPANI

The old town

In the large Piazza Vittorio Emanuele, laid out in the mid-19th century, is a monument (1882) to Vittorio Emanuele II by Giovanni Dupré, one of the great Florentine sculptor's last works. From here Viale Regina Margherita skirts the north side of Villa Margherita, a charming garden laid out in the late 19th century, to Piazza Vittorio Veneto, the administrative centre of the city, with early 20th-century buildings including the fine post office (1924). Close by is the Castello di Terra, a castle of ancient origin reconstructed during the centuries and converted into a barracks in the 19th century. The outer walls now surround the modern police station. Streets to the north give access to the seafront, with a good view of the old town on the promontory.

Via Garibaldi leads towards the old centre past the 18th-century Palazzo Fardella Fontana, with an elaborate window above its portal, and the 18th-century Palazzo Riccio di Morana decorated with stuccoes. The 17th-century church of **Santa Maria dell'Itria** has a façade completed in 1745. Inside is a sculptural group of the *Holy Family* by Andrea Tipa (1725–c. 1776), one of the family of sculptors that revitalised art in Trapani in the mid-18th century. Beyond is the 19th-century red-brick Palazzo Staiti opposite the 18th-century Palazzo Milo.

The Salita San Domenico (with steps and cobbled paving) leads up to the church of **San Domenico**, with a blind 14th-century rose-window. The interior contains a remarkable wooden Crucifix (thought to date from the 14th century) in an 18th-century chapel by Giovanni Biagio Amico in the left aisle. Near the entrance is a 15th-century fresco fragment. The sanctuary preserves the sarcophagus of Manfred, son of Frederick III of Aragon. A chapel behind has more recently discovered fresco fragments of the 14th and 15th centuries. The Baroque frames, pulpit and organ (in good condition), bear witness to the wealth of the city in the 18th century, thanks to the importance of its salt and fishing industries.

Nearby, downhill to the south, is the church of **San Nicolò Mirense**, which has a little garden. Inside is a 16th-century marble tabernacle on the sanctuary wall and in the left transept a striking sculptural group of *Christ Between the Two Thieves*, a realistic 18th-century work in wood and papier-mâché by a local sculptor. Via delle Arti and Via della Badia lead back to Via Garibaldi and the 17th-century façade of Santa Maria del Soccorso (or the **Badia Nuova**), with a fine interior decorated in pink and grey marble and elaborate organ lofts. A short way back along Via Garibaldi is the church of the Carminello (or San Giuseppe), with an 18th-century portal with bizarre twisted columns. It was built in 1699 and the statue in the apse of *Joseph and the Young Christ Child* is a charming 18th-century sculpture by Antonio Nolfo (an earlier version of the statue, used for processions, is kept in the sacristy). A wooden Crucifix in the church is attributed to Giacomo Tartaglio, one of the group of 18th-century Trapanese sculptors that modelled many of the statues carried in the Procession of the *Misteri*.

From the Badia, Via Torrearsa leads right, past the 16th-century church of the Carmine with a fine exterior with tall pilasters and a high cornice, to the seafront pass-

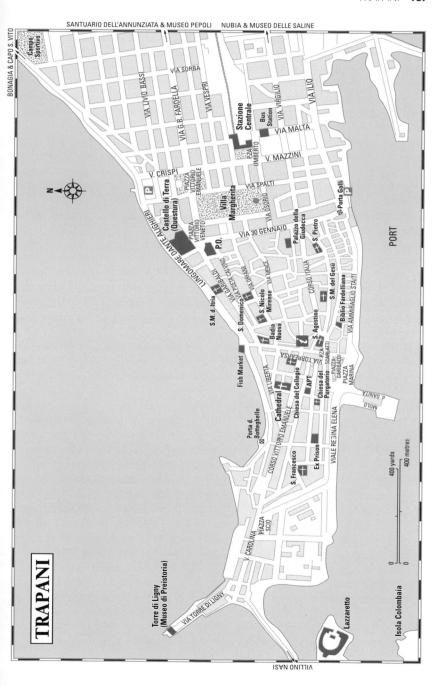

TRAPANI

SANTUARIO DELL'ANNUNZIATA & MUSEO PEPOLI   NUBIA & MUSEO DELLE SALINE

BONAGIA & CAPO S. VITO

Campo Sportivo

VIA SORBA

VIA LIVIO BASSI

VIA G.B. FARDELLA

VIA VESPRI

VIA VIRGILIO

VIA ILIO

Stazione Centrale

Bus Station

VIA MALTA

P.ZA UMBERTO

V. MAZZINI

V. CRISPI

PIAZZA VITTORIO EMANUELE

VIA SPALTI

Castello di Terra (Questura)

Villa Margherita

Porta Galli

LUNGOMARE DANTE ALIGHIERI

PIAZZA VITTORIO VENETO

P.O.

VIA OSORIO

VIA 30 GENNAIO

Palazzo della Giudecca

S. Pietro

VIA GARIBALDI

VIA POETA CALVINO

VIA ORFANE

VIA MERCÈ

CORSO ITALIA

S.M. d'Itria

S. Domenico

S. Nicolo Mirense

Bada Nuova

S. Agostino

Biblio Fardelliana

S.M. del Gesù

VIA AMMIRAGLIO STAITI

Fish Market

VIA LIBERTA

VIA TORREARSA

PIAZZA SBARBATI

PIAZZA GARIBALDI

PIAZZA MARINA

Porta d. Botteghelle

Cathedral

Chiesa del Collegio

APT

Chiesa del Purgatorio

MOLO d. SANITA

CORSO VITTORIO EMANUELE

VIALE REGINA ELENA

S. Francesco

Ex Prison

V. CAROLINA

PIAZZA SCIO

PORT

Torre di Ligny (Museo di Preistoria)

VIA TORRE DI LIGNY

VILLINO NASI

Lazzaretto

Isola Colombaia

400 yards

400 metres

N

ing an attractive market building (1874). Fish is sold under the portico and other produce is sold around a fountain with a statue of *Venus* in the piazza. Via Torrearsa leads
in the other direction to Palazzo Senatorio, used as municipal offices, built in 1672,
which has an unusual façade with statues on the upper part.

Near the southern end of Via Torrearsa is the restored Templars' church of
Sant'Agostino, with its 14th-century rose-window and portal (now used as a concert
hall). The Saturn fountain here (a reference to the mythical foundation of the city by
the god) is on the site of a 14th-century fountain. Nearby is the Biblioteca Fardelliana
(*open 10–1 & 4–7; Sat 9–1; closed Sun and holidays*), the prestigious civic library of the
province, housed in the former church of San Giacomo, with a fine Mannerist façade.
Opened to the public in 1830, it contains many important manuscripts, a collection
of etchings, and some 118,000 volumes.

In the rebuilt district of San Pietro, back towards Villa Margherita, is **Santa Maria
del Gesù**, a church with a transitional 16th-century façade and a Renaissance south
doorway in Catalan-Gothic style bearing an Annunciation. The fine simple interior,
golden in colour, contains a decorative niche with a very beautiful *Madonna and Child*
in enamelled terracotta by Andrea della Robbia (1435–1525), under a marble baldachin by Antonello Gagini. The work of Andrea di Marco della Robbia, nephew and
student of the great Florentine sculptor Luca della Robbia (d. 1482), their name
derived from the red dye used in the family textile business, shows the influence of
Verrocchio.

Further east in the former Jewish district, is the unusual Palazzo della Giudecca,
usually called 'lo Spedaletto', with an embossed tower, rusticated walls and 16th-cen-
tury windows recalling the highly decorated plateresque style of Castile.

Along Corso Vittorio Emanuele

The broad, handsome Corso Vittorio Emanuele leads west from Via Torrearsa towards
the end of the promontory. On the right is the church of the Collegio dei Gesuiti, built
c. 1614–40 and designed by the Jesuit architect from Messina, Natale Masuccio
(1568–1619), with a Baroque façade added later. The interior has been closed for
restoration for many years. Beyond the monumental former Collegio dei Gesuiti (now a
school), preceded by a portico, is the **Cattedrale di San Lorenzo**, built by Giovanni
Biagio Amico in 1743. Amico (fl.1684–1754) was the theologian and self-taught architect from Trapani who wrote the influential treatise *L' Architetto Prattico* (1726) and
designed many sacred and secular buildings in the city. On the fourth altar in the south
aisle is a *Crucifixion* attributed to the local 17th-century artist Giacomo Lo Verde. On the
second altar of the north aisle is a painting of St George by Andrea Carreca and (fourth
altar) a fine painting of the Deposition, showing Flemish influence.

In front of the cathedral Via Giglio leads to the church of the **Purgatorio** (*open
4–6.30; in the morning by arrangement, T: 0923 562882*) where the figures of the
Misteri, statuary groups made of wood, cloth, papier-mâché and glue, are kept in
between the Good Friday processions. The church has a fine tiled dome and elaborate façade by Giovanni Biagio Amico.

Nearby in Via San Francesco is a 17th-century prison house, with four caryatids on its façade, and, further along, on the opposite side of Via San Francesco, the church of the Immacolatella with a delightful apse by Giovanni Biagio Amico (1732). At the end of the street, the church of San Francesco (13th–17th centuries) can be seen, with a green dome next to a fine doorway. Inside, on the left, is a curious 17th-century tombstone dedicated to the 'death of the nation of Armenia', with a bilingual inscription.

The corso continues past (left) the 18th-century Palazzo Berardo Ferro, which has an inviting courtyard, and then Palazzo Alessandro Ferro (1775), decorated with a clock and busts in medallions. Beyond on the right is the little Porta delle Botteghelle (13th century), outside which the defensive fortifications, which protected the town from the sea, can be seen. The promontory ends at the Torre di Ligny, a fortress built in 1671 by the Spanish viceroy, on the tip of the promontory. It has been well restored to house the **Museo del Mare e di Preistoria** (*open 9–1*), with a particularly interesting section devoted to submarine archaeology, displaying Phoenician, Greek, Roman, Spanish and Egyptian amphorae, and a bronze helmet of 241 BC, probably lost at sea during the First Punic War. Many of the objects on display were recovered by local fishermen.

From beside the Torre di Ligny there is a view across the bay to the Isola Colombaia, the base for the Romans' siege operations in 241 BC. An Aragonese castle here, the **Castello di Mare**, was restored in later centuries, and in 1714 the octagonal lantern was added by Giovanni Biagio Amico. It was used as a prison until the 1960s.

Santuario dell'Annunziata

Inland, in the modern part of town, at no. 179 Via Conte Agostino Pepoli (c. 4km from the centre; *bus nos 1, 10 and 11*) is the Santuario dell'Annunziata (*open 9–12 & 4–7; July, Aug late closing at 8; www.madonnaditrapani.com*), founded in 1315 and rebuilt in 1760. Little remains of the 14th-century structure except the west front with a rose window which overlooks a garden. The bell-tower dates from 1650.

The unusual grey and white interior was redesigned in the 18th century by Giovanni Biagio Amico. Off the south aisle is the beautiful Cappella dei Pescatori (the fishermen's chapel), built in 1481, perhaps an adaptation of an earlier chapel. On the left of the presbytery is the Cappella dei Marinai (the seamen's chapel), another attractive chapel built in the 16th century in a mixture of styles. From the sanctuary, which has a pretty apse, two fine 16th-century doorways lead into the **Cappella della Madonna**; here another arch, with sculptures (1531–37) by Antonino Gagini and a bronze gate of 1591 (by Giuliano Musarra), gives access to the inner sanctuary containing a highly venerated 14th-century statue of the Madonna and Child, known as the *Madonna di Trapani*, a very fine work by Nino Pisano or his workshop. The master of the cathedral works at Orvieto, where he succeeded his celebrated father Andrea, Nino Pisano (from Pisa, as the name suggests) was one of the most confident and skilful sculptors of free-standing Gothic figures in the mid-14th century. His school had great influence in both Pisa and Venice. Below the statue is a tiny silver model of Trapani by the 17th-century silversmith Vincenzo Bonaiuto, who also made the silver statue in the chapel of *St Albert*, to the right of the Cappella della Madonna.

Museo Regionale Pepoli

Open Tues–Sat 9–1, Sun and holidays 9–12.30, closed Mon. Entrance to the right of the façade of the church. T: 0923 553269.
The museum, housed in the former Carmelite convent, holds a municipal collection formed in 1827; a group of Neapolitan paintings which belonged to General Giovanni Battista Fardella; and a large fine and applied art collection donated by Count Agostino Pepoli in 1906. The exhibits are beautifully arranged and well labelled. The entrance is through the paved 16th–17th-century cloisters, with palm trees.

Two rooms on the ground floor contain architectural fragments and Arab funerary inscriptions (10th–12th centuries), and a wooden ceiling salvaged from a chapel, along with a sculpted 16th-century portal by Bartolomeo Berrettaro, a stoup of 1486 from the Santuario dell'Annunziata, and works by the Gagini, notably a figure of *St James the Great* (1522), by Antonello Gagini.

The first floor is devoted to the museum's collections of paintings and decorative arts. Paintings range from Roberto di Oderisio's *Pietà* (c. 1380) and the early 15th-century Master of Trapani's polyptych, *Madonna and Child with saints* (from the church of Sant'Antonio Abate), and *St Francis Receiving the Stigmata*, attributed to Titian, to a portrait of the politician Nunzio Nasi (c. 1902) by the Futurist artist Giacomo Balla. Cases of wooden figurines by Giovanni Matera (1653–1718) illustrate the *Massacre of the Innocents* in 16 tableaux.

The superb collection of decorative arts, the work of local craftsmen in the 17th–19th centuries, includes scenes of the *Adoration of the Magi* and *Nativity* by Andrea Tipa in wax, alabaster, and coral; a late 17th-century salt cellar; magnificent 18th–19th-century Sicilian coral jewellery and a 17th-century chalice. Particularly important are the charming crib figures, the best by Giovanni Matera, and Nativity scenes. Elaborate 17th-century objects in red coral, a skill for which Trapani is particularly famous, include a *Crucifixion* and a candelabra.

The archaeological collection contains finds from Erice, Selinunte and Mozia, and coins of the 5th century BC. At the top of the stairs, in the first corridor, are majolica tiled floors, including one with a splendid scene of tuna fishing (the *mattanza; see box, p. 174*). The small prints and drawings collection here includes works by the printmaker Stefano Della Bella (1610-1664) and Jacopo Callot (1592–1635). The flag of *Il Lombardo*, the ship sailed by Garibaldi and the 'Thousand', is owned by the museum.

The salt pans of Trapani

The *saline* or salt pans of Trapani can be seen from the secondary road which runs from the port to Marsala. A number of windmills survive, turning Archimedes' screws in order to raise the seawater from one pan to the next in spring, and to grind the salt in summer. Much of the area is now a nature reserve (*WWF Riserva Naturale delle Saline di Trapani e Paceco, www.salineditrapani.it*), and flamingoes, great white herons, avocets and black-winged stilts are frequently seen. At **Nubia**, on the coast c. 5km south of Trapani, is the **Museo del Sale** (*open 9.30–1.30 & 3.30–6.30; Sun and holidays; call first to make sure T: 0923 867442*). Here an old wooden mill is now used to

Salt pan windmills near Trapani.

illustrate the ancient salt-extracting industry, started here by the Phoenicians and still working a a number of pans between Trapani and Marsala. Piles of salt, protected by tiles, are a common sight in the area, the salt being exported all over Europe. The wind and sun here favour evaporation, while the seawater has a naturally high level of salinity. From February to March seawater is pumped by the windmills from a canal into the salt pans. The water level is gradually decreased, encouraging the evaporation process and the water assumes a reddish colour as the mineral content becomes more concentrated. The harvest begins in July, before total evaporation, avoiding the deposit of harmful minerals; the salt is then raked from the pans into mounds to dry.

ERICE

Erice is a medieval walled town perched on top of an isolated limestone spur, high above the sea. It can be reached in ten minutes by cableway from Via Fardella (Raganzili district) in Trapani. The resident population is diminishing rapidly, and many of its houses are now occupied only in the summer months by residents of Trapani or Palermo who come here on holiday to escape the heat: the number of inhabitants in August rises to about 5,000. By far the most populous part of Erice is at the foot of the hill, close to Trapani. The locals call their town '*u Munti*', the mountain. It is often shrouded in a mist, known as '*il velo di Venere*' (the veil of Venus), and it can be very chilly here, the steep cobbled streets slippery, even snowy in winter, which, along with the often deserted streets, contributes to the feeling of isolation.

The perfect triangular shape of the town makes it difficult to find one's bearings, despite the fact that it is so small. The view to the north of Monte Cofano, one of the most beautiful promontories on the coast of Sicily, is exceptional. To the southwest there is another remarkable view of Trapani and the Egadi Islands, and, on a clear day, Cape Bon in Tunisia can be seen, and looking east, even Mount Etna.

HISTORY OF ERICE

Eryx, an Elymian city of mythical origin, was famous all over the Mediterranean for the magnificent temple of the goddess of fertility, known to the Romans as Venus Erycina. This splendid site, naturally defended and visible for miles around, was a noted landmark for navigators from Africa. An altar to the goddess was first set up here by the Sicans and the sanctuary became famous during the Elymian and Phoenician period. Every year, the Carthaginians (who venerated her as Astarte) released hundreds of white doves and one red one to represent the goddess, which arrived nine days later at the temple of Sicca Veneria at Carthage. This ceremony took place in mid-August (by a strange coincidence, the feast of the patron saint of Erice, Our Lady of Custonaci, was always held on 16th August). In 415 BC the inhabitants of nearby Segesta took the visiting Athenian ambassadors to see the rich treasury of the temple, which convinced Athens to take their side against Selinunte and Syracuse, a decision which led to the fatal attack on Syracuse in 413 BC and the consequent defeat of the Athenians. Captured by Pyrrhus in 278 BC it was destroyed in 260 by Hamilcar Barca. The Roman consul Lucius Junius Pullus took the hill in 248 and was besieged by Hamilcar, who was himself blockaded by a Roman army, until the Carthaginians were defeated by the Romans, led by Catulus. The cult of Venus Erycina reached its maximum splendour under the Romans and the sanctuary was restored for the last time by Tiberius and Claudius. The Saracens called the place *Gebel Hamed*, which Count Roger—who had seen St Giuliano in a dream while besieging it—changed to Monte San Giuliano, a name it kept until 1934. The city thrived in the 18th century (with a population of around 12,000) and there were many religious communities. The town is now world famous for its Ettore Majorana Cultural Centre, founded by the local physicist Antonino Zichichi in 1963.

EXPLORING ERICE

The grey stone houses of Erice (mostly dating from the 14th–17th centuries), hidden behind their high walls, and the beautiful stone-paved streets, give the town an austere aspect. But behind the walls are many charming courtyards, some of which have little gardens. There are no fewer than 60 churches in the town, testifying to the once large population. The entrance to the town is by Porta Trapani, beyond which Via Vittorio Emanuele climbs steeply uphill. Just to the left is the **Matrice** (Assunta) (*open 9.30–12 & 3.30–6*), which has a beautiful fortified Gothic exterior. The porch dates from 1426. The splendid detached campanile was built as an Aragonese look-out tower c. 1315 by Frederick III, several years before the foundation of the church. The interior received its impressive neo-Gothic form, with an elaborate cream-coloured vault, in 1852. The apse is filled with a huge marble altarpiece (1513) by Giuliano Mancino from Carrara. In the sanctuary, through a small round opening on the left wall, a fresco fragment of an angel can be seen, the only part of the 15th-century decoration of the church to have survived. In a chapel on the left, the 16th-century painting of the *Madonna of Custonaci* (the venerated patron of Erice) was replaced in 1892 by the present copy when the original was taken back to the sanctuary of Custonaci on the coast. The next chapel, with a beautiful dome, dates from 1568. In a chapel on

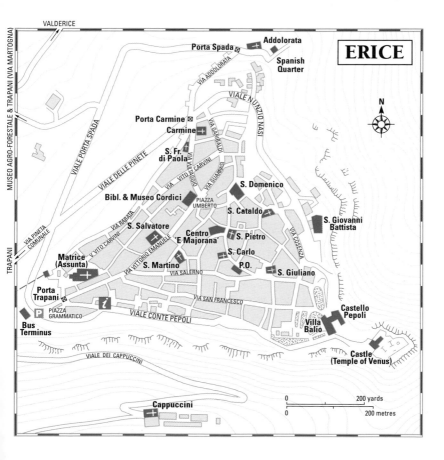

the south side is a marble *Madonna* (1469) by Domenico Gagini, with a finely carved base. Outside, on the south wall, there are nine iron crosses, said to come from the Temple of Venus (*see below*).

Via Vittorio Emanuele continues steeply uphill past several old shop fronts and characteristic courtyards. At a fork Via Vittorio Emanuele continues left past the old ruined Gothic church of San Salvatore beside a lovely old narrow street which leads downhill (and has a distant view of the sea). To the right Via Bonaventura Provenzano ends at a house with a Baroque doorway and window near the church of **San Martino** (*open 3–6*), with another Baroque portal, and an interesting 15th-century statue of the Madonna in the interior. Just before reaching Piazza Umberto, beside a charming café in a 19th-century palace, a flight of steps leads down left to the monumental doorway with four columns of San Rocco (*closed*).

Piazza Umberto

The central Piazza Umberto is the only large open space in the town. An elegant palazzo is now used by a bank, and a long 19th-century building houses the town hall and the **Biblioteca Comunale e Museo Civico Cordici** (*open Mon–Fri 8.30–1.30; Mon and Thur also 2.30–5*), named after the local historian Antonino Cordici (1586–1666). The library was founded in 1867 with material from the suppressed convents of the city. It now has c. 20,000 volumes. In the entrance hall is a beautiful relief of the Annunciation by Antonello Gagini, one of his finest works (1525), and a number of inscriptions. Upstairs in the small museum are interesting local archaeological finds (including a small Attic head of Venus, 5th century BC), church vestments, paintings, and a 17th-century wooden Crucifix. Close by is the tiny opera house, Teatro Gebel el Hamid.

Via Guarrasi leads ahead out of the piazza and immediately on the left a stepped street (Via Argentieri) leads down across Via Carvini into Via Vultaggio which continues to wind down past the 17th-century church of **San Francesco di Paola** (*open 10.30–12.30*) with a Classical façade. The delightful interior was restored in 1954 by an American benefactor. It has white stucco decoration in very low relief on the walls and the barrel vault, a worn tiled floor in the sanctuary, fine woodwork, and popular votive statues.

Lower down on the right is the 14th-century Palazzo Militari with Gothic traces next to the Gothic church of the Carmine (*closed*). Porta Carmine stands nearby, with a worn, headless statue of Beato Alberto, a patron of Erice, in a niche, on its outer face.

The town walls

The magnificent walls here, which stretch from Porta Spada to Porta Trapani, protected the only side of the town which has no natural defences: on all the other sides the sheer rock face made the town one of the most impregnable fortresses on the island. The walls are constructed on huge blocks of rough stone which probably date from the Elymian period (c. 1200 BC), above which the square blocks added by the Carthaginians can be seen. The masonry in the upper parts, with stones of smaller dimension, date from the 6th century BC. The defences were strengthened in the Roman era and in the Middle Ages, and six postern gates and 16 medieval towers survive. Inside the gate the stepped Via Addolorata leads down past a well-preserved stretch of the walls, with a distant view ahead of Monte Cofano, to the church of the Addolorata (or Sant' Orsola; *closed*), surrounded by a little garden. It has an interesting 15th–16th-century plan. The 18th-century *Misteri* sculptures are kept here, which are taken in procession through the streets of Erice on Good Friday.

In this remote and picturesque corner of the town is the Norman Porta Spada. Outside Porta Spada is the so-called **Quartiere Spagnolo**, a desolate group of buildings on a spur, intended by the Spanish to be the barracks for their troops in the 17th century, and for some reason, never finished. Plans to complete the structure and transform it into a hostel will probably never materialize, because the local people say the place is haunted—particularly by *Birrittu Russu* or 'Red Cap', a mysterious phantom who has been spotted over the centuries in various parts of the city, but especially in the Spanish Quarter—and it is easy to believe it on damp foggy winter nights.

From Porta Carmine Via Rabatà leads back to Porta Trapani following the walls where there are a number of postern gates. Tiny narrow alleyways, designed to provide shelter from the wind, lead up left to Via Carvini and Piazza Umberto.

Piazza San Domenico and environs

From Piazza Umberto, in front of the museum, Via Antonio Cordici leads up out of the piazza past a few shops to Piazza San Domenico. The former church of San Domenico, with a Classical porch, has been restored as a lecture hall for the Ettore Majorana Centre (*see below*). From the right side of the church Via San Cataldo leads downhill (and right) past a neo-Gothic electricity tower to the bare façade of San Cataldo (open for services only) on the edge of the old town. It was founded before 1339, and rebuilt in 1740–86. It contains a stoup of 1474 by the workshop of Domenico Gagini.

Further downhill and to the right is the church of San Giovanni Battista (deconsecrated; *opened on request by the religious community here*) on the cliff edge, with a 15th-century dome whose shape recalls Arab architecture, and an ancient side doorway. It contains a statue of St John the Evangelist by Antonello Gagini, and of St John the Baptist by Antonino Gagini.

From Piazza San Domenico, Via Guarnotti leads up right to the church of **San Pietro** (*open for services only*) with an 18th-century portal. The beautiful white interior by Giovanni Biagio Amico (1745) has a worn tiled floor. Beside it is an arch over the road and on the right (at no. 26) a convent has been restored as the headquarters of the Ettore Majorana International Centre for Scientific Culture. Founded in 1963, this has become a famous centre of learning where courses and seminars are held for scientists from all over the world.

Via Guarnotti continues past the former convent and orphanage of San Carlo next to the bare façade of the church of **San Carlo** (*open 10.30–12.30*). It has a pretty majolica floor, and on a side altar there is a statue of *Our Lady of Succour* with a tiny

Castello di Venere, site of the Temple of Venus, Erice.

relief of St Michael Archangel on the base. The nuns' choirs are protected with carved wooden screens. On the right is the post office and downhill on the left is a pleasant raised piazza with the statue of Beato Alberto in front of the church of San Giuliano (deconsecrated and used by a religious community), which has an elegant 18th-century campanile.

The road continues down past two very old shop fronts and crosses Via Porta Gervasi (with a view left of the church of San Giovanni Battista with its dome, see above). A ramp leads up right to **Villa Balio**, delightful public gardens laid out in 1870 by Count Agostino Pepoli on the summit of the hill with wonderful views. It has a monumental entrance with a double staircase on Via San Francesco. Above is the **Castello Pepoli** (still privately owned by the Pepoli; *no admission*), a Norman castle reconstructed in 1875–85 by Count Pepoli, with a 15th-century tower restored in 1973. The excellent view from the terrace on the left encompasses Monte Cofano, the coast, and San Giovanni Battista on the side of the hill. Below, among the trees you can see the abandoned neo-Gothic Torretta, also built by Count Pepoli.

The Temple of Venus

A ramp leads down from the gardens beside the castle to Viale Conte Pepoli, on the southern edge of the hill, which continues left to end beside the 17th-century steps up to the **Castello di Venere** (*opened daily by volunteers 8.30–1.30, and sometimes in* *the afternoon*), on the edge of the rock. Above the entrance to the castle is the coat-of-arms of Charles V and a Gothic window. In the disappointing interior, the ruined Norman walls surround the sacred area which was once the site of the famous Temple of Venus, many fragments of which are embedded in the masonry of the castle. A few very worn Roman fluted column drums can be seen here and the so-called *Pozzo di Venere*, once thought to be a ceremonial pool but more probably a silo or a water cistern. The view is breathtaking, extending to Mount Etna, Enna, and Caltabellotta.

THE TEMPLE HIERODULES

As in Corinth and at Sicca Veneria in Tunisia, sanctified prostitution was prac-tised by the Romans at the temple of Venus Erycina. In his *Geography* (c. 7–23 AD) Strabo writes that many people, residents and foreigners, in fulfilment of vows, came here to dedicate girl slaves at the temple to become *hierodules* or holy slaves. Quintus Fabius Gurges was possibly the first Roman to dedicate a temple to Venus, in 295 BC, in thanksgiving for his father's victories against the Samnites. The temple here may in fact have been re-dedicated during the Punic Wars; certainly the fame of the shrine became great enough to prompt the founding of a temple to Venus Erycina near the Porta Collina in Rome. The slaves started their career at the age of 12 or 13, were trained in the art of love-making, and retired at 21, rich and much sought after as wives. Visitors to the temple were expected to leave gifts for the girls in exchange for the act of love, during which it was believed they assumed the guise of the goddess herself. The girls were fed on large quantities of milk and honey to make them pleasantly fat. They seldom conceived, perhaps because they were made to drink a concoction specially prepared by the priests.

Environs of Erice

On the hillside below the town is the interesting **San Matteo Forest Museum** (*open* 8–2). It is reached from the Raganzili road. About 3km below Erice a signposted turn leads in c. 500m to the gates of the estate, run by the Azienda Forestale. A rough road (c. 1km) continues to the museum in the lovely old Baglio di San Matteo, arranged in rooms around the courtyard. The exhibits include wine- and olive-presses, farm carts, saddle and tack, agricultural implements and household objects. There is also a nat-ural history section. The beautifully kept farm of c. 500 hectares may also be visited, where workhorses (a Sicilian breed known as San Fratello) are raised. It occupies a spectacular site with fine views towards Capo San Vito, and the vegetation includes dwarf palm trees, cypresses, fruit trees and forest trees. Experimental replanting is being carried out here.

THE NORTH COAST OF THE PROVINCE

North along the coast from Trapani, at the foot of Monte San Giuliano, is **San Cusumano** where a salt-pan windmill (now a beautiful hotel; *see p. 179 below*) can be seen. Ships are alerted to the low-lying islands offshore here by a lighthouse. **Pizzolungo** is the spot where, according to Virgil, Aeneas came ashore, welcomed by King Acestes of *Eryx*, and where his father Anchises died, obliging Aeneas to bury him here (an event commemorated by a white column).

Tonnara di Bonagia is a picturesque tuna fishery which has been restored as a hotel (*see p. 179 below*). Beside the little fishing port are hundreds of rusting anchors and an impressive tall tower.

Just inland, **Custonaci** has a sanctuary church, a frequent pilgrimage destination, because of the venerated 16th-century panel painting of the Madonna. The economy, once based on agriculture, is now supported by a number of marble quarries where the beautiful red stone called *perlato di Custonaci* is excavated. On the outskirts, a road (signposted *Grotte Mangiapane*) leads past an old quarry to the enormous **Grotta di Scurati** at the foot of Monte Cofano. The cave contains a little hamlet, now no longer inhabited. On either side of the paved street are little houses with courtyards, bread ovens, and workshops, and high above, the vault of the cave serves as a second roof. The village comes to life at Christmas, in a very successful venture called *Presepe vivente*, or 'Living Crib', when local people demonstrate the various trades and crafts of the area in the old houses. The initiative has been so popular that a similar event, the 'Living Museum', is held in summer (*mid June–mid September Fri, Sat and Sun 8pm–midnight; entrance ticket can include dinner; information from the Associazione Culturale Presepio Vivente, T: 0923 973553, www.mcsystem.it/presepe*).

Surrounded by barren hills, **Castelluzzo** has a picturesque sloping main street with one-storey houses and palm trees, and outside the town are groves of almonds and olive trees on the plain which descends to the seashore. There is a fine view of the beautiful headland of Monte Cofano, with Erice in the distance. **Monte Cofano** (659m), a perfect pyramid in shape, is now a nature reserve run by the Azienda Forestale; apart from its sheer beauty, it is interesting for the abundant spring wildflowers, several of which are endemic. On the main road stands the little 16th-century domed Cubola di Santa Crescenzia, derived from Arab models.

San Vito lo Capo

At the tip of the headland, San Vito lo Capo has been developed as a seaside resort, with gorgeous beaches of vanilla-coloured sand. Laid out on a regular plan in the 18th–19th centuries, the houses are bright with geraniums and bougainvilleas. The unusual church, a square fortress, was a 13th-century sanctuary, fortified by order of Charles V in 1526 as a defence against pirate raids. On the eastern side of the lovely promontory of Monte Monaco is a disused tuna fishery overlooking the Gulf of Castellammare.

A deserted road (signposted Calampiso) continues high above the shore across bare hills through a North African landscape, with dwarf palm trees and giant carobs, where broom and wild flowers blossom in spring, to the northern entrance to the Riserva Naturale dello Zingaro (*see below*).

RISERVA NATURALE DELLO ZINGARO

Open daily Oct–May 10–4; June–Sept 8–8; for park wardens T: 0924 35108, www.riservazingaro.it

The coast road soon ends at the southern entrance to the Riserva Naturale dello Zingaro, a beautiful nature reserve, with 7km of unspoilt coastline that can be explored on foot along marked paths. There are also several beaches where you can swim. Dwarf palms, Mediterranean maquis, ilex, carob, olive and cork oak flourish here amid wide swards of grass. No motorized transport of any kind is allowed inside the park; the keepers use mules to carry out their work. Traditional farming methods are also preserved: durum wheat is sown and reaped by hand, and threshed by mules, before being ground into flour at the old mill inside the reserve.

The museum, about 500m from the Scopello entrance, illustrates the life of the peasants who once lived in the area, and also traditional fishing methods. The **Grotta dell'Uzzo**, also in the reserve (about 5km from the Scopello entrance), was inhabited in the Palaeolithic era and is now home to six different species of bat. Among the birds, nesting species include Bonelli's eagle, peregrine falcon, and the Sicilian form of the rock partridge; among the mammals are fox, rabbit, porcupine, and the garden dormouse. An important part of the reserve also are the coastal waters, where no fishing is allowed. There is another entrance to the park on its northern border, approached by the road from San Vito lo Capo.

CASTELLAMMARE DEL GOLFO

Surrounded by mountains, Castellammare del Golfo lies on the bay, a jumble of small houses in pink, cream, yellow and orange. The fishing fleet is still active here, and there are few shops aimed solely at tourists. The charm of the place has attracted many second-homeowners from Northern Italy, drawn by the different pace of life, to enjoy summer evenings watching the sun drop behind the mountain and the fishermen sit on the quay preparing the *conzu*, the bait for the night's fishing, while tempting cooking aromas waft from open doorways.

The town was originally founded by the Elymians, as the harbour for the city of Segesta. The 18th-century Chiesa Madre houses a life-size majolica statue of *Our Lady of Succour* in the act of threatening the enemies of the town with her distaff, balancing the Christ Child on her left arm. The statue has been attributed to the 16th-century Della Robbia workshop in Tuscany. The castle, built by the Saracens in the 9th

Panorama of Castellammare dell Golfo.

century and then enlarged by the Normans and later again by the Swabians, is now the seat of the Museo Civico (*open Mon–Fri 9–1; summer also Sat and Sun*), dedicated to life in the area, displaying antique clothes, furniture, tools, pots and pans, and equipment for making wine and olive oil. The old tunnery warehouses on the seafront are very attractive; some of these, too, are being restored and turned into summer homes and comfortable, welcoming hotels.

North of Castellammare

A byroad follows the coast north of Castellammare for **Scopello**. Paths lead down to Cala Bianca, Cala Rossa and Baia Guidaloca, beautiful bays on the rocky coast, where the sea is particularly clear. Baia Guidaloca is the fabled spot where Nausicaa found the shipwrecked Ulysses, and led him back to her father's court. Scopello itself is a tiny picturesque village (although it is in the process of being developed with hotels to provide some 8,000 extra rooms). From the little piazza, with its large drinking-trough, an archway leads into the old paved courtyard of an 18th-century *baglio*, with a few trees surrounded by one-storey houses, a number of them now used as cafés or restaurants.

Just beyond the village is the **Tonnara di Scopello**, sometimes called *Marfaraggio*, an important tuna fishery from the 13th century up to the middle of the last century. It is easily visible on the sea below the road, beside fantastically shaped rocks on which ruined defence towers are situated. The buildings have been beautifully preserved (now private property, but accommodation can be rented, *see p.183 below*). A footpath leads down to the seafront where hundreds of anchors are piled up beside the picturesque old buildings. The sea is very clear in the small cove, where feral cats teach their kittens the art of survival. The life of the fishermen who used to live here was vividly described by Gavin Maxwell in *The Ten Pains of Death* (1959).

SEGESTA

The temple and theatre of Segesta are two of the most magnificently sited Classical monuments in the world. From the old road, the view of the Doric temple, on a bare hillside in deserted country amid the rolling hills west of the Gaggera, has been admired by travellers for centuries. The theatre is on a second, higher hill to the east. The surrounding countryside is impressive, with extensive vineyards, tiny olive trees and old farmhouses or *bagli*, and it is peaceful, despite the proximity of the motorway.

HISTORY OF SEGESTA

Segesta, also originally known as *Egesta*, was the principal city of the Elymians, who are now thought to have come from the eastern Mediterranean, probably Anatolia. Legendary survivors of the Trojan war, they were led here by Aeneas, which recent studies of their language appear to confirm. The city was rapidly Hellenized, and was continually at war with Selinunte from 580 BC, seeking an alliance with Athens in 426. After the destruction of Selinunte in 409, Segesta became a subject-ally of Carthage, and was saved by Himilco (397) from the attacks of Dionysius of Syracuse. In 307, however, Agathocles sacked the city, changed its name to *Dikeopolis*, and from the flat area behind the temple catapulted some 8,000 of the inhabitants into the ravine below, over the course of three days. The city resumed its old name under the protection of Carthage, but treacherously murdered the Carthaginian garrison during the First Punic War, after which it became the first city in Sicily to announce allegiance to Rome. The city's fortunes declined during the Arab period and by the late 13th century it was abandoned.

The site

Open 9–4; shuttle bus tickets (every 30mins) to the theatre can be purchased.
The ancient city which covered the slopes of Monte Barbaro is now being extensively excavated, but the location of the necropolis has not yet been identified. Sporadic excavations have in fact taken place since the end of the 18th century, when the temple was first restored. The theatre was brought to light in 1822. An important sanctuary at the foot of Monte Barbaro was discovered in 1950 and the entire area has been declared an archaeological park

The temple at Segesta, seen from the southeast.

The temple

The temple is situated on a low hill (at 304m) on the edge of a deep ravine formed by the River Pispisa, across which is a hillside covered with pinewoods. One of the grandest extant monuments of Doric architecture, a series of entases, often only a few millimetres in depth, are sufficient to correct the optical illusion that would otherwise deform the temple when seen from a distance. It was almost certainly an unfinished building, because there is no trace of a cella, the columns have not been provided with the grooves typical of Doric, and the bosses used for shifting the blocks of stone have not been removed. Although it may have been constructed in a hurry, in order to impress the ambassadors from Athens whom the Segestans were anxious to win over to help protect them from Selinunte, it is certainly the work of a great Athenian master and can tentatively be dated c 426–416 BC. It is peripteral and hexastyle, with 36 unfluted columns (c. 9m high, 2m wide at base) on a stylobate 58m by 23m. The high entablature and the pediments are intact. The building is inhabited by a colony of jackdaws, their garrulous call adding to the mystery of the site.

The theatre

A road leads up to the theatre from the car park. At the foot of the hill conspicuous excavations of part of the walls (and gate) of the ancient city can be seen. Above a sheepfold, yellow signs mark various excavations including an upper line of walls (2nd century BC) and a cave dwelling (re-used in Roman times; protected by a wooden roof). Beside the bus stop near the top of the hill are two enclosures, the higher one with remains of medieval houses built over public buildings from the Hellenistic era and the lower one with a monumental Hellenistic edifice, reconstructed in the Roman period. A path continues towards the theatre with a fine view of the temple below. On the right is an enclosure with a ruined church (12th–15th centuries). On the summit of the hill are the remains of a 12th–13th-century castle and, on the opposite side of the hill, a 12th-century mosque (destroyed by the owners of the castle in the 13th century).

The theatre occupies a spectacular position near the summit of Monte Barbaro (415m), facing the Gulf of Castellammare beyond Monte Inici (1064m) while more high mountain ranges rise to the east. It is one of the best-preserved ancient theatres in existence, built in the mid-3rd century BC or possibly earlier. With a diameter of 63m it could hold 3,200 spectators. The exterior of the cavea was supported by a high polygonal wall, which is particularly-well preserved at the two sides. Beneath the cavea a grotto with late Bronze Age finds was discovered in 1927 by the archaeologist Pirro Marconi. Classical drama productions are presented here in summer.

In Contrada Mango at the foot of Monte Barbaro, to the east near the Gaggera river, is a large Archaic sanctuary (not fully excavated), of great importance, thought to date from the 7th century BC. The temenos measures 83m by 47m. A huge deposit of pottery sherds dumped from the town on the hill above has also come to light here.

Calatafimi

The nearest town to Segesta is Calatafimi, frequently visited by the writer Samuel Butler between 1893 and 1900. He identified in this corner of Sicily all the places described in Homer's *Odyssey*, and in *The Authoress of the Odyssey* he reveals his belief that the epic was really written by a woman, Nausicaa.

Southwest of the town (signposted Pianto Romano, off the SS 113) an obelisk commemorates Garibaldi's victory against the Bourbon troops on 15th May 1860. A cypress avenue leads to the monument by Ernesto Basile (1892) on which Garibaldi's words on reaching the hill after his disembarkation from Marsala are inscribed: *'Qui si fa l'Italia o si muore'* ('here we will create Italy or die'). There are fine views from the hilltop.

ALCAMO

At the eastern extremity of the province of Trapani is the agricultural town of Alcamo, with numerous fine 18th-century churches. Founded at the end of the 10th century, it derives its name from the Arabic *manzil al qamah*, possibly interpreted as 'the farm of bitter cucumbers'. It was the birthplace of the 13th-century poet Cielo or Ciullo, short for Michele, one of the earliest exponents of the Sicilian School (*see box overleaf*), and a forefather of Italian literature. The town has a strongly Saracen flavour in its regular plan, with many attractive cobbled streets.

THE SICILIAN SCHOOL

A group of poets writing for the court of the Holy Roman Emperor Frederick II in the first half of the 13th century, the Sicilian School was first identified as such by Dante. He regarded his own work as an attempt to transcend their achievements, which included the adaptation of Provençal forms, largely lyrical celebrations of courtly love, into the local vernacular. One of their number, Giacomo da Lentini, is also generally credited with inventing the sonnet, later perfected by Petrarch, with his *Io m'aggio posto in core* (I have a place in my heart...). Little is known about the life of Ciullo d'Alcamo, but his work *Contrasto Amoroso*, probably written c. 1230, was cited by Dante in *De Vulgari Eloquentia*. Frederick II's court would have exercised a severe restraining influence on the poets' subject matter, something which Ciullo is believed to have subverted, with his bright and earthy parody of the School's conventions. His poem begins *Rosa fresca aulentissima* (Sweetest smelling fresh rose...) and tells of a young man's illicit seduction of a high-born lady, displaying such intimate acquaintance with life at court that some scholars have suggested that Ciullo was the *nom de plume* of a senior member of the nobility, close to the Emperor himself.

EXPLORING ALCAMO

Corso VI Aprile

In Piazza Bagolino the terrace offers a fine panorama of the plain stretching towards the sea. Beyond the 16th-century Porta Palermo, Corso VI Aprile leads into the town. On the left is the church of **San Francesco d'Assisi**, founded in 1348 and rebuilt in 1716. It contains a beautiful marble altarpiece attributed to Giacomo Gagini (1568), statues of *St Mark* and *Mary Magdalene* by Antonello Gagini and a 17th-century painting of the *Immaculate Virgin* by Giuseppe Carrera.

The corso continues past the former church of San Tommaso (c. 1450) with a carved Gothic portal. Opposite, next to a convent, is the church of Santi Cosma e Damiano (usually closed), a domed centrally planned building of c. 1721 by Giuseppe Mariani. It contains two stucco statues by Giacomo Serpotta, and two altarpieces by Guglielmo Borremans; the interior is among the finest examples of Baroque architecture in Sicily.

The corso crosses Via Rossotti with a view left of the castle and right of San Salvatore. The **Castello dei Conti di Modica** (*open daily 9–1 & 4–8*) was built c. 1350, on a rhomboid plan with four towers. For many years it was used as the local prison. Now it has been lovingly restored and is the seat of the Civic Historical Library and the Oenological Museum dedicated to local production of the prize-winning *Bianco d'Alcamo*, one of Sicily's 21 wines guaranteed by the *Denominazione d'Origine Controllata* (DOC) label (*see p. 518*). Not far from the castle, tucked away in this part of town, is Torre De Ballis (1495), one of the few surviving tower-houses in Sicily. It is now a private home with no public access.

The corso continues past the former church of the Madonna del Soccorso (15th century) with a portal attributed to Bartolomeo Berrettaro, to the Chiesa Madre. Founded in 1332, it was rebuilt in 1669 by Angelo Italia, with a fine dome. In the interior are columns of red marble quarried on Monte Bonifato. The frescoes in the vault, cupola and apse are by Guglielmo Borremans. In the second chapel of the south aisle is a Crucifix by Antonello Gagini (1523); in the fourth chapel a late 16th-century sarcophagus with portraits of two members of the De Ballis family; in the fifth there is a marble relief by Antonello Gagini. In the chapel to the right of the choir is a 17th-century painting of the Last Supper. In the adjoining chapel (right) are two fine Gothic arches and a beautiful fresco fragment of the Pentecost (1430). In the chapel to the left of the choir is a wooden statue of the Madonna (1721). On the altar of the north transept, the statue of St Peter is by Giacomo Gagini (1556).

The inner door of the sacristy (beyond the wooden door in the north aisle) is decorated with carvings of fruit attributed to Bartolomeo Berrettaro. In the third chapel of the north aisle there is a high relief of the Transition of the Virgin by Antonello Gagini.

Piazza Ciullo and environs

The corso continues to the elegantly curved Piazza Ciullo, at the centre of town and the market place in the Middle Ages. On the corner is the church of **Sant'Oliva**, built by Giovanni Biagio Amico in 1724. It was restored in 1990 after a fire in 1987 destroyed the 18th-century frescoes and stuccoes in the vault of the nave. The interior has altars beautifully decorated with marble. In the fourth chapel of the south aisle is a statue of St Oliva by Antonello Gagini (1511). One of the four patron saints of Palermo, St Oliva was a beautiful young girl from the 9th century who is supposed to have been captured by the Saracens and taken to Tunis where she converted many to Christianity before finally being tortured and beheaded. Her soul was seen to escape in the form of a dove. The high altarpiece is by Pietro Novelli (*see p. 81*) and on the left wall is a 16th-century marble tabernacle. On the left side are 18th-century statues and a marble group of the Annunciation (1545) by Antonino and Giacomo Gagini. Piazza Ciullo is dominated by the magnificent **Collegiate Church** (1684–1767) containing 18th-century stuccoes and altarpieces. On Sunday mornings a large proportion of the population—the wine farmers and their families, the women elegantly dressed, the men wearing black serge jackets and cloth caps—tends to congregate in front of this church.

Corso VI Aprile continues from Piazza Ciullo past 18th-century and Neoclassical palaces to the church of **Santi Paolo e Bartolomeo** (1689) with a splendid interior decorated by Vincenzo and Gabriele Messina and Antonino Grano. The oval *Madonna del Miele* (Our Lady of Honey), so-called because she is shown with a honeycomb symbolizing her sweetness, dates from the late 14th or early 15th century.

In Via Amendola, the road leading out of the square to the north, opposite the church of Sant'Oliva, is the church of the Rosario (San Domenico) which contains a fresco attributed to Tommaso de Vigilia, one of western Sicily's more celebrated 15th-century artists, whose work often displayed Genoese and Catalan influences.

Beyond the castle and the large Piazza della Repubblica is the church of **Santa Maria del Gesù** (1762). Beneath the portico is a portal attributed to Bartolomeo Berrettaro (1507). The church also contains a 16th-century altarpiece, the *Madonna and Saints with the Counts of Modica*, and a statue of the Madonna and Child attributed to Bartolomeo Berrettaro or Giuliano Mancino. The cloister of the adjoining convent is especially beautiful.

In Via Caruso is the church of **San Francesco di Paola**, rebuilt in 1699 by Giovanni Biagio Amico. The pretty interior has eight statues modelled in stucco by Giacomo Serpotta (*see p. 56*), commissioned in 1724, and an altarpiece of *St Benedict* by Pietro Novelli. The church is only open for services, but it is possible to ask for admission at the Benedictine convent next door.

Environs of the town

On **Monte Bonifato** (825m), south of the town, in a pinewood, a ruined Norman castle of the Ventimiglia is situated, with the chapel of the Madonna dell'Alto (superb view). The medieval **Fontanazza** here is a huge reservoir or thermal edifice dating from the 14th century. Most of the mountain is a nature reserve (*Riserva Bosco di Alcamo*), run by the provincial administration.

To the north, between the town and the sea, the spectacular castle on a spur known as **Calatubo** (no access) adequately protected Alcamo on that vulnerable side; probably Byzantine, the fortress was rebuilt and renamed by the Arabs in the 9th century. Close to the railway station is a spa, *Stabilimento termale Gorga*, where water from hot springs flows into a pool prepared, according to Diodorus Siculus, by the local nymphs for Hercules 'to refresh his body'.

THE WEST COAST

The west coast of Sicily from Trapani to Mazara del Vallo is flat, with many salt marshes, which have given rise to one of the oldest salt-extracting industries in the world. Between Trapani and Marsala they are now protected, in part because of the interesting birdlife, and also as important sites of industrial archaeology. The coastal plain is reminiscent of North Africa, dotted with white cube-shaped houses, palms and Norfolk Island pines. Four private islands lie close offshore in the beautiful shallow lagoon of Lo Stagnone, which has an average depth of just over one metre, and is abundant in fish. Isola Longa is the largest, with a charming small hotel (*see p. 180*), while the smallest is Isola Scola, site of an ancient academy where Cicero is said to have taught oratory. The only island fully accessible to visitors is San Pantaleo, the site of ancient Mozia. Further south is Marsala, and beyond a plain densely cultivated with olives, low vineyards, and gardens of tomatoes, melons and cantaloupes, stretching as far as colourful Mazara del Vallo, an important fishing port.

MOZIA

On the edge of the lagoon (signposted from the coastal road), there are several jetties from which boats ferry visitors to the island of San Pantaleo. The long-established boatmen, who have been doing this for many years, are Arini e Pugliese (*T: 347 3430329 and 347 7790218*). There are splendid views of the other islands from the water's edge and on the far right the mountain of Erice is prominent beyond salt pans, windmills and piles of salt. San Pantaleo itself is an oasis of luxuriant vegetation, a sanctuary for birds, with sweet-smelling plants, palm trees and pinewoods. The ruins of Phoenician Mozia are unenclosed (*open summer 9–7; winter 9–5*).

HISTORY OF MOZIA

Motya was founded in the mid-8th century BC by Phoenicians as a commercial base and industrial area (the name means 'mills'). By the mid-6th century BC the island was entirely surrounded by defensive walls, 2400m long and over 2m thick. It became an important Carthaginian station, controlling a large part of the western Mediterranean. In his determination to remove the Carthaginians from Sicily, the tyrant Dionysius I of Syracuse brought a large army, formed partly of mercenaries, here in 398 BC. During the fierce battle which ensued, he used wooden towers that enabled his men to shoot over the walls, and served as mounts for catapults. When his fleet became trapped in the lagoon, Dionysius escaped by dragging his ships over an isthmus, 4km wide, using logs as rollers, to the open sea, where he finally defeated the enemy. By the following year the Carthaginians had moved their headquarters to *Lilybaeum*.

Villa Whitaker

Open May–Sept 9–12.45 & 3–6.45; Mar–May Sept–Oct 9–12.45 & 3–6; Nov–Mar 9–3.
The island was owned from 1888 by Joseph (Pip) Whitaker (1850–1936), a distinguished ornithologist and amateur archaeologist, and member of the famous family of Marsala wine merchants. The low vineyards here still produce an excellent wine. He began excavations around 1913. Since the death of his daughter Delia in 1971, the island has been the property of the Joseph Whitaker Foundation (*167 Via Dante, Palermo, T: 091 6820522*). Excavations continued until around 1993. The boat docks near a stretch of the fortifications of the Punic city, from which a path leads to the crenellated Villa Whitaker, founded as a museum in 1925. Some of the showcases brought at that time from Edinburgh and Belfast are still in use. The material on display comes from the excavations at Mozia, Lilybaeum and Birgi, carried out by Whitaker and (in the last few years) by the Italian State. It includes Phoenician ceramics, the earliest dating from the 8th century BC, and Greek ware including proto-

Il Giovane di Mozia (c. 440 BC) in the Villa Whitaker, Mozia.

Corinthian and Corinthian vases, and Attic black- and red-figure vases. Other finds from the island include Phoenician glass, alabaster and jewellery.

Among the sculptural fragments is an extraordinarily vivid metope from the North Gate showing two lions attacking a bull, distinctly Mycenaean in style (end of 7th century or early 6th century BC), and a marble krater with bas-reliefs (Augustan period). The expressive statue of a young man in a finely pleated linen tunic, **Il Giovane di Mozia**, was found at Cappiddazzu on the northeast side of the island in 1979. In the the stance of a victor, with hand on hip, the pose of the statue expresses great confidence in youth, beauty and power. This remarkable work, made of white marble, is thought to be the work of a Greek master, perhaps Pheidias, and to date from c. 440 BC. One theory suggests that the statue may represent Melqart (a Phoenician god identified by the Greeks as Heracles), the titular divinity of Tyre, who was probably wearing a lion's skin made of bronze, which would have partially covered the head, and a bronze band around the chest, although the beardless chin does not support this identification. The statue was found buried under a layer of stones, face up in the road by the sanctuary. The face and the front are abraded, possibly by the bronze accoutrements being torn from the statue during Dionysius' attack. The fact that the statue was not recovered and replaced in a temple, in spite of its enormous value, would be explained if the shocked survivors of the battle had thought the statue profaned. Other theories suggest that the statue may represent a charioteer, or an unknown Carthaginian hero.

Nearby is a small building used up until the 1970s for wine-making. During reconstruction work in 1995 remains of houses (called *Zona E*), dating from 7th–4th centuries BC, were found beneath the pavement: the excavations can now be viewed from a walkway.

The map shows:

MOZIA

Archaic necropolis — causeway to Birgi
Zona K
North Gate
'Industrial' zone
'Cappiddazzu' site
Tophet
East Tower
Urban zone
House ot the Anforae
Bar
Zona E
Museum (Whitaker Villa)
Landing Stage
Cothon
South Gate
'Casermetta'
Punic Walls
N
0   200 yards
0   200 metres

The excavations

In front of the museum a path leads towards the lagoon to the **House of the Mosaics**, surrounded by a fence and rich vegetation, with bases of columns and pebble mosaics showing a panther attacking a bull and a griffin chasing a deer, among other designs (4th–3rd centuries BC).

A longer path (c. 400m) leads from the custodian's house across the southern part of the island to the waterfront at the southeast corner, beside the **Cothon** and **South Gate**. The Cothon is a small basin (50m by 40m) within the walls, thought to have been an artificial dock used for repairing ships or for harbouring small craft. A paved canal with ashlar walls of the 6th century BC, thought to be its seaward entrance, has also been excavated. A path leads back towards the villa along the edge of the south shore past an enclosure near a clump of pine trees. Excavations here have unearthed a building that was probably used for military purposes, known as the **Casermetta**.

The path continues along the water's edge below the villa, passing the jetty and the impressive fortifications (late 6th century BC), the best-preserved stretch on the island, along the eastern shore, reaching (after 400m) the **East Tower**, which preserves its flight of steps. Beyond some recent excavations (protected by a roof) is the imposing **North Gate**, with a triple line of defences. It defended a submerged causeway (meant to be invisible from land, but perfectly practicable for a horse and cart), which was built in the late 6th century BC to link the island to the mainland and a necropolis at Birgi. Several kilometres long, just wide enough for two carts to pass each other, it can still be seen at low tide and crossed on foot.

A path leads inland through the north gate to **Cappiddazzu**, the site of an important sanctuary, perhaps dedicated to Melqart, where *Il Giovane di Mozia* was first found. Above the level of the path is a building with mosaic remains. To the right is a field with low vines and two enclosed areas, the farthest of which, on the edge of the sea, is the Archaic necropolis with tombs dating from the 8th–6th centuries BC. Nearby a fence surrounds an 'industrial area', known as Zona K, with interesting kilns, similar in design to some found in Syria and Palestine. The largest enclosure is the **Tophet**, a Punic sacrificial burial ground dedicated to the goddess Tanith and to her husband god Baal Hammon, where children, possibly the male first-born, were sacrificed (replaced after the 5th century BC by animal sacrifices). Excavations here produced cinerary urns, votive terracotta masks, and stelae (some with human figures).

From the Tophet a path leads round the western shore to the Cothon and South Gate (after c. 700m). Another, marked by low olive trees, leads back through a vineyard in the centre of the island towards the museum (c. 400m). It passes (right) an enclosure with remains of the **House of the Anforae**, so-called because a huge deposit of amphorae was found here. On the edge of the lagoon, near the jetty, is an old salt mill which is now a museum with a small hotel, Saline Ettore e Infersa (*open summer 9–8.30; winter 9.30–1.30 & 3–7.30*). The various phases of obtaining salt from sea water are explained, and a film illustrates the method of production.

MARSALA

Marsala is a pleasant town with a 16th-century aspect, and an attractive open seafront on Capo Boeo, the site of the Carthaginian city of *Lilybaeum*. The town gives its name to a famous dessert wine still produced here in large quantities from the vineyards along the coast. Much like sherry and port, Marsala owes its worldwide fame to the British. In the late 18th century an English merchant tasted it and noted a striking similarity to the wines of southwestern Andalucia. By adding brandy to the base wine, he created a fortified liquor which he sold in England with enormous success (*see box opposite*). Production of top quality Marsala began in 1880, when Paolo Pellegrino founded his winery and dedicated his life to the wine. The wine is stored in huge *bagli*, fortified farmhouses or wineries. The name derives from the Latin *balium* or *vallum*, being a group of buildings forming a square or a rectangle around a central courtyard, with one entrance, sometimes lavishly decorated, in the front wall. In the courtyard there is often a well-head above the rainwater cistern. On entering, the house immediately in front is that of the owner, usually with a private chapel to one side. . Other buildings house the farmworkers, the wine or olive presses and the stables.

HISTORY OF MARSALA

Lilybaeum, founded by the Carthaginians in 396 BC, near the headland of Capo Boeo, the western extremity of Sicily, was peopled from *Motya* (*see above*), and became their strongest bulwark in Sicily after the sack of that city by Dionysius. It succumbed to the Romans only after a siege of ten years (250–241 BC). The historian Polybius describes the extraordinary siege in detail: a Carthaginian called Hannibal 'the Rhodian' made a considerable contribution by regularly running the Roman blockade of the city's famous harbour. During the Second Punic War, Scipio (later to become Africanus) set sail from Lilybaeum on his way to defeat Hannibal near Carthage itself at the battle of Zama (202 BC). As the seat of the Roman governor of Sicily, the city reached the zenith of its importance. Cicero, made quaestor here around 70 BC, called it '*civitas splendidissima*'. In 47 BC Julius Caesar also pitched camp here on his way to Africa. A *municipium* during the Augustan age, it was later raised to the status of *colonia*. It kept its importance as an avenue of communication with Africa during the Saracen dominion under the name *Marsa Alí*, the harbour of Ali, but declined after 1574 when Don John of Austria (illegitimate son of Charles V) almost completely blocked its port to protect it from Barbary pirates.

The wine trade was founded by John Woodhouse in 1773 when he made the first shipment of local white wine to Liverpool, conserving it on its month-long journey by adding alcohol. In 1798, after the Battle of the Nile, Nelson placed a large order of Marsala for his fleet. In 1806 Benjamin Ingham and his nephew Whitaker also took up trading in Marsala with great success; by 1812 they were exporting the wine to North America. Production on an even grander scale was undertaken by Vincenzo Florio (d. 1868), one of Sicily's most able businessmen. In 1929 the establishments of Woodhouse, Ingham Whitaker and Florio were taken over by Cinzano, and merged under the name of Florio. The house of Florio continues to flourish along with many other companies, including **Pellegrino** (*open Mon–Fri 9–12 & 2.30–5.30; Sat 9–12; 39 Via del Fante, T: 0923 719911, www.carlopellegrino.it*), **Donnafugata** (*18 Via Lipari, T: 0923 724200, www.donnafugata.it*), and **Montalto**.

Garibaldi and the 'Thousand' landed here on 11th May 1860, being unobtrusively assisted by two British warships which had officially been assigned to protect the wine merchants. In 1943, Marsala was heavily damaged by Allied air attacks during preparations for *Operation Husky*.

Exploring Marsala

The centre of town is entered from the port and southwest by the monumental Porta Garibaldi, formerly the Porta di Mare, reconstructed in 1685. On the left is the church of the Addolorata, with a fine circular domed 18th-century interior, and a venerated popular statue of the Madonna wearing a black cloak. Opposite, municipal offices occupy a restored 16th-century military building, behind which is the market square. Via Garibaldi continues to the central **Piazza della Repubblica** with the idiosyncratic Palazzo Comunale (town Hall) which has original lamps on its upper storey. Opposite on Via XI Maggio, is a wall and dome of the 17th-century church of San Giuseppe, with a lovely interior and a fine organ.

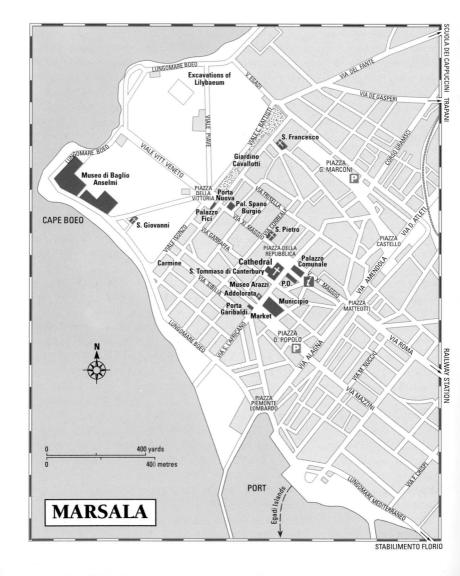

The duomo and town centre

The duomo (San Tommaso di Canterbury) has a Baroque front completed in 1957. The first church on this site was built in 1176–82 and dedicated to St Thomas Becket. A new building, begun in 1607 and completed in 1717 was ruined when the dome collapsed in 1893, and it was partly rebuilt in the 20th century.

The interior contains some important 17th-century paintings and sculptures. On the south side in the first chapel there is an unusual statue of the *Assunta* and two reliefs on the side wall, all by Antonino Gagini. The delicately carved tomb slab dates from 1556. In the second chapel there is a 15th-century statue of the Madonna, and a tomb with the effigy, attributed to Domenico Gagini, of Antonio Grignano (d. 1475) who fought with honour in the wars of King Alfonso. In the third chapel is an elaborate statue of the *Madonna dell'Itria* (of the kind usually depicting the Child standing, representing Our Lady the protector of wayfarers) and the tomb of Giulio Alazzaro with an amusing effigy, both by Antonino Gagini. The fifth chapel has a 15th-century Crucifix and an expressive, popular statue of the *Virgin in mourning*. In the south transept is a striking altarpiece of the *Presentation in the Temple* by Antonello or Mariano Riccio, and the tomb of Antonio Lombardo, who donated the tapestries to the cathedral (now in the Museo degli Arazzi, *see below*). In the chapel to the right of the sanctuary is an unusual statue of the Madonna (wielding a distaff), attributed to Giuliano Mancino, and a tomb with an effigy of Antonio Liotta (d. 1512), also attributed to Mancino. On either side of the sanctuary are two statues, one of St Vincent Ferrer attributed to Giacomo Gagini and one of St Thomas the Apostle by Antonello Gagini. In the apse is a 17th-century painting of the Martyrdom of St Thomas in the original frame. In the chapel to the left of the sanctuary is a beautiful gilded marble altarpiece of the Passion begun in 1518 by Bartolomeo Berrettaro and finished by Antonello Gagini (1532; four of the panels have been set into the walls). On the north side, in the sixth chapel is a charming polychrome wooden statue of *Our Lady of Carmel*, and in the second chapel is another wooden statue (1593) of the Madonna, and two frescoed ex-votos with scenes of Marsala.

Behind the duomo, at no. 57 Via Giuseppe Garraffa, is the small **Museo degli Arazzi** (*open 9–1 & 4–6; Sun 9–1*), opened in 1985 to display eight precious tapestries given to the duomo in 1589 by Antonio Lombardo, archbishop of Messina (1523–95), born in Marsala and buried in the duomo. He became ambassador to Spain, and the very fine tapestries, depicting the capture of Jerusalem, were made in Brussels between 1530 and 1550 and are known to have come from the royal palace of Philip II in Madrid. They are displayed on three floors. Since their careful restoration they have to be kept in darkened rooms.

Via XI Maggio runs off Piazza della Repubblica. The 15th-century convent of **San Pietro** (*open 9–1 & 4–8; Sun and holidays 9.30–1.30 & 4–8; closed Mon*), in Via Correale, with a massive pointed tower, is now used as the town library, cultural centre and Civic Museum. The museum has sections on ancient history, the exploits of Giuseppe Garibaldi, and popular traditions.

Beyond, a street to the left leads towards the former church and convent of the **Carmine** (*open 10–1 & 5–7; closed Mon; www.pinacotecamarsala.it*), now used to house the municipal archives and an interesting contemporary art gallery, with paintings by 20th-century Italian masters such as Alberto Sughi (b. 1928), Bruno Caruso, Franco Gentilini (1909-1981), and the mythopoeic painter and sculptor Mirko (Basaldella, 1910–1969). The detached campanile was designed by Giovanni Battista Amico. The former convent was founded in the late 14th century and has an 18th-century cloister.

Back on Via XI Maggio, just before Porta Nuova (on Piazza della Vittoria), is the façade (left) of Palazzo Fici with a tall palm tree in its delightful Baroque courtyard. Opposite is the 19th–20th-century Palazzo Spanò Burgio (no. 15). Outside the gate is the entrance (right) to the **Giardino Cavallotti**, lovely public gardens with huge ficus trees, magnolias and ornamental Norfolk Island pines.

Capo Boeo and Insula Romana

Between Piazza della Vittoria and the seafront extends Capo Boeo, an open area with lawns and trees. Some picturesque old *bagli* on the seafront are still used as warehouses for wine, others have been converted into restaurants, and one of them houses the Archaeological Museum. Capo Boeo was the site of *Lilybaeum*, the excavations of which are reached by steps from Viale Piave, or by a path from Porta Nuova. The area, known as the Insula Romana, is now an archaeological park (*open 9–1.30; Wed, Fri , Sat & Sun also 4–6.30*). A marble *Venus Anadyomene*, similar to the *Landolina Venus* (*see p. 352*) at the Paolo Orsi Museum in Syracuse, has recently been uncovered here. In a well-restored house are diagrams of the site, which includes a sumptuous Roman villa (surrounded by a fence and covered for protection) dating from the 3rd century AD, which was built over in the Arab period. Around the *impluvium* are four mosaics of wild beasts attacking each other (thought to represent circus animals), probably the work of African craftsmen. There are remains of baths and other rooms with mosaics, including a head of Medusa, the symbol of Trinacria (*see p. 204*), and the four seasons. Nearby are more recent excavations including part of the walls, a necropolis, a Roman road, and a Roman *vomitorium*. A *hypogeum* with painted walls where a certain Crispia Salvia was buried in the 2nd century AD has also been discovered.

Baglio Anselmi Museo Regionale Archeologico
Open 9–1.30; also 4–6.30 Wed, Fri, Sat and Sun.
On the tip of the promontory is the Baglio Anselmi, a former Marsala distillery and wine cellar, which has been restored as the Baglio Anselmi Museo Regionale Archeologico, with a very interesting collection. From the entrance hall the spacious courtyard is visible; the museum is arranged in two huge vaulted warehouses. The display begins in the hall on the left with prehistoric material from the Marsala area, in particular from Mozia and also Phoenician articles from the Tophet (sacrificial burial area) of Mozia, along with some exquisite Hellenistic gold jewellery found in Marsala.

The finds from the Phoenician necropolis of Lilybaeum are displayed chronologically with explanatory diagrams and photographs, and include ceramics, funerary monuments, sculptures, terracottas, and Tanagra figurines (graceful female figures, so called because their type was first found at Tanagra in Greece). On the end wall are fragments of funerary monuments, stele and edicole with carved inscriptions or paintings (3rd–2nd centuries BC) from Mozia and Lilybaeum. Also here are fragments from a large mausoleum in local stone covered with a fine layer of white and polychrome stucco (its hypothetical form has been reconstructed in a drawing). Finds from Roman Lilybaeum (3rd–4th centuries AD) follow, along with a model of the excavations on Capo Boeo, including fragments of wall paintings, a hoard of coins, lamps and a fragment of a female statuette. The displays conclude with photographs of Palaeo-Christian finds, and a case of ceramics including Siculo-Norman ware. The last case illustrates the discovery of a Norman wreck offshore in 1983, with a few finds from the boat.

The other hall on the right contains the **Punic ship**, discovered by Honor Frost in 1971 off the Isola Longa, in the Stagnone lagoon. The well-preserved poop was recovered from the seabed and the rest of the hulk, 35m long, was carefully reconstructed in 1980. Manned by 68 oarsmen, it is thought to have been sunk on its maiden voyage during the First Punic War. The only warship of this period so far discovered, it is not known how the iron nails resisted the corrosion of the sea. The ship has been partly reconstructed around the original wood, which is conserved beneath a huge tent, which makes viewing awkward. Drawings illustrate the original appearance of the ship. Objects found on board are also displayed, including remains of ropes, a sailor's wooden button, a bone needle used for making nets, corks from amphorae, a brush, some ceramic fragments, and cannabis leaves and stalks—possibly an aid to the oarsmen during battle. The underwater finds include numerous amphorae, of which the contents, place of origin and date offer an interesting insight into trade in the Mediterranean in the Ancient World.

Nearby is the little church of **San Giovanni** (*kept locked, enquire for the key at the tourist office*), covering the so-called Grotto of the Sibyl, with a spring of water which later became an early Christian baptistery. There are still faint traces of ancient 5th-century AD frescoes.

THE SIBYL OF LILYBAEUM

Prophetesses or sibyls were popularly believed to be able speak for the gods, and hence foretell the future. Apollo was especially generous in this respect, and is often referred to as 'the far-seeing one'. There were several places where these oracles could be consulted, such as Delphi or Cumae, but the sibyl of Lilybaeum had a particularly good reputation for accuracy. The person requiring the information would enter the grotto where the priestess lived and put their question; she would then bathe their face and her own with water from the little pool. The pair would then take turns in sipping wine from a golden cup, after which the sibyl would enter a trance-like state and read the future in the dregs of wine remaining in the cup. The custom died out here when Sicily became a province of Rome in the 3rd century BC.

Stabilimento Florio

Open Mon–Thur 3–5; Fri 11–12; www.cantineflorio.com.
On the road which continues along the seafront back towards town, lined with palms, is the former Baglio Woodhouse (the entrance is marked by two round towers in front of a jetty and next to a chapel built by the English). In the harbour only the base remains of the monument commemorating the *Landing of the Thousand*, by Ettore Ximenes. It was destroyed in the Second World War. The road passes a number of old *bagli*, and, beside two tall palm trees, is the Stabilimento Florio. The monumental buildings designed by Basile surround an inner courtyard planted with trees. Visitors are shown the historic cellars and invited to taste the wine (free of charge). In the small museum a letter is preserved from Nelson, Duke of Bronte to John Woodhouse in 1800 with an order for Marsala for his fleet.

The Neoclassical villa built by Benjamin Ingham can be seen a little further along the waterfront.

Environs of Marsala

North of the town, in the Scuola dei Cappuccini, are the remains of a Punic-Roman necropolis (*open in summer*). To the south, on SS 115, the former Baglio Amodeo, one of the oldest Marsala wineries, is surrounded by a beautiful garden and is open as a hotel and restaurant (Villa Favorita, *see below p. 180*).

MAZARA DEL VALLO

Mazara del Vallo, at the mouth of the Mazaro, is the most important fishing town in Italy, with a large proportion of Tunisians who work on the farms and in the fishing fleet. It has a colourful waterfront and busy canal-port. The town, built in golden tufa, has a distinctly Arab flavour. Animated and attractive, with elegant shops and graceful squares, Mazara is one of the most lively towns in western Sicily.

HISTORY OF MAZARA

Mazara, once a Phoenician trading post, became an *emporium* of Selinunte and fell with it in 409 BC. It was held by the Carthaginians until 210 BC when it came under Roman rule. Here in 827 AD the Arabs, called in by the governor Euphemius to assist his pretensions to the imperial purple, gained their first foothold on the island. There followed the most important period in the town's history, when it became the capital of the Val di Mazara, one of the three administrative districts into which the Arabs divided Sicily. It was captured by Count Roger in 1075; and it was here in 1097 that the Sicilian parliament, one of the oldest in the world, was convened for the first time.

Exploring Mazara

The **cattedrale** was founded in 1093 and rebuilt in 1690–94. Above the main door, which faces the sea, is a 16th-century sculpture of Count Roger on horseback. The interior contains a *Transfiguration* in the apse by Antonello Gagini (finished by his son Antonino, 1537). The statues of St Bartholomew and St Ignatius are by the Palermitan sculptor Ignazio Marabitti (1719–97). In the south aisle is a sculpted portal by Bartolomeo Berrettaro. In the vestibule of the chapter-house are two Roman sarcophaghi. Off the north aisle is a chapel with a 13th-century painted Cross, and in the chapel of the *Madonna del Soccorso* is a Byzantine fresco (in a niche) of *Christ Pantocrator*.

Near the cathedral, at no. 14 Via San Salvatore, is the **Museo Ornitologico** (*open 9–12 & 3–6.30*), a collection of 373 stuffed birds, some of them extremely rare, and a few mammals, prepared by a local taxidermist in 1924. Between the cathedral and the seafront is a public garden with fine trees on the site of the Norman castle, one ruined wall of which faces the busy Piazza Mokarta at the end of the main Corso Umberto. On the other side of the cathedral is the 18th-century Piazza della Repubblica, with a statue by Marabitti (1771) and the handsome Seminario Vescovile (1710) with a double portico.

The **Diocesan Museum**, entrance from Via dell'Orologio (*open Tues–Sat 9–1*) contains the tomb (1495) of the Bishop Giovanni Montaperto, who ordered the construction of the cathedral in Agrigento, by Domenico Gagini, as well as paintings, vestments, and church silverware, including a processional Cross from Salemi dated 1386, by a Pisan artist, and another 15th-century Cross, along with numerous 18th-century reliquaries.

Via San Giuseppe leads to the church of **Santa Caterina** decorated in 1797 by Giuseppe Testa, with a statue of the saint by Antonello Gagini (1524). On the other side of Piazza della Repubblica, Via XX Settembre leads to Piazza Plebiscito with the two 16th-century churches of the Carmine and Sant'Egidio,

Museo del Satiro

Open Tues–Sun 9–6; holidays 9–1; closed Mon. T: 0923 933917.

The church of Sant'Egidio now contains the Museo del Satiro. In 1998 some local fishermen found a bronze statue of a satyr caught in their nets, while fishing in the Sicilian Channel. By returning to the same area a few weeks later they found the left leg of the statue and a bronze elephant's foot, perhaps from the same statuary group; they are still trying to find the missing arms and the other leg. It is encouraging that the statue was not sold on the clandestine antiquarian market; those involved are extremely proud of their discovery. It has been suggested that the Satyr could be Dionysus himself: he is shown with his body twisted in a dance of drunken ecstasy, his head thrown back, wild hair and pointed ears. A little larger than life size, the statue is made of bronze about 7mm thick, the weight, including the stand, about 140kg. Judging from other works of art on the same subject (statues, reliefs, cameos), the Satyr would have been carrying an empty wine cup in his left hand and a long rattle in his right. A panther skin would have been thrown over his left arm with its legs and tail flailing, and this, plus his donkey tail behind him, would have increased the effect of his frenzied whirling. Restoration and research on the statue is still being carried out, but a tentative date for it can be set between 404 and 280 BC. One authority has declared that the statue could even be the work of Praxiteles.

Close by is the church of Sant'Ignazio and the Collegio dei Gesuiti (1675–86), which now houses the municipal library and archives, and the **Museo Civico** (*open 9–1; Tues and Thur also 3.30–5.30; closed Sat, Sun and holidays*) which has Roman finds from the area and two interesting sculpted elephants which once bore the columns outside the west porch of the Norman cathedral. Many drawings by the local sculptor Pietro Consagra are displayed here.

The harbour nearby lies at the mouth of the River Mazaro which is normally filled with the fishing fleet during the day, except on Saturdays. This is the more picturesque part of the city, together with the Tunisian district around Via Porta Palermo and Via Bagno. A short way upstream stands the little Norman-Byzantine church of San Nicolò Regale with a crenellated top. The Lungomazaro continues along the river past the fish market to the bridge from which there is a splendid view of the boats.

The church of the Madonna dell'Alto, erected in 1103 by Juliet, daughter of Count Roger, is 2km outside the town.

SELINUNTE

One of the more impressive Classical sites in Sicily because never subsequently redeveloped, the extensive ruins (270ha) of the ancient city of Selinunte (sometimes called *Selinus*) are in a superb position overlooking the sea. On the coast nearby the simple fishing village of Marinella has been developed as a small resort. The beautiful coast to the east, around the mouth of the Belice river (and as far as Porto Palo), with its sand dunes, has recently been preserved as a nature reserve (*Riserva Naturale Foce del Fiume Belice*). The ancient town with its acropolis occupied a raised terrace between the River Selinon, or Modione, and the marshy depression now called Gorgo di Cottone or Galici, and possessed a harbour at the mouth of each valley. An important group of temples lay to the east of this site, and a necropolis to the north. The sandy soil is overgrown with wild celery, lentiscus, mandrake, acanthus and capers. The site has been enclosed, and is now the largest archaeological park in Europe.

PARCO ARCHEOLOGICO DI SELINUNTE

The site

Open summer 9–6.30; winter 9–4; re-entry permitted with ticket on the same day.

The site was rediscovered in the 16th century; but systematic excavations were begun only in 1822–3 by the Englishmen William Harris and Samuel Angell, after a fruitless dig had been made in 1809–10 by Robert Fagan, British consul-general in Sicily.

HISTORY OF SELINUNTE

Selinunte was a colony of Megara Hyblaea, probably founded as early as 651 BC. It takes its name *Selinus* from the wild celery, *Apium graveolens* (Greek, *selinon*), which still grows here in abundance, and which appears on its coins. The colony's most prosperous period was the 5th century BC, when the great temples were built and the city was laid out on a rectangular plan. After the battle of Himera in 480 BC Selinunte took part with Syracuse in an alliance against Carthage, and in 409 BC the Carthaginians, summoned to the help of Segesta, the mortal enemy of Selinunte, sent an army of 100,000 under Hannibal, son of Gisco, which captured Selinunte before the allied troops of Acragas and Syracuse could arrive. The city, which fell in only nine days, was sacked and destroyed, and its inhabitants sold as slaves. A later settlement, led by Hermocrates, a Syracusan exile, was dispersed by Carthage in 250 BC, and the population resettled at Lilybaeum. It is thought, however, that the utter destruction of every building, scarcely a single column being left upright, could also have been due to earthquakes. In fact, around and under the columns of Temple C are the ruins of a Byzantine settlement, and a later, Arab village called *Rahal al Asnaam*, or 'village of the columns', which must have been destroyed by an earthquake in the Middle Ages.

Temple E (490–480 BC), reconstructed in 1958, on the East Hill at Selinunte.

Harris and Angell found the famous metopes of Temples C and E, but Harris died of malaria, contracted while excavating here, and Angell was killed by bandits on a successive visit. In 1956–68, 12 streets were excavated, and in 1973 excavations were begun to the north, on the site of the ancient city. There have also been recent excavations in the area around the Sanctuary of Demeter Malophoros. A bronze statue (Phoenician, 12th–11th centuries BC) of Reshef (kept in the Museo Archeologico in Palermo), found in the vicinity, is the first archaeological confirmation that the Phoenicians traded here before the foundation of Carthage. A large modern dyke isolates the temples from the buildings of Marinella near the entrance to the park.

A visit, best started early in the morning, takes at least two or three hours, to include the three quite widely separated areas of the site: the East Hill temples; the Acropolis; and the Sanctuary of Demeter Malophoros.

The majority of the temples are distinguished by letters as their dedications are still under discussion. Among the few temples in Sicily to have had sculptured metopes, many of these beautiful works are now displayed in the Museo Archeologico in Palermo. All except Temples B and G are peripteral and hexastyle and all are orientated. The measurements given in the following descriptions refer to the temple stylobates. Many architectural fragments bear remains of plaster, and throughout the site are underground cisterns, built to collect rainwater. Beside most of the temples are sacrificial altars.

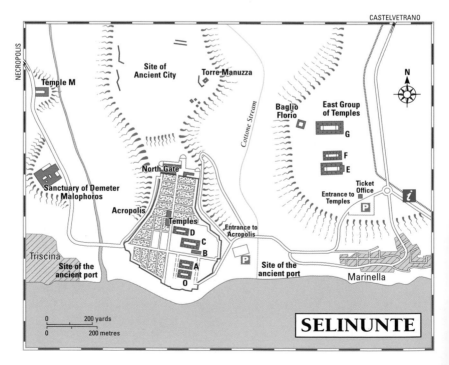

THE EAST HILL TEMPLES

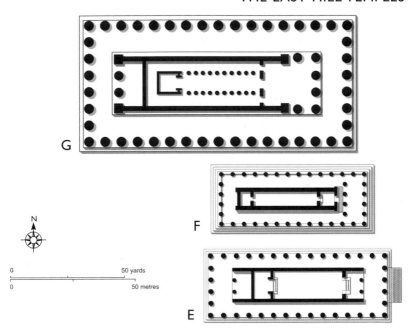

G

N

0   50 yards

0   50 metres

F

E

The East Hill

The East Hill shows the ruins of three large temples. Beyond the modern dyke and tunnel is **Temple E**, which measures 67.7m by 25.3m, and was probably dedicated to Hera. A Doric building of 490–480 BC, the temple had beautiful sculpted metopes, four of which were discovered in 1831 and are now in Palermo. Toppled by an earthquake, its colonnades were reconstructed in 1958. **Temple F**, the oldest on this hill (c. 560–540 BC), possibly dedicated to Aphrodite, is almost completely ruined. It once had a double row of columns in front and 14 at the sides. Part of one column rises above others which are now only a few metres high. The farthest north is **Temple G**, probably dedicated to Zeus; octastyle in form, it is the second largest (110m by 50m), after the Olympieion at Agrigento, among Sicilian temples. The columnar arrangement (8 by 17) is matched only by the Parthenon. Laid out in the 6th century and left incomplete (with unfluted columns) in 480 BC, it is now an impressive pile of overgrown ruins. One column still stands, called by the local people *'u fusu d'a vecchia* (the old lady's distaff). The columns, over 16m high with a base diameter of 3.4m, were built up of drums, each weighing c. 100 tons, from the quarries at Cusa (*see below*). The cella, preceded by a pronaos of four columns, had three aisles, the central aisle being open to the sky. The fallen capitals give some idea of the colossal scale of the building and the stylobate is in itself a marvel of monumental construction.

THE TEMPLES OF THE ACROPOLIS

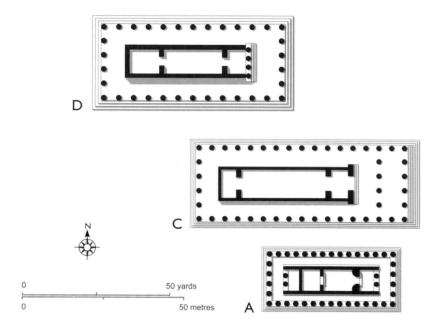

The Acropolis

From the first car park a road continues downhill across the Gorgo di Cottone (site of one of the ancient harbours) and up to the Acropolis, where there is a second car park (*see plan on p. 162*). From here a path continues up between the sea and massive double walls, constructed after the Carthaginian attack, in which five towers and four gates have been located, dating from c. 307–306 BC. In front of the custodian's house is a plan and explanation of the site, beside the stylobate of Temple O, whose superstructure has disappeared, and, next door, the stylobate of **Temple A** (40m by 16m; 36 columns), with some fluted drums. The cella was one step higher than the pronaos and the adytum one higher still. Between the cella and pronaos two spiral staircases led up to the roof. Fragmentary ruins of a monumental entrance exist to the east. Temples A and O, both built in 490–480 BC, and identical in form and dimension, were the latest and probably the most perfect of the Selinuntine temples. In front of Temple O a sacred area has been excavated, thought to date from after the destruction of the city in 409 BC. A castle that was constructed on this site was probably early 9th-century Arabic.

The ruins of the Acropolis are crossed by two principal streets at right angles, with lesser streets running parallel in a grid pattern. To the north are the remains of the great **Temple C**, on the highest point of the knoll, and the most conspicuous monument on the Acropolis. It measured 63.7m by 24m, and dates from the early 6th century, when it would have replaced a more simple megaron. Probably dedicated to Apollo, it was once adorned with metopes found here in 1823, now in the Palermo archaeological museum. In order to accommodate the sacrificial altar, the temenos was artificially extended some way eastwards, supported by monumental steps. The colossal columns (6 x 17), some of which were monolithic, are nearly 2m in diameter at the base, except for the corner-columns which are even thicker; they fell during an earthquake in the Middle Ages, burying a Byzantine village that had grown up in the 5th century (a crucifix and a Christian bronze lamp were found here) and a later Arab village. The north colonnade, now the temple's most salient feature, was re-erected in 1925–27. Part of the sacrificial altar remains.

To the south of the temple is a megaron (17.6m by 5.5m), dating from 580–570 BC. In the east corner of the temenos a stoa has been excavated which was probably built at the same time as the acropolis walls (late 6th century). To the southeast is the small Temple B, a prostyle aediculum with pronaos and cella, once famous for being very brightly coloured.

The path leads left, following the east–west thoroughfare of the city, passing in front of the pronaos of Temple A. Near a solitary ancient ilex tree is a crude mosaic floor depicting an image of the Punic goddess, Tanith.

The wide main northern thoroughfare of the city (the north gate can be seen at its end) leads away from the sea, past the stylobate of **Temple D** (570–554 BC) which stands beside the road: it carried 34 columns, measures 56m x 24m, and was the second temple to be built on the Acropolis. Some of its blocks still have their bosses. Beyond, by a small pine tree is a row of modest constructions, thought to have been shops, each with two rooms, a courtyard, and stairs up to the living quarters on the first floor. Nearby are the foundations of the **Temple of the Small Metopes**, named after the six small metopes found here, now in the Palermo Museum. It had a simple cella and adytum and measured 15.2m x 5.4m.

Just before the North Gate there is a good view east of the splendid Temple E (*see above*) on its hill. The **North Gate**, one of the main gates of the city, is well preserved. Beyond is a sophisticated defence system once thought to date from the time of Hermocrates, but probably constructed by Agathocles in 307–306 BC. The fortifications include three semicircular towers, and a second line of walls c. 5m outside the earlier ones which were reinforced after their destruction by Hannibal in 409 BC using material from the acropolis, including capitals. The imposing remains are explained in a diagram at the site.

A sandy path continues through the low vegetation to the most recent area of excavations of the ancient city (not yet open to the public), near another well-restored farmhouse. The city was orientated north–south and recent research has suggested it may originally have extended beyond the (later) perimeter wall to the north, and into the valleys of the Cottone and Modione rivers. Another area of the city farther north, on the sand-covered hill of Manuzza, may have had a slightly different orientation. Further north was a necropolis (probably on the site of a prehistoric burial-place).

Sanctuary of Demeter Malophoros

Outside the North Gate, to the west, can be seen the excavations on the right bank of the Modione. These can most easily be reached by the rough road (c. 1km, used by the custodians) which branches off from the main crossroads near Temple C. Here the interesting Sanctuary of Demeter Malophoros (the Bearer of Fruits) consists of a sacred area enclosed by walls. It is now approached by a monumental entrance (late 5th century) and portico. In the centre is a huge sacrificial altar, and beyond, the temple (a megaron), thought to have been built c. 560 BC, with a Doric cornice. Nearby are the scant remains of two other sacred precincts, one of them dedicated to Zeus Meilichios with two altars, where numerous stelae carved with a male and female head were discovered. More than 5,000 terracotta figurines have been found in the vicinity. Another temple is being excavated to the south.

Near a spring, some 200m north, a sacred edifice has recently been excavated and called **Temple M**. This may, in fact, be an altar or a monumental fountain of the 6th century BC. The necropolis proper extends for some kilometres to the west: several tombs and heaps of bones are still visible, behind the unattractive modern holiday village of Triscina, but at least another two burial grounds have been located.

THE CAVE DI CUSA

Off the road between Selinunte and Castelvetrano a country road (signposted) leads through extensive olive groves and vineyards to Campobello di Mazara, a wine-producing centre. A Crucifix in the church here is by fra' Umile da Petralia (*see p. 287*). From Campobello a road (signposted) leads south towards Tre Fontane on the coast. At a crossroads by the ruins of the Baglio Ingham, a right turn continues past a disused sewage plant to end at the Cave di Cusa (*open from 9 until 2hrs before sunset*), the ancient quarries used for excavating the stone used for the construction of the temples of Selinunte.

The quarries have not been worked since the destruction of Selinunte in 409 BC and no excavations have ever been carried out here. Ancient olive trees grow among the peaceful ruins, and the beautiful site, inhabited by birds, is surrounded by olive and orange groves and vineyards. Only some 120m wide, the quarries extend for 2km, unenclosed, unannounced and often, especially in winter, utterly deserted and romantic. The various different processes of quarrying can be studied here, from the first incisions in the rock to the empty spaces left by the removal of the completed drums for columns. One block, still attached to the rock, seems to have been intended for a capital. Around each column carved out of the rock a space of c. 50cm allowed room for the stonemason to work. Four drums stand close together, carved along the whole of their length and apparently waiting simply to be detached at their bases. The large cylindrical masses of stone (c. 3m by 2m) were probably intended for Temple G. It is thought that wooden frames were constructed around the columns and that they were transported to Selinunte, about 18km away, on wheels of solid wood strengthened by iron bands and pulled by oxen.

CASTELVETRANO

Castelvetrano is a farming community in the centre of a wine- and oil-producing area. The olive trees are very small, the fruits being gathered by hand for preserving or for making oil, thought to be the finest in Sicily; the local bread is particularly good, too, and has been indicated by the Slow Food Organization as worthy of protection. To the south the view falls away across the cultivated plain towards the sea and the ruins of Selinunte. The simple architecture of many of the houses, with internal courtyards, is interesting, although the town was damaged in the Belice earthquake of 1968. The body of the bandit Salvatore Giuliano was 'found' here in 1950.

EXPLORING CASTELVETRANO

The town centre

In the centre of town is the cramped and oddly shaped Piazza Garibaldi, which is planted with trees. The **duomo** (usually entered by the side door in Piazza Umberto) is a 16th-century church with an unusual ornately decorated portal. The central roof beam has preserved its painted decoration. Two triumphal arches are bedecked with white stuccoes of cherubs, garlands and angels, by Antonino Ferraro, the accomplished Mannerist decorator from Giuliana, and Gaspare Serpotta (who also carved the four saints in the nave). In the presbytery there is gilded decoration by Antonino Ferraro and an *Assumption* (1619) by his son Orazio Ferraro. The chapel to the right of the sanctuary has a 16th-century wooden Crucifix. The chapel to the left of the sanctuary has a marble Gaginesque statue, and, on the wall, a painting attributed to Pietro Novelli. Off the north aisle, the Cappella della Maddalena has fine decoration, especially in the dome, by Tommaso Ferraro. The detached campanile dates from the 16th century.

On the corner of Piazza Umberto is an elaborate fountain (1615, by the Neapolitan designer Orazio Nigrone) with a statue of a nymph. The church of the Purgatorio, which has a decorative 18th-century façade (now used as an auditorium), and the Neoclassical **Teatro Selinus** (*open 9–1*), of 1870 by Giuseppe Patricolo, are also both in the piazza. The little opera house, with 350 seats, looks like a miniature Doric temple, with four columns in front; in the entrance is a marble sculpture of children playing by Mario Rutelli. From the top of Via Garibaldi, Via Fra' Pantaleo leads downhill southeast to Piazza Regina Margherita, where there is a little public garden and two churches. **San Domenico**, which has a plain façade, contains a riot of 16th-century Baroque terracotta figures, coloured and stuccoed, by Antonino Ferraro, who included his self-portrait in the choir, and unusual funerary monuments. Ferraro's meticulous work was commissioned by Don Carlos of Aragona, the first prince of Castelvetrano and later Governor of Milan. The richly decorated tombs of his family can also be seen. On another side of the piazza is the 16th-century church of **San Giovanni Battista**, newly restored after the earthquake, with an elaborate façade and a green cupola. The interesting interior contains a remarkable statue of St John the Baptist by Antonello Gagini (1522), and three 17th-century paintings.

Madonna and Child (c. 1460), by the workshop of Francesco Laurana, in the Museo Civico.

Museo Civico

Open 9–1 & 3.30–7.30; Dec–Mar 9.30–1.30 & 2.30–6.30.

Via Garibaldi continues downhill southeastwards past Via Francesco la Croce, on the corner of which is the Biblioteca Comunale, which houses the Museo Civico displaying objects excavated at Selinunte. On the ground floor is an unusual little room, well-designed in an intimate arrangement to display the interesting bronze statuette known as the **Efebo di Selinunte** (5th century BC), stolen from the town hall in 1962 and subsequently recovered in 1968. It was restored and displayed in the Archaeological Museum at Palermo, before returning here. Found by a nine-year-old boy at Selinunte in 1882, it is thought to be a locally produced work of c. 480–460 BC, made using the lost-wax method. The small, but well chosen collection also includes the *Lamina Plumbea*, a 5th-century BC transcription of a sacred law on a thin sheet of lead, coming from the archives of one of the Selinunte temples. It is the largest of its kind in existence, and was recently returned from the Paul Getty Museum in Malibu, to whom it had been sold by clandestine diggers. Among the other finds from Selinunte are: a red-figure krater with four satyrs (470–460 BC); Corinthian ware; terracottas; coins; and a two-headed stele from the Sanctuary of Demeter Malophoros. The tawny alabaster statue of the *Madonna and Child* by Francesco Laurana and his workshop (c. 1460) comes from the ruined church of the Annunziata. The tourist office is on the first floor, over the museum.

Environs of Castelvetrano

About 3km west of the town is the church of the **Santissima Trinità di Delia**. It is reached by taking Via Pietro Colletta downhill from Piazza Umberto and continuing straight ahead (signposted Trinità di Delia). After c. 1km, at a fork, the road (unsignposted) continues left past a gravel works and straight on (signposted Lago di Trinità). It passes a small eucalyptus wood and then follows the white wall of the farm, which incorporates the church. The key is kept at the modern house on the right. The chapel, dating from the 11th–12th centuries, is a very fine building derived from Arab and Byzantine models. It was beautifully restored in 1880, and contains 19th-century family tombs. The crypt beneath is entered by an outside staircase. In the churchyard in a little wood is a romantic tombstone by the Palermitan sculptor Benedetto Civiletti (1845–99), erected by the Saporito family. Beneath the hill is the beautiful reservoir Lago della Trinità.

THE BELICE VALLEY

The Belice is one of Sicily's most important rivers; once known as the *Hypsas*, it is formed by the union of the Belice Destro (the ancient *Crimisus*) from the mountains of Piana degli Albanesi, and the Belice Sinistro, or River Frattina, from Rocca Busambra. The two rivers meet near Poggioreale, forming the boundary between the provinces of Trapani and Agrigento. The Belice Valley, east of Castelvetrano, together with the parallel Mazaro, Modione, and Carboj valleys, lie upon natural fault lines in the earth's crust, and earthquakes are therefore to be expected. That of 15th January 1968 was exceptionally destructive though. The inhabitants are still recovering from the impact. At least 370 people died and some 70,000 people were made homeless.

Gibellina

The town of Gibellina was the worst affected. It stood below a ridge of sulphur-bearing hills and was abandoned completely after its destruction. The new town of Gibellina, relocated some 20km to the west, occupies a position that becomes unpleasantly hot in summer. Several of Italy's most prominent artists and sculptors provided the new town with striking works of art, some of which are now already dilapidated. In 1994 the new church collapsed without warning. The new houses have no balconies and the streets few trees. At the entrance to Gibellina is the Porta (1980) designed by Pietro Consagra. Born in Mazara del Valla, Pietro Consagra (1920–2005), one of Italy's leading abstract sculptors, dedicated much of his activity to the town and the post-earthquake reconstruction. In the central Viale Segesta is the **Museo Civico di Arte Contemporanea** (*open 8–2 & 4–7; closed Sun and holidays*), which houses the models for the monuments of the new city, and paintings by Renato Guttuso, Fausto Pirandello, Mario Schifano.

The ruins of the old town, **Rovine di Gibellina**, were covered with white cement as a work of 'Land Art' by the Tuscan sculptor Alberto Burri. During the summer, open-air theatrical performances called *Orestiadi* are held here; for the first production, in 1983, the sculptor Arnaldo Pomodoro made items of scenery in wood and fibreglass, decorated with gold leaf. These have recently been restored and are displayed in a special museum called the **Museo delle Trame Mediterranee** (*open 9–1; www.fondazione.orestiadi.it*), in the old wheat farm known as Baglio Di Stefano, c. 2km from Gibellina. It houses a collection of local Elymian and Greek archaeological material, and there is also an ethnographical section, with costumes, jewellery from Maghreb, and more than one hundred 14th-century majolica dishes from Spain. The gallery displays works donated to Gibellina by contemporary Italian artists such as Scialoja, Consagra, Pomodoro and Schifano.

Santa Ninfa, Poggioreale and Partanna

Santa Ninfa was rebuilt where it stood even though the 1968 earthquake caused the collapse of a large majority of the housing stock. Near the town is a cave with splendid stalactites and 'cave pearls', and a necropolis of the Elymians, called **Grotta di Santa Ninfa**, protected as a nature reserve (*www.legambiente.sicilia.it*).

On the eastern border of the province is the old town of **Poggioreale** (also destroyed in the earthquake and later rebuilt), to the east of which excavations in 1970 revealed part of an ancient city and a necropolis (with 7th- and 6th-century BC tombs). **Salaparuta**, famous for its vineyards belonging to the Corvo family, was abandoned after the earthquake and a new town partially reconstructed.

Partanna is an agricultural centre which was also badly damaged. The Norman castle (rebuilt in the 17th century) survives; in its courtyard is a damaged coat of arms sculpted by Francesco Laurana who visited here in 1468. The Chiesa Madre has been partially reconstructed after being almost totally destroyed in the earthquake. It contains stuccoes by Vincenzo Messina, an organ by Paolo Amato, and a statue of the Madonna by the workshop of Francesco Laurana. Nearby are numerous rock-hewn tombs and caves which have revealed the presence of a group of Beaker People, c. 5,000 years ago.

Salemi

North of Castelvetrano is Salemi, probably the site of *Halicyae*, a town of the ancient Sicans or Elymians, and later an important Arab city. Even now the town's layout is clearly Islamic in character. When Philip of Spain signed the famous edict on 31st March 1492 banishing Muslims and Jews from Sicily, Salemi was one of the few places to offer them refuge. On 14th May, 1860, Salemi became capital of the new Italy under Garibaldi, for three days. The town was badly damaged in the 1968 earthquake when a third of the population (about 4,000 people) were housed in huts on the edge of the town. The Chiesa Madre and the Capuchin Monastery were destroyed.

The church of the Collegio (near the summit of the hill), with its twisted Baroque columns either side of the entrance, became the new Chiesa Madre. The steep and slippery Via Garibaldi leads up to the impressive golden 13th-century castle, with fine vaulted rooms and a characteristic round tower. The enormous Collegio dei Gesuiti in Via D'Aguirre was restored to house the **Museo Civico** (*open 9–1 & 3–7*). Divided into four sections, it contains paintings and sculptures attributed to Domenico and Antonello Gagini and Francesco Laurana, brought here after the earthquake of 1968 from the damaged churches; an archaeological section, with material excavated at Mokarta and Monte Polizzo; and a section on the Risorgimento and memorabilia of Garibaldi's time in Sicily in 1860. On the outskirts of the town is the early Christian basilica of San Miceli, with mosaic floors.

THE EGADI ISLANDS

The Egadi Islands, Favignana, Levanzo and Marettimo, lie 15km–30km off the west coast of Sicily. They are connected by boat and hydrofoil services from Trapani or Marsala. The inhabitants, famed as skilled fishermen, are now turning to tourism to earn a living. The varied birdlife includes migratory species in spring and autumn and the islands now form a marine nature reserve, the largest of its kind in Italy. The waters around the islands are popular with divers, and those between Favignana and Marsala are also of great interest to marine archaeologists because of the many sea battles fought here. Sometimes called the Aegadian Islands in English, these islands were the ancient *Aegades* or *Aegates*, off which Lutatius Catulus routed the fleet of Hanno in 241 BC, one of the most resounding Roman victories over Carthage. In the mid-16th century the islands were given to the Genoese Camillo Pallavicini, from whom they were purchased in 1874 by the Florio, a family from Calabria, who settled in Palermo (*see p. 71*) and became important entrepreneurs on the west coast of Sicily.

FAVIGNANA

The island

Favignana, 17km southwest of Trapani, is the largest island of the group and is mostly flat with a rather bare landscape, used mainly as pastureland. The best swimming is at the rocky bay of **Cala Rossa**, on the north coast; there are more crowded sandy beaches on the south coast between Grotta Pergiata and Punta Longa where there is a tiny port and fishing village. In the eastern part of the island are numerous disused tufa quarries (the white tufa found here provides excellent building stone). The small quarries are now mostly used as orchards, although one quarry still operates, supplying the local market. Near the cemetery, several wells with huge wooden water wheels of Arab origin survive, once used for irrigation. At **Punta Marsala** there is a view of Marsala and (on the left) the low, green island of Mozia. The prettiest part of the island is to the west beyond Monte Santa Caterina (where a Norman castle is now used by the armed forces).

The town

The little medieval town, where most of the inhabitants live, and where all the island's shops are situated, was refounded in 1637 by the Pallavicini family. **Palazzo Florio**, a large Art Nouveau palace near the port, was built in 1876 for Ignazio Florio by Giuseppe Damiani Almeyda. It is now used as a police headquarters. Nearby is a smaller 19th-century palace, now the town hall, with a statue of Ignazio Florio in front of it. The little church of Sant'Antonio da Padova is close by. **Via Vittorio Emanuele**, the main street, leads to Piazza Matrice where there is the main church with a green dome and the tourist office. Numerous shops sell smoked tuna fish and *bottarga* (dried tuna roe).

The town has a peaceful, rather run-down atmosphere, with a number of the cube-like houses half-restored, half-built, or for sale. The passenger boats and hydrofoils dock at the picturesque harbour, filled with fishing vessels. Here the **Stabilimento Florio** is an enormous old tuna-canning facility built in 1859 by Giulio Drago for the Pallavicini. The tuna fisheries here used to be among the most important in the Mediterranean. The bluefin tuna (*Thunnus thynnus*), renowned for its excellent quality, is still caught here, although the fishermen now have to look for sponsorship in order to keep the *tonnara* in activity; the commercial value of the catch is no longer economically viable because of the depleted stock. Before the cannery was built the fish were salted, hung up by the tail, then cut in pieces to be smoked, cooked or preserved in oil. Every piece of the fish was used: the skin was used as sandpaper; the tail and fins became brooms; some bones were used to make tools; and other parts either boiled to make glue or fishmeal. The industry thrived and in 1874 Drago ceded his contract to the Florio who ran this factory until 1937. By 1977 it had closed down owing to competition from tuna fishing (yellowfin) in the Atlantic. The fine buildings are now owned by the region of Sicily and are undergoing restoration to house a restaurant, theatre, auditorium, artisans' workshops, a marine research centre, and the Archaeological Museum. This last will display an intriguing collection of objects found on the sea bed. A few years ago some fishermen discovered the wreck of an Arab ship dated c. 1000, with its storage jars still intact. More recently, four young divers found shards of pottery among the seaweed not far offshore, and also an enormous octopus, guarding a pewter wine bottle (which they retrieved with some difficulty). Still sealed with the wine inside, it is believed to be the oldest bottle of wine in the world, dated to the 14th century, and can now be seen in the window at the Banca di Credito, 1 Piazza Castello (*open Mon–Fri 8.30–1.30*).

LEVANZO

Levanzo, 15km from Trapani, has no natural springs, and also virtually no cars. The ancient *Phorbantia* or Pliny's *Bucinna*, its austere, windbeaten landscape is set in a transparent, turquoise and cobalt blue sea. The island is particularly interesting for botanists: many of the plants are endemic. It is also famous for its caves, notably the **Grotta del Genovese**, which has the most interesting prehistoric wall art in Italy, discovered by chance in 1950. The cave paintings, comparable with those at Lascaux in France or Altamira in Spain, date from the Neolithic period; the primitive paint is made of animal fat, ochre and charcoal; fish and people are represented. The stunning incised drawings of bison and deer date from the Upper Palaeolithic period, when the island was still joined to Sicily. A footpath leads across the island from the port to the cave, which can also be reached by boat; enquire for directions at the port, or ask the custodian (at least the day before), signor Natale Castiglione, 11 Via Calvario (*T: 0923 924032*) who has the key and can arrange transport. The walk takes c. 2hrs. The cave is now locked since vandals damaged some of the graffiti.

A capsized Roman cargo-ship was recently located close to the island, with its cargo of *garum* amphorae still intact, and in 2004, submarine archaeologists discovered

Neolithic cave paintings in the Grotta del Genovese, Levanzo.

some wrecks of military vessels on the seabed, going back to 241 BC; several anchors, a bronze helmet, and an impressive bronze rostrum from a Roman ship have so far been brought to the surface.

GARUM

In Roman times, Levanzo was noted for the production of *garum*, a fish sauce much appreciated by connoisseurs. Garum was widely used in ancient times for preparing dishes of meat, fish, or vegetables, as well as in fruit recipes and drinks. The flavour of the sauce varied according to the type of fish used in its manufacture, and gourmets would distinguish between different provenances. There were famous garum factories in Sardinia, Tunisia, Morocco, Lebanon, Spain and Sicily. The garum produced on Levanzo was one of the most highly prized. To make the sauce, small fish, or the intestines of big fish, or both, were placed in terracotta pots or stone vats, together with salt, sea water, and aromatic herbs. After a week in the sun, the mixture was stirred and again left to ferment. After 20 more days, the garum, or *liquamen*, was strained off into amphorae. The solids, called *allec*, left in the vats, were not thrown away, but sold in the markets, where the poor were only too glad to eat them with bread.

LA MATTANZA

In the deep channel between Levanzo and Favignana the traditional method of tuna fishing known as *la mattanza* has been practiced in spring since prehistory. A series of net traps form a corridor leading to a square pen called the *camera della morte* (death chamber), which is activated under the instructions of the head fisherman, called the *rais*. The wind called the Favonio which brings the fish here for spawning, starts to blow at the end of May or in early June; choosing the right moment for fishing is all important. The females, already fertilized by the males, escape the trap because they swim deep down, about 20m below the surface, while the males are much closer to the surface. When there are around 100 fish in the pen the area is encircled by boats, with that belonging to the *rais* in the centre, and the nets are slowly hauled in, accompanied by the ancient haunting chants of the fishermen, called *cialome*: '*aja mola, aja mola, aja mola e iamuninni ... Gesù Cristu cu' li Santi ... nianzò ... nianzò ...*', to maintain the correct rhythm. It is very heavy work; one fish caught in 1974 weighed 600 kg. Tuna tend to dive when in danger so that during this operation they often collide with one another and hit their heads: by the time the net reaches the surface (the whole operation takes about an hour) many of them are wounded and stunned. They are then harpooned and pulled into the boats. The sea runs red with blood; it is a horrid but fascinating spectacle which has changed little since the Bronze Age. The catch has drastically declined in recent years, due in part to modern fishing techniques carried out by super-efficient Japanese and Korean boats, using huge nets (illegal for EU fishermen) and consequently quite indiscriminate in what they catch. The fish is frozen on board, taken to Malta and flown to the Far East. Sicily once had many tuna fisheries: they have nearly all closed now but there is strong local determination to save the Favignana tunnery (*info: T: 0923 873200 (Consorzio Pesca), www.favignanaweb.it/mattanza.asp*).

MARETTIMO

Marettimo, once known as *Hiera* or *Hieromesus* (the sacred), is the most isolated of the Egadi Islands, 38km from Trapani. Wild, beautiful and mountainous, it is rich in natural springs and grottoes, and is the best preserved of the three islands, mainly because it was once a notorious pirate stronghold, which discouraged settlers. There are many birds, especially during the migratory passage, and the nesting species include Bonelli's eagle, peregrine falcon, kestrel, lesser kestrel, buzzard, black wheatear as well as many interesting sea birds, including the storm petrel, gannet, and Cory's shearwater. In the interior of the island there are even boars and mouflons. The island is cared for by the Azienda Forestale, and there are well-signposted tracks to the various points of interest. With a charming little Moorish-looking village, there are no cars or hotels. Samuel Butler suggested that this was the island described as Ithaca in Homer's *Odyssey*, the islets of Le Formiche being the rocks hurled by Polyphemus at Ulysses. On the harbour there is a small Museo del Mare. A rewarding and spectacular hike leads to the ruins of the ancient castle at Punta Troia. Some Roman ruins and a small Palaeo-Christian church can also be found. Boat trips around the island and its sea caves can be arranged at the harbour. At the end of the 19th century many islanders from Marettimo found their way to Monterey in California, where they established a successful canned fish enterprise, immortalized by John Steinbeck in his *Cannery Row* (1945).

PANTELLERIA

Far away to the southwest, about 110km from the Sicilian mainland (and only 70km from Tunisia) lies Pantelleria (83 square kilometres, population 8,000), the largest of Sicily's offshore islands. The wild scenery of the island includes volcanic phenomena such as hot springs (the last eruption was in 1891). The central conical peak rises to a height of 836m. The sea bathing and scuba diving is exceptionally good here and the island is also a sanctuary for migratory birds. Capers, thought to be the finest in the world, figs, and sweet raisin grapes called *zibibbo* are cultivated here, despite the lack of spring water, and it is especially famous for its wines, *Moscato di Pantelleria* and *Moscato passito*. The cube-shaped white-washed cottages, called *dammusi*, with thick walls and domed roofs, are of Arab origin.

HISTORY OF PANTELLERIA

The island was the legendary home of Calypso, the nymph who was able to keep Ulysses from his travels for seven years. Archaeological evidence has proved the island was inhabited in the Neolithic era, when the obsidian on the southern shores would have been particularly useful, and later it was home to a Phoenician settlement called *Hiranin*, meaning 'place of the birds'. The Greeks called it *Cossyra*, meaning the small one, a name it maintained under the Romans, who took it in 217 BC. The Arabs gave it the name it still bears, *Bint errhia*, or 'daughter of the wind'. After conquest by Count Roger in 1123 it remained a Sicilian possession. During the Second World War it was used as a base for harrying Allied convoys. Reduced by heavy bombardment during May 1943, it was taken from the sea on 11th June with 11,000 prisoners, Allied casualties being reported as 'one soldier bitten by a mule'. The island was once used as a place of exile for political prisoners. It is now popular with the rich and famous: Gerard Depardieu, Sting and Giorgio Armani, among others, own properties on the island.

EXPLORING PANTELLERIA

Now protected as a nature reserve run by the Azienda Forestale, the island is particularly attractive to lovers of the sea. There are no beaches, but swimming from the rocks is very pleasant, because the water is clean and clear. Dolphins are common, and the rare nun seal is once again occasionally being spotted, after many years of absence from Italian waters. It is a good place for birdwatching too, especially during the migratory passage, when herons, cranes, flamingoes, geese and ducks can be seen. During the summer the hoopoe is resident, as is the cattle egret, the Tunisian chaffinch and the rock thrush. Among the mammals, the wildcat is still present.

The inhabitants of Pantelleria are farmers rather than fishermen, showing considerable patience and fortitude in caring for their plants in the difficult, windswept volcanic terrain, they produce superb wines, capers, olive oil and citrus.

The port of Pantelleria was completely rebuilt after the Second World War; the little houses around the harbour are relatively new. The oldest building is the forbidding Spanish **Castello Barbacane** (*open daily 6–8, and for exhibitions*).

In località **Mursia** 58 prehistoric tombs known as *sesi*, were discovered by Paolo Orsi in the 19th century. These large domed tumuli were built in blocks of lava. Only 27 have survived, notably the **Sese Grande**, the others having either fallen into ruin or been engulfed by new buildings. Several of them still contained human remains, buried in the foetal position, with their personal possessions close by. More recent excavations at *Cossyra* have brought to light an exceptional series of finely-carved Roman heads. Two of them, a portrait of Julius Caesar and another of Antonia the Younger, daughter of Mark Anthony, sister-in-law to Tiberius and mother of Claudius, are of Paros marble, and were found in a cistern, where apparently they had been placed with care; the third (also found in a cistern) is a stunningly realistic portrait of Titus, son of Vespasian. The finds are evidence of the vitality of Cossyra in the 1st–2nd centuries AD.

Among the villages of the island, **Scauri** is high on the edge of a cliff, with a spectacular view down to its little fishing harbour. **Nicà** is a fishing village, on a narrow inlet, while the inland village of **Rekhale**, close by, is still intact, with the typical stone cottages and tiny, luxuriant gardens. Spectacular views can be had at Saltalavecchia and the ancient landing-place of Balata dei Turchi, both on the south coast. The most famous view is at Punta dell'Arco, where there is good swimming and the rock formations look like the head and the trunk of an elephant extending into the sea. **Gadir** is another fishing village, where the sea is easily accessible even for inexperienced swimmers. The extinct volcanoes in the middle of the island, Montagna Grande (836m) and Monte Gibele (700m) offer rewarding treks through vineyards and pinewoods; the wobbly song-flight of the fan-tailed warbler can be observed, even in the middle of the day, and the Algerian form of the blue tit can also be spotted. The old volcanic cones are called *cuddie*. The beautiful inland crater lake of Bagno dell'Acqua (or the Lago di Venere) is about 6km from the port. It is fed by a hot water spring and is 500m in diameter and 2m above sea-level.

PRACTICAL INFORMATION

GETTING AROUND

• **By train:** The central railway station in Trapani is in Piazza Umberto, with services to Palermo, Marsala (c. 40 mins), Mazara del Vallo (c. 1 hr) and Castelvetrano (c. 2–3hrs). Trains stop at Ragattisi, the nearest station for the boat to Mozia; about a 1km walk from the station. Segesta is on the Palermo–Trapani line (infrequent services) but it is a 20-min walk from the site;
• **By bus:** AST buses from Trapani (T: 0923 23222, www.aziendasiciliana-trasporti.it) run to Trapani airport, also Erice, Castellammare, San Vito Lo Capo, Selinunte, Marsala, Mazara del Vallo, Nubia Salt Museum, Alcamo and Segesta. SAU (T: 0923 550011) also has services to Erice in c. 40mins.
Lumia (T: 0922 20414) connects Marsala to Mazara del Vallo and Agrigento.
Salemi (T: 0923 981120, www.autoservizisalemi.it) runs buses to/from Trapani, Mazara del Vallo and Palermo, and connects Castelvetrano with Palermo Airport and Campobello di Mazara..
There are buses from Castelvetrano to Selinunte (the stop is a 5-min walk from the entrance).
Inter-city services from Piazza Malta in Trapani are run by Segesta (T: 0923 21754, www.segesta.it) to/from Palermo and Palermo Airport; Bari; Taranto; Lecce and Rome.
• **By air:** Daily flights to Pantelleria are run by Easy Islands, T: 091 6622224, www.easy-islands.it, from Palermo.
• **By sea:** For up-to-date information on ferries and hydrofoils, times, tariffs and bus connections, consult www.bookingitalia.it. Ferries from Trapani to Pantelleria (4–5 hrs) and to the Egadi Islands (Favignana and Levanzo 4 daily, c. 50 mins; Marettimo twice weekly, 3 hrs) from Molo della Sanità by Siremar (T: 0923 540515). The fast ship *Guizzo* run by Siremar (T: 0923 545411) goes from Mazara del Vallo daily, except Wed, mid June–mid Sept, in 2hrs to Pantelleria.
Hydrofoils (more expensive) for the Egadi Islands, run by Siremar (T: 0923 27780), leave from Molo Dogana, those run by Ustica Lines (T: 0923 22200, www.usticalines.it) leave from Via Ammiraglio Staiti several times a day in summer: services also for Pantelleria, Naples, Ustica and San Vito Lo Capo, leave from Via Ammiraglio Staiti.

INFORMATION OFFICES

Trapani APT Trapani, 27 Via San Francesco d'Assisi, T: 0923 545511, www.apt.trapani.it; for information on the whole province.
Tourist Information Bureau: Piazza Scarlatti, T: 0923 29000.
Alcamo Aliante Piazza della Repubblica, 5, T: 0924 23898 www.alcamo.it, www.comune.alcamo.tp.it
Calatafimi Pro Loco Calatafimi Segesta: 16 Via Vittorio Emanuele, T: 0924 954680, www.calatafimisegesta.com
Castellammare del Golfo 6 Via de Gasperi, T: 0924 592303/304, www.castellammaredelgolfo.com, www.castellammareonline.it;

Information Point: 1 Viale Umberto, Castellammare del Golfo, T: 0924 31320.

Erice 1 Via Guarrasi, T: 0923 869388, www.erice.net

Favignana Consorzio Turistico Egadi: c/o Residence Tempo di Mare, Via Giuseppe Garibaldi, Favignana, T: 0923 922121, www.egadi.com
Riserva Marina Egadi (marine nature reserve): Palazzo Florio, 1 Via Florio, Favignana, T: 0923 921086.

Gibellina Piazza XV Gennaio 1968, T: 0924 67877, www.comune.gibellina.tp.it; Pro Loco: 53 Viale Indipendenza Siciliana, T: 0924 69949.

Marsala Palazzo VII Aprile, Piazza Repubblica, T: 0923 714097, www.comune.marsala.tp.it; Pro Loco: 100 Via XI Maggio, T: 0923 714097.

Mazara del Vallo Azienda Turismo: 2 Piazza Santa Veneranda, T: 0923 941727, www.comune.mazara-delvallo.tp.it, www.mazaradelpesce.it; Pro Loco: 14 Piazza Mokarta, T: 0923 944610.

Pantelleria Associazione Turistica Pantelleria: T: 0923 912948, www.isoladipantelleria.com; Pro Loco: Via San Nicola, T: 0923 911838, www.pantelleria.com, www.infopantelleria.org; Promozione Turistica di Pantelleria: T: 0923 912257, www.viverepantelleria.it

Salemi Pro Loco: 8 Piazza Libertà, T: 0924 981426, www.comune.salemi.tp.it

San Vito Lo Capo Azienda Autonoma: Via Savoia, T: 0923 972464, closed winter. www.comune.sanvitolocapo.tp.it, www.sanvitolocapo.org, www.sanvitoweb.com

Santa Ninfa c/o Municipio, Piazza Libertà, T: 0924 992111.

Selinunte by the entrance to the archaeological park and car park, T: 0924 46251; Pro Loco: c/o Hotel Alceste, 21 Via Alceste, T: 0924 46184.

HOTELS

Trapani
€€ **Relais Antiche Saline**. Beautifully restored *baglio* in the salt marshes, lovely rooms, good restaurant. Via delle Saline, Nubia, T: 0923 868029, www.antichesaline.it
€€ **Nuovo Albergo Russo**. Bright and comfortable, in the old town in front of the cathedral, car park. 4 Via Tintori, T: 0923 22166.
€ **Moderno**. Good position in the old city. 20 Via Tenente Genovese, T: 0923 21247, hotelmodernotrapani@virgilio.it
€ **Maccotta**. In the old city, small guesthouse with comfortable rooms and friendly management.4 Via degli Argentieri, T: 0923 28418, www.albergomaccotta.it

Alcamo
€€ **Centrale**. Restored palazzo with car park, internet, restaurant serving vegetarian meals on request, centrally situated. 24 Via Amendola, T: 0924 507845, www.hotelcentrale.sicilia.it
€€ **La Battigia**. On the beach, with 26 rooms, many with sea views, perfectly comfortable, at the pleasant resort close to town. SS 187 km 46.850, Alcamo Marina, T: 0924 597259, www.labattigia.it
€ **La Principessa**. Clean, comfortable, recently refurbished and central. 5–9 Via Canapè, T: 0924 507789, www.albergolaprincipessa.it
€ **Terme Gorga**. Simple little hotel at the spa down by the railway station.

Open all year, it has a good restaurant. Contrada Gorga, T: 0924 23842, www.termegorga.com

Bonagia

€€ **La Tonnara di Bonagia**. Beautifully restored tuna fishery on a tiny harbour. Lovely rooms, some with private garden, and apartments. Good restaurant, tennis, children's play area and scuba-diving centre. Piazza Tonnara, T: 0923 431111, www.framonhotels.com

€€ **Saverino**. Family-run hotel, with an excellent restaurant. 3 Via Lungomare, T: 0923 592727, www.saverino.it

Calatafimi

€ **Mille Pini**. Well-organized small hotel, with good restaurant. 4 Piazza Francesco Vivana, T: 0924 951260, www.hotelmillepini.com

Castellammare del Golfo

€€€ **Cetarium**. On the harbour, a beautifully restored tuna fishery; restaurant serves vegetarian food on request. Car parking. 45 Via Zangara, T: 0924 533401, www.hotelcetarium.it

€€ **Al Madarig**. Close to the castle and the old city, with a restaurant and car park. 7 Piazza Petrolo, T: 0924 33533, www.almadarig.com

€€ **Cala Marina**. Attractive little hotel, on the harbour, in a converted warehouse. Internet point, no restaurant, car park. 1 Via Zangara, T: 0924 531841, www.hotelcalamarina.it

€€ **Belvedere**. Spectacular position on the mountain overlooking the bay, on the road to Scopello. Restaurant and car park. SS187 km 37.350, T: 0924 33330, www.hotelbelvedere.net

Custonaci

€ **Cala Buguto**. Tiny hotel in an old house not far from the cave which encloses the hamlet of Scurati. Delicious meals on request. 1 Via D, Contrada Scurati, T: 0923 973953, www.calabuguto.com

€ **Il Cortile**. Delightful little hotel in a *baglio* close to the Sanctuary, with restaurant serving excellent simple local dishes (also vegetarian on request) and good local wine. The owner, signor Andrea Oddo, is founder-member of the Living Crib Association. 67 Via Scurati, T: 0923 971750.

Erice

€€ **Elimo**. Small and comfortable, on the main street, with a rooftop terrace, and lovely little courtyard garden; nice restaurant. 23 Via Vittorio Emanuele, T: 0923 869377, www.elimohotel.com

€€ **Moderno**. Fascinating old hotel with exceptionally good restaurant. 63 Via Vittorio Emanuele, T: 0923 869300, www.hotelmodernoerice.it

€ **Edelweiss**. Very small, early booking is essential; breakfast on the terrace is a delightful experience. 5 Cortile P. Vincenzo, T: 0923 869420, a.edelweiss@libero.it

Erice Mare (Pizzolungo)

€€ **L'Approdo** Small hotel right on the coast in a peaceful spot where Aeneas supposedly disembarked. Restaurant and garden. 3 Via Enea, T: 0923 57155, www.hotelapprodotrapani.it

€€ **Tirreno**. Plain but comfortable hotel with its own little harbour. Organizes sailing and excursions. 37 Via Enea, T: 0923 571078, www.tirrenohotel.com

Erice Mare (San Cusumano)

€€ **Baia dei Mulini**. One of the oldest salt-extraction plants in Italy has been restored and transformed into a lovely peaceful hotel. Good restaurant, private sandy beach, pool, tennis, pétanque, minigolf, children especially welcome.

Car parking. Lungomare Dante Alighieri, T: 0923 562400 www.baiadeimulini.it

Favignana

€€ **Aegusa**. Delightful little hotel, very welcoming. 11 Via Garibaldi (at the port), T: 0923 922430, www.aegusahotel.it

€€ **Egadi**. Very small, usually fully booked because of the renowned restaurant, which is probably one of the most famous in Sicily. Closed in winter. 17 Via Colombo (at the port), T: 0923 921232, www.albergoegadi.it

€ **Bouganville**. Small but comfortable, family run, convenient situation in the town centre. 10 Via Cimabue, T: 0923 922033, www.albergobouganville.it

€ **Hotel delle Cave**. A quiet little place with a delightful little hidden garden in the quarry. Contrada Torretta, T: 0923 925423.

Levanzo

€ **Pensione dei Fenici**. A well-run little hotel with a good restaurant. 18 Via Calvario, T: 0923 924083.

€ **Paradiso**. Simple hotel with good restaurant, on the terrace in summer. Via Lungomare, T: 0923 924080, www.isoladilevanzo.it

Marettimo

There are no hotels on Marettimo, but rooms can be rented in private houses, the fishermen will meet you on the quay to propose this kind of accommodation. Islanders offering rooms or apartments and other services, such as boat excursions and fishing trips: **Rosa dei Venti**, 4 Via Punta San Simone, Contrada Crocilla, T: 0923 923249, www.isoladimarettimo.it and **Simmar**. 1 Piazza Scalo Nuovo, T: 0923 923392, www.vacanze-marettimo.it

€€ **Marettimo Residence**. Offers comfortable little apartments in cottages for stays of one week or more. Via Telegrafo, Località Spatarello, T: 0923 923202 , www.marettimoresidence.it, www.marettimoresidence.com

Marsala

€€ **New Hotel Palace**. Delightful 19th-century building, recently restored, lovely hall. Garden, good restaurant, excellent wine list. 57 Lungomare Mediterraneo, T: 0923 719492, www.newhotelpalace.com

€€ **Ecoresort Sole Mare Vento**. Closed Nov-Feb. Restored salt mill for nature-lovers who like their creature comforts. In summer the coast is covered with sweetly-scented sea lilies, and there are breathtaking views. Restaurant has a marvellous chef—the legendary Zeffirino of Genoa—who owns restaurants in Portofino, Las Vegas, Hong Kong and on board the *Costa Victoria*. Isola Longa, T: 0923 733072.

€€ **Resort Baglio Oneto**. Former castle in a splendid panoramic position, surrounded by olive groves and vineyards, not far from Marsala. Good restaurant. Pool, private beach; scuba diving, water-skiing and fishing trips are organized. 55 Contrada Baronazzo Amafi, T: 0923 746222, www.framonhotels.com

€€ **Delfino Beach**. 2km south of town, recently renovated, elegant hotel with renowned restaurant, nice beach. 672 Lungomare Mediterraneo, Contrada Berbaro, T: 0923 751076 www.delfinobeach.com

€€ **Villa Favorita**. Beautiful old winery, excellent restaurant and wine list, comfortable accommodation; garage, gardens, tennis, bowls and pool. 27 Via Favorita, T: 0923 989100, www.villafavorita.com

€ **La Finestra sul Sale**. Comfortable

accommodation in an old salt mill, right in front of the island of Mozia. Saline Ettore e Infersa, 55 Contrada Ettore Infersa, T: 0923 733142, www.salineettoreinfersa.com

Mazara del Vallo

€€€ **Giardino di Costanza**. Situated among palms, olive groves and orchards, this is the only Kempinski hotel in Italy, and is also part of the 'hotels of silence' chain. Spa centre offers beauty treatments using the local salt, milk and honey. 7km on Via Salemi, T: 0923 675000, www.kempinski-sicily.com

€€ **Hopps**. The old *baglio* of the Hopps family is a reliable hotel, recently restructured. Garage, pool, disco, garden, good restaurant, private beach. 29 Via Hopps, T: 0923 946133, www.hoppshotel.it

Pantelleria

€€ **Cossyra**. Close to a prehistoric settlement called Sesi. Comfortable hotel with pool, diving centre, and a very good restaurant. Località Cuddie Rosse, Mursia, T: 0923 911217, www.cossyrahotel.it

€€ **Khamma**. Overlooking the harbour, with a pleasant open-air bar. 24 Lungomare Borgo Italia, T: 0923 912680, hotelkhamma@supereva.it

€€ **Mursia**. Very comfortable; under the same management as Cossyra. Famous restaurant. Pool and diving centre. Località Mursia, T: 0923 911217, www.mursiahotel.it.

€€ **Papuscia**. 180m above sea level, a family-run hotel in a 200-year-old *dammuso*, with good restaurant serving simple meals. Località Tracino, 28 Contrada Sopra Portella, T: 0923 915463, www.papuscia.com www.papuscia.it

€€ **Club Cala Levante**. Exclusive

accommodation in comfortable *dammusi*, panoramic position. Closed Nov–Mar. 11 Cala Levante, T: 0923 915582.

€€€ **Monastero**. Five ancient *dammusi* (stone cottages) have been restored to create this unusual and exclusive hotel. For peace and tranquillity in a precious setting with a pool modelled on the Lago di Venere. Excellent meals. Contrada Kassà, Scauri Alta, T: 0923 916304, www.monasteropantelleria.com

San Vito lo Capo

€€ **Capo San Vito**. Right on the beach. Garden, candlelight dinners on the terrace, well-furnished rooms, car park. 29 via Principe Tommaso, T: 0923 972122, www.caposanvito.it

€€ **Egitarso**. Pleasant location close to the beach, with restaurant. 54 Via Lungomare, T: 0923 972111, www.hotelegitarso.it

€€ **Mediterraneo**. Small, elegant and comfortable, with a restaurant. 61 Via Generale Arimondi, T: 0923 621062, www.hotelmediterraneonline.com

€€ **Miraspiaggia**. Family hotel close to private beach, with good restaurant. 6 Via lungomare, T: 0923 972355, www.miraspiaggia.it

€€ **Pocho**. Tiny hotel out of town, in a spectacular position. Pool and good restaurant; car park. Contrada Makari, T: 0923 972525, www.sicilian.net/pocho

€ **Halimeda**. Very small, comfortable hotel. No restaurant. 100 Via Generale Arimondi, T: 0923 972399, www.hotelhalimeda.com

€ **Riva del Sole**. Dependable little hotel, close to private beach, with restaurant. 11 Via Generale Arimondi, T: 0923 972629.

€ **Vecchio Mulino**. Small hotel 300m from the beach; central. Via Vecchio

Mulino, T: 0923 972518, www.hotelvecchio-mulino.com

€€ **Vento del Sud**. Beautiful small hotel but no restaurant. 157 Via Duca degli Abruzzi, T: 0924 621450, www.hotelventodelsud.it

Selinunte (Marinella)

€€ **Admeto**. In a lovely position overlooking the fishing harbour, modern hotel with comfortable rooms, good restaurant. Via Alceste, T: 0924 46184, www.hoteladmeto.it

€€ **Alceste**. Small, modern, family-run hotel with one of the best restaurants in Sicily; walking distance from the archaeological park. 21 Via Alceste, T: 0924 46184, www.hotelalceste.it

€ **Lido Azzurro**. Central position, good restaurant, pizza in the evenings. 98 Via Marco Polo, T: 0924 46256, email: lazzurro@freemail.it

BED & BREAKFAST

Trapani

€ **Ai Lumi**. Five minutes from station, in the old quarter, lovely 18th-century palazzo with courtyard, air conditioning, also restaurant and self-catering apartments, English, French and German spoken. 71 Corso Vittorio Emanuele, T: 0923 872418, www.ailumi.it

€ **All'Angolo Fiorito**. In a quiet area of town, airport transfer on request, with a little garden. 29 Via Pietro Mascagni, T: 0923 538633, www.allangolofiorito.it

€ **Il Cortiletto**. Comfortable self-catering apartments in pedestrian area of town. Patio, air conditioning. 2 Vicolo dei Compagni, T: 0923 872625, www.ilcortilettotrapani.it

€ **Baglio Case Colomba**. Open Apr–Oct. Delightful old house with kind owners: English, French and Spanish spoken and an EU certificate for eco-friendliness. 185 Via Maggiore Toselli, T: 0923 852729 www.casecolomba.com

Castellammare del Golfo

€ **Rais**. Friendly family. 2 Via Tobruk, T: 0924 30685, www.bedrais.it

Castelvetrano

€€ **Torre Pignatelli**. Stylish accommodation in Castelvetrano's most aristocratic palace, very central. Palazzo Pignatelli, Piazza Garibaldi, T: 348 8029359 (Gabriella Becchina), info@becchina.com

€€ **Villa Mimosa**. About half-way between Castelvetrano and Selinunte, in the countryside. Very attractive self-catering rooms, garden full of dogs and cats, pergola and veranda. The home of Jacky Sirimanne, a sommelier who knows all about wine and olive oil. Contrada La Rocchetta, Castelvetrano, T: 0924 44583. sirimanne@libero.it

Marsala

€€ **Andrea's**. On the lagoon, very welcoming. 216 Contrada Spagnola, T: 328 4849399.

Salemi

€ **Conte Umberto**. Self-catering, but Signora Armata prepares breakfast and there is a restaurant close by. The house is in the heart of the old city. 172a Via Giovanni Amendola, T: 0924 982062, conte.umberto@virgilio.it

San Vito Lo Capo

€ **Ai Dammusi**. Comfortable accommodation. 83 Via Savoia, T: 0923 621494, www.aidammusisanvito.it

€ **Chiedi la Luna**. Very central. 37/b Via del Santuario, T: 0923 621401, www.chiedi-la-luna.it

Selinunte (Marinella)

€ **Il Pescatore**. Self-catering rooms but there is an excellent breakfast. 31 Via

Castore e Polluce, T: 0924 46303.
€ Selinon di Selinunte. Comfortable old farmhouse, all rooms with private bath; air conditioning; baby sitter available; credit cards accepted. Nice breakfasts, bicycles for hire, English, French & Spanish spoken. 8 Via della Cittadella, T: 0924 903744.
€ Sicilia Cuore Mio. Open year round, comfortable rooms. 44 Via della Cittadella, T: 0924 46077, www.siciliacuoremio.it
€ The Holiday House. In the modern part of town and convenient for the archaeological site. 23 Via Apollonio Rodio, T: 0924 46035, guispar@libero.it

ROOMS & APARTMENTS TO RENT

Trapani
€ Alle Due Badie. Beautiful apartments of various sizes in a restored building in old city, for short-term rental; internet, satellite TV and car park. 33 Via Badia Nuova (corner Via Arti), T: 0923 24054, www.duebadie.it
Erice
€ Agorà. Lovely medieval house within the ancient walls. Air conditioning. 11 Via Vittorio Emanuele. T: 0923 860133, www.agoraerice.com;
Favignana
€€ Residence Punta Longa. On the south coast, apartments of various sizes, lots of amenities (tennis, snorkelling, water-skiing), run by Italy's prestigious Touring Club. 1 Via Costiera di Mezzogiorno, Contrada Punta Longa, T: 0923 925417, www.touringclub.it
€ Villa Antonella. Nice rooms, garden. SP Punta Marsala, T: 0923 921073, www.egadi.com/villantonella
Marsala

€ Il Molo, 55 via Molo Caito, T: 0923 941116, www.formusa.it, self-catering apartments on the canal-port.
Mazara del Vallo
€ Residence Mediterraneo. Air-conditioned rooms and apartments; car park, garden, self-catering or restaurant nearby. 31 Via Hopps, T: 0923 932688, www.residencemed.it
Pantelleria
€€ Dammusi Sciuvechi. Self-catering in comfortable, typical *dammusi* (little stone cottages). Località Sciuvechi, T: 0923 916174, www.dammusisciuvechi.it
Scopello
€€€ La Tonnara di Scopello. Rooms or apartments in the beautiful old 13th-century tuna fishery, close to the Zingaro wildlife reserve, regularly used as a film location. Call Signora Foderà, T: 347/3243789 (English spoken).

FARMHOUSE ACCOMMODATION

Trapani
€€ Duca di Castelmonte. A comfortable old olive farm, close to Trapani, with a good restaurant. 3 Via Salvatore Motisi, Contrada Xitta, T: 0923/526139, www.ducadicastelmonte.it
€€ Vultaggio Misiliscemi. Hilltop farm between Erice and Marsala, producing wine, olives, cereals and fruit. Medieval castle nearby. Bowls and clay pigeon shooting. 4 Contrada Misiliscemi, Guarrato, T: 0923 864261, www.misiliscemi.it
Alcamo
€€ Tarantola. Wine farm belonging to the Conte Testa family, famous for their Gorgo del Drago wines; very nice food. Contrada Tarantola, T: 329 2713073, www.gorgodeldrago.it

Calatafimi

€ **Villa del Bosco**. Small farm producing olive oil, wine and honey, close to an ancient oak wood. Hilltop position, view of Segesta. Vegetarian food on request. Archery and excursions on foot or by 4WD vehicle. English and French spoken. Contrada Marzuco, T: 330 849216, www.neomedia.it/personal/degaeta

Castellammare del Golfo

€ **Camillo Finazzo**. Small farm, well-placed for exploring the surrounding area. Self-catering or restaurant. 1 Contrada Badia Molinazzo, T: 0924 38051, www.camillofinazzo.com

Castelvetrano

€€€ **Antica Tenuta dei Principi Pignatelli**. Suitably regal accommodation on this vast estate, olive trees as far as the eye can see, producing the world-famous Olio Verde. Via Santissima Trinità, T: 348 8029359, olioverde@centrocomp.it

€€ **Baglio Vecchio**. Lovely old building surrounded by olive groves, overlooking the river. Contrada Zangara, SP 13, T: 0923 28890; www.tenutazangara.it

Erice

€€ **Belvedere San Nicola**. Converted farmhouse, beautiful views, under the same management as Hotel Moderno. Good restaurant and wine cellar. Horse-riding, pool and bowls. Children welcome. Contrada San Nicola, T: 0923 860124, www.pippocatalano.it

Marsala

€€ **Tenuta Volpara**. Beautifully-restored and furnished farmhouse; very good restaurant and pizzeria. Contrada Volpara Bartolotta, T: 0923 984588, www.delfinobeach.com

€€ **Baglio Vajarassa**. Beautiful old winery, lots of atmosphere, near the lagoon;

relaxing holiday. 176 Contrada Spagnola, T: 0923 968628, www.bagliovajarassa.com

€ **Samperi**. Farm south of Marsala producing wine, olive oil, citrus and cereals. Guests are welcome to take part in the harvesting or other day-to-day activities. Good restaurant, vegetarian dishes on request. Horse-riding, minigolf and tennis. Località Strasatti, 308 Contrada Samperi-Fornara, T: 0923 741733, www.agriturismosamperi.it

Mazara del Vallo

€€ **Poggio Gilletto**. Peaceful farm producing wine and carobs, bordering on two WWF nature reserves, Gorghi Tondi and Preola. The beach can be reached by bicycle. Cookery, painting and pottery courses. SP 86, Gorghi Tondi, Contrada San Nicola Sottano, T: 0923 711551, www.poggiogiletto.com

Pantelleria

€€ **Santa Teresa**. The lovely old *dammusi* of this farm are surrounded by cultivations of capers, lentils, vineyards and fruit trees. Three pools, golf practicing course, horse-riding. Località Monastero Alto, T: 0923 916389, www.santateresa.it

Petrosino

€€ **Baglio Spanò**. Delightful old winery with garden; excellent restaurant reserved for guests, with good house wine. Contrada Triglia-Scaletta, T: 348 8822095, www.bagliospano.com

Pizzolungo

€€ **Adragna Pizzolungo**. In a stunning position between Mt San Giuliano and the sea. The farm produces wine, olives, vegetables and cereals; delightful rooms, good food and wine, or self-catering.Contrada San Cusumano, T: 0923 563710 www.pizzolungo.it

Salemi
€€ **Settesoldi**. Friendly farm within walking distance from Salemi, good restaurant. Vineyard and olive grove. 111 Contrada Settesoldi, T: 0924 982011, www.agrisettesoldi.it

RESTAURANTS

Trapani
€€€ **Da Peppe**. The home-made pasta is delicious. Closed Mon. 50 Via Spalti, T: 0923 28246.

€€ **Cantina Siciliana**. Excellent trattoria. Try chef Pino's *bruschette con uova di tonno* (croutons with tuna roe) as a starter, perhaps followed by fish cous cous, then *cassatelle di ricotta*, an irresistible dessert. Next door there is a well-stocked wine shop run by the same management. 36 Via Giudecca, T: 0923 28673.

€€ **La Bettolaccia**. One of the best seafood restaurants in Trapani; excellent cous cous. Choose orange sorbet for dessert. Closed Sun. 23 Via Fardella, T: 0923 21695.

€€ **La Perla**. Outside the city to the south, by the salt pans where the flamingoes go in winter, is this simple restaurant indicated by the local people as being the very best place for seafood. Closed Mon. Viale Motya, Contrada Marausa, T: 0923 841577.

€€ **Taverna Paradiso**. Elegant restaurant on the sea front, offering absolutely delicious traditional fish dishes. Typical Sicilian desserts. 32 Lungomare Dante Alighieri, T: 0923 22303.

€€ **Trattoria del Porto**. Close to the dockside, a family-run restaurant preparing good simple food. Closed Mon. 45 Via Ammiraglio Staiti, T: 0923 547822.

€ **Trattoria del Sale**. Open for lunch only, very tasty dishes prepared using 'on the spot' ingredients: fish from the salt pans, Nubia garlic, intensely flavoured tomatoes from the dunes. 44 Via Garibaldi, Nubia, T: 338 3915967.

€ **Trattoria Miramare**. In front of the ferry terminal, a down-to-earth, family-run trattoria where tourists never come; excellent fish cous cous and grilled squid; one of the best restaurants in town. 30 Viale Regina Elena, T: 0923 20011.

Alcamo
€€ **Salsapariglia**. Good pasta dishes and grilled fish. Closed Mon. 1 Via Libertà, T: 0924 508302.

€ **Trattoria dei Mille**. Inexpensive robust meals. Closed Tues. 10 Via delle Rose, T: 0924 26232.

Castellammare del Golfo
€€ **La Cambusa**. Excellent grilled fish. Closed Thur in winter. 67 Via Zangara (Cala Marina), T: 0924 30155.

€ **Kalos**. Excellent pizzeria near the castle. Closed Tues. 4 Piazza Petrolo, T: 0924 35210.

€ **Sandwicheria**. Tasty Palermo-style snacks, sandwiches, pasta. Piazza Petrolo, T: 0924 30889.

Custonaci
€€€ **Stele d'Anchise**. This little village is 20km from Trapani but it is well worth the journey. The shellfish are exceptionally good: oysters, clams, mussels, razor-shells, shrimps and prawns, also lobster and sometimes crab. Closed Mon. Piazza Riviera, Contrada Cornino, T: 0923 971053.

Erice
€€€ **La Pentolaccia**. The best cous cous in Erice. 17 Via Guarnotti, T: 0923 869362. Closed Tues.

€€€ **Moderno**. The restaurant of the hotel is exceptionally good, and is part of the Buon Ricordo chain. 63 Via Vittorio Emanuele, T: 0923 869300.

€€ **Caffè San Rocco**. Welcoming bar and restaurant, crowded with scientists from the nearby Majorana centre. Closed Wed. Tasty pasta.23 Via Guarnotti, T: 0923 869337.

€€€ **Egadi**. Thought to be one of Sicily's finest restaurants; the fish is excellent and so fresh it can also be eaten raw as carpaccio; also spaghetti with lobster. Closed in winter. 17 Via Colombo, T: 0923 921232.

€€€ **El Pescador**. This tiny restaurant (booking essential) is popular with the locals, and also Giorgio Armani, a regular client. Donna Rosa is a fantastic cook; try her spaghetti with ricci (sea urchins), or the excellent cous cous. Closed Feb and Wed in winter. 38 Piazza Europa, T: 0923 921035.

€€ **La Bettola**. Quite elegant. There is a nice courtyard for eating al fresco; excellent octopus salad. Closed Nov. 47 Via Nicotera, T: 0923 921988.

€€ **La Tavernetta**. Good meals with a pleasant area outside for al fresco dining. 54 Piazza Matrice, T: 0923 921639.

Levanzo

€€ **Paradiso**. Simple little restaurant, marvellous food, prepared with the freshest fish. Closed winter. 8 Via Lungomare, T: 0923 924080.

Marettimo

€€ **Il Pirata**. Serves appetizing seafood risotto, lobster soup, and grilled fish. Also rooms to rent. By the harbour, T: 0923 923027. Closed Jan.

€€ **Il Timone**. Signora Maria prepares home-made pasta and wonderful tuna dishes. Via Garibaldi, T: 0923 923142.

€€ **Il Veliero**. Meals served on the terrace; try Peppe's legendary lobster soup in which he cooks spaghetti; the pasta dressing, *pesto di Trapani*, made with raw tomato is also memorable. 22 Via Umberto (by the harbour), T: 0923 923274.

€ **Al Carrubo**. Good pizzeria and trattoria, with a panoramic terrace. Above the town in Contrada Pelosa, T: 0923 923132.

Marinella di Selinunte

€€ **Hotel Alceste**. This restaurant is the ideal place for grilled fish, local sourdough bread, perfect seafood risotto, spaghetti with clams or shrimps, *pasta cu' le sarde* (macaroni with fennel and sardines), all served with excellent local wines.

€ **Lido Zabbara da Jojò**. Lunch here is a delightful experience; summer only, swimming facilities. On the beach under the Acropolis, T: 0924 46194.

Marsala

€€€ **Villa Favorita**. This is the place for lunching or dining in style; the cous cous is exceptional. Good wine list, lovely surroundings. 27 Via Favorita (on the southern outskirts), T: 0923/989100.

€€€ **'A Ciaramira**. 8km out of town on the road to Salemi (SS 188) is this extraordinary restaurant, where a fixed-price menu covers everything. The menu varies daily. Cous cous with snails, home-made macaroni, excellent local wines. 182 Contrada Misilla, T: 0923 967767. Closed Mon.

€€ **Trattoria Garibaldi**. Popular with the locals. Excellent fish, good local wines. Closed Sat midday, Sun evening. 35 Via Rubino, Piazza Addolorata, T: 0923 953006.

€€ **Capo Lilybeo**. Close to the archaeological museum. Excellent pasta dishes, pizza is served in the evenings. Closed Mon. 40 Lungomare Boeo, T: 0923 712881.

€ **Bizzy**. Appetizing, inexpensive and fast. 143 Corso Gramsci, T: 0923 711168.

Mazara del Vallo

€€€ **Il Casale**. Very elegant restaurant, specializing in fish dishes, also pizza in the evening. Closed Mon. 31 Viale Africa, T: 0923 942535.

€€€ **Il Pescatore**. On the outskirts of Mazara, an elegant restaurant which attracts gourmets coming from all over Italy, especially for the fish. Very good pasta dishes and cous cous, delicious desserts, good wine cellar, impeccable service. Closed Mon in winter. 191 Via Castelvetrano, T: 0923 947580.

€€ **Alla Kasbah**. In the heart of the old city, intriguing little restaurant offering Tunisian and Sicilian cuisine, cous cous prepared with fish, vegetables or meat. Closed Mon in winter. 10 Via Itria, T: 0923 906126.

€€ **La Bettola**. Very good local fare and wines. Closed Wed. 32 Via Francesco Maccagnone, T: 0923 946422.

€€ **Al Pesciolino d'Oro**. A favourite with the locals; the grilled and fried fish are superlative, so is the *zuppa di pesce* (fish soup). Delicious meat and local sausages also available. Closed Thur. 109 Lungomare San Vito, T: 0923 909286.

€ **Lo Scoiattolo**. Delicious pasta, cous cous, and fish; exceptional antipasti; pizza in the evenings. Closed Thur. 9 Via Tortorici, T: 0923 946313.

€ **Il Gambero**. Friendly, crowded restaurant on the seafront. Closed Tues. 3 Lungomare Mazzini, T: 0923 932932.

Pantelleria

€€€ **I Mulini**. The restaurant is famous for a delicious dessert called *baci*, crispy pastry layered with sweet creamy ricotta; the chef is from Milan, so he also prepares good risotto. Closed winter. 12 Via Krania, Contrada Tracino, T: 0923 915398.

€€€ **Castiglione**. Elegant restaurant serving excellent antipasti; the spaghetti with *ammogghiu*, the local raw pesto (ripe tomatoes, basil, mint, oregano, chilli and lots of garlic), is exceptional; chef Franco also prepares good fish soup. 24 Lungomare Borgo Italia, T: 0923 911448.

€€€ **Le Lampare**. Try *ravioli amari* (the local ravioli, filled with ricotta cheese and mint), spicy cous cous, *sciakisciuka*, a popular local dish made with vegetables and capers, and fresh sheep's milk cheese called *tumma*; good assortment of robust desserts. At the Hotel Mursia, T: 0923 911217.

€€ **Trattoria Favarotta**. Serves very tasty rabbit. Open evenings only, closed winter. T: 0923 915347.

€€ **Il Cappero**. Among the best restaurants of Pantelleria, delicious tuna dishes; pizza in the evenings; crowded on Saturdays. Closed winter. 31 Via Roma (at the port), T: 0923 912601.

€€ **La Risacca**. Open evenings only in summer, on a pretty terrace, serves excellent meals with good antipasti, also pizzas; very good spaghetti with lobster. 65 Via Milano, T: 0923 912975.

€€ **Trattoria di Bugeber**. Offers all the local specialities and has a panoramic veranda, on a high point of the island. Ballroom dancing in the evenings in summer. Contrada Bugeber, T: 0923 914009.

San Vito lo Capo

€€ **Gna' Sara**. Welcoming trattoria, for the very best local cuisine. Closed Mon. 6 Via Abruzzi, T: 0923 972100.

€€ **Tha'am**. Delightful North African and Sicilian dishes, including kebabs, and Moroccan mint tea; also rooms to rent. Closed Wed in winter. 32 Via Duca degli Abruzzi, T: 0923 972836.

Scauri

€€ **Scauri**. One of the oldest establishments of the island, with an excellent reputation for local ravioli, fresh fish and cous cous. T: 0923 916101.

€€ **La Nicchia**. Restaurant and pizzeria in an Arab garden; very good food, including *focaccia al paté di capperi*, soft bread with caper paste; you can buy their products to take home. Closed winter. T: 0923 916342.

€€ **La Vela**. Imaginative cuisine and excellent pizzas. Closed winter. T: 0923 916566.

Scopello

€€ **Torre Bennistra**. The best restaurant in Scopello. 9 Via Armando Diaz, T: 0924 541128.

CAFÉS, PASTRY SHOPS & ICE CREAM

Trapani

Antica Gelateria Beninvegna. Ice cream with a delightfully fluffy consistency; try *croccantino* flavour. Closed Mon in winter. 375 Via Fardella.

Caffè Aiuto. Excellent espresso; jasmine ice cream; *caldo freddo*, vanilla ice cream with hot chocolate sauce and other delights. 209 Via Vespri,

Colicchia. Great place for Sicilian breakfast, *cannoli di ricotta*, excellent ice cream, including granita made with jasmine flowers—*granita al gelsomino*. 6 Via delle Arti.

Alcamo

Extra Bar. Very good ice cream and pastries. 29 Viale Italia.

Erice

Caffè Maria. Old-fashioned coffee house in a beautifully furnished 19th-century house. Maria Grammatico, immortalized by Mary Taylor Simeti in *Bitter Almonds* and *On Persephone's Island*, is one of the most accomplished pastry-cooks in Sicily. Ask for *genovesi*, tiny shortcrust-pastry pies filled with confectioner's custard, served warm. 4 Via Vittorio Emanuele.

Favignana

Bar del Corso. The best place for Sicilian breakfast; unusual snacks. 40 Via Vittorio Emanuele.

Bar Due Colonne. Fresh fruit juices and tasty snacks. 68 Piazza Matrice.

Levanzo

The *cannoli di ricotta* are excellent everywhere; they are freshly prepared every day with milk from the goats which roam the island.

Panetteria di Levanzo. The town bakery, where Signora Olimpia (who is also an artist) makes delicious currant biscuits. 5 Via Pietre Varate (going towards lighthouse), T: 0923 924024.

Marettimo

Caffè La Scaletta. The best home-made ice cream, and fresh fruit juices. 4 Via del Telegrafo (at the port).

Caffè Tramontana. On the road above the port, is the perfect place for relaxing and admiring the view; nice cocktails.

Marsala

Bar Saviny. Busy coffee and snack bar, ideal for breakfast, lunch, or a leisurely ice cream. 25/F Piazza Piemonte e Lombardo.

Enzo e Nino. Home-made ice cream,

freshly prepared each day. Closed Wed in winter. 130 Via XI Maggio.

Vito. One of the best places in town for ice cream. 16 Corso Gramsci.

Mazara del Vallo

Pasticceria Lamia. Delicious local pastries. Ask for the local biscuits: *muccunate* and *mazaresi al pistacchio*. 44 Via Val di Mazara.

Pantelleria

Goloso. On the harbour, is just right for an evening aperitif.

Cicci's Bar. Prepares very good snacks. Piazza Cavour.

Tikirriki. On the harbour, for splendid ice creams.

San Vito lo Capo

Il Gabbiano. This is where Cristoforo prepares his delicious home-made ice cream, using fresh fruit and nuts; he has recently opened a branch in Detroit. Closed Mon in winter. 10 Via Gen. Arimondi.

La Piazzetta. For the famous *caldo freddo*: ice cream and biscuits covered with hot chocolate sauce.

Scopello

Bar Scopello. For Sicilian breakfast and the very best *cannoli di ricotta* or *genovesi*. 13 Via A. Diaz.

Selinunte

Enoteca Siciliana. Right in front of the entrance to the archaeological park. Excellent espresso, Sicilian breakfast, or wine-tasting; they also have good olive oil. 155 Via Caboto.

LOCAL SPECIALITIES

Alcamo

The Ceuso farm produces good red wine, which they call Fastaia; very nice with pasta, grilled steak or cheese. A good label for the famous white, Bianco d'Alcamo, is Rapitalà.

Belice Valley

The Settesoli estate near Menfi (T: 0925 77111), produces the prize-winning Mandrarossa wine, while Fiano vines on the Planeta estate (T: 0925 80009, www.planeta.it) produce a marvellous white wine called Cometa, a perfect accompaniment to rich fish dishes.

Campobello di Mazara

This area produces excellent olive oil. **Tenuta Ducale**, 86 Via Marconi, www.tenutaducale.it, is an excellent address, they will ship on request.

Castelvetrano

A prize-winning olive oil company is SO.VI.CA, 55 Via Seggio, T: 0924 905079. They will ship abroad on request (also wine). Olives are gathered by hand from the tiny trees of the Nocellara del Belice variety, and pressed the same day. There are several bakeries which make the local sourdough loaves. The bread is a characteristic coffee-brown colour, with a delicious flavour, and it keeps well. Try **Rizzo**, 85 Via Garibaldi (opposite the museum).

Erice

The pastries made here are unique in Sicily, and were once made by the nuns of the many convents in the town. The women of Erice also weave the bright cotton rugs called *frazzate*. **Pasticceria Grammatico** at 14 Via Vittorio Emanuele, for Maria Grammatico's little cakes and marzipan. One of her Easter lambs, made of marzipan and filled with candied citron, was shown at the American Craft Museum, New York.

Marsala

There are several good places for buying wines or other local products. **Enoteca**

La Ruota and **Enoteca Luminario** are close to each other on Lungomare Boeo, near the Archaeological Museum.
Enoteca Fazio, at 99 Via S. Bilardello, is a good example of how the younger generation is injecting new energy into long established industries; their wines and olive oil are winning recognition.
Cantine Mothia is a small winery on the outskirts of Marsala at 12 Via Sappusi, T: 0923 737295, www.cantine-mothia.com.

Mazara del Vallo
The Benedictine nuns at the **Monastero di San Michele Arcangelo**, Piazza San Michele, have been making delightful little almond sweets to the same recipe since 1600.

Pantelleria
Pantelleria wines are made using a high proportion of white Zibibbo grapes. Although they are usually considered to be dessert wines, they work as aperitifs when drunk icy cold. The kinds to look out for are Moscato di Pantelleria, a sweet, strong wine, best drunk chilled, excellent with cheese; Moscato passito di Pantelleria, made with grapes which have been allowed to shrivel in the sun before harvesting; Tanit, or Nikà, from the Case di Pietra cellars (www.casedipietra.it) are good names, and Ben Ryé, from the Donnafugata Rallo estate (www.donnafugata.it) has won several awards.

Salemi
The town is famous for its decorative loaves of bread, baked to celebrate the feasts of St Blaise (3 February) and St Joseph (19 March); they are also sold, and the proceeds go to charity. Prices are high, and can exceed 50 euros for one small, albeit very intricate, loaf. All the women of the town take part in the baking, which begins about ten days before the feasts.

Trapani
Platimiro Fiorenza, at 36 Via Osorio (behind Villa Margherita) is one of the few coral craftsmen in Trapani, once famous for this art. He makes exquisite jewellery, using silver and coral. **Saverio D'Angelo**, 19 Via Cuba, is an old-fashioned shop specializing in antique coral jewellery.

FESTIVALS & EVENTS

Trapani *Procession of the Misteri*, Groups of life-size figures made in the 17th–18th centuries by local artists. Each group represents an episode in the Passion of Christ, and is carried by the representatives of the 20 corporations, or *mestieri*—hence the name. The procession starts at three in the afternoon, and continues all night long, passing through the narrow streets, never decreasing in intensity. Good Friday. www.imisteriditrapani.it
Luglio Musicale, opera in the gorgeous setting of the public gardens, Villa Margherita. July. T: 0923 29290, www.lugliomusicaletrapanese.it
Castelvetrano The Aurora festival is celebrated with a traditional procession and an enactment of the meeting of the Madonna with her risen Son, Easter Sunday morning.
Erice Procession of the *Misteri*. Good Friday.
Estate Ericina, festival of music and art, July–Aug.
Feast of Our Lady of Custonaci, the patron saint, with a magnificent procession organized by the women, who wear medieval dress, last Wed in Aug.

La Zampogna d'Oro, international bag-pipes and folk music competition, Christmas–New Year.

Gibellina Orestiadi at plays, concerts and ballet. Aug–Sept. Info T: 0924 67844, www.orestiadi.it

Marsala A magnificent procession representing the Via Crucis. The little girls dressed as Veronica are particularly impressive, as traditionally they must wear all the family jewels. Maundy Thursday

Mazara del Vallo *'U Fistinu di San Vitu*, celebrations for St Vitus, during which the fishermen pull a cart with his statue through the streets. T: 0923 941777. Third Sun in Aug.

San Vito lo Capo International Cous Cous Fest, with cooks from all around the Mediterranean, Sept. www.sanvito-couscous.com
The patron St Vitus is celebrated, culminating with firework displays and a competition among the fishermen who try to walk along a slippery pole suspended over the water to get a flag at the far end, 13–15 June.

Scurati (near Custonaci) The 'Living Crib' takes place at Christmas, and the 'Living Museum' in summer. Local crafts and trades are on show in the houses of the now uninhabited village in the Mangiapane Cave. 13–15 June. T: 0924 30217, www.mcsystem.it/presepe

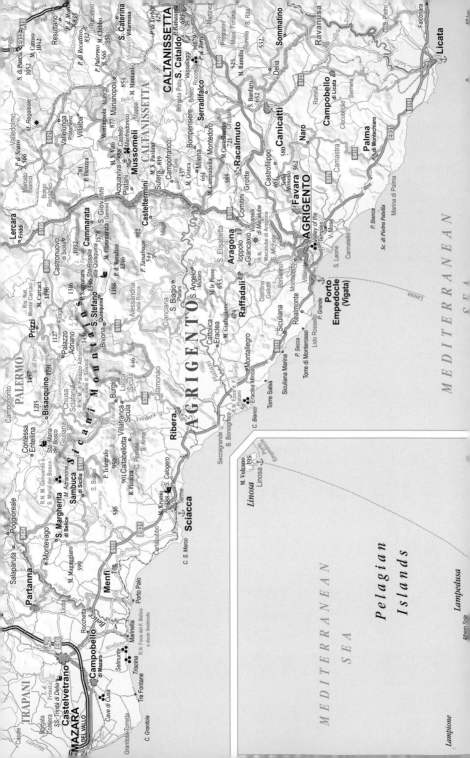

THE PROVINCE OF AGRIGENTO

AGRIGENTO

A grigento, once one of the most prosperous of the ancient Greek cities on the island, preserves a remarkable series of Doric temples of the 5th century BC, unequalled except in Greece itself. The medieval and modern city, on the site of the ancient acropolis, crowns a narrow ridge overlooking a valley which stretches towards the sea, in the midst of which, on a second lower ridge, stand the superb Classical ruins.

The province of Agrigento, which after the collapse of the sulphur industry became one of the poorest regions in Italy, is now reaping the benefits from tourism and its export of high quality agricultural produce; wines, oranges, olive oil and vegetables. The town and its surroundings have also become an important international centre for the study of almond trees.

HISTORY OF AGRIGENTO

Agrigento, the *Acragas* of the Greeks and the *Agrigentum* of the Romans, claims Daedalus as its legendary founder, but seems almost certainly to have originated as a colony of Gela (580 BC), founded about a hundred years earlier by settlers from Rhodes. From 570 to 555 the city suffered under the tyranny of Phalaris; the bull-cult he introduced was perhaps Cretan (*see p. 205*). The great poet Pindar (who lived here) described Acragas as 'the fairest city of mortals'. Its population was then about 200,000. The local breed of horses was renowned, and the racing-chariot found on many coins minted here may derive from their frequent successes at the Olympic games. It was the birthplace of the philosopher Empedocles (*see p. 210*). Acron, the physician, who invented fumigation and succeeded in stopping the plague in Athens in 430 BC was also a native of the city.

Conflict with Syracuse led to defeat in the field, after which Theron's dynasty gave place to a republican government. In 406 BC the Carthaginians, under Hannibal Gisco and Himilco, took the city and burned it after a siege of eight months. Timoleon (*see p. 338*) defeated the Carthaginians (340) and rebuilt the city, but it was taken by the Romans in 261 and again in 210, and remained in their possession until the fall of the Empire. It fell to the Arabs in 827 AD, and then to Count Roger's Normans in 1087, when the bishopric was founded.

The present town, long known as Girgenti, occupies the acropolis of the Greek city. The name, abandoned in 1927, derives from *Kerkent*, an Arabic corruption of *Agrigentum*.

THE MEDIEVAL & MODERN CITY

The old part of Agrigento occupies the summit of Monte Camico (326m); its modern suburbs extend along the ridge to the east below the Rupe Atenea, and the city is expanding down the hillsides to the north and south. Three connected squares effectively divide the centre of the town; the area to the west contains the old city.

Santo Spirito and the Museo Civico

Via Atenea, the long main street of the old town, leads west from Piazzale Aldo Moro. Just out of the Piazza on the right is the Palazzo Celauro, where Goethe stayed on his visit during his Grand Tour of the island. Via Porcello (right) and the stepped Salita Santo Spirito lead steeply up to the abbey church of **Santo Spirito** (*if locked, ring for the custodian at no. 2 or 11 Salita Santo Spirito, offering expected, or at the convent*), founded c. 1290 for Cistercian nuns. The nuns still make delectable sweets (*frutti di martorana*, marzipan fruits; *cous cous dolce*, with pistachio and cocoa; and marzipan shells filled with pistachio) which may be purchased here. The façade has a Gothic portal surmounted by a rose window; inside are lovely stuccoes (c. 1693–95), by Giacomo Serpotta (*see p. 56*) and his school. The statue of the *Madonna Enthroned* is by the workshop of Domenico Gagini.

Part of the convent was restored in 1990 to house part of the Museo Civico (*open 9–1 & 3–6; Sat morning only; closed Sun and holidays*), formerly in Piazza Luigi Pirandello, with a miscellany of objects, poorly labelled. It is approached through an over-restored cloister, and up a modern flight of stairs. The two rooms on the top floor contain a local ethnographical collection of agricultural implements and domestic ware. On the floor below, archaeological material and remains of frescoes are displayed. Steps lead down to the *Stanza della Badessa* in a tower with a Gothic vault and a painted 15th-century Crucifix. The beautiful dormitory has fine vaulting and an exhibition of international folk costumes, as well as a collection of butterflies, beetles and shells. On the ground floor a chapel with a Gothic vault has a crib, with charming domestic scenes, made by a local craftsman (1991). The chapter-house (now used for weddings) is also shown. The paintings include works by Pietro Novelli, Luca Giordano and Fra' Felice da Sambuca.

Towards the duomo

Further along Via Atenea is the unfinished façade of Santa Rosalia beside the **church of the Purgatorio** or San Lorenzo (containing elegant statues of the Virtues by Serpotta). The lion to the left of the church sleeps above the locked entrance to a huge labyrinth of underground water channels and reservoirs, built by the Greek architect Phaiax in the 5th century BC. Beyond the neo-Gothic exchange building the street widens at the undistinguished Piazza Nicola Gallo, once the centre of the old city. Beyond the church of San Giuseppe, at the top of the rise, Via Atenea descends to Piazza Luigi Pirandello (formerly Piazza del Municipio). On the right is the Baroque façade of San Domenico; while occupying the former convent (mid-17th century) are the town hall and the fine Teatro Pirandello opera house (Ernesto Basile, 1870).

To the right of San Giuseppe, Via Bac Bac leads to the stepped Via Saponara (signposted for Santa Maria dei Greci). From here it is a steep climb up the Salita Eubernatis and Salita Santa Maria dei Greci to (right; inconspicuous entrance) **Santa Maria dei Greci** (*usually open 8–12 & 3–dusk except on Sun and holiday afternoons. The custodians live at no. 1 Salita Santa Maria dei Greci, opposite the church; donation expected*), preceded by a charming little courtyard with a palm tree and a cypress. This small basilica was built with antique materials, on the site of a Doric temple, perhaps that of Athena, begun by Theron in the 5th century BC. The interior preserves fragments of charming 14th-century frescoes. Parts of the temple may be seen here, and in a passage (*entered from the churchyard; unlocked by the custodian on request*) below the north aisle are the stumps of six fluted columns on the stylobate.

The duomo

The alleys on the north side of the church join Via del Duomo. A magnificent old staircase leads to the duomo, dedicated to the Norman bishop of Agrigento St Gerland. It is mainly a 14th-century building with an unfinished campanile (to the southwest) that shows in its Gothic windows a mixture of Arab-Norman and Catalan influences. Inside, a single round arch divides the nave into two parts: at the entrance the tall polygonal piers support an open painted roof of 1518; in the sanctuary is a coffered ceiling of 1603 decorated with the two-headed royal eagle of the House of Aragon. At the end of the south aisle is the Chapel of St Gerland (who refounded the see after the Arab defeat), with a lovely 17th-century silver reliquary by Michele Ricca. Opposite, in the left aisle is the tomb of the merchant Gaspare de Marino, by Andrea Mancino and Giovanni Gagini (1492), and other Baroque funerary monuments, and fragments of 15th-century frescoes. A curious acoustic phenomenon (*il portavoce*) permits a person standing beneath the cornice of the apse to hear every word spoken even in a low voice near the main doorway, though this does not work in reverse.

The **Seminary** (17th–18th centuries) has an arcaded courtyard, off which (*shown on request*) is a Gothic hall with a double vault, remains of the 14th-century Chiaramonte Steri (*hosterium*), one of several castles in Sicily built by the powerful Chiaramonte family.

The extensive façade of the **Biblioteca Lucchesiana** lines Via del Duomo. This fine building was founded here in 1765 as a public library by the bishop of Agrigento. Its treasures number 40,000 volumes (including Arab MSS still housed in the original presses of 1765).

THE VALLEY OF THE TEMPLES & THE ANCIENT CITY

The ancient city, encircled by a wall, occupied the angle between the rivers *Hypsas* and *Acragas* (now the rivers Sant'Anna and San Biagio) which meet near the coast to flow into the sea. The temples should, if possible, be seen at several different times of the day, especially in the early morning and at sunset; and at night when floodlit. In early

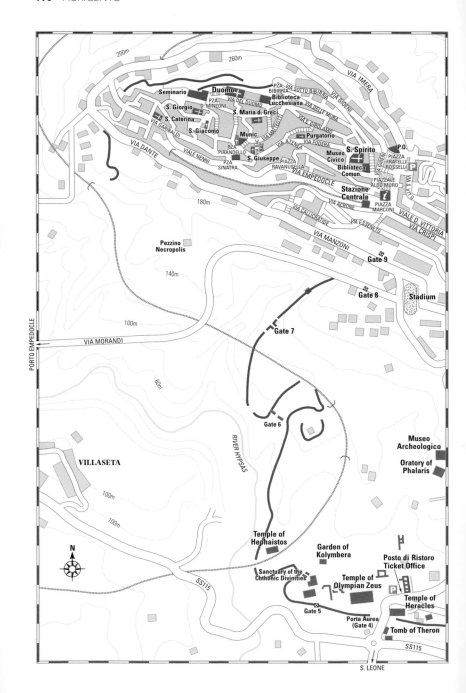

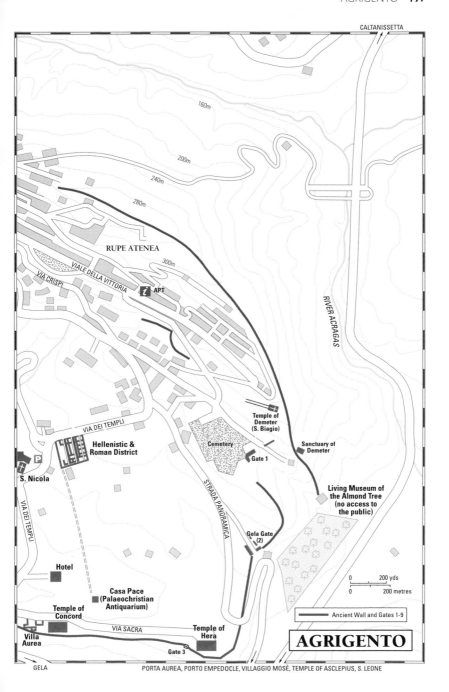

CALTANISSETTA

160m

200m

240m

280m

RUPE ATENEA

VIALE DELLA VITTORIA

VIA CRISPI

300m

APT

RIVER ACRAGAS

VIA DEI TEMPLI

Temple of
Demeter
(S. Biagio)

Cemetery

Sanctuary of
Demeter

Hellenistic &
Roman District

Gate 1

P

S. Nicola

VIA DEI TEMPLI

STRADA PANORAMICA

Living Museum of
the Almond Tree
(no access to
the public)

Gela Gate
(2)

Hotel

Casa Pace
(Palaeochristian
Antiquarium)

0   200 yds
0   200 metres

Temple of
Concord

VIA SACRA

Temple of
Hera

Ancient Wall and Gates 1-9

Villa
Aurea

Gate 3

AGRIGENTO

GELA

PORTA AUREA, PORTO EMPEDOCLE, VILLAGGIO MOSÈ, TEMPLE OF ASCLEPIUS, S. LEONE spring, when the almond trees are in bloom, they are particularly beautiful. Butterflies are in the valley in abundance. The temples are a World Heritage Site, and the archaeological area is a regional park. Haphazard, illegal building is no longer possible and several modern structures in the vicinity of the temples have already been demolished.

Planning a visit to the temples

Temples and Hellenistic and Roman district open daily 8.30–7 (sometimes until midnight in summer). Tickets available at the entrance to the Temple of Zeus (near the car park) or at the other end of the Via Sacra, by the Temple of Hera. One ticket allows entry to all the temples or a combined ticket is available for temples and museum.

The museum and the main ruins are linked by road. At least a whole day should be allowed if on foot as the site covers a large area (ancient Acragas and its temples measured 4.5km by 3km). Buses run from Piazza Marconi (next to the railway station) along Viale Crispi, past the Hellenistic and Roman districts and the museum to the car park and the Posto di Ristoro (probably the site of the agora, excavations are currently being carried out here) where there is the main ticket office and a café. Those with less time should not miss the museum, the temples on the Via Sacra (it takes at least an hour to walk to the Temple of Hera and back) and the Temple of Zeus. Just below the Posto di Ristoro the main road (the ancient road to the sea) descends through the rock on the site of the Porta Aurea (Gate Four). This was the main gate of the ancient city of Acragas, built over in Byzantine times.

Temple of Heracles

The Via Sacra (*closed to cars*) traverses the ridge on which stand the temples of Heracles, Concord and Hera. Beyond the Temple of Concord it leads through delightful countryside, here undisturbed, with beautiful groves of almonds and ancient olive trees. At the beginning on the right is a footbridge above a deep street of tombs carved into the rock which leads to the Temple of Heracles, a heap of ruins showing traces of fire, with nine upright columns, eight of them re-erected in 1922–3 by the munificence of Captain Alexander Hardcastle (*see below*).

This is probably the oldest visible temple of Acragas (built c. 500 BC). Peripteral hexastyle in plan, its 38 columns were 9.9m high and 2m in diameter, and it had a cella (perhaps roofless) with pronaos and opisthodomos both distyle in antis. In ancient times it was famed for its statue of Heracles, which Verres (*see box opposite*) attempted to steal. It also contained a painting of the infant Heracles strangling the serpents, by Zeuxis, the famed artist from Heraclea whose painted grapes were so lifelike that birds came to peck at them.

The Villa Aurea

Beyond, on the Via Sacra is the Villa Aurea (now used as offices; *admission only with special permission*) surrounded by a luxuriant and beautifully kept garden. Visible from the road, in the forecourt, is a memorial bust set up in 1984 of Captain Alexander

Hardcastle. This eccentric Englishman repaired the villa in 1921 and lived here with his brother Henry until his death in 1933. The Captain provided substantial funds to restore and excavate the ancient city, supporting the work of Pirro Marconi. He also took an interest in the modern city, providing an aqueduct from there to the temple valley. In gratitude, the Italian government awarded him the important honorary title of *Commendatore della Corona d'Italia* and the Home Office allowed him to wear the insignia. The villa now contains an antiquarium (material from the Pezzino Necropolis, and excavations in Contrada Mosè), and in the garden are tombs and underground cisterns.

Further up on the left is a Palaeo-Christian necropolis. Here there are Christian tombs cut in the surface of the rock, as well as extensive catacombs with subterranean passages extending below the road. In the field here are two tholos tombs thought to date from the 5th century BC.

VERRES THE ART THIEF

In 73 BC Caius Verres, influential in Rome, was made Governor of Sicily. No sooner was he installed in the governor's palace at Syracuse than he began pillaging works of art to adorn it. At first, he requisitioned beautiful objects from private homes, but later he stole cult statues and paintings from the temples: a statue of Ceres from Catania, the chryselephantine doors of the Temple of Athena at Syracuse, together with paintings and the effigy of the goddess, whose face and hands are said to have been of gold. In Acragas, the magnificent bronze statue of Apollo, signed by Myron, was again stolen from the Temple of Asclepios (it had once before been carried away by the Carthaginians, in 406 BC, and returned by Scipio in 146). Verres sent a group of soldiers to steal the statue of Heracles from the temple at Acragas at dawn one day, but word of the raid got out and the soldiers were overpowered by furious citizens. Cicero, who had been called by the Sicilians in 71 BC to plead their cause in front of the senate, described the statue as the most beautiful work of art he had ever seen, and the effect of Verres on the island as more devastating than war. Cicero won his case, which launched his political career, but Verres was only nominally punished: he went into voluntary exile to Marseilles, where he died in 43 BC. The stolen artworks were never recovered.

Temple of Concord

The Temple of Concord (*pictured overleaf*) at Agrigento is the best preserved of all Greek temples except the Temple of Hephaistos at Athens, which it recalls in its majestic symmetry and rich colour. It is currently undergoing thorough restoration. The name occurs in a Latin inscription found here, but has no real connection with the temple (although there is a tradition among the inhabitants of Agrigento that the

temple should be visited by a husband and wife on their wedding day to ensure a future free from marital strife).

The building, which probably dates from about 430 BC and was only slightly harmed by the Carthaginians, stands on a stylobate of four steps and is peripteral hexastyle in plan. Its 34 Doric columns are 6.8m high including the capitals, with a diameter of 1.4m at the base. The intercolumniations of the façades become narrower towards the sides (to accommodate the corner metopes); this is one of the earliest instances in Sicily of this refinement in temple design. The cella has a pronaos and an opisthodomos, both distyle in antis. From the east end of the cella two spiral staircases mount to the architrave. The complete entablature survives at both ends.

The excellent state of preservation of the temple is explained by the fact that it was converted into a church by San Gregorio delle Rape ('St Gregory of the turnips'), bishop of Agrigento, in the 6th century AD. It was restored as a temple in the 18th century, but the arches of the nave remain in the cella walls. The material of this and of the other temples is easily eroded sandstone, formerly protected by white stucco made of marble dust, which was once brightly painted, and has now almost completely disappeared; the stone is now burnt by the sun to a rich tawny gold.

The Antiquarium

From the temple the attractive Hotel Villa Athena can be seen. A little gate on the road gives access to the Casa Pace, an old building restored to house a Palaeo-Christian Antiquarium (*officially open at the same time as the temples, but if closed ask at the ticket office*). The exhibits illustrate the history of the three early Christian churches so far found in Agrigento: one outside the walls at the eastern edge of the temple ridge; one built inside the Temple of Concord; and one excavated beside the Hotel Villa Athena. Finds include a finely carved sarcophagus (5th century AD), left unfinished. Upstairs are photographs and plans of the necropoleis excavated in the area.

The Via Sacra, now more peaceful, continues parallel to the ancient city walls, the inner face of which contains many Byzantine tomb recesses. There is a view on the left of the cemetery, to the right of which San Biagio can be seen beside a clump of trees. On the skyline, radio masts mark the Rupe Atenea.

Temple of Hera

About 1km further east stands the much ruined but picturesque Temple of Hera, called the Temple of Juno Lacinia, from a confusion with a temple dedicated to Hera on the Lacinian promontory at Crotone, in Calabria. It resembles the Temple of Concord in form, but is slightly smaller and older (c. 450 BC). Since a landslide in 1976 threatened its stability the entrance has been fenced off. The stylobate, on a massive artificial platform, measures 38m by 16.8m. Of its 34 columns (6 by 13), 6.4m high with a base-diameter of 1.3m, nine have fallen. Traces of a fire (which probably

The Temple of Concord, Agrigento, seen from the east, framed by an almond tree.

occurred in 406) are still visible. The work of the Roman restorers was ruined by an earthquake. To the east is the sacrificial altar; to the west an ancient cistern.

Looking west there is a good view of the outer face of the wall, in some places carved out of the natural rock, clinging to the brow of the hill. Nearby are the scant remains of Gate Three (one of the ancient city gates), and outside the city walls, an ancient roadway used for transporting the stones for the temples: the deep wheel-ruts can still be seen.

Temple of Olympian Zeus

NB: The custodians of the ancient monuments of Agrigento, whose offices are here, are help-ful and informed. Enquire here for admission to areas found closed or for the key to sites normally kept locked.

The entrance to the Temple of Olympian Zeus is next to the Posto di Ristoro. Excavations extend to the westernmost edge of the temple ridge, and the Garden of Kolymbetra (*see below*). Beside the entrance is the vast, complicated heap of ruins of the Temple of Olympian Zeus, or Olympieion, thought to have been begun by the Carthaginian prisoners taken at Himera in 480 BC, and left unfinished in 406: its destruction, partly due to earthquakes, was completed by quarrying in the 18th cen-tury, much of the stone going into the foundations of Porto Empedocle.

This huge Doric temple (110.1m by 52.7m, virtually a double square), is the largest Doric temple known, and is unique in form among Greek temples. It was built of comparatively small stones (each capital was composed of three blocks) and then cov-ered in stucco. It is heptastyle and pseudoperipteral, i.e. the seven columns at each end and the 14 on each side were engaged in the walls, being rounded externally and presenting a square face towards the interior. In between the semi-columns, 16.7m high and 4m thick at the base, were 38 colossal telamones set on the outer wall; their exact arrangement is still under discussion. In the east pediment a *Gigantomachia* was represented, and in the west pediment the *Capture of Troy*. The cella was divided into three aisles, separated by square pillars (to support the vast roof).

Little remains in position except the stereobate, but this alone is sufficient to con-vey an impression of the immensity of the monument. Part of the north wall survives (note the outer face), and the foundations of the aisle pillars. To the east, beyond the wall which (curiously) 'blocked' what is thought to have been the entrance, are the foundations of the altar platform. All around the temple is a heap of ruins, amid which lies a copy of a giant (7.6m high), one of the telamones; the original 19th-cen-tury reconstruction is displayed in the Archaeological Museum. The U-shaped inci-sion visible on many stones is believed to have facilitated their being raised by ropes. Near the southeastern corner, below one of the colossal fallen capitals, is a small tem-ple of Archaic date with a cella divided by piers. The agora of the ancient city is thought to have been to the east (under the car park by the Posto di Ristoro).

Sanctuary of the Chthonic Divinities

Further to the west is a complicated area of excavations including remains of houses, and traces of an L-shaped portico, which enclosed a sanctuary and a tholos on a spur

The Temple of Castor and Pollux in the Sanctuary of the Chthonic Divinities.

beside Gate Five. The carriageway is obstructed by masonry which apparently fell in Greek times. It was probably a double gate defended by a tower. On the other side of the gate are various shrines that together formed the Sanctuary of the Chthonic Divinities (the gods of the earth—Dionysus, Demeter and Persephone). The shrines were entirely enclosed by a precinct wall, a portion of which is visible on the west side. The misnamed **Temple of Castor and Pollux** is here. The four columns bearing a portion of the architrave, which have been used as the picturesque symbol of Classical Sicily, are a reconstruction of 1836 now known to incorporate elements from more than one building on this site.

Superimposed ruins show the existence of shrines dedicated to the cult of the earth gods as early as the 7th century BC. The structures on the north side, notably the pairs of altars, one circular and one square, date from this period. To the south of these are the remains of two unfinished 6th-century temples; the third is that formerly misascribed to Castor and Pollux, which was probably to the same plan as the Temple of Concord. A fourth temple was built just to the south, in Hellenistic or Roman times. Many of the fallen column drums belong to the last temple and the well-preserved altar east of the platform.

The Garden of Kolymbetra

Beyond the custodians' house is an Archaic Sanctuary, recently excavated on the edge of the hill. From here two columns of the Temple of Hephaistos (*see p. 210*) can be seen on the hill across a delightful fertile little valley where there are orange trees. This is the Garden of Kolymbetra (*open May–Oct 9–7; Nov–Jan 10–5; Feb–Apr 9–6; closed Mon, Jan and during the Almond Blossom Festival*), recently restored and opened to the public by the FAI, the Italian conservation agency. The garden was originally an artificial lake, dug by the Carthaginian prisoners taken by the tyrant Theron after the Greek victory at Himera in 480 BC. It was intended for use as a reservoir and a source of freshwater fish for the king's table. Historians describe it as a place of great beauty with swans, ducks and many other birds. After a relatively short time, probably little more than a century, the lake was filled in, perhaps because of malaria, and it became a flourishing garden where the Arabs cultivated oranges. Abandoned for centuries, it will be cared for by the FAI for 25 years. From the garden it is easy to cross the railway line to reach the remains of the Temple of Hephaistos.

Beneath the viaduct of the Via Morandi the Pezzino Necropolis (*admission from Via Dante*) has been excavated.

Museo Regionale Archeologico

Open 9–7.30; Sun, Mon and holidays 9–1.30; sometimes open until midnight in summer; last tickets 30mins before closing.

On the main road (Via dei Templi), about 1km uphill from the Posto di Ristoro, is the Museo Regionale Archeologico, one of the finest museums in Sicily, spaciously arranged in a 1960s building designed by Franco Minissi. It is approached through a garden and the 14th-century cloisters of the convent attached to the church of San Nicola. In the cloisters is a long stone bench carrying an inscription to Heracles and Hermes found in the agora zone of the city.

Room I: Early and Late Bronze Age material from sites near Agrigento, including a small Mycenaean amphora (probably found at Porto Empedocle), and painted vases. Also prehistoric objects found in Agrigento beneath the Classical area.

Room II: Objects from nearby Gela (6th–7th centuries BC), including Corinthian and Rhodian ware (note the head of a bull), as well as locally made vases; votive statuettes from Licata (late 4th century BC). There is a small dish with the three-legged symbol of Sicily, the **Trinacria** or Triskele, one of its earliest known depictions (7th century BC). A relatively common sun symbol, related to the Sanskrit swastika, the Phoenician sun-god Baal, and the Greek Apollo, the legs signify the sun's course through the skies. Probably the Greeks dedicated the island to Apollo. Snakes were sacred to the god (he gave two entwined on a stick to Asclepios) and this has prompted the erroneous assumption that the head represents the Gorgon Medusa. The device became official when Frederick II of Aragon had himself crowned King of Trinacria, adopting the ancient Greek name for the island. It is famously also used by the Isle of Man, perhaps chosen by Alexander III of Scotland and Man in 1266, when all things Sicilian were considered worthy of emulation.

THE BULL-CULT OF ACRAGAS

Daedalus the skilled inventor was in the employ of Minos of Crete. When Minos' wife conceived a blind passion for a beautiful bull, Daedalus built a wooden cow for her to climb inside. Consequently the bull had his way with her, resulting in the birth of the Minotaur, half-man, half-bull, whom Minos shut up in a labyrinth also devised by Daedalus. The inventor emerges as legendary founder of Acragas, whose tyrant ruler Phalaris also had bullish associations. He is said to have had a hollow bronze bull built, into which he would force his victims and then light a fire underneath. As they roasted, their shrieks would issue from the bronze bull's mouth, reverberating against the metal to sound like a bull in full bellow. Ethnographers believe that much of this is bound up with cults of sacrifice. The Phoenician god Baal (Zeus Atabyrius) was worshipped at Rhodes; the temple of Zeus contained brass bulls, which were said to bellow when danger threatened the island. It was Rhodian colonists who are thought to have founded Acragas, from Gela, which was founded by settlers from both Rhodes and Crete. The worship of Baal involved human sacrifice, usually of children. Children were sacrificed to the Minotaur. The Bull of Phalaris is likely to have been an instrument of ritual sacrifice.

Room III: Superb collection of vases, including a group of outstanding **Attic vases** from the mid-6th to the early 3rd centuries BC. Black- and red-figured kraters from the 4th–3rd centuries BC include a lekythos with Nike sacrificing (460–450 BC), and kraters depicting Dionysiac scenes (c. 440 BC) and Perseus and Andromeda in polychrome on a white ground, a rare example of c. 430 BC; a stamnos (440–430 BC) shows a sacrifice to Apollo; a small red-figured krater with a bull being led to sacrifice, and several kraters and stamni with banqueting scenes (some by the Painter of Lugano, c. 400 BC). At the end of the hall is a fine marble **statue of a warrior** (c. 480 BC), belonging to the Early Classical period, that may have adorned part of the pediment of the Temple of Heracles. Also in this room are an Attic red-figured vase of the early 5th century BC, two kraters by the Harrow Painter, and a krater showing the burial of a warrior, as well as black-figured Attic vases of the end of the 6th century BC including a lekythos with Heracles and the Hydra. From the same period is a large amphora with four gods and a quadriga by the Painter of Dikaios.

Room IV: Architectonic fragments including a remarkable variety of lion-head water spouts from various buildings (including the Temple of Heracles and the Temple of Demeter) and a huge statue of Telamon.

Room V: Statuettes and heads in terracotta, notably, female votive statues; the mask of a black African of the 6th century BC; two cases of moulds; head of

Athena with a helmet (c. 490 BC); head of a kouros (500 BC). On the end wall are delicate bas-relief friezes, including some showing the telamones. Beyond the steps which descend to Room VI, a case on the balcony displays the head of a kouros of c. 540 BC, and a female bust of the end of the 6th century BC. Other cases here contain finds from the area near the Temple of Heracles, including architectonic fragments in terracotta.

Room VI: Devoted to **finds from the Temple of Zeus**. Here the remarkable giant (7.6m high) is displayed, one of the telamones from the temple, which was recomposed from fragments in the 19th century; along the wall are three colossal telamon heads illustrating three different ethnic types. The blocks of stone were originally covered with plaster. Plans and models suggest possible reconstructions of the temple, and the controversial position of the telamones. The discovery of a leg attached to a block of stone of one of the statues has shown that their feet must have been further apart than is indicated here.

Room VII: Fragments of wall paintings and mosaics from the Roman district.

Rooms VIII and IX (*opened only on special request*): Contain inscriptions and coins.

Room X (reached from Room V): In the first part three statuettes are displayed: the 5th-century BC **Ephebus of Agrigento** (*pictured opposite*), a marble statue of a young man, found in a cistern near the Temple of Demeter, which was transferred during the Norman period to the Church of San Biagio (*see p. 208 below*), thought to represent an athlete from Agrigento victorious in various events at the Olympic games and a significant milestone in Greek sculpture, being suggestive of a body in motion; a statuette of Apollo, or the river-god Acragas (c. 480 BC); and a fragment of a kneeling statue of Aphrodite (2nd–1st centuries BC). In the second part material found in the bouleuterion is displayed, including coins. A corridor, overlooking a little garden with two Roman statues, has panels illustrating the political history of Acragas.

Room XI: Finds from various necropoleis, notably that at Contrada Pezzino. It is the oldest necropolis in Agrigento and the one that has produced the richest finds (early 6th–3rd centuries BC). The miniature vases were found in children's tombs. At the end of the room, the fine alabaster **sarcophagus of a child**, with poignant childhood scenes (ended by illness and death), a Hellenistic work of the 2nd century BC, was found near Agrigento. Nearby is another Roman sarcophagus. From the window here recent excavations can be seen.

Room XII: An introductory display of prehistoric material, and finds from Sciacca.

Room XIII: Objects from the province of Agrigento, including finds from the Grotto dell'Acqua Fitusa and from Sant'Angelo Muxaro. The fragments of ochre are thought to have been used to colour vases.

Room XIV: Material from **Eraclea Minoa** (*see p. 210*), and Greek and Roman helmets; busts from Licata; also bronze cooking utensils.

Room XV: Contains a single magnificent **red-figured krater** from Gela (5th century BC). In perfect condition, it displays an episode from the Trojan War: the battle with the Amazons on one side, and on the other Achilles falling in love with Penthesilea queen of the Amazons as he strikes her to death. It could be the work of Polignotus of Athens. Photographs on the walls show other vases, now in the Gela museum.

Room XVII: Finds from Caltanissetta (notably a fine red-figured krater showing horsemen of 450–440 BC).

Room XVIII (*opened only on special request*): Houses the contents of the cathedral treasury: especially noteworthy are two reliquaries of Limoges-enamelled copper, a portable altar-stone with Byzantine enamels (13th century), an ivory crozier, and a *Madonna* attributed to Guido Reni.

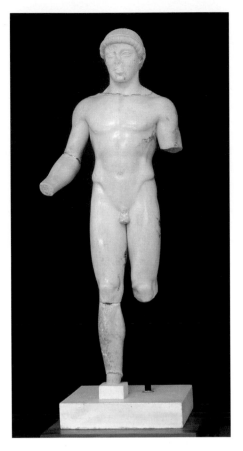

The Ephebus of Agrigento (5th century BC)

The Oratory of Phalaris and Church of San Nicola

Outside the museum is the entrance to an area of excavations. The bouleuterion (or *ekklesiasterion*) was built in the 4th–3rd centuries BC and transformed into an odeon in the Imperial era. It was used for the meetings of the *boulé*, a political ruling body. It could hold some 300 people; the participants are thought to have stood. The narrow divisional rows are carved into the rock. In one corner is the so-called **Oratory of Phalaris**, a prostyle building in antis, probably a late-Hellenistic shrine, which was transformed into a Gothic chapel. A footbridge crosses an area with remains of late-Hellenistic houses, and Imperial Roman buildings (mosaics).

The early 13th-century church of **San Nicola** (*open 8–1 & 3–7*) has a curious façade made up of a Gothic doorway in strong relief between antae with a Doric cornice (the material probably came from a Roman edifice nearby). The architecture of the interior, reconstructed in 1322, and altered in 1426, is interesting. In the second south chapel there is a magnificent sarcophagus of white Parian marble, which with great delicacy and purity of style portrays four episodes in the story of Hippolytus and Phaedra, son and second wife of Theseus. Phaedra fell in love with Hippolytus, hanged herself in despair and blamed her death on her step-son, who was killed by Poseidon as a favour to Theseus. It could be a Greek work of about 450 BC, or a later Roman copy of the original. The front panel shows Hippolytus with his male companions and numerous horses and dogs, and the side panel illustrates Phaedra with female companions. The angle figures are particularly skilful, as well as the delicate frieze at the top and bottom of the scenes. The last two sides do not appear to have been completed, possibly because the sarcophagus was placed in the corner of a building. In 1787, when it was in the duomo, it was much admired by Goethe as the best-preserved Classical relief carving he had seen. The church also contains a venerated wooden Crucifix, a statue of the Madonna and Child by the Gagini school (*see p. 423*), and an unusual stoup supported by a grey marble hand, bearing two dates (1529 and 1685). From the terrace there is a fine view of the Valley of the Temples.

The Hellenistic and Roman district

On the opposite side of the Via dei Templi is the entrance to the enclosure (behind a green fence) with the conspicuous remains of the Hellenistic and Roman district of the city. Here an area of c. 120 square metres has been excavated, exposing four *cardines*, running north and south, with their complex of buildings sloping downwards from east to west in a series of terraces. The district was first developed towards the end of the 2nd century BC and its civic life lasted probably to the 4th or 5th century AD. The drainage system is elaborate, and traces of stairs show that buildings were of more than one storey. Houses, of sandstone blocks, are built around a peristyle, or with an atrium; many of their rooms have good floors (the best, which include the Casa della Gazzella and the Casa del Maestro Astrattista, are covered for protection).

San Biagio and the Rock Sanctuary of Demeter

From Viale Crispi a road to the left crosses a main road and continues to the cemetery. Captain Alexander Hardcastle, who was responsible for excavating the ancient walls here, was buried in this cemetery beside a 'window' in the wall. A gate on the left (signposted) is officially open at the same time as the temples but it is often locked. Beyond it an unsurfaced road (c. 200m) leads (on foot) to the edge of the cliff.

On the hillside above is **San Biagio**. This Norman church was built on the cella of a small temple begun after the victory at Himera in 480, and dedicated to Demeter and Persephone. The pronaos and stylobate of the temple protrude beyond the apse of the church. To the north are two large round altars. The temple was approached by the ancient track with deep wheel ruts, still clearly visible, mounting the side of the hill. On the rock face a marble plaque records Captain Hardcastle's excavations here.

On the edge of the cliff the line of the ancient city walls can clearly be seen running from the Rupe Atenea, above San Biagio, to the Temple of Hera; beyond, the view extends along the temple ridge and to the sea. Just outside the walls and below the cliff edge is the entrance gate to the **Rock Sanctuary of Demeter**, reached by long, steep flights of steps (20th century) built into the rock face which lead down through a delightful garden. Beside two natural caverns in the rock (in which numerous votive busts and statues dating from the 5th–4th centuries BC were found) is a tunnel which carries a terracotta aqueduct from a spring far inside the hill. In front is a complex series of cisterns on different levels and remains of what may have been a monumental fountain. The sanctuary was formerly thought to antedate the foundation of the city by some two centuries, but some scholars now believe it was constructed in the 5th century BC.

Another unsurfaced road (signposted) leads along the wall of the cemetery to (200m) an interesting wedge-shaped bastion built to guard this vulnerable spot where a valley interrupts the natural defence line. To the north is Gate One.

The **Rupe Atenea** (351m), a rocky hill, the highest part of the town, was part of the acropolis of Acragas. It is reached by a road which runs beyond the hospital, but as it is now military property the ruins of a large ancient building found here are inaccessible.

Strada Panoramica

Viale Crispi continues downhill from the Hotel Della Valle, and the Strada Panoramica forks left, passing near Porta Gela (Gate Two) and continues to the Temple of Hera. Just before the roundabout on the high ground to the left is a Roman funerary monument, miscalled the Tomb of Theron, a two-storeyed edifice with a Doric entablature and Ionic corner columns, according to local legend the place where Theron buried his favourite horse, which had won several Olympic competitions. It stands on the edge of a huge Roman cemetery (1st century BC–5th century AD) which extends eastwards below the line of the walls.

Temples of Asclepios and Hephaistos

The Gela road (SS 115) runs east from the roundabout beneath the temple ridge and walls, past a park of 4 hectares which has recently been designated to protect some 300 varieties of almond tree. This Living Museum of the Almond Tree (*no public access*) is run jointly by the province and the university.

The first unsurfaced road on the right (signposted) leads through another almond orchard to a farm beside the little **Temple of Asclepios** on the bank of the San Biagio river (near a medicinal spring). Excavations are in progress here and the site has been enclosed (*usually unlocked on request at the custodian's office, at the entrance to the Temple of Olympian Zeus; see p. 202*). This is a small Doric temple in antis with a pronaos, cella and false opisthodomos. In spite of its size, it shows the advanced techniques of con-

The Temple of Hephaistos and beyond, the medieval and modern city of Agrigento.

struction (including entasis) associated with the (contemporary) Parthenon. The stairway is preserved between the cella and pronaos. This is the temple mentioned by Polybius in his account of the Roman siege of 262, and it once contained the statue of Apollo by Myron (looted by Verres in 72 BC; *see box p. 199*).

In the other direction, the Porto Empedocle road (SS 115) leads (c. 500m) westwards from the roundabout to the bottom of a little valley where, just before a bridge, an unsurfaced road (not signposted) forks right. Follow it as far as the high railway viaduct. Here, steps (signposted) lead up past agave and aloe plants to the **Temple of Hephaistos** (or Vulcan), beyond an orchard of contorted almond trees and beside an old farmhouse. The temple, hexastyle and peripteral, was built c. 430 BC and two columns remain upright. The cella was partly built over a small Archaic temple of the early 6th century. A marble stone beneath the stylobate on the south side records excavations here in 1930 by Alexander Hardcastle. From here the irregular line of walls leading up to the Rupe Atenea is pierced by Gates Six, Seven, Eight and Nine.

Porto Empedocle Vigata and Kaos

Porto Empedocle takes its name from the poet, physician, philosopher and democrat Empedocles (c. 495–430 BC), the most famous native of ancient Acragas. For Empedocles cosmic history was a cyclical process of union and division under the alternating influences of Love and Strife and the four immutable elements. He believed in metempsychosis, and declared that he had been a boy, a girl, a bud and a fish. 'O ye who inhabit the great city of holy Acragas, who harbour worthy strangers, who know not how to do ill, all hail! I move among you an immortal god...' he wrote in his *Fragments*. 'It is not possible to apprehend god with the eyes, nor to grasp him with our hands, which in truth is the truest way to persuade the mind of man; for he has no human head nor body, nor feet, nor legs, nor hair, but he is ineffable mind alone, moving through the cosmos with swift thoughts...'

With a cement works and a declining fishing port, Porto Empedocle is the port for the remote Pelagian Islands: Lampedusa, Linosa and Lampione, which lie nearer to Tunisia than Sicily. In 2003 the town officially also assumed the name Vigata, in honour of Andrea Camilleri, the immensely popular writer of the Inspector Montalbano stories, who names it thus in his books.

On the inner quay, built using stone from the temples of Agrigento between 1749 and 1763, is a massive tower. On the western outskirts a Roman villa, the **Villa Romana di Durrueli**, dating from the 1st century AD, has been excavated. Nearby at Punta Grande is the Scala dei Turchi, remarkable white rocks of limestone and sandy clay which have been eroded by the sea into fantastic shapes.

Just outside Porto Empedocle is **Kaos**, Luigi Pirandello's birthplace, now with a delightful small museum (*open summer 8.30–1 & 2–8; winter 9–1 & 2–7*), with books, manuscripts, paintings and photographs. In his honour, the Taviani brothers made a film called *Kaos* (1984) based on a synthesis of the writer's short stories. Under a wind-blown pine, the ashes of the dramatist and novelist were finally buried according to his wishes, beneath a 'rough rock in the countryside of Girgenti'.

LUIGI PIRANDELLO (1867–1936)

Luigi Pirandello was the son of a sulphur dealer in Girgenti. He became famous as a playwright after the First World War, making his name in 1921 with the first performance of *Sei personaggi in cerca d'autore* (*Six Characters in Search of an Author*), which caused a scandal in Rome. Quickly produced in Milan, Paris, London and Berlin, it was much admired by G.B. Shaw and was followed the next year by the equally successful *Henry IV*, dealing with themes of illusion, insanity and reality. From 1925, with the backing of Mussolini, Pirandello established and directed the Art Theatre. His short three-hander *The Man with a Flower in his Mouth* was the first ever broadcast TV drama, being used by the BBC for test transmission in 1930. Four years later he was awarded the Nobel Prize for literature.

In his writings Pirandello conveys an idea of man suffering from solitude, disillusioned by his ideals. With a strong element of irony he suggests that his characters frequently reveal the necessity of 'wearing a mask', and this has been credited with inspiring the Theatre of the Absurd. Pirandello was a prolific writer (some 40 plays, six novels, many novellas and hundreds of short stories, many of which are still in print), and was widely acclaimed in his lifetime: one of his most famous novels is *Il Fu Mattia Pascal* (*The Late Mattia Pascal*), published in 1904, but it is as a playwright and short-story writer that his genius fully emerged. Much against his own wishes ('When I am dead, do not clothe me. Wrap me naked in a sheet... Burn me.'), the Fascist government gave him a full state funeral.

THE PELAGIAN ISLANDS

The Pelagian Islands (from the Greek *pelagos*, meaning sea) lie about 205km south-west of the Sicilian mainland (and 113km from Tunisia). Hauntingly beautiful, they lie tossed into a sea which varies in hue from pale green through to turquoise and deep cobalt. There are three islands, Lampedusa, Linosa and Lampione, all quite individual and different in character. They fell to the Allies without resistance in June 1943; Lampedusa surrendered to an English airman who landed there by accident, having run out of fuel. All three islands now enjoy protected status as a nature reserve: Lampedusa's is run by Legambiente (27 *Via Vittorio Emanuele, T: 0922 971611, www.legambiente.sicilia.it*); Linosa's and Lampione's by the Azienda Forestale. The collective name of the reserve is Area Marina Protetta Isole Pelagie (*T: 0922 975780, www.isole-pelagie.it*).

LAMPEDUSA

Lampedusa is the largest of the three islands, some 20 square kilometres populated by about 6,000. On the African continental shelf, it is a flat limestone rock, similar to the Tunisian coast behind it, with crystal-clear waters and lovely sandy beaches, especially to the south, while the north coast forms a steep cliff. It is impossibly crowded in July and August with holidaymakers from northern Italy, attracted by the clean sea and the memorable seafood. Italians really do love crowded beaches. The island's popularity means that it can be rather dirty and untidy, and not particularly well kept. Whale-watchers should come in March when the rorqual, or fin whale, passes along the south coast of Lampedusa and mates off the east coast (*for details see www.cetacean-watching.com*).

The Isolotto dei Conigli, just offshore, is protected by Legambiente, because of the loggerhead turtles (*Caretta caretta*) which still lay their eggs on the beach. There is a small museum and library on the turtles at 27 Via Vittorio Emanuele (*T: 0922 971611*).

Lampedusa has important US and Italian military installations; the Libyans made an unsuccessful attack in 1986, and two missiles fell 2.5km short of the island. Lampedusa is notorious today as the preferred landing place for illegal immigrants from North Africa. In April 2002 an unfinished illegal village called Villaggio Sindona, built in the wildlife reserve of Cala Creta, was demolished.

LINOSA & LAMPIONE

Linosa, about 5 square kilometres in extent, 42km north of Lampedusa, is stunningly beautiful, formed of dark volcanoes, with cobalt-blue waters, and tidy little houses painted in bright, contrasting colours. It is quite hilly, and the most fertile of the islands. The people are not all fishermen, most of them were once cattle farmers; but they have been forced to stop this because there is no slaughter-house between here and Agrigento. They have also stopped extracting *pozzolana*, the stone formed by hardened volcanic ash (much in demand on the mainland for building), in order to preserve the landscape. The economy is now based on agriculture and tourism. The bright colours of the houses, with contrasting borders around the doors and windows, were traditionally to help the fishermen recognize their own home when they were far out at sea. The atmosphere is very peaceful on Linosa; just the place for a restful holiday. The small beaches are of black volcanic sand; there are lovely secluded rocky coves. Visitors are not permitted to bring cars to the island, but they are not necessary; the island is so small. You can walk all the way round Linosa in about 3 hours (trekking boots, water, sunhat, sunblock all advised), or hire a motor-scooter or a bike. Sea daffodils cover the eastern slopes of Monte Nero in summer.

It has been suggested that Linosa is the lost Atlantis: offshore to the east there are great rectangular blocks of basalt on the seabed, and what appears to be a primitive divinity carved in stone, now covered with seaweed. The loggerhead turtle also lays her eggs on one of the beaches here (*no access*).

Lampione
Lampione, with an area of just 1.2 square kilometres, is uninhabited; formed of white limestone like Lampedusa, its deep waters are frequented by scuba divers in the summer. Practically inaccessible, it is home to an important colony of Cory's shearwaters.

SCIACCA

Sciacca, thought to be the oldest spa in existence, has been known since Greek times, when it was the *thermae* of Selinunte. It took the name of Sciacca after the Arab domination (9th–11th centuries AD): the town rises in front of a white limestone cliff, that looks rather like an iceberg when seen from the sea, and the name probably derives from the Arabic *as-saqqah*, meaning ice. It has an important and very picturesque fishing harbour, where every day about 5,000 tonnes of fish are disembarked, most of it for processing. The people here build their own boats. Along the tiny streets of the old centre, both men and women clean sardines and anchovies ready for salting. A local ceramics industry flourished here in the 16th and 17th centuries, and there are several artisans' workshops in the town. The colours and the patterns are quite different from those seen elsewhere in Sicily; often the bright floral designs or human figures stand out against a black or dark blue background.

EXPLORING SCIACCA

Porta San Salvatore
The centre of town is still reached by most traffic through the fortified Porta San Salvatore (1581), a fine work in sandstone by local masons. Beside it in Piazza Carmine is the arresting façade of the **Carmine**, with a half-finished Neoclassical

lower part and an asymmetrical 13th-century rose window. The dome, with green tiles, dates from 1807. The church contains a fine *Transition of the Virgin*, the last work of Vincenzo da Pavia, completed by another artist in 1572.

A short way up Via Geradi (left) is the Steripinto, a small fortified palace in the Gothic-Catalan style. It has an interesting façade, with diamond-shaped stone facing, erected in 1501. Opposite the Carmine, on the other side of Via Incisa, is the north portal of the church of **Santa Margherita**, sculpted in 1468 by Francesco Laurana and his workshop. The church was deconsecrated many years ago, and is now used for concerts and exhibitions. The polychrome stuccoes and marble reliefs (1623) by Orazio Ferraro in the chapel of the titular saint are impressive. Beyond is the Gothic portal of the former church of St Gerland and the abandoned Ospedale di Santa Margherita. Opposite are the late-Gothic Palazzo Perollo-Arone and the 15th-century Torre di Pardo.

Corso Vittorio Emanuele

Corso Vittorio Emanuele continues into the central Piazza Angelo Scandaliato, planted with trees. From here there is a view of the pastel-coloured old houses rising in terraces above the fishing harbour. The former Collegio dei Gesuiti (now the town hall), begun in 1613, has a fine courtyard.

The corso continues to the dilapidated Piazza Duomo where the **duomo**, called the Basilica and dedicated to Mary Magdalene, has statues by Antonino and Gian Domenico Gagini on its façade. It was rebuilt in 1656, and the vault fresco was completed in 1829. It has some good sculptures including a statue of the Madonna (1457), a marble altarpiece with reliefs by Antonino Gagini, and (on the high altar) the *Madonna del Soccorso* by Giuliano Mancino and Bartolomeo Berrettaro, two sculptors from Carrara. In Piazza Don Minzoni next to the duomo, there is the **Scaglione Museum** (*may be closed for repairs, T: 0925 83089*), the private collection of paintings, ceramics and *objets d'art*— lovingly displayed—of Francesco Scaglione, a local 19th-century nobleman.

The corso continues to Piazza Friscia, in a pleasanter part of the town, which has pretty 19th-century public gardens with tropical plants Via Agatocle leads past the new theatre to the edge of the cliff. Here, the Nuovo Stabilimento Termale (*open June–October*), a pink spa building in Art Nouveau style (1928–38), offers thermal swimming pools with a temperature of 32°C and mud baths.

The upper town

From Piazza Friscia, Via Valverde leads up to the gardens in front of the church of Santa Maria delle Giummarre (or Valverde), its façade tucked in between two castellated Norman towers; the restored chapel in the left tower has an interesting interior. The elaborate 18th-century Rococo decoration in the main church is remarkable. The vault was frescoed by Mariano Rossi (1768). Also in the upper town is San Nicolò La Latina, a simple 12th-century church. Above is the ruined castle of the Spanish Luna family. Their feud with the Perollo clan in the 15th–16th centuries became notorious under the name of *caso di Sciacca* (the Sciacca affair); it was resolved only after the population of the town had been reduced to almost half its size.

The outskirts

Above Sciacca (signposted) is **Monte Kronio** (or Monte San Calogero; 388m), which has caves (*closed Dec–Mar*) with steam vapours, known since Roman times, and now a little spa. The sanctuary church of San Calogero (1530–1644) has a statue of the saint by Giacomo Gagini. One of the most popular saints in Sicily, he is often invoked against sickness, especially cholera, plague and leprosy. His name means 'good old man' in Greek, so probably many bearded hermits were called Calogero. The saint is supposed to have discovered the vapours' healing properties, provided accommodation here for the sick and possibly lived in the largest of the caves. There is a small museum, Antiquarium Kronio (*T: 0925 28989*), with a collection of vases and fragments found in the grottoes and dating from the Neolithic to the Copper Age.

On the Agrigento road (SS 115) east of Sciacca is the well-signposted **Castello Incantato** ('enchanted castle'; *T: 0925 993044*), a park with olive and almond trees where thousands of heads were sculpted in wood and stone by a local farmer, Filippo Bentivegna (d. 1967). After being hit on the head during a robbery in the USA (where he had emigrated), Bentivegna returned home and carved heads wherever he could find space in his garden. A room is dedicated to his work at the Museum of Art Brut, Lausanne, originally Jean Dubuffet's collection of 'outsider' or pathological art.

ISOLA FERDINANDEA

Twenty-six nautical miles southwest of Sciacca, in July 1831, a volcanic island appeared, rising through the water with fountains of volcanic mud and clouds of ash. It was spotted by HM sloop *Rapid* from Malta under the command of Captain Charles Henry Swinburne, who reported the phenomenon: 'It gradually increased in dimensions, magnificent eruptions of cinders with white vapours rising to the height of from 400 to 1,000 feet, accompanied by a noise like thunder.' By 17th July the island was 9m high, and on 11th August it was 25m with a circumference of nearly 2km. An enterprising captain, Commander Senhouse, passing close by the island with his ship at the beginning of August, surveyed the island, planted the Union Jack and claimed it as British territory, naming it Graham Island after the then First Lord of the Admiralty. Adventurous people started organising boat trips and picnics, one such being the novelist Sir Walter Scott in the year before his death. The claim, however, was contested by the Bourbon king Ferdinand II, who also sent warships to the spot. On 17th August the island was named Isola Ferdinandea and annexed by the Kingdom of the Two Sicilies; but the victory was short-lived. By November the island was seen to be gradually sinking, and it disappeared completely on 8th December. Renamed the Graham Shoal, it remained some seven metres below the surface, until in 2002 it was announced that Isola Ferdinandea was once more on the rise.

INLAND IN THE WEST OF THE PROVINCE

MENFI & ENVIRONS

Northwest of Sciacca is Menfi, a town laid out on a regular plan in 1698, with the houses arranged around courtyards off the main streets, many of which were made uninhabitable by the Belice earthquake in 1968. The beautiful Torre Federiciana, however, has been completely restored—it is the only remaining fragment of a Swabian castle built here by Frederick II in 1238. A new town now rises on the higher ground above.

On the coast, beyond lots of condominiums and holiday villas, is the fishing village of **Porto Palo**. There are still some unspoilt stretches of coast here, adjoining the nature reserve at the mouth of the River Belice, in the province of Trapani (which extends to Marinella and Selinunte); the Menfi beaches have been awarded the European Union Blue Banner for quality.

North of Menfi is **Santa Margherita di Belice**, where the country house described by Lampedusa in *The Leopard* as Donnafugata, Palazzo Filangeri di Cutò, was destroyed together with most of the town in the 1968 earthquake, but has now been completely restored and can be visited by appointment (*T: 0925 940217, donnafugata@parcotomasi.it.*). In the new church of the town the stained glass is the work of Americo Mazzotta from Florence. Santa Margherita is renowned for prickly pears and for *Vastedda* sheep's milk cheese.

A vineyard in the countryside around Menfi.

Montevago, close by, was also completely destroyed; the inhabitants have rebuilt the town close to where it was before, leaving a poignant heap of ruins as a perpetual memory of old Montevago. This was the town with the highest number of victims. Many contemporary artists have donated works of art to Montevago, such as the stone sculpture by Giò Pomodoro of the *Deposed Sun*, and the bronze group by Lorenzo Cascio of the *Embrace*. There is a new spa centre, with a pool into which thermal mineral waters gush constantly at a temperature of 40°C; mud baths are also available.

GIUSEPPE TOMASI DI LAMPEDUSA (1896–1957)

Giuseppe Tomasi di Lampedusa, whose family were princes of Lampedusa and dukes of Palma di Montechiaro, wrote his famous novel *Il Gattopardo* (*The Leopard*, translated into English in 1960) at the end of his life. It was published posthumously in 1958. The book recounts the life of his great-grandfather Giulio Tomasi (1815–85), renamed Don Fabrizio Corbera, Prince of Salina, in the novel, who reacted with instinctive resignation to the turmoil produced by the landing of Garibaldi on the island in 1860. Set over three periods in the course of half a century, Don Fabrizio awaits the fall of his class and the ruin of his family, approving of the desire of his young nephew Tancredi Falconeri to marry the daughter of a newly wealthy rogue, Calogero Sedara. Invited to join the Senate of the new Kingdom of Italy, the prince declines, proposing in his place Calogero. Disenchanted, he waits for death. The novel had enormous success, which was confirmed when it was made into a film by Luca Visconti in 1963, with Burt Lancaster and Claudia Cardinale. The palace of Donnafugata described in the novel is not that of Palma di Montechiaro, but a villa in Santa Margherita Belice, which was destroyed in the earthquake of 1968. Another villa, which was bought by Tomasi di Lampedusa's great-grandfather around 1845 survives on the Piana dei Colli outside Palermo. Also described in the book is the Villa Niscemi, the family home of Tancredi. Tomasi di Lampedusa also wrote a book of short stories *I Racconti*, translated in 1962 as *Two Stories and a Memory*. In Palermo, Palma di Montechiaro, and Santa Margherita, 'Literary Parks' (*T: 091 6160796 www.parcotomasi.it*) have been established in his honour.

Sambuca and Monte Adranone

Northeast of Menfi, Sambuca di Sicilia has an old centre which has the best-preserved Islamic layout (near Piazza Navarro) in Sicily. Known as Sambuca Zabut until 1921, this town escaped the 1968 earthquake unscathed. The economy is based on the production of wine (Planeta), on the banks of nearby Lake Arancio (*see below*).

On entering the town, to the right is the main street, Corso Umberto, which leads up to the old district. On the right is the little opera house, Teatro L' Idea (1850); to the left Via Marconi leads to the church of the Concezione, with a 14th-century portal. Back on the corso, on the left is the church of Santa Caterina, of which the convent is an Antiquarium, housing a well displayed collection of finds from the archaeological area of Monte Adranone (Adranon). In Piazza Vittoria is the Neoclassical church of the Carmine (or Santuario della Madonna dell'Udienza), with 19th-century stuccoes and a much-revered statue of the Madonna attributed to Antonello Gagini. Corso Umberto continues up to Palazzo degli Archi, the town hall, and then Via Belvedere to Piazza Navarro. On the left is a little street leading to the Arab quarter, called Vicoli Saraceni, and the Renaissance-style Palazzo Panitteri. Inside is a collection of 19th-century wax figures, arranged to represent a political meeting. The Chiesa del Collegio and that of the Cappuccini have works by Fra' Felice da Sambuca (1704–1805), who was born here.

The Planeta family runs one of the most successful wineries in Sicily in the village of **Ulmo**, on the shores of Lake Arancio near Sambuca. Here they make their famous oak-aged Chardonnay, a yardstick for Chardonnay growers all over Italy. There is another Planeta winery near Menfi, where only red wine is made.

About 7km north of Sambuca is **Monte Adranone**, site of a Phoenician city refounded by Selinunte in the 6th century BC; excavations have brought to light traces of the walled city and the necropolis, with some impressive stone tombs (*see p. 107*).

Caltabellotta

Northeast of Sciacca, Caltabellotta is a little town in a beautiful and commanding position, on a southeastern slope of its mountain, and visible from vast distances around. Some historians believe this to be ancient *Camico*, the Sican kingdom of Cocalos, who befriended Daedalus, after he came to Sicily from Crete (*see box on p. 221*). Slaves in rebellion against Rome took refuge here from 104–99 BC. The Arabs erected a fortress, which they called *Qal'at al Ballut*, or Fortress of the Oak Trees. Here the peace treaty ending the war of the Sicilian Vespers (*see p. 73*) was signed in 1302. In 1194 the castle sheltered Sibylla of Acerra, widow of King Tancred, her two daughters, and her infant son who reigned for a few months as William III, shortly before they were imprisoned in Germany by the new king of Sicily, Henry VI. The little boy was never seen again; it is said that he was blinded and castrated, and ended his days in a monastery. The same castle inspired Wagner, who imagined it as the dwelling of Klingsor in his *Parsifal*.

The Norman Chiesa Madre has Gagini statues, and an isolated square bell tower to the left, probably once a watch tower, while in the church of San Francesco there is a splendid panel painting of the Madonna. The church of the Salvatore, below the rock face, has a late Gothic portal. From here is the narrow path and steps to the fortress, worth the climb for the marvellous views over much of Sicily.

On the outskirts of town is the old monastery of **San Pellegrino** (17th–18th centuries; now derelict). To the left of the church are two caves, one on top of the other, used by early Christians as churches. Many prehistoric rock-hewn tombs were used as dwellings through the centuries, noticeably near the church of Santa Maria della Pietà, which is itself also partly carved into the rock.

BURGIO & ENVIRONS

Across the valley of the Verdura from Caltabellotta, Burgio is an agricultural town with a local ceramics industry founded in the 16th century, and the only remaining bell foundry of Sicily. The town has developed around the remains of a castle built by the Saracens. In the Chiesa Madre, where the third altar is dedicated to the Madonna of Trapani, among frescoes, stuccoes and marble reliefs, there is a *Madonna* by Vincenzo Gagini, signed and dated 1566, and a 13th-century wooden Crucifix, much revered, and carried in procession every year to the sanctuary, 8km away, of Santa Maria di Rifesi, built in the 12th century by Ansaldo, steward of the royal household of Palermo. The 17th-century **Convento dei Cappuccini** has recently been restored and opened to the public; during the works a painting by Zoppo di Gangi (Giuseppe Salerno) was discovered, complete with the original early 17th-century frame, considerably the worse for wear after being exposed to the elements for several years. A small museum, called *La dimora delle Anime*, the Dwelling-place of the Souls, or more frequently the **Museo delle Mummie** (*call at the town hall or tourist office to request a visit*) has been created to display a small collection of mummies, once carefully preserved by the monks, then allowed to decay after the convent was abandoned, and now refreshed and rearranged. Mummification was once a privilege of the members of the Church and wealthy citizens, and in Sicily the art of preserving bodies was almost exclusively confined to the Capuchins. Mummification was something that people planned and paid for while still in good health, even stipulating the clothes in which they should be dressed on their death. The best examples of preserved bodies can be seen at the Capuchin convent of Palermo, but there are plenty more elsewhere in Sicily, such as at Savoca near Taormina.

Another museum, the **Museo della Ceramica** (*call at town hall or tourist office to request a visit*), dedicated to the production of local pottery through the centuries, has been opened in the former railway station, just west of the town. The attractive pottery, business-like in function (floor and wall tiles, jugs, dishes and pharmacy vases) is decorated with medieval designs. The predominating colours are delicate yellow, green and cobalt blue, on a white background.

Villafranca Sicula and Ribera

A couple of kilometres south of Burgio, Villafranca Sicula, founded in 1499 by the Alliata family from Pisa, was damaged in the Belice earthquake. In 1609 Francesco Alliata was made prince of Villafranca, and given the right of life or death over the population, a privilege which lasted until 1812.

On the road back to the coast south of Burgio is **Ribera**, lying in an agricultural area of olive groves, vineyards, strawberry fields and orange groves. The town was founded in 1627 by Luigi, Prince of Paternò, and named in honour of his Spanish wife, Maria de Ribera. It was the birthplace of Francesco Crispi (*see box overleaf*). The beautiful coastline to the south of the town, which includes Torre Salsa, has interesting flora and fauna, and parts of it are protected.

FRANCESCO CRISPI (1818–1901)

The statesman Francesco Crispi, instrumental in establishing the nation of Italy, with many streets named after him across the country, was born in Ribera. He trained as a lawyer in Naples, and was forced to flee the island after his involvement in the failed uprising of 1848 against the Bourbons, travelling to Piedmont where he was implicated in the Mazzini conspiracy of 1853 in Milan. After seeking refuge in first Malta, and then Paris, he eventually joined Mazzini in London. In 1859 he returned to Sicily in disguise to prepare the ground for the landing of Garibaldi's 'Thousand' in the next year. He was a deputy in the first national parliament and twice prime minister of Italy (from 1887–91 and 1893–96), thanks to the support of the right wing, which many of his colleagues regarded as a betrayal of his radical principles. His authoritarian style established order in the new nation, for example using the army to put down the Sicilian *fasci* movement, which carried out agrarian strikes and largely peaceful demonstrations, part of a deepening economic crisis that resulted in mass emigration from the island to America. The onset of blindness forced Crispi to retire from politics towards the end of the decade. His complex political career is comprehensively treated in Christopher Duggan's *Francesco Crispi, 1818–1901: From Nation to Nationalism* (OUP, 2002).

ERACLEA MINOA & THE COAST

The excavations of Eraclea Minoa are in a magnificent, isolated position on the sandy coast at the mouth of the ancient river *Halykos* (now the Platani). The road off the main coast road follows the lovely meandering river valley as it climbs the hill, passing vineyards. Beyond the turning for the seaside village an unsurfaced road continues for the last 500m. Here part of the town defences can be seen.

Above the dirt road on the left are the foundation of a circular Greek tower and a section of well-preserved wall (ending in a square Roman tower). The continuation of the walls has been lost in landslides. A splendid view extends along the wooded shore, the vanilla-coloured sand, and the white limestone cliffs to Capo Bianco, beyond the river.

The excavations
Open 9–3; until 4 in summer. The main entrance is beside the ruins of Hellenistic houses.
A small antiquarium houses finds from the site, and has informative plans of the area so far excavated. A path leads on through the beautifully kept site where the visible remains (excavations in progress) date mainly from the 4th century BC. The well-preserved theatre was built at the end of the 4th century. The soft sandstone is now pro-

tected by a perspex cover. The site of the city is on the hillside in front of the theatre. Under cover is the so-called governor's house: part of the wall decoration and mosaic floor survives. Also here is a little sacrificial altar (under glass). Outside excavations have revealed three levels of destruction; the level of the Archaic city is at present being uncovered. The second line of the walls (built when the eastern part of the town was abandoned) is visible nearby. A path (or steps) leads up to the top of the hill above the theatre and a paved path leads over the hillside to the line of walls to the northeast, with square towers, built in the 4th century BC.

HISTORY OF ERACLEA MINOA

The name *Eraclea Minoa* suggests that this was originally a Minoan colony; a legend that Minos pursued Daedalus from Crete (after the Athenian inventor had helped Theseus and Ariadne escape from Knossos) and founded a city here was reiterated by Diodorus who records that Theron of Acragas found the bones of Minos close to this spot. The Cretan King is supposed to have been murdered in his bath with boiling oil poured through a pipe in the roof by the daughters of the Sican King Cocalos. A colony was founded here by the inhabitants of Selinunte in the 6th century BC, and the name *Heracleia* was probably added later in the century by Spartan emigrés. The town thrived during the 4th century BC when it was resettled by Timoleon, but it seems to have been uninhabited by the end of the 1st century BC, perhaps because of malaria. The first excavations took place in 1907 (and were resumed in 1950–61).

The coast towards Agrigento

The little town of **Montallegro** was rebuilt in the 18th century below its abandoned predecessor on the hill, where a grotto has produced finds dating from the Early Bronze Age to the Copper Age. The ruins, which look very enticing from a distance, are in fact practically inaccessible, due to a mud slide which has obliterated the path.

Further inland, **Cattolica Eraclea** was founded in 1610, close to the Platani. Originally called Cattolica (*Kata Halykos,* close to the Halykos), it took the second name Eraclea in 1874, by order of Vittorio Emanuele II. The town, with its regular 17th-century street plan, is particularly attractive.

Siculiana, on a low hill between Eraclea Minoa and Agrigento, has a prominent domed church (1750–1813), and is very picturesque. The castle on the top of the hill dates from 1350. A byroad leads down to the pretty coast (with good beaches) beside the Torre di Monterosso where there is also a nature reserve open to the public.

Closer to Agrigento is **Realmonte**, with the only salt mine still functioning in Sicily. It can be visited on request (*open Mon–Fri 7–11; call first to book, T: 0922 816244)*; the patterns formed by the layers of rock look like a gigantic piece of abstract art.

THE PLATANI VALLEY

This part of the province consists of remote countryside, studded with small, sun-baked towns, a landscape defined by the River Platani, the ancient *Halykos*, 84 km long, which formed the boundary between the Greek and Carthaginian territories in Sicily. Sulphur was mined in the hills here up until the mid-19th century (*see box on p. 225*).

ARAGONA & AROUND

Aragona, c. 12km from Agrigento, was founded in 1606. It has an interesting street plan: straight, regular streets delimiting blocks of houses, which reveal a host of tiny alleys and little courtyards, Saracen in style. The tiny central square, Piazza Umberto, is dominated by the 17th-century Palazzo Feudale, now the town hall, and the Baroque façade of the church of the Purgatorio. Close by is the 17th-century Chiesa Madre, which houses a rare 18th-century crib with large wooden statues. Almonds and pistachios are cultivated in the surrounding fields. It is the centre which has suffered the most in this area from depopulation.

Four kilometres southwest of the town are the **Vulcanelli di Macalube**, tiny conical volcanoes, only 0.5–1m high, filled with salty bubbling mud, now part of a nature reserve (*Riserva naturale integrale Macalube di Aragona, c/o Legambiente, 53 Via La Rosa, T: 0922/699210, macalube@oasi.net*). They fascinated Guy de Maupassant when he visited the area in the course of his journey to Malta and Sicily, in the late 19th century: 'If Satan has an abode, it is here, here in this monstrous sickness of nature, amid these pustules which in every respect resemble some loathsome suppuration of the soil, abscesses of the earth which from time to time burst noisily, spewing stones, mud and gas high into the air...'

Due east of Aragona, on the other side of the main highway, is the village of **Comitini**, in a panoramic position on a hill. There are numerous sulphur mines around the town, and in the centre is a museum, Palazzo Bellacera, on the subject— Museo della Storia delle Solfare (*open 8.30–1.30 & 3–8; closed Sun and holidays*).

West of Aragona

Raffadali has a Roman sarcophagus depicting the *Rape of Proserpine* in bas-relief, in the 16th-century Chiesa Madre. The myth of Persephone, with its themes of rebirth and resurrection, was a popular burial motif in the Classical world; worshippers, especially participants in the Ancient Greek cult of the Mysteries of Eleusis, believed that the goddess would bring them renewal in the afterlife (*see box on p. 281*). A prehistoric necropolis on the hill of **Busone** has yielded finds including a number of statuettes of a female divinity made from pebbles, now in the Archaeological Museum of Agrigento. **Joppolo Giancaxio**, to the south of Raffadali, is a pretty village in a fine position with an 18th-century castle and church.

A *vulcanello* in the Macalube reserve near Aragona.

North of Raffadali is **Sant'Angelo Muxaro**, in the heart of the Platani valley, surrounded by rugged farming country, possibly the site of the ancient *Kamikos*. Prehistoric tombs pepper the hillside. Those near the foot of the road which mounts to the village date from the 11th–9th centuries BC; the higher domed tombs were used in the 8th–5th centuries BC. These tombs have revealed interesting finds, some of which are in the Museo Archeologico at Agrigento (a gold dish, with a pattern of animals in relief, is at the British Museum in London). At the foot of the mountain is an interesting cave, Grotta dei Ciavoli, extending for over 1200m, and a flourishing population of bats; it is protected as a nature reserve.(*For information on access, ask Legambiente, 2 Via Messina; T: 0922 919669, grottaciavoli@virgilio.it*).

Across the River Platani is **San Biagio Platani**, with white stone houses glittering in the sun; its Easter festivities (*see p. 237*) are unique in the Mediterranean.

THE NORTH OF THE PROVINCE

Casteltermini

To the east, above the narrow Platani Valley with its odd-looking sulphurous hills, is Casteltermini, once a sulphur-mining town, which has an interesting festival on the last Sunday in May known as the *Tataratà*. The name refers to the sound of the drums which accompany the colourful processions. The celebrations commemorate the miraculous discovery of an ancient Crucifix in the 17th century: a cow kept on kneeling down in a particular spot, in spite of her owner's attempts to move her; out of curiosity, he dug a hole in the ground where she sat and revealed the Crucifix. The Cross, carbon-dated to the 1st century AD, is made of wood, about 3.5m high and just over 2m wide. It is thought to be the oldest in the world and is kept in a little church 3km from the village, which is where the processions go on the Friday and the Sunday of the last week in May. The participants wear magnificent costumes, and even the horses are richly arrayed. The last procession, on Sunday evening, is a frenetic dance of hordes of 'Moors', accompanied by the drums. It is said that the Muslims in this area were miraculously converted when the Cross was discovered.

Cammarata

Cammarata is a little medieval town on the northeastern slopes of **Monte Cammarata** (1578m), the highest peak of the Sicani Mountains. The town is surmounted by the ruins of its 13th-century castle. Many of the streets are very steep, and some of them are steps, which makes the religious processions particularly exciting to watch. There are several ancient churches housing precious works of art.

The town is surrounded by the Sicani Mountains and their extensive forests, which abound with indigenous flora and fauna, and are protected in this area as a regional nature reserve (*Riserva Naturale di Monte Cammarata*), run by the Azienda Forestale Regionale di Sicilia.

SULPHUR MINING

The sulphur mines in central Sicily (some 5,000 square kilometres, in the provinces of Agrigento, Enna and Caltanissetta), which were worked throughout the 19th century, gave Italy a world monopoly of the mineral by 1900. Among its many uses are in the manufacture of sulphuric acid, electrical insulators, and match heads, and in the vulcanisation of rubber. Some 16,000 miners were employed by 1860, and of the 700 or so mines in operation, steam engines were used in only four, and horses in only ten; the formation of the seams of mineral allowed for nothing else. In most mines sulphur was extracted manually from an average depth of 60m, and many of the workers, known as *carusi*, were children under 14. Working conditions were shocking: little children were used because they were small enough to crawl through the galleries; many of them only saw the light of day once a week. By the end of the century American sulphur was dominating the market, being much cheaper (a more economical method of refining, using steam, had been discovered, but the system was impossible to use in the Sicilian mines). The consequent collapse of this part of the economy is one of the reasons for the mass emigration at the end of the 19th century, from Sicily to Australia, Venezuela, Canada and the USA. It was not until 1934 that legislation was introduced forbidding employers to use women or boys under 16 as miners. The destiny of these people influenced many native writers, including Pirandello and Sciascia. The last mines in the province of Agrigento were closed down in 1988 (some of them may yet become museums), while those in the province of Caltanissetta were abandoned in the 1970s. You can see models of the mines in the Museum of Mineralogy in Caltanissetta (*see p. 241*). It may have been tough work, but the miners earned more than the peasants. The girls used to sing: '*cu surfuraru m'haju a fari zita, ca iddu lu sciallu mi lu fa di sita*', 'I must choose a sulphur-miner for a fiancé, because he will buy me a silken shawl.'

Santo Stefano Quisquina and Bivona

Santo Stefano Quisquina is a sleepy town in a panoramic position, where the Chiesa Madre has a lovely altarpiece of the *Resurrection of Lazarus* by the Carracci school. Four and half kilometres east of the town, a track leads from the Cammarata road for c. 2km to an oak wood, where the 17th-century **Santuario di Santa Rosalia** (986m) is situated. Decorated with modern frescoes, it has a cave where St Rosalia is said to have lived before she went to Mt Pellegrino near Palermo.

Bivona, where renowned peaches are cultivated, also has a number of fine churches, though most of them are in bad repair. The schoolchildren of the village have recently got involved in an initiative to save at least the beautiful portals of the churches of Carmelo, Santa Rosalia, San Paolo, San Sebastiano, Santa Maria di Loreto and the Immacolata Concezione.

THE EASTERN PROVINCE

LICATA

A plain surrounds Licata, a seaside town that was once a busy port, first for the shipping of wheat, and later for Sicilian sulphur, but became isolated after that industry collapsed, cut off as it is from world trade routes. Frederick of Hohenstaufen pronounced it *dilettissima* in 1234, and gave it the imperial eagle as coat of arms. It occupies the site of *Phintias*, the Greek city founded by the eponymous tyrant from Gela, and is situated between the sea and a low hill, with the Bourbon **Castel Sant'Angelo** (*open Mon–Sat 9.30–1.30 & 4–7; Sun 9–12.30*) of 1640 on the top, and the mouth of the River Salso (*see box opposite*) to the east; the new section of town is on the far side of the river. *Phintias* was a prosperous town with a series of wells, water-cisterns and aqueducts; among these, the Pozzo della Grangela well can still be seen, a short distance from the town hall.

In the central **Piazza Progresso**, where the main streets of the town converge, is the Art Nouveau-style town hall, Palazzo del Municipio (1935, Ernesto Basile), with a small collection of antique reliefs, a gorgeous early 17th-century triptych, the *Madonna with Saints*, and a white marble *Madonna*, known as the *Madonna della Mazza*, by Domenico Gagini (1470). The Art Nouveau opera house, Teatro Comunale Re Grillo (19th century) has recently been restored. Corso Roma leads north, passing (left) two palaces: Palazzo Canarelli, which is decorated with grotesque heads, and Palazzo Urso-Ciarcià. To the right is the church of **San Domenico**, which has two paintings by Filippo Paladini (*see p. 253*); one is the splendid *St Anthony Abbot and Stories of his Life*, a masterpiece of *trompe l'oeil*. The kindly saint, dressed in freshly pressed robes, appears to be stepping out from his niche, which is surrounded by little 'theatre settings', each one with a different episode to narrate. The other painting by Paladini shows the *Holy Trinity with Saints* (1611). A little further along the street is the convent and church of the **Carmine**, designed by Giovanni Biagio Amico in 1748 on 13th-century foundations, which houses ten beautifully modelled medallions, with stories of the Old and New Testaments. The 16th-century cloister is interesting, with a double-lancet window and Gothic portal.

Going towards the sea, Corso Vittorio Emanuele passes Palazzo Navarra and the church of the Purgatorio to the 16th-century church of **San Francesco**; its fine convent (now a school) was reconstructed in the 17th century and the marble façade added in 1750 by Giovanni Biagio Amico, the theologian and self-taught architect from Trapani. It is also possible to see the peaceful cloister. In the single-nave interior are a handsome 18th-century organ, elaborately carved wooden choir-stalls, and some interesting old tombs.

Behind the church is the favourite meeting-place of the people of Licata, **Piazza Sant'Angelo**, surrounded by imposing 18th-century buildings. The 17th-century church of Sant'Angelo has an unfinished façade and elegant cupola attributed to Angelo Italia. Inside, the 17th-century silver urn contains the bones of St Angelo, the patron saint of Licata, who was martyred in 1225. The 16th-century Cistercian abbey (entrance from Via Dante) houses in the cloister the important **Museo Archeologico della Badia** (*open Mon–Sat 9–1; closed Sun and holidays*), which contains local archaeological material from the prehistoric and Greek periods, including Hellenistic votive statuettes, ceramics and red-figure vases from a necropolis of the 5th century BC, also a beautiful 5th-century BC statue of a female divinity, probably Hera, in Greek marble; and a curious boat-shaped oil lamp.

The corso ends at the 15th-century Chiesa Madre, or Santa Maria La Nuova. The interior, a central nave and two side aisles, has glowing 19th-century frescoes on the vault. An elaborately decorated chapel in the south transept, with a magnificent coffered ceiling, has an unusual wooden Crucifix with a black Christ, which narrowly escaped destruction at the hands of the raiding Turks in 1553. On 11th July, the notorious Anatolian corsair Dragut and a handful of pirates overpowered the garrison, crucified the chatelaine, and enslaved his two young sons and 600 citizens but failed in their attempts to burn the Crucifix, which would not catch fire. The side aisles are adorned with several canvases by the Capuchin Fra' Felice da Sambuca (1734–1805). Born Gioacchino Viscosi in Sambuca, he took orders in 1755 and trained initially in Sciacca at the school of Francesco Avervi before working with Olivio Sozzi in Palermo and also with Vito D'Anna. His deeply devotional works adorn many of the Capuchin convents in Sicily. On the main altar is a 17th-century Flemish panel painting of the *Nativity of the Virgin*.

From Piazza Progresso, by taking Via Santa Maria up the hill, you reach the old church of **Santa Maria La Vetere**, probably built in 580 by Benedictine monks together with their abbey. In the 16th century, it passed to Franciscan friars.

THE RIVER HIMERA

There are several Salso rivers in Sicily, so called because of their slightly salty waters. The one known as Himera enters the sea just east of Licata and is the second longest river on the island (112km). It springs from Bafurco in the Madonie Mountains, meets up with the River Gangi, and then joins the Imera Meridionale at Ponte Cinque Archi. It passes through the sulphur-rich interior, flowing north–south, neatly dividing Sicily into two parts. It once separated Sicans from Sicels, while for the Normans it was the dividing line between the diocese of Syracuse and that of Agrigento. It forms deep gorges as it winds its way towards the plain of Licata and the sea. Subject to frequent, abundant floods, the river was only provided with a bridge to replace the ferry in the mid-20th century. Off the mouth of the river in 256 BC, Attilius Regulus defeated the Carthaginian fleet, but in 249 a convoy of Roman merchant ships for Africa was driven ashore by the Carthaginians during a tempest (the wrecks are still being located from time to time).

INLAND OF LICATA

Palma di Montechiaro, Campobello and Naro

On the edge of remote countryside west of Licata, planted with almond trees, olives and vineyards, is Palma di Montechiaro, founded in 1637 by the prince of Lampedusa, ancestor of novelist Giuseppe Tomasi di Lampedusa (*see p. 217*). The town is surrounded by hundreds of half-constructed houses (now abandoned concrete shells), begun in 1960s by emigrants, some of whom are are returning, because the wine, table grapes, almonds, cherry tomatoes, and especially cantaloupe melons of the area have achieved fame on the international market. The conspicuous 17th-century Chiesa Madre, by the Jesuit architect Angelo Italia, is a fine building with twin bell-towers, approached by a long flight of steps. The *Living Nativity* tableau takes place here at Christmas. The 17th-century Palazzo Lampedusa, now owned by the town council, has been partially restored and is sometimes open in summer at weekends. The famous pastries known as *mandorlati del Gattopardo*, a favourite with Tomasi di Lampedusa, are still made by the Benedictine nuns in the Santissimo Rosario Convent.

Campobello di Licata was founded in 1681. In the Parco delle Pietre Dipinte (Park of the Painted Stones), a series of 110 blocks of local stone have been polished and painted by a local artist, Silvio Benedetto, with scenes from the *Divine Comedy*, creating an unusual open-air museum.

The town of **Naro**, which bases its economy on the production of table grapes, stands on a hilltop, once defended by battlemented walls (1263). It has an assortment of old churches, ranging from the ruined Norman Duomo to early 17th-century churches, and a Chiaramonte castle (13th–14th centuries). The simple restaurants are well worth a lunch break, while the coffee bars serve exquisite almond biscuits. In the main street, Corso Vittorio Emanuele, near the church of San Francesco, is the 15th-century Palazzo Giacchetto-Malfitano, which houses the Museo della Grafica (*open Mon–Fri 9–1; entrance from 54 Via Piave*), opened in 2000 with a display of some 250 works by artists ranging from Goya through to the Expressionism of Renato Guttuso. The displays are based on a gift of works by the artist Bruno Caruso, born in Palermo in 1927, widely travelled, acquainted with many great artists of the 20th century and a vociferous supporter of the local farmers' struggle for land rights.

Racalmuto, Canicattì and Favara

The little town of Racalmuto, named from the Arabic *rahal-maut*, village in ruins, surrounded by barren, hilly countryside, is imbued with the spirit of Leonardo Sciascia, now considered one of Italy's most important writers (*see box opposite*). The quiet streets present a typically Arabian pattern, with blocks of houses facing onto narrow alleys, where people pass much of their time, in the open air, with stepped streets, and the occasional tall palm tree. At the top of the hill is the main square, Piazza Umberto, with the 17th-century Chiesa Madre, or Annunziata. The interior is decorated with stuccoes, and there are five paintings by the local artist Pietro d'Asaro, who achieved excellence in spite of the fact that he was blind in one eye. Also facing onto the square are the 17th-century church of San Giuseppe, and the 13th-century Castello Chiaramontano (*open 9–1 & 3–6*), with two large cylindrical towers. It is now the seat of the Sciascia Foundation, although his books and papers are in the specially re-designed old Electricity Board at no. 3 Viale della Vittoria.

Steep steps lead up from the left of the Chiesa Madre to the former monastery of Santa Chiara, now the town hall; close by in Via Sciascia is the beautiful little 19th-century opera house (a miniature version of the one in Palermo), Teatro Regina Margherita (*www.teatroracalmuto.com*). The stairs end at the sanctuary church of Santa Maria del Monte (1738), with a Gaginesque statue of the Virgin on the main altar; an important feast takes place here in July, attracting pilgrims from many nearby towns.

Canicattì is a market town of some importance and a railway junction. It is sur-rounded by vineyards, pergolas of a table grape called *Italia*, which can be marketed during the winter months thanks to the technique of covering the vines with thick plastic in August, when the grapes are just beginning to ripen. This blocks the ripen-ing process indefinitely. When the farmer wants to sell his grapes, he takes off the plastic three or four days before picking. When covered with the plastic sheeting, the vineyards look like an endless silver sea. Peaches, nectarines and plums are also grown in this area.

There is a recently restored castle of the Chiaramonte family (1275; enlarged in 1488) in **Favara**, not far from Agrigento on the old SS 122 from Canicattì. The town is dominated by the 18th-century church of the Rosario, with a beautiful blue-tiled dome. The pastry shops prepare famous marzipan lambs at Eastertide.

LEONARDO SCIASCIA (1921–89)

Sciascia, one of the best-known Italian novelists of the last century, was born in remote Racalmuto, and lived there for most of his life. He is commemorated by a life-size bronze statue (1997), on the pavement in the main street near the Chiesa Madre, by a local artist (the cigarette, which never left his fingers when he was alive, is repeatedly replaced by a fan). His simple white marble tomb, surrounded by jasmine, is in the little cemetery nearby. His best novels, includ-ing *Il giorno della civetta* (*The Day of the Owl*, 1961), *A ciascuno il suo* (*To Each His Own*, 1966), *Il Consiglio d'Egitto* (*The Council of Egypt*) and *Todo modo* (1974) (*One Way or Another*, both 1974), written in a particularly simple and direct style, are detective mysteries with a distinctive Sicilian flavour. In a number of essays and articles he also wrote about the problems which afflict the island, and exposed political corruption and the insidious power of the Mafia long before these two evils of Italian society were widely recognized. Sciascia was very reserved and often pessimistic, but had a high standing in Italy in the 1970s as an intellectu-al figurehead. His 'Literary Park' (*www.regalpetra.it*) is in Racalmuto.

PRACTICAL INFORMATION

• **By train:** From Agrigento (railway station T: 0922 25055) there are services to and from Palermo, Syracuse, Catania and Caltanissetta, as well as some through trains to Rome and Milan. Cammarata, Casteltermini and Aragona are on the Agrigento–Palermo line but services are infrequent. In the eastern part of the province the nearest station for Racalmuto is Aragona (14km); Canicattì is a railway junction, from which Campobello and Licata can be reached. Sciacca can be reached from Palermo.

• **By bus:** In Agrigento small buses run by TUA (T: 0922 412024) cross the upper town along Via Atenea. Nos 1, 2 and 3 run from Piazza Marconi to the Valle dei Templi (request stops at the museum and, lower down, for the temples at the Posto di Ristoro). Buses from Piazza Marconi: bus no. 1 to Kaos (Pirandello's house) and Porto Empedocle. Bus no. 2 to San Leone on the coast.
Inter-city buses: Tickets and information for all lines are available from Omnia, Piazza Fratelli Rosselli, Agrigento, T: 0922 596490.
SAIS (T: 0922 595933), Cuffaro and Lumia (T: 0922 20414, www.autolinee-lumia.it) have frequent services from Agrigento for Sciacca, Licata and Caltanissetta. Autolinee Licata (T: 0922 401360, www.autolineesal.it) runs services for Porto Empedocle, Racalmuto and Palma di Montechiaro.
Buses from Sciacca run by SAIS and Cuffaro sometimes stop at Porto

Empedocle. Autolinee Licata (T: 0922 401360, www.autolineesal.it) run three buses a day connecting Porto Empedocle (and Agrigento) and Palermo Punta Raisi Airport with ferries to Lampedusa.
There are frequent services to Sciacca from Agrigento and Palermo. There is no direct public transport to Eraclea Minoa, but Lumia (Agrigento office, T: 0922 20414) runs a service from Agrigento (Piazzale Fratelli Rosselli) for Cattolica Eraclea, and from there (June–Sept only), Cacciatore (T: 0922 39016) runs buses the rest of the way, about a 15 min. bus ride.
The towns of the northern province are connected to Agrigento by Panepinto, T: 0922 901998, www.panepintobus.it, and Lattuca, T: 0922 36125, www.autolineelattuca.it
Sicilbus (T: 091 346376) runs services from Palermo to Aragona; Cuffaro (T: 091/6161510) has services from Palermo to Racalmuto; ATA (T: 0922 401360) to Licata; and SAIS (T: 0935 524111) from Catania to Canicattì.

• **By air:** To the Pelagian Islands, direct daily flights to Lampedusa from Palermo and Catania run by Meridiana.

• **By sea:** To the Pelagian Islands, car ferries from Porto Empedocle to Linosa (6 hrs) and Lampedusa (8 hrs) run by Siremar (T: 0922 636683, www.siremar.it) every day except Fri in winter; visitors are not allowed to bring cars to Lampedusa in July and August, and never to Linosa. Hydrofoils from Porto Empedocle are run by Ustica Lines twice daily (T: 0923 22200, www.usticalines.it) to Linosa (4 hrs) continuing on to Lampedusa (5 hrs). Ferry and hydrofoil ticket offices: Lampedusa: Siremar, Lungomare Rizzo, T: 0922 970003; Ustica Lines, c/o Strazzera, Lungomare Rizzo, T: 0922 970003. Linosa: Siremar and Ustica Lines, c/o Cavallaro, 46 Via Re Umberto, T: 0922 972062. www.bookingitalia.it. Inter-island transport: hydrofoil connections twice a day between Lampedusa and Linosa in summer, once a day the rest of the year, run by Ustica Lines.

It is risky to leave cars parked unattended in the port area when visiting the islands. Alfonso Stagno (T: 0922 636029) has two garages near the port and will take care of your car: call him a few days beforehand to secure a place.

INFORMATION OFFICES

Agrigento APT Agrigento: 225 Viale della Vittoria, T: 0922 401352, www.apt.agrigento.it, www.agrigento-sicilia.it, www.valleyofthetemples.com Tourist Information Bureau, Piazzale Aldo Moro, T: 0922 20454.
For information on the whole province: Azienda Autonoma Turismo, 73 Via Empedocle, T: 0922 20391; Parco Archeologico della Valle dei Templi: T: 0922 26436, www.regionesicilia.it
For helpful and detailed information on Agrigento and the rest of Sicily, consult www.siciliainfo.it
Burgio c/o Municipio, T: 0925 65011, www.comune.burgio.ag.it; Pro Loco Terra di Burgio: 135 Corso Vittorio Veneto, T: 0925 64239.
Caltabellotta c/o Municipio, 1 Piazza Umberto, T: 0925 951104, www.comune.caltabellotta.ag.it

Lampedusa Pro Loco: 3 Via Anfossi, T: 0922 971390; www.isoladilampedusa.com, www.lampedusa.it. Sogni nel Blu: Via Bonfiglio, T: 0922 973566, www.sogninelblu.it. The agency can assist in finding accommodation and organise car, scooter or boat rental.
Licata Corso Campobello, T: 0922 891173; Municipio, Piazza Progresso, T: 0922 868111.
Linosa www.linosa.info, www.isolalinosa.com and www.linosa.too.it provide a wealth of information on the island.
Menfi Torre Federiciana, Piazza Vittorio Emanuele, T: 0925 70202, www.comune.menfi.ag.it, www.unionedeicomuniterresicane.it
Sambuca di Sicilia c/o Municipio, 226 Corso Umberto, T: 0925 940111, www.agrigento-sicilia.it/sambuca_di_sicilia
Santa Margherita di Belice Piazza Matteotti, T: 0925 30234, www.agrigento-sicilia.it/santa_margherita_di_belice
Sciacca 94 Corso Vittorio Emanuele, T: 0925 20111, www.comune.sciacca.ag.it, www.termedisciacca.it (not only information on spas); Azienda Autonoma: 84 Corso Vittorio Emanuele, T: 0925 21182, www.aziendaturismosciacca.it; The towns along the **River Platani**, among the Sican Mountains, have formed an association: **Terre di Halykos**, San Biagio Platani, T: 0922 918911, www.terredihalykos.it

BOAT TRIPS

Linosa
Stefano Errera (T: 0922 972106) and Piero Bonadonna (T: 0922 972077) will

take you out in their boats.

Porto Empedocle
Empedocle Mar Service, T: 333
1660864, for excursions along the coast
on the Mirtillo motor boat; charter possible for Lampedusa, Linosa or Malta.

DIVING CENTRES & BOAT CHARTER

Lampedusa
Forza Dieci Diving Center, T: 0922
975462.
Lo Verde Diving, 118 Via Roma, T: 0922
971986, also rents boats;
Linosa
Linosa Diving Center, T: 0922 972061.
Marenostrum, T: 0922 972042,
www.marenostrumdiving.it
Sciacca
Nautica Gerardi, ,T: 0925 22002 Porto
di Ponente, next to the Capitaneria del
Porto (Port Authority). Fishing boats or
sailing boats available.

HOTELS

Agrigento
€€€ **Baglio della Luna**. A small converted castle, just outside Agrigento,with
comfortable rooms, a very good restaurant, and a view. Contrada Maddalusa, T:
0922 511061, www.bagliodellaluna.com
€€€ **Domus Aurea**. Enchanting house,
on the outskirts, built in 1781, with
beautiful Mediterranean garden provided
with hydro-massage tub; the old-fashioned red-plush sitting room is irresistible. Contrada Maddalusa, SS 640 km
4.150, T: 0922 511500,
www.hoteldomusaurea.it
€€ **Akrabello**. One of the Hollywood-
style hotels built here in the 1970s;
friendly staff and nice pool. Villagio

Mosé, Contrada Angeli, T: 0922 606277,
www.akrabello.com
€€ **Colleverde**. Comfortable, straight-
foward hotel close to the town and within walking distance of the temples.
Beautiful garden and very good restaurant. Passeggiata Archeologica, T: 0922
29555, www.colleverdehotel.it
€€ **Grand Hotel dei Templi**. A long
tradition for hospitality. Garden with
pool. Villagio Mosé, Via Leonardo
Sciascia, Contrada Angeli, T: 0922
606144, www.grandhoteldeitempli.com
€€ **Villa Athena**. Once the finest hotel
in Agrigento, it is shabby now but people still come for the position, right in
front of the Temple of Concord, and
there is a garden and pool. Località
Templi, T: 0922 596288,
www.athenahotels.com
€ **Belvedere**. Charming little hotel with
garden and tennis court, no restaurant,
close to the old city centre. 20 Via San
Vito, T: 0922 20051.
Cammarata
€ **Falco Azzurro**. 66 Via Venezia, T:
0922/900784, and
€ **Rio Platani**. Via Scalo Ferroviario, T:
0922 909051, are two basic inns, both
with excellent restaurants.
Comitini
€ **U' Cavalleggeri**. A charming hotel in
the main square, over their excellent
restaurant. 22 Piazza Umberto, T: 0922
600062.
Lampedusa
Accommodation on the Pelagian Islands
is considerably more expensive than in
similar establishments on the mainland.
The hotels usually demand a minimum
stay of three nights or a week; many
close in winter.
€€€ **Cupola Bianca**. The rooms are in

dammusi (stone cottages); peaceful position with a lovely garden and palm trees; open-air dining, tennis, run by the same people as Hotel Medusa. Contrada Madonna, T: 0922 971274. www.hotelcupolabianca.it

€€€ **Medusa**. Elegant hotel on Guitgia Bay, good central position, all rooms with sea view, tennis, private catamaran for excursions to Lampione and Linosa. Open year round. Via Rialto Medusa, T: 0922 970126. www.lampedusahotelmedusa.com

€€€ **Paladini di Francia**. Very comfortable, well situated, this hotel has two-room apartments sleeping four with cooking facilities, ideal for families, also four little restaurants, each with its own particular style. Via Alessandro Volta, T: 0922 970550. www.paladinidifrancia.it

€€ **Il Gattopardo**. A quiet house on the cliff, rooms in *dammusi*, boat excursions are organized, no children, no TV. Open June–Sept. 6 Via Beta, T: 0922 970051.

€€ **Martello**. One of the oldest hotels on the island, completely refurbished, very good restaurant, good value for money. Open mid Mar–mid Nov. 1 Salita Medusa, T: 0922 970025, www.hotelmartello.it

€€ **La Perla**. Close to the port, good restaurant, reasonable value for money for the island. 1–3 Lungomare Luigi Rizzo, T: 0922 971932, www.laperlahotel.net

€€ **U' Piddu Club**. Charming little hotel in a quiet street, with lovely terrace and patio; good restaurant, private motor boat for excursions with lunch on board. Open June–Sept. 10 Via Madonna, T: 0922 970901.

Linosa

€ **Linoikos**. This little hotel is also a cultural centre and organizes art shows. Via Alfieri, T: 0922 401810, www.sanlore.it

Porto Palo di Menfi

€€ **Da Vittorio**. Simple rooms on the lovely unspoilt beach of Porto Palo, very quiet. Incredible restaurant, one of the best in Sicily, if you like fish. Closed Nov–Feb. 9 Via Friuli-Venezia Giulia, T: 0925 78381, www.futuralink.it/vittorio

Sciacca

€€ **Grande Albergo delle Terme**. Rather gaunt 1950s building next to the spa, good restaurant. Via delle Nuove Terme, T: 0925 23133, www.grandhoteldelleterme.com

€€ **Villa Palocla**. Country villa built in 1750, panoramic position over the city; excellent restaurant, pool. Contrada Raganella, T: 0925 902812, www.villapalocla.it

BED & BREAKFAST

Agrigento

€€ **Camere con vista**. Comfortable rooms and lovely bathrooms, this is really an exclusive little hotel. English French German spoken. Views over the temples. 4 Via Porta Aurea, Contrada Bennici (nr hospital), T: 0922 554605, www.cameraconvista.net

€ **Corte dei Greci**. In the medieval city near the cathedral. Cortile Leopardo, T: 0922 21329, www.cortedeigreci.it

€ **Villa Goethe**. The villa where Goethe stayed in 1787. 7 Via Celauro, T: 0922 23190, www.villagoethe.it

Caltabellotta

€ **Badia**, 16 Via Colonnello Vita, T: 0925/951121. A beautiful convent in the old centre of the little town with a lovely garden, run by nuns who use the proceeds to help young people. Stunning views; comfortable rooms, each with private bath. The nuns organize excursions from time to time.

Montallegro
€ Capitolo 1. A welcoming family home in a strategically situated village, good cooking.1 Via Trieste, T: 0922 8451771 capitolo1@hotmail.it;

Sciacca
€ Al Moro. A 13th-century house, with patio, internet, excursions organized. 44 Via Liguori, T: 0925 86756, www.almoro.com

FARMHOUSE ACCOMMODATION

Agrigento
€ Fattoria Mosè. Between the Valley of the Temples (about 2km from the Temple of Juno), and the sea at San Leone, the farm produces almonds, oranges, wheat and olive oil. 4 Via Pascal, villaggio Mosè, T: 0922/606115, www.fattoriamose.com

Cammarata
€€ Casalicchio. The farm has belonged to the same family since 1816. Comfortable rooms or self-catering apartments, pool, lake, tennis, sauna, good restaurant, vegetarian food on request.Contrada Casalicchio, T: 0922 908144, www.casalicchio.info

Campobello di Licata
€€ Baglio Lauria. This beautiful farm was once a Franciscan hermitage; now the land is cultivated with vineyards, olive groves and almond orchards; self-catering accommodation, or you can eat the delicious food prepared by the family; pool. SP 63, Contrada Crocifisso Ciccobriglio, T: 0922 419749, www.bagliolauria.it.

Menfi

€€ Tenuta Baglio San Vincenzo. The farm produces olive oil and the prize-winning *Lanzara* wines; conveniently situated for Selinunte. Contrada San Vincenzo, T: 0925 75065, www.bagliosanvincenzo.net

Sambuca
€ Lago Arancio Vacanze. Rooms and apartments in a lovely farmhouse overlooking Lake Arancio; great for bird-watching. Contrada Arancio, T: 0925 941371, lagoaranciovacanze@tiscali.it

RESTAURANTS

Agrigento
€€€ Il Dehors—Hotel Baglio della Luna restaurant. Very high standard in beautiful surroundings, recently voted one of the four best restaurants in Sicily. Lunch on the terrace overlooking the valley is a delight. Contrada Maddalusa, T: 0922 511061.
€€€ Kokalos. In the countryside near the town. Excellent antipasti and *cavatelli*, local home-made pasta, and pizza in the evenings. 3 Via Cavalieri Magazzini, T: 0922 606427.
€€ La Trizzera. Good grilled fish or mussel soup, inexpensive set menu. Pizzas in the evening. Closed Mon. Via delle Fosse Ardeatine, Contrada Kaos, near Pirandello's house, T; 0922 597427.
€€ Ruga Reali. For a subtle mix of country cooking and marine cuisine, local wines. Open evenings only, Closed Sun. 8 Cortile Scribani, Piazza Pirandello, T: 0922 20370.
€€ Trattoria dei Templi. Good pasta, fish, local wines; choose *spumone all'arancia* for dessert. 15 Via Panoramica Dei Templi, T: 0922 403110.

Canicattì

€€ Di Franco Vincenzo. Friendly restaurant, famous around these parts for its delicious home-made pasta, often served with shrimps. 172 Viale della Vittoria, T: 0922 853546.

Castrofilippo

€ Osteria del Cacciatore. A country inn serving the local pasta, *cavati*, and delicious thick vegetable soups in winter; grilled meat; fruit pizza for dessert. Contrada Torre, SS 122 Agrigento-Caltanissetta, T: 0922 829824.

Lampedusa

On the Pelagian Islands eating out is expensive; a popular dish served by many of them is *siluri di Gheddafi* (Gheddafi's missiles), a filling version of stuffed squid. Dishes are often spicy and cous cous is frequently on the menu. Most restaurants are closed in winter.

€€€ Gemelli. For the best cous cous, also bouillabaisse and paella; irresistible desserts. Closed winter. 2 Via Cala Pisana, T: 0922 970699.

€€ Il Polpo Escondido. Try the lasagne made with fish instead of meat, or grilled prawns. The restaurant is also a wine bar. 2 Via Stazzone, Porto Vecchio, T: 0922 973574.

€€ Trattoria Pugliese. A cosy and quiet trattoria. The chef is from Apulia; this guarantees excellent pasta dishes. Open evenings only in summer. 17 Via Cala Francese, T: 0922 970531.

Licata

€€€ La Madia. Excellent fish, well prepared to original recipes and beautifully served, accompanied by their own home-made bread and served with Sicilian wines; central position—a meal here is certainly worth the trip to Licata. Closed Sun evening, all day Tues. 22

Corso Capriata, T: 0922 771443.

€€ Logico. Family-run seafront restaurant, using ancient recipes for preparing fish. Via Salvo D'Acquisto, T: 0922 773002.

€ Il Gabbiano. Charming little restaurant, close to the museum, either meat or fish for the main course. 1 Via Dante, T: 0922 774521.

€ Oasi Beach. Closed Mon. On the beach, this restaurant serves fantastic seafood *antipasto*. Contrada Plaja, T: 0922 803494.

Linosa

€€ Errera. Close to the sea, wonderful pasta or cous cous; delicious fruit granita for dessert.Via Scalo Vecchio, T: 0922 972041.

€€ Trattoria da Anna. Her lentil soup is famous, or try the *pasta con gli sgombri* (pasta with mackerel). 1 Via Veneto, Belvedere, T: 0922 972048.

Montallegro

€€ Monteletus. This restaurant is so good it is worth a long detour. Absolutely wonderful pasta dishes, the best Sicilian wines. Closed Mon. 13 Via Roma, Contrada Caracciolo, T: 0922 845177.

Porto Empedocle

€€ San Calogero. This is the little restaurant immortalized by the author Andrea Camilleri in his stories about police inspector Montalbano, who likes his food, especially *spaghetti al nero di seppia* (spaghetti with squid ink).Via Roma 32, T: 0922 637255.

Porto Palo di Menfi

€€ Da Vittorio. Family-run restaurant of long standing, on the beach, renowned for the sumptuous fish soup and seafood salads; rooms also available. Vittorio hails from Bergamo, but he has a real flair for cooking fish. House wines are excellent. 9 Via Friuli-Venezia Giulia, T: 0925 78381.

Racalmuto

€€ **Lo Zenzero**. Close to the opera house, a historic restaurant run by the same family for many years. Closed Mon. 18 Via Sciascia, T: 0922 941087.

€ **La Taberna**. In the centre, a friendly trattoria serving all the best local dishes, including *stigghiole*, intestines of lamb or kid, seasoned, wound around a cane and grilled. 108 Via Garibaldi, T: 0922 948043. Closed Wed.

San Leone

€€€ **Leon d'Oro**. The cuisine blends the flavours of land and sea: home-made pasta with swordfish, tomatoes and pistachio, or the delicious *bavette ai filetti di triglia e macco di fave* (fresh egg noodles with red mullet fillets and crushed broad beans). Closed Mon. 102 Viale Emporium, T: 0922 414400.

Sciacca

€€€ **Hostaria del Vicolo**. Well-cooked fresh fish, with some very special dishes: *spaghetti frutti di mare e finocchietto* (spaghetti with shellfish and wild fennel), *merluzzo ai fichi secchi* (cod with dried figs), or swordfish ravioli. Closed Mon. 10 Vicolo Samaritano, T: 0925 23071.

€€ **La Lampara**. Closed Mon. 33 Vicolo Caricatore, Lungomare Cristoforo Colombo, T: 0925 85085.

€€ **Vecchia Conza**. Picturesque little restaurant liked by local people. 37 Via Conzo, T: 0925 25385. Closed Mon.

CAFÉS, PASTRY SHOPS & ICE CREAM

Agrigento

Caffè Concordia. An old-fashioned café on the main street. 349 Via Atenea.

Infurna Tempting pastries and ice cream, try the strawberry flavour made with wild strawberries from Ribera. 96 Via Atenea.

La Promenade dei Templi. The perfect place for breakfast or a snack, close to the museum. 12 Via Passeggiata Archeologica.

Ragno d'Oro. Fantastic ice cream, all freshly made on the spot. 25 Via Nettuno, San Leone.

La Sosta. On the SS 115 to Sciacca, after Porto Empedocle and before Realmonte, keep an eye open for this coffee bar, said to be the best place in the province for ice cream, which comes in 80 flavours, all home-made.

Tempio di Vino. A wine bar, the most delightful place to spend a summer evening, sitting in the square in front of the church, listening to music. 11/13 Piazza San Francesco.

Aragona

Cacciatore. Excellent *cannoli di ricotta*. 1 Via Venezia.

Racalmuto

Pasticceria Taibi. For the delicious local pastries: *taralli racalmutesi*, delicate lemon biscuits. 127 Via Garibaldi.

Raffadali

Di Stefano. Home-made ice cream, freshly prepared every day, some unusual flavours, such *as pecorino* made with sheep's milk. Closed Wed. 23 Via Murano.

Sciacca

Bar Sant'Angelo. 66 Corso Vittorio Emanuele. An excellent choice for home-made ice cream and granita, this coffee shop hasn't changed at all since 1963, when it was chosen by Pietro Germi as a film-set for his *Sedotta e abbandonata*.

Bar Scandaglia. Art Nouveau ice cream parlour, which opened in 1919. 456 Piazza Scandagliato.

LOCAL SPECIALITIES

Agrigento
At the **monastery of Santo Spirito**, Via Santo Spirito, T: 0922 20664, the nuns make unique confectionery, including *cous cous dolce*; the recipe hasn't changed in 500 years. **Dalli Cardillo**, 32 Piazza Pirandello, bakery for all kinds of local bread, including the special rolls for the feast of St Calogero. **Sammartino 1961**, 24 Via Pirandello, to buy olive oil, wines, liqueurs, the local pesto made with wild fennel, anchovies with chilli pepper, swordfish paté.

Lampedusa
Cose Buone. A very up-market bakery at 8 Via Cavour. **Famolaro** at 41 Via Terranova, also 43 & 112 Via Roma, for all kinds of local fish, smoked or in olive oil, and sponges. **Titti Sanguedolce**, at 98 Via Roma, has a vast array of sponges, and wooden model boats.

FESTIVALS & EVENTS

Agrigento
First week in February: *Sagra del mandorlo in fiore*, an international folklore festival, held at the temples www.mandorloinfiore.net
First week in July: Feast of *San Calogero* with processions and fireworks; when the procession goes along Via Atenea, it is pelted with decorative loaves of bread.

Cammarata
First Sunday in May: unusual and picturesque feast with procession of the Cross of St Anthony called *Crocifisso di Tuvagli*.
Last Sunday in May: procession of the Cross of the Angels, with a cavalcade.
Last Sunday in August: procession of the Cross of the Rain.

Casteltermini
Last week in May: *Tataratà* (*see p. 224*).

Licata
3rd–6th May: *Festa di Sant'Angelo*, including a traditional fair, parades of Sicilian carts, crafts, fireworks and music in honour of St Angelo, who was martyred in the 13th century. In years of good harvest, the farmers take a mule with flowers into the church; in dry years the statue of the saint is taken out to sea on a boat in the hope that he will send rain.

Palma di Montechiaro
May: *Festa della Madonna del Castello*, a procession of barefoot devotees, accompanied by richly bedecked mules and musicians.

Racalmuto
Second Sunday in July: Colourful procession of riders on festooned horses goes up the stairway to Santa Maria del Monte.

San Biagio Platani
Easter: *Gli Archi di Pasqua* dates back to the early 17th century; special bread is baked and streets are decorated with flowery arches made of branches of palm leaves, fruit, bread and dates.

Sciacca Carnival
February: processions with allegorical floats, thought to be the oldest in Sicily; info: www.carnevaledisciacca.com

THE PROVINCE OF CALTANISSETTA

Caltanissetta, the province between Enna and Agrigento, is neatly divided into two parts by the River Imera Meridionale (the ancient *Himera*). The town of Gela, on the south coast, dominates the southern part, while Caltanissetta, the capital, presides over the northwest. Particularly favourable in position and conformation for human settlement, the entire area has been inhabited since the early Bronze Age. Giuseppe Tomasi di Lampedusa caught the resemblance between 'these bare, wild hills, stretching as far as the eye can see, and the tumultuous waves during a tempest, suddenly frozen into immobility by a capricious god'. In the 16th century much of the land was divided up among the more powerful aristocratic families, in order to farm it more efficiently, and many new towns were founded. The economy is now based on the production of wheat, fruit and vegetables, especially artichokes, table grapes, peaches and plums, and also one of the island's largest oil refineries at Gela. Caltanissetta was once the centre of the most important sulphur industry in the world. The famous bitter liqueur *Amaro Averna* is still produced near the capital, according to a secret recipe owned by the Averna family for more than 150 years.

CALTANISSETTA

The capital of the province is a small but prosperous provincial town, built of golden-yellow sandstone. It has a charming, dilapidated old centre, inviting displays in the shop windows, and a small but vibrant daily fish and vegetable market.

HISTORY OF CALTANISSETTA

The name of the town was, for many years, thought to have derived from that of the ancient Sican city of *Nissa*, with the Arabic prefix *kal'at* (castle); but the name could also derive from *kal'at el nissaat*, or 'castle of the young women'. Excavations in 1989 on Mt San Giuliano (or del Redentore) yielded 7th–6th-century BC finds. The site was then abandoned until the Roman period. After its conquest by Count Roger in 1086 it was given as an appanage to his son Jourdain, and passed subsequently into the hands of Corrado Lancia (1296) and the Moncada family (1406). The province was an extremely important centre of sulphur mining from the 18th century up until the early 20th century (the last mines were closed down in the 1970s).

Piazza Garibaldi

In Piazza Garibaldi is an amusing fountain depicting two bronze sea-monsters squirting water at a triton and a hippogryph by Michele Tripisciano (1860–1913), a talented native sculptor, whose statues also decorate Corso Umberto, the town hall and the public gardens. Here is the honey-coloured façade of the **duomo** or Santa Maria La Nova e San Michele (1570–1622), much damaged by bombing raids in 1943. In the luminous interior, decorated with white and gold stuccoes and bright frescoes, the vault painting (1720), a brilliant, swirling triumph of *trompe l'oeil*, is thought to be the Flemish artist Guglielmo Borremans' masterpiece. In the second south chapel is a wooden statue (covered with silver) of the *Immacolata* (1760). In the chapel to the right of the sanctuary is a charming polychrome wooden statue of the Archangel Michael by Stefano Li Volsi (1625), flanked by marble statues of the Archangels Gabriel and Raphael by Vincenzo Vitaliano (1753). St Michael is particularly venerated in Caltanissetta, because he is thought to have saved the people from epidemics of the plague. The high altarpiece of the *Madonna with Saints* is by Borremans, and the richly painted, carved and gilded organ dates from the 17th century. In the left transept is a painting of the *Madonna of Carmel* by Filippo Paladini, and in the second north chapel is a Crucifix attributed to Fra' Umile da Petralia. One of the altars is taken up by an elaborate gilded urn, containing a very realistic *Dead Christ*, made by Francesco Biangardi in 1896.

The church of **San Sebastiano**, opposite, has an unusual façade (1891), painted bright red, and a blue campanile. It is said to have been founded in the 16th century in thanksgiving to St Michael and St Sebastian.

Another side of the piazza is occupied by a large former convent which now houses the town hall (with statues by Tripisciano) and the opera house, **Teatro Regina Margherita**, which houses a collection of the local sculptor's works in a side gallery—the Mostra Permanente Michele Tripisciano (*T: 0934 74111 to request visit, possible Mon–Fri 9–12; Mon–Thurs also 4–6*).

Corso Umberto

Beside the town hall, Corso Umberto leads up to a statue of Umberto I (the second King of Italy, wearing a flamboyant hat) by Tripisciano, outside the former Jesuit collegiate church of **Sant'Agata** (1605), painted red, and preceded by an outside stairway. The Greek-cross interior is finely decorated with inlaid marble, especially the two side altars. The north altar (with a delightful frontal with birds) is surmounted by a relief of St Ignatius by the Palermitan sculptor Ignazio Marabitti (1719–97). The high altarpiece, the *Martyrdom of St Agatha*, is by Agostino Scilla (1654). A painter from Messina, Scilla published *Vain Speculation Undeceived by Sense* (1670) arguing the organic origin of fossils, an important contribution to palaeontology. With this ground-breaking publication, Scilla placed himself in the tradition of natural philosopher artists stretching back to Leonardo, demonstrating that his skill as a painter allowed him to see fossils in their true light, as once living creatures rather than stone copies of natural forms. His work here is framed in black marble adorned with cherubs by Marabitti. The first left chapel has frescoes by Luigi Borremans, the son of Guglielmo (including an *Assumption* in the vault, and a *Nativity* on a side wall).

Off the right side of Corso Umberto is the grand Palazzo Moncada (1635–38), left unfinished. A street on the left side of the duomo leads downhill to Via San Domenico, which continues to the church of **San Domenico** with a sinuously curving Baroque façade, fitting an awkward site, in the oldest district of the city. The stuccoes inside have recently been repainted in bright blue (the pastel shades in the nave instead date from 1961). The fine canvas of the *Madonna of the Rosary* (1614) is by Filippo Paladini (*see p. 253*).

From here the 14th-century church of Santa Maria degli Angeli (*closed*), the first Chiesa Madre, can be reached in ten minutes. Sadly ruined, the church's west door survives. Beyond, on a rocky outcrop, stand the scattered ruins and lonely tower of the Arab Castello di Pietrarossa, so-called because built of red stone, residence of Frederick III of Aragon.

Near Villa Amedeo, the beautiful public gardens, at no. 51 Viale Regina Margherita is the Seminary which houses the **Museo Diocesano** (*open 9–1, closed Wed, Sun and holidays*), with 17th- and 18th-century vestments and a fine collection of paintings, including two by Luigi Borremans, who was employed in Caltanissetta as a fresco painter; also a very expressive *Martyrdom of St Flavia* by Fra' Felice da Sambuca. At no. 73 Viale della Regione, in a school, is the **Museo Mineralogico Paleontologico e della Zolfara** (*T: 0934 591280 to request visit, possible Mon–Fri 9–1*), an interesting collection of some 3,000 minerals, and scale models of many of the sulphur mines once operating in the provinces of Caltanissetta and Agrigento.

ENVIRONS OF CALTANISSETTA

The **Abbazia di Santo Spirito**, 3km north from Caltanissetta, is the oldest church in the province, founded by Count Roger and his wife Adelaide (probably between 1086 and 1093), and consecrated in 1153. It was attached to a fortified building, parts of which now form the sacristy. The church has a fine triple apse, recently restored. The charming small interior (*open 11–12 & 5–6; ring at the door on the right marked Abbazia*) contains a large font, where people were baptized by immersion, below a painted Crucifix dating from the 15th century. On the walls are three detached 15th-century frescoes. The striking 17th-century fresco of *Christ in Benediction* was repainted in 1974. On the arch of the apse is the dedication stone (1153), and nearby is a little Roman cinerary urn (1st century AD), with rams' heads, birds and a festoon. A 17th-century sedan chair, with its original fittings, which was once used as a confessional, has been removed to the priest's house (*shown on request*).

Close by, at 57 Via Santo Spirito, is the new building housing the **Museo Archeologico** (*open 9–1 & 3.30–7; closed last Mon every month*). The museum has a particularly interesting archaeological collection from pre- and post-Greek colonization sites in the province, including objects from tombs at *Gibil Gabib*; some fine kraters (many with animal illustrations); black- and red-figure vases; and figurines found recently on Mt San Giuliano (on the northern outskirts of Caltanissetta) which represent the earliest portrayal of the human figure so far discovered in Sicily, after the Palaeolithic graffiti in the Addaura caves near Palermo. Dating from the early Bronze

A farmstead in the countryside near Delia, southwest of Caltanissetta.

Age, they are thought to have been used in a prehistoric sanctuary. Finds from the Arab period date from AD 996 to 1020. Other displays contain material from Sabucina, Capodarso and Mt Mimiani, including a bronze 6th-century BC helmet.

Off the Enna road, beneath Mt Sabucina, is the site of **Sabucina** (*to request visit T: 0934 504240*). The approach road climbs up past several disused mines, and there is a view up to the right above an overgrown mine of the line of walls of *Sabucina*, just below the summit of the hill. After 2km the asphalted road ends beside recent excavations of a necropolis. An unsurfaced road continues downhill for another 500m to a gate by a modern house at the entrance to the site, in a fine position with wide views. Mt Sabucina was first occupied in the Bronze Age. A thriving Iron Age village was then settled by the Greeks in the 6th century BC. The city declined after the revolt of Doucetius in 450 BC. The long line of Greek fortifications with towers and gates were built directly onto the rock. Sacred edifices can also be seen here.

In the valley below Caltanissetta to the east, the River Salso is crossed by Ponte Capodarso, a graceful bridge built in 1553 by Venetian engineers. A legend says that once a year the devils hold a market on the bridge; anyone lucky enough to see it, may purchase just one fruit, which next day will turn into solid gold. Nearby is the archaeological zone of *Capodarso*, an ancient city which had disappeared by the beginning of the 3rd century BC. Part of the walls and necropolis survive. Finds from the site are kept in the museum in Caltanissetta, and the area is now part of a large nature reserve, Monte Capodarso e Valle dell'Imera Meridionale (*open 9–1 & 4–7;*

www.riservaimera.it). There are many caves in the reserve, some of which have thriving populations of various species of bat.

Just south of Caltanissetta is the site of the ancient city of *Gibil Gabib* (*to request visit T: 0934 504240*). The name derives from the Arabic *Gebel Habib* (pleasant hill), and it was discovered in the 19th century. A necropolis here has yielded finds from three periods of occupation, in the 7th, 6th, and 4th centuries BC.

Southwest from Caltanissetta

Some 20km southwest of Caltanissetta, close to the border with the province of Agrigento, are two little-visited towns. **Delia**, twinned with Vanguard in Canada (where many of its inhabitants emigrated between 1890–1910), was re-founded as a farming community in the early 17th century, on an older medieval settlement. The name derives from the Arabic *daliyah*, meaning vineyard. A regular street plan divides the town into rectangular blocks, which in turn present a typical Arabian network of tiny alleys, serving also as courtyards for the dwellings, often built of blocks of yellow sandstone. There are many of the old fountains where the families used to collect their supply of water, and life is still lived largely in the open air, in a very sociable manner. The southern part of the town is recognizably the old centre, gathered around the Palazzo del Principe and the 16th-century Chiesa Madre, dedicated to the Madonna of Loreto. The painting of St Rosalia of Palermo over the altar is by Pietro d'Asaro 'Monocolo di Racalmuto'.

Turreted ruins of the Castellazzo, the old castle (11th century) of Delia, still stand, 1km from the town. The deliciously crunchy *cuddureddra* biscuits, to be found only here in Delia, look like little golden knots of twisted dough. It is said they were invented to cheer up the *castellane*, noble ladies who took refuge here during the Sicilian Vespers (*see p. 73*).

Close to Delia is **Sommatino**, a bright little town founded in the 14th century as the feu of the Del Porto family, who populated it with peasant farmers. Here too, the older quarter of the town is clearly recognizable in the eastern part.

NORTH & WEST OF CALTANISSETTA

North of Caltanissetta is **Santa Caterina Villarmosa**, founded in 1572 by Giulio Grimaldi, baron of Risigallo. The centre of this quiet agricultural town is Piazza Garibaldi, with the 18th-century Chiesa Madre. Many of the women are expert at embroidery and lace-making; you will see them sitting in front of their doorways in the early afternoon, hard at work.

About 2km northeast of the town, on the slopes going down to the Vaccarizzo stream, an area of particularly interesting geology is protected as a nature reserve (Riserva Geologica di Contrada Scaleri; *T: 0934 534122*). Slabs of limestone have collapsed through the centuries, eroded by the streams of water; resulting in formations that are unique in Sicily.

Resuttano stands above the Imera in a northernmost pocket of the province. An Arab farming village, it was re-founded in 1625 by the Di Napoli family, to whom it belonged until feudalism came to an end here in 1812. The ruins of the **Castello di Resuttano** are c. 5km east of the town, on the left bank of the river. The castle, which is incorporated into a 19th-century farmhouse (offering farm accommodation; *see p. 256 below*), can be reached by a little road which branches off to the left from the country road to Alimena. It was probably built by the Arabs (*rahlsul tan* meaning fortified house, hence the name of the town), and was important during the Middle Ages because of its position on the river, controlling the southern part of the Madonie Mountains. In 1337, the last year of his reign, Frederick II of Aragon, while travelling from Palermo to Enna and Catania, stayed the night here and is supposed to have written the will that sparked off the feud between the Ventimiglia and Chiaromonte families.

Archaeological sites of Marionopoli

West of Santa Caterina, along the old road to Palermo, which skirts the southern foot of Mt Chibbò (951m), is **Marianopoli**, founded in 1726 by Baron Della Scala, who brought a group of emigrants from Montenegro here to farm the land. The town centre is built on a checkerboard street plan around Piazza Garibaldi. On the west side is the 18th-century church of San Prospero (or Santa Maria Addolorata); the body of the saint, patron of the town, is in the main altar. At the town hall (1 Piazza Garibaldi) is the interesting **Museo Archeologico** (*open 9–1 & 3.30–5; closed Mon*), on two floors, with a collection of finds from the nearby archaeological sites of Monte Castellazzo (Neolithic, early Bronze Age, Iron Age, Greek), Balate and Valle Oscura (Vallelunga culture, early Bronze Age), and from the 6th-century BC necropolis of Valle Oscura.

East of Marianopoli is the rocky summit of Monte Castellazzo, where excavations (signposted) have brought to light a prehistoric necropolis with both rock-hewn tombs and signs of burial in large pots, and Greek tombs. On top of the crest are the remains of a city with walls (6th–3rd centuries BC), probably the ancient *Mytistraton*, which put up fierce resistance to the Romans in the First Punic War and was built on top of an earlier settlement.

Continuing south along the road, after c. 7km is a private road on the right, leading to an ancient town on Monte Balate; parts of the walls and the acropolis have been explored, the material is at the museum in Marianopoli. Still further south is the valley signposted Valle Oscura, where the inhabitants of an early Bronze Age village buried their dead by placing them into cracks in the rock; the same tombs were used again by the Hellenistic population in the 6th century BC. In town they may tell you that the three sites are closed to the public (because of difficult access), but they are not fenced; trekking boots required.

Southeast of Mt Mimiani and Marianopoli, c. 8km from the town, is a nature reserve (Lago Sfondato, *for information T: 0934 564038*), created to protect a small lake and the surrounding area.

Villalba and **Vallelunga Pratameno** are north of Marianopoli, in a particularly spectacular part of the interior of Sicily and in another isolated northern pocket of the province. Villalba was a Roman colony in the 3rd century BC, and later a Muslim village, while Vallelunga is an important agricultural centre.

Mussomeli

Mussomeli is a waterfall of ochre houses on the southern slopes of Mt San Vito, dominating a fertile and well-watered territory. The valley was formed by the River Platani (the ancient *Halykos*), 84km long, which enters the sea near Capo Bianco. It was founded by Manfredi III Chiaramonte in the late 14th century with the name *Manfreda*, near a Muslim farming community. Very soon the name Manfreda was forgotten, in favour of the Arabic toponym *Menzil al emir*, the house of the emir.

On the north side of the central Piazza Umberto is the palace of Barone Mistretta; close by, preceded by a stairway, is the 16th-century church of San Francesco. The west side of the square gives onto the old district of Terravecchia, with quiet little streets surrounding the Chiesa Madre, which was founded in the late 14th century by Manfredi, and dedicated to St Ludwig. In the church of the **Madonna dei Miracoli** is a splendid fresco (1792) on the vault, by Domenico Provenzano (1736–1794), showing *Heretics Being Flung into Hell*. The son of a carpenter, Provenzano was born in Palma di Montechiaro, and trained in Palermo under arch rivals Gaspare Serenario and Vito D'Anna, eventually showing more of the influence of the latter. In the crypt is a stone with an old painting of the Madonna, found near the spot where a cripple suddenly, and miraculously, regained the use of his legs.

By taking the road for Villalba, after c. 2km you reach the magnificent, gravity-defying **Castello Manfredonico** (*open 9.30–12 & 3–6; closed Mon*), a good example of medieval military architecture, recently restored, and one of the most beautiful in Sicily; it seems to have grown out of the rock it was built upon. Manfredi built it on top of an older fortification. It is said to be haunted by the ghosts of three sisters, walled up in a small triangular room by their brother for their own safety when he went away to fight in a war. Leaving plenty of food and water, he was forced to stay away longer than expected, returning to find the corpses of his unfortunate sisters and the half-eaten soles of their shoes. On the 1st and 2nd September, for the *Corteo Storico*, the inhabitants dress up in medieval costumes for a pageant and the old castle comes back to life again.

Acquaviva Platani is c. 8km west of Mussomeli. The name, meaning 'living water of the Platani', is a reference to the abundant springs in the area. With panoramic views, facing north and west over the upper Platani valley towards Mt Cammarata, and of ancient origin, the town was re-founded in 1635 by Francesco Spadafora as an agricultural centre. Many years of depression and mass emigration are now giving way to new hopes for the future, thanks to the production of high quality olive oil and wines.

Sutera

To the south of Mussomeli, in a spectacular hilltop position, is Sutera, standing on the chalky-white slopes of steep Mt Paolino, dominating the wide, hilly interior of the island. Its ancient castle (now completely destroyed) was once of fundamental importance for the defence of this strategic point. Probably founded by the Byzantines, the town was developed by the Muslims. The typically Arab district of *Rabato* is the oldest part of town, with its tiny alleys and courtyards, while the Chiesa Madre, dedicated to the Assumption, stands on the site of the mosque. In 1366 the village was assigned to Giovanni Chiaramonte, count of Caccamo, son of Manfredi III. After a period of stability, in the 16th century development ground to a halt, because many inhabitants left the town to live in the nearby settlements of Acquaviva, Campofranco and Casteltermini, where it was easier to farm the land.

Entering Sutera from the north, after a district of new houses Via del Popolo leads to Piazza Umberto, with the town hall, the 15th-century church of St Agatha, and the monastery of Santa Maria delle Grazie. Continuing along Via Sant'Agata, you reach Piazza San Giovanni, with the church of San Giovanni; inside there are some very good stuccoes of the Serpotta school. From here, Via del Carmine leads from the Rabatello district to Rabato. From the square (Piazza Carmine), Via San Paolino leads up on the left by the church of the Carmine to the top of the hill via many flights of steps, where there is an old convent and the sanctuary church of **San Paolino**, built in the 14th century for Giovanni Chiaramonte, in place of the old castle, with far-reaching views. Back in the village, Via del Carmine continues up to the ancient Chiesa Madre (1370).

Campofranco

Close to Sutera is Campofranco, a friendly village, founded in 1573 by Baron Giovanni del Campo, which prospered during the sulphur-mining period in the 19th century. The Chiesa Madre, dedicated to St John the Baptist, was completed in 1575, but considerably modified in later centuries. Inside is a dramatic 17th-century canvas depicting the beheading of St John the Baptist, by Pietro d'Asaro. In the central Piazza Vittorio Veneto is an incongruous bronze fountain, the *Fontana della Rinascita*, with a 5m diameter and abundant jets of water. It was a gift from the Sicilian Regional Government in 1955 because 99% of the population had turned out to vote in the elections. The statue of the patron St Calogero is kept in the church of San Francesco d'Assisi, and is carried around the town twice a year, on the shoulders of 20 stalwarts.

Frequently seen in the countryside in this area are little stone 'igloos' in the fields, some in good condition, some not. Called *cubuli,* they were used by the peasants as emergency dwellings, for storing equipment, or to protect sick animals. Try to look inside one, you will be amazed at the intelligent use of space. Smaller ones were built to cover wells.

Milena

South of Campofranco is the saline, small River Gallo d'Oro, the 'Golden Cockerel', a tributary of the Platani. On the other side of the valley is Milena, a farming community formed of the central village and 13 hamlets, called *robbe*, distributed on the hills around it: San Martino, Vittorio Veneto, Cavour, Piave, Crispi, Roma, Monte Grappa, Cesare Battisti, Masaniello, San Miceli, Mazzini, Garibaldi and Balilla, most of which are now abandoned. The area shows signs of human settlement going back to the Copper Age and even the Neolithic, and Milena itself was certainly an important Arab village. For many centuries known as *Milocca*, it became a feu of the monastery of San Martino delle Scale near Palermo, which held it until 1866. The monks granted the peasants perpetual lease of the land, which along with the abundant water, allowed the inhabitants to enjoy relative prosperity. In one of the hamlets, Masaniello, is the **Casa-Museo della Civiltà Contadina** (*open daily July, Aug, Sept 9–12 & 3–6; closed Sun afternoon*), a collection of objects and equipment used by the farmers.

In Milena town centre, on the Piazza Europa, is the sleek new **Antiquarium Comunale Arturo Petix** (*open Mon–Fri 9.30–1*), exhibiting some of the archaeological finds from the area. The slopes of Mt Conca, degrading down to the Gallo d'Oro stream, with many caves, are now protected as a nature reserve (*For information T: 091 322689*). The river is fringed by tamarisks, a haze of pale pink in spring, and a paradise for many small birds—Cetti's and fan-tailed warblers and the penduline tit, as well as kingfishers, little ringed plovers, black-winged stilts, kestrels and buzzards. Two caves here are of great speleological interest.

West from Caltanissetta

San Cataldo, is a farming community, 5km to the west of Caltanissetta, founded in 1607 by Baron Nicolò Galletti, who named it after the Irish St Cathald, a disciple of St Patrick, who later became the first bishop of Taranto. During the 19th century the economy prospered, thanks to the sulphur mines, and the town grew considerably. Time stands still on the quieter back streets, where you will occasionally see women embroidering or making lace, sitting in front of their homes, working away at their threads with deft fingers.

On the road to Serradifcalco, after c. 5km a path on the right leads to the archaeological site of **Vassallaggi**, five small rocky hills, where excavations have brought to light the remains of the Sicel town of *Motyon*, scene of a tremendous battle in 450 BC between Doucetius and his Sicels against the Greeks of Agrigento and Syracuse. So far some streets have been located, a sanctuary and a necropolis. The finds are in the archaeological museum of Caltanissetta.

Serradifalco is a neat and tidy town in a strategic position controlling the major roads, and with abundant sources of water. This too was once an important centre for the sulphur mines. Not far from the town is the strange Lago Soprano, a small, beautiful natural lake, set like a gemstone in the arid highlands. No streams can be seen to lead in or out of Lago Soprano, which is fed by underground springs. It is now protected as a nature reserve.

Across the valley of the Gallo d'Oro, **Montedoro** stands on a small plateau on the slopes of Mt Croce, which was known as *Montedoro* (Golden Mountain), overlooking the river of the same name. Founded in 1635 by Don Diego Tagliavia Cortes, prince of Castelvetrano, for agricultural purposes, the town flourished in the 19th century thanks to its sulphur and potassium salt mines. One of these has been opened as a museum, the Museo della Zolfara (*open 9–1, T: 0934 934404*). At Montedoro, and in the nearby farming village of **Bompensiere**, near Milena, several house fronts have been decorated with murals, illustrating the history of the community.

GELA & THE SOUTH

Gela is an important port and the fifth largest town in Sicily. Renowned for its splendour in the past, it was the home of the dramatic poet Aeschylus. Now it is frankly unattractive, thanks to uncontrolled building activity in the late 20th century and the presence of the local oil refinery. Mafia, here called *'a stidda*, is unfortunately still very powerful, and its influence has forced many honest tradesmen into bankruptcy; spasmodic struggles between rival clans sometimes result in a spate of violent murders. Visitors should not be deterred: among the town's many fine qualities are the exceptional courtesy of the inhabitants; the archaeological museum; and the splendid Greek fortifications at Capo Soprano. Recent excavations at Bosco Littorio, site of the tradesmen's quarters and the harbour of the old city, have brought to light some warehouses buried under six metres of sand, untouched since the 5th century BC; among the material recovered are three unique terracotta altars which can be seen in the museum.

HISTORY OF GELA

The modern city, known until 1927 as Terranova, was founded by Frederick II in 1230, on the site of *Gela*, a colony of Rhodians and Cretans established in 689 BC. Gela soon rose to importance, founding the colony of *Acragas* (Agrigento) in 580 and contributing to the Hellenization process of the indigenous settlements in the interior of the island. Under Hippocrates (498–491 BC) the city reached its greatest prosperity, but Gelon, his cavalry commander and successor, transferred the seat of government and half the population to Syracuse in 485. Aeschylus, the great 5th-century BC playwright, died in Gela in 456, supposedly because an eagle flying above him dropped a tortoise on his bald head, mistaking it for a stone. In 405 the town was destroyed by the Carthaginians, but Timoleon refounded it in 339. The new city was larger than the earlier one and was provided with a new circle of walls. Phyntias, tyrant of Acragas, transferred its inhabitants in 282 BC to his new city at the mouth of the *Imera* (now Licata), and Gela disappeared from history.

EXPLORING GELA

Museo Archeologico Regionale
Open 9–1 & 2 until one hour before sunset.
At the east end of the town, on Corso Vittorio Emanuele, is the sumptuous Museo Archeologico Regionale, with beautifully displayed material. This includes some of the painted vases for which Gela is best known and which are exhibited in many archaeological museums in Europe and the USA, the three famous terracotta altars recently excavated in the emporium area of the city, and a superb coin collection.

Section I: Dedicated to the acropolis area (east of the modern city) which was inhabited from prehistoric times up to the 5th century BC.

Section II: Displays later material from the acropolis (4th–3rd centuries BC) when it was an artisans' district. There is also material salvaged from an Archaic Greek ship found off the coast of Gela in 1988.

Section III: Devoted to Capo Soprano, now at the western extremity of the modern city, where there was a residential area and public edifices were erected in the late 4th century BC; this is followed by an exhibit illustrating the production of various potteries, including some pots with dedicatory inscriptions on their bases.

Terracotta altar relief of Medusa (early 5th century BC)

Section IV: More than 50 amphorae (7th–4th centuries BC) attest to the importance of Gela's commerce with other centres in the Mediterranean.

Section V: Dedicated to sanctuaries found outside Gela, most of them dedicated to Demeter and Persephone, with numerous votive statuettes.

Section VI: Displays finds from the surrounding territory, dating from the prehistoric to the Hellenistic era.

Section VII: Roman and medieval material found during the restoration of the Castelluccio (*see p. 254 below*) is displayed here. In front of the coin room are three terracotta altars, with images on the front in relief, found in the emporium part of the ancient city. Dating from the early 5th century BC, the two larger ones are unique for their size, artistic quality, subject matter, and state of conservation. That on the left represents a magnificent **Gorgon Medusa** (*pictured above*), running with her babies in her arms, Pegasus the winged horse and the warrior Chrysaor, and tightening her snake belt as she goes. The smaller central altar shows a slender lioness attacking a bull in the top part, and underneath the goddess of dawn, Eos, making away with the huntsmen Cephalus, husband of Procris, who in revenge seduced King Minos of Crete. The altar on the right shows three goddesses, probably Hera, Demeter (smoothing her braids) and Aphrodite. Also on display is the exceptional numismatic collection of more than 2,000 pieces, found in or around Gela, including a magnificent hoard of some 600 silver coins, minted in Agrigento, Gela, Syracuse, Messina and Athens, between 515 and 485 BC, one of the most important such collections in existence. Discovered in Gela in 1956, the coins were stolen in 1973, but most of them have now subsequently been recovered.

Section VIII: Important 19th-century Navarra collection of ancient Sicilian vases (with a fine group of Attic black-and-red figure vases, and Corinthian ware from the 8th–6th centuries BC). Also here is the smaller Nocera collection and two cases of finds from the necropolis, including (in case F) an Attic lekythos on a white ground showing Aeneas and Anchises (460–450 BC) and (in case G) an exquisite Attic red-figure lekythos, by the Nikon painter.

Molino a Vento Acropolis

Outside the museum is the entrance to the Molino a Vento Acropolis (*open 9–7, closed last Mon every month; same ticket as museum*), which now overlooks the oil refinery. This was part of Timoleon's city, on a terraced grid plan with shops and houses (c. 339–310 BC), above the ruins of a small sacred enclosure. In the garden on the site of the acropolis of the earliest city, stands a single (re-erected) column of a temple probably dedicated to Athena (6th century BC), and the basement of a second earlier temple also dedicated to Athena. This area had been abandoned by 282 BC.

Capo Soprano and the coast

Corso Vittorio Emanuele crosses the long, untidy town, but the most pleasant way of reaching Capo Soprano and the Greek fortifications (which are over 3km from the museum) is along the seafront. The remarkable **Greek fortifications** (*open 9–1hr before sunset; same ticket as museum*) of Capo Soprano have been excellently preserved after centuries beneath the sand: they extend for several hundred metres, and reach a height of nearly 13m. They were first excavated in 1948. The walls were begun by Timoleon in 333 BC and completed under Agathocles. Their height was regularly increased to keep ahead of the encroaching sand, a danger today removed by the planting of trees. In the peaceful site close to the sea, with eucalyptus and acacia trees, a path (right) leads past excavations of battlements to a circular medieval kiln (under cover). From here there is a view of the coast.

The path follows walls (partly under cover) and foundations of the brick angle towers to the west gate, and then descends to the most complete stretch of walls: the lower course is built of sandstone, while the top is finished with plain mud bricks. A small postern gate in the walls can be seen here, dating from the time of Agathocles (filled in with mud bricks soon after it was built), near a well-preserved drain. Steps lead up past a little house which contains photographs of the site.

About 500m from the fortifications (signposted *Bagni Greci*), now engulfed by modern apartment blocks, are remains of Greek baths (4th century BC). The baths, including hip baths (with seats) are protected by a roof, but are always open, surrounded by a garden behind railings.

Behind the sand dunes, along the coast east of Gela, is a shallow coastal lake (the largest of the kind in Sicily), now protected as a nature reserve, and particularly interesting during bird migration periods in early spring and late summer: the Biviere di Gela (*T: 0933 926051 to book visit, www.ntv.it/lipu.gela*). Short-toed eagles, spoonbills, pratincole, Audouin's and slender-billed gulls, Terek and buff-breasted sandpipers, red-necked grebes, black-tailed godwits, slender-billed curlews, purple herons, glossy ibis (symbol of the reserve), even mute swans (very unusual for Sicily) have been seen here, and many duck species, while the black-winged stilt nests in the marshy area near the lake; another nester is the collared turtle dove, until recently, for Sicily, only found on Pantelleria and Linosa (it has started nesting even in downtown Gela). Birds which winter here include the jack snipe, short-eared owl, marsh harrier, hoopoe and bluethroat.

On the coast west of Gela is **Falconara**, with its well-preserved, spectacular 14th-century castle on the sea, now a beautiful hotel (*see p. 255 below*). There is an inviting sandy beach. Beyond are vegetable and melon fields, protected from the wind by cane fences, and often covered with plastic sheeting, which gives the countryside a strange, watery aspect, like a billowing sea.

NORTH & EAST OF GELA

Butera

Some 30km north of Gela is Butera, perched up on a flat rock in a strategic position, with fine views towards the sea, and dominated by the bell-tower of the sanctuary church of the patron, San Rocco. Important excavations of the Bronze Age settlement (perhaps the Sican town of *Omphake*) have been carried out nearby; the finds are in the archaeological museum in Gela. As *Butirah* it was one of the largest cities in Arab Sicily, later becoming a Lombard centre under the Normans (for the followers of Roger's Lombard wife Adelaide). William I destroyed the town in 1161 when he suspected its baron to have taken part in a plot against his person. Later rebuilt, it became the seat of the Santapau family, Catalans who became the first feudal lords on the island to receive the title of prince in 1563 from Philip II of Spain.

In Piazza Duomo (approached from the north) is the plain, elegant 17th-century Chiesa Madre, dedicated to St Thomas the Apostle, with a Latin-cross interior surmounted by a dome and decorated with stuccoes, and housing an exquisite 13th-century enamelled copper Crucifix from Limoges, and a collection of paintings, including a fine canvas by the Mannerist artist Filippo Paladini (*see p. 253*) of *St Mary of the Angels* (1606).

From here the main street, Via Principe di Piemonte, winds its way through to Piazza Dante, with a spectacular view over the hills to the Madonie Mountains and Mount Etna. Here is the interesting 15th-century triangular town hall, surmounted by a clock tower, and the 18th-century church of **San Giuseppe**, a simple façade with a large window, and an unusual 16th-century painted wooden Crucifix. Via Aldo Moro leads to Piazza della Vittoria, where the romantic and imposing 11th-century castle (*open 9–1 every day except Sat*) was once thought to be impregnable, and the donjon is still in good condition.

From the castle, Viale Diaz leads to the eastern crest of the hill, overlooking the plain, and the 18th-century sanctuary church of **San Rocco**, dedicated to the patron saint of Butera. A French nobleman, St Roch (1295–1327) tended to the sick in a plague-stricken town while on pilgrimage before contracting the disease himself. Retiring to the woods to die, he made a miraculous recovery thanks to the devotion of a dog which brought him food from its master's table. The single-nave interior is richly decorated with stucco and 18th- and 19th-century canvases by local artists, representing episodes of the life of the saint, who is frequently invoked against the plague.

Southwest of Butera is an artificial reservoir (signposted from the railway station), **Lago Comunelli**, used as a resting-place by many species of migratory bird in spring and autumn, while the sand dunes along the coast are still intact, a wealth of typical vegetation, including the rare, sweet-scented white broom, *Lygos raetam*.

Mazzarino

North of Butera is Mazzarino, the ancient Sicel city of *Maktorion*, which in the 14th century became the seat of the Branciforte family from Piacenza, who were renowned throughout Europe for their culture, learning, and magnificence. In 1507 King Ferdinand II of Aragon invested Niccolò Branciforte with the title of Count of Mazzarino. His descendant, Prince Carlo Maria Carafa Branciforti (1651–95), embellished and enlarged the town, and built an enormous residence, a miniature royal palace, with its own theatre and printing shop. Parts survive, though much neglected. Around the palace, convents and monasteries were built by all the major religious orders—Jesuits, Carmelites, Benedictines, Franciscans, Capuchins, Dominicans—and there were 25 churches.

The attractive main street, Corso Vittorio Emanuele, runs west to east for c. 1km, passing numerous aristocratic palaces in decay. At the west end is the 16th-century church and convent of **Santa Maria del Gesù**, containing the funerary monument of Prince Carlo Maria Carafa Branciforte.

In the middle of the corso is the Carmelite complex. The convent is now the Town Hall, while the church of **Santa Maria del Carmelo** houses notable works of art, including a Branciforte funerary monument and paintings by Filippo Paladini. Another Branciforte funerary monument, by the Gagini school, is in the courtyard of the town hall, once the cloister of the monastery.

Nearby is Via Consolazione, which leads up to the church of **San Francesco**, or Immacolata; on the main altar is a splendid canvas by Filippo Paladini of the

Immaculate Virgin and St Francis, signed and dated 1606. Paladini died in Mazzarino in 1615. From here there is a view over the valley. In the spacious Piazza Crispi, in front of Palazzo Branciforte, is the wide Baroque façade of the Chiesa Madre (Angelo Italia), dedicated to the Madonna of the Snow; inside are some paintings of the Paladini school.

Close by is Piazza Colajanni, with the Dominican complex; in the church is a masterpiece by Filippo Paladini, signed and dated 1608, the *Madonna of the Rosary (pictured below)*. Pink, white, mauve and dark green are the dominant colours; in the top corners, while cherubs toss down pink roses, and in the bottom left-hand corner is the astonished-looking donor, a certain Pasquale Rondello.

At the eastern extremity of the corso is the 18th-century church of **Santa Maria del Mazzaro**; the 15th-century triptych on the main altar, showing the *Madonna with Sts Agatha and Lucy*, has been damaged by two fires, and poorly restored.

Filippo Paladini (1544–1615)
Filippo Paladini, or Paladino, arrived in Sicily from Malta in 1601, at the invitation of Counter-Reformist religious orders. In Mazzarino, he lived at the court of Don Fabrizio Branciforte. Born in Casi, near Rufina, in Tuscany, he was convicted of assault in 1586 and sent as a galley-slave to Malta. Only one work is extant from his late-Mannerist period. His cool, elegant colour schemes and careful positioning of figures owes much to his Tuscan origins though, while also displaying Flemish influences. His work also shows that he had met Roman artists working during the Counter-Reformation as well as the new generation of Florentine artists, suggesting that he may have briefly returned to northern Italy.

Detail from the *Madonna of the Rosary* by Filippo Paladini (1608).

In Sicily, he was tutor to the two Zoppo di Gangi, and his later works, in particular those for Enna cathedral and the *Martyrdom of St Ignatius* in Palermo, display the marked influence of Caravaggio.

Environs of Mazzarino

Mazzarino is dominated by the ruins of its pre-13th-century castle, north of the town, on an isolated hill, with a round tower; it is known as *'U Cannuni*, the cannon; not far away are the ruins of yet another, called *Grassuliato*. These fortresses, and ancient *Maktorion* itself, on Mt Bubbonia, were built to defend the vast plain of Gela, and the valleys leading out of it towards the interior of the island.

About 12km east of Mazzarino are the remains of a Byzantine village called **Sofiana** (signposted *Statio Philosophiana—Itinerarium Antonini*), probably representing a rest-ing-point on the Roman road from Catania to Agrigentum, when it was known as *Philosophiana*. A small bath-house has been excavated, and a Palaeo-Christian basilica.

At **Riesi**, a simple town to the west of Mazzarino, where sulphur miners and farm workers have always led a hard existence, a kind of trade union uniting them all became strong enough for the town to declare itself a Socialist Republic in 1893. Although short-lived, the episode remains a source of local pride.

Northeast of Gela

On the Caltagirone road is the 13th-century **Castelluccio** (*open at the same times as the archaeological museum in Gela, accessible with the same ticket*), a castle said to be haunted by the ghost of a mysterious lady who sometimes entices travellers inside; when this happens they are never seen again. It occupies a prominent site dominat-ing the surrounding plain, now cultivated with artichokes. On the approach road there is a war memorial to the battle of 1943, which followed the landings of the American assault forces on the beaches in the Gulf of Gela, appropriately sited beside two pill-box defences.

There is a **prehistoric necropolis** on Monte Disueri or Dessueri (no signs, but exactly 7.4km along the SS 190 to Mazzarino from the junction with the SS 117 bis to Gela; on the left-hand side) with more than 2,000 tombs carved into the rock. It is the most important ancient necropolis in Sicily after Pantalica (*see p. 375*), and dates from the 11th–9th centuries BC. The paths have all but disappeared, and there are no explanatory information boards; trekking boots are advisable for exploring. In spring the mountain is covered with wildflowers.

Also northeast of Gela is **Niscemi**, on a plateau in a panoramic position facing west over the plain of Gela. Like others in the area, the town bases its economy on the pro-duction of artichokes. It was completely rebuilt, following a regular street plan, after the 1693 earthquake. In the rectangular central square, Piazza Vittorio Emanuele, to the east is the 18th-century Chiesa Madre (Santa Maria dell'Itria)—with a fine por-tal—while opposite is the interesting, octagonal church of the Addolorata (18th cen-tury, Rosario Gagliardi). Another side of the square is occupied by the elegant Neoclassical town hall.

East of the town is a small forest of cork, kermes and holm oaks, with tree heath, now protected as a nature reserve: the Sughereta di Niscemi (*for information T: 0933 954308*). The reserve boasts a small nesting colony of bee eaters; until recently these handsome, colourful birds were only spotted here during their migratory flights.

PRACTICAL INFORMATION

GETTING AROUND

• **By train:** The station at Caltanissetta (T: 0934 21104), in Piazza Roma, has services via Canicattì to Agrigento, Gela, Ragusa and Syracuse. The station of Caltanissetta Xirbi, 7km north (bus connection with the town), is on another line connecting Palermo, Enna and Catania. **Gela** is on the Syracuse, Ragusa, Canicattì, Agrigento line.

• **By bus:** There are frequent services (usually faster than the trains) from the bus station in Caltanissetta, in Via Rochester, for Palermo, Catania and Agrigento (SAIS, T: 0934 564072, ticket office 22 Via Colajanni); for Piazza Armerina, Gela and San Cataldo (ASTRA, T: 0934 573315) and for towns in the province. Electric city buses leave from Piazza Roma (SCAT, T: 0934 29576, www.scattrasporti.com). Etna Trasporti (T: 095 532716) runs services to and from Gela to Catania; SAIS (T: 0922 595260) has services from Gela to Agrigento and Licata; ASTRA (T: 0934 573315), runs services connecting Caltanissetta, Gela, Piazza Armerina and San Cataldo. Yellow city buses leave from Gela station to Capo Soprano and the Archaeological Museum; information and tickets from the booth opposite the station.

INFORMATION OFFICES

Caltanissetta APT Caltanissetta: 109 Corso Vittorio Emanuele, T: 0934 530411, www.aapit.cl.it, for informa-tion on the entire province; 20 Viale Conte Testasecca, T: 0934 21089, www.caltanissetta-sicilia.it
Campofranco c/o Municipio, Via Piave, www.comune.campofranco.cl.it; ProLoco: Via Vittorio Emanuele, T: 0934/959412, www.lavocedicampofranco.it
Gela APT Gela, 31 Via Morello, T: 0933 911509, www.comune.gela.cl.it; 73 Via Pisa, T: 0933 553788.
Mazzarino 410 Corso Vittorio Emanuele, T: 0934 381940.
Mussomeli Via Santa Maria dei Monti, T: 0934 993105, www.prolocomussomeli.it
Sutera c/o Municipio, T: 0934 954235; Pro Loco: 3 Piazza Carruba, T: 0934 954461.

HOTELS

Caltanissetta
€ **Hotel Giulia**. Charming small hotel, friendly service, central and comfort-able. 85 Corso Umberto, T: 0934 542927 www.hotelgiulia.it
€€ **San Michele**. Elegant, clean and efficient hotel with 122 rooms in the outskirts. Reliable service, good restau-rant. Via Fasci Siciliani, T: 0934 553750, www.hotelsanmichelesicilia.it
Campofranco
€ **La Fazenda**. Only a simple inn, but there is a car park, the food is fantastic, the position on the main Palermo-Agrigento highway is very convenient. SS 189 km 36, T: 0934 959212.
Falconara
€€€ **Castello di Falconara**. Quiet position on a lovely beach, antique fur-

niture; the whole castle and staff can also be rented for up to 2 weeks (sleeps 35). The castle has its own railway station; the nearest town is Licata (11km). Contrada Falconara, T: 091 329082, www.castellodifalconara.it
€ **Stella del Mediterraneo**. Small 1960s' building close to the sea, with views of the sea or Castello di Falconara, private beach and restaurant. SS 115, Contrada Faino, T: 0934 349004, www.stelladelmediterraneo.it

Gela
€ **Sileno**. In the suburbs at Giardinelli, not far from museum. Strada statale 117 bis, T: 0933 911144, giorgiabracchitta@virgilio.it
€ **Sole**. Spartan, but all rooms have sea views; restaurant. 32 Viale Lungomare, T: 0933 9244400, www.hotelsole.sicilia.it

Mazzarino
€ **Hotel Alessi**. Comfortable modern hotel, central, with restaurant. 20 Via Caltanissetta, T: 0934 381549.

San Cataldo
€ **Helios**. Close to centre. Contrada Zubbi San Leonardo, T: 0934 588207, hotelhelios@pgol.it

BED & BREAKFAST

Caltanissetta
€ **Piazza Garibaldi**. English and French spoken, in the middle of the town, with some distinctly curious wall decorations. 11 Piazza Garibaldi, T: 0934 26436, www.piazza-agaribaldi.it
€ **Serra dei Ladroni**. An old stone farmhouse in the middle of an olive grove, all rooms with private bath. English and French spoken. South of the town. Contrada Serra dei Ladroni,

SS 640 Caltanissetta–Agrigento, T: 0934 568688 & 333 1630938, www.serradeiladroni.it
€ **Casa Messana**. Pool, countryside location, English spoken, Sicilian meals on request with the family. Borgo Petilia, t 339/5971179 & 320/1957066, email: scascino@libero.it

FARMHOUSE ACCOMMODATION

Caltanissetta
€ **Canicassè**. 9km from Caltanissetta, panoramic position, air conditioning, breakfast with fresh milk and home-made bread. Contrada Cozzo di Naro, T: 0934 568307, lombardoluigi@virgilio.it

Butera
€€ **Farm Ospitalità di Campagna**. A fine example of Sicilian farmhouse accommodation, to which the owner, Andrea, has conferred an artistic atmosphere. Set in spectacular countryside, where Bonelli's eagle flies, its position is ideal for exploring the local towns. Contrada Strada, T: 0934 346600.

Resuttano
€ **Al Castello**. In the north of the province, an old fortified farmhouse, easy to reach, close to the Madonie Park and the Valle dell'Imera Wildlife Reserve. Carefully-prepared food. The farm produces durum wheat, olive oil and almonds. There's also a pool. Contrada Castello, T: 0934 673815.

RESTAURANTS

Caltanissetta
€€ **Cortese**. Elegant restaurant serving Mediterranean cuisine. 166 Viale Sicilia, T: 0934 591686.

€€ **Vicolo Duomo**. Local dishes in romantic old building in tiny alley, menu includes the authentic *farsumagru*. Closed all day Sun and mid-day Mon. 3 Piazza Garibaldi, entrance from 1 Vicolo Neviera, T: 0934 582331.

Gela
€€ **Casanova**. Interesting ravioli and noodles prepared with fish, local wines. Closed Mon in winter and Sun in summer. 89 Via Venezia, T: 0933 918580.

€€ **Centrale da Totò**. Very good seafood. 39 Via Generale Cascino, T: 0933 913104.

€€ **Il Delfino**. By general agreement, the finest restaurant in Gela, good menu and wine list. Closed Mon. 1 Via Giulio Siracusa, T: 0933 924513.

Mazzarino
€€ **Villa Rosangelo**. Delightful seafood dishes. Contrada Pileri, T: 0934 381437.

Mussomeli
€ **Il Giullare**. A simple trattoria, very good *'mbriulata*. 50 Via Barcellona, T: 0934 993992.

Sutera
€ **Civiletto**. Trattoria serving delicious local food, in a 12C convent, good wine list. 7 Via San Giuseppe, T: 0934 954587.

LOCAL SPECIALITIES

Caltanissetta
Calogero Garzia, at 2 Via Calabria, is a traditional bakery with stone oven, sourdough bread. **Salvatore Amorelli**, 424 Via Xiboli, www.amorelli-italy.com, has a famous smoking pipe workshop with a shop on site.

Delia
Pasticceria del Corso, at 183 Corso Umberto, for the best *cuddureddra* biscuits, indicated by the Slow Food Foundation as one of the finest food products of Sicily.

Mussomeli
In Mussomeli they are famous for a tasty and very filling winter snack called *la 'mbriulata*, found in the bakeries.

EVENTS

Caltanissetta
Holy Week: Procession of *I Misteri*, impressive scenes describing the Passion of Christ.

Butera
15th Aug: *'U Sirpintazzu*, on the eve of the day dedicated to the patron San Rocco.

Campofranco
17th Jan: Feast of St Anthony with a traditional procession and fireworks.

11th Jan and last weekend in July: Feast dedicated to the patron St Calogero, and to bread—*Sagra dei Pupi di Pane*—modelled into 'bread men', rather like gingerbread men, but bigger.

Delia
Good Friday: *La Scinnenza*, a dramatic Easter procession involving almost all the inhabitants.

Gela
18th & 19th March: *Festa di San Giuseppe*, many families spend weeks preparing the lavish *altari di San Giuseppe*, feasts for three poor people chosen to represent the Holy Family; one 'family' for each altar. For information T: 0933 911423 or 0933 913788.

THE PROVINCE OF ENNA

Enna is the capital of the only entirely landlocked province of Sicily. Its vast castle, dominating practically the whole island, was an almost impregnable stronghold for centuries. The view of the medieval hill town of Calascibetta from Enna is exceptional, while nearby Villarosa houses two interesting museums: one in a train, and the other in a baron's villa. The province is the most important in Sicily for the production of cereals, and provides a large proportion of the durum wheat used by the Italian pasta industries; the wheat-fields on the dramatically hilly landscape provide a palette of ever-changing colours.

ENNA

Enna, at 931m, is the highest provincial capital in Italy, often called the Belvedere of Sicily because of its position on the top of a precipitous hill that dominates the whole island. Enna Alta is the old city on the mountaintop, gradually being abandoned because of the harsh climate (even in August the nights are chilly). The new districts on the southern slopes and on the plateau of Pergusa are known as Enna Bassa.

HISTORY OF ENNA

The city occupies the site of *Henna*, a Sicel stronghold subjected to Greek influences, perhaps from Gela, as early as the 7th century BC. Before the arrival of the Greeks, according to the historian Diodorus Siculus, the Sicels and Sicani had already agreed to divide the island between them with its centre at Enna. The legendary scene of the rape of Persephone, and the centre of the cult of Ceres or Demeter, her mother, to whom Gelon of Syracuse erected a temple in 480 BC, Enna fell by treachery to Dionysius of Syracuse in 397. The Romans conquered it in 258 during the First Punic War. In 214, in the course of the Second Punic War, the Roman Consul feared a rebellion here in support of Syracuse and ordered a large part of the population to be executed before sacking the city. In 135 the First Servile War broke out under the slave Eunus (*see box on p. 264*), and the town was taken in 132 by the Roman army only after two years' siege. The Saracens took it in 859 AD and named it *Kasr Janni* (from the Roman name *Castrum Ennae*); and it was not captured by the Normans until 1087. From then on the town was known as *Castrogiovanni* until 1927, on the decision of Mussolini, it became the capital of a new province, in spite of the fact that Piazza Armerina had a larger population and was easier to reach.

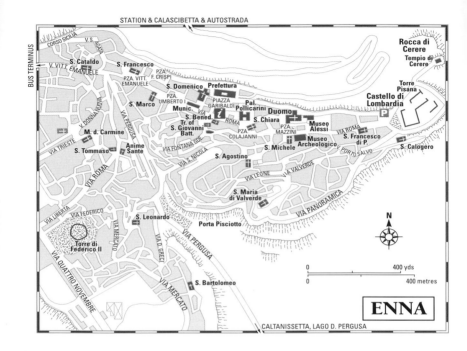

EXPLORING ENNA

Piazza Vittorio Emanuele

The centre of the city is Piazza Vittorio Emanuele. On the north side is the church of San Francesco, with its fine 16th-century tower. On the left is Piazza Crispi, which has an excellent view across the valley to Calascibetta, and, on a clear day, to Etna. The bronze statue on the fountain is a copy of Bernini's celebrated *Rape of Proserpine* (now in the Galleria Borghese in Rome). West of the square is Piazza Cataldo, with the newly restored church of **San Cataldo** (*open 9–1 & 4–7*), rebuilt in the 18th century on a preceding construction. The font (1473) is the work of Domenico Gagini, a decorative sculptor from Lombardy, thought to have served as an apprentice under Brunelleschi, who came to Sicily and founded an important dynasty of sculptors and carvers (*see p. 423*). The vast 16th-century marble polyptych, the *Annunciation*, the *Nativity*, and *Madonna and Child with Sts Cathald and Blaise*, is by an unknown sculptor. Saint Cathald, to whom the church is dedicated, was a 6th-century Irish missionary saint, who preached widely in southern Italy and Sicily.

Via Roma

The main street of the town, Via Roma continues uphill traversing a series of squares. In Piazza Umberto is the Neoclassical *Municipio* (Town Hall), which incorporates the opera house, Teatro Garibaldi (*T: 0935 26034*). The Baroque façade of San Benedetto (or San Giuseppe) decorates Piazza Coppola, off which is the 15th-century tower of San Giovanni Battista with Gothic arches, and crowned by a Moorish-style cupola.

On the north side of Via Roma the tower of the Prefettura (1939) rises from piazza Garibaldi. Santa Chiara, in Piazza Colajanni, is a war memorial and burial chapel. Two majolica pictures (1852) decorate the tiled floor, one celebrating the advent of steam navigation, and the other the triumph of Christianity over Islam. The bronze statue in the piazza outside commemorates Napoleone Colajanni (1847–1921) a politician and social reformer born in Enna. It is the work of the great Palermo-born eclectic sculptor Ettore Ximenes.

On the north side of the square is the massy Palazzo Pollicarini, which with its impregnable-looking stone walls and tiny windows retains one or two Catalan-Gothic features. Via Roma continues up towards the duomo past several narrow side streets on the left which lead to the edge of the hill, with views over the valley to Calascibetta.

The duomo

Open 9–1 & 4–7.
The duomo, founded on the site of a temple to Persephone in 1307 by Eleonora, wife of Frederick II of Aragon, and damaged by fire in 1446, was slowly restored in the 16th century. The façade, with a 17th-century bell-tower, covers its Gothic predecessor. The transepts and the polygonal apses survive in their original form (they can be seen from the courtyard of the Museo Alessi; *see below*). The Gothic-Catalan south door was walled up in 1447, after Pope Nicholas V declared it holy and only for the use of popes.

The **interior** has dark grey basalt columns with splendid bases, carved with grotesques, and Corinthian capitals (1550–60), the work of various artists including Gian Domenico Gagini, grandson of Domenico, who carved the symbols of the *Evangelists* on the first two at the west end. The nave ceiling is by Scipione di Guido, who also carved the walnut choir-stalls. On either side of the west door are 16th-century statues of the Annunciation. The two stoups in the nave date from the 16th century, and at the east end of the nave are richly carved 16th-century organ lofts. The altarpieces on the south side (c. 1722) are by the Flemish artist Guglielmo (Willem) Borremans (the painting *Sts Lucille and Hyacinth* on the second altar is particularly good). In the presbytery are five paintings (1613) of New Testament scenes by Filippo Paladini (*see p. 253*) which clearly show the artist's late phase, when he had rejected his earlier Mannerism in favour of *Caravaggismo*. In the chapel to the right of the sanctuary is 18th-century marble decoration and a painting of the *Visitation* also attributed to Paladini. There are more works by Borremans in the north transept and on the fourth north altar.

Museo Alessi and Museo Archeologico

The Museo Civico Alessi (*open 8–8; closed Mon; T: 0935 503165*) is in a building behind the east end of the Duomo. It is named after Canon Giuseppe Alessi (1774–1837), a native of Enna, who left his remarkable collection to his brother intending that he should donate it to the Church. Instead, the Church had to buy it in 1860, and the museum was first opened to the public in 1862. The main highlights are on the first floor, where the cathedral treasury is exhibited. There are splendid 16th- and 17th-century works, including four reliquaries (1573) by Scipione di Blasi (a Neapolitan silversmith who brought a new Mannerism to reliquaries in Sicily and influenced a generation of the Gagini family); a precious gold crown (*pictured opposite*), encrusted with jewels and enamels, made for a statue of the Madonna in 1653; and a beautiful 16th-century jewel in the form of a pelican (symbol of Christ's sacrifice). Alessi's important numismatic collection is displayed here. The Greek, Roman and Byzantine coins are arranged topographically and include many in bronze used in everyday transactions. A charming archaeological collection (with some of Alessi's original labels) is also displayed here. It includes missiles (*glandes*) used in the Servile War (*see p. 264*), bronzes and pottery. In the last room the Egyptian *ushabti* figurines (664–525 BC), which also formed part of the Alessi collection and were presumably found in Sicily, are of the greatest interest.

Across Piazza Mazzini the attractive 15th-century Palazzo Varisano, where Garibaldi made the speech in August 1863 that climaxed with the famous phrase '*o Roma o morte*', houses the **Museo Archeologico Varisano** (*open 9–6.30; closed Mon; T: 0935 528100 or 24720*). The collection is well displayed and includes finds from Calascibetta and Capodarso; the prehistoric rock tombs of Realmese; Enna (Greek, Roman, and medieval ceramics, including an Attic red-figure krater); Cozzo Matrice (where the necropolis was in use from the Bronze Age up to the 5th century BC); prehistoric material from the lake of Pergusa; and a collection of coins.

Castello di Lombardia

Open 9–1 & 3–6.

Via Roma continues up to the 13th-century Castello di Lombardia or Cittadella, adapted as a residence by Frederick II of Aragon. One of the best-preserved medieval castles on the island, six of the 20 towers remain. Outside is a First World War memorial by Ernesto Basile (1927), and a bronze statue of the rebel slave Eunus.

Steps lead up to the entrance to the castle. The first courtyard forms a permanent open-air theatre used in summer. Beyond the second court, planted with trees, the third has remains of a church, and (beneath a roof) tombs carved in the rock. Here is the entrance to the Torre Pisana, which can be climbed by a modern flight of stairs. The view from the top encompasses Etna, Centuripe on its hill and Lake Pozzillo. In the other direction, Lake Pergusa and Calascibetta can be seen. At the edge of the hill, beyond the castle, are the unenclosed remains of the Rocca Cerere, where old hewn stones mark the site of the Temple of Demeter (Ceres). Steps lead up to the summit with a view of Etna straight ahead.

The lower town

The lower town is reached by following the other branch of Via Roma, which takes a sharp turn to the south below Piazza Vittorio Emanuele. On the right are the church-

The crown of the Madonna (1653) in the Museo Alessi, Enna.

es of San Tommaso, with a 15th-century tower and a marble altarpiece by Giuliano Mancino (1515), and the Carmine (behind San Tommaso), with another 15th-century campanile and a curious stair-tower. On the left, near the southwest end of Via Roma, rises the octagonal **Torre di Federico II**, thought to have been built by Frederick II of Hohenstaufen in the 13th century. Frederick, King of Sicily and later Holy Roman Emperor, was famously born in a public square in Jesi, near Ancona. His mother, Constance d'Hauteville, daughter of the Norman ruler Roger II, was deemed by most to be past child-bearing age when she conceived. In order to demonstrate to sceptics that the pregnancy was not a hoax, and that the successor to the throne was legitimate, a pavilion was constructed in a public square, and in it, on 27th December, 1194, Frederick was born. This tower, 24m high, is surrounded by a public garden, all that remains of Frederick's former hunting reserve. At night it is said to be haunted by the sound of thundering hoofbeats, as Frederick rides hell-for-leather around the perimeter of the park. Not all scholars accept its 13th-century date: another theory suggests that it might in fact be much older, and symbolically represent the exact centre of the island.

EUNUS & THE FIRST SERVILE WAR

Eunus, originally from Syria, and a slave in Enna, organized a rebellion in 139 BC which led to the First Servile War. Sicilian slaves were notoriously badly treated; branding with a horseshoe was commonplace. The best near-contemporary accounts we have are by Diodorus of Sicily (90–30 BC) and Florus, quoting Livy. They say that Eunus claimed to be acting in the name of the Syrian goddess Atargatis, the equivalent of Ceres (Demeter). This made a great impression on the field workers, for whom Ceres, in this grain-growing area, was an important deity. He is said to have convinced his followers that the goddess spoke through him by breathing out fumes from a sulphur-filled nut secreted in his mouth, a trick that he also used to entertain his master and guests at dinner parties. Having convinced his colleagues to murder their Roman owners but to respect the farms, he set himself up as a king (Antioch I), and even minted coins. His forces put the majority of the citizens of Enna to the sword, sparing only the metalworkers. Joined by the ex-herdsman Cleon from Agrigento, they put together an army of some 200,000 men, and took Taormina before laying siege to Messina. The revolt was only eventually suffocated by the Roman consul Publius Rupilius in 132 BC, who laid siege to Taormina and starved the rebel slaves into submission. The slaves (15,000 of them) were thrown over the battlements of Taormina Castle (other sources say crucified). Cleon committed suicide. Pursued by Rupilius, Eunus fled from Enna. His men turned on each other in desperation and he died in prison at Morgantina, after atrocious torture; and (obviously) the conditions of the slaves worsened.

ENVIRONS OF ENNA

CALASCIBETTA

Calascibetta is perched on a flat-topped hill opposite Enna. It is particularly pictur-esque when seen from a distance (and provides one of the most delightful views from Enna). The narrow main street leads up to the main square, with its Fascist-era mon-uments and the Chiesa Madre (*open 9.30–1 & 4.30–7*), built between 1310–40 for Peter II of Aragon, who replaced the castle with this church; the façade, surmounted by the bells, was rebuilt after the 1693 earthquake. The spacious interior, with a cen-tral nave and two side aisles, is divided by ten magnificent columns of the local hard red stone called *di cutu*; three of them are monolithic. The bases are cube-shaped, with faces and animals carved on the corners, the fourth north-aisle base shows Peter of Aragon, his queen, his son, and the anonymous sculptor.

A one-way street leads back down to Piazza Umberto where the signposted road to Enna leads downhill past the church and convent of the Cappuccini, on the edge of the hill. In the church is a splendid large altarpiece of the Epiphany by Filippo Paladini (*see p. 253*), in the enormous original wooden frame.

Environs of Calascibetta

No fewer than ten archaeological areas have been located around Calascibetta, a region which has been inhabited continuously since prehistoric times. One of the eas-iest to visit is the **Realmese necropolis** (*unenclosed*), c. 3km northwest of Calascibetta, well signposted; the road suddenly finishes on the brink of an old quar-ry, and paths lead down into the valley, where some 300 rock-hewn tombs (9th–4th centuries BC) have been found (stout boots needed in winter). In summer the moun-tainside is covered with deep purple thyme and yellow mullein; there are many shrikes in this area.

VILLAROSA

Villarosa, in the sulphur-rich hills west of Enna, was founded in 1762 by Placido Notarbartolo, who asked the painter Rosa Ciotti to design the town for him; the result is an octagonal central square with four main streets. Villarosa became quite prosperous in the 19th century, thanks to the sulphur mines. On the subject is an intriguing museum housed in a train in the railway station: the **Museo di Arte Mineraria e Civiltà Contadina** (*open 9.30–12 & 4.30–8, closed Mon; T: 0935 31126 or 338 4809721, www.trenomuseovillarosa.com*). One carriage is dedicated to the his-tory of steam trains in Sicily, the others to mining activities and farming methods. Outside the town, on the SS 121, is the local baron's home, Villa Lucrezia, where another small museum has been opened: the **Museo della Memoria** (*T: 0935 567095 or 338 4809721 to request visit, www.museodellamemoria.it*) with a collection of 19th-century clothes and furniture.

LAGO DI PERGUSA

Lago di Pergusa, 9km south of Enna, is one of the few natural lakes in Sicily. It is said to occupy the chasm from which Pluto emerged to carry Persephone down to the underworld (*see p. 281*), as mentioned by Milton in *Paradise Lost*:

> *Not that fair field*
> *Of Enna, where Proserpin gath'ring flow'rs*
> *Herself a fairer Flow'r by gloomy Dis*
> *Was gather'd, which cost Ceres all that pain*
> *To seek her through the world...*
> Paradise Lost, Book IV

Today the lake has no visible inlet or outlet and is apparently disappearing, perhaps because building activity nearby has damaged its supply channels. The vegetation on the shores, as well as the bird-life, have suffered greatly since the 1950s, when it was decided to build a motor-racing track around it. Though the lake has been declared a nature reserve, a small—and vocal—part of the population is insisting on the continuation of the motorcycle competitions, and is even dreaming of the eventual return of Formula 1.

On a hill above the lake (signposted) excavations (*not open to the public*) were begun in 1878 of the necropolis, city and walls of **Cozzo Matrice**, a Bronze Age settlement. About 10km southwest of the lake in Località Gerace, a Roman villa with polychrome mosaics was discovered in 1994: the excavations have since been covered over.

A short way southeast of Pergusa is the neat and tidy farming town of **Valguarnera Caropepe** (the name means 'Valguarnera expensive pepper'; the second part is now usually dropped). It was founded by the Valguarnera family in 1628, and reached prosperity thanks to its sulphur mines. There is a textile factory here now.

In the countryside east of Valguarnera are the isolated, desolate ruins of the medieval castle of **Gresti**, on an enormous rock split in two—a very rough track for the last part of the way, but incredibly beautiful at sunset.

PIAZZA ARMERINA

The town of Piazza Armerina has a medieval character, with dark cobbled streets and interesting Baroque monuments. The inhabitants are of Lombard origin; many of them have blue eyes and blond hair, and they have their own particular dialect. The town is divided into four districts: Monte (on the highest point of Monte Mira, where the new town was built in 1163); Castellina (the district around the church of San Francesco d'Assisi, so-called because of a small castle which once protected it); Canali (once the Jewish Ghetto; the church of Santa Lucia was once the synagogue); and Casalotto (a separate village, which became part of the city only in the 16th century).

Though it was once far more important and more populous than Enna (which was named capital of the province by Mussolini), it was little known to travellers before the discovery of the Roman villa nearby at Casale (*see p. 268 below*). It has suffered considerably from depopulation throughout the 20th century.

HISTORY OF PIAZZA ARMERINA

The town was probably founded by the Sicels near Casale, where the Romans would later build their luxurious villa, a well-watered, fertile area, which was conquered by the Arabs in 861, and named *Iblatasah*. The name may derive from *palatia*, a reference to the imperial villa, whose imposing ruins were visible for many centuries. In 1091 Count Roger gave it to his Lombard troops, who had taken it after a particularly ferocious battle; the Lombards called their new home *Plutia*. Less than a century later, in 1161, William I (the Bad) discovered that Ruggero Sclavo of Plutia was a ringleader in a rebellion against him; he sent Saracen troops to destroy the city and scatter the inhabitants (barely a hundred survived). When his son William II (the Good) came to power in 1163, the Lombards begged him to allow reconstruction; he replied that he could not disobey his father's edict, but they could build a new town 3km away, on Monte Mira (now the Monte quarter); it was called *Plutia Armoria*, now Piazza Armerina. After the Sicilian Vespers (*see p. 73*), Piazza Armerina was vocal in demanding independence for the island. At a meeting of the Sicilian Parliament convened here in December 1295, Frederick II of Aragon was declared king. The townspeople stoutly resisted the attempts of Robert of Anjou to reclaim the island for his family. In recognition of this loyalty, King Frederick granted the town many privileges, which are listed in a manuscript, *Il Libro dei Privilegi*, still in the civic library.

THE TOWN CENTRE

A number of streets converge on the central Piazza Garibaldi, a favourite meeting place, with tall palm trees. Here is the 18th-century Palazzo di Città next to the church of the Fundrò (or San Rocco), with a carved sandstone doorway. Between them Via Cavour leads up past the former seat of the electricity board, restored as the law courts. Further uphill is the former convent of San Francesco with an elaborate Gagini balcony high up on the corner.

The road continues past the 17th-century Palazzo del Vescovado to Piazza del Duomo, at the top of the hill, with a pretty view from its terrace over the district of Monte. Here is a statue (1905) of Baron Marco Trigona, who was responsible for financing the rebuilding of the duomo in 1627. The fine brick façade of the large 18th-century Palazzo Trigona is also in the piazza. The façade was added in 1719 and the dome in 1768. The lovely bell-tower (c. 1490) survives from an earlier church.

The entrance to the **duomo** is by one of the side doors. In the interior the crossing and transepts, decorated in white and blue, are unusually light and spacious. On the high altar is a copy of a venerated Byzantine panel painting, the *Madonna of the Victories*; the original is preserved behind in a 17th-century silver tabernacle. The painting was given by Pope Alexander II to Count Roger in 1063, after the battle of Cerami, and entrusted to the group of Lombards who took the city from the Muslims. Three of the 17th-century paintings in the sanctuary are by Zoppo di Gangi (Gaspare Vazano, *see p. 102*). In the little chapel to the left of the sanctuary (above the door of which is the *Martyrdom of St Agatha*, 1600, by Jacopo Ligozzi) is a Cross, painted on wood, attributed to a Provençal artist (1485).

The altarpiece of the *Assumption of the Virgin* (1612) in the north transept is by Filippo Paladini (*see p. 253*). The organ is by Donato del Piano (1760). The font is surrounded by a Gaginesque portal in mottled beige marble, decorated with monsters' heads, which survives from the earlier church. An equestrian statuette of Count Roger and a late 14th-century reliquary by Paolo d'Aversa are among the cathedral's treasures, which may one day be exhibited in a museum.

The Lower Town

The picturesque Via Monte leads downhill through an interesting part of the town, while Via Floresta leads down past the back of Palazzo Trigona with its Renaissance loggia and ends in Piazza Castello. Here is the 14th-century castle, overgrown with creepers, and four small 17th-century palaces. From here Via Vittorio Emanuele continues down past the Jesuit College on the right, now housing the Biblioteca Comunale. This is one of the most important libraries in Sicily, with a small museum of antiquities including some swords, First World War shotguns, terracotta and bronze statuettes, and the *Libro dei Privilegi*, a list of concessions granted by the kings of Sicily from 1300 to 1760.

To the east of the centre, in Piazza Umberto, is **San Giovanni dei Rodi**, the plain 13th-century chapel of the Knights of St John, with lancet windows. Nearby are the eccentric façades of Santo Stefano and the opera house, Teatro Garibaldi (1905). Downhill are the fine public gardens, Villa Garibaldi, near the 16th-century church of San Pietro. On the rise to the south the church of the Carmine preserves a campanile and cloister of the 14th–15th centuries.

VILLA ROMANA DEL CASALE

Open 8–6; T: 0935 680036 or 0935 683000
This famous villa lies 5.5km southwest of Piazza Armerina, in the *contrada* of Casale. The road from Piazza Armerina (signposted *Mosaici*) leads under a high road viaduct and then along a pretty valley. The complex, which has some of the most extensive and most beautiful Roman mosaics known, is a World Heritage Site and receives thousands of visitors a day. It is beginning to show signs of strain, especially in spring when the school groups go through.

HISTORY OF THE VILLA

There is still no certainty as to the origin of the villa. The most cogent theory is that it was the retreat of a Roman emperor, possibly Diocletian's co-emperor Maximian. It lay in a wooded and secluded site at the foot of Monte Mangone (where the plundered tombs of the villa's necropolis have been found); the nearest Roman settlement was *Philosophiana* (Soffiana), 5km south, a station on the route to *Agrigentum*.

In richness and extent the villa is comparable to Hadrian's Villa at Tivoli or Diocletian's Palace at Split, but while enough remains of the walls to give an idea of the elevation (and many of them are still covered with painted decoration, both inside and out), it is the extent of the polychrome floor mosaics (3,500 square metres), of the Roman-African school, that makes the building unique. The owner was a person of great wealth; the variety and quality of the marble and the coloured tesserae are unparalleled elsewhere; some of the marble was certainly recuperated from earlier buildings, because the quarries it came from were already exhausted at the time the villa was built. Several groups of craftsmen must have been working on the floors at the same time, in order to complete the assignment within a reasonable schedule. The signs on some of the cupids' foreheads, 'x', 'v' or a small diamond, were perhaps the 'signatures' of the craftsmen, and sometimes appear on North African floors of the same period. It is possible that some of the floors were prefabricated in North Africa and brought here in 'panels'; the geometric designs would have been particularly suitable for this. The mansion is a single-storey building, made of rubble-and-mortar concrete faced with irregular brown stones, in some places painted to imitate marble.

Built between the 2nd and 4th centuries AD, the villa, which consists of four distinct though connected groups of buildings on different levels, was perhaps inhabited for about 150 years, before being partly destroyed by a flood in Byzantine times, when much of it was covered with a thick layer of mud. Some rooms were reused by the Arabs or the Normans, who set up a furnace there, but after the destruction wreaked on the town by William the Bad in 1161 (*see p. 267*), the villa was completely abandoned. The buried ruins remained unexplored until 1761 and it was not until 1881 that any but spasmodic excavations took place. In 1929, when Paolo Orsi brought the triclinium to light, and again in 1935–39, the work was continued, and finally, in three campaigns from 1950–54 (too quickly) the main structure of the building was exposed, under the direction of Vinicio Gentili. The slaves' quarters and the outbuildings are only now being explored. Apart from the floors themselves, any archaeological evidence (such as coins or pottery) discovered during the excavations remains unpublished. The mosaics were extensively restored after flood damage in 1991.

VILLA ROMANA DEL CASALE

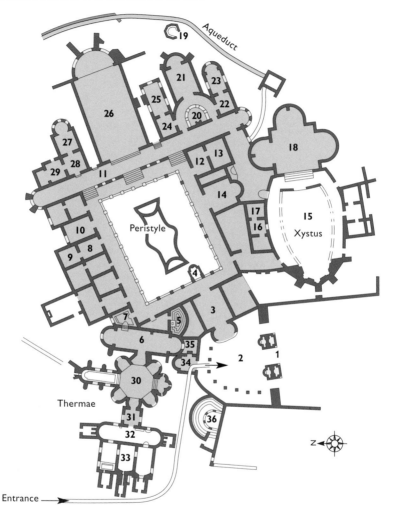

1 Monumental Entrance	10 Room of the Small Hunt	19 Latrine	28 Antechamber
2 Atrium	11 Corridor of the Great Hunt	20 Atrium	29 Bedchamber
3 Tablinum	12 Anteroom	21 Room of Arion	30 Frigidarium
4 Aediculum	13 Room of the Ten Girls	22 South vestibule	31 Massage Room
5 Small Latrine	14 Music Room	23 Bedchamber	32 Tepidarium
6 Circus Room	15 Xystus	24 North vestibule	33 Calidarium
7 Vestibule	16 Cupids	25 Bedchamber	34 Aediculum
8 Four Seasons	17 Cupids	26 Basilica	35 Vestibule
9 Cupids Fishing	18 Triclinium	27 Bedchamber	36 Great Latrine

Most of the site has been protected against the weather by a plastic shelter, causing an uncomfortable hothouse atmosphere in summer, but designed also to give some idea of the shape of the original villa. The following description follows the order in which the rooms can be viewed from the platforms and elevated walkways constructed along the lines of the villa's walls; the plan (*opposite*) is numbered in the same order, showing the layout of the villa, with the enclosed areas shaded.

1: From the ticket office a path leads to a courtyard and the **main entrance**, recalling in its massive form the Roman triumphal arch. It had two fountains on each face, probably fed from a reservoir.

2: The **atrium** is an ample polygonal courtyard surrounded by a portico of marble columns; the capitals are identical to those at Diocletian's villa near Split, coming from the same workshop, and made at the same time.

3: The villa proper is entered through the **tablinum** (or reception hall, which now contains a scale model of the site) leading to steps which descend into the **peristyle**, a quadriporticus of ten columns by eight, interrupted on the east side by an arch, and forming a garden with a fountain in the centre. Archaeologists have found that the garden was originally full of sweetly perfumed flowers such as roses, sage, marjoram, lavender and rosemary, surrounded by climbing plants (climbing roses covered the latrines). On the mosaic floor of the reception hall, members of the household can be seen receiving their guests, with olive branches and torches; they are wearing garlands of flowers on their heads to indicate their joy.

Steps lead up on to the raised walkway, from which the peristyle walks can be seen to be divided by geometrical borders into panels, in which animal heads are framed in laurel wreaths, with birds native to Sicily in the corners, and a recurrent ivy-leaf motif, popular with Maximian.

4: Immediately opposite the entrance is an **aediculum**, the shrine of the patron deity of the house.

5: On the left below the walkway is the **small latrine**, the floor decorated with pictures of animals, including an ocelot. Just beyond, it is possible to look down into the **circus room** (**6**), an exercise-room intended for use before entering the baths, and so-called from the scenes of the chariot races at the Roman Circus Maximus depicted on the floor.

7: Steps lead up past a **vestibule** (this was formerly another entrance to the thermae). Its mosaic, showing the lady of the house with a girl and boy (wearing a yellow tunic, he squints, a characteristic of Maxentius, son of Maximian), and two slave-girls carrying bathing necessities and clean clothing, is doubly interesting because it reveals their style of dress, and because it probably represents the imperial household in a family scene.

8–10: The majority of the rooms (probably for use by guests) on the north side of the peristyle have geometrical mosaics, several of them damaged by Arab or Norman structural alterations; one has an outside kitchen. One floor shows young people dancing very vivaciously. Representations of the seasons figure in another (**8**); yet another (**9**) shows cupids fishing. Of most interest is one called the small hunt (*piccola caccia*) (**10**), where a number of hunting scenes are depicted in great detail. On five 'levels', we see different techniques for catching and killing birds and animals, using dogs, falcons, nets, lime-sticks and double-pointed lances. Some of the dogs (upper left-hand corner) are *cirnechi*, originally imported by the Phoenicians from Cyrene in Libya, and still bred at Adrano on Mount Etna. A dangerous accident during a boar-hunt is vividly portrayed in the bottom right-hand corner, while in the centre, under a red awning (the colour of the emperor),

a sacrifice to Diana is being held, and slaves are emptying baskets in preparation for the picnic, while others drink a toast to the organiser of the day's sport. Notice also the restless, agitated horses, and the attention to shadows. Some of the characters in the scene would appear to be portraits of the owner of the house and his guests. As this room could not be closed by a door, it is thought that it was a sitting room or small dining room.

11: From here steps ascend to the **Corridor of the Great Hunt** (*grande caccia*), 64m long, running the width of the building to isolate the private apartments, and closed at either end by an exedra. An arcade would have overlooked the peristyle. This is certainly the focal point of the whole building, the original idea from which all the

Detail from the Corridor of the Great Hunt, depicting an ostrich being embarked from Africa.

other floors derive; it has been carried out with admirable skill. The corridor (reached from the walkway by a curving stair) is paved throughout with a wonderful series of hunting scenes (*venationes*), one of the finest Roman mosaics known. By the stair is a dignified figure robed in Byzantine splendour, protected by two 'bodyguards' holding shields, who appears to be the overseer. In the apses are personifications of two Provinces, flanked by wild beasts, representing perhaps the two poles of the Roman world, Africa (left) and India (right). The landscape between is divided in the centre by a fish-filled sea on which large galleys sail, transporting exotic animals. The hunting scenes are remarkable for the number and detail of the species of wild animal (African elephants along the corridor, and an Indian elephant and tiger in the right-hand apse) and for the accuracy with which they are depicted in action: the mosaics of the leopard on the antelope's back, and the tigress rescuing her cub are particularly skilful.

12–13: At the southeast corner of the peristyle steps lead back up to an anteroom, and, beyond, the **Room of the Ten Girls** (**13**), whose mosaic shows young women in bikinis, performing gymnastic exercises, and receiving prizes. In one corner is part of an earlier geometric pavement that was covered over.

14: Adjacent is a **music room** with a damaged mosaic representing the Orphic myth; again the animals are lovingly depicted. There was a statue of Apollo here, and a fountain to cool the air.

Detail from the triclinium, depicting a snake-footed giant mortally wounded by Hercules.

15: Steps descend from the building, and, outside, a path skirts an apse of the triclinium to enter the **xystus** (uncovered), a large elliptical court surrounded on three sides by a portico and closed at the west end by a wide exedra.

16–17: Two rooms adorned with mosaics of vintage and fishing scenes; other rooms here are usually covered.

18: From the east end, steps lead up to the *triconchos* or **triclinium**, the ceremonial banqueting-hall, 12m square with deep apses on three sides (hence the name). The theme of the superb central pavement is the Labours of Hercules, the violent episodes being combined into a single turbulent composition. Ten of the Labours can be distinguished, those missing being the man-eating Stymphalian Birds and the Girdle of Hippolyte, the Amazon Queen. In the apses can be seen the *Glorification of Hercules, Conquered Giants (detail pictured on previous page)* and a particularly beautiful portrait of Lycurgus and Ambrosia. The tonal shading of the figures is remarkable.

A path (signposted for the exit) leads round the outside of the triclinium and back towards the main building follow- ing the line of the aqueduct and past a small **latrine (19)** to enter the private apartments. Here Pompeian-style fres- coes on the wall imitate marble. The nar- row doorway, in complete contrast to the sumptuous spaciousness of the villa, was for the slaves, and the widening at the top was to allow the passage of whatever they were carrying on their heads.

20: The original approach, for the householder and his guests, was through the semi-circular **atrium** (with a mosaic of cupids fishing), divided by a tetrastyle portico into a nymphaeum and an ambulatory.

21: On either side a vestibule leads into a bedchamber, while the centre opens into a **living room**, whose walls were

MOSAICS

The richly tessellated floor mosaics which were such a feature of Roman villa life throughout the empire originally developed from Greek models of the Hellenistic period (323–27 BC) when for the first time ordinary homes adopted some comfort and luxury. In Sicily the first mosaics of the 3rd century are crude: chips of stone placed in pavements of crushed tile and mortar. One example is the floor of Temple A at Selinunte (*see p. 160*) where the decorative motifs appear to have been copied from local Carthaginian examples. By the end of the 3rd century there is more local experimentation, as in the House of Ganymede at Morgantina (*see p. 279*) where a mixture of styles include patterned floors and figures (notably Ganymede) with shaped tesserae now in several colours. However, home-grown experiments are eclipsed in the later Hellenistic period by wider Mediterranean influences as Sicily adopted styles and motifs from the Aegean, notably Delos, and then transmitted them on to Italy. Then, in the early centuries AD, Italian styles in black and white fed back into Sicily and by the 2nd century AD there seems to have been an influx of mosaicists from the prosperous workshops of North Africa. The great period of Sicilian mosaics was the 4th century AD, above all here at the opulent villa at Piazza Armerina where a wealthy family with connections to official life in Rome flaunted their status with an amazing array of themes and subjects. It is assumed that the mosaic teams were from North Africa and there is some evidence, from the villa on the River Tellaro (*see p. 369*), for instance, that they settled in Sicily in order to exploit the island's prosperity. As so often in Sicily, the island becomes part of a wider Mediterranean culture, sus- tained in this case by the underlying stability of the empire.   **C.F.**

decorated with marble; the overcrowded, *horror vacui* mosaic shows the poet Arion riding on a dolphin, surrounded by naiads and marine creatures—sealions and sea-horses among them—and is the best known representation of this myth. The inventor of dithyrambic poetry, and famous at the court of King Periander of Corinth, Arion was rescued by a dolphin after being held up for his prize money on board the boat back to Greece after winning a musical contest in Sicily.

22–23: The **south vestibule**, decorated with nursery scenes, leads into a **bedchamber** (**23**) in which the mosaic shows scenes of drama; the musical instruments and the indication by Greek letters of musical modes are of unusual interest.

24–25: Off the **north vestibule**, with its scene showing the contest between Eros and Pan, is a bedchamber (**25**) with scenes of inexperienced young hunters, those in the centre already amusingly routed by their quarry.

26: Steps lead down past the large **basilica** (covered and seen only through windows), the throne-room in which guests were received. The apse is decorated with inlaid marble.

27–28: Steps lead up on the right to the northern group of private apartments which consists of a bedchamber with a decorative mosaic depicting a variety of fruit, and an **antechamber** (**28**) with a large mosaic of *Ulysses and Polyphemus*, showing Odysseus offering the Cyclops wine.

29: The adjoining **bedchamber** has well-preserved, colourful frescoes on the walls, and a famous erotic scene in the 12-sided centre floor panel.

Return down the same steps and follow the path which leads round the outside of the buildings to a group of trees (there is a strawberry tree here, if you are lucky enough to come when they are ripe), and the remains of the bath-suite or **thermae** (partly covered).

30: The **frigidarium**, an octagon with radiating apses of which two served as vestibules and two, larger than the rest, as plunge baths, was covered with a dome. The mosaics show slaves helping people to dress or undress, and in the centre, marine myths (some of these show signs of having been clumsily repaired at a later date). Those in the adjoining room (**31**), show the massage of bathers by slaves, a function consistent with its position between the cold baths and the tepidarium (**32**) and calidaria (**33**), which lie beyond.

34: The **aediculum** designed for a statue of Venus, was the original entrance to the baths.

35: The **vestibule** was the entrance to the long **narthex** (or Circus Room). In both these the partial disappearance of the floor has exposed the hypocaust beneath.

36: Near the atrium of the villa are the remains of the **great latrine**, the marble seats of which are lost; the water-channel for washing and the niches for sponges can be seen.

NORTH & WEST OF PIAZZA ARMERINA

To the north of Piazza Armerina is the Norman church of **Sant'Andrea** (*open on Sun mornings; at other times enquire locally for the key*). Dating from 1096, the austere interior contains 12th–15th-century frescoes, including one of the crucifixion of St Andrew, making this church particularly important for the history of Sicilian medieval art. The abbey was one of the oldest religious communities in the area. The prior was elected by the local Aleramici counts and the nomination approved by the King of Sicily. After final ratification by the pope, the appointed prior had a permanent seat in the Sicilian Parliament and was one of the most powerful men in the kingdom.

West of the town, reached from the road to Casale, a rough track climbs the Piano Marino (or Armerino; so called because from there you can sometimes see the sea) to the church of **Santa Maria di Platea** where the Byzantine *Madonna of the Victories* (*see above, p. 268*) was found in 1348, during an epidemic of plague, which miraculously stopped. Apparently the precious little painting, carefully packed in a cypress-wood box, had been hidden in 1161 to protect it from the Saracen sack. Nearby are the ruins of a castle, traditionally thought to have been founded by Count Roger. The views are delightful.

At **Montagna di Marzo**, northwest of Piazza Armerina, there was a Sicel settlement, possibly the 8th-century BC *Herbessos*, where recent excavations have revealed an extensive sanctuary of Demeter and Persephone, in use from the 6th–3rd century BC. Votive statuettes and even coins have been found. Due west of Piazza Armerina is **Barrafranca**, a farming community of ancient origin; some historians believe that this could be *Hybla Heraia*, an important Sicel town which has not yet been located with certainty. Still further west, dominated by its ruined castle, is **Pietraperzia**, a town of medieval character, especially in the old district at the foot of the castle, which was built by the Normans in 1088 on top of an existing (probably Arab) structure, and which is said to be haunted by the ghosts of three women, who went inside the ruins to look for a treasure and were never seen again. The façade of the 16th-century Chiesa Madre, Santa Maria, is incomplete, but inside there are some Gagini statues, and over the main altar is a masterpiece by Filippo Paladini (*see p. 253*), the *Madonna with Saints*.

MORGANTINA & AIDONE

The extensive and thoroughly absorbing remains of the ancient city of Morgantina lie on a high ridge surrounded by open, wooded countryside. With its superb views, the usually deserted and very peaceful site is one of the most memorable places on the island. The huge site (c. 20 hectares) occupies the long ridge of Serra Orlando to the west, once a Greek and Sicel city loyal to Hieron II of Syracuse, separated by a deep valley from the conical hill of Cittadella to the east, where the original settlement of the Sicels under their leader Morges had stood several centuries earlier.

Morgantina: the theatre.

HISTORY OF MORGANTINA

Here, in the centre of a rich agricultural plain near the source of the River Gornalunga, a group of Sicels called Morgetians (from the name of their leader Morges) founded a town c. 850 BC on the Cittadella hill, the site of an early Bronze Age settlement. They probably came from the Aeolian Islands, judging by their similar pottery. Morgantina would have been an important point on the route through to Agira and southern Sicily. Groups of Greek settlers, from both Gela and Catania, fought over the site in the 6th century BC, and rebuilt the city, which however was not abandoned by the Sicels, who continued living there, side by side with the newcomers. In 459 BC Doucetius, King of the Sicels, seeing Sicels and Greeks living peacefully together as inimical to his dream of expelling the Greeks from Sicily, sacked the city. The Cittadella was abandoned, and a new city was built on Serra Orlando, which probably reached its zenith under the protection of Hieron II of Syracuse (307–215 BC; he came to power in 276 BC). Almost all of Sicily was under Roman rule when he died, but his young successor chose to side the Carthaginians, causing the city's inevitable vindictive destruction following the fall of Syracuse to Rome in 212 BC. By the time of Augustus, Morgantina had lost its importance.

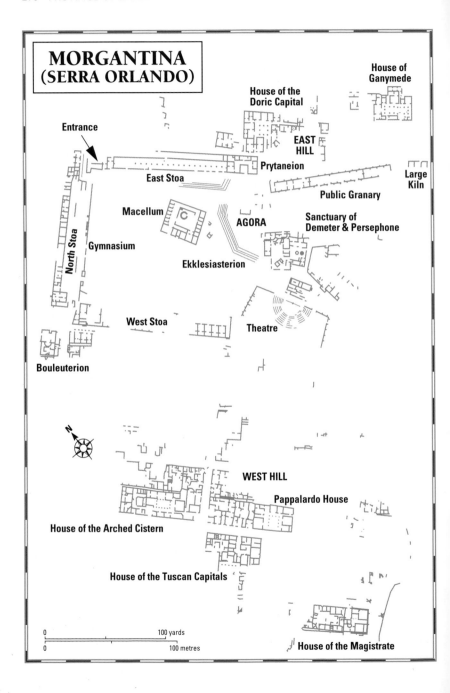

MORGANTINA (SERRA ORLANDO)

House of Ganymede

House of the Doric Capital

Entrance

EAST HILL

East Stoa

Prytaneion

Large Kiln

Public Granary

Macellum

North Stoa

AGORA

Sanctuary of Demeter & Persephone

Gymnasium

Ekklesiasterion

West Stoa

Theatre

Bouleuterion

N

WEST HILL

Pappalardo House

House of the Arched Cistern

House of the Tuscan Capitals

0   100 yards

0   100 metres

House of the Magistrate

The site
Open 9–6; T: 0935 87955.

The site was excavated for the first time by the Swedish archaeologist Erik Sjoqvist in 1955 for Princeton University; he was under the impression that the city was *Erbessa*, until a wooden die carved with the initials MGT and coins proved conclusively that he had found Morgantina. Precious objects of gold and silver found during the excavations are in the Metropolitan Museum of New York, while a large stone statue of *Persephone* is in the Paul Getty Museum at Malibu. The main excavations consist of the area of the agora laid out in the 3rd century BC and the residential areas on the two low hills to the east and west of the agora. The entrance is through the gap between the east stoa and north stoa, where the remains of the gymnasium can be seen. A number of lava millstones, used for grinding wheat, have been placed here—most of them were found in the residential quarters. This area of the upper agora was also enclosed on the west and east side by a stoa. At the extreme right-hand corner, at the foot of the hill, are remains of shops and a paved street near the **bouleuterion**, where the city council met. In the centre of the upper agora, surrounded by grass, is the large rectangular **macellum**, added in 125 BC, a covered market with shops, around a tholos.

The long **east stoa** (87m) consisted of a narrow portico. A monumental fountain (under cover) with two basins has been excavated at its north end, and at its extreme south end is the chief magistrate's office. In the centre of the piazza is a monumental three-sided *ekklesiasterion*, a flight of steps unique in the Greek world, 55m wide, which descends to the lower polygonal agora. It served as a meeting-place for public assemblies. Beside the steps is a **Sanctuary of Demeter and Persephone**, with two round altars (under cover), and the pottery kilns used for manufacturing the votive offerings. Behind this, built into the hillside, is the **theatre** (*pictured p. 277*), still with appreciably good acoustics, with room for an audience of over 1,000. To the right, beyond a long terracotta conduit (provided with little lids to allow cleaning), are shops in the hillside, part of the west stoa.

Opposite the theatre, across the valley, is the **public granary**, a long, narrow storehouse for wheat, with a small pottery kiln (under cover), which was added later, and at the other end (by the fence), a larger kiln for tiles and bricks with elaborate ovens (under cover). From the granary a stepped street zig-zags up the East Hill, passing on the left a large building paved in brick, the **prytaneion**, or residence of the magistrates, which could also be used as a reception-centre for visiting dignitaries. The three large holes you can see carved in a stone were to accommodate the amphorae used for wine or water; the house was also provided with an oven. Just below the summit is the elegant **House of the Doric Capital**, so-called because one was found incorporated into a wall. It has the word EYΞEI, meaning 'welcome' in Greek, inlaid into one of its floors, at the right of the entrance.

Leaving the house by the passage on the south side, and walking c. 50m along the summit, you reach the **House of Ganymede** built c. 260 BC, and destroyed in 211 BC, with two columns and mosaic fragments in two little huts (seen through glass doors).

The Ganymede mosaic is particularly interesting as one of the earliest known made with cut-stone tesserae, which also incorporates natural pebbles. There is a fine view of the agora and, on a clear day, of Etna to the east. A lane leads back past the farmhouse and down towards the exit.

In front of a conspicuous ruined house in the centre of the site, a rough lane leads up along the fence (with fine views) in c. 15 minutes to the West Hill, with a residential district at the intersection of two streets, one orientated east–west, the other north–south, where a number of houses have been excavated. To the right, on the north–south street, is the **House of the Tuscan Capitals**, completely rebuilt in the 2nd century BC. Part of the house has been reconstructed to protect the walls and floors.

Across the street, near a large olive tree, is the **Pappalardo House**, paved with early mosaics, and named after the engineer who first discovered it in 1884. Built in the 3rd century BC, the most prosperous period for Morgantina, the house measures c. 500 square metres, and had a peristyle with 12 columns. It would have been one of the more luxurious in the city. In 1966, in one of the houses in this district, a pot containing 44 gold coins was found, probably buried hastily during an attack. Returning to the intersection and heading north, you will see the largest house in Morgantina (partly covered), the **House of the Arched Cistern**, with a cistern beneath a low arch, and several mosaics. On the north side of the hill (near the approach road to the site) new excavations are in progress of another house. The views from the West Hill over the agora are incomparable.

The Cittadella

To the east of the site can be seen the conical hill of the Cittadella (reached from here by a rough road, at least an hour's strenuous walk), which was separately fortified. On the summit is a long narrow temple of the 4th century BC. Here a hut village of the Morgetians (850–750 BC) was excavated, and rock-hewn tombs of Sicel type on the slopes have yielded considerable finds of pottery. Parts of the walls (7km in circumference) of Serra Orlando, and the west gate, can be seen near the approach road to the site.

AIDONE

The little red-stone town of Aidone stands in a panoramic position on the Heraean Mountains, close to lovely woods of pines, oaks and eucalyptus, where the fallow deer has returned; part of the forest is protected as a nature reserve: Riserva Naturale Russomanno (*Azienda Demaniale Foreste, T: 0935 680428 or 0935 525111*). In the heart of the reserve is a photogenic group of large, mysterious stones, called the *Pietre Incantate*—the 'enchanted stones'. Legend says they are a petrified band of maniacal St Vitus dancers.

Aidone was founded by Count Roger for the families of the Lombard troops from Monferrato, who accompanied his third wife Adelaide, mother of Roger II. In 1282 the town took a leading role in the famous uprising against the Angevins, the Sicilian Vespers (*see p. 73*).

In the upper part of the town, in Piazza Torres Truppia, is a restored 17th-century Capuchin convent, now the **Museo Archeologico** (*open 8–6; T: 0935 87307*), with a well-displayed collection of finds from Morgantina. The entrance is through a charming little church with wooden statues. The ground floor has Bronze Age and Iron Age finds from the Cittadella, including material from huts inhabited by the Morgetic colony. Upstairs are Corinthian and Attic ceramics, antefixes with gorgons' heads (6th century BC), a large red-figure krater by the Euthymides painter, an Attic Corinthian krater with birds, and lekythoi. There is also a fine collection of ceramics from the agora zone of Serra Orlando (including a plate with three fish), and from the houses excavated on the west and east hills (including statues), as well as fine large busts of *Persephone* (3rd century BC) from the three sanctuaries of Demeter and Persephone so far found in the district. Another room on two levels has a display of household objects, cooking utensils, agricultural implements, toys and masks, all found at Morgantina.

THE CULT OF DEMETER

The goddess Demeter, patroness of the sowing of seed and the harvesting of corn, was already ancient when first recorded in the 8th century BC. 'Blonde Demeter separates fruit and chaff in the rushing of the winds' in Homer's *Iliad*. Demeter's daughter by Zeus is Persephone. There is the legend, sometimes placed in Eleusis in Greece but more often by Lago di Pergusa near Enna in Sicily, that Persephone and her companions are gathering flowers in a meadow when the earth opens and Hades, the god of the underworld, charges out in his chariot and seizes Persephone. The Sicilian legend says that he re-enters the earth with his captive at the Cyane spring near Syracuse: there are records that there were drowning sacrifices at that site in ancient times which may be linked to the myth. Demeter wanders the earth desolate but eventually finds and rescues Persephone. However, by now Persephone is part of the underworld and must always return there for a third of the year. While she is underground, Demeter is in despair and nothing can germinate or grow. This myth, of the cycle of death and rebirth, is an ancient one with echoes in many different cultures. As Sicily was an oasis of fertility compared with the home cities of the Greek colonists, it is not surprising that the legends surrounding Demeter should become so well rooted here. They may have been introduced by the Greeks specifically because of the importance of gaining the goddess' support when they first established their settlements. Demeter's most important festival, the *Thesmophoria*, was held in secret in autumn at the sowing season and restricted to women whose personal fertility was linked in ritual to the fertility of the land. 						C.F.

NORTHEAST OF ENNA

The River Salso, so-called because of its slightly salty water, springs from Monte Bauda in the Madonie Mountains, and flows east, forming Lake Pozzillo, before it joins the Simeto. The countryside along its course is particularly spectacular, and there are numerous interesting and very ancient little towns.

LEONFORTE

Leonforte is a delightful little town founded in 1610 by the local overlord Nicolò Placido Branciforte. He saw the potential of all the rivers and mills, and founded a city here, naming it after the lion on his family coat of arms. Today the town bases its economy on the production of lentils, broad beans, and late-ripening peaches. Via Porta Palermo leads to the main street, Corso Umberto or Cassaro, just before which, below the road to the left, is the Chiesa Madre (17th–18th centuries), with a striking façade in a mixture of styles. It contains numerous interesting wooden statues.

A very short steep road, Via Garibaldi, can be followed on foot downhill past the church of Santo Stefano to the church of the Carmelo, beside the delightful Granfonte (built in 1651 by Nicolò Branciforte) an abundant fountain of 24 jets. The water is collected in a stream which follows a picturesque lane downhill. Beside it is the gate of an overgrown botanical garden, with palms and orange trees.

Just beyond the Chiesa Madre is Piazza Branciforte with the impressive façade of the 17th-century Palazzo Baronale, and, at the end, a stable block built in 1641 (the town used to be famous for horse-breeding). The well-proportioned corso leads gently up through a pretty circular piazza. Beyond, a side street (left) leads to the convent and church of the **Cappuccini**. It contains an enormous canvas of the *Calling of St Matthew* by Pietro Novelli (*see p. 81*). On either side are niches with Gaginesque statues. A finely carved arch (1647) precedes the Branciforte funerary chapel, with the sumptuous black marble sarcophagus (1634) of Caterina di Branciforte, supported by four lions.

Fifteen kilometres to the west of Leonforte is **Monte Altesina** (1193m), thought by the Arabs to be exactly in the centre of the island; it is said that on this spot they decided the division of Sicily into three administrative districts, the Val Demone, Val di Noto, and Val di Mazara. Set in a nature reserve run by the Azienda Forestale (*T: 0935 638520 or 0935 646637*), it is a pleasant trek through the woods to the top, where the remains of a Sicel village are to be found, and panoramic views.

ASSORO

To the east of Leonforte is Assoro, a town founded by the Sicels. Ally of Syracuse until 260 BC, it changed sides, became a Roman stronghold, and was even prosperous enough to mint coins. In 72 BC the notorious Roman governor Verres (*see p. 199*) was forced by the indignant inhabitants to abandon his attempt to steal the statue of Crisa, the town's patron god, from the temple. Assoro was taken by the Arabs in 939, who fortified it, and by the Normans in 1061; during the Middle Ages, Assaro was particularly fortunate, eventually becoming the fiefdom of the Valguarnera family.

The old centre, once surrounded by walls, is medieval in character. The main street, Via Crisa, leads up to Piazza Marconi (Piazza Matrice) and the 12th-century Chiesa Madre (San Leone), a national monument, with a square bell-tower. It is entered by a Gothic-Catalan doorway and has an unusual interior with five aisles and three apses, twisted columns and a carved and painted wooden roof. The gilded stucco decoration dates from the early 18th-century. In the raised and vaulted presbytery is a fine marble altarpiece of the Gagini school (1515) with statues and reliefs, and two early 16th-century Valguarnera funerary monuments on the side walls. Over the nave hangs a Crucifix (late 15th-century), painted on both sides. The high altar has three Gothic statues. To the left of the presbytery is a double chapel, the first with Gothic vaulting and bosses, and the second with Baroque decoration. Here is a carved processional Crucifix attributed to Gian Domenico Gagini, and two 17th-century sarcophagi. In the nave are some particularly interesting 16th-century polychrome gilded wooden statues. The porch of the church is connected by a Gothic arch to Palazzo Valguarnera, which has a balcony supported by grotesque heads. The Baroque portal of an oratory is also in the square.

On the top of Monte Stella is the **Castello Valguarnera**, separated from the town by a steep slope. It is only accessible from the west. Some of the stones used for building the walls show Greek inscriptions—probably an example of recycling building material in the past. Most of the visible ruins go back to the 14th century, when the Valguarnera family took over Assoro. It is said that Queen Blanche of Castile, granddaughter of Eleanor of Aquitaine, mother of 'Saint Louis IX' King of France and also of Charles I of Sicily, once stayed here.

AGIRA & ENVIRONS

The little town of Agira is perched on a conical hill. The ancient *Agyrion* was a Sicel settlement, important for its position between Sicel territory and that of the Sicans. It was colonised with Greeks in 339 BC by Timoleon of Corinth (the parent-city of Syracuse), who came to Sicily to oust the tyrant Dionysius II. Games were regularly organized in honour of Heracles, for whom there was a strong cult. Traces have been found here of Roman houses with mosaic pavements, a temple on what must have been the acropolis, and necropoleis of the 4th–3rd centuries BC. Diodorus Siculus, the historian (90–20 BC), was born in Agira: in his description of Timoleon's city he declares the theatre to be the most beautiful in Sicily after that of Syracuse. Diodorus was the first historian to use the chronology of the Olympic Games to date historical events. The town was the scene of the miracles of the apocryphal St Philip of Argirò, a hermit from Syria, who is said by the local people to have imprisoned the devil in a nearby cave, where he can be heard wailing on stormy nights. Pope Leo II (682–83), who instituted the kiss of peace during High Mass, was probably born here.

Exploring Agira

The highway SS 121 becomes Via Vittorio Emanuele, leading to Largo Mercato, with the church of **San Filippo** (12th and 14th centuries). The interior has a central nave and two side aisles; on the main altar is a Crucifix by Fra' Umile da Petralia (*see p. 287*). The walnut choir-stalls, carved with *Scenes of the life of St Philip*, are the work of Nicola Bagnasco (1818–22). In the left aisle are two paintings by Olivio Sozzi (*see p. 314*) and three panels of a 15th-century polyptych. There is a crypt with two statues of St Philip, and a relief of the Gagini school.

Piazza Garibaldi is in the centre, with the large church of **Sant'Antonio da Padova** (1549); inside there is a 16th-century polychrome wooden statue of St Sylvester, a beautiful painting on marble by Guglielmo Borremans, with a precious silver frame, and a 16th-century Flemish-School canvas of the *Deposition*. Via Diodorea continues steeply up to Piazza Immacolata and the 13th-century church of **Santa Margherita**, the largest in the town, with 13 sumptuous altars and several paintings by Olivio Sozzi. By taking the street to the right of the church, passing under an arch, and going through Largo Raccommandata, you reach Piazza Roma, with the Norman church of the Santissimo Salvatore; it has a beautiful bell-tower. Inside the church is a fine Aragonese portal from the oratory of Santa Croce (once the Jewish synagogue), and a 15th-century panel painting *St Philip of Agira*.

By returning to Largo Raccommandata and taking via Sant'Antonio Abate, you reach the top of the hill, and the romantic ruins of the castle. Just below it is the church of Santa Maria Maggiore (11th century), with an unusual interior: two asymmetric naves divided by three arches on columns, with decorated capitals; immediately in the right nave, a 16th-century wooden Crucifix, and a 16th-century polychrome marble statue of the Madonna. In the chapel at the end of the left nave is a 15th-century wooden Crucifix, painted on both sides. A short distance away is the 16th-century church of **Sant'Antonio Abate**, with a modern façade. Inside there are some remarkable works of art: a painted wooden Crucifix by Pietro Ruzzolone, 14 small 17th-century canvases of the Venetian School, and a dramatic *St Andrew* by Polidoro da Caravaggio (*see p. 452*). Polidoro was an artist in Raphael's workshop, who had escaped poverty to go to Rome to carry plaster. After the Sack of Rome in 1527, he worked in Naples and Messina where, it is said, he was murdered by his servant on the eve of his return to Rome.

On the road to Regalbuto, outside Agira (left; signposted) is a Canadian Military Cemetery (490 graves), beautifully kept in a clump of pine trees on a small hill; Canadian forces were engaged in heavy fighting here in 1943. Close to Agira is the beautiful, wooded Lake Pozzillo, the largest artificial lake in Sicily, measuring 6km by 1.6km, usually with cattle and sheep grazing around it. There are plans to build a vast recreation area here, with a golf course and enormous hotels.

South of Agira is a beautiful, remote valley in the central Heraean Mountains known as **Piano della Corte**, where a stream, flowing to join the River Dittaino, has created formations in the rock. It is protected as a nature reserve (*T: 095 312104, www.cutganambiente.it*). The vegetation is typical Mediterranean maquis, together with poplars, willows and tamarisks; there are rabbits, foxes, porcupines and hedgehogs, while the birds include the woodchat shrike, barn owl, buzzard, and the Sicilian sub-species of the long-tailed tit.

Regalbuto

Regalbuto was the ancient *Ameselon*, destroyed by Hieron II of Syracuse in 270 BC, and later re-founded as an Arab village. The people historically feuded with the inhabitants of nearby Centuripe, who completely destroyed their town in 1261. Fortunately, the appeals of the townsfolk to King Manfredi were crowned with success, and Regalbuto was rebuilt the following year at his expense. The curving medieval streets, with narrow side streets and courtyards, are particularly attractive.

Via Ingrassia leads north to the vast Piazza Re, with the Chiesa Madre dedicated to St Basil. The church has a sumptuous curving Baroque façade, and a tall campanile crowned by a spire. Inside is a towering altar, 10m high, with a wooden statue of St Vitus (Giuseppe Picano, 1790). The little town has some fine 18th-century buildings and a public garden. Beyond red and ochre hills on the left there is a splendid view ahead of Etna. The plain is filled with lustrous green citrus groves, many of them protected by 'walls' of olive trees, and Centuripe can be seen on its hill to the right.

CENTURIPE & ENVIRONS

Centuripe is lonely and remote, a cascade of coloured houses surrounded by harsh countryside; hills dappled with light, an occasional prickly pear, a few almond trees. The city has grown out in five directions on the top of its ridge, like a starfish. Centuripe was founded by the Sicels, who called it *Kentoripa*. It occupies a superb commanding position facing Etna, at a height of 719m; when Garibaldi saw it in 1862 he aptly named it *'il balcone della Sicilia'*. With the advent of Greek colonisation, the city maintained good relations with the newcomers, but later it discovered that its true sympathies lay with Rome, an alliance that brought prosperity, wealth, power and the gratitude of Augustus, who rebuilt the town after the destruction wreaked by Pompey during the Civil War in the 1st century BC. In the early Middle Ages decadence set in, although it remained an important strategic stronghold. The people made the mistake of rebelling against Frederick II of Hohenstaufen in 1232, who forcibly removed the entire population to the southeast coast, founding the city of Augusta, after razing Centuripe and its castle to the ground. Some trickled back, however, and started rebuilding; but it was a forlorn effort. Crushed once more in 1268 by Charles I of Anjou, it was not until 1548 that it was re-founded by Francesco Moncada. Its capture by the Allies in 1943 caused the Germans to abandon Sicily.

Exploring Centuripe

The town centre is the piazza near the 16th-century pink and white Chiesa Madre, with an attractive symmetrical façade, with a clock in the middle and bell-tower above. On the edge of the cliff an avenue of pines leads to the remains of a monument possibly of Roman (2nd century AD) origin. Locally it is known as *Il Corradino* in allusion to the Swabian, Corrado Capace, who is thought to have built a castle here. There are impressive views from here.

Close by in Via Giulio Cesare is the **Museo Archeologico** (*open 9–7, closed Mon; T: 0935 73079*), housing a display of some 3,000 objects discovered in the area, including a few of the famous **Centuripe vases**. Unfortunately, a large part of the collection was stolen while the museum was being built. The vases are unique in Sicily for their shape and decoration. The terracotta itself has a particularly rich hazelnut colour, and the ceramicists decorated them further by picking out details in relief before firing, and adding brightly coloured painted motifs afterwards. In the 4th and 3rd centuries BC this pottery was prized right across the Mediterranean. More recently, in the 19th century, and particularly after the Second World War, its particular beauty gave rise to a rash of illegal, clandestine excavations for the black market, supported by unscrupulous collectors. Several local craftsmen also proved to be adept at faking old vases, some of which apparently still hold pride of place in important museums of the world. Today, however, the craftsmen are limiting their activities to making souvenirs for tourists. *Tombaroli* (clandestine looters of ancient burial sites) are still a significant problem in Sicily thanks to the ready market for the artefacts abroad.

The museum is conveniently situated in the archaeological area and the remains are all within walking distance. The local people are extremely friendly, proud of their town, and more than willing to show visitors around. In the valley (Vallone Difesa), east of the town, excavations beneath and near the church of the Crocifisso have revealed an important Augustan edifice, known as the *Sede degli Augustali*. On Monte Calvario (Contrada Panneria) is a Hellenistic house, and to the northwest in Vallone dei Bagni, is a large Roman thermal edifice with five niches. Close by in Via Genova in what used to be the slaughterhouse, is the **Anthropological Collection** (*open 9–1; Sun 10–1 & 3.30–5.30; T: 0935 919093*), a well-arranged collection of tools, furniture, and equipment used until quite recently by farmers, artisans and labourers.

On the road to Adrano, near the Ponte del Maccarone, a large aqueduct (31 arches) constructed in 1761–66 by the Prince of Biscari can be seen.

Catenanuova

South of Centuripe and close to the motorway is the prosperous farming community of Catenanuova, overlooking the River Dittaino, and founded in the 18th century in a strategic spot for travellers going to Palermo from Catania, and vice-versa. Goethe stayed here during his travels in Sicily in 1787, and appreciated the hospitality of the people. This hospitality is legendary. In 1714: when the Duke of Savoy (proclaimed King Vittorio Amedeo II of Sicily the year before, although forced by the Great Powers to drop the title in exchange for Sardinia), and Queen Anna were passing through Catenanuova, a local knight ordered his farm workers to pour all that day's milk into a nearby stream, thus creating for their majesties a river of milk. The royal pair were suitably impressed, and the knight was made captain of the Royal Guard. As a boy in Turin, King Vittorio had breadsticks or *grissini* invented for his delicate appetite.

NICOSIA & THE NORTH

Nicosia, founded by the Byzantines with the name meaning 'victorious', became a place of some importance in the Middle Ages, and was given by Count Roger to his Lombard troops, hence the noticeable local dialect. The beautiful stone-built medieval city was damaged by a landslide in 1757, by an earthquake in 1968 and a flood in 1972. It is known locally as the town with two cathedrals and two Christs, because for a time the churches of Santa Maria Maggiore and San Nicola took turns in being the cathedral, and therefore two processions for Good Friday were organized, with two crucifixes, and considerable rivalry between the two groups.

EXPLORING NICOSIA

The cathedral

The cathedral of San Nicola di Bari has an elegant 15th-century portico with six slender marble columns. The Arab-Norman bell-tower is one of the most important in Sicily: 40m high, it consists of three sections, in three different architectural styles. The base of the tower once formed part of a defensive structure, devised by the Arabs to protect the castle. The decorative 14th-century main door is in extremely poor repair; the entrance is by the north door.

In the Latin-cross interior, a new vault was erected in the early 19th century, unfortunately covering the important 15th-century painted wooden ceiling. Over the second south altar is a *Martyrdom of St Placidus* by Giacinto Platania of Acireale. The 16th-century pulpit is attributed to Gian Domenico Gagini. In the right transept is a Gaginesque statue of the *Madonna della Vittoria*. Over the crossing, in the octagonal vault, surrounded by 17th-century paintings, is an unusually large statue of St Nicholas by Giovanni Battista Li Volsi. In the chapel to the right of the high altar, is a venerated wooden Crucifix by Fra' Umile da Petralia, one of the two carried in procession through the town on Good Friday and called *Padre della Provvidenza*. Fra' Umile was born Giovanni Francesco Pintorno, the son of a woodcarver, in c. 1601. To escape a marriage brokered by his family, he became a Franciscan friar, and from then on devoted his life to prayer and fasting, and to carving and painting crucifixes. Thirty-two extant are certainly known to be his work. In the presbytery the intricately carved choir-stalls (c. 1622; with a relief showing the old town of Nicosia) are by Giovanni Battista Li Volsi and his son Stefano, while the altarpiece is a *Resurrection* by the Palermitan painter Giuseppe Velasquez. In the chapel to the left of the high altar is delightful polychrome marble decoration. On the left side is a font by Antonello Gagini (*see p. 423*) and, in the base of the bell-tower, the funerary monument of Alessandro Testa by Ignazio Marabitti. In the chapter house (*opened by the sacristan on request*) are some more fine paintings, including the *Madonna with St John and St Rosalia* by Pietro Novelli, the *Martyrdom of St Sebastian* by the Neapolitan Salvator Rosa, and the *Martyrdom of St Bartholomew* by the Spanish Caravaggist Jusepe de Ribera, 'Lo Spagnoletto', whose work had some influence on Novelli.

The town

Further uphill is the imposing **Santa Maria Maggiore**, with a handsome Baroque portal. The campanile crashed to the ground in 1968, and the bells were re-hung on a low iron bracket beside the façade. The interior, a central nave and two side aisles separated by pilasters, contains a huge carved marble pyramid-shaped polyptych (*pictured below*) by Antonello Gagini (1512), over 10m high, behind the main altar. A statue in the left transept of the Madonna is thought to be by Francesco Laurana. There is a view from the terrace of the modern buildings of the town, and the church of San Salvatore perched on a rock. Via Carlo V and Via del Castello lead up behind Santa Maria Maggiore to the ruins of the Norman castle. Views from here are splendid.

From Piazza Garibaldi, Via Fratelli Testa, a narrow alley with lots of steps, leads up

to a rocky outcrop at the top of the hill, and the 13th-century church of San Salvatore, rebuilt in the 17th century, with an attractive portico and bell-tower. On the outside wall of the tower are the *Calendari delle Rondinelle*, carved stones giving the arrival dates of the house-martins, from 1737–98 and from 1837–45. In the opposite direction, it leads down past the closed churches of San Calogero (with a fine ceiling and works by Filippo Randazzo) and Sant'Antonio Abate, ending at Via Li Volsi with (left) the church of the Carmine which contains two statues of the *Annunciation* attributed to Antonello Gagini. At the top of Via Li Volsi, which is lined with trees, the Baroque façade of Palazzo Speciale can be seen, now propped up with concrete pillars.

Marble polyptych by Antonello Gagini (1512) in the church of Santa Maria Maggiore, Nicosia.

In the 14th-century church of **San Michele** (just east of the town) is a 16th-century font and two wooden statues by Giovanni Battista Li Volsi; the marble statue of *St Michael Archangel* is a youthful work by Antonello Gagini.

The landscape is particularly beautiful east of Nicosia, with frequent glimpses of Etna in the distance. In the rugged countryside at the foot of the Nebrodi mountains the fields are dotted with *pagliari*, conical huts of straw and mud, used by the shepherds as temporary refuges.

SPERLINGA

To the west of Nicosia is Sperlinga, the only Sicilian town which took no part in the Vespers: on an arch inside the castle are inscribed the words *Quod Siculis placuit, sola Sperlinga negavit* ('What pleased the Sicilians, was shunned only by Sperlinga'). By offering refuge to the Angevins, Sperlinga earned itself a reputation for betrayal which is still remembered today. The approach road offers beautiful views over the valley. The village is a delightful little place at the foot of the conspicuous castle rock; part of the town and all of the castle are carved into the stone. The people base their economy on raising cattle and sheep. The road enters the town past the 17th-century church of Sant'Anna and on the right you will see some cave dwellings, inhabited until recently.

Further along the main road, a road (signposted right) leads up past the large 17th-century Chiesa Madre to a car park just below the entrance to the castle (*open 10–1 & 4–7; T: 0935 643265; if closed apply at the town hall T: 0935 643177*), which probably goes back to the days of the Sicels. Two grottoes are used as local ethnographical museums with agricultural implements. Steps lead up across a small bridge (on the site of the drawbridge) through the double entrance. Stables, carved out of the rock in the Middle Ages, were later used as prisons. In one room are old photographs of Sperlinga, some taken during Operation Husky in 1943 by the great Hungarian-born documentary photographer Robert Capa (1913–54). From a terrace a flight of high steps hewn out of the rock leads up to the battlements from which there are wonderful panoramic views.

TROINA & ENVIRONS

Troina, on a steep ridge, is the highest town in Sicily (1121m). Its early capture by the Normans in 1061 is recalled by Norman work (1078–80) in the Chiesa Madre which has a 16th-century campanile, and a Byzantine panel painting of the Madonna. According to the historian John Julius Norwich, Count Roger and his young bride Adelaide spent a very cold winter in the castle in 1061, with little food, sharing one blanket between them, while they were besieged by Greeks and Arabs who had improvised an alliance. Count Roger also instituted the first of his Basilian monasteries here, and in 1082 made it the first diocese of the island, entrusting it to a bishop of his own choice. Nothing much remains of the castle, which must have been imposing; the Normans maintained the Royal Treasury here for many years, even after taking Palermo. Parts of the Greek walls remain, and the Belvedere has a fine view.

In a breathtaking position among the mountains, south of Troina, is **Gagliano Castelferrato**, a picturesque village dominated by a huge rock which incorporates the castle. The numerous tombs carved into the rock show that the mountain has been inhabited continuously since the early Bronze Age. Though the castle resisted the Arab onslaughts, the town acquired importance under their domination, and later under the Normans. The town today is struggling to achieve economic prosperity, thanks to a textile factory (which closed down) and a methane gas and petroleum extraction plant (which has not fulfilled the dreams it awoke in the population in the 1960s). The Chiesa Madre (1304), by the castle ruins, has a plain façade and a spire covered with brightly coloured majolica tiles, and is dedicated to the Irish saint Cathald, who preached widely in Sicily; inside is an old organ and a lovely 16th-century carved wooden choir; the celebrations dedicated to Cathald in August are almost certainly of pagan origin. In the southern part of the village is the church of Santa Maria di Gesù, which contains an impressive wooden Crucifix by Fra' Umile da Petralia (*see p. 287*).

West of Troina, **Cerami** is a little medieval town on a crest, built on top of a series of earlier settlements; it was the scene in July 1063 of a decisive victory of Count Roger's Lombard troops over the Muslims. Four camels taken from the enemy were presented to Pope Alexander II. The name derives from the Greek *Keramion*, meaning terracotta. The church of the Carmine houses a Crucifix by Fra' Umile da Petralia.

To the north of Cerami, **Lake Ancipa** or Sartori, at a height of 949m and full of fish, was formed in 1952 when the Troina river was dammed for hydro-electric works; the dam itself is 120m high. There is a nature reserve (*T: 0935 638520 or 0935 646637*), where the two peaks of the Nebrodi chain, Monte Sambuchetti (1559m) and Monte Campanito (1514m), are protected for the flourishing beech forest, the southernmost in Europe. Other trees include chestnuts, varieties of oak (including the cork oak), holly and maple; the wildlife includes the endemic form of the marsh tit and also wildcat and pine marten.

PRACTICAL INFORMATION

GETTING AROUND

• **By rail:** The railway station for Enna (T: 0935 55091, www.trenitalia.com) is in the valley, 5km from the town centre, on the Palermo–Catania line. On the same line are Villarosa, Leonforte (Stazione di Pirato) and Centuripe (nearest Stazione Catenanuova at 15km).

• **By bus:** The bus station (T: 0935 500902) in Enna is in Viale Diaz. Services run by SAIS (T: 0935 524111, www.saistrasporti.it.) and Interbus (T: 0935 565111, www.interbus.it) to Calascibetta, Catania (via the motorway in 1hr 20mins), Syracuse, Palermo, Messina, Caltanissetta and Agrigento, Caltagirone, Piazza Armerina (in 45mins), Nicosia, Leonforte, Adrano, and Paternò; Centuripe has poor connections: very few buses run from Catania and Enna (Romano, T: 0935 73114); Sperlinga can be reached from Nicosia (ISEA, T: 0935 931103), and there is also a bus to and from Palermo (SAIS). also mainland destinations, such as Rome, Naples, and Bologna. Localities within the province can be reached by ASIS bus from Enna, AST or Etna Trasporti buses from Catania.

INFORMATION OFFICES

Enna APT Enna, 411 Via Roma, T: 0935 528228 & 0935 528288, www.apt-enna.com, www.ennaonline.com; for information on the whole province.
For the town and environs: Tourist Information Bureau, 6 Piazza Colajanni, T: 0935 26119 and 0935 500875.

Aidone c/o Municipio, 1 Piazza Umberto, T: 0935 691677 & 0935 600531; Pro Loco Aidone: 1 Via Mazzini, T: 0935 86557.
Calascibetta Pro Loco Calascibetta, 9 Via Conte Ruggero, T: 0935 569111.
Centuripe c/o Municipio, 28 Piazza Vittorio Emanuele, T: 0935 919411, www.centuripe.com; Pro Loco Centuripe: 18 Via Nino Bixio, T: 0935 73445.
Leonforte c/o Municipio, 231 Corso Umberto, T: 0935 665111, www.comuneleonforte.it; Pro Loco: 265 Corso Umberto, T: 0935 901681.
Morgantina Tourist Information Bureau: T: 0935 86777.
Nicosia Tourist Information Bureau: c/o Municipio, Piazza Garibaldi, T: 0935 638139, www.cormorano.net/nicosia; Pro Loco Nicosia: Via IV Novembre (under the portico next to the Tribunal).
Piazza Armerina APT Piazza Armerina: 12 Via Floresta, T: 0935 85200, www.piazza-armerina.it; Pro Loco Piazza Armerina: c/o Municipio, 1 Atrio Municipio, T: 0935 982246 244. Tourist Information Bureau: 15 Via Cavour, T: 0935/680201.
Regalbuto Pro Loco: 118 Via Ingrassia (Centro Lasalliano), www.regalbutonline.com
Sperlinga Pro Loco Sperlinga: 3 Via Crispi, T: 0935 643025 and 0935 643177, www.comune.sperlinga.en.it
Troina Pro Loco Troina: 71/73 Via San Silvestro, T: 0935 656981. Tourist Information Bureau: La Sorgente, 5 Via Schifani, T: 0935 653666.

HOTELS

Enna
€ **Demetra.** Close to the railway station and to the motorway exit. Simple but very comfortable. Contrada Misericordia, SS 121, T: 0935 502300, hoteldemetra@tin.it

€ **Grande Albergo Sicilia.** Popular, central hotel with good breakfasts, a restaurant and terrace, and comfortable rooms many with views. 7 Piazza Colajanni, T: 0935 500850, www.hotelsiciliaenna.it

Aidone
€ **Morgantina.** Very friendly and welcoming, in the centre of Aidone with 27 rooms (some with views of the mountains) refurbished in 1997, including a good restaurant, and also a car park. 42 vico Adelasia (piazza Cordoba), T: 0935 88088 and 0935 88111, www.hotelmorgantina.it

Nicosia
€ **Pineta.** Pleasant hotel with garden. 35/A Via S. Paolo, T: 0935 647002, 4 0935 646927.

€ **Vigneta** Out of town, but with a good restaurant very popular with the locals, car park. Contrada Basilio, T: 0935 646074.

Pergusa
€ **La Giara Park.** Small hotel built in the late 1960s with air conditioning and pool, in a quiet position; good restaurant with views over the lake. 125 Via Nazionale, T: 0935 541687, www.parkhotellagiara.it

Piazza Armerina
€ **Gangi**. The oldest hotel in town, recently renovated with 19 rooms, central position, no restaurant. 68/70 Via Generale Ciancio, T: 0935 682737, www.hotelgangi.it

€ **Mosaici da Battiato**. Within walking distance of the Roman Villa, car park, very good restaurant. 11 Contrada Casale Paratore, T 0935 685453.

Pietraperzia
€ **Marconi.** Small and simple, restaurant. 5 Via Kennedy, T: 0934 461983.

Regalbuto
€ **Castel Miralago.** Country hotel in panoramic position overlooking Lake Pozzillo, restaurant. Contrada Pettoruta, SS 121, T: 0935 72810.

Troina
€ **Eden.** Welcoming little hotel 800m from town, good restaurant, car park. Contrada Piano Fossi, T: 0935 656676.

BED & BREAKFAST

Enna
€ **Il Mandorleto.** In the countryside with a swimming pool and comfortable rooms. Contrada Gerace, T: 06 50917089 and 333 2923930;

Aidone
€ **Pintura.** Pool, car park, internet point, helpful people, English and Spanish spoken. Contrada Pintura, T: 338 3706220 and 333 6983472, angeloscopzzo@hotmail.it

Assoro
€€ **Casa Museo Elio Romano**. Accommodation in the fascinating home of a local anthropologist. Contrada Murra, T: 338 1137595.

Calascibetta
€ **Longobardi.** On the hillside just under the town. Contrada Longobardi, T: 0935 33647 and 340 2765763.

Nicosia
€ **Umberto I**. In the heart of town. 34 Corso Umberto, T: 0935 361135 and 347 1535382.

Piazza Armerina

€ **Dolce Casa Mia**. Comfortable and welcoming B&B in the centre of town, run by the same people as the Hotel Morgantina in Aidone. 14 Piazza Boris Giuliano, T: 0935 88088 www.hotelmorgantina.it

€ **La Casa sulla Collina d'Oro**. Comfortable rooms with private bathrooms, meals on request, shuttle service to/from Catania airport or station, car park. Via Mattarella, T: 0935 89680, www.lacasasullacollinadoro.it

FARMHOUSE ACCOMMODATION

Enna

€€ **Bannata**. Well-run farm offering excursions to archaeological areas on horseback or in off-road vehicles. Organic food; in summer films are shown in their own cinema. SS 117 bis km 41, T: 0935 681355 & 329 6274918, www.agriturismobannata.it

Aidone

€ **Cammarata**. Spectacular views, organic methods, free shuttle service to/from Catania station or airport for at least four people staying at least a week. Contrada Pintura, San Giovanni, T: 0935 88144, www.agricammarata.com

Cerami

€ **Pancallo**. A farm producing organic food and olive oil, 12km from Cerami, close to the Nebrodi Mountains Regional Park, belonging to the aristocratic Cutrona family; pool. Very good food. Contrada Pancallo, T: 0935 931903, 333 5622691, www.agriturismopancallo.com

Nicosia

€€ **Mercadante**. Beautiful farmhouse belonging to an aristocratic family; good restaurant for simple local dishes;

archery, minigolf, obstacle course, library, bowls, darts, play area for children; donkeys are raised on the farm. Contrada Mercadante, T: 0935 640771, 347 1535382, www.agrimerc.com

Troina

€€ **'A Mecca i Crisafi**. in a panoramic position 4km from Troina, an old-fashioned farm with lots of farmyard animals, guests can help; all food is home-grown and home-made. Pool, horse-riding, children welcome. Contrada Crisafi, T: 0935 656350, confagritroina@virgilio.it

Piazza Armerina

€ **Torre di Renda**. Old farmhouse once the summer residence of a bishop, relaxing atmosphere, children welcome, excellent food. Contrada Torre di Renda, T: 0935 687657, www.torrerenda.it

€ **Villa Alida**. Beautiful old farmhouse with comfortable rooms, the farm produces fruit, vegetables and wheat using organic methods; children welcome. Contrada Colla-Casale, T: 0935 683011, www.villaalida.it

Villarosa

€ **San Giovannello**. 4km from Villarosa, the farm offers comfortable rooms and an apartment, all with TV and air conditioning, some once used by the sulphur miners. Using organic procedures, the farm produces durum wheat and, in alternate years, vegetables and pulses. Contrada San Giovannello, T: 0935 31260 and 328 8677270, www.sangiovannello.it

RESTAURANTS

Enna

€€ **Centrale**. Sicilian cuisine; long-established family-run restaurant; terrace for summer lunches. Closed Sat lunchtime. 9 Piazza VI Dicembre, T: 0935 500963.

€€ **Liolà**, Cosy restaurant with frescoes on the walls inspired by the works of Pirandello; good Sicilian cooking, also pizza in the evening. Closed Tues. 2 Via Duca d'Aosta, T: 0935 37706

€ **Fontana**. Family-run establishment, very tasty Sicilian dishes; open-air lunches in summer, with panoramic views. 6 Via Volturo, T: 0935 25465. Closed Fri.

Aidone
€ **Il Rifugio**. Restaurant serving simple, delicious food, such as tagliata di carne (beef salad), and pizza in the evenings. Closed Mon. 17 Via Martiri della Libertà, T: 0935 88119.

Leonforte
€ **La Piramide**. Homely atmosphere, simple food; excellent grilled meat, vegetables, also pizza. Closed Mon. 26 Via Pirandello, T: 0935 902121.

Nicosia
Vigneta. Just outside the town, a spacious place with a veranda, doing Sicilian dishes and also rooms to let. Closed midday Tues. Contrada Basile, T: 0935 638940.

Pergusa
€ **Da Carlo**. Excellent grilled meat or vegetables; pasta and good local wine. Closed Tues. 34 via Nazionale, T: 0935 541030.

Piazza Armerina near Casale
€€ **La Ruota**. Shortly before reaching the Roman villa, this place will be seen on the left; very good food, simple preparations, the trademark dish of the house is *coniglio alla stemperata* (rabbit with tomatoes, olives and capers). Contrada Paratore Casale, T: 0935 680542.

Piazza Armerina outskirts
€€ **Al Fogher**. Imaginative blend of tradition and new ideas; very good extrovert chef, Angelo Treno. Closed Sun evening & Mon, Contrada Bellia, T: 0935 684123.

€€ **Bellia**. Excellent mushroom risotto and grilled meats. 60 Via Mazzoni, T: 0935 680622 or 0935 685524.

€€ **Coccinella**. Just outside the city to the north. Simple, tasty dishes that are typical of this area. Closed Mon. 2 Via Renato Guttuso, T: 0935 682374.

CAFÉS, PASTRY SHOPS & ICE CREAM

Enna Bassa
At Bivio Sant'Anna, the main crossroad on the way down to Pergusa, is the **Bar Di Maggio**, known throughout Italy, for cakes and biscuits, snacks and excellent ice cream.

Aidone
Cammarata. For Sicilian breakfast, ice cream, snacks, pastries, very good coffee. 23 Piazza Cordova

Centuripe
Pasticceria Centrale. Very special confectionery, unique to the town. 11 Piazza Sciacca.

Piazza Armerina
Pasticceria Diana. For tiramisù, nougat and morning coffee. 34 Piazza Generale Cascino.

Pasticceria Zingale. For the local nougat, made with hazelnuts and covered with chocolate 8 Via Generale Muscarà.

Sperlinga
A special cake is made here called *tortone*, with durum-wheat flour, olive oil, cinnamon and sugar. Try it at **Bar Li Calzi**, 1 Piazza Marconi.

LOCAL SPECIALITIES

Enna

Campisi. A bakery where they still make ciabattina, miners' bread which lasts a week. Also simple local biscuits. 22 Piazza Umberto.

Lina Messina. Embroiders and makes lace, as her family has been doing for generations. 23 via Passione.

Centuripe

Salvatore Stancanelli, of *Keramos*, Zona Artigianale, T: 0935 919126, makes perfect replicas of antique pottery; you will find him in the new craft centre 3km from town.

FESTIVALS & EVENTS

Enna

Holy Week: the religious ceremonies culminate with a Procession of the Confraternities on Good Friday; probably the eeriest of the Easter celebrations in Sicily, because it takes place in total silence. Starting in the afternoon, 2,000 hooded representatives of the 15 corporations solemnly escort the symbols of the Passion through the town, from the church of San Leonardo to the duomo, then to the Addolorata. They wear a wooden number around their necks which is inherited from father to son. First week of June until 2nd July: Festivities for the *Madonna della Visitazione*, which almost certainly go back to the ancient rites for Demeter and Persephone. The celebrations begin a month before, finishing with 124 bearers carrying the statue of the Madonna in procession, on a magnificent float called the *nave d'oro*, the golden ship, made by Scipione di Guido in 1590.

Agira

Christmas Eve: A *Living Crib*, the only one in Italy to take place on Christmas Night, a play and procession involving hundreds of locals, starting in the old town and finishing under the castle.

Aidone

Palm Sunday: *I Santuni*, procession of 12 giant figures representing the Apostles, each carrying his symbol—keys for St Peter, a fish for St Andrew, a sword for St Matthew.

Cerami

27th–28th August: Procession for St Sebastian, including a cavalcade of riders in Roman costume.

Gagliano Castelferrato

29th–31st August: Feast of the patron St Cathald, with a procession of farmers riding horses, donkeys and mules carrying branches of laurel to the church for blessing on the first day; the urn with the relics is carried through the town on the second; and finally the statue of the saint.

Piazza Armerina

19th March: San Giuseppe, with the traditional banquets and ornamental loaves. 12th–14th August: the *Palio dei Normanni*, medieval jousting to celebrate Count Roger's victory over the Saracens, T: 0935 680201.

15th August: Our Lady of the Victories procession: the banner given to Count Roger returns to the cathedral.

Pietraperzia

15th August: an hour after midnight, Mass is held in a cave for the Madonna della Cava, followed by an open-air feast.

Troina

2nd January: Feast of St Sylvester, during which the crowd is pelted with hazelnuts. This much-loved saint is also celebrated in May, June and September.

THE PROVINCE OF RAGUSA

R agusa, smallest of the Sicilian provinces, is also one of the wealthiest areas of the island. Off-shore oil wells provide a large proportion of the national requirement. The hill towns of the area, devastated by earthquake in the late 17th century, were rebuilt with splendid late Baroque churches and *palazzi*, a concerted architectural accomplishment that represents, in its quality and consistency, a vivid final flowering of the style in Italy. The landscape is a limestone plateau, deeply scored by its waterways, which have formed canyons and gorges luxuriant with vegetation in their depths. The uplands provide smooth green pastures, a checkerboard of tidy dry-stone walls, dotted with the intense green, almost black, of the shady carob trees, the shimmering foliage of ancient olives, and the contorted almonds which surround old stone farmhouses, low on the horizon. The limestone rises to form the Monti Iblei (Hyblaean Mountains), named after a great king of the Sicels, Hyblon.

RAGUSA SUPERIORE & RAGUSA IBLA

In the southern part of the Hyblaean mountain range, the town of Ragusa Superiore is an elegant provincial capital laid out after the earthquake of 1693, on a spot chosen by a group of survivors as being more suitable for their new city—the others stayed where they were, and rebuilt Ragusa Ibla. It occupies a ridge that runs from west to east between two deep gorges, and has expanded across the river gorge to the south, where three breathtaking bridges now connect it to the modern town. On another hill just below it to the east is Ragusa Ibla, a finely carved old town of golden stone, one of the best preserved in Sicily. An intricate maze of stepped streets, it is connected to the upper town by a steep winding road. The two centres have many exceptionally fine Baroque palaces and churches, 18 of which are UNESCO World Heritage Sites.

EXPLORING RAGUSA SUPERIORE

The cathedral

The monumental, creamy-gold cathedral of **San Giovanni Battista**, built after 1694 by Mario Spada of Ragusa and Rosario Boscarino of Modica, has a wide façade with a pretty campanile and spire. It dominates Piazza San Giovanni, at the centre of the well-kept upper town, Ragusa Superiore. The Latin-cross interior, suffused with light from the cupola, houses richly decorated chapels and many works of art: paintings, including a canvas of St Philip Neri by Sebastiano Conca (c. 1680–1764), known as 'Il Cavaliere', pupil of the Neapolitan Francesco Solimena; gilded stuccoes; marble and wooden statues; and a monumental organ. Fronting the cathedral is a terrace and small garden.

HISTORY OF RAGUSA

Ragusa Ibla occupies the site of the Sicel *Hybla Heraea*; the Romans called it *Heresium*, and the Byzantines *Reusia*; during their rule it was attacked continuously by Vandals, Goths and Visigoths, and practically abandoned, until the arrival of the Arabs, who refounded it as *Rakkusa*, an important centre for trade and agriculture. The county of Ragusa, created in 1091 by Count Roger for his son Godfrey, was united in 1296 by Manfredi Chiaramonte with that of Modica. The Chiaramontes were succeeded by the Cabrera family, who were disliked by the people of Ragusa, resulting in a rebellion in 1448. Because of this the seat of government was transferred to Modica, which became one of the most important towns in Sicily until 1926. After the earthquake of 1693, which killed 5,000 inhabitants, the wealthy aristocracy, who were devoted to St George, decided to rebuild the town where it was (Ibla), while the equally wealthy middle class, who were devoted to St Joseph, decided they wanted a modern city with a rational street plan, and chose a new site to the west (Ragusa Superiore). The two groups, with the encouragement of the clergy, competed in building a large number of beautiful churches (in 1644 there were 41 churches for a population of 15,000), but considerable controversy arose over which of the two could legitimately house the cathedral. Rivalry continued for centuries, and because of the friction, the upper and lower towns became separate communities from 1695 to 1703, and from 1865 to 1926, when they were united again as a new provincial capital.

The area is known for its asphalt mines. The limestone impregnated with bitumen hardens quickly in contact with the air, providing an attractive black stone which can be easily worked, while the bitumen itself has been used for paving the streets of many Italian and European cities. Oil was found here in 1953, and there used to be oil wells scattered about the upper town. Drilling now takes place offshore, and the oil is piped from Marina di Ragusa to Augusta. Numerous small farms in the area provide durum wheat, olives, fruit, vegetables, and also milk from the local breed of cattle, *Modicana*, used for making excellent cheese, especially the famous *caciocavallo*. Close to the sea, where the Arabs cultivated sugar cane, are market gardens, protected by plastic frames in winter, hence in production year-round.

Around the cathedral

Next to the cathedral is the **Museo Diocesano** (*open 9–12 & 3.30–8*) with a precious collection of works of art from the churches, many dating back to before the earthquake. Just beyond the east end of the cathedral is the elegant 18th-century Casa Canonica. Across Corso Italia is the imposing façade of the collegiate church of Santa Maria Addolorata (1801), next to its convent. **Corso Italia**, the handsome, long main street, lined with trees, descends steeply to the edge of the hill above Ibla. Uphill, above the cathedral, it crosses Via Roma, which to the right ends in a belvedere, La Rotonda, with a view of Ibla and the San Leonardo canyon. Via Roma leads south of the cathedral towards Ponte Nuovo (1937), which crosses the little Santa Domenica stream high above the public gardens of Villa Margherita. From the bridge, there is a good view (left) of Ponte dei Cappuccini (1835) and Ponte Papa Giovanni XXIII (1964) beyond. Across the bridge is Piazza Libertà, with Fascist-era buildings, and the modern town.

Museo Archeologico Ibleo

Open 9–1.30 & 4–7.30. T: 0932 622962
Just before the Ponte Nuovo bridge, in a building beneath the road viaduct which also houses the Hotel Mediterraneo, is the Museo Archeologico Ibleo. The poorly labelled collection here displays finds from the province, dating from prehistory to Roman times. In the prehistoric section, the Bronze Age civilization of Castelluccio is particularly well represented. Pride of place in the museum is given to a unique sculpture known as the **Warrior of Castiglione**, discovered by a farmer in 1999 while ploughing his field north of Ragusa. Made to fit over a door, this carved stone probably stood over the entrance to the warrior's tomb. Castiglione would have been a Sicel centre when this warrior died at the end of the 7th century BC. The relief, carved from a single block of local limestone, shows the warrior on horseback with his shield in front, at one side a bull and at the other a sphinx, probably symbolizing his nobility (horse), strength (bull) and wisdom (sphinx). The carving bears an inscription with the name of the warrior, '*Pyrrinos son of Pyttikas*', and is even signed by the sculptor, Skyllos, very unusually for the times.

Another section displays objects dating from the Archaic to the Classical period found at Camarina, while yet another is dedicated to the inland indigenous centres inhabited by the Sicels, such as those at Monte Casasia and Licodia Eubea; in case 15 is a rare Ionic vase with an inscription in the Sicel language. Further on, a potter's workshop from Scornavacche (corresponding to the ancient city of *Akrillae*, near Chiaramonte Gulfi) has been reconstructed, and the terracotta figurines are particularly interesting. The Roman section includes finds from Kaukana, and early Christian mosaics from Santa Croce Camerina.

Towards Ragusa Ibla

From Piazza San Giovanni, Corso Italia descends steeply to Piazza Matteotti, passing on the right at no. 90 the 18th-century Palazzo Lupis, with ornamented balconies and corbels. Here is the town hall (1880; enlarged 1929) opposite the monumental post office (1930), with colossal statues on the top. In the centre of the square is a large fountain with bronze dolphins. Corso Italia next crosses Via San Vito in which, on the right, is the fine Baroque **Palazzo Zacco**, with the magnificent family coat-of-arms on the corner of the building and elaborate balcony corbels.

Further down Corso Italia is the late 18th-century **Palazzo Bertini** (no. 35),

famous for its three grotesque gargoyles known as *i Tre Potenti*. They are usually interpreted as representing 'poverty', 'aristocracy', and 'wealth'. The corso ends at Via XXIV
Maggio, with two palaces at the corner, which narrows and becomes steeper as it
begins the descent to Ragusa Ibla (called *iusu* by the local people, meaning down),
now seen in its magnificent position on a separate spur. At the foot of an elegant
Baroque palace, a small tabernacle recalls a cholera epidemic here in 1838; in front,
wide steps descend to an appealing group of houses with courtyards, overlooking the
valley. The road continues downhill, passing the pretty Via Pezza (left), which runs
along the hillside, and Via Ecce Homo which climbs uphill to the left, passing a handsome little Baroque building, the Villa del Lauro, that has been carefully restored and
transformed into apartments for short-term rental (*see p. 332 below*). Via XXIV Maggio
ends at the balcony beside the bell-tower of Santa Maria delle Scale, where there is a
superb bird's-eye view of Ragusa Ibla, with its beautiful expanse of tiled roofs, in various shades of terracotta, grey and gold. The large building on the top of the hill is an
old military barracks occupying the site of the castle of the Chiaramonte family. Many
fragments of the 15th-century structure of the church of **Santa Maria delle Scale**
(*open for Mass only, 7.30, holidays also 11*) survived the 1693 earthquake. Outside,
beneath the campanile, is part of a Gothic doorway and the remains of an outside pulpit. Inside is an elaborate Gothic arch decorated with sculptures and (over a side altar)
a recently restored relief of the *Dormition of the Virgin* in coloured terracotta, by the
Gagini school (1538).

RAGUSA IBLA

Crumbling away on its hilltop, with a maze of mysterious, inviting little stepped
streets, Ragusa Ibla lends itself to exploration on foot. UNESCO recognition, a new
university, and use as a film set for an extremely popular TV series on the adventures
of Chief Inspector Montalbano, have saved it from depopulation, which was becoming a problem in recent years. Ibla can be reached from Ragusa Superiore by the zig-
zag Corso Mazzini, or on foot by various flights of steps. By the road is a relief of the
Flight into Egypt (15th–16th century), probably once part of a votive tabernacle. Also
on the way is the delightful **Palazzo Nicastro** (or *Vecchia Cancelleria*), erected in 1760
and once the seat of government, with tall pilasters, a decorative doorway, and windows with large balconies.

To the left is the bell-tower and little dome decorated with blue majolica tiles of the
church of **Santa Maria dell'Idria**, or San Giuliano (*pictured opposite*), built in 1626 for
the Knights of Malta: the cross of the Order can be seen over the doorway. The interior is sumptuously decorated. The Salita Commendatore (once the main street of the
town, with 240 steps) continues down, passing (left) the 18th-century **Palazzo
Cosentini**, with splendid Baroque pilasters, capitals, and more fantastic balconies, the
corbels illustrating scenes from daily life, such as a group of travelling minstrels. In
one corner St Francis of Paola can be seen travelling over to Sicily on his cloak. In
1464 the saint had been refused passage by the boatmen and used his cloak and staff

The bell-tower of Santa Maria dell'Idria in Ragusa Ibla.

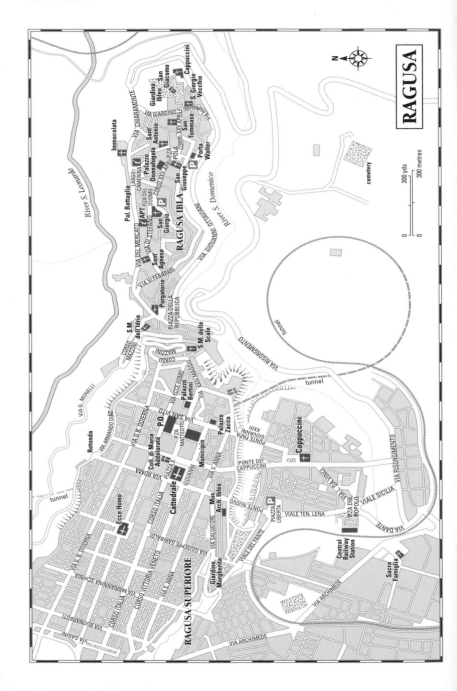

RAGUSA

N

RAGUSA IBLA

RAGUSA SUPERIORE

cemetery

300 yds

300 metres

River S. Leonardo

River S. Domenico

Cappuccini
San Giorgio Vecchio
San Giacomo
Giardino Ibleo
Duomo
VIA CHIARAMONTE
VIA GIARDINO
Sant' Antonio
CORSO XXV APRILE
San Tommaso
Porta Walter
VIA INNOVAZIONI
Immacolata
LARGO CAMERINA
Palazzo Donnafugata
PZA DEL DUOMO
PZA POLO
CORSO XXV APRILE
San Giuseppe
Pal. Battaglia
APT
VIA DEL MERCATO
VIA DI STEFANO
San Giorgio
P
Sant' Agnese
VIA X FEBBRAIO
Purgatorio
PIAZZA DELLA REPUBBLICA
S.M. delle Scale
VIA RISORGIMENTO
VIA GIOVANNI OTTAVIANI
tunnel
tunnel
CORSO MAZZINI
S.M. dell'Idria
VIA G. MONELLI
VIA ARMANDO DIAZ
Rotonda
Palazzo Bertini
CORSO ITALIA
VIA B. EREDIA
P.O.
VIA SAN VITO
PZA MATTEOTTI
Palazzo Zacco
PONTE PAPA GIOVANNI XXIII
Cappuccini
Coll. di Maria Addolorata
PZA S. GIOVANNI
Municipio
VIA S. ANNA
PONTE DEI CAPPUCCINI
VIA RISORGIMENTO
VIA ROMA
Cattedrale
Mus. Arch. Ibleo
PONTE NUOVO
VIALE DEL FANTE
PIAZZA LIBERTA
VIALE TEN. LENA
PZA DEL POPOLO
VIA DA VINCI
VIALE SICILIA
VIA DANTE
Ecce Homo
CORSO ITALIA
CORSO VITTORIA VENETO
VIA SALVATORE
Giardino Margherita
VIA S. ANNA
VIA ARCHIMEDE
Central Railway Station
Sacra Famiglia
VIA S. R. ODIERNA
VIA MARIANNA SCHININA
CORSO ITALIA
VIA BUONARROTI
VIA GAGINI
VIA ARCHIMEDE
VIA GIUSEPPE GARIBALDI
tunnel

to sail safely across the Straits of Messina with his companions. Franz Liszt composed a piece inspired by the miracle. The main façade is on Corso Mazzini, which now continues right to Piazza della Repubblica at the foot of the hill of Ragusa Ibla.

To the left of the 17th-century church of the **Purgatorio** (the bell-tower was built on top of the old walls of the pre-earthquake city). Via del Mercato leads up around the left side of the hill with a view of the massive Baroque Palazzo Sortino Trono above the road. Further on it continues left past the old market building and has splendid views over the unspoilt San Leonardo valley. Via XI Febbraio, peaceful and well paved, forks right off Via del Mercato for the centre of Ibla. On a bend there is a view (left) of the hillside covered with characteristic dry-stone walls. Via Sant'Agnese continues left, and then steps lead up to the wide Via Tenente Di Stefano near the church of Sant'Agnese. It continues uphill and soon narrows with a good view ahead of the cathedral's dome. On the left are the six delightful balconies of **Palazzo La Rocca**, now the tourist office. It has an interesting double staircase in black asphalt stone, and a little garden with citrus trees.

Duomo San Giorgio

Via Di Stefano continues round the side of the cathedral into the charmingly asymmetrical Piazza del Duomo, planted with a row of palm trees, and then slopes up to the magnificent three-tiered golden façade of the Duomo San Giorgio, designed by Rosario Gagliardi in 1744, standing above a flight of steps enclosed by a beautifully crafted 19th-century balustrade, the work of Angelo Paradiso of Acireale. The Neoclassical dome (hidden by the façade but visible from the road behind or from the extreme left side of the piazza), 43m high, was constructed in 1820 by Carmelo Cutraro, a local craftsman, who modelled his design on that of the Pantheon in Paris.

The interior (entered by one of the side doors), with a central nave and two side aisles, is lit by the impressive dome which rises above its high drum with

FAÇADE OF THE DUOMO SAN GIORGIO

windows between the coupled columns. The stained glass dates from 1926. In the south aisle, above the side door (and behind glass), is an equestrian statue of *St George*; on the third altar is *The Immaculate Virgin* by Vito D'Anna (c. 1729–69), a leading figure in the art world of Palermo; and on the fourth altar, *Rest on the Flight into Egypt* (1864) by Dario Guerci. In the north transept is St *George and the Dragon*, also by Dario Guerci. In the sacristy is a lovely stone tabernacle with the equestrian statue of *St George between Sts Hippolyte and Mercurius*, with ruined reliefs below; and Rosario Gagliardi's original plans for the cathedral. By the west door is a stone statue of *St George* by the Gagini school. The organ in the nave is by the Serassi brothers of Bergamo.

Along Corso XXV Aprile

Palazzo Arezzi forms an attractive corner of the Piazza Duomo, with a wide arch passing over a side street. At the lower end of the piazza is a charming little fountain and the handsome Palazzo Veninata (early 20th century). The Neoclassical **Circolo di Conversazione** (c. 1850), at 5 Via Alloro (*open 9–1 & 3–9*), which preserves an interesting interior, houses an exclusive private members club. The carved sphinxes, symbolizing wisdom, over the doorways supposedly refer to the intelligent conversations being held within. Next to it is **Palazzo Donnafugata** (*admission only with special permission*) with its delightful little Arabian-style wooden balcony, from which it was possible to watch the passers-by in the road below without being seen. The palace contains a private art collection formed in the mid-19th century by Corrado Arezzo de Spuches (*see p. 325*) and a little theatre built in the late 19th century (150 seats) where public performances are sometimes held.

The wide Corso XXV Aprile continues to **Piazza Pola**, with the splendid tall Baroque façade of the church of **San Giuseppe** (1590, probably re-designed in the 18th century by Gagliardi). In the oval domed interior there are still the raised galleries once used by the nuns. The beautiful floor is made with black asphalt, mined locally, while the unusual altars along the sides are made of shiny painted glass. In the centre of the dome is a painting of the *Glory of St Benedict* by Sebastiano Lo Monaco (1793). Above the high altar, in an elaborate frame, is the *Holy Family* by Matteo Battaglia. The side altarpieces include a *Holy Trinity* by Giuseppe Cristadoro.

Corso XXV Aprile continues to wind downhill past the closed church of the Maddalena and the high wall of the church of **San Tommaso**, which has a pretty bell-tower. In the oval interior is an unusual font in black asphalt (1545), and a masterpiece by Vito D'Anna—*Our Lady of Carmel*.

Giardino Ibleo

Open 8–8.

Just beyond San Tommaso, beside the church of St Vincent Ferrer (or San Domenico, or of the Rosario), is the entrance to the Giardino Ibleo or Villa Communale, a delightful public garden laid out in 1858, with a splendid palm avenue, goldfish pool, flower beds, and wide views over the Irminio valley. It contains three small churches. Beyond the colourful campanile of St Vincent Ferrer is the church of San Giacomo, founded in the 14th century with a façade of 1902. At the bottom of the garden is the 17th-century church (closed) of the **Cappuccini**, with a simple interior, and a very fine altarpiece, a triptych by Pietro Novelli of the *Madonna with Angels and Saints*. Pietro Novelli had fled to Ragusa after offending the court of Philip IV of Spain; the monks, far from supportive of the monarchy having been 'voted to poverty', gave him refuge, and in return the artist created this masterpiece for them, including the imprisoned Sts Barbara and Agatha in his painting, perhaps reflecting his own concerns. It is still in its original minutely carved frame. The attached convent is now the seat of a restoration laboratory and of the Diocesan Museum (*closed*); the city library occupies part of the building. There are good views from here, and, beyond the war memorial, the church of San Giorgio can be seen on the skyline, with the large church of the Immacolata on the right.

In an orchard below the balustrade are ancient Sicel tombs carved out of the rock. Outside the entrance to the gardens, in Via Normanni, is the 15th-century Gothic side portal of the church of **San Giorgio Vecchio** (in very bad condition), with a relief of St George, behind a little garden. The church, which was very large, was completely destroyed in the earthquake of 1693, but this portal has become the symbol of the town of Ibla.

North of Piazza Pola

From Piazza Pola, with a view of the top of the façade of San Giorgio and its dome, Via Orfanotrofio leads past the church of **Sant'Antonio** with remains of a Gothic portal next to a little Baroque side doorway. Just beyond is the 18th-century **Palazzo di Quattro** with a balcony along the whole length of its façade.

A road descends on the left past Santa Teresa to reach the **Immacolata**, with a fine campanile. It contains interesting works in asphalt stone. Its Gothic portal stands in Piazza Chiaramonte, in a little garden of orange trees.

The narrow Via Chiaramonte leads up past the campanile to the back façade of **Palazzo Battaglia** (no. 40), a very original building, with two completely different façades. You can see the main façade beyond the arch on the left, on Via Orfanotrofio, leading to the church of the Annunziata. This church houses the oldest bell in the city, dated 1501. Just uphill from Largo Camerina, Via Conte Cabrera leads back past more interesting palaces, to Piazza del Duomo.

A road leads out of the other side of the Piazza del Duomo, under the arch of Palazzo Arezzi, to (left) the Salita Ventimiglia (steps) which lead down to the simple façade and the rich portal of the church of the **Gesù**. The interior has stuccoes and frescoes by Matteo Battaglia (1750).

Behind the church is the **Porta Walter** (1644), the only one of Ibla's five ancient gates to have survived the earthquake and subsequent developments. It is a Romanesque arch, about 5m high and 3m wide, with a very faded Latin inscription. The origin of the name is uncertain. Along the road outside it are some old houses carved into the rock.

MODICA

Modica is an unusual town divided into two parts, Modica Bassa (lower town) and Modica Alta (upper town), with decorative palm trees and elegant Baroque buildings, which bases its economy on the rich agriculture of its hinterland. The lower town occupies a valley at the confluence of two rivers, which were channelled and covered over in 1902 after a disastrous flood. On the steep spur between them the upper town rises in terraces above the dramatic church of San Giorgio. There is a sharp contrast between the ample main streets, built over the rivers, and the tiny alleys and court-yards of the six ancient city districts, still perfectly intact, each with its own distinctive character: Francavilla, behind the castle, a populous district reminiscent of an Arab kasbah; Cartellone, once the Jewish Ghetto, between Corso Umberto and Via Vittorio Veneto; Corpo di Terra, the district around St Peter's, with handsome houses and gardens; Malvaxia, a very poor district, also called Vignazza, on the Gigante hill opposite Porta d'Anselmo; Casale, the 'modern' district, with steep cobbled streets, behind Piazza Matteotti; and Porta d'Anselmo, a poor district, under the castle, where until recently many people still lived in cave-houses.

HISTORY OF MODICA

The site of Modica was first occupied by the Sicels, then by the Greeks and the Romans; becoming an important centre in Byzantine times. Under the Normans it became a county, one of the most powerful fiefs of the Middle Ages, and passed from the Chiaramonte in 1392 to the Spanish Cabrera family. It controlled Noto, Ragusa, Comiso, Chiaramonte Gulfi, Scicli, Spaccaforno (now Ispica), Pozzallo, Vittoria, Monterosso and Giarratana, and reached its maximum splendour in the 16th century; at the end of the 17th century Modica was the fourth largest town in Sicily. It owed its prosperity to a particular form of renting out the land to the peasants on a long-term basis, which was to prove extremely profitable, both for the landowners, who were assured of a regular income, and for the farm-workers themselves, who found they could make improvements and invest for the future. Like many towns in this corner of Sicily it had to be rebuilt after the earthquake of 1693. There has always been considerable rivalry between the two churches of San Giorgio and San Pietro, both of which aspired to the role of Chiesa Madre; after the earthquake, the king had expressly forbidden the people from rebuilding both churches, in the hope they would build only one, dedicated to both saints, but in the course of time the ban was forgotten, and so, fortunately, was the rivalry. After 1704 Modica came through Spanish connections to the seventh Duke of Berwick and Alba. For many centuries Modica was known as the 'Venice of Sicily', both for its rivers, then in use as waterways, and for the intellectual fervour of its inhabitants.

Statues of the Apostles flanking the steps leading up to the church of San Pietro.

EXPLORING MODICA

Corso Umberto

The main street of Modica Bassa is Corso Umberto, unusually wide because it occupies the bed of a river, covered over in 1902. Lined with handsome 18th- and 19th-century palaces, it provides a splendid view of the monumental church of San Giorgio (*see below*), half-way up the hillside between the lower and upper town. On the extreme right, on top of a bare rock face, the round tower surmounted by a clock is all that remains of the castle of the counts of Modica. Secret tunnels (*not accessible*) run from the castle to the river and to the church of Santa Maria di Betlemme.

A monumental flight of steps, decorated with statues of the apostles, leads up from the corso to the elegant flat façade of the church of **San Pietro**, rebuilt after the earthquake of 1693, and provided with a balcony. The vast interior presents a central nave and two side aisles, separated by 14 columns with Corinthian capitals. In the south aisle is a large chapel, with a splendid *Madonna of Trapani* by the Gagini school, while a little further along on the same aisle is a sculpted group by Benedetto Civiletti (1846–1899) of *St Peter and the Paralysed Man* (1893). To the right of the church is the inconspicuous entrance to a grotto used for many years as a storeroom. Three layers of frescoes were discovered here in 1989, the earliest of which may date from the 11th century. They decorated the ancient church of **San Nicolò Inferiore** (*open 10–1 & 4–7; closed Mon*); the baptismal font carved into the rock is very unusual.

By turning right along Corso Umberto after coming down the steps in front of San Pietro, you will see the late Baroque façade of the opera house, **Teatro Garibaldi**, recently restored and embellished with paintings (inside) by the contemporary artist Piero Guccione. Born in Scicli in 1935, Guccione was the first president of the *Movimento Culturale Vitaliano Brancati* founded in 1980 in that town to encourage and promote artists in the province of Ragusa.

In the centre of the town, at the former confluence of the two rivers, the corso forms a fork with the broad Via Marchesa Tedeschi, also on the site of a riverbed. Here is the town hall, ex-convent of the church of **San Domenico** (*crypt open 9–1 & 4–8, closed Sun afternoon*) which contains a 16th-century painting of the *Madonna of the Rosary*. On the other side of the corso, in Via De Leva, is a fine Arab-Norman doorway in a little garden, probably once part of a 13th-century palace. Also in Via Marchesa Tedeschi is the simple façade of a national monument, the church of **Santa Maria di Betlemme**, which incorporates four preceding churches, including a beautiful chapel built in the 15th century by the Cabrera, called the Cappella Palatina. At the entrance is a stone with an inscription, indicating the level reached by the flood waters in 1902. The elaborate crib (1881) in the left aisle, was modelled to represent Modica by a Capuchin friar named Benedetto Papale; he entrusted the important task of making the 60 terracotta figurines to the well known boutique of Vaccaro in Caltagirone.

On the other side of the town hall, Corso Umberto continues past Piazza Matteotti with its decorative palm trees. Here is the fine rose window and Gothic portal of the 13th-century church of the **Carmine**, which contains a superb marble group of the *Annunciation* by Antonio Gagini. On the other side is the Art Nouveau ex-Cinema Moderno, soon to be transformed into a concert venue.

Museums of the Palazzo dei Mercedari

Corso Umberto ends at Viale Medaglie d'Oro above which, in Via Merce, is the majestic, but unfinished, sanctuary church of **Santa Maria delle Grazie** next to its huge former convent, the Palazzo dei Mercedari, restored as the seat of the civic museums. On the ground floor the **Museo Archeologico Belgiorno** (*open 9–1; Tues and Thur also 3.30–6; closed Sun and holidays*) has an archaeological collection arranged in chronological order from the Neolithic onwards, with finds from Cava d'Ispica and Modica; pride of place is given to the *Ercole di Cafeo* (the 'Heracles Alexikakos', 3rd century BC), a bronze statuette of high artistic value, found locally in 1966, and only recently returned from Rome, where it had been sent for restoration. The hero's lion-skin cloak is marvellously portrayed; so well, in fact, that many scholars believe that the author could be Lysippus, or one of his school. On the top floor, in the lovely vaulted rooms of the old convent, is the **Museo Ibleo delle Arti e delle Tradizioni Popolari S.A. Guastella** (*Via Mercè, open 10–1 & 4–7; closed Mon*). This fascinating ethnological collection of artisans' tools and utensils is displayed in reconstructed workshops (such as a smithy, shoemaker's shop, basketworker's store, chocolate laboratory, cartwright's shop, saddlery, and carpenter's workroom). Local artisans give demonstrations of their skills, a typical farmhouse has also been faithfully reconstructed, and there is a collection of Sicilian carts.

San Giorgio

The imposing church of San Giorgio (11th century–1848, mostly the work of local stonemasons, followed later by the architect Paolo Labisi), dedicated to the patron saint of Modica Alta, is reached from Corso Garibaldi which runs parallel to Corso Umberto. Some 250 steps (completed in 1834) ascend to the church, built in pale honey-coloured stone. The façade is one of the most remarkable Baroque works in Italy. It has five original doorways and a very tall, central bell-tower. In the interior, with double side aisles and a central nave, the apse is filled with a large polyptych on *Episodes of the Gospel and the life of St George*, attributed to the local painter Bernardino Niger (1573). The silver high altar was made in 1705. In the south aisle is a 16th-century painting of the *Nativity* and (on the second altar) an *Assumption* (1610) by Filippo Paladini (c. 1544–1615), comparable in quality with his canvases in the cathedral at Enna *(see p. 261)*. In the chapel to the right of the presbytery is a much-venerated equestrian statue of St George, while in that to the left of the presbytery is a statue of the *Madonna of the Snow* (1511) by Giuliano Mancino and Bartolomeo Berrettaro. There is a meridian on the floor of the transept, traced by the mathematician Armando Perini in 1895. The fine Serassi organ dates from 1886–88. Among the treasures of the church is a silver ark with the relics of St George, made in Venice in the 14th century. On completion in 1848, the happy parishioners placed a plaque over the main doorway with the words *Mater Ecclesia*, Chiesa Madre, to put an end once and for all to the rivalry with San Pietro.

On the left side of San Giorgio is the 18th-century **Palazzo Polara** which houses the civic art gallery, and from which there is a fine view of the lower town and the hillside beyond. Uphill behind San Giorgio, on Corso Francesco Crispi, is the Baroque Palazzo Tomasi-Rossi, with attractive carved balconies—the caryatids are said to be portraits of the owner.

The Nobel Prize-winning poet Salvatore Quasimodo (1901–68) was born at no. 84 Via Posterla, just under the castle clock. It is possible to visit his house at no. 5, **Casa-Museo Salvatore Quasimodo** *(open 10–1 & 4–7; closed Mon)*. He worked for many years in Milan as a surveyor where his intense homesickness for Sicily inspired many of his most beautiful poems, which are written in a characteristic lyrical style.

Modica Alta

Roads and steps continue steeply uphill to the highest point of Modica Alta. The main street, Corso Regina Margherita, is lined with handsome 18th- and 19th-century palaces. At the highest point of the hill another monumental flight of steps leads up to its most important church, **San Giovanni Battista**, which occupies the site of a preceding church and Benedictine monastery, one of the six founded in Sicily in the 6th century by St Gregory. The top of the bell-tower represents the highest point in Modica (449m), from where it is possible to spot Malta on a clear day. The Baroque façade was erected in 1839. In another part of the upper town, Piazza del Gesù at the end of via Don Bosco, which can be reached by taking the alley to the right of San Giovanni, is the elaborate doorway (1478) of the ruined church of Santa Maria di Gesù.

SOUTHEAST OF RAGUSA

The attractive countryside southeast of Ragusa and Modica is well cultivated, with low dry-stone walls between fields of pastureland and crops, and small farmhouses built of the local grey stone. Scicli is a bustling Baroque market town. Ispica is built on chalk, which has been tunnelled over the centuries for tombs and dwellings.

SCICLI

Described by Elio Vittorini, author of the lyrical anti-Fascist novel *Conversations in Sicily* (1941), as 'the most beautiful town in the world', Scicli has occupied the floor of its valley, surrounded by rocky cliffs, since the 14th century. From Modica a country road runs down the valley alongside the railway. In a little wood under the high Gurrieri viaduct is the simple little church of San Giacomo (14th-century), probably the oldest in the area. Before descending to Scicli, the road passes the site of the old medieval town (destroyed by the 1693 earthquake), marked by the ruined, incomplete church of San Matteo (11th-century), once the Chiesa Madre. The hill was almost certainly used as a stronghold by the Sicels when they rose up against the Greeks in the 5th century BC; there are still two underground tunnels which pass under the church and reach the valley bottom. It is a good place for some gentle trekking, especially in spring. There are many caves, once used as homes. Prosperous under the Saracens (when it was known as *Sikli*), it was taken by the Normans after a tremendous battle, in which, according to legend, the Madonna herself took part. Prosperous again today thanks to its production of vegetables, especially cherry tomatoes, and flowers, it is another of the region's charming Baroque towns rebuilt with numerous churches after the 1693 earthquake.

In **Piazza Italia**, planted with trees and surrounded by Neoclassical buildings, a favourite meeting-place for the people of Scicli, is the richly ornate façade of the 18th-century duomo, dedicated to St Ignatius and to St William of Noto, who is the patron saint of the town. The interior, a central nave with two side aisles, is bright with gilded stuccoes and frescoes by local artists. Here also you will find the brilliantly coloured papier-mâché statue of the *Madonna of the Militias* which is carried in procession in May (*see p. 336 below*).

Opposite is the Baroque **Palazzo Fava**, with a large entrance, flanked by elaborate columns on plinths, surmounted by Corinthian capitals crowned with cherubs. On top of the arch is a mysterious face, with acanthus leaves for hair. The balconies are splendid, especially those looking out over Via San Bartolomeo, with corbels shaped into galloping horses, winged dragons, and mythical creatures ridden by cherubs. The area which opens out in front of the church of **San Bartolomeo** (15th century; the

Baroque decorative detail on the top corner of Palazzo Beneventano, Scicli.

only church in Scicli to survive the earthquake), in front of a rock face, was created in 1824 when the river was covered. The pastel-coloured façade, crowned with a cupola, was built at the beginning of the 19th century by Salvatore Alì; the single-nave interior was decorated with stuccoes by the Gianforma, father and son. There is a monumental crib with 29 almost life-size statues by Pietro Padula (1773–75), the only one of its kind in Sicily. It comes in fact from Naples and the figures (some of them dating back to 1573; there were originally 65) are carved in lime wood.

Via Nazionale leads uphill and on the right, at the end of a short street, is the corner of **Palazzo Beneventano** (*pictured on previous page*). The most famous building in Scicli, arguably one of the most interesting examples of Baroque architecture in the province, it was designed not by an architect but by the local master builders. It too has elaborate balconies supported by fantastic creatures, as well as the unusual addition of a richly decorated zig-zag design running up one corner: on the top are two Moors and at the bottom is St Joseph.

Off the other side of Via Nazionale is the decorative central street, Via Mormino Penna. The relatively sombre town hall (1906) stands next to the elegant church of San Giovanni, with a fine façade. Via Penna winds on past the oval church of San Michele, past Palazzo Spadaro (*open 10.30–12.30 & 4–7*), with its splendid wrought-iron balconies and elegant carved stone window frames, and the stupendous façade of the church of Santa Teresa, now used as an auditorium. The street continues to Piazza Busacca, planted with palm trees, with a 19th-century statue in the middle by Benedetto Civiletti, of the rich local merchant and philanthropist Pietro Di Lorenzo Busacca (d. 1567). Here is the church of the Carmine (1751–69), beside its convent (1386) with a decorative balcony. **Palazzo Busacca** (1882), surmounted by a clock between two mermaids, is now used as council offices. Inside, the rooms are still decorated with wonderful frescoes and stuccoes, and 18th-century paintings. Beyond, to the right, is the elegant church of **Santa Maria della Consolazione**, once dedicated to St Thomas; with a wooden statue (1560) of *Christ at the Column*.

Still further on, surrounded by a rocky crag in an interesting part of the old town, is the large church of **Santa Maria la Nova** (15th century). The Neoclassical façade dates from 1816. In the interior, decorated with stuccoes, there is a high altarpiece of the *Birth of the Virgin* by Sebastiano Conca (1680-1764), one of the most successful painters in Rome during the early 18th century, with a distinctive style that introduced elements of academic Classicism into the grandeur of late Baroque. The presbytery was designed by the Neoclassical architect Giuseppe Venanzio Marvuglia (1729–1814). Among the paintings is a particularly beautiful *Immaculate Virgin* by Vito D'Anna; there is also a Gaginesque marble statue of the Madonna. On the second left-hand altar is a highly venerated statue of *Our Lady of Pity*, made of cypress wood and thought to be Byzantine.

From Scicli to the sea

On leaving Scicli and going towards the coast, after c. 1.5 km you will see the sanctuary church of the **Madonna delle Milizie**, an ancient temple of Bacchus transformed into a church by Count Roger after his victory in 1091. The building was enlarged in 1391, and rebuilt in 1721. Inside is a stone with the hoof-marks of the Madonna's horse. The bell-tower, adapted in 1470, is in reality one of the best-preserved Byzantine towers in Sicily.

Southwest of Scicli is the town's natural harbour, the charming, simple little fishing village of **Donnalucata**, often used as a film set. The name refers to the appearance of the Madonna one night in 1091 'bathed in light'. To the east, near Cava d'Aliga, is a sandy bay.

LATE BAROQUE

The dominant European style of architecture during the 17th and early 18th centuries, characterised by a strong sense of movement and the theatrical handling of space, the Baroque achieved distinctive and concerted expression in southeastern Sicily after the earthquake on 11th January 1693 which killed more than 60,000 people. Within half a century, more than 100 towns and villages, including some 600 churches, were re-built in this triumphant and exaggerated style, an exceptional legacy thanks to the experience and traditions of the native craftsmen, the flair of the architects and the beautiful colour of the hard, local limestone. Formerly dubbed 'Sicilian Rococo', it has more recently been recognised as late Baroque, an idiosyncratic continuation of the mid-17th-century Italian style perfected in Rome by Bernini and Borromini. The streets and squares are arranged as theatre settings for the population to act out their lives. Carefully detailed carvings on the balcony corbels and around the windows attest to the skill of the stonemasons and sculptors. Faces can be portraits of members of the family, or enigmatic monsters. Garlands of flowers and leaves, birds and animals, dragons, hippogryphs, cherubs and harpies, jostle for space, each with their own significance. The churches have imposing façades, playing daring games with convex and concave curves, light and shade, the lines drawing our gaze up from the opulent stairways to the highest pinnacles; the dazzling interiors are decorated with gold and silver, inlaid marble, paintings, stuccoes and statues; the people of southeast Sicily certainly did their best for the saints whom they hoped would ward off further catastrophes.

ISPICA

Parco della Forza

The small town of Ispica was rebuilt on its present site after the earthquake of 1693 destroyed the former town on the valley floor, and has fine 18th- and 19th-century buildings. Known in the Middle Ages as *Spaccaforno*, derived from *Ispicae Fundus*, it re-adopted its old name in 1935. The chalk eminence on which it stands is pierced with tombs and cave dwellings. These can best be seen in the Parco della Forza (*open daily 9–6.45; mornings only in winter. T: 0932 951133*) at the south end of the Cava d'Ispica (*see p. 316 below*). It has lush vegetation, of considerable botanical interest, various water-cisterns, tombs and churches, all carved out of the rock, and a remarkable tunnel known as the *Centoscale* (hundred stairs), 60m long, formerly used by those carrying water from the river to the town centre. Before the 1693 earthquake, at least 5,500 people lived here in the valley, and about 2,000 in the citadel which stood on the top of the rock. The museum here displays a notable collection of finds from the site, including amphorae, fragments of pottery and neolithic tools. Further along the valley is the area still known as **Ispicae Fundus**, with yet more interesting caves and churches, and part of the old main street, which was paved with limestone.

Just east of Ispica is a group of 4th-century AD Christian catacombs, the **Catacomba di San Marco** (*for information contact Senatrice Marisa Moltisanti, 16 Via Dante, Ispica, T: 0932 951124*), the largest in Sicily after that of San Giovanni in Syracuse; consisting of a man-made cave 45m long, with over 300 tombs. Boots and a torch recommended.

The town centre

In the new town centre, Piazza Regina Margherita is dominated by the elegant lines of the Chiesa Madre, dedicated to St Bartholomew. Nearby is a national monument, the church of **Santa Maria Maggiore**, an attractive building by Vincenzo Sinatra of Noto (or perhaps Rosario Gagliardi), with a semi-elliptical loggia around it inspired by the columns in front of St Peter's in Rome. The startling interior is decorated with 18th-century frescoes painted by Olivio Sozzi (1690–1765) during the last two years of his life. Born in Catania, Sozzi married a wealthy bride and used her dowry to put himself through his studies, going to Rome to work in the *bottega* of Sebastiano Conca in Rome and as a student of the great fresco decorator Corrado Giaquinto. His paintings are largely in the Roman Classicist style. He also worked in Palermo and Catania, but was buried here, having included in his scheme a self-portrait as one of the elderly Apostles admiring the Ascension, in the central apse. The large (40 square metres) fresco on the vault, with scenes from the Old and New Testaments, is considered his masterpiece, while the whole group of 26 frescoes is one of the most important in Sicily. Over the main altar is a luminous canvas by Vito D'Anna of the *Madonna*, while to the right of the altar is a panel painting of the *Madonna of the Rosary*, dated 1567, by an unknown follower of Polidoro da Caravaggio or Vincenzo da Pavia. The most venerable chapel is that dedicated to Christ at the Column, in the left transept, with a very ancient Crucifix, thought to be miraculous, and brought from the preceding church after the 1693 earthquake, which it survived. The rather kitsch-looking soldiers, made of wood and papier-mâché, were added in 1729 by Francesco Guarino, a sculptor from Noto. Near the main door is the *casa della cera*, a room containing many of the wax figurines which it is customary to offer Christ at the Column, as ex-voto; there is also a glass case containing the body of Olivio Sozzi.

Fresco (1763–65) by Olivio Sozzi entitled *The Madonna in Glory and St Michael expelling Lucifer from Paradise with his Fiery Sword* in the south aisle of Santa Maria Maggiore.

Palazzo Bruno di Belmonte, an Art Nouveau building (the finest in the province) by Ernesto Basile (1906) has been restored as the town hall. The most imposing building in the town is the church of the Annunziata (1704), with its theatrical façade; it is filled with stuccoes carried out in the mid-18th century by Giuseppe Gianforma. In the sacristy is a painting attributed to Caravaggio, *St Andrew of Avellino*; notice the cleverly depicted hands, and the expressive face. Mounted on one of the side walls is the head of a bull, supposedly the cause of a miraculous event in the 18th century: a child wearing a red cloak was attacked and carried off on the horns of this bull, which suddenly stopped and knelt down in front of the church, allowing the little boy to escape unscathed.

CAVA D'ISPICA

The Cava d'Ispica (*open 9–6.30*) lies 11km east of Modica (signposted). It is a deep gorge 13km long which follows a river (now usually dry) with luxuriant vegetation— many rare terrestrial orchids in early spring. It is also an interesting place for bird-watchers, who might see sparrow hawks, buzzards, kestrels, jays, and colonies of ravens. The sides of the canyon are honeycombed with prehistoric tombs, early Christian rock-hewn churches, and medieval cave dwellings; here the presence of man can be traced from the earliest times to the most recent, although the valley was greatly damaged in the earthquake of 1693.

A ruin in the Cava d'Ispica.

Just below the entrance are extensive Christian catacombs known as Larderia (4th–5th centuries AD). They extend for some 36m inside the rock, and contain 464 tombs. Across the main road is the little church of **San Nicola** (*unlocked on request*), which contains very damaged traces of late Byzantine (possibly early Norman) frescoes. A path near here leads along the dry riverbed to **Baravitalla**, with Sicel tombs dating from the Castelluccio period (1800 BC), and one with a design of pilasters on its façade.

From the entrance (*see above*) a gravel road (c. 400m) leads past numerous caves, including some on more than one storey, ruined by the earthquake. Outside the enclosure an overgrown path runs along the valley passing numerous rock tombs and dwellings, including the so-called *castello* on four floors. At the far end is the Parco della Forza, best approached from Ispica (*see p. 313 above*).

POZZALLO

Pozzallo, the southernmost municipality in Italy, is a busy port with a prominent square tower built by the Cabreras to protect it from pirate raids in the 15th century, reconstructed after 1693, and now a national monument, **Torre Cabrera**. The port, already well known in Roman times for the abundant springs of fresh water in the vicinity, in the Middle Ages was used as the loading point for shipping to various destinations the enormous quantities of wheat grown in the county. Giorgio La Pira, the *sindaco santo* (saintly mayor), who for many years was mayor of Florence, was born in Pozzallo. A great politician, he played an important role in the preparation of the Italian Constitution after the Second World War; but it was his intense efforts to secure conciliation among different religions, and his strong ideas about guaranteeing dignity to the poor, that won him the reputation of being a saint (his case is being examined at the Vatican). Now the area is acquiring importance for the production of carobs, while the harbour is increasingly used both for trade and tourism—there is a useful daily catamaran service for Malta. The lovely beaches, awarded the EU Blue Banner for quality, are hidden behind tree-covered dunes where cane fences control the sand.

WEST OF RAGUSA

The small towns of Vittoria, Comiso, and Santa Croce Camerina have fine Baroque and Art Nouveau buildings and the surrounding countryside is beautiful. Traditional ways of life have been preserved here, involving the production of wine, olive oil, vegetables and limestone for paving.

VITTORIA & ENVIRONS

Vittoria is a prosperous agricultural town (machinery for agriculture, market-garden produce and flowers), and centre of the wine trade, especially for the famous

Cerasuolo di Vittoria. It was built for, and named after the wife of Luigi III Enriquez, Count of Modica and the daughter of the viceroy Marcantonio Colonna, in 1607. Constructed according to a grid plan on a large plain overlooking the Ippari, a small river bordered by pine forests, it escaped the 1693 earthquake with little damage, but a tragic death-toll: the Chiesa Madre collapsed, killing 40 children at a prayer service.

Exploring Vittoria

In the main square, Piazza del Popolo, the elegant Neoclassical **Opera House** (1869–77), particularly admired by the critic Bernard Berenson, stands next to the church of the **Madonna delle Grazie**, with an attractive Baroque façade of 1754, complete with a clock. The simple interior has polychrome marble altars along the sides, with 18th-century wooden statues and canvases.

From here, the central Via Cavour, with its Art Nouveau buildings and enticing shop windows leads to the rectangular, shady Piazza Ricca, and the Chiesa Madre, **San Giovanni Battista**, dedicated to the patron saint of Vittoria, with an unusual Moorish façade and dome (18th–19th centuries). The four bells in the tower are dedicated to St John the Baptist, Our Lady of Carmel, St Rosalia and St Victoria, all of whom were thought to be suitable patron saints for the town when it was founded; the four names were placed in an urn, and drawn out by a blindfolded child. John the Baptist came out three times running. The Latin-cross interior, divided into a central nave and two side aisles by Corinthian columns, is richly decorated with gilded stucco, marble inlay, statues, and 17th–19th-century paintings. The marble floor in front of the main altar was completed with an interesting ex-voto in the 19th century, two vases of grapes: the one on the right, dated 1798, is a withered vine, that on the left, dated 1801, is flourishing; a reference to a terrible blight which destroyed the local vineyards, and the miraculous recovery only three years later, thanks to the intercession of the saint. The wooden statue of St John the Baptist, over the main altar, is by an unknown sculptor who has depicted him as black, and wearing camel skins. To the right of the main altar, under the large canvas of the *Beheading of St John the Baptist* (1600, Mario Minniti?), is an urn with the remains of Vittoria Colonna, brought here from Spain in 1991. The magnificent organ (1748) is by Donato Del Piano.

The **Museo di Arte Sacra Monsignor Federico La China** (*open 9–1; closed Sun and holidays*) at no. 51 Via Cavour, contains a collection of material from the Chiesa Madre (stone carvings, sculptures and fragments of altars), together with fine examples of 18th-century Sicilian gold and silver work.

Among the Art Nouveau palaces in the town, perhaps the finest is Palazzo Traina, on Via Rosario Cancellieri, in the Venetian-Gothic style, a good example of the skill of the local stonemasons. The **Museo Civico Virgilio Lavore** (*open summer 9–12 & 4–6; winter 9–12 & 3–5; closed Sat, Sun and holidays; T: 0932 864038*) is at no. 15 Piazza Enriquez, in the oldest building in town, once the castle of the Countess Vittoria. It has an interesting exhibit on the 19th-century equipment used for obtaining sound effects for the opera house, as well as a picture gallery with a section devoted to modern art, a collection of Sicilian carts, archaeological finds, and some stuffed birds.

In Via Garibaldi, the former prisoner-of-war camp, where some 20,000 Austro-Hungarian soldiers were imprisoned in 1916, the largest of such camps in Sicily, is now the EMAIA trade fair centre and the interesting **Museo Storico Italo-Ungherese** (*open 9–12; closed Sun and holidays*). The museum was prepared with the help of the Budapest Museum of Military History. In the local cemetery is a chapel dedicated to the Hungarian soldiers who died here in Vittoria. The **Villa Comunale**, public gardens, once the garden of the Capuchin monastery, offers a beautiful view over the Ippari valley. Along the River Ippari, between Vittoria and the sea, is a pinewood protected as a nature reserve (Riserva naturale Pino d'Aleppo; *T: 0932 675526/5*). The trees are the last remaining examples of a species of Aleppo pine, endemic to Sicily. Other species have benefited from the protective measures too, including typical Mediterranean trees and flowers, mammals such as the hare and the garden dormouse, the tortoise, and a wide variety of birdlife.

Acate

About 8km northwest of Vittoria is Acate, so-called because of the agate which was once abundantly found along the banks of the River Dirillo. It is surrounded by olive groves and vineyards, some of which produce excellent Chardonnay. In the central Piazza Libertà is the impressive 15th-century Castello dei Principi di Biscari, flanked by the church of San Vincenzo, opposite the Chiesa Madre, rebuilt in 1859.

COMISO

On the slopes of the Hyblaean Mountains, the pretty Baroque town of Comiso is unmistakable for its skyline of church domes. The handsome paving on the streets of the old centre is made from the local stone, which has the appearance of marble. Comiso has a strong economy, based on the quarrying of the stone and the year-round production of vegetable crops and carobs. There is an old Fascist-era airport which is being transformed for civil use.

HISTORY OF COMISO

Nearby, at Cozzo di Apollo, are the ruins of an old city identified by scholars as *Casmene*, a sub-colony of Syracuse founded in 644 BC to protect the route from Acrai to Camarina, and destroyed by the Roman general Marcus Marcellus in 212 BC. The survivors rebuilt their town not far away, and the settlement was fortified by the Byzantines, who called it *Jhomiso*, or 'fountain of water'. It became a fief of various aristocratic families, until 1453 when it passed to the Naselli, who held it until 1812; Comiso flourished under their intelligent, far-seeing administration. Many inhabitants died during the 1624 plague epidemic, and the 1693 earthquake destroyed much of the town.

THE HONEY OF HYBLA

An important preservative as well as sweetener, honey was an indispensable ingredient in the Classical kitchen. Along with the bees of Mount Hymettus and Mount Ida in Greece, the wild bees of Mount Hybla were the most celebrated source of honey in Antiquity. They and their produce became a literary byword for all things exceptionally sweet and good, eventually coming to represent poetry itself. Citing Theocritus (c. 300 BC), the founding father of the pastoral idyll, the American 19th-century nature writer John Burroughs expanded on the subject in his *Locusts and Wild Honey*: 'Sicily has always been rich in bees. The idylls of Theocritus are native to the island in this respect, and abound in bees, 'flat-nosed bees' as he calls them in the Seventh Idyll, and comparisons in which comb-honey is the standard of the most delectable of this world's goods. His goatherds can think of no greater bliss than that the mouth be filled with honeycombs, or to be inclosed in a chest like Daphnis and fed on the combs of bees; and among the delectables with which Arsinoe cherishes Adonis are 'honey-cakes', and other tidbits made of 'sweet honey'. In the country of Theocritus this custom is said still to prevail: when a couple are married, the attendants place honey in their mouths, by which they would symbolize the hope that their love may be as sweet to their souls as honey to the palate.' In his first *Eclogue*, Virgil described the ideal lullaby for old age to be the murmuring of Hybla bees. Ovid compared women's hairstyles to their numberlessness. In Shakespeare's *Julius Caesar*, with some sarcasm Cassius remarks that Mark Antony's fine words 'rob the Hybla bees and leave them honeyless'. In one sonnet John Keats longs to sweeten his song by sipping the dew on 'Hybla's honied roses' in the moonlight. Fanny Trollope, disappointed in business in the US, made euphemistic use of the honey's proverbial qualities in her *Domestic Manners of the Americans* (1832): 'During nearly two years that I resided in Cincinnati, or its neighbourhood, I neither saw a beggar, nor a man of sufficient fortune to permit his ceasing his efforts to increase it; thus every bee in the hive is actively employed in search of that honey of Hybla, vulgarly called money; neither art, science, learning, nor pleasure can seduce them from its pursuit.' That pursuit was possibly not far from the mind of James Leigh Hunt when he published a popular volume of Sicilian *divertimenti* simply entitled *A Jar of Honey from Mount Hybla* in 1848. The actual thing can in fact still be purchased, in different varieties according to the flora of the season: the *satra* honey is derived from wild thyme; *zagara* honey from citrus flowers.

Exploring Comiso

Three palm trees stand outside the church of the **Santissima Annunziata**, with a spectacular stairway in front, and a beautiful blue dome above. It was rebuilt in

1772–93 on the ruins of the Byzantine church of St Nicholas. The plans, which can be seen in the sacristy, were drawn up by Rosario Gagliardi. The luminous interior has stucco decoration in blue, grey and white. It contains a wooden 15th-century statue of St Nicholas on the first right-hand altar, and an impressive Crucifix attributed to Fra' Umile da Petralia in the right transept. On the second north altar is a panel painting of the *Transition of the Virgin* (1605) by local artist Narciso Cidonio. The font (1913) is a fine piece in marble and bronze by the Palermo-born sculptor Mario Rutelli (1859-1941) whose monumental public works include the Fountain of the Naiads in Rome's Piazza Repubblica. In the apse is a painting of the *Nativity and Resurrection of Christ* by native artist Salvatore Fiume (1915-97).

Via Papa Giovanni XXIII leads downhill in front of the church, and via degli Studi leads right to the central **Piazza Fonte Diana** with its amusing fountain (1937). The waters of this spring were said to refuse to mix with wine when poured by unchaste hands; in Roman days they supplied a bath-house, with a mosaic of Neptune, the remains of which are visible beneath the town hall. Nearby, in Piazza delle Erbe, which was the old market place, rises the imposing Chiesa Madre, **Santa Maria delle Stelle**, also with a dome. The fine 18th-century façade is attributed to Rosario Gagliardi. The interior has a wooden ceiling painted in the 17th century with scenes of the Old Testament, attributed to Antonio Alberti 'Barbalunga', and interesting altars with the statues protected by curtains.

The square has a fountain, on to which faces the handsome market building, with a raised portico, built in 1867. It has been restored as the seat of the civic library and museums, entered from the delightful courtyard, also with a fountain. The collection of paintings includes 19th-century portraits. The library is now officially known as the **Museo Bufalino** (*open 9–2 & 4–8*), because it houses the private collection of more than 6,000 books once belonging to the local writer Gesualdo Bufalino (1920–96), one of Italy's most important contemporary writers, born in Comiso. He achieved recognition relatively late in life, at the age of 61, with his novel *Diceria dell'Untore* (1981), published in English seven years later as *The Plague Sower*. Semi-autobiographical, it is set during and immediately after the Second World War, and chronicles the disturbing reflections of the sole survivor of a Sicilian TB clinic upon life, death, and the Christian faith. Writing in a highly literary, allusive style that critics quickly described as 'baroque', Bufalino shares with other contemporary Italian authors a playful distrust of his own narrative. The museum also has newspaper articles written by or about Bufalino, photographs and other memorabilia. The same building houses the **Museo Civico di Storia Naturale** (*open 9.30–1 & 3.30–7.30; Sun and holidays mornings only; closed Mon*), with a collection of fossils and an interesting exhibit on rare creatures found after being washed up on the beaches of Sicily and Calabria. Opposite the library is the church of **Gesù** (San Filippo Neri), with a magnificent wooden ceiling into which paintings by Olivio Sozzi (*see p. 314*) have been inserted, with *Stories of the life of St Philip Neri*.

From Via Giovanni XXIII, Via degli Studi leads shortly (right) to the lovely church of **San Francesco**, or the Immacolata (*if locked, ring at the convent*), founded in the early 14th century, and a national monument. The present church was built in 1478, and the very interesting **Cappella Naselli** (1517–55) was added at the east end by Gaspare Poidomani, using an imaginative pastiche of architectural styles. Arab-Norman squinches support the dome, and classical details are incorporated in the decoration. It contains the sandstone funerary monument of Gaspare Naselli, Count of Comiso, attributed to Antonello Gagini. At the west end is a 15th-century wooden choir loft. It is also worth asking to see the beautiful 15th-century cloister.

At the entrance to the town, and from a similar period, is the **Castello Feudale** (*closed*). Once owned by the Naselli family, it has been much altered over the years, but traces of an octagonal tower, probably once a Byzantine baptistery, and the square 15th-century keep, can still be seen. In 1841 a Neoclassical opera house, **Teatro Naselli** (*T: 0932 963933*) or Teatro Diana, which brought fame to the town and is still in use, was built on the east side of the castle.

SOUTH OF COMISO

Santa Croce Camerina

A direct descendant of the ancient settlements of *Camarina* and *Kaukana*, Santa Croce Camerina is a little town which has never fulfilled its true potential, thanks to pirate attacks, malaria, cholera, and other lethal setbacks, but after the 1693 earthquake, many refugees from badly hit centres came to live here, giving the town new energy. Today the economy is based on cattle-rearing and the cultivation of flowers (especially roses, tulips, and gladioli) for export. Many of the buildings in the centre are in Art Nouveau style.

In the central Piazza degli Studi is the **Museo Civico** (*open Mon–Fri 9–1; Sat, Sun open by prior request*) with interesting collections of objects coming from the nearby archaeological sites, and tools and equipment used by farmers and craftsmen until the 20th century. On the coast south of the town several ruined watchtowers against pirate attacks can be seen, now surrounded by chaotic holiday homes.

The sandy headland of **Punta Secca** on Capo Scalambri, has a series of coves, one of which was the site of a Byzantine settlement—*Kaukana* (*T: 0932 622150 to request visit*), a large harbour town mentioned by Procopius, where the fleet of Belisarius put in on the way to Africa, and where Roger II departed for the conquest of Malta. The remains are protected as an archaeological park, with three distinct groups of ruins, corresponding to the different districts of the town. Unfortunately the site, although screened with trees, has been surrounded by unattractive holiday bungalows.

Marina di Ragusa

South east of Santa Croce, Marina di Ragusa is a crowded resort, with palm trees along the seafront, which grew up in the 1950s on the site of an old Arab port. A fast *super-strada* connects it to Ragusa. Oil is drilled offshore and piped from here to Augusta. The beach is sandy, once continuing into extensive sand-dunes many of which are now covered with holiday homes or market gardens. The well-preserved reedy sand-dunes around the mouth of the River Irminio near Playa Grande are protected as a nature reserve (*Riserva Macchia Foresta dell'Irminio, T: 0932 675526/5, entrance c. 2km from Marina di Ragusa on the road to Donnalucata*), where black-winged stilts and avocets nest and historical remains include a Sicel bee-farm and a Greek forge.

Camarina

Further west along the coast, Camarina is an archaeological park, and a very interesting archaeological museum, on the site of an important Greek city.

HISTORY OF CAMARINA

Camarina was a colony founded c. 598 BC, by Syracusans and perhaps Corinthians, which suffered alternate sacking and repopulation by Syracuse, Gela and Carthage, because the inhabitants were of a particularly rebellious nature, and tended to take sides with the Sicels. They first rose up against Syracuse only 45 years after their founding, in 552 BC. Glaukos (6th–5th centuries BC) a boxer who won at the Olympic Games in 520 BC, and later became commander-in-chief of his city, was a citizen of Camarina. The angry citizens assassinated him in 484 BC when his arrogance became overbearing. Other Camarina athletes victorious at the Olympics include Parmenides, who won at the 63rd games, and Psaumis, who perhaps in 488 (the 73rd) won the triple crown, for the chariot races using four mules and that using two mares, and the horse race ridden with a saddle. At the height of the city's splendour, about 460 BC, it had a population of 30,000 people. It was finally taken by the Romans in 258 BC, and the inhabitants sold as slaves, although there are signs of occupation in the Republican and Imperial eras and also of a late Arab-Norman settlement. Camarina was a nymph, daughter of the god Oceanus, who lived in a nearby lake and in the river *Hypparis* (now Ippari). She can be seen on the 5th-century BC coins minted in the city, riding on a swan and holding her dress out of the water, while fish jump around her. This was a good place to build a city, with a large flat area protected by mountains and rivers, and in a strong strategic position on the south coast of the island. Archaeologists have discovered traces of prehistoric settlements here, and some scholars believe the Phoenicians established a trading-post here; the cult of Heracles, corresponding to the Phoenician Melqart, had a strong following in Camarina. The city was famous in the Greek world for the Games, which were held periodically like those at Olympia or Corinth; the most exciting competitions here were the races, with heavy chariots drawn by mules or mares competing for the purely symbolic, but greatly appreciated, prizes. The historian Tommaso Fazello located the site in the 16th century. Sporadic digs took place in the 18th and 19th centuries, followed by the scientific excavations carried out by Paolo Orsi from 1896–1910.

Museo Archeologico and the excavations
Open 9–2 & 3–7.
The road passes several enclosures with excavations (*if closed, usually unlocked on request at the museum*) before reaching the Museo Archeologico. The museum is housed in a restored 19th-century farmhouse built above the remains of the Temple of Athena. A room displays underwater finds made offshore where nine shipwrecks have so far been identified. These include a Greek bronze helmet (4th century BC), and objects from Punic and medieval boats. In 1991 a hoard of 1,272 bronze coins was found from the treasure chest of a Roman cargo ship which sank offshore in 275 AD. The headland by the city is surrounded by treacherously sharp rocks: an entire Roman fleet foundered here in 255 BC.

One of the most interesting exhibits shows a rare set of 3rd–2nd-century BC square lead weights, the *pesi campione*, found under the sea in front of the acropolis in 1993, allowing experts to calculate the metric system used by the inhabitants of this area. Outside in the courtyard, beneath a porch, are sandstone sarcophagi and a circular stone tomb. Beyond, part of the temple's sanctuary wall can be seen. Another building contains a plan of the site and explanatory diagrams, and Bronze Age finds from the area. Material from the 6th century BC includes a beautiful Corinthian black-figure vase with a hunting scene.

In another building the foundations of the temple, dating from the early 5th century BC, have been exposed (it was re-used as a church in the Byzantine era). A room on two floors has a splendid display of amphorae (mostly Corinthian and Carthaginian), around one thousand of which were found in the oldest necropolis of Camarina, known as *Rifriscolaro*. The various excavated areas overlooking the sea, include fragments of the walls, part of the street layout and houses with three or four rooms opening on to a courtyard (built after 405 BC) and part of the agora. The necropoli have yielded a great number of tombs, revealing different methods of burial and cremation, varying through the years: it was customary for a time, for example, to provide the corpses with pillows made of seaweed. Studies of skeletons show that the inhabitants were stocky and robust, with good teeth, but some had serious back problems. Traces of the canal-port have been found at the mouth of the River Ippari, once *Hypparis*.

On the coast to the north of Camarina is **Scoglitti**, the beach resort of Vittoria. It overlooks the Gulf of Gela, a long shallow bay whose beaches provided the chief landing-place for the American assault forces on 10th July 1943, during *Operation Husky*.

Castello di Donnafugata
Open 9.30–12.30; Sun and holidays also 3.30–6.30; closed Mon.
A quiet byroad (signposted Santa Croce Camerina) leads southwest from Ragusa through lovely countryside with numerous farms to the Castello di Donnafugata. On the site of a 17th-century building, the present castle was constructed by Baron Corrado Arezzo De Spuches in the 19th century. It is a large country villa, built in an eclectic style, with a Venetian-Gothic loggia. In 1893 the owner was able to have the

Syracuse–Licata railway line diverted, to bring his guests and himself right up to the entrance by train. Its delightful setting survives, with its farm and a large park. In the exotic gardens with splendid old Morton Bay fig trees, are a stone maze entered over a miniature drawbridge guarded by a stone soldier, a coffee-house, a little Neoclassical temple above a grotto and an amusing little chapel with a papier-mâché friar inside, which pops up to frighten people. The asphalt-stone monument to Corrado Arezzo De Spuches (2005) is the work of the Anglo-French artist Peter Briggs. Many of the 122 rooms of the castle have been recently restored, the most interesting of which are the *Salone degli Specchi*, displaying some paintings of the Neapolitan school, and the *Salone della Musica*, containing three pianos and with frescoes on the walls, and also the tiny theatre. In the oldest part of the building, a small chamber is indicated as the prison of Bianca di Navarra, widow of King Martin of Sicily. She was captured (in 1410?) after being chased across Sicily by Count Bernardo Cabrera who was aiming to improve his claim to the throne by forcing her into marriage.

BARON CORRADO AREZZO DE SPUCHES (1824–95)

Baron Corrado Arezzo De Spuches was several times mayor of Ragusa, member of the Sicilian parliament in 1848, and later senator of the Kingdom of Italy, besides editing a ferociously satirical magazine, and being a very good farmer. Nicknamed *Terremoto* (earthquake), he married Concettina Trifiletti and had one daughter, Vincenzina, who at the age of 16 married a prince and had two daughters, before the prince absconded with another woman. Vincenzina died of a broken heart, followed soon after by her mother. De Spuches became the legal guardian of his granddaughters. The youngest, Maria, abandoned him to marry a commoner and live in Messina (where she died in the 1908 earthquake), and the other, Clementina, fell in love with a Frenchman and escaped from the family home with him on board a ship. A gardener saw them going and raised the alarm. Another ship was sent to intercept the lovers, who were taken back to the castle. They were allowed to wed, in Malta to avoid scandal, and it was a happy marriage, but Clementina was never forgiven by her grandfather, who cut her out of his will. On his death she brought a court case against distant relatives, and succeeded in gaining possession of the castle. Her daughter was the last of the De Spuches line.

CHIARAMONTE GULFI & THE NORTH

Chiaramonte Gulfi was founded by Manfredi Chiaramonte for the survivors of *Gulfi*, an Arab town destroyed in 1299 by the Angevins, who killed most of the inhabitants, including the women and children, in a massacre still remembered for its ferocity. Called the 'Balcony of the Hyblaean Mountains' and the 'City of Museums', of which it has eight, it is also famous for its top quality olive oil, officially recognized by the DOP (*Denominazione d'origine protetta*) seal, as well as excellent bread, pasta, pork, salami and cured hams. At the foot of the hill, at Scornavacche, remains have been found of the Greek colony of *Akrillae*, founded 70 years after Syracuse, and destroyed in the 9th century by the Arabs.

In the central Piazza Duomo is the Gothic-style Mother Church dedicated to **Santa Maria la Nova** (15th century; finished 1800), and nearby is the 18th-century church of **San Filippo**, which houses a beautiful chapel dedicated to St Philip of Argirò, the work of Nicolò da Mineo (1542–1625), a sculptor of the Gagini school (*see p. 423*), and considered his masterpiece. The stonework is very ornate; just over the doorway is a highly unusual naked mermaid, and up above, two winged sphinxes. Nicolò da Mineo lived until he was 83 and is buried by the altar.

In the highest part of town is the Gothic **Arco dell'Annunziata**, the northwestern doorway to the castle, and the only one to survive the 1693 earthquake. Through the archway is a lovely view of the simple church of San Giovanni, with Doric columns on either side of the portal.

Chiaramonte museums

The efficient civic administration has led to the opening of eight museums, some of which have been set up in the historic Baroque Palazzo Montesano (in Via Montesano), the others close by in the town centre.

All museums open June–Sept Mon–Fri 9–1, Sat 7–10, Sun 10.30–1 & 7–10; Oct–May Sat 5–8, Sun 1–1 & 3–7, but on request they can be visited on any day of the week, T: 0932 928049 (town hall) or T: 0932 711239 (Tourist Information Bureau).

Museo di Arte Sacra (Piazza Duomo) is considered to be one of the finest collections of its kind in Italy. Among the rare and precious objects from the churches of the town there is a crib of 40 terracotta figures about 30cm high, dressed in the traditional 19th-century costumes of the people of Modica.

Pinacoteca Giovanni De Vita (Corso Umberto) houses about 60 paintings of this local Impressionist artist, donated by his family when he died.

Museo di Liberty (Art Nouveau), at Palazzo Montesano, is the latest museum and illustrates with photographs, paintings and furniture the fervid period between 1895 and 1913 when this style was fashionable in Sicily.

Museo dell'Olio d'Oliva (Olive Oil Museum; also Palazzo Montesano) gives information about the town's most precious product, with a complete collection of presses and tools used through the ages. Things have not changed very much; today the excellence of this oil is due to the fact that the olives are gathered by hand and processed the same day, using only stone presses.

Museo del Ricamo e dello Sfilato Siciliano (Via Lauria, one of the tiny alleys off the stairway to the church of San Giovanni) is a display of beautiful embroidery and lace made by local women, together with the tools used in their craft. Its success has led to the creation of the first Town School for

Embroidery in Sicily, where more than 60 experts teach whoever wants to learn, so that this precious skill is not lost. Many of the traditional designs can be traced back to the pottery of the Middle Ages or even further back to prehistoric art, showing fishing nets, honeycombs, flowers, leaves, ears of wheat and birds. **Collezione Ornitologica Fratelli Azzara** (Palazzo Montesano) shows about 500 stuffed birds of Sicily and Italy (some now extinct), prepared by the Azzara brothers, expert taxidermists. **Collezione di Strumenti Musicali Etnici** (Palazzo Montesano) is a beautiful arrangement in seven rooms of more than 600 rare musical instruments from all over the world. **Collezione di Cimeli Storici Militari F. Gulino** (ex-Casa del Fascio, Piazza Duomo) contains about 1000 interesting mementoes, most of them relating to the two World Wars.

Around Chiaramonte

A short walk (c. 2km) from Chiaramonte Gulfi, in the pinewoods on the slopes of Mt Arcibessi, is the sanctuary church of the **Madonna delle Grazie**, built in 1576 by the local population as thanksgiving for being spared a terrible epidemic of the plague. The people chose this spot because a spring of water had miraculously appeared. The views towards Mt Etna from here are spectacular.

Near the site of ancient Akrillae, c. 4km from Chiaramonte, is the **Eremo di Gulfi**, a very ancient church and convent, parts of which go back to the earliest days of Christianity; it was visited on pilgrimage in 576 by St Gregory the Great before he became pope. Gregory was Roman, of a very wealthy family, which owned huge estates in Sicily. Over the altar in the cave which forms part of the church, is a crudely carved bas-relief of the *Nativity* (? late 3rd–early 4th century), with angels and palm trees, thought to be the oldest representation of the episode in the world. Local lore has it that the cave was used by a group of Christians who had heard St Paul speak at Syracuse (? AD 66).

GIARRATANA

East of Chiaramonte Gulfi is Giarratana, the smallest town in the province, basing its economy on the production of wheat, almonds, and vegetables, especially the large flat onions, to which a feast is dedicated every August (*see p. 336 below*). Rebuilt after the earthquake of 1693 on a site once occupied by the Sicel town of *Erbessa*, it is dominated by three Baroque churches: San Bartolomeo has a fine façade, perhaps the work of an apprentice of Gagliardi; Sant'Antonio Abate, on the top of the hill contains gold stuccoes and a beautiful 18th-century floor of asphalt stone and bright ceramic tiles; and the Chiesa Madre, similar in appearance to the cathedral of Noto. The highest part of the town, around the ruins of the castle built in 1703, and centred on via Galilei, is the **Museo a Cielo Aperto** (*open 9–1; Sun and holidays by prior arrangement*), an open-air museum providing an interesting opportunity to see how the local houses once looked inside, and how the tradesmen and craftsmen carried on their occupations. In 1988 the remains of an Imperial Roman villa were discovered close by, at **Orto Mosaico** (*although not normally open to the public, worth calling the Sovraintendenza Monumenti T: 0932 622150 or 0932 976012 to request a visit*), with fine mosaics. At 10km from the town is a dam on the River Irminio, which forms the beautiful artificial lake of Santa Rosalia.

MONTEROSSO ALMO

North of Giarratana is Monterosso Almo, the highest town (at 691m) in Ragusa, and very ancient; it was a centre of the Sicels. Monterosso is renowned in Sicily for cherries and ricotta, both remarkably good. The inhabitants are currently under study by an international group of scientists, for their exceptionally long lives, and the low incidence of cancer. Because of its quaint atmosphere, it is often used as a film set.

In the large central Piazza San Giovanni is the church of San Giovanni Battista (attributed to Vincenzo Sinatra), preceded by an immense stairway. Inside there is a precious glass chandelier from Murano. Over the main altar is a 15th-century wooden statue of St John the Baptist, viewable only on the first Tuesday of each month. Via Roma leads down to the golden-brown and red neo-Gothic church of the Assunzione, sometimes called the Matrice, founded in the 11th century—this is the oldest parish in the diocese of Ragusa, and the building suffered little damage during the 1693 earthquake. On entering, to the south you will see the original Norman baptismal font, and by the side entrance is an 11th-century holy-water stoup on a 5th-century Palaeo-Christian column—a national monument.

Opposite the Matrice is another national monument, surmounted by an attractive triple belfry, the church of Sant'Antonio Abate (12th century), or Sanctuary of Our Lady of Dolours, the patroness of Monterosso Almo. This part of town was the centre before the earthquake. Inside the church are some important works of art, including paintings by the schools of Antonello da Messina, Vito D'Anna, and Caravaggio, and a poplar-wood Crucifix by Fra' Umile da Petralia.

In the public gardens is a small astronomical observatory, with a telescope available to the public; the clear skies and low light interference guarantee good visibility.

PRACTICAL INFORMATION

GETTING AROUND

• **By rail:** Ragusa is on the Caltanissetta–Gela–Ragusa–Modica–Noto–Syracuse line; www.trenitalia.com for destinations, schedules and fares.
• **By bus:** AST operates services in this area; Giamporcaro runs services between Catania and Comiso and to/from Ragusa/Comiso. Etna Trasporti (T: 095 532716 & 095 7465402) and Tumino (T: 0932 623184) both have services from Ragusa railway station to Santa Croce Camerina, and in summer to Camarina.

INFORMATION OFFICES

Ragusa APT Ragusa, 33 Via Capitano Bocchieri, Ragusa Ibla, T: 0932 221529 or 0932 221511, www.comune.ragusa.it; www.ragusa-sicilia.it; www.ragusa.net; www.copai.it
For information on nature reserves and parks in the province, Assessorato Ambiente, Settore Riserve, 175 Via Di Vittorio, T: 0932 675526 or 0932 675525.
For further information on southeast Sicily (the Val di Noto), try www.sudesttraveltour.it; they also offer a tourist discount card.
The agency Discovering Sicily, 152 Via Schininà, T: 0932 655566, www.discoveringsicily.com; can supply a wealth of information and advice on the area, and assist in organizing itineraries, accommodation, guides etc.
Chiaramonte Gulfi 65 Corso Umberto, T: 0932 711239, www.comunechiaramontegulfi.it

Comiso c/o Municipio, Piazza Fonte Diana, T: 0932 722521, for guided tours T: 0932 748286, www.comune.comiso.rg.it
Pro Loco: 6 via Di Vita, T: 0932/961586, www.comiso.it
Ispica Pro Loco: 21 Via Bellini, T: 335 1224962, www.comune.ispica.rg.it, www.ispicaweb.it
Modica 72 Corso Umberto, T: 0932 753324 & 0932 759204, www.conteadimodica.com, www.comune.modica.rg.it
Scicli c/o Municipio, 2 Via Formino Penna, T: 0932 839111, www.comune.scicli.rg.it; Pro Loco: 4 via Castellana, T: 0932/932782, www.scicli.com
Scoglitti www.scoglitti.it/storia for information on the 1943 Allied landings.
Vittoria Pro Loco: 53 via Cavour, T: 0932 810260, www.comune.vittoria.rg.it

HOTELS

Ragusa Superiore
€ **Rafael**. Small family-run hotel, with 28 straightforward, clean, comfortable rooms in a fairly central renovated 19th-century building, with restaurant and bar. 40 Corso Italia, T: 0932 6540808, www.hotelrafael.it
Ragusa Ibla
€€ **Locanda Don Serafino**. Elegant family-run accommodation in a charming old palace; internet access in each of the ten rooms, and the added attraction of a private beach with excellent restaurant at Marina di Ragusa. 15 Via

XI Febbraio, T: 0932 220065, www.locandadonserafino.it

€ Il Barocco. Beautifully restored old building, close to the cathedral and once a carpenter's workshop, with rooms that are very clean and well looked after, some overlooking a central courtyard garden. Reputable restaurant, out of which the hotel has grown. 1 Via Santa Maria La Nuova, T: 0932 663105, www.ilbarocco.it

€ Palazzo degli Archi. Comfortable little hotel in easily accessible part of the old town, near Piazza della Repubblica, with restaurant. 6 Corso Don Minzoni, T: 0932/685602, www.hotelpalazzodegliarchi.it

South of Ragusa

€€€ Eremo della Giubiliana. Hard to classify according to Italian standards; it is really a *relais*. A restored villa with authentic antique furniture, once a convent and then a fortified farmhouse. Private airport. Excursions (on request) by private plane to Malta, Lampedusa, Aeolian Islands, Etna, and Tunis, or by private boat. Very good restaurant, excellent wine list. 8km south of Ragusa, on the SP25 Ragusa–Marina di Ragusa, Contrada Giubiliana, T: 0932/669119, www.eremodellagiubiliana.it

Cava d'Ispica

€ Villa Teresa. 4km from Cava d'Ispica, a convivial and hospitable little country hotel, with restaurant. Via Crocevia Cava d'Ispica, Contrada Bugilfezza, T: 0932 771690, www.villateresaweb.it

Chiaramonte Gulfi

€ Villa Nobile. Tiny, efficient hotel with basic rooms but splendid views, garage, friendly service, no restaurant.

168 Corso Umberto, T: 0932 928537.www.albergovillanobile.com

Comiso

€ Cordial. Simple but very clean, with restaurant and pizzeria, out-of-town position. 284 Contrada Deserto, T: 0932 967866, www.cordialhotel.com

Donnalucata (Scicli)

€€ Acquamarina. A decent place for a holiday by the sea, a quiet hotel right on the beach, with a good restaurant. 9 Via della Repubblica, T: 0932 937922, www.acqua-marina.com

Ispica

€ Villa Principe di Belmonte. An isolated old country villa with lovely terraced gardens. Some of the relatively spartan but clean rooms have splendid views. A popular venue for wedding receptions. Contrada Crocevia, T: 0932 700127, www.principedibelmonte.it

Modica

€€€ Palazzo Failla. Newly refurbished grand old town house in the centre of Modica Alta with rooms individually decorated in a 'baroque' style. 5 Via Blandini, T: 0932 941059, www.palazzofailla.it

€€ Principe D'Aragona. Modern, and rather corporate in feel, but clean and functional with the added attraction of an outdoor swimming pool. Right in the middle of Modica Bassa on Corso Umberto. 128 Corso Umberto, T: 0932 756041, www.hotelprincipedaragona.it

€ I Tetti di Siciliando. Tucked away close to the cathedral, the friendly owners of this tiny hotel will help organize handicraft and photography courses, and excursions on horseback or bicycles. 24 Via Cannata (entrance from 292 Corso Umberto), T: 0932/942843, www.siciliando.it

€ **Torre Palazzelle**. Just outside town, fairly basic but enormous rooms in a lovely old national monument fortified farmhouse with an ancient defensive tower; tennis. Contrada Torre Palazzelle, T: 0932/901200, www.torrepalazzelle.it

Pozzallo

€ **Villa Ada**. Charming, elegant little hotel in a centrally located 1920s building, with a restaurant and car park, close to the beach, quiet rooms. 3 Corso Vittorio Veneto, T: 0932/954022, www.hotelvillaada.it

Santa Croce Camerina

€ **Kaukana Inn**. On a lovely stretch of beach on the Scarámia headland south of Santa Croce, an unassuming little hotel with a good restaurant and tennis. Località Punta Secca, T: 0932 915377.

Scoglitti (Vittoria)

€€ **Al Gabbiano**. Great little hotel with a good restaurant, right on the beach. 52 Via Messina, T: 0932 980179, www.hotelsulmare.it

BED & BREAKFAST

Ragusa Ibla

€ **Casa del Belvedere**. Signor and signora De Blasi will take good care of you in this old town-house overlooking a spectacular gorge; with four bedrooms upstairs and an apartment on the ground floor; easy to park, also with a garage, only minutes on foot to the centre. 78 via del Mercato, T: 0932 868263 & 347 0963669, www.casadelbelvedere.it

€ *Discesa Santa Maria*. Comfortable, clean rooms in a heart-stopping position, poised on the brink of Ibla with spectacular views from the tiny terrace

for breakfast. 3 Corso Mazzini, T: 0932 624402 & 335 6025865, www.bbdiscesasantamaria.com

Comiso

€ **Balcone di Sicilia**. Perched high in the Hyblaean Mountains, a stone-built farmhouse with breathtaking panoramic views towards Mount Etna and the sea. Delicious breakfasts. English and French spoken. Contrada Margitello, T: 0932 625992 & 320 0141674, www.balconedisicilia.it

Donnalucata (Scicli)

€ **Natura e Barocco**. Straightforward, well-run bed & breakfast. The same management also has rooms to rent in the old centre of Scicli. Contrada Barone, T: 338 4258474, www.naturaebarocco.com

Ispica

€ **Palazzo Zuccaro**. Comfortable, old-fashioned and elegantly furnished bed & breakfast in a handsome early 1900s building. 14 Via Vittorio Veneto, T: 0932 952385 & 0932 952888. www.bedandbreakfastpalazzozuccaro.it

Modica

€€ **L'Orangerie**. Superior accommodation in the heart of town, with an estimable restaurant under the same ownership on the Corso Umberto, the Fattoria delle Torri. 5Vico de Naro, T: 347 0674698, www.lorangerie.it

€ **Dei Ruta**. Very clean, comfortable and welcoming accommodation in a tiny alley near St George's. 9 Via Moncada, T: 0932/755600, www.deiruta.it

Scicli

€ **Conte Ruggero**. Lovely renovated rooms (all with air conditioning, en suite bathrooms & TV), in the 18th-century palace of the local nobles overlooking the town's main square; English spoken.

24 Piazza Italia, T: 0932 931840 & 335 8218269, www.conteruggero.it

€ **Torre Camarella**. Six km from Scicli towards the sea, a friendly family home in the countryside with clean, simple rooms; excellent home-grown food, fresh milk and ricotta from the farm. Contrada Mosca, SP 64 2km, T: 339 5277855, www.torrecamarella.it

ROOMS & APARTMENTS TO RENT

Ragusa Superiore
Villa del Lauro Comfortable accommodation in a beautifully restructured old palace; steep little cobbled street close to Ibla. 11 Via Ecce Homo, T: 0932 655177.

FARMHOUSE ACCOMMODATION

Ragusa
€ **Girlando**. Very simple and friendly farm (cattle and olives), pool, open fireplaces, English spoken, beautiful surroundings. Contrada Girlando Ragusa, Frigintini, T: 0932 774109, www.agriturismo-girlando.it

Acate
€ **Il Carrubo**. Hillside position 13km from the sea and 4km from Acate. All rooms with air conditioning & private bath. A fascinating ancient farm producing citrus, olives and forage; good, simple restaurant, organic food. Contrada Bosco Grande Canalotti, T: 0932 989038, www.ilcarrubo.it

€ **Villa Mogghi**. Old fortified farmhouse surrounded by an Arab garden and pines. Guests can help prepare jam, sun-dried tomatoes and sauces. T: 0932

988711, 2km from the sea.
Chiaramonte Gulfi
€ **Villa Zottopera**. Old fortified farmhouse with swimming pool and tennis court, surrounded by olive groves. The farm regularly wins prizes in international competitions for its olive oil. Some self-catering apartments in outbuildings; meals are available on request. Contrada Roccazzo, T: 335 6633052 or 338 5258902, www.villazottopera.it

Comiso
€ **Tenuta Margitello**. Large farm with accommodation for up to 17 people, producing carobs, almonds and olives, in a panoramic position with a swimming pool. SS 115 km 310.700, T: 0932 722509, www.tenutamargitello.com

€ **Torre di Canicarao**. Fifteenth-century farmhouse and palace in which Rosaria Gagliardi had a hand, with its own Buddhist temple. Stunning countryside; quiet peaceful atmosphere. Excellent wine and organic food. Contrada Canicarao, Comiso, T: 0932 731167, www.agriturismo.com/canicarao/default_uk.htm

Modica
€€ **Nacalino**. Quiet farm producing organic products; dairy cattle; carobs. 19C farmhouse. Contrada Nacalino, T: 0932 779022 & 0932 904988, www.nacalinoagriturismo.it

Vittoria
€€ **Azienda Cos**. Prize-winning wine farm using interesting ancient methods, offers accommodation in luxurious suites; English spoken. T 0932 876145 and 392 7691549, www.cosvittoria.it.

RESTAURANTS

Ragusa Superiore

€€€ **La Fenice**. Elegant restaurant in the new town, with garden and pool; excellent, imaginative cuisine, good wine list. Closed Mon. 3 Via Gandhi, T: 0932 252070.

€ **Ragusa al Forno**. Self-service, also bread, pizza and biscuits baked in a wood-fired stone oven, snacks. 498 Via Archimede (new town), T: 0932 252266.

Ragusa Ibla

€€€ **Locanda di Don Serafino**. Fine dining in the converted stables of an old palace. Run by the same people as the eponymous hotel. Attentive service, excellent local dishes, using ingredients such as pistachios from Bronte and bacon from local pigs, with considerable flair; vast wine cellar. Closed Tues. 39 Via Orfanotrofio, T: 0932 248778.

€€€ **Ristorante Duomo**. One of Sicily's best restaurants, awarded Michelin star, presided over by famous award-winning chef Ciccio Sultano; excellent wine cellar; ideal for a special dinner, including superb sorbets. Closed all day Mon & Sun evening in winter, all day Sun & Mon lunchtime in summer, Aug open every day. 31 Via Bocchieri, T: 0932 651265.

€€ **Antica Macina**. Specializes in fish; the appetizers might include whitebait patties, oysters, shrimps and mussels, while *spaghetti alla Sortino*, with crayfish, shrimps and borage is a good starter. Closed Mon. 129 Via Giusti, T: 0932 248096.

€€ **Il Mulino**. Ask someone to help you find this old water-mill in the valley, now a delightful trattoria, delicious home-made bread and pasta. Closed Mon. Vallata Santa Domenica, T: 0932 228866.

€€ **La Rusticana**. Pleasant atmosphere in this busy restaurant which specializes in pasta dishes, including the celebrated local ricotta-filled ravioli. 68 Corso XXV Aprile, T: 0932 227981. Closed Tues.

€€ **'U Saracino**. A favourite with the locals. Excellent ravioli, delicious soups in winter; inexpensive set menu. Closed Wed. 9 Via del Convento, T: 0932 246976.

Chiaramonte Gulfi

€€ **Majore**. Excellent local dishes, using the best ingredients Sicily can offer; pork is a speciality. Closed Mon. 16 Via Olivares, T: 0932 928019.

€ **Pizzeria D'Amato**. Open in the evening for delicious pizza. Closed Mon. 52 Via Vittorio Emanuele, T: 0932 928500.

Donnafugata

€€ **Il Gattopardo**. Good home-made pasta. Next to the castle. Closed Mon. T: 0932 619313.

€ **Al Castello**. Simple trattoria offering local dishes, also next to the castle. Closed Mon. T: 0932 619260.

Donnalucata (Scicli)

€€ **Al Molo**. On the sea front, a friendly trattoria serving imaginative fish dishes; try the local version of blancmange for dessert—*biancomangiare alle mandorle abbrustolite*. Open every day in summer, closes Mon in winter. 90 Via Perello, T: 0932 937710.

Ispica

€€ **Hotel Ispica**. If you are in or near Ispica, don't miss this exceptionally good restaurant—the cook is gifted. Closed Fri in winter. Contrada Garzalla (railway station), T: 0932 952010 or

0932 951652.
Marina di Ragusa
€€ **Lido Azzurro da Serafino**. Long-standing reputation for fish dishes. Closed Mon & Tues lunchtime in winter. Lungomare Andrea Doria, T: 0932 239522.
Modica
Modica is famous for the excellent quality of its cuisine. A local cook, Piero Selvaggio (www.pieroselvaggio.com) runs a hugely successful restaurant in the USA, the Valentino of Santa Monica.
€€€ **Fattoria delle Torri**. Local ingredients prepared with an imaginative twist, excellent wines. Summer open every day, winter closed Mon & Sun evening. 14 Vico Napolitano, T: 0932 751286.
€ **L'Arco**. Good home-made pasta, ravioli, and fried fish, accompanied by wine from their own vineyard. Closed Mon (July & Aug open every day). 11 Piazza Corrado Rizzoni, T: 0932 942727.
€ **Taverna Nicastro**. An old-fashioned trattoria serving exceptionally good pasta and meat dishes, tasty *arancini* (fried rice balls), lentil or chick-pea soups in winter, friendly and relaxed. Open evenings only from Tues to Sat, booking advisable. 28 Via Sant'Antonino (Modica Alta), T: 0932 945884.
Pozzallo
€€ **Il Delfino**. Central and on the sea, absolutely delicious fish dishes, good value for money. Closed Mon. 4 Piazza delle Sirene, T: 0932 954732.
Scicli
€€ **Monzù Millennium**. Ground floor lively café and ice cream parlour, downstairs good restaurant. Closed Wed. Via Francesco Mormino Penna, T: 0932

842620.
€€ **Pomodoro**. Delightfully innovative dishes, intensely Sicilian atmosphere. Closed Tues. 46 Corso Garibaldi, T: 0932 931444.
Scoglitti (Vittoria)
€€€ **Sakalleo**. In the centre of the village. Fresh fish and good wine; the appetizers are very special; renowned for cous cous and fish soup. Closed Mon lunchtime in winter. 12 Piazza Cavour, T: 0932 871688.
Vittoria
€€ **Hostaria delle Grazie**. In beautiful surroundings, the opportunity to savour the top quality local ingredients, prepared by a good chef. Closed Aug. 127 Via Cavour, T: 0932 862018.

CAFÉS, PASTRY SHOPS & ICE CREAM

Ragusa Superiore
Di Pasquale, 104 Via Vittorio Veneto, one of the finest confectioners in Italy, Di Pasquale has won many prizes. Try *testa di turco* (Turk's head), a creamy confection, or *cannoli di ricotta*, or the excellent ice cream.
Chiaramonte Gulfi
Pasticceria del Corso, at 136 Corso Umberto, traditional confectionery and ice cream.
Giarratana Gelatomania, at 52 Via XX Settembre, has the best ice cream in town.
Marina di Modica
Bar Gelateria Pasticceria, in Piazza Mediterraneo, very nice long drinks, wide variety of ice creams and granita.
Modica
Antica Dolceria Bonaiuto, at 159 Corso Umberto, sells delicious local sweets including 'mpanatigghi (light pas-

try filled with mincemeat, chocolate, and spices), *cedrata* (honey and citron rind), *cobaita* (honey and sesame seeds), and Modica chocolate. Founded 1880. **Bar Napoli**, 43 Corso Principessa Maria del Belgio, Modica Alta, an amazing pastry shop, where you will find ricotta ice cream served in the wicker *cavagne* in which the cheese is made.
Pasticceria Chantilly, 76 Corso Umberto, for good coffee and a wonderful array of the fine local confectionery—don't miss the strips of candied orange rind dipped in dark chocolate.

Monterosso Almo
Terranova, in Piazza San Giovanni, here you will find the exquisite ricotta ice cream, served in the little wicker *cavagne* where the cheese is prepared.
Pozzallo
Dolce Stil Novo, at 55 Lungomare Pietre Nere, overlooking the sea, ideal for brunch, home-made ice creams.
Gelateria Fede, 29 Corso Vittorio Veneto, exquisite sorbet and granita—chocolate granita was invented here.
Scicli
Le Coccole, at 6 Via Perello, delicious home-made ice cream; try the *zuccotto*.

MODICA CHOCOLATE

During the 16th century, cocoa beans imported from Mexico by the Cabrera family were made into chocolate by the confectioners of Modica, using the ancient Aztec method of slowly grinding the beans between two stones, to avoid overheating, and then adding maize. Elsewhere in Europe the method of manufacture evolved rapidly to industrialize the product, improve the flavour, and lower the cost. In Modica, however, the method is still basically the same, the only difference being that sugar instead of maize is added towards the end of the grinding operation, giving a typical grainy consistency to the finished product. Natural flavourings are also added, such as cinnamon, vanilla, orange essence or chilli pepper.

LOCAL SPECIALITIES

Ragusa
Casa del Formaggio Sant'Anna, 387 Corso Italia, T: 0932 227485, for local cheeses, including the superb *caciocavallo*. **Maddalena**, 86 Via Lombardia, T: 0932 254014, for traditional sourdough bread, baked in a stone oven. **Forno San Paolo**, 121 Via Giusti, T: 0932 681420, is a traditional baker.

Modica
Rizza, 128 Corso Umberto, for olive oil, fresh roasted coffee, herbs, pepper, and Modica chocolate, including *cioccolato al peperoncino* (chilli-flavoured chocolate).
Casa del Formaggio, 3 Via Marchesa Tedeschi, T: 0932 946192, for typical cheeses, hams and salami, Modica chocolate, carob products and liqueurs.

Ragusa Superiore
29th Aug: *Festa di San Giovanni*, the patron saint; colourful celebrations, typical sweets and fireworks.
Ragusa Ibla
Last Sun in May: *Festa di San Giorgio*, procession for the patron saint, fireworks.
October: Ibla Buskers, street musicians from all over the world meet up to perform. www.iblabuskers.it
Acate
Good Friday: *Scinnenza*, a procession of the statue of Christ, accompanied by little girls dressed in white, representing Veronica.
Third Sunday after Easter: Feast of the patron St Vincent the Martyr, with the exciting horse race called *Cavalcata di San Vincenzo*.
Chiaramonte Gulfi
February: A spectacular carnival called *Carnevale della Contea*, including a celebration for the local sausages.
Comiso
3rd February: Feast of the patron St Blaise, with fireworks and distribution of blessed loaves.
First week of June: *L'Isola dei Mestieri*, a fair dedicated to Sicilian handicrafts.
Giarratana
14th August: *Sagra della Cipolla*, special celebrations for harvesting the large, flat, very tasty onions.
21st & 22nd August: *Fiera di San Bartolomeo*, a cattle-market held in the street, according to an ancient tradition, followed by a festival on the 24th August with the Feast of St Bartholomew.

Modica
Easter Sunday: *La Maronna Vasa-Vasa* (The Kiss-Kiss Madonna) the culmination of Easter week with the meeting of the Madonna and her Son, the two statues exchanging joyful kisses.
Sunday of or after 23rd April: *Festa di San Giorgio*, patron saint of Modica Alta.
End of June: *Festa di San Pietro*, patron saint of Modica Bassa, with a fair.
Pozzallo
Second Sunday in August: *Sagra del Pesce*, when fish of many different kinds are cooked and served in Piazza Rimembranza, using a pan 4m wide.
Santa Croce Camerina
19th March: splendid celebrations for St Joseph.
Scicli
Mid-March: *Cavalcata di San Giuseppe*, bonfires on street corners light the Flight from Egypt.
Palm Sunday: impressive procession culminating where decorative woven palm leaves are offered to the Madonna.
Easter Sunday: *Festa dell'Omu Vivu*, a dramatic procession of young people carrying the statue of the Risen Christ, shouting 'Gioia! Gioia!' (Joy! Joy!).
Last Sunday of June: the *Madonna of the Militias* is celebrated in commemoration of the famous battle between the Normans and Saracens.
Vittoria
18th March: The little town is famous for the *Tavolata di San Giuseppe*, when a banquet is prepared by those inhabitants who have reason to be grateful to the saint.

THE PROVINCE OF SYRACUSE

SYRACUSE

Syracuse, as the city is usually known in English, is the successor of the magnificent *Syracusae*, which rivalled Athens as the largest and most powerful city of the Greek world; at the height of its splendour the population probably numbered around 150,000. The beautiful island of Ortygia suffered from depopulation up until a few years ago, but this peaceful part of the town, which has many monuments of great interest, is once again the heart of the city, with good restaurants and a lively atmosphere in the evenings. The principal ruins of the Greek city, including the famous theatre, and the splendid archaeological collection, are higher up on the hill of the mainland. Cicero noted that Syracuse knew no day without sun, and it does indeed enjoy a mild marine climate throughout the year. It is now a World Heritage Site and one of the more popular destinations in Sicily.

NB: This chapter is covered by the map on p 296.

ORTYGIA

The island of Ortygia, just under 1 square kilometre, is joined to the mainland by three short bridges. The charming old town, best explored on foot, has delightful narrow streets of Baroque houses with pretty balconies and numerous trees. Ortygia recently faced serious decline, but is once more becoming a fashionable place to live. Several hotels have also been reopened here in the last few years; it is certainly the most pleasant place to stay in Syracuse.

Exploring Ortygia

From **Ponte Umbertino**, the main bridge connecting the island to the mainland, numerous colourful small boats can be seen and part of the fishing fleet moored in the channel. On the left, the monumental post office by Francesco Fichera (1934) has a handsome interior with Neoclassical and Art Nouveau decorations. At the foot of the bridge is Piazza Pancali, the island's main taxi rank, with shady ficus trees, leading into Largo XXV Luglio. To the left, a daily fresh fish market is held every morning in the streets surrounding the old covered market place, a fine turn of the century building, now sadly abandoned. Nearby is the fishermen's district, a small area of interesting narrow streets, once the old Arab quarter, centred on Largo della Graziella.

On the right, on Via XX Settembre, are the remains of the Porta Urbica, a gateway in the fortifications constructed in the 4th century BC by the tyrant Dionysius against the Carthaginians. Nearby, in Largo XXV Luglio, are the ruins of the Temple of Apollo.

HISTORY OF SYRACUSE

The city of Syracuse was founded on Ortygia, literally 'the island of the quail' after its shape, an island so close to the mainland that it would later be joined to it by a causeway. The island had a famous spring, Arethusa, and it helped provide shelter for a superb harbour (the Great Harbour, 640 hectares in area). The city was founded in 733 BC by Corinthian settlers, led, tradition says, by one Archias, and links remained close with Corinth whose pottery dominates in the early settlement. As with other Greek cities the native Sicels were scattered or used as cheap labour. The city grew fast and its wealth channelled into major temples and expansion onto the mainland. Much of the new settlement, the districts of Achradina, Tyche and Neapolis, were on the slopes of the Heights of Epipolae which were to provide an outer defence line for the city. Soon the city was expanding its territory in southeastern Sicily through the smaller colonies of *Acrae*, *Casmenae*, *Helorus* (or *Eloro*) and *Camarina*.

The early government of Syracuse was by landed aristocrats and, when challenged by an emerging democratic movement, these called on a 'tyrant' from the outside, Gelon, ruler of the city of *Gela*, who forcibly settled much of Gela's population in Syracuse and made it his capital in 485. In 480 he defeated the Carthaginians at Himera. The Temple of Athena, built to celebrate this victory, is now the cathedral. Gelon was succeeded by his brother Hieron I (478–c. 467), who married Gelon's beautiful widow Damarete and defeated an Etruscan fleet off Italy (474). He won a chariot race at the Olympics, and patronized the arts, welcoming the poets Aeschylus, Pindar, Simonides and Bacchylides to his court. Much of the expansion to the city dates from this period of cultural splendour.

Following Hieron's death, the city became a democracy (a common response in Greek cities to a long period of tyranny), with an assembly, administrative council and elected generals. Even when Dionysius I seized power as 'general with full powers' in 405, he preserved the democratic institutions. By this time Syracuse, with help from Corinth and Sparta, had fought off the great Athenian invasion fleet of 415. The Athenians had tried to close off the city with a double row of walls and blockade it, but eventually their fleet was trapped inside the Great Harbour and annihilated. Dionysius I made sure that the city was made invulnerable by constructing defences along the heights of Epipolae. Although none of the four wars Dionysius fought against Carthage drove the Carthaginians from the island, under his rule Syracuse became a major power in Sicily and southern Italy.

It all collapsed under Dionysius' son, Dionysius II, when Syracuse was forced to ask its mother city for help to restore order. The Corinthian Timoleon (ruled 334–336) did have some success in confronting the Carthaginians and setting up an oligarchic government, of some six hundred leading citizens, modelled on that in Corinth, but Timoleon's constitution was overthrown by one Agathocles who established his own tyranny in 417. Agathocles was an opportunistic adventurer who led campaigns to Africa and southern Italy and proclaimed himself a king as if he were a Hellenistic monarch. However, he brought no long term stability to Syracuse which lapsed once again into anarchy after his assassination in 289. In fact, Syracuse's security was compromised by a group of his mercenaries, the Mamertimes. The city had to call on the ambitious ruler of Epirus, Pyrrhus, who was already supporting Greek cities in southern Italy against the Romans, for help against both the Mamertimes and a resurgent Carthage. It was from this weak position that Syracuse enjoyed an unexpected revival. When the Mamertimes called for help from Rome, a new king of Syracuse, Hieron II, realised the advantages of allying with, rather than resisting Rome, and for the next 60 years he exploited his favoured position to bring about an Indian summer of prosperity. Once again trading links extended across the Mediterranean. One of the largest theatres of the Greek world, with a major stoa above it, and a massive altar to Zeus, were among the grand building projects of his day. Such grandeur masked the city's reliance on Rome though and when, after Hieron's death in 215, his successor unwisely moved towards the Carthaginians who, under their general Hannibal, were threatening Rome from inside Italy, Rome's retaliation was inevitable. Even the genius of Archimedes (*see box on p. 383*) could not save Syracuse after two years of siege in 212.

The Romans made Syracuse a provincial capital under a praetor (a magistrate elected annually in Rome) and adopted Hieron's system of gathering a tax in grain to feed Rome and their armies. Some praetors, notably the notorious Verres (praetor 73-71), used their rule to despoil the city further but evidence of Roman building, an amphitheatre, a triumphal arch and a new forum, attest to a steady prosperity. The city remained a stopping point for any voyager coming to Italy from the east (the apostle Paul spent three days in the city on his way to Rome), and it had some status as a tourist attraction. Catacombs show the growth of Christianity (they date from a century before Constantine's Edict of Toleration of 313 and then expand rapidly after it). After the Roman period, Syracuse's power declined rapidly although the Byzantine Emperor Constans II resided there in 662–68. Syracuse was badly damaged by the Saracens in 878, but freed from Arab rule for a time by George Maniakes (1038–40), the general of Basil II of Byzantium. The temporary importance Syracuse regained between 1361 and 1536 by holding the quasi-independent seat of the *Camera Reginale* or Queen's Chamber, a kind of miniature Parliament, did not last. In 1837, having rebelled unsuccessfully against the Bourbons, it was punished by losing its role as provincial capital. After the Italian conquest of Libya the port expanded again but during the Second World War it was a target first for the Allied air forces, and, after its capture on 10th July 1943, for German aircraft.

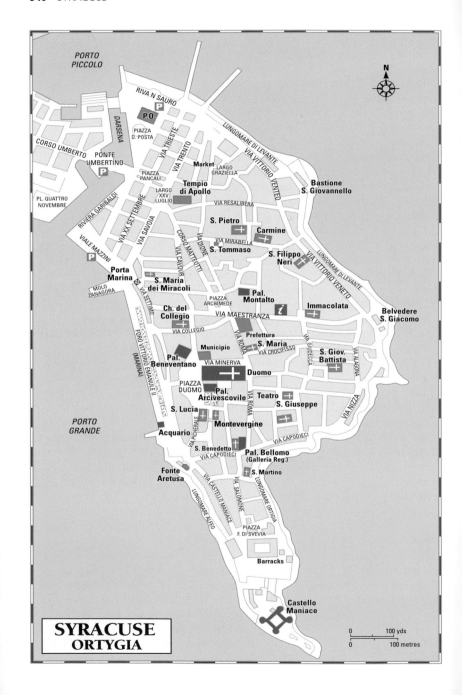

PORTO PICCOLO

RIVA N SAURO

P.O.

PIAZZA D. POSTA

DARSENA

CORSO UMBERTO

PONTE UMBERTINO

PIAZZA PANCALI

PL. QUATTRO NOVEMBRE

RIVIERA GARIBALDI

VIA TRIESTE

VIA TRENTO

Market

LARGO GRAZIELLA

Tempio di Apollo

LARGO XXV LUGLIO

VIA RESALIBERA

LUNGOMARE DI LEVANTE

VIA VITTORIO VENETO

Bastione S. Giovannello

VIA XX SETTEMBRE

VIA SAVOIA

CORSO MATTEOTTI

VIA DIONE

S. Pietro

VIA MIRABELLA

Carmine

S. Tommaso

S. Filippo Neri

VIA VITTORIO VENETO

LUNGOMARE DI LEVANTE

VIALE MAZZINI

Porta Marina

MOLO ZANAGORA

VIA CAVOUR

S. Maria dei Miracoli

VIA SETTIMO

Ch. del Collegio

PIAZZA ARCHIMEDE

Pal. Montalto

VIA COLLEGIO

VIA MAESTRANZA

Immacolata

Belvedere S. Giacomo

FORO VITTORIO EMANUELE II (MARINA)

Municipio

Prefettura

VIA ROMA

S. Maria

VIA CROCIFISSO

S. Giov. Battista

VIA GIUDECCA

VIA ALAGONA

Pal. Beneventano

VIA MINERVA

Duomo

Teatro

S. Giuseppe

VIA NIZZA

PIAZZA DUOMO

Pal. Arcivescovile

VIA ROMA

PORTO GRANDE

S. Lucia

VIA PICHERALE

Montevergine

Acquario

S. Benedetto

VIA CAPODIECI

Pal. Bellomo (Galleria Reg.)

VIA CAPODIECI

Fonte Aretusa

S. Martino

VIA CASTELLO MANIACE

VIA SALOMONE

LUNGOMARE ORTIGIA

LUNGOMARE ALFEO

PIAZZA F. DI SVEVIA

Barracks

Castello Maniace

SYRACUSE
ORTYGIA

0   100 yds

0   100 metres

N

The **Temple of Apollo**, surrounded by lawns, papyrus plants and palm trees, is the earliest peripteral Doric temple in Sicily, built of local limestone in the late 7th century BC and attributed to the architects Kleomenes, responsible for the project, and Epicleos, who designed the columns. Some scholars have identified it with the Artemision recorded by Cicero, but the dedication to Apollo cut in the steps of the stereobate (on the eastern side) seems conclusive. Transformed through the centuries, first into a Christian church, then an Arab mosque, and lastly into a Spanish prison, it was freed in 1938 from overlying structures, and two monolithic columns and part of the cella walls remain intact. Fragments of its polychrome terracotta cornice are preserved in the Museo Archeologico Regionale (*see p. 349 below*).

Via Savoia leads to the waterfront overlooking the Porto Grande, near the elaborate Chamber of Commerce building. Here is **Porta Marina**, a plain 15th-century gateway to the Great Harbour with an aedicule in the Spanish-Gothic style. The long promenade by the water's edge, planted with splendid *Ficus benjamin* trees, called Foro Vittorio Emanuele, is known locally as the Marina. There is a lovely view across the harbour to the wooded shore on the Maddalena headland, the ancient *Plemmyrion*.

Within the gate to the left (in the street of the same name) is the attractive little church of Santa Maria dei Miracoli, with a fine doorway resting on little lions, with a sculptured lunette, and a worn tabernacle in the Gothic-Catalan style. Straight on from the gate, Via Ruggero Settimo emerges on a terrace above the trees of the marina, and Via del Collegio leads away from the sea skirting the high walls of the imposing **Chiesa del Collegio** with its Corinthian pilasters and overhanging cornice (1635–87), whose incomplete façade (undergoing restoration) recalls that of the Gesù in Rome. The interior (now a temporary exhibition venue) contains altars from the former Jesuit college in Palermo, moved here in 1927–31. The church faces Via Cavour, off which parallel streets run down towards the sea to the left on the return downhill to Largo XXV Luglio.

To the right is Piazza Duomo, where there are some fine Baroque buildings: to the left the town hall occupies the former Seminary (begun in 1628 by Giovanni Vermexio). Under the building lie the remains of an Ionic temple. Probably never finished, and probably dedicated to Artemis, it was found in 1963. An ancient Sicel necropolis, with tombs hewn in the rock, was discovered a few years ago while the square was being repaved.

The duomo

Open 8–8.
Across Via Minerva is the duomo, or Santa Maria del Piliero or delle Colonne. Bishop Zosimus in the 7th century repaired the Byzantine church built from the ruins of the Doric Temple of Athena, erected by Gelon in 480 BC to celebrate the victory of Himera, and declared it the cathedral of the city. The present façade of the cathedral is a powerful Baroque composition erected 1728–54 and designed by Andrea Palma. The marble statues of *Sts Peter and Paul* flanking the steps are the earliest known works of Ignazio Marabitti; he also sculpted the other statues (1754) on the façade.

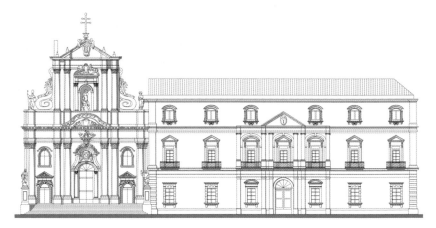

FAÇADES OF THE DUOMO & PALAZZO ARCIVESCOVILE

The interior
Stripped of Baroque decoration between 1909 and 1927, the nave arcades were reduced to the plain massive piers formed by the eight arches opened by the Byzantine Christians in the side walls of the cella, which is the original 480 BC construction. The stained glass windows are modern. On the internal entrance wall two columns from the opisthodomos of the cella are preserved, and 19 columns of the peristyle are incorporated in the aisles, those on the left side being engaged. Along both sides of the nave, more or less where the roof of the temple would have been, is an inscription in Latin describing this as the oldest Christian church in Europe: *Ecclesia syracusana prima divi Petri filia, et prima post Antiochenam Cristo dicata.*

South aisle
A The first chapel is for baptisms. The font is a 5th-century BC krater, carved from Paros marble, with a Greek inscription (found in the catacombs of San Giovanni (*see p. 354*) where it had been used as a burial urn), standing on seven miniature bronze lions (13th century); on the wall are fragments of mosaics which survive from the earlier Byzantine church.

B In the second chapel (1711), with wrought-iron gates by Pietro Spagnuolo (1605), is a silver statue of St Lucy by Pietro Rizzo (1599; shown only on certain religious festivals and carried in procession on 13 December). The two marble medallions are attributed to Ignazio Marabitti.

C The third chapel, also with magnificent wrought-iron gates (1811), was designed in 1650–53, probably by Giovanni Vermexio. The **frescoes** in the vault are by the natural scientist and artist Agostino Scilla (1657; *see p. 240*). The altar frontal bears a beautiful relief of the *Last Supper* by the Florentine sculptor Filippo Della Valle (1762). Above is a ciborium by Luigi Vanvitelli (1752), designer of the royal palace of Caserta for Charles VII of Bourbon.

D At the end of the aisle, in the **Cappella del Crocifisso**, is a panel painting (left) of *St Zosimus* attributed to Antonello da Messina. Opposite is a damaged early 16th-century panel painting of *St Marcian*. In the sanctuary is a Byzantine Crucifix and 13 panels from a polyptych by the school of Antonello (or early work by Antonello himself?). Other paintings exhibited here include two works by Marco di

Costanzo (*St Jerome* and the *Annunciation*).

E The bronze candelabra in the chancel date from 1513, while the splendid main altar is the work of Giovanni Vermexio (1659), incorporating a monolith originating from the temple of Athena. The altarpiece, by Agostino Scilla (1653), is the *Nativity of the Virgin*. The two paintings over the choir, of *St Paul Preaching to the Christians of Syracuse* and *St Peter Sending Marcian to be Bishop of Syracuse*, were carried out by Silvio Galimberti in 1950.

North aisle
F In the Byzantine apse (*closed*) is a *Madonna of the Snow* by Antonello Gagini (1512). The end of the pronaos wall of the temple with its column can be seen here. The noticeable irregularity

SYRACUSE DUOMO

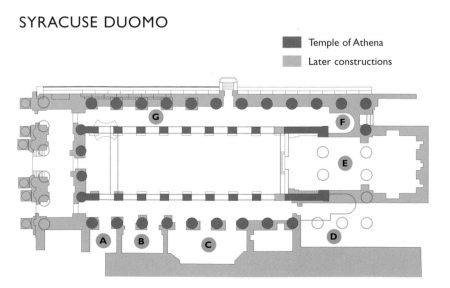

■ Temple of Athena

■ Later constructions

of the pillars on this side is due to earthquakes.

G Close by are three arresting statues in white Carrara marble: *St Lucy* by Antonello Gagini; *Madonna and Child* by Domenico Gagini; and *St Catherine of Alexandria* by the Gagini school.

HISTORY OF THE DUOMO

The victorious Gelon returned home with thousands of prisoners-of-war to be used as slaves. In celebration of his victory, the finest craftsmen among them were selected to build a new Temple of Athena on the summit of the island of Ortygia. Work probably continued for some 10 years, although scholars have also suggested that it took only two years to complete. Doric peripteral, with 14 columns on the long sides and six on the short, the temple had doors inlaid with ivory and gold. Inside, the statue of Athena, larger than life-size, was made of Paros marble, with face, hands, feet and weapons of gold. Paintings by Zeuxis lined the walls of the cella. The magnificence of the building and these works of art were famous throughout the Mediterranean. The golden shield on the top, which reflected the rays of the sun, was a landmark for sailors. All these treasures were later stolen by the proconsul Verres (*see p. 199*).

Under Byzantium the temple was converted into a Christian church: arches were cut in the wall of the cella, the entrance was moved to the west, and the space between the columns closed by a wall. Under the Arabs it became the Great Mosque. The Normans raised the height of the roof and added the side chapels. The Spanish added the ceiling of chestnut wood from Mt Etna in 1518. Damaged by several earthquakes, it was rebuilt after 1693 when the Norman façade fell.

In Via Minerva 12 columns of the temple, with their architrave and triglyphs, punctuate the medieval north wall of the church, their cornice replaced by Muslim battlements while the church was a mosque. Excavations beneath the cathedral carried out by Paolo Orsi in 1912–17 revealed details of an Archaic temple, demolished to make way for the later temple, and, at a lower level, pre-Greek huts of the 8th century BC; more recently, while re-paving, an ancient Sicel necropolis of rock-cut tombs was discovered under the square.

Piazza Duomo

Next door to the duomo, forming part of the Palazzo Arcivescovile (Archbishop's Palace; c. 1750, Louis Alexandre Dumontier), is the prestigious **Biblioteca Alagoniana** (Alagonian Library, *not open regularly to the public*; *T: 0931 67968 or 0931 60248*), with 13th-century Greek, Latin and Arabic manuscripts. It has a pretty hanging garden with palm trees. Archbishop Alagona, who founded the library in 1780, loved books so much that he excommunicated anyone caught stealing them. A doorway opening onto the square allows access to the subterranean passages under the cathedral, some carved out in the Byzantine era, which house an exhibition on their use as an air-raid shelter during the Anglo-American bombing in the months before the Armistice. The self-guided route through dry and dripping caverns emerges at sea level on Foro Vittorio Emanuele II.

On the other side of the piazza, opposite the town hall, is Palazzo Beneventano del Bosco (*accommodation available, see p. ???*), a very fine building by the local master-builder Luciano Alì (1778–88) concealing a particularly attractive courtyard. Next to it is the curved, pink façade of Palazzo Gaetani e Arezzo, and, beyond, the building of the Soprintendenza ai Beni Culturali e Ambientali which once housed the Museo Archeologico (*see p. 349 below*), and now contains one of the finest numismatic collections in the world (*open by appointment; call at least the day before T: 0931 481111; open Mon–Fri 9.30–1; Wed also 3.30– 5.30*).

At the end of the piazza, with a balcony on the corner, is Palazzo Impellizzeri and the church of Santa Lucia alla Badia, which has a fine façade of 1695 by Luciano Caracciolo with a balcony used by the nuns to watch the festivities for St Lucy. Just out of the piazza is the church of Montevergine (*closed*) with a façade by Andrea Vermexio; the convent next door is the gallery of Modern Art, **Galleria Civica d'Arte Contemporanea Montevergini** (*open 9–12 & 4–8; www.montevergini.it*), with works by local artists.

Fonte Aretusa to Piazza Archimede

From Piazza Duomo, Via Picherale passes the Hotel des Etrangers, which incorporates part of the medieval Casa Migliaccio, and leads down to a charming terrace in a quiet spot on the waterfront surrounding the **Fonte Aretusa**, one of the most famous fountains of the Hellenic world. The spring of the nymph Arethusa was celebrated by Pindar and Virgil: when Arethusa was bathing in the River Alpheus near Olympia the river god fell in love with her. Making her escape from Alpheus, Arethusa plunged into the Ionian sea and reappeared here. Transformed by the goddess Artemis into a spring, she was pursued here by Alpheus, who mingled his river water with that of the spring: it was believed that the river in the Peloponnesus was connected, via the sea, to the fountain of Arethusa. A freshwater spring, called the Occhio della Zillica, still occasionally wells up in the harbour. The spring of Arethusa diminished after the erection of the Spanish fortifications. Nelson claimed to have watered his fleet here before the battle of the Nile in 1798. The fountain now flows into a pond (built in 1843), planted with papyrus, abounding in fish and inhabited by white ducks, under a splendid old Morton Bay fig tree.

By the spring is the **Aquarium** (*open 10–8*), with some of the fish to be found in the Ionian Sea. The attractive seafront here with its magnificent shady *Ficus benjamin* trees, is the favourite spot for the *passeggiata*.

The end of the promontory, beyond Piazza Federico di Svevia, is occupied by the 13th-century **Castello Maniace** (*open 8.30–1*), built c. 1232 by Frederick II of Hohenstaufen but named after the Byzantine general George Maniakes, supposed (in error) to be its founder. The keep, c. 51 square metres, with cylindrical corner towers, has probably lost a third of its original height. On either side of the imposing Swabian doorway are two consoles, formerly bearing splendid 4th-century BC bronze rams, one of which is now in the Museo Regionale Archeologico in Palermo, and thought to be the work of Lysippus. Overlooking the harbour are the remains of a large three-light window. Beneath the castle is the so-called *Bagno della Regina*, an underground chamber once probably a reservoir.

Via Salomone and Via San Martino return past (right) the church of **San Martino**, founded in the 6th century, with a doorway of 1338. The interior, dating from Byzantine times, contains a fine triptych by a local 15th-century master. At the end of the street (left) stands the church of **San Benedetto**, with a huge canvas of the *Ecstasy of St Benedict* by Mario Minniti, a local painter, follower of Caravaggio. Adjacent is **Palazzo Bellomo**, seat of the Galleria Regionale (*closed for refurbishment and rearrangement*). The building combines elements of its Swabian construction (c. 1234) with alterations of the 15th century. The collection includes some great masterpieces, including works by Caravaggio (*Burial of St Lucy*) and Antonello da Messina (*Annunciation* from Palazzolo Acreide).

Via Roma, with delightful overhanging balconies, leads away from the sea front, north past the Opera House (*under repair*). On the corner of Via Crocifisso is the church of Santa Maria della Concezione (1651) which has a fine interior with a tiled floor. On the vault is a late 18th-century fresco by Sebastiano Lo Monaco, while the altarpieces on the left side and on the first right altar are by Onofrio Gabrielli (1616–1706), depicting the *Madonna della Lettera*, patroness of Messina, Gabrielli's home town, *the Martyrdom of St Lucy* and the *Massacre of the Innocents*.

Piazza Archimede was laid out between 1872 and 1878 in the centre of Ortygia, where there is the cement Fountain of Diana by Giulio Moschetti (1910). Palazzo Lanza is on the south side and the courtyard of the Banca d'Italia on the west side preserves medieval elements. Off the square, reached by Via Montalto, is the façade of Palazzo Montalto in the Gothic-Chiaramonte style of 1397; it has been propped up with concrete bastions. From the car park behind, the shell of the building is visible, with a fine loggia.

The interesting Via Maestranza, once seat of the wealthy city corporations, leads east from the square towards the sea, past several Baroque palaces and the church of San Francesco (or Immacolata) with an attractive little convex façade. It has a fine late 18th-century interior, with 12 small paintings of the Apostles in the apse. Two Gothic portals have been exposed. Via Giudecca, to the right, recalls the Jewish district of the city. Last turning on the right is Via Alagona, where at no. 41 you will find Palazzo Cordaci which houses the Museo del Cinema (*open Tues and Thur 9.30–12.30; Mon 7–8; www.cinemuseum.it, T: 0931 65024 to book visit*). Besides a vast library of books about cinema and theatre, there is a collection of more than 2,600 films. Cameras and posters going back to the early days of cinema are also on view.

Close by, at no. 52 Via Alagona, is an intact medieval *miqva*, a spring for ablutions: Bagno Ebraico (*open Mon–Sat 9–12.30*).

Via Vittorio Veneto, lined with smaller 17th–18th-century Spanish palaces, emerges on the sea by the church of **San Filippo Neri** (once a synagogue), which bears the lizard symbol and signature of the architect Vermexio, next to the fine restored Gothic Palazzo Interlandi, a convent. Ring here and the nuns will open the church for viewing. Via Mirabella (with Palazzo Bongiovanni on the corner) leads away from the seafront past the church of the Carmine, which preserves part of its 14th-century structure.

ACHRADINA & TYCHE

The area on the mainland opposite Ortygia corresponds to the ancient district of Achradina, and to the northeast that of Tyche where the Museo Archeologico Regionale is situated. From Piazza Pancali, buses run across the bridge along Corso Umberto to the **Foro Siracusano**, a large and busy square with a Fascist-era war memorial (1936), and fine trees. Here are some remains of the ancient agora; recent excavations have revealed other parts of the agora near Corso Umberto and Corso Gelone, where dwellings of the late 8th century BC have also come to light, the earliest of the Greek period so far found in Syracuse.

From the adjacent Piazza Marconi, Via Crispi forks right to the station, while Via Elorina (left) leads to the so-called **Ginnasio Romano** (*open 9–1; closed Sun and holidays*), a complex ruin surrounded by lawns and palm trees, with a portico surrounded on three sides, an altar, a temple and a small theatre. The portico on the north side, and part of the high temple podium remain. The theatre's orchestra is now under water, but a few of the lower steps of the cavea are visible. The buildings, all of Imperial date, probably formed part of a *serapeum*, a Roman temple dedicated to Serapis.

From Foro Siracusano, the Viale Diaz leads towards Borgo Santa Lucia. On the left are two excavated sites: the first (straddled by a brown modern block of flats) includes a small bath house of Roman origin, possibly the **Baths of Daphne** in which the Emperor Constans II was assassinated in 668; the second, just beyond, behind railings, marks the Arsenale Antico, where the foundations of the mechanism used by the Greeks to drag their ships into dry dock can be seen. In a simple house at no. 11 in Via Orti di San Giorgio, a little plaster image of the Virgin is supposed to have wept in 1953 (plaque in Piazza Euripide; the sanctuary of the Madonna delle Lacrime is described below). The long, narrow Riviera Dionisio il Grande continues north, seaward of the railway, through the district of Santa Lucia.

A long way northeast is the large piazza, surrounded by an avenue of ficus trees, in front of the church of **Santa Lucia**. The façade, which relatively recently collapsed without warning, has been faithfully reconstructed. It was begun in 1629 on a plan by Giovanni Vermexio, and completed in the 18th century (perhaps by Rosario Gagliardi), on the spot where St Lucy (?281–304), patron saint of Syracuse, was buried. The portal, the apses and the base of the campanile are Norman work and the rose window is of the 14th century. Outside can be seen the chapel of the Santo

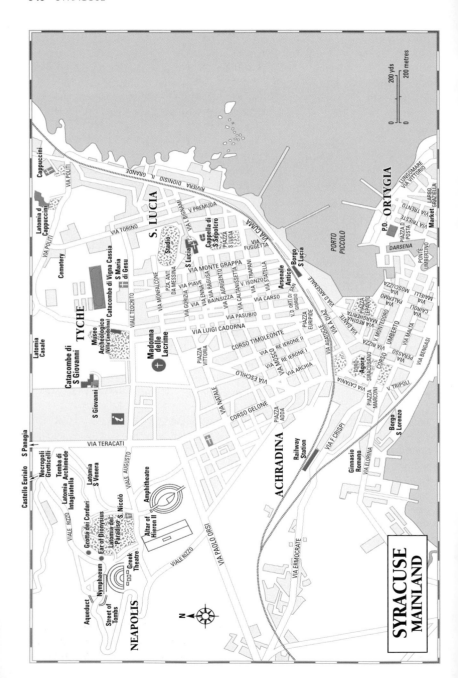

SYRACUSE MAINLAND

NEAPOLIS

Aqueduct
Street of Tombs
Nymphaeum
Greek Theatre
Ear of Dionysius
Latomia del Paradiso
Altar of Hieron II
Amphitheatre
Grotta dei Cordari
Latomia Intagliatella
Latomia del Paradiso S. Nicolò
Latomia S Venera
Tomba di Archimede
Necropoli Grotticelli
Castello Eurialo   S Panagia

VIALE RIZZO
VIALE AUGUSTO

Latomia dei Cappuccini
Cappuccini

S. LUCIA

VIA POLITI
RIVIERA DIONISIO IL GRANDE

Cemetery

TYCHE

Latomia Casale
Catacombe di S Giovanni
Museo Archeologico (Villa Landolina)
S Maria di Gesù
Catacombe di Vigna Cassia
S Giovanni

VIA TORINO
VIA TEOCRITO

Madonna delle Lacrime

VIA TERACATI

Stadio
S Lucia
V PREMUDA
V BIGNAMI
Cappella di S Sepolcro
PIAZZA S LUCIA
VIA CIMA
VIA FUGGETTA

VIA MONTE GRAPPA
PZA ANT. DA MESSINA
VIA MONFALCONE
VIA GORIZIA
VIA PIAVE
VIA ENNA
VIA BAINSIZZA
VIA AGRIGENTO
VIA RAGUSA
VIA CALTANISSETTA
V. ISONZO
VIA TRAPANI
VIA STATELLA
VIA CARSO
VIA PASUBIO

Arsenale
Antico Borgo
S Lucia

PORTO PICCOLO

P.O. ORTYGIA

LUNGOMARE VIA VITTORIO

BARBO GRAZIELLA
Market
PIAZZA D. POSTA
VIA TRIESTE
DARSENA
PONTE UMBERTINO

VIA DANTE
VIA REGINA MARGHERITA
VIA MONTEDORI
VIA ELEFANTO
VIA PALERMO
VIA MESSINA
VIA MOSCUZZA
VIA MAIELLI
VIA CAIROLI

VIA LUIGI CADORNA
CORSO TIMOLEONTE
VIA MOSCO
RE IERONE II
RE IERONE I
VIA ARCHIA

PIAZZA VITTORIA
VIA NATALE
CORSO GELONE
VIA ESCHILO

PIAZZA EURIPIDE
V.D. ORTI DI S GIORGIO
VIA D ARSENALE
VIA AGATOCLE

Agorà
SIRACUSANO
PIAZZA MARCONI
CORSO UMBERTO
VIA RIZZA
VIA PERASSO
VIA MALTA
VIA BENGASI
V. TRIPOLI

Borgo S Lorenzo

PIAZZA ADDA
VIA CATANIA
VIA AGATOCLE DIAZ
VIA F CRISPI

Railway Station

ACHRADINA

Ginnasio Romano
Gimnasio Romano
VIA ELORINA
VIA A. DIAZ

VIA PAOLO ORSI
VIA ERMOCRATE

N

Sepolcro, which has a pretty exterior. Inside the church, in a chapel off the left side, are two ancient Crucifixes (one T-shaped).

A tunnel from the church leads past the entrance to the catacombs, which are closed indefinitely. These are the oldest in Sicily and the most extensive in existence, after those in Rome. Caverns in the limestone existed here before the Christian era; there are Christian remains of the 2nd century and fragmentary Byzantine paintings. The tunnel emerges in Santo Sepolcro, the domed octagonal chapel by Giovanni Vermexio, partly below ground. This was the burial place of St Lucy (the empty tomb remains behind the altar) and from here her body was taken to Constantinople in 1038; it was later rescued by the doge and carried off to Venice, where her intact body can still be seen in the church of San Geremia. The 17th-century statue of the saint is by Tedeschi.

SAINT LUCY

According to Vatican files, Lucy of Syracuse would have been about 24 years old when she was martyred in 304, during the persecution of Diocletian. She had accompanied her wealthy, ailing mother to Catania to pray at the tomb of St Agatha. Having obtained a miraculous recovery, the two women returned to Syracuse, where they proceeded to donate all their possessions to the poor, as testimony of the miracle. Lucy was denounced by her betrothed for practising Christianity, and imprisoned. As punishment for her refusal to make sacrifices to the gods, the consul Pascasius sentenced her to be taken to the brothel, stripped, and raped. The soldiers, however, could not move her; she seemed rooted to the ground. Not even a team of oxen was sufficient. By now the people of the city were rejoicing, and calling out her name. Pascasius told the soldiers to burn her, but even with the help of generous quantities of oil, the pyre would not catch. She was finally beheaded. Portrayals of Lucy show the saint with her eyes in a dish or cup, about which the Vatican says nothing, but she is constantly invoked by people with eye problems, and also by the Swedish, to whom the light is so important. Swedish girls traditionally take part in her procession in Syracuse on 13th December, once thought to be the shortest day in the year, harbinger of Spring. Her name derives from *lux*, 'light', and by a curious coincidence, the goddess Artemis, bringer of light, was once worshipped in Syracuse.

Museo Archeologico Regionale Paolo Orsi

Open Tues–Sat 9–7, Sun and holidays 9–2, last tickets an hour before closing.

In Viale Teocrito, once the district of Tyche, is the park of Villa Landolina surrounding the modern museum. The Museo Archeologico Regionale Paolo Orsi is dedicated to the great archaeologist Paolo Orsi, superintendent for antiquities from 1895–1934.

The museum, among the finest in Europe, has one of the most interesting archaeological collections in Italy, especially representative of the eastern half of Sicily. The material from excavations made by Paolo Orsi is outstanding. It is beautifully displayed in an unusual, low-level functional building in the shape of a broken triangle designed by Franco Minissi in 1967 and opened to the public in 1988.

The approach is through the garden, with splendid trees and some antique remains, which was once used as a Protestant cemetery. Among the 19th-century British and American tombstones (reached by the upper path which encircles the garden) is that of the Classicist German poet and scholar August von Platen (1796–1835).

Beyond the entrance hall the centre of the building has a display illustrating the history of the museum and the collocation of the exhibits, which are in three sections: **(A) Geology, Palaeontology** and **Prehistory**; **(B) Greek colonies in Eastern Sicily**; and **(C) sub-colonies and Hellenised centres**. On the upper floor the Hellenistic, Roman, Palaeo-Christian, Christian and Medieval material is to be presented.

Section A

Prehistory: An enlightening display illustrates the geology and the palaeontology of Sicily, with models of the famous dwarf elephants, the skulls of which, casually found in the past, gave rise to the legend of the Cyclops giants with only one eye.

Neolithic Period: Represented by the Stentinello culture, characterized by fortified villages and the use of impressed pottery.

Early Bronze Age: Display relating to the site of Castelluccio (between Noto Antica and Palazzolo Acreide), with objects recovered by Paolo Orsi, including brown painted pottery and carved stone doors from rock-cut tombs, each presenting spirals, yin-yang signs and male-female motifs, presumably symbolizing death, rebirth, and eternity.

Middle Bronze Age: Material from Thapsos on the Magnisi peninsula, a metropolis of the Mycenaean world, with inhabitants from various parts of the Mediterranean. The necropolis was excavated by Paolo Orsi, but the inhabited area (1500–900 BC) has only recently been excavated. Finds include imported pottery (from Mycenae, Cyprus and Malta) and some splendid large storage jars, made using the 'coil of clay' method (some of these had been recycled as tombs). There are also some fascinating lebetes, water-bowls with a pedestal underneath, and strangely modelled upright backs, with what could be eyes and ears, or nipples and upheld arms, perhaps recalling a divinity who protected water. They had handles behind, so they could be carried from one place to another. People of this culture used long-stemmed dishes for serving food, indicating that they were probably reclining on the floor while eating.

An absorbing display is dedicated to **Pantalica**, the most important Late Bronze Age site in Sicily, which was naturally defended by its position, and

Running Gorgon with Pegasus (7th century BC): the earliest known representation of Medusa.

inhabited by the Sicels who are thought to have migrated here from the Italian peninsula c. 1700 BC, their culture remained virtually unchanged until the arrival of the Greeks. There are many of the handsome, characteristic red vases, made this time by using a potter's wheel, and some of them (the heart-shaped jugs for carrying water) are reminiscent of Mycenaean ware, with shiny glaze. One found in the so-called 'Prince's Tomb', looks almost modern. Nearby are some of the numerous bronze artefacts found at Pantalica. Interesting reconstructed tombs, illustrating different burial methods, and a fine hoard of bronze fragments from Mendolito near Adrano, complete this part of the museum.

Section B

Greek colonization: This period began mid 8th century BC, when settlers from Naxos, Corinth and Chalcis arrived on the island. Among the finds shown here is a superb kouros (late 6th century BC) from Leontinoi, the head of which is in the Civic Museum of Catania.

Megara Hyblaea: Ample space is dedicated to this colony founded a little later than the others (728 BC) by Lamis of Megara; late-comers successful enough to found Selinunte in their turn, exactly 100 years later. The objects displayed include imported Greek ware and local products, a fusion of the two cultures.

The most interesting sculptures include a marble statue of a **young man** (c. 560–550 BC), thought to be a funerary monument, with an inscription on the leg naming him as the physician Sambrotidas, son of Mandrokles, and a headless statue made from painted local limestone of a seated mother goddess suckling twins (550 BC). When found in the 1950s it was smashed into more than 900 pieces by workers building the oil refineries for fear of having their employment stopped.

Syracuse: By the entrance to this next section is the gorgeous headless statue of *Venus Anadyomene*, 'emerging from the water', an Imperial Roman copy of a 2nd-century BC Hellenistic original (eventually to be moved upstairs). Found in Syracuse in 1804 by the aristocrat Saverio Landolina, she was greatly admired by Guy de Maupassant, who came purposely to see her in 1885 and left a vivid description of his emotions when he saw her: 'It is not woman poeticised, idealised, divine or majestic like the Venus de Milo; it is woman as she is, as she is loved, desired and

Venus Anadyomene (? c. 1st century AD)

should be embraced.' Of the type derived from the Venus of Cnidos by Praxiteles, whose mistress's breasts became famous for providing him with such perfect models, and posed in the conventional Anadyomene way, although with unusual billowing drapery protecting her modesty, it is clearly an individual woman: tall, broad-hipped, with long, slender fingers and sometimes described as being best appreciated from behind, with two small dimples at the base of her back.

Finds from **Ortygia** are arranged topographically, giving an idea of the continuous habitation of the island: Arab pottery shards along with Roman glass and Greek vases, and a very lifelike 5th-century BC marble fragment of a male figure.

Achradina is represented by material from excavations in Piazza della Vittoria (when building the new church of the Madonna delle Lacrime), where a sanctuary of Demeter and Persephone of the 5th–4th centuries BC was found, with hundreds of votive statuettes and an exceptional polychrome terracotta bust of Artemis. The necropoleis of the city have revealed much of interest, arranged here in chronological order, and displayed as they were found in the tombs. They include an exquisite proto-Corinthian lion-shaped perfume vase (725–700 BC, case 190) and a fine bronze 8th-century BC geometric style statuette of a horse, now the symbol of the museum (case 188). Artefacts imported from all over the known world, mostly of exceptionally high artistic value, demonstrate the wealth, influence and power of Syracuse.

Models of the Temples of Apollo and Athena have been reconstructed and terracotta fragments from them are exhibited. The frieze of seven lion-faced gargoyles comes from the **Temple of Athena**. The stunning polychrome marble relief of the *Running Gorgon with Pegasus* (*pictured on p. 351*), the earliest known representation (7th century BC), was part of the older temple on the same site, replaced by Gelon's magnificent new building in 478 BC.

Section C
Sub-colonies and Hellenized centres
Eloro, **Acrae** and **Casmenae** These sites

are represented by a high-relief in limestone (570–560 BC) of Persephone holding a dove, and weapons left as ex-votos.

Kamarina: Finds include a large terracotta horse and rider (6th century BC), perhaps one of the Dioscuri, used as part of the roof decoration of a temple.

Grammichele: A fine marble **torso** by a Greek artist (c. 500 BC) and a terracotta *Goddess Enthroned* (late 6th century BC).

Francavilla di Sicilia: A remarkable series of *pinakes*, little terracotta pictures in relief (470–460 BC), which previously had only been found at the sanctuary of Persephone at Locri, in Calabria.

Centuripe: A beautiful little clay miniature altar bears a relief from the 6th century BC showing a lion attacking a bull.

Adrano: The bronze statuette known as the Ephebus of Mendolito dates from c. 460 BC.

Gela and **Agrigento:** The last section is devoted to Paolo Orsi's work here, with architectural terracottas, cinerary urns and sarcophagi. The vases from Gela include a krater signed by Polygnotus (440 BC); part of a cup signed by Chachyrylion (520–510 BC); a lekythos with a Nike, signed by Douris (470–460 BC), and a bronze dish with relief of horses, 7th century BC. Also, a fragment by the Painter of Panaitos, and fine bronze kraters. The finds from Agrigento include three rare wooden statuettes of archaic type dating from the late 7th century BC, found by a sacred spring at Palma di Montechiaro (case 309).

Madonna delle Lacrime

Open 8–12 & 4–7.

South of the museum is the vast circular sanctuary of the Madonna delle Lacrime (Our Lady of Tears), begun in 1970 to enshrine a small mass-produced plaster image of the Madonna, and inaugurated in 1994. The figure is supposed to have wept for four days in 1953 in a nearby house. The church (by Michel Andrault and Pierre Parat), where the miraculous image is preserved, incorporates some remains of Byzantine buildings. The huge conical spire (98m high, including the statue) towers incongruously above the buildings of the city. In the crypt below are numerous ex-votos.

Adjoining it to the south, in Piazza della Vittoria, extensive excavations begun in 1973 during the construction of the church of the Madonna delle Lacrime have revealed a group of Hellenistic and Roman houses, a sanctuary of Demeter and Persephone (late 5th or early 4th century BC), and a monumental 5th-century BC fountain. 5,000 terracotta votive statuettes were found here, some of which are now exhibited in the Museo Archeologico Regionale.

Church and Catacombs of San Giovanni

Open 9–12.30 & 2.30–5.30.

Off Viale Teocrito, just to the northwest of the Museo Archeologico, Via San Giovanni leads right. Here, amidst modern buildings, are the ruined church and catacombs of San Giovanni. The façade is preceded by three arches constructed of medieval fragments. To the right is the main entrance and ticket office, beyond which are the entrances (right) to the catacombs and (left) to the ruined church and crypt. The catacombs were probably in use from the 3rd century to the end of the 6th. They are among the most interesting and extensive in Italy outside Rome, with thousands of loculi. From the *decumanus maximus*, or principal gallery, adapted from a disused Greek aqueduct, smaller passages lead to five domed circular chapels, one with the rock-cut tombs of seven nuns, members of one of the first religious houses established after the persecutions in Syracuse, and one containing a sarcophagus bearing a Greek inscription.

On the left of the main entrance, a garden with palms and cacti and flowering shrubs now occupies the ruins of the roofless church which was built into the western portion of an old basilica, once the cathedral of the city. It was reconstructed by the Normans in 1200, and reduced to ruins in 1693 by earthquake. A fine 14th-century rose window survives, as well as its 7th-century apse.

Steps lead down to the crypt, in the form of a Greek cross, with three apses, the site of the martyrdom of St Marcian (c. 254 AD), first bishop of Syracuse: the sanctuary was transformed into a basilica at the end of the 6th or the beginning of the 7th century and was probably destroyed by the Arabs in 878. The visible remains (which include faded frescoes) date from a Norman reconstruction. The fine Byzantine capitals, with symbols of the Evangelists, are thought to have been reused from the earlier basilica. In one apse are traces of 4th- and 5th-century frescoes from a hypogeum. The column against which the saint was martyred (he was flogged to death), and his tomb, surrounded by some of the earliest catacombs, can be seen. An altar is said to mark the site of St Paul's preaching in Syracuse.

To the east of Villa Landolina and the Museo Archeologico is the **Vigna Cassia** (*T: 0931 64696 & 0931 69966, possible every day*) with 3rd-century catacombs, which may be visited with permission.

To the northeast, near the sea is the **Latomia dei Cappuccini** (*open 9–1, closed Sun and holidays; bus no. 4 from Corso Umberto*), to the right of the former Capuchin convent. One of the most extensive of the twelve ancient quarries that surrounded the city, it is now overgrown by plants and trees. Adjacent is Villa Politi, the hotel where Winston Churchill stayed on his painting holidays in Syracuse. From Piazza dei Cappuccini, in front of the 17th-century church, is a fine view of Ortygia.

Viale Teocrito crosses Via Teracati Neapolis. At the end of Viale Augusto (500m) is the entrance to the archaeological park.

Neapolis: Parco Archeologico

Open 9–two hours before sunset. A visit can take at least two hours; a single entrance gives access to the Latomia del Paradiso, the Greek theatre and the Roman amphitheatre; combined tickets with the Museo Archeologico are available.

Beside a splendid giant magnolia tree and a group of ficus trees is the little Norman church of **San Nicolò**. The funeral service of Jourdain de Hauteville, son of Count Roger, was held here in 1093. The church has been restored but is kept locked. Below it, part of an aisled piscina can be seen, a reservoir used for flushing the amphitheatre, to which it is connected by a channel.

A short path, overlooking the Latomia del Paradiso on the right and the Altar of Hieron on the left, continues to the ticket office. The monuments were pillaged in 1526 to provide stone for the Spanish fortifications. Another path leads down through the beautiful garden with lemons, oleanders and pomegranates of the **Latomia del Paradiso**, the largest and most famous of the quarries excavated in ancient times, and since then one of the great sights of the city. Their size testifies to the colossal amount of building stone used for the Greek city, for export throughout the Mediterranean, and for Dionysius' famous fortifications. Following the northern limit of Achradina from here to the Cappuccini near the sea, they also served as a defensive barrier. They were used as concentration camps and according to Thucydides some 7,000 Athenians were incarcerated here in 413 BC.

The right-hand path reached by steps from the ticket office ends at the **Orecchio di Dionisio** (Ear of Dionysius), a curved artificial cavern, 65m long, 5–11m wide, and 23m high, in section like a rough Gothic arch. Its name was given to it by Caravaggio in 1608. Because of the strange acoustic properties of the cavern, it has given rise to the legend that Dionysius used the place as a prison and, from a small hole in the roof at the far end, heard the whispers of his captives. Before Caravaggio, local people called the cave the 'grotto of the noises'. It amplifies every sound and has an interesting echo, which only repeats each sound once. Now it is filled with the strange echoes of noises made by the pigeons which nest here. Once your eyes get accustomed to the

dark you can walk to the far wall. The entire surface bears the marks of the slaves' chisels.

To the right of the Ear of Dionysius is the **Grotta dei Cordari**, named after the rope-makers who used to work here. It is a picturesque cavern supported by huge pillars and covered with maidenhair ferns and coloured lichens. Access, unfortunately, is prohibited because of its perilous state.

The Greek theatre

Another path leads to the Greek theatre, the most celebrated of all the ruins of Syracuse, and one of the largest Greek theatres known (138m in diameter). Archaeological evidence confirms the existence on this spot of a wooden theatre as early as the 6th century BC, and here it was that Epicharmus (c. 540–450 BC) worked as a comic poet. In c. 478 BC Gelon excavated a small stone theatre, engaging the architect Damokopos of Athens. This was inaugurated by Aeschylus in 476 BC with the first production of *Women of Aetna*; his *Persian Women* was performed shortly afterwards. The theatre was enlarged in the 4th century BC, under Timoleon, by excavating deeper into the hillside; it was again enlarged under Hieron II (c. 230 BC) by extending the cavea upwards, using blocks of stone. It could thus hold an audience of 15,000; some scholars think even more.

Under the Romans the scena was altered several times, eventually to make it suitable for gladiator battles and the circus. The Romans probably also cut the trapezoidal lines around the orchestra, when creating a *kolymbetra*, an ornamental garden with fish pool, but it was abandoned in the 1st century AD in favour of the elegant new amphitheatre.

The existing cavea, with 42 rows of seats in nine wedges, is almost entirely hewn out of the rock. This is now believed to represent Hieron II's auditorium of 59 rows, less the upward extension, which has been quarried. The extent of Timoleon's theatre before Hieron's excavations is marked by the drainage trench at the sixth row, above the larger gangway. Around the gangway runs a very worn frieze bearing, in large Greek characters, the names of Hieron (II), Philistis (his queen), Nereis (his daughter-in-law, wife of Gelon II), and Zeus Olympius, which served to distinguish the blocks of seats. The foundations of the scena remain, but successive alterations make it difficult to identify their function, except for the deep recess for the curtain. The view from the upper seats was especially good in the early morning (the hour at which Greek drama was performed). Above the theatre were two porticoes, to provide shelter from the weather, and to serve as foyers. The little house which dominates the cavea is a medieval watch tower against pirates.

Steps at the far end of the Greek theatre, or a path near the entrance (which passes behind the medieval watch tower perched on a rock) lead up to the rock wall behind the theatre. Here there are recesses for votive tablets and a nymphaeum or grotto in which the Galermi aqueduct ends after traversing Epipolae bringing water from the River Bottigliera near Pantalica, 33km away. At the left-hand end of the wall

The cavea of the Greek theatre at Syracuse.

the **Via dei Sepolcri** (Street of Tombs) begins, rising in a curve 146m long. The wheel ruts in the limestone were made by carts in the 16th century serving the mills which used to occupy the cavea of the theatre. The Byzantine tombs and Hellenistic niches in its rock walls have all been rifled. Its upper end (*no admission*) crosses the rock-hewn Acquedotto Galermi.

Immediately to the west of the theatre a Sanctuary of Apollo Temenites has been dis-covered. A smaller, and probably older theatre lies to the southwest, the Teatro Lineare. Across the road from the ticket office (*see above*) is a good view of the foundations of the huge **Altar of Hieron II**, hewn out of the rock. The altar, built between 241 and 217 BC, was used for public sacrifices to Zeus, when as many as 450 bulls could be killed in one day. It was 198m long and 22.8m wide (the largest altar known), and was destroyed by the Spaniards in the 16th century for stone for harbour fortifications (1526); it was presumably about 15m high, and elaborately decorated.

The Roman amphitheatre
Near San Nicolò and the main entrance is the Roman amphitheatre, approached past stone sarcophagi from necropoleis in Syracuse and Megara Hyblaea. An imposing Roman building probably of the 1st century AD, partly hollowed out of the hillside, in external dimensions (140m by 119m) the amphitheatre is only a little inferior to the one in Verona. The perfection of the masonry is probably attributable to a Syracusan architect. Beneath the high parapet encircling the arena runs a corridor with entrances for the gladiators and wild beasts; the marble blocks on the parapet have inscriptions (3rd century AD) recording the ownership of the seats. In the centre is a rectangular depression, probably for the machinery used in the spectacles. The original entrance was at the south end, outside which a large area has been exposed, including an enclosure thought to have been for the animals, and a large fountain. Excavations have revealed an earlier roadway and the base of an Augustan arch here.

A short way to the north of the church of San Nicolò is the beautiful, verdant Latomia di Santa Venera (*closed*), the walls honeycombed with niches for votive tablets. At the far end is the **Necropoli Grotticelli**, a group of Hellenistic and Byzantine tombs, one of which, with a triangle over the entrance, is arbitrarily known as the Tomb of Archimedes (*see p. 383*). The recent excavations here can be seen from the fence along the main road, Via Teracati.

ENVIRONS OF SYRACUSE

At the western limit of the ancient city, on the open, barren plateau of Epipolae, is Castello Eurialo. The approach road crosses the great **Walls of Dionysius**, which defended the Epipolae ridge. Begun by Dionysius the Elder in 402 BC, they were fin-ished by 397 and were 30km long. Just before the main road to Belvedere crosses the walls, a path (50m) leads right to the **Latomia del Filosofo** (or Bufalaro). Philoxenus of Cythera was supposedly confined here for expressing too candid an opinion of the verses of Dionysius. The quarry supplied stone for the walls and the castle.

DIONYSIUS THE ELDER

Dionysius was one of the most remarkable rulers of his day. He exploited tensions in his native Syracuse after the failure of a campaign against the Carthaginians in order to seize control of the city and declare himself 'general with full powers' in 405 BC. He was clearly a charismatic speaker; several accounts tell of the theatres emptying as the citizens rushed to greet his arrival in a city. Dionysius was flamboyant in his personal life (one story tells of him consummating two marriages on the same night) but equally open to Greek culture. He loved making a display, flaunting the wealth of his city at the Olympic games of 384. He supported Sparta against Athens but then was wooed back by the Athenians and even won first prize for a play at the city's drama festival. It is said that he was so excited by the news that he drank himself to death.

Ultimately, however, his position rested on a large force of mercenaries drawn from all over Sicily and Italy which sustained him in power even against popular uprisings. While his central mission to rid Sicily of the Carthaginians was never achieved, he came to control much of the island and extended his rule to the Greek cities of the mainland. An important innovator in siege warfare at a time when Greek armies usually gave up as soon as they met city walls, his capture of the Carthaginian stronghold of *Motya* in 397 was a major achievement. It is sometimes argued that if Dionysius had defeated the Carthaginians he might have conquered much of Italy and stayed the growing power of Rome. The most visible legacy of Dionysius is the fortifications around Syracuse which he completed between 401 and 397, culminating in the Castello Eurialo.   C.F.

Castello Eurialo

Open summer 9–7; winter 9–5. See plan overleaf.
The main road winds up towards the town of Belvedere; just after the signpost for the town, a narrow road (signposted) leads right for the Castello Eurialo.

Three ditches precede the west front: the outermost is near the custodian's house. Between the second and the third are the ruins of an outwork, the walls of which have partly collapsed into the second ditch. On the left, steps lead down into the innermost ditch, the principal defence of the fortress, which gave access to a labyrinth of casemates and passages. On the right the three piers of the drawbridge are prominent. There are 11 entrances from this main ditch to the gallery parallel with it; from here three passages lead east; the longest, on the north (174m long; *closed since 1983*) connects with the Epipolae Gateway (*see below*). Prominent in this part of the castle are the remains of five towers, originally 15m high, and surmounted by catapults invented by Dionysius.

The dark corridor to the south leads to a ditch outside the south wall of the castle. At the end, steps (which were concealed from the enemy) lead up to the outer ward

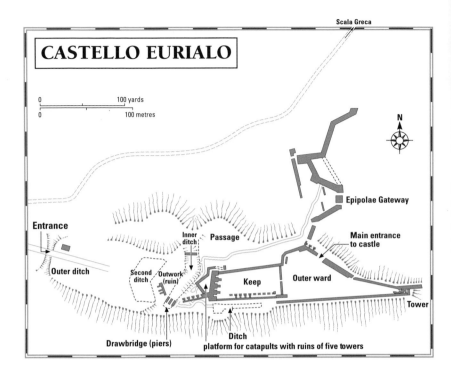

of the castle proper, which consisted of a keep with an irregular outer ward on the east. The barracks and cisterns were located in these parts of the castle. On the northeast side of the outer ward was the main entrance from the town; on the southeast rose a tower connected with the south wall of Dionysius. From here there is a good view of the Epipolae gateway below, a 'pincer' type defence work on the spur of the north wall of Dionysius (*described above*), which can be seen, broken at intervals by towers and posterns, stretching towards the sea. It was united to the keep by a complicated system of underground works, notable for their ingenious provisions for shelter and defence. An arch leads back towards the entrance into the keep. On the left a few steps lead down to a path which follows the edge of the site back to the entrance.

The Olympieion

The Olympieion or Temple of Zeus is on the right bank of the Ciane. On the approach the two remaining columns of the temple can be seen among trees on the skyline of a low hill, the **Polichne**, a point of great strategic importance, invariably occupied by the besiegers of Syracuse. About 1km after the bridge over the Ciane, at the top of the rise, a road (right; signposted) leads in less than 1km (keep right) to the temple in a cypress grove. Built in the 6th century, just after the Temple of Apollo, it was the second Doric temple in Sicily, hexastyle and peripteral with 42 monolithic columns, two of which remain standing on part of the stylobate. There is a view from here of the island of Ortygia.

Fonte Ciane

The Fonte Ciane, source of the river and now a nature reserve (Riserva naturale orientata Fiume Ciane e Saline di Siracusa) is reached by a turning off the Canicattini Bagni road SP 14. After crossing the Anapo, a byroad (left; signposted) leads for 3km through a fertile valley with orange and lemon groves and magnificent old olive trees. Beyond a tributary of the Ciane, a road (signposted) continues left to end in a grove of eucalyptus and cypress trees beside the romantic spring (the ancient *Cyane*), overgrown with reeds and thick clumps of papyrus. This plant grows only here and along the River Fiumefreddo in Sicily, and in no other part of Europe. The name of the spring (in Greek, blue) describes the azure colour of its waters, but a myth relates how the nymph Cyane, who tried to prevent Hades from carrying off Persephone (*see p. 281*), was changed into a spring and condemned to weep forever. Beyond the bridge a path follows a fence along the reeds to the large pool, inhabited by numerous waterfowl. Both springs, the Testa della Pisma, and the smaller Pismotta have pools with papyrus.

Plemmyrion and the coast to the south

The ancient district of Plemmyrion, now known as the peninsula of the Maddalena, was on the headland opposite Ortygia on Syracuse's Great Harbour. The headquarters of Nicias were established here after his defeat on Epipolae by Gylippus, in the famous battle between Athens and Syracuse in 415 BC. Although tragically disfigured by concrete villas and holiday apartment blocks, the coast is still intact and is protected as a marine nature reserve (*T: 0931 709734, www.plemmirio.it*), one of six such reserves around the coast of Sicily. You can book a guide for an immersion to do some sea-watching, or you can birdwatch along the 7km of protected coastline—the many interesting birds include kingfishers, here adapted to fishing in the sea.

Neolithic settlements have been found further south on the offshore islet of **Ognina** where Neolithic and Early Bronze Age pottery finds suggest that it may have been a Maltese trading outpost. There is a little port here and sea-bathing at Capo Sparano, just to the north.

The bay to the south, Fontane Bianche, used to be one of the best bathing beaches on the island; it has now been spoilt by hundreds of ugly concrete holiday homes. Nearby is **Cassibile**, where a huge Bronze Age necropolis and hut village yielded extremely interesting finds, now in the Museo Archeologico Regionale in Syracuse. In an olive grove near the bridge over the river, close to the road, on the afternoon of 3rd September 1943, Generals Bedell Smith and Castellano signed the military terms of surrender of the Italian army to the Allies. Several pill-boxes survive along the road and on the bed of the river. At the mouth of the Cassibile, the ancient *Kakyparis*, the Athenian general Demosthenes, covering the rear of Nicias' forces during the retreat from Syracuse, was cut off and forced to surrender. The countryside here is particularly lovely, with old olive trees, carobs, almonds and citrus groves.

NOTO

Noto is perhaps the most fascinating of the 18th-century Baroque cities of Sicily. It was built after the earthquake of 1693 when the former town (now known as Noto Antica) on Monte Alveria was abandoned. An excellent example of 18th-century town planning, the local limestone has been burnt gold by the sun. The inhabitants call their city *il giardino di pietra*, the garden of stone. The surrounding vineyards produce an exquisite dessert wine, *Moscato di Noto*, also rich gold in colour. Made from white Muscat grapes, the wine comes in three varieties: *naturale*, *spumante* and *liquoroso*.

HISTORY OF NOTO

This was ancient *Neas*, founded in 448 BC by Doucetius; a city which enjoyed several privileges under the Romans, who called it *Netum*, and was chosen by the Arabs in 903 to be the centre of the *Val di Noto*, one of the three administrative areas of the island. The economy flourished, thanks to the introduction of citrus, mulberry trees for the silk industry, almonds, rice, sugar-cane and cotton; there were wool mills and tanneries. Trade was encouraged and there was a flourishing Jewish community.

These happy conditions continued through the successive dominations of Sicily, until 1492, when the Jews were expelled, and 1693, when the great earthquake struck, followed by epidemics of cholera. The town on the Alveria was so severely damaged that a new site about 14km away was chosen by the Spanish government, against the wishes of the Church and the majority of the inhabitants, making reconstruction slow. Only in 1702 was the old town abandoned for the rational new town, planned and built by some of the greatest engineers, architects and master-builders of the time.

In 1817 Syracuse was preferred by the Bourbons as provincial capital (briefly returned to Noto from 1837–65), and the economy languished. A further blow was the governmental decision in 1866 to expropriate the monasteries and convents; Noto, seat of a bishopric, had always had a very strong religious community, which had a considerable influence on the economy. People started to abandon the city, in favour of new districts to the south. In 1986 many buildings were propped up with scaffolding, and closed. A serious earthquake in 1990 did further damage, and in 1996 the dome of the cathedral collapsed. A World Heritage Site, the town and cathedral are still in the process of being restored.

EXPLORING NOTO

At the east end of the main street of Noto is the bronze statue of the patron San Corrado Confalonieri (*see box on p. 367*), near the public gardens, where the thick evergreen *Ficus benjamin* trees form an impenetrable roof over the road. To the south is the Neoclassical church of Ecce Homo (*open for Mass Sun morning 8, 10.30*), now a sanctuary for local soldiers who died in the Second World War.

Porta Reale, surmounted by the three symbols of the people of Noto, a tower for strength, dog for loyalty, and pelican for self-sacrifice, was erected for the visit of Ferdinand II of Bourbon in 1838. It leads into **Corso Vittorio Emanuele** along which the town rises to the right and falls away to the left. By skilful use of open spaces and monumental flights of steps, this straight and level street, 1km long, has been given a lively skyline and provides successive glimpses of the countryside. The main streets are paved with blocks of stone, while the side streets are cobbled. On the right, a grandiose flight of steps leads up to San Francesco all' Immacolata (1704–48), by Vincenzo Sinatra, with a decorative façade and an interior of lavish white stucco by Giuseppe Gianforma; there are two canvases here by Olivio Sozzi: over the first left-hand altar, *Ecstasy of St Francis*, and opposite, *St Anthony Preaching to the Fish*. The convent of **San Salvatore** (now a high school) faces Via Zanardelli with a fine long 18th-century façade and attractive tower (possibly designed by Rosario Gagliardi); part of it is the Museo Civico (*closed for rearrangement*), with an interesting archaeological collection, representative of the area (including finds from the Greek city of *Eloro*, on the coast) and many poignant remains from the old pre-earthquake city.

Opposite San Salvatore is the church of **Santa Chiara** (*open for Mass 8.30*), with an oval interior by Gagliardi (1730–48), and a *Madonna* by Antonello Gagini, from Noto Antica. The convent now houses the Galleria di Arte Moderna (*open 9–1 & 4–8*), a collection of sculptures and drawings by the local artist Giuseppe Pirrone (1898–1978), responsible for the impressive bronze doors of the cathedral.

Around the cathedral

At the heart of the town, the immense façade of the cathedral, rising above a dramatic stairway, looks down on **Piazza Municipio** with its symmetrical horseshoe hedges of ficus. The Cattedrale San Nicola (18th century, Rosario Gagliardi and Vincenzo Sinatra) is under repair after part of the dome, which was rebuilt in the 19th century, collapsed in 1996. Beside the cathedral is the Neoclassical Bishop's Palace, and Palazzo Sant'Alfano Landolina, once the residence of this privileged local family, the only one to have a palace on the main street, and the only one allowed to offer hospitality to visiting kings and queens. Beyond the Bishop's Palace is the basilica of **San Salvatore**. The façade was designed by Andrea Gigante of Trapani and probably built by Antonio Mazza (1791). The polychrome interior, with a vault painting by Antonio Mazza, contains 18th-century paintings by Giuseppe Velasquez.

On the south side of the piazza, facing the cathedral, is the town hall, Palazzo Ducezio (*open Mon–Fri 8.30–2 & 3–7*), a splendid building of 1746 by Vincenzo Sinatra. The upper floor was added in 1951. To the right of the town hall is the **Chiesa del Collegio** (*open 10–1 & 3.30–7*), with a curved façade probably by Gagliardi (1730; restored by Vincenzo Sinatra in 1776). It has a luminous interior, with frescoes on the vault. It is possible to climb up the bell-tower, for a view over the rooftops.

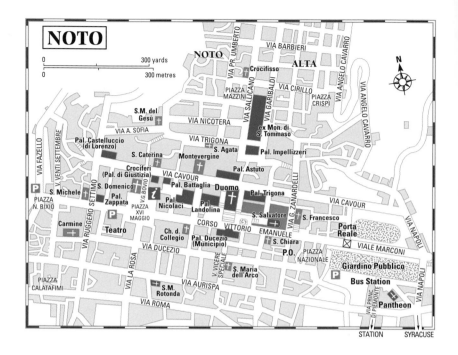

San Domenico, Via Ducezio and Via Cavour

The long façade of the former Collegio dei Gesuiti (now a school) stretches as far as Piazza San Domenico (or Piazza XVI Maggio), with the opera house, **Teatro Vittorio Emanuele** (*open Mon–Sat 9–12 & 4–6, Sun 10–12*), a perfectly preserved building of 1861, with a beautiful interior and 330 seats. In front of the building, in a little garden is a 17th-century Baroque fountain from Noto Antica with a statue of Hercules, thought to be Roman. In the pavilion behind is the Tourist Information Bureau. Above to the left is the soaring, glorious golden façade of **San Domenico** (1737–56) by Gagliardi, perhaps his most successful building in the town. In Via Bovio above is the former convent of the Casa dei Crociferi by Paolo Labisi (1750), finished by Vincenzo Sinatra. It has been restored for use as the law courts.

From Piazza XVI Maggio, Corso Vittorio Emanuele continues to the rather severe Palazzo Zappata. To the left Via Ruggero Settimo leads past an aristocratic palace to the pretty Via Ducezio, which runs parallel to the corso to the south. It is closed at the west end by the fine concave Baroque façade (with Rococo details) of **Santa Maria del Carmine** (or Carmelo), a late work by Gagliardi with a charming elliptical interior. At the other end of the street, on Via Viceré Speciale, is the church of **Santa Maria dell'Arco** (1730), also by Gagliardi, with an elegant portal, and a decorative stucco interior with two stoups from Noto Antica; the organ is dated 1778, and the wooden Crucifix over the altar is 14th century. Nearby is an attractive Art Nouveau house. Via

Aurispa, parallel to Via Ducezio on the south, is another pretty street with simpler buildings and the church of Santa Maria Rotonda, which has a Baroque façade.

From Santa Maria dell'Arco, Via Vicerè Speciale leads up to the splendid rear façade of the town hall. To the left is Palazzo Rau della Ferla, which has a handsome front and a courtyard covered with jasmine. Part of the palace houses the Costanzo pastry shop. At the end the impressive wall of the Collegio dei Gesuiti can be seen, which a road now follows uphill back to the corso, straight across which Via Corrado Nicolaci continues uphill towards the church of Montevergine. Via Nicolaci is overlooked by the delightful Baroque balconies of **Palazzo Nicolaci Villadorata** (*open 10–1 & 3–7*), built between 1737 and 1765, once the residence of Don Giacomo Nicolaci, a patron of the arts. He donated part of his collection of books to the important City Library, housed here, consisting of 80,000 volumes, incunabula, rare editions and manuscripts.

The façade of the church of **Montevergine** is attributed to Vincenzo Sinatra. Deconsecrated, it has a magnificent 18th-century floor of majolica tiles from Caltagirone, and paintings by Costantino Carasi. The church is on the handsome Via Cavour, another 18th-century street, with views of the countryside at either end. It leads west past Palazzo Battaglia (1735), on the corner of Via Rocco Pirri, in which a charming little market-place, with a loggia supported on iron pillars surrounding a fountain, has been restored and used for open-air concerts in the summer. Via Cavour continues west past the former Oratorio di San Filippo Neri (1750) and the church of Santa Caterina (right; attached to the oratory, on Via Fratelli Ragusa). Beyond, near the end of Via Cavour, is the large Neoclassical Palazzo di Lorenzo (Castelluccio) built for the Knights of Malta. Opposite is a basket-maker's workshop.

At the other end of Via Cavour, to the right of Montevergine, is the beautiful **Palazzo Astuto** (late 18th century; Vincenzo Sinatra or Paolo Labisi). Further on, on the right, is Palazzo Trigona (1781), part of it renovated as a congress centre, exhibition room and auditorium.

Noto Alta

Via Mariannina Coffa (partly stepped) leads uphill to the upper part of the town known as Noto Alta. This simpler district was laid out facing north and south, on a different plan and orientation from the lower monumental area, with its four long, straight, parallel streets running from east-west. There is a view of the battlemented former Convento di Sant'Antonio di Padova on the top of the hill. The road continues left past Palazzo Impellizzeri San Giacomo (1752) with a balcony along the whole length of the first floor. Part of the palace is now used to house the city archives (*open Mon–Fri 9–1 & 3–7, Sat morning only*), often used for exhibitions, and in one room there is a splendid 18th-century crystal chandelier. The corner and bell tower of the former Ospedale Trigona are visible here. Via Trigona leads past the former convent to the deconsecrated church of **Sant'Agata**, attributed to Gagliardi and completed by Paolo Labisi. It contains stuccoes by Labisi and paintings by Costantino Carasi. Opposite is Santissima Annunziata e Badia, another church dating from 1720. Just beyond, approached by a double stairway, is Santa Maria del Gesù, next to its convent.

Via Trigona leads back to the impressive former **Monastero di San Tommaso** (1720), with an attractive façade and double stairway. It is now used as a prison, which extends as far as Piazza Mazzini. On the summit of the hill, at the centre of Noto Alta, is the enormous church of the **Crocifisso** (1715, Gagliardi), which contains a number of works of art from Noto Antica, including (in the right transept) a beautiful statue of the *Madonna della Neve* (Our Lady of the Snows) signed by Francesco Laurana (1471), and two Romanesque lions. A Dalmatian-born Venetian sculptor who absorbed a variety of influences in France and Naples as well as Sicily, where he worked in the late 1460s and early '70s, he is recognised as one of the more complex sculptors of the 15th cen-

Madonna della Neve (1471) by Francesco Laurana, in the church of the Crocifisso, Noto Alta.

tury. In his most famous works, often quiet and austere busts of women, there is a pursuit of abstract formal perfection that has led to comparisons with Piero della Francesca. The Cappella Landolina contains paintings by the school of Costantino Carasi. On the high altar is an 18th-century reliquary designed by Gagliardi which contains part of a venerated Crucifix from Noto Antica. A relic of the Holy Thorn also belongs to the church (only shown on Good Friday).

ENVIRONS OF NOTO

San Corrado di Fuori

The most beautiful road from Noto to Noto Antica (12km, signposted for Palazzolo Acreide) leads uphill to the left from the public gardens, crossing Noto Alta, a prosperous district of low-lying Art Nouveau houses and passing through the village of San Corrado di Fuori, with more attractive early 20th-century houses. Outside the town, in the Valle dei Miracoli, amid fertile vegetation, is the hermitage of San Corrado Confalonieri, who lived here in the 14th century. The 18th-century sanctuary contains a painting of the saint by Sebastiano Conca. The road continues across a fine upland plain with old olive trees. It then descends to cross a bridge decorated with four obelisks.

SAN CORRADO CONFALONIERI

Corrado Confalonieri was born an aristocrat in Piacenza in 1284. While unsuccessfully hunting a white deer, he set a fire in the forest to flush the animal, the blaze doing a great deal of damage to the countryside and the villages. A vagabond was blamed, who confessed after atrocious torture. On the point of the man's execution by hanging, Corrado saved his life by admitting his responsibility. All Corrado's possessions were confiscated to make good the damage, but he saw in this episode a sign that he should change his way of life. He told his young wife to enter a monastery, while he joined the Franciscans. After a few years he came down to Sicily, where he lived as a hermit in the hills between Noto and Avola, gaining a reputation for wisdom and sanctity. It is said that he could conjure loaves of bread from the air, whenever he was hungry. On his death, on 19th February 1351, his body was hotly contested by the two towns, so was placed on an ox-cart with no driver, allowing Corrado to choose the place of his burial. He ended up in Noto and is portrayed with a flame on his right hand, and a white deer by his side.

Noto Antica

Open 9–1 hr before sunset.
The byroad (left) for Noto Antica is lined with early 20th-century Stations of the Cross on the approach to the large sanctuary of **Santa Maria della Scala** (*open 9.30–12.30 & 3 or 4–6 or 7*), next to a seminary with an elegant façade (1708) surmounted by three statues and a balcony. The road now descends to cross another bridge over a ravine before reaching Noto Antica, abandoned since the earthquake of 1693 and now utterly deserted. The scant ruins, reduced to rubble and overgrown, are very romantic, and provide inspiration for artists, photographers and writers. This was a settlement that long antedates its legendary foundation by the Sicel chief Doucetius in 448 BC, and was the only Sicilian town to resist the depredations of Verres (*see box on p. 199*). The last stronghold of Muslim Sicily, it gave its name to the *Val di Noto*, one of the three areas into which the Arabs divided up the island. It fell to the Normans in 1091, and became a flourishing medieval city. After the terrible earthquake of 1693, the city of Noto was rebuilt on its present site.

The entrance is through the monumental Porta della Montagna with remains of the high walls on either side. A rough road leads up past a round tower and along the ridge of the hill. The conspicuous wall on the left (the highest one to survive) belonged to the Chiesa Madre. After 1km, beside a little monument, the right fork continues (and the road deteriorates) to end beside the Eremo della Madonna, a small deserted chapel, with a good view of the surrounding countryside.

Some distance to the west is the remote prehistoric village of **Castelluccio** (c. 18th–14th centuries BC), which has given its name to the most important Early Bronze Age culture of southeast Sicily. The rock tombs had carved portal slabs (now in the Museo Archeologico at Syracuse).

Cava Grande del Cassibile

Open Apr–Sept 8–8; Oct–Mar 8–4.
The Cava Grande, formed through the centuries by the River Cassibile, where centuries-old plane trees and colourful oleanders grow, is a nature reserve, the Riserva naturale orientata Cavagrande del Cassibile. A spectacular gorge nearly 10km long, it reaches a depth of 300m, and is the deepest canyon in Europe: a series of rock pools, waterfalls, and ancient cave-homes. The river was the first in Sicily to be exploited to produce hydroelectric energy, in 1910. Thousands of tombs (11th–9th centuries BC) have been identified here (finds in the Museo Archeologico at Syracuse). The easiest approach to the gorge is via Villa Vela, a little village with some Art Nouveau villas on the road between Noto and Palazzolo Acreide. The gorge can be entered from here, or from the belvedere (where you will find a restaurant and an Azienda Forestale information kiosk) at the end of the very winding road to **Avola Antica**, the site of the pre-earthquake town c. 6 km inland. The deserted and desolate streets can also be explored here, overgrown with vegetation, the buildings destroyed, as at Noto Antica, in 1693. The path here is steep and overgrown with vegetation, but it is the most impressive approach to the gorge (trekking boots advisable). Birds that may be heard or spotted include dippers, ravens, kingfishers, Cetti's warblers, blue rock thrushes, spotless starlings, shrikes, nightingales and owls; but the Cava Grande is particularly important for the resident populations of different varieties of bat.

Avola

Avola is a prosperous agricultural town and an important centre for almond cultivation. It has expanded in a disorderly way around its centre, which retains the hexagonal plan to which it was designed after 1693 by Angelo Italia. The central square is Piazza Umberto, where the Chiesa Madre, dedicated to St Nicholas and St Sebastian, is situated. The interior, a central nave and two side aisles, houses two splendid canvases, the *Madonna of the Rosary* by Sebastiano Conca, and the *Wedding of the Madonna* by Olivio Sozzi. In the choir is an 18th-century organ by Donato Del Piano, while the chapel of the Sacrament is richly decorated with stuccoes in Rococo style. Near the church is one of Sicily's most famous cafés, the Caffè Finocchiaro. Four smaller squares open off the outer edge of the hexagon, one of which, Piazza Vittorio Veneto, has an early 20th-century fountain with three lions stooping to drink, by Gaetano Vinci. The 18th-century churches include Sant'Antonio Abate in Piazza Regina Elena, which houses a wooden statue of Christ at the Column from Avola Antica, and, in Via Manzoni, the Santissima Annunziata (with a façade by Giuseppe Alessi), which is a national monument. There are a number of Art Nouveau buildings, evidence of the flourishing economy here in the early 20th century. The 16th-century church of the Cappuccini, outside the hexagonal centre, in Piazza Francesco Crispi, has a lovely 17th-century altarpiece, a painting by an unknown artist of *The Invention of the Cross.*

THE GULF OF NOTO

Noto Marina (or Lido di Noto) is a little resort on the sea, which has some of the best beaches on the east coast of the island. The beautiful landscape here has huge old olive, carob, almond and citrus trees. The River Asinaro, which reaches the sea near Calabernardo, a fishing village and popular spot for bathing, is the ancient *Assinaros*, where the retreating Greeks, trying to reach *Heloros*, were overtaken while drinking at the river and killed after the great battle between Syracuse and Athens in 412 BC.

Near the mouth of the Tellaro river, on a low hill, in peaceful countryside, are the remains of **Eloro** (*open 9–1.30*), the first sub-colony to be founded by Syracuse, also called *Heloros*, probably at the beginning of the 7th century BC. The excavations are in a lonely, deserted position by the sea and there is a good view inland of the Pizzuta column (*see below*), with Noto seen beyond green rolling hills. The view along the unspoilt coastline extends to the southern tip of the island.

The road passes the basement of a temple dedicated to Asclepios. To the right of the road, in a large fenced enclosure sloping down to the canal, is the **Sanctuary of Demeter** consisting of a larger temple and a monumental stoa. A theatre has been partially excavated nearby. To the left, beyond the custodian's house, is another enclosure of recent excavations. An ancient road continues to the walls and north gate. Outside the walls another later (Hellenistic) **Temple of Demeter and Persephone** has been found and reconstructed in the museum of Noto.

The so-called **Pizzuta**, a column over 10m high, can be reached by returning to the approach road beyond the railway bridge. This is now known to be a funerary memorial of the 3rd century BC; the archaeologist Paolo Orsi found the burial chamber underneath it, with three funerary couches complete with skeletons.

Villa del Tellaro
Open 8–7.30.
From the main road (SS 115), just by the bridge across the Tellaro river, a road leads inland towards a farmhouse (conspicuous to the right of the road) in the locality of Caddeddi, less than 1km from the main road. Beneath the farmhouse in 1972 a Roman villa of the late 4th century AD, known as the Villa del Tellaro was discovered. The splendid polychrome mosaics, reminiscent of those at Piazza Armerina, can at last be seen, after many years of careful restoration.

OASI FAUNISTICA DI VENDICARI

Open 9–dusk, further information and guides are available on entry.
The eight-kilometre stretch of coast south of the mouth of the River Tellaro was one of the first areas on the island to become a nature reserve. This beautiful wetland, of the greatest interest for its wildlife, has been protected since 1984 after opposition led by the Ente Fauna Siciliana succeeded in halting the construction of a vast tourist village here. More than 250 different species of birds have been recorded, some nesting (including black-winged stilts), some migratory (many ducks, herons, cormorants, flamingoes).

From the main road, beyond the railway, a track closed to cars continues for c. 1km through lemon groves to the entrance. At the south end is the 18th-century farmhouse of **San Lorenzo Lo Vecchio**, with remains of a Hellenistic temple transformed into a Byzantine church. On the edge of the shore are ruins of a Norman tower, and an old tuna fishery. The landscape from here to the southern tip of the island is less striking. In the shallow bay by the fishing village of **Marzamemi**, a wonderful place for diving, excavations begun in 1959 have brought to light 14 ancient shipwrecks (four Greek, five Roman and five Byzantine ships), as well as more modern wrecks, such as the *Chillingham*, a British cargo ship that sank in the 19th century; a Hurricane fighter plane which came down in 1943; and a submarine, the *Sebastiano Veniero*, which sank in 1925 after colliding with a merchant ship.

Pachino and Portopalo

Pachino is a wine-producing centre, renowned for its sweet white *Moscato* and also the red *Nero d'Avola* also known as *Calabrese*. The latter is grown all over the island, but the best vineyards are in the warm southeast. In the north of the island Nero d'Avola does not ripen easily, and it is common to find it blended with Syrah or Merlot, varieties which ripen readily at higher altitudes. The Melia family are producing wonderful blends of Nero d'Avola with Cabernet Sauvignon and Merlot at their winery on the outskirts of Alcamo. When fully ripe, Nero d'Avola has an incredibly high sugar content, and acid is often added during vinification to balance the sweetness.

In recent years Pachino has also acquired world-wide fame for cantaloupe melons, and especially for the exquisite cherry tomatoes with which the town has now become synonymous, especially in Italy.

Beyond almond and olive trees near the sea and an inland lagoon is the southernmost municipality in Europe, the untidy fishing port of **Portopalo di Capo Passero**. The ruins of an imposing watch-tower stand on the eastern end of the island of **Capo Passero** (*custodian T: 338 4054855*), the ancient *Pachynus*, the southeast horn of Sicily. A Roman necropolis has been excavated here, and the island, once joined to the mainland by an isthmus, is of interest to naturalists.

The southernmost point of Sicily is the little **Isolotto delle Correnti**, with a lighthouse, where sea turtles and pelicans can still frequently be spotted on the shore. West of Pachino, on the border with the province of Ragusa, several marshy areas now form a nature reserve for the protection of migrating birds, known as the Pantani Cuba e Longarini.

Rosolini

Between Pachino and Noto, Rosolini is a town of very ancient origin, re-founded in 1713 by the aristocrat Francesco Moncada. In the spacious central Piazza Garibaldi is the elegant town hall, surmounted by a clock, and the sturdy Chiesa Madre, which dominates all the buildings around it. Commenced in 1720 on the orders of Moncada, it was only finished in the late 19th century, thanks to the town carters, who transported the blocks of stone from the quarry to the site, free of charge. A rock-hewn Palaeo-Christian basilica lies beneath the **Castello del Principe** (1668) amid extensive catacombs (now used as a garage). The rivers of this area have formed deep gorges, very interesting to explore; many of them, besides prehistoric tombs, have churches and homes carved into the rock, used up until quite recently, and immersed in luxuriant vegetation. Along the road to Noto can be found examples such as **Cava Stafenna**; while on the road to Modica is the **Cava di Croce Santa**.

PALAZZOLO ACREIDE

Successor to the Greek city of *Acrae*, of which the impressive remains can be seen on the outskirts, Palazzolo Acreide is a charming town with a good climate. Acrae was a sub-colony founded by Syracuse in 663 BC, in a strategic point for dominating southeast Sicily and the route to the interior. In a treaty between Rome and Hieron II in 263 BC, Acrae was assigned to Syracuse. Its period of greatest splendour followed, and its main monuments, including the theatre, were built at this time. Hieron built himself a magnificent summer residence here, hence the name Palazzolo. Under Byzantium it had a conspicuous and vocal Christian community, which probably caused its destruction in the 9th century by the Arabs. Count Roger assigned the town to his son Godfrey and from 1374 it was governed for two centuries by the Alagona family. Its finest buildings were erected after the earthquake in 1693, in Baroque style, for which the town is a World Heritage Site.

EXPLORING PALAZZOLO ACREIDE

The lower town

The Chiesa Madre (San Niccolò, 13th century, 18th-century façade by Vincenzo Sinatra) is in the lower town, in the central Piazza Moro. Inside there are two late 19th-century carved thrones used for transporting the 16th-century statue of the saint in procession. The charming sacristy with its painted vault dates from 1778 and retains its original furniture. Opposite is the extremely elegant church of San Paolo (18th century, Vincenzo Sinatra), with statues on the façade and the bell tower on the top. The interior is richly decorated with stucco.

From San Paolo a road leads down to Piazza Umberto, and the red 18th-century Palazzo Zocco, with a decorative long balcony supported by grotesque heads, all different. Via Annunziata leads downhill from the piazza towards the edge of the town and the unfinished church of the **Annunziata**, one of the oldest churches in town, with a lovely 18th-century portal decorated with four twisted columns and vines and festoons of fruit. In the dazzling, luminous interior, covered with stuccoes, is a fine high altar in marble. The *Annunciation* by Antonello da Messina that is now in the Palazzo Bellomo Regional Gallery in Syracuse, was commissioned for this church in 1474.

From Piazza Moro, Via Garibaldi leads uphill past **Palazzo Caruso** (or **Judica-Cafici**) at no. 127, with monsters' heads beneath its balconies, the longest Baroque balconies in the world. Further uphill, after a flight of steps, is Palazzo Ferla (no. 115) with four graceful balconies. Close by, at no. 36 Via Gaetano Italia, is the Art Nouveau Palazzo Cappellani which will one day house the Archaeological Museum, with a rich collection formed by the local historian, Baron Gabriele Judica, who was the first to excavate the monuments of Acrae, in 1809.

The upper town

The centre of the busier upper town is Piazza del Popolo. Here is the 18th-century church of **San Sebastiano**, which is approached by a flight of steps and has a splendid façade and portal by Paolo Labisi. In the interior are a painting of *St Margaret of Cortona* by Vito D'Anna (fourth north-aisle altar), and a pre-earthquake statue of St Sebastian. The handsome town hall, with the municipal clock on the top, dates from 1808. In Corso Vittorio Emanuele the 19th-century Palazzo Judica has an imaginative façade, and vases on the roof.

Just off the piazza, at 19 Via Macchiavelli, entered through a courtyard, is the **Casa-Museo Antonino Uccello** (*open 9–1; ring the bell*), a delightful local ethnographical museum created by Antonino Uccello (1922–79) and displayed in his 17th-century house. The interesting material from the provinces of Syracuse and Ragusa includes farming utensils and tools, household objects, puppets, and terracotta statuettes.

At the top of the road, Via Acre continues uphill to Piano Acre and the church of the **Immacolata**. Its convex façade is difficult to see as the church is now entered through the courtyard at the east end (*ring at the central door, at the house of the custodian of a school*). It contains a very fine statue of the *Madonna* by Francesco Laurana.

The ruins of Acrae

Beyond the Immacolata a road continues westwards up to the entrance to the Greek remains of Acrae (*9–7; winter till 5*), the first colony founded by Syracuse (663 BC). It is a well-kept site, although part of it is at present inaccessible. A *strada panoramica* (above the entrance gate) circles the top of the acropolis, with traces of its fortification walls. It gives a splendid idea of the site, and offers excellent views. Excavations began here in 1824, and were continued in the last century.

The small theatre (seating for 600), built in the late 3rd century BC, is well preserved, and now used regularly for Greek drama presented by students. The scena was altered in Roman times, and in 600 AD a mill with round silos was built over the ruins. Nearby is an altar for sacrifices. Behind the theatre is the bouleuterion, a tiny council chamber (connected to the theatre by a passageway). From here (through a locked double gate) there is a good view of the recent excavations of the ancient city. There is a long stretch of the *decumanus*, the main street, constructed in basalt (altered by the Romans), and parts of another road at right-angles which passes close to a circular temple. Probably dedicated to Persephone, it is thought to date from the 3rd century BC. It was covered by a cupola with a circular opening in the centre, supported on girders of terracotta (no longer *in situ*, but preserved); the holes for them are visible in the circular walls, and the pavement survives. Excavations continue here in the area thought to have been the agora.

The rest of the enclosure consists of a depression between two latomies, or stone quarries, with traces of a Heroic cult and of later Christian occupation. On the face of the smaller latomy, nearest to the path, niches can be seen (formerly closed with commemorative plaques carved with reliefs and inscriptions) and an interesting funerary bas-relief of c. 200 BC, showing two scenes, one Roman, with a warrior sacrificing, and one Greek, with a banquet scene. Further on (at present kept locked) are extensive Byzantine catacombs carved into the rock (some of them adapted by the Arabs as dwellings). The larger family chapels are decorated with unusual lattice-work transennae. From the other path the larger latomy can be seen, and near the theatre a monumental gateway. Beyond a locked gate is the basement of a Temple of Aphrodite (6th century BC).

Until recently it was possible to visit the so-called Santoni, interesting statues of Cybele, carved in a rock face. The road goes down the hill to the Ragusa road, off which a paved byroad (left) ends beside a gate (*locked for new archaeological research*). Steps continue down past 12 remarkable life-size statues dating from around the 3rd century BC representing the Earth goddess Cybele (Rhea or Mother of the Gods), hewn out of the rock (protected by wooden huts). The goddess is shown between the two dioscuri (Castor and Pollux) on horseback; with Marsyas, Hermes and other divinities; with her daughter Persephone; seated and flanked by two little lions. They are extremely worn, and were vandalized in the 20th century. There was a sanctuary here near a spring on the road to the necropolis across the valley from the city. It was reached via the Templi Ferali, on the east side of the hill, in a vertical cliff. These temples of the dead, containing Greek inscriptions and votive niches, are also at present inaccessible.

ENVIRONS OF PALAZZOLO ACREIDE

East of Palazzolo Acreide, on the fast road to Syracuse, is **Canicattini Bagni**, now surrounded by new buildings. Founded in 1678, it contains interesting early 20th-century houses decorated in the local stone in Art Nouveau style, and a beautiful 18th-century bridge, known as Ponte di Sant'Alfano, over the Cava Cardinale stream. Nearby is Grotta Perciata, the largest cave so far discovered in Sicily, where prehistoric artefacts have been found.

Across the Anapo valley north of Palazzolo Acreide is the attractive little town of **Buscemi**, rebuilt after 1693. The main road runs uphill past its four impressive churches. Sant'Antonio di Padova has an 18th-century façade which incorporates ten splendid large columns on its curving front (with three bells hung across the top). Higher up is San Sebastiano, preceded by a stairway, and then the elliptical 19th-century church of San Giacomo, high up on a terrace. At the top of the town is the 18th-century Chiesa Madre, which houses a wooden statue of *Our Lady of Dolours* by Filippo Quattrocchi (1732). A number of artisans' workshops and houses in the town can be visited, along with a water-mill in Palazzolo Acreide, making up a museum of 19th-century life in the Hyblaean Mountains: I Luoghi del Lavoro Contadino (*open 9–12.30; T: 0931 878528, www.museobuscemi.org*).

On the barren Piana di Buccheri, with views to Monte Lauro (986m), the highest point of the Hyblaean Mountains, and of Etna to the north, some pinewoods have recently been planted. **Buccheri** was another town destroyed in 1693, and rebuilt in Baroque style. Corso Vittorio Emanuele passes the 18th-century church of Santa Maria Maddalena, which contains a statue of Mary Magdalen by Antonello Gagini (1508). From Piazza Toselli a steep flight of steps rises to the towering façade of the church of Sant'Antonio Abate; the rich interior, a central nave and two side aisles, is decorated with stuccoes by Giuseppe Gianforma (1760), and houses two signed and dated (1728) paintings by Guglielmo Borremans: *Sts Vitus, Modestus and Crescenza* in the right aisle, and *Ecstasy of St Anthony the Abbot* over the main altar.

THE ANAPO VALLEY

The plateau above the Anapo valley to the south is beautiful open countryside, with attractive farmhouses and low dry-stone walls. Dark carob trees provide welcome shade, and the olive groves are renowned for the high-quality of their oil. Shepherds pasture their flocks and small herds of cattle wander around apparently untended; the sound of their neck bells lingers after their passage. Byzantine tombs and caves in the area show evidence of Neolithic and Bronze Age occupation.

Near the village of **Cassaro**, famous for excellent olive oil from the *tonda iblea* variety, and a very picturesque place, is the **Valle dell'Anapo** (*open 8–1 hr before sunset*). A beautiful deep limestone gorge, and a protected area since 1988, it is run by the Azienda Forestale. A map of the paths in the area is available at the entrance. No private cars are allowed: a van takes visitors for 8km along the rough road on the course of the disused narrow-gauge railway track (and its tunnels), which runs along the floor of the valley, once the Syracuse–Vizzini line. The interesting vegetation here includes ilexes, pines, figs, olives, citrus trees and poplars, and the only buildings to be seen are those once used by the railway company. Horses are bred here and may soon provide horse-drawn transport along the old railway line. Picnic places are provided with tables. The van stops in the centre of the valley from where there is a good view of the tombs of the necropolis of Pantalica (*see below*) high up at the top of the rock face. There is another entrance to the valley from the Sortino road, where another van takes visitors along the valley for some 4km before joining this road.

On the Ferla road is the site of the destroyed town of Cassaro which was moved after the earthquake of 1693 up to the top of the cliff face (seen above the road). Orange trees, prickly pear and pomegranates have been allowed to grow wild on the approach to **Ferla** itself. A small stone-built town, it is traversed by one long main street sloping steeply uphill past four Baroque churches with imposing facades, lined with interesting early 20th-century houses, and makes the best approach to Pantalica.

Pantalica

A lonely road leads from Ferla for 12km along a ridge through beautiful remote farming country and pinewoods to the extraordinary prehistoric necropolis of Pantalica (marked by a yellow sign), in deserted countryside, now a nature and archaeological reserve (Riserva naturale orientata Pantalica, Valle dell'Anapo e Torrente Cavagrande; *www.archeologia.com/pantalica*). All around rock tombs carved in the cliffs (*see plan*) can be seen. The road runs through this huge unenclosed site and ends here.

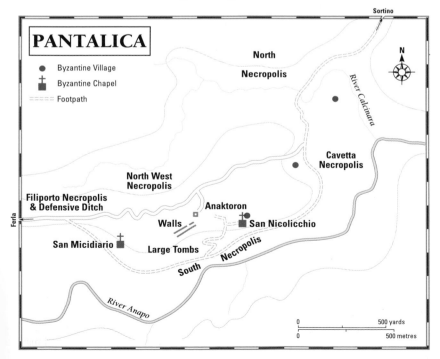

NECROPOLEIS

A necropolis is literally 'a city of the dead' where bodies are buried outside the community. Often existing caves are used or soft rock is tunnelled to make tomb chambers. Necropoleis are of immense importance to archaeologists as they usually contain fine objects which can be dated and used to confirm the status of those buried. The chambers may be in a local style or influenced by neighbouring cultures while the way a chamber is used, to contain one or many burials, or a sequence of burials can illustrate how kinship groups work and are sustained over time. About a hundred burials have been recovered from the thousand tombs cut into the limestone rocks of Pantalica and there is some sign in the early ones (13th century BC onwards) of Mycenaean influence in the way that the tombs have been cut, with corridors embellished with masonry leading to the grave entrance, while some of the pottery is either directly imported from Mycenaean Greece or copied from Mycenaean models. Although the size and importance of graves vary, women are given some status and one of the wealthier tombs of c. 1200 contained a female body with an array of golden goods. A common feature is a basin placed on a large pedestal, evidence of some kind of feasting rite at the time of burial, with the basin left after the sealing of the tomb. In the Late Bronze Age (1200–900 BC) a few larger tombs connected by corridors suggest a stratified society at Pantalica based on strong kinship groups. Clearly the local Sicel community was an effective and self-supporting one with some limited contact in earlier times with the Mycenaeans. However, with the coming of Greek settlement in the 7th century the community was dispersed and burials at Pantalica cease.   C.F.

The necropolis

The deep limestone gorges of the Anapo and Cava Grande rivers almost encircle the plateau of Pantalica, occupied from the 13th–8th century BC. In this naturally defended site Sicels from the Italian mainland settled c 1270 BC. Their way of life remained virtually unchanged until the arrival of the Greeks in the second half of the 8th century BC. The cliffs of the vast necropolis, one of the largest and most important in Europe, are honeycombed with some 1,000 tombs of varying shapes and sizes. Each cell held a family tomb, and there appears to have been an arrangement of the cells in groups. The objects discovered in them, including fine pottery, are displayed in the Museo Archeologico in Syracuse. The city disappeared after the foundation of the Greek colony of *Acrae* in 663 BC, and some of the tombs were converted into cave dwellings during the Barbarian invasions, and later inhabited by Christians.

An easy footpath (signposted Villaggio Bizantino) at the beginning of the road leads to a tiny Byzantine oratory carved in the rock (with traces of frescoes) known as **San Micidiario**, and the southern necropolis. Off the road, further on, a track leads up to the top of the hill and the so-called **Anactoron**, or Palace of the Prince, a megalithic building dating from the late Bronze Age, the foundations of which survive (35m by 11m); it was the only stone construction in the settlement. Nearby are short sections of wall and a defensive ditch, the only remains of the city, recently identified with the legendary *Hybla*, whose king, Hyblon, allowed the Megarese colonists to found Megara Hyblaea.

Far below, the Anapo Valley can be seen, with a white track following the line of the old railway. Further on, downhill, near the end of the road a signpost indicates the **Cavetta** necropolis (9th–7th centuries BC), and another Byzantine village.

A path leads towards the northern necropolis, beyond the stream in the valley. The road ends abruptly here and the road from Sortino, which will now never be completed, can be seen across the valley. There is a view of Sortino in the distance. In the early months of the year, flocks of ravens can sometimes be seen here, performing a mysterious mating flight, almost like a dance, during which they fly upside down and link feet for a moment, apparently enjoying it immensely.

SORTINO & FLORIDIA

Reached from Solarino, on the main road between Ferla and Syracuse, **Sortino** is well known for the production of honey, delicious oranges, and traditional puppet theatre. The town was rebuilt after the earthquake of 1693, and contains some elegant 18th-century churches and palaces. At no. 9 Piazza San Francesco, is the **Museo dei Pupi** (*open 10–12 & 3.30–5.30; closed Sun and holidays*), the collection of puppets, posters and scenery accumulated by the Puglisi family, illustrious *pupari*. At no. 5 Via Gioberti is a museum dedicated to the production of honey (*see p. 320*), the **Museo dell'Apicoltura a casa d'o Fascitraru** (*open Sat, Sun 10–1 & 3–6*), which explains all the secrets of this fascinating craft.

Floridia

Near Solarino is Floridia, a Sicel stronghold (in 1909 Paolo Orsi found a Mycenaean vase in a necropolis here, indicating Bronze Age trade activities), re-founded in 1628, and rebuilt after 1693. The Madonna delle Grazie, now in disrepair, was built by the Spaniards to celebrate their victory over the Austrians in 1720. A supposedly miraculous image of the Madonna, painted on sandstone, was stolen from this church in 1970, and never recovered.

About 3km from Floridia is the **Cava di Spampinato**, one of the deepest gorges in the area. The road leaving the town from the south, signposted Canicattini Bagni, immediately crosses the gorge and goes to the right. At the first crossroad, where the road curves left, take the byroad right (it becomes a track after 800m) to reach the entrance to this beautiful and little-known gorge. There are many caves here, and tombs carved into the rock. It was through this gorge that the defeated Athenians, in 413 BC, tried to retreat inland, as the plateau was defended by Syracusan forces; they eventually reached the Assinaros, where they were defeated in 412.

THAPSOS & THE GULF OF AUGUSTA

Capo Santa Panagia, the headland north of Syracuse, has been identified with ancient *Trogilus*. Fossils are found in the limestone caves, and in the over-lying clays are remains of Neolithic habitation. The flat Magnisi peninsula, a little further north along the coast, was the ancient *Thapsos*, under whose northern shore the Athenian fleet anchored before the siege of Syracuse. It is almost an island (2km long and 700m wide), connected to the mainland by a sandy isthmus 2.5km long and little more than 100m wide at one point. The fleet of Marcellus also moored near here during the Roman siege of Syracuse. Finds from the settlement and its vast necropolis have given the name to a Bronze Age culture (see the Museo Archeologico in Syracuse) and interesting domed rock tombs line the shore west of the lighthouse.

The excavations at Thapsos show three periods of occupation: c. 1500–1400 BC, characterized by round huts; c. 1300–1200 BC, where the square houses are of the Mycenaean type (a bronze bar with figures of a dog and fox, unique in prehistoric Sicily, and thought to be of Aegean origin, was found here); and a final period c. 1100–900 BC, with finds of remarkable large terracotta vases (now in the Museo Archeologico in Syracuse). The Magnisi peninsular and the coast alongside are protected as a nature reserve (Riserva Saline di Priolo e Penisola Magnisi; *for information T: 0931 735026; www.lipusicilia.it*). The coastal wetland, once exploited as salt-pans, is an ideal resting-place for migrating birds; about 215 different species have been spotted, including some rarities: greater sand plover (the only sighting for Italy), shoveler, ferruginous duck, and Caspian tern.

MEGARA HYBLAEA

Near the port of Priolo, a fast road, signposted *Zona Industriale and Catania Via Litorale* (the old SS 115 coast road to Catania) branches off towards the sea. Yellow signposts indicate the way to the excavations of the ancient city of Megara Hyblaea.

The excavations
Open 9–5.30.
The excavations are approached by a byroad which runs alongside a citrus grove behind a line of cypresses. The road continues right (signposted *scavi*) and here in a group of pines is a stretch of Archaic walls (6th century BC) with four semicircular towers (a fifth has been destroyed). The walls can be followed on foot for some 250m as far as the west gate. A number of tombs have been placed near the walls, salvaged from excavations of the two necropoleis which are now covered by industrial plants. The third necropolis was located in the vicinity of these walls. Further on, below ground level, is an oblong construction with seven bases for columns. Excavated in 1880, it is of uncertain significance. Just before the little bridge over the railway is a car park; cars can continue over the narrow bridge along a rough road past some abandoned farmhouses.

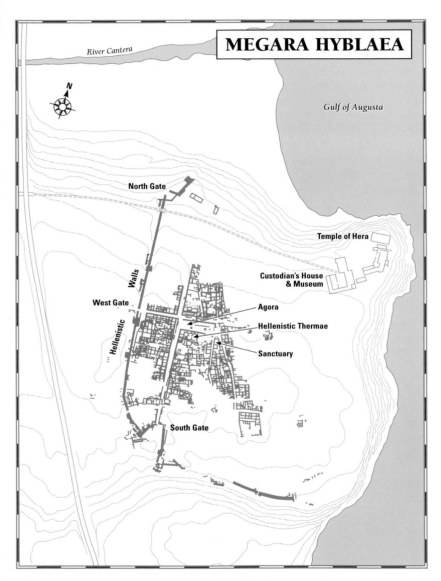

The road passes over the second line of Hellenistic walls built around the Hellenistic town (they follow a line of cypresses). To the left of the road here the Hellenistic north gate of the city has been identified near the remains of Archaic walls. The road ends at the custodian's house in a little garden. The farmhouse here is used as a small museum to house the finds (*to arrange a visit T: 0931 481111*), including a tomb with a decorative frieze, although the most important Archaic sculptures excavated here are now in the Museo Archeologico Regionale at Syracuse.

A path leads across a field to the main area of excavations: the complicated remains include buildings from both the Archaic and Hellenistic periods (the red iron posts indicate the Archaic areas, and the green posts the Hellenistic buildings). At the intersection of the two main roads is the agora, near which are a sanctuary, interesting Hellenistic thermae with intact floors, and a poorly-preserved small Doric temple of the 4th century (protected by a roof). The main east–west road leads from the agora to the narrow Hellenistic west gate in the walls (with two square towers) along the line of cypresses. Near the gate, on a lower level to the south, are ovens and houses of the Archaic period. The main north–south road ends at the Hellenistic south gate, a 'pincer'-type defence work.

HISTORY OF MEGARA HYBLAEA

The city was founded by Lamis of Megara in 728 BC. Having delayed their departure, his settlers found no land available for them in the area, beaten to it by the Corinthians of Syracuse and the Chalcidian sub-colony of *Leontinoi*. After uncomfortable sojourns at Leontinoi and then at Thapsos, where Lamis died, King Hyblon of the Sicels magnanimously donated a small but choice stretch of land still under his control, at the mouth of the River Cantera; the grateful people remembered this when choosing a name for their new home, Megara Hyblaea.

A century later, wanting to found a sub-colony of their own, again they found no room, and were forced all the way to southwestern Sicily in order to found Selinunte. Megara Hyblaea was destroyed by Gelon in 483. A second city was founded here by Timoleon in 340, which in its turn was obliterated by the Romans in 214, after which the site was abandoned. Excavations of the site were begun by the French School in Rome in 1949. The site is enchanting in spring, when wild chrysanthemums (*fiori di maggio*) carpet the surrounding countryside with gold.

AUGUSTA

The shores of the Gulf of Augusta, once lined by the ancient cities of Syracuse, Thapsos and Megara Hyblaea, are now a jungle of oil refineries, and oil tankers anchor offshore. The industrial zone extends from here to Priolo and Augusta, and has the largest concentration of chemical plants in Europe. The industries here are going through a bad period and many workers have been laid off. After years of pollution problems, and criticism from many quarters, the hoped-for solution to the economic woes of southeastern Sicily is revealing shortcomings. After the Second World War, the industrial area seemed the answer to many peasants' prayers, and the population of Syracuse rocketed from 44,000 to 135,000 people, attracted by the opportunity to avoid emigration. The most important oil and military port in Italy, Augusta stands on a rocky islet connected to the mainland by a long bridge. To the east and west are two capacious harbours, the Porto Xifonio, and the Porto Megarese with two old forts.

HISTORY OF AUGUSTA

Augusta was founded by Frederick II in 1232 as a refuge for the inhabitants of Centuripe and Montalbano, which he himself had destroyed. In 1269 it was sacked by Philip and Guy de Montfort. It was taken by the French in 1676 after the defeat in the bay of a Dutch fleet under De Ruyter by Admiral Duquesne. De Ruyter was mortally wounded in the action and died a few days later at Syracuse, where he still lies.

Augusta was completely destroyed by the earthquake of 1693, and the modern town suffered severe damage from air raids in World War II. Another earthquake hit the town and the provinces of Syracuse, Catania and Ragusa on 13 December 1990 (St Lucy's Day; hence the name by which it is commonly remembered, *Terremoto di Santa Lucia*), leaving 13,000 people homeless.

The town and environs

The main road enters the town through the old Spanish bastions (1681); on the left is the battered, but still imposing, Castello Svevo, built by Frederick of Hohenstaufen 1232–42, and surrounded by a double circle of walls. Until recently it was used as a prison, but there are plans to restore it for use as a museum and a library. Further ahead on the left, are the public gardens. From here Via Principe Umberto leads south through the city. It crosses Via Garibaldi, with some fine churches and convents. Via Umberto continues to Piazza Duomo, with the severely damaged Chiesa Madre (Santa Maria Assunta, 1644). The north side of the square is taken up by the Municipio (1699), with a long balcony, and the Swabian eagle under the cornice. The sundial was erected to record the total eclipse of the sun in 1870. On the first floor is the Opera House (1730).

On the coast to the north is the ruined castle of **Brucoli**, erected by Giovanni Bastida in 1468, near a beautiful little fjord used by the fishing-boats. *Trotilon*, one of the oldest Greek settlements on the island, probably stood on the bay of Brucoli, which now has a large holiday village.

A poorly signposted road leads to the site of the Greek city of **Leontinoi** (*T: 095 7832962 to book visit*). Founded by the Chalcidians of Naxos in 730–728 BC, on the site of an earlier Sicel settlement. In the 6th century BC Panaetius set himself up as tyrant of Leontinoi, the first such ruler in Sicily. In the early 5th century BC it was taken by Hippocrates of Gela, and soon afterwards succumbed to the Syracusans. In

427 BC the city despatched the orator Gorgias (480–c. 380) to invoke the assistance of Athens against her tyrants. Hieronymus, the last native tyrant of Syracuse, grandson of Hieron II and barely 14 years old, was assassinated at Leontinoi in 215 BC, a month or so after coming to power, for having dared declare allegiance to Hannibal and the Carthaginians. Archimedes (*see box opposite*), famously absent-minded, was unaware of the event. The Roman general Marcellus captured *Leontinoi* in the same year.

The excavations are in a nicely planted and well-kept site. A path leads down from the entrance to the elaborate south gate. Across the valley steps lead up to a path which follows the walls to the top of the hill, from which there is a fine view of the site and the surrounding hills. The site of the prehistoric settlement, with a necropolis (6th–4th century BC), and hut village, are not at present open to the public.

LENTINI & ENVIRONS

Lentini is a busy agricultural centre. The medieval town was destroyed in the earthquake of 1693, and the modern town was again badly shaken in 1990. The Chiesa Madre preserves an icon thought to date from the 9th century and the churches of San Luca and Santa Trinità have interesting 16th-century paintings.

Piazza Studi, at the far end of Via Piave, a street leading from close to the cathedral, is Via del Museo, at no. 1 is the small **Museo Archeologico** (*open Tues–Sun 9–6*) with a well-arranged collection of local finds including three fine calyx kraters, and a reconstruction of the south gate of the ancient city.

Northwest of Lentini is a large artificial lake, the Biviere or Lago di Lentini (*T: 095 901477 to book visit*), a vast wetland thought to have been created by the Templars in the Middle Ages, which was drained in the 50s, with disastrous effects on the climate, so it was filled again in the late 90s. Potentially, this is the most important area in Sicily for waders and water birds, both as a resting place during migration, and as a nesting site; but the level of the water in the lake varies constantly, as water is siphoned off for agriculture and for nearby industries, and this damages plant life, and sometimes nests. However, there is an important colony of white storks, which seem to be doing well. Princess Borghese, who lives in a villa close to the lake, will show you her beautiful gardens if you book beforehand (*T: 095 7831449, biviere@sicilyonline.it*); besides being a good gardener, she is a competent botanist, and will provide lunch or brunch, on request.

Southwest of Lentini is the hill town of **Francofonte**, also damaged in 1990, whose town hall occupies the 18th-century Palazzo Palagonia adjoining the medieval castle. Local orange groves produce the *tarocco di Francofonte*, voted by an international jury recently the finest orange in the world. Quite large, it peels easily and the flesh is tinged with red. The flavour is reminiscent of strawberries. Opera lovers will remember that in *Cavalleria Rusticana* this is the place where the teamster Alfio came to get his wine.

Closer to Augusta, and clearly visible on the hill to the right when approaching Syracuse, is **Melilli**, destroyed and rebuilt after the 1693 earthquake, famous in the past for its production of wild thyme honey (*see box on p. 320*), highly prized both by Greeks and Romans; the coat-of-arms shows three honey-bees on a shield. This town has suffered a lot for the proximity of the industrial area, which has also affected the health of the population. In the centre is the **Chiesa Madre**, dedicated to St Nicholas, with a beautiful wooden ceiling into which paintings by Olivio Sozzi have been set, representing the *Triumph of Faith*.

In the lower part of the town, to the east, is the church of **San Sebastiano** (1751, Louis Alexandre Dumonier), approached by a large square with a portico. The church is decorated inside with a remarkable series of frescoes by Olivio Sozzi, carried out between 1759 and 1763. Tombs along the nearby rivers Mulinello and Marcellino (the ancient *Mylas*) have both revealed extremely interesting archaeological remains (now in the Museo Archeologico, Syracuse), proving that trade with the Greeks existed before the colonization of mid 8th century BC. Melilli also has some really beautiful caves to explore, in the district of **Villasmundo** (signposted from Villasmundo village, c. 12 km north of Melilli, on the Carlentini road); they are now protected as a nature reserve (Riserva naturale integrale complesso speleologico Villasmundo-Sant'Alfio; *for information T: 095 317097, www.unict.it.cutgana*). The caves extend for a total of 2km (the longest in Sicily), with a series of narrow tunnels on different levels, with magnificent stalagtites and stalagmites, underground streams and a small lake. The bats are extremely interesting; outside the caves several different kinds of snake and unusual reptiles live; birds include the buzzards, kestrels, blue rock thrushes and tawny owls. In May a festival dedicated to St Sebastian takes place in Melilli, attracting thousands of pilgrims from all over the world.

ARCHIMEDES (?287–212 BC)

The mathematical genius Archimedes may have been a close friend or relative of King Hieron II of Syracuse; certainly it was Hieron who sponsored his journey to the great library of Alexandria, where he was able to discuss many of his theories with his peers. Among the discoveries attributed to Archimedes are the cogged wheel (hence the winch); the relationship between the circumference and the diameter of a circle; the lever; the displacement of liquid method for ascertaining the composition of metals (which he famously discovered in the bath); and the calculation of the volume of a sphere contained inside a cylinder. In 240 BC he designed a luxurious cruise ship for Hieron, called the *Syrakosia*, described by one of the engineers, Moschyon, who took part in the construction. The great ship was a catamaran, built of timber from Mt Etna, rope from Iberia, ivory and rosewood from Africa, and weighed 4,000 tons. Intended to demonstrate the power of Syracuse in the Mediterranean, the ship was in fact impractical, being too large for most ports. Hieron made the generous gesture of sending it to Egypt loaded with wheat, as a gift to Ptolemy during a famine.

PRACTICAL INFORMATION

GETTING AROUND

• **By rail:** Trains run from Syracuse north to Lentini, Melilli and Augusta on the Syracuse–Catania line, and southwest to Noto on the Syracuse–Gela line. For details www.trenitalia.com

• **By bus:** In Syracuse take city bus no 1 for Neapolis; no 4 for the Archaeological Museum; no 2 for Santa Lucia and no 11 for Castello Eurialo and Belvedere. Inter-city buses run by AST and SAIS/Interbus offer services to Noto, Pachino and Avola; Ferla and Sortino; Lentini, Melilli and Augusta; Palazzo Acreide, as well as the main centres of Catania and Messina.

INFORMATION OFFICES

Syracuse APT Siracusa: 45 Via San Sebastiano, T: 0931 481211 & 0931 461477, www.apt-siracusa.it for information on the whole province.
Useful information on Syracuse, Noto, Palazzolo Acreide and Pachino at www.sudesttraveltour.it
Tourist Information Bureau: 33 Via Maestranza, Ortygia, T: 0931 65201, www.comune.siracusa.it, www.siracusa-sicilia.it
Syrako Tourist Point: under Porta Marina has lots of information and can arrange walks on the old walls, T: 0931 24133.
Augusta Viale Eroi di Malta, T: 0931 52112288; Pro Loco: 325 Via Epicarmo.
Avola Palazzo Modica, Via Milano; Pro Loco: 48 Via San Francesco d'Assisi,

T: 0931 834270.
Buccheri 1 Piazza Roma, T: 0931 873566, www.comune.buccheri.sr.it; Pro Loco: Piazza XXIV Maggio, T: 0931 880428.
Canicattini Bagni Pro Loco: 96 Via Vittorio Emanuele, T: 0931 947434, www.comune.canicattinibagni.sr.it, www.sistemia.it/canicattini_b.it
Carlentini 76 Via Etnea, T: 095 7846418; Pro Loco: 26 Piazza Diaz, T: 095 991108, www.prolococarlentini.it
Floridia c/o Municipio, 12 Piazza del Popolo, T: 0931 920111; Pro Loco: 160 Via Archimede, T: 0931 944524, www.comune.floridia.sr.it
Melilli c/o Municipio, T: 0931 552111, www.comunemelilli.it; Pro Loco: 2 Via Nocera, T 338 3529638.
Noto Piazza XVI Maggio, T: 0931 573779, www.comune.noto.sr.it, www.notobarocca.com For information on nature reserves in the area, call Ente Fauna Siciliana, T: 0931 813273.
Palazzolo Acreide 11 Piazza Sant'Antonio, T: 0931 871286; Pro Loco: 2 Corso Vittorio Emanuele, T: 0931 881354 & 329 6198962, www.palazzolo-acreide.it
Portopalo di Capo Passero 33 Via Lucio Tasca, T: 0931 848011; Pro Loco: 78 Via Vittorio Emanuele, T: 0931 848035, www.prolocoportopalo.it
Sortino c/o Municipio, Viale Giardino, T: 0931 917000, www.comune.sortino.sr.it; Pro Loco Pantalica Sortino: T: 333 2076206 & 333 6958211, www.proloco.net/pro-sortino/menu/html

HOTELS

Syracuse

€€€ **Etrangers et Miramare**. Beautiful 19th-century hotel, luxurious, overlooking the historic old harbour. Two restaurants, beauty & fitness centre, sauna, indoor pool. 10–12 Passeggio Adorno, T: 0931 62671, www.johansens.com/etrangersetmiramare

€€ **Grand Hotel**. First of the glorious historical hotels to be restored,. 12 Viale Mazzini, T: 0931 464600, www.grandhotelsr.it

€€ **Panorama**. This hotel has always been much-loved by travellers, because its position is ideal for the archaeological park (and very panoramic); it has now been beautifully refurbished. 33 Via Necropoli Grotticelle, T: 0931 412188, www.hotelpanoramasr.it

€€ **Roma**. Delightful, on Ortygia, right next to the cathedral, with restaurant and private beach. 10 Via Minerva, T: 0931 465626, www.hotelroma.sr.it

€€ **Villa Politi**. On the Latomy of the Capuchins, a bit tired but Winston Churchill's favourite. 2 Via Politi, T: 0931 412121, www.villapoliti.com

€€ **Domus Mariae**. The nuns who run it have turned part of their 15th-century convent to good use. 76 Via Vittorio Veneto, T: 0931 24854, www.sistemia.it/domusmariae

€€ **Gran Bretagna**. Charming little hotel on Ortygia, beautifully restored, some rooms with 19th-century frescoes, plate-glass floor in the lounge reveals 16th-century Spanish bastions, no restaurant. 21 Via Savoia, T: 0931 68765, www.hotelgranbretagna.it

€€ **Gutkowski**. Medieval palazzo on seaward side of Ortygia, a small hotel

for travellers of taste. 26 Lungomare Vittorini, T: 0931 465861, www.guthotel.it

€€ **Posta**. In a pleasant quiet part of Ortygia near the central post office, no restaurant. 33 Via Trieste, T: 0931 21819, www.hotelpostasiracusa.it

€ **Archimede**. Close to railway station. 67 Via Francesco Crispi, T: 0931 462458, www.hotelarchimede.sr.it

€ **Milano**. Basic accommodation close to Ortygia. 10 Corso Umberto, T: 0931 66981.

€ **Pantheon**. Good value for money at this small, family-run hotel; friendly people. 22 Via Foro Siracusano, T: 0931 21010.

Augusta

€€ **La Cavalera**. Small hotel surrounded by a garden, panoramic views, pools, fitness centre, good restaurant and pizzeria. Via delle Palme, Contrada Cavalera, T: 0931 997414, www.lacavalera.it

Buccheri

€ **Monte Lauro**. Good service, nice rooms, with garage and restaurant. 62 Via Cappello, T: 0931 880362, montelaurohotel@virgilio.it

Noto

€ **Borgo Alto**. Small hotel in countryside, no restaurant. Contrada Piano Cugni, T: 0931 753778, www.borgoalto.com

€ **Della Ferla**. Rather spartan; garage but no restaurant. 5 Via Gramsci, T: 0931 576007, www.hoteldellaferla.com

€ **La Fontanella**. Very small, central, no restaurant. 3 Via Rosolino Pilo, T: 0931 894724.

€ **Oasi Don Bosco**. Old country farmhouse hotel run by religious community, hillside position, pool, tennis. Contrada

Arco Farina Pianette, T: 0931 946275, www.oasidonbosco.it

Noto Marina

€€ **La Corte del Sole**. Country hotel in a point overlooking the Vendicari nature riserve, once an olive mill; beautiful rooms, good restaurant. Località Eloro-Vendicari, T: 0931 820210, www.lacortedelsole.it

Pachino

€€ **Villa Giulia**. Eighteenth-century farmhouse surrounded by vineyards, north of Pachino; pool, good restaurant, air-conditioning. SP Noto-Pachino, Contrada San Lorenzo, T: 0931 591688.

Palazzolo Acreide

€ **Senatore**. Modern hotel with good restaurant, garage and bar, in the lower city. 5 Largo Senatore Italia, T: 0931 883443, www.hotelsenatore.it

Portopalo di Capo Passero

€ **Il Castello**. A quiet hotel with garden, pool and good restaurant.Via Tonnara, T: 0931 842025.

BED & BREAKFAST

Syracuse

€ **Arcobaleno**. On the main street of Ortygia, air conditioning, English spoken and very professionally run. 45 corso Matteotti, T: 334 3831840 info@arcobalenosiracusa.it

€ **Artemide**. Well-restored 16th-century palazzo, air conditioning, internet, garage. 9 Via Vittorio Veneto, T: 0931 69005, www.bedandbreakfastsicily.it

€ **Belvedere San Giacomo**. Panoramic position overlooking the sea. 1 Piazza Belvedere San Giacomo, T: 0931 32582 & 0931 462082, www.bb-bsg.it

€ **Giuggiulena**. Clifftop villa south of city, air conditioning, en suite baths, internet, access to sea, car park.35 Via Pitagora da Reggio, T: 0931 468142, www.giuggiulena.it

€ **Minerva**. Excellent rooms; central position; English spoken. 56–60 Via Roma, T: 0931 22606.

€ **Viaggiatori Viandanti e Sognatori**. Gorgeous view from rooftop terrace, air conditioning; on request they will take you sailing. 156 Via Roma, T: 0931 24781, www.bedandbreakfastsicily.it

Augusta

€ **Ulisse**. Close to the beautiful Capo Sbarcatore cliff, Art Nouveau house with comfortable rooms and patio. Contrada Serpaolo, Capo Sbarcatore, T: 0931 998381, www.holidayinsicily.it

Avola

€ **Villa Urso**. On the sea, English spoken.Via Lungomare Lido Tremolo, Traversa Metastasio 11, T: 0931 822316 or 338 6244360.

Buccheri

€ **Casazzurra**. Beautiful countryside position. 8 Contrada Piana Sottana, T: 349 6529962 or 348 3402646, gvojvod@tin.it

Buscemi

€ **Al Vicoletto**. In the old town centre. 7 Via Dante Alighieri, T: 0931 878134.

Canicattini Bagni

€ **Palazzo Iargia**. Lovely old house. 38 Via La Vecchia, T: 0931 541166 or 339 4810153.

Ferla

€ **Pantalica**. Simple but comfortable, friendly owners, ideal for Pantalica, mountain bikes rented.98 Via Roma, T: 0931 879183, or 333 3920839, pantalicabb@libero.it

Lentini

€ **Al Giardino dei Cavalieri**. Central

position. 13 Salita Pisano, T: 347
8062801, www.giardinodeicavalieri.it
Noto
€ **Centro Storico**. Eighteenth-century
palazzo on the main street, air condi-
tioning, private bath. 64 Corso Vittorio
Emanuele, T: 0931 573967,
www.centro-storico.com
€ **Viceré Speciale**. Comfortable rooms
behind town hall, air conditioning, private bath.14 Via Viceré Speciale,
T: 0931 835789, www.vicerespeciale.com
€ **Sierra Vento**. Outside Noto, in a
wonderfully panoramic position.
Contrada Sierra del Vento, Belvedere,
T: 0931 573722, www.sierravento.it
Rosolini
€ **Casa & Verde**. Central position,
comfortable rooms, private bath, air
conditioning, garden. 10 Via Mazzini,
T: 0931 857028, 0931 841097 & 347
8660247, elenasessa@hotmail.com,
verdecasa@libero.it

ROOMS & APARTMENTS TO RENT

Syracuse
€€€ **Palazzo Beneventano di Bosco**
Antique apartment on Piazza Duomo,
available through Lanza and Baucina,
44 20 7738 2222.
www.lanzabaucina.com
€ **Alla Giudecca**. A whole group of
medieval houses, part of the Giudecca
or Jewish Quarter, for short-term rentals
(even one night). 52 Via Alagona,
T: 0931 22255, www.allagiudecca.it
€ **Le Antiche Siracuse**. Newly restored
palace overlooking Piazza Archimede.2
Via Maestranza, T: 0931 483003,
www.leantichesiracuse.it
Noto
€ **Casa vacanze Liberty**. Beautiful,

completely self-contained apartments. 2
Via Francesco Ferruccio, T: 0931
839548, 338 2304042 or 333
5080570, www.villacatera.com
€ **Villa Canisello**. Comfortable accommodation in a quiet old farmhouse, a
short walk from centre. 1 Via Pavese,
T: 0931 835793, www.villacanisello.it
€ **Carmine**.In a picturesque alley. 5
Vico Curtatone, T: 0931 891895,
www.carminehotel.com

FARMHOUSE ACCOMMODATION

Syracuse
€ **Villa dei Papiri**. Beautiful old farmhouse in the Ciane Nature Reserve, self-
catering apartments. Contrada Cozzo
Pantano, Fonte Ciane, T: 0931 721321
& 335 6064735, www.villadeipapiri.it
Augusta
€ **Tenuta San Calogero**. Delightful
farm surrounded by citrus and olive
groves, raising their own breed of horses, offers self-catering apartments and a
villa, pool. Contrada San Calogero,
T: 095 990085 or 095 7252109,
www.tenutasancalogero.it
Avola
€ **Crisilio Castello**. Lovely building on
large estate, close to sea, pool, tennis.
Contrada Petrara, T: 0931 561906 &
0931 564576, www.crisiliocastello.it
Buscemi
€€ **Casmene**. 3km from Buccheri,
very well organised farm (organically-
raised cattle), restaurant, pool, mountain bikes. Contrada Guffari, T: 0931
880055 or 368 3754287.
Canicattini Bagni
€ **Casale La Conversazione**.
Comfortable old farm, interesting organic food (even snails in season), children

welcome, hay therapy in summer. Contrada Bosco di Sopra (SS 14 Maremonti), T: 0931 947100, www.turismoruralesicilia.it

Carlentini

€€ **Casa dello Scirocco**. The farm produces oranges, and raises ostriches. Accommodation is in an old farmhouse, or *baglio*, in an ancient complex of caves, entirely carved out by hand thousands of years ago, with Moorish style décor, or in a pretty country cottage. Very high standard. Excursions are arranged, also cookery courses with an aphrodisiacal slant—*La cucina dell'Eros*. Contrada Piscitello, T: 095 447709, www.casadelloscirocco.it

€ **Le Chiuse**. Comfortable, well-run farm producing oranges and olives; hospitality in rooms with en suite baths and air conditioning; wonderful home-grown food; pool, bowls, embroidery and lace-making courses on request. Contrada Contado, T: 095 990388, www.lechiuse.net

€ **Tenuta di Roccadia**. In panoramic hillside position, this 13th-century farm produces citrus; pools, internet access, garden, famous restaurant. Contrada Roccadia, T: 095 990362, www.roccadia.com

Noto Antica

€ **Il Carrubo**. Dairy farm in the mountains overlooking the Tellaro Valley. Organic food.Contrada Castelluccio, SS 115 Noto–Rosolini bivio Giarratana, T: 0931 810114.

€€ **Monte Alveria**. Old farm, self-catering facilities and restaurant. Bicycle-trekking and horseriding. The farm raises horses and donkeys. Very peaceful. Contrada Noto Antica, T: 0931 810183 or 0931 838132, www.agriturismo.com/fattoriamontealveria

Noto-Palazzolo Acreide

€ **Masseria degli Ulivi**. Comfortable rooms in a beautiful old farmhouse, olives and carobs, good restaurant run by an enthusiastic young chef. Contrada Porcari, SS 287 Noto-Palazzolo Acreide, T: 0931 813019 or 0931 812330, www.masseriadegliulivi.com

Palazzolo Acreide

€ **Borgo degli Ulivi**. Self-catering apartments for four on this hillside farm, pool, garden, children welcome. Contrada Bibbia, T: 0931 883866, www.borgodegliulivi.com

€ **Fattoria Giannavì**. Wonderful isolated position in the Hyblaean Mountains not far from the town. The farm raises sheep for milk. Facilities for campers, also accommodation in the farmhouse. Contrada Giannavì, T: 0931 881776, www.fattoriagiannavì.it

Sortino

€ **Il Giardino di Pantalica**. In a breathtaking position in the heart of the nature reserve, by the Anapo stream, the only farm within the park boundaries. Contrada Savary, Valle dell'Anapo, T: 095 7122680, www.pantalica.it

MONASTERY ACCOMMODATION

Belvedere

Villa Mater Dei. Rooms with private bath, air conditioning, restaurant and large park. Via delle Carmelitane, contrada Sinerchia, SP 77, T: 0931 744044, www.villamaterdei.it

Brucoli

Santuario Santa Maria Adonai. Guests sleep in the monastic cells of this very ancient religious institution, a beautiful

place.Contrada Gisira, T: 329 6199452, www.coop-koinonia.com
Noto Antica
Eremo Santa Maria Scala del Paradiso. A beautiful, isolated monastery. Contrada Scala, T: 0931 813141.
San Corrado di Fuori
Eremo di San Corrado. Accommodation in the old hermitage near where St Conrad lived. T 0931 813111 or 0931 813350.

RESTAURANTS

Syracuse
€€€ **Le Terrazze del Grand Hotel**. One of the finest restaurants in the city, beautiful rooftop setting. Closed Tues in Aug. 12 Viale Mazzini. T: 0931 464600.
€€€ **Don Camillo**. Superb pasta dishes, but Giovanni, the brilliant chef, gives an innovative touch to his antipasto and main courses too; excellent wine cellar. This is one of the few restaurants where you will find (when in season) *zuppa di mucco*, soup of tiny new-born fish; definitely worth a visit. Closed Sun. 96 Via Maestranza, T: 0931 67133.
€€ **La Foglia**. Very unusual restaurant, principally vegetarian; the experience is rather like eating in someone's front parlour, hospitable owners but nothing matches—all odd crockery, tablecloths and cutlery. Superb grilled vegetables and famous soups; it should not be missed. 29 Via Capodieci, T: 0931 66233.
€€ **Darsena da Jannuzzo**. On the harbour front; very good fish. Closed Wed. 6 Riva Garibaldi, T: 0931 66104.
€€ **Il Cenacolo**. In one of Ortygia's most beautiful squares; Syracuse fish soup (unique); pizza is served also at lunchtime. Closed lunchtime Sat & Sun. 9–10 Via del Consiglio Reginale, T: 0931 65099.
€€ **L'Ancora**. Superb fresh fish restaurant next to the market and the bridge to the mainland, popular with locals. 7 Via Perno, T0931 462369.
€€ **Il Veliero da Piero**. Booking essential as this restaurant is very popular with local patrons, excellent fish dishes, local wines. Closed Mon. 6 Via Savoia, T: 0931 465887.
€€ **La Rambla**. An old-fashioned, delightful restaurant, serving exceptionally good antipasto and seafood risotto. 8 Via dei Mille, T: 0931 66638.
€€ **Minerva**. Lovely position, outside tables. Pizza available at lunchtime, thick satisfying soups in winter. 20 Piazza Duomo, T: 0931 69404.
€€ **Osteria da Mariano**. Tiny restaurant specializing in Hyblaean mountain food. Closed Tues & July. 9 Vicolo Zuccalà, T: 0931 67444.
€€ **Sapori di Sicilia** (ex-La Stalla). This family-run restaurant, now used as a banqueting hall, does excellent food, especially the seafood risotto, mixed fried fish, breaded swordfish. Local wines. Contrada Circuito (out of town, turn left at traffic light after cemetery), T: 0931 66570.
€ **Paradiso da Pinello**. In front of the Roman amphitheatre, a simple, friendly trattoria where you can eat outside for most of the year; all the food is made on the spot and is very tasty. 2 Largo Anfiteatro, T: 0931 61099.
€ **Spaghetteria d'o Scogghiu**. Popular locale on Ortygia, renowned for spaghetti. Closed Mon. 11 Via Scinà.

Augusta
€€ **Osteria della Mattonella**. The oldest inn of Augusta, the menu offers traditional fare, including (in season) snails, salt cod, thick vegetable soups: in summer you eat outside. Sicilian and Italian wines. Closed Mon & Aug. 88 Via Garibaldi, T: 334 3660649 & 368 7777747.

Avola
€ **Trattoria Cava Grande**. This little restaurant is the ideal lunch stop while exploring the area. Closed Mon. Belvedere sul Cava Grande, T: 0931 811220.

Brucoli
€€ **La Lanterna**. Charming restaurant and pizzeria in an old tuna-fish factory. Closed Tues in winter. 56 Via Libertà, T: 0931 981980.

Buccheri
€€ **'U Lucale**. Very good food; boar meat (*cinghiale*). Closed Tues. 14 Via Dusmet, T: 0931 873923.

Floridia
€€ **Il Veliero**. Simple, family-run restaurant, serving delicious food; wonderful spaghetti, and mixed fried fish. Good wine list. Choose green tangerine and lemon sorbet for dessert. Viale Vittorio Veneto (corner Viale Paolo VI), T: 0931 940576. Closed Mon.

Lentini
€€€ **'A Maidda**. Owner-chef Salvo Bordonaro really cares about Sicilian food and wine. Worth a detour. 2 Via Alfieri (corner Via Alaimo), T: 095 941537. Closed Thur & Aug.

Marzamemi
€€ **La Cialoma**. A restaurant famous for fish; try smoked tuna and swordfish; you eat outside in the square. 16 Via Nuova, T: 0931 8401772.

Noto
€€ **Il Barocco**. In the old stables of Palazzo Astuto-Barresi with a lovely patio. Try chef Graziella's prize-winning *spaghetti ca pateddi d'a roccia* (spaghetti with limpets). Via Cavour, T: 0931 835999.
€€ **Neas**. Delightful old-fashioned little restaurant, good wine list, nice home-made desserts. Closed Mon in winter 30 Via Rocco Pirri (corner Via Cavour), T: 0931 573538.
€ **Trattoria del Carmine**. Serves pizza in the evenings, and sandwiches during the day, if you prefer these to a plate of delicious pasta. Closed Mon. 1 Via Ducezio, T: 0931 838705.
€ **Trattoria Il Buco**. Excellent *caponata* (mixed vegetable starter) and ricotta-filled ravioli, near San Francesco. Closed midday Sat. 1 Via Zanardelli, T: 0931 838142.
€ **Al Terrazzo**. Near central square, tables outside, surrounded with flowers. Closed Tues. 4 Via Alfredo Baccarini, T: 0931 839710.

Noto Marina
€€ **L'Ulivo**. Excellent, imaginative cuisine prepared by chef Sebastiano Miceli; the fish is perfect, so are the desserts. Open for dinner only, closed Wed. Località Falconara, T: 0931 812193.

Portopalo di Capo Passero
€€ **Il Castello**. Delicious spaghetti with seafood. Via Tonnara, T: 0931 842025.
€€ **La Giara alla Tavernetta del Porto**. On the dockside, this delightful restaurant serves only the freshest-possible fish. Try the *brezza marina* (sea breeze), spaghetti with 8 different kinds of fish; a meal in itself. Closed Mon. Porto, T: 0931 843217.

€€ **Maurì 1987**. Reliable restaurant that never closes in summer (Tues in winter); good value for money. 22 Via Tagliamento, T: 0931 842644.

€ **Locanda del Borgo**. Simple establishment serving delicious food. Closed Mon. 11 Via Controscieri, T: 0931 850514.

Palazzolo Acreide

€€ **Il Portico**. Hyblaean mountain food, but they are also known for their fish-filled ravioli; pizza in the evenings. Vegetarian dishes on request. Good wine list. Closed Tues. 3–6 Via Orologio, T: 0931 881532.

€€ **La Trota**. Beautiful park and pools where the trout are raised (smoked trout for sale). The restaurant is in an ancient cave. Closed Mon. 7km from town on the SS 287, contrada Pianette, T: 0931 883433.

€ **Il Camino**. Cosy. Delicious pasta, local sausage, pizza in the evenings. Closed Tues. 11 Via Martiri di Via Fani, T: 0931 881860.

€ **Pappalardo**. Simple trattoria specialized in snails (when in season). 24 Via Galeno, T: 0931 881558.

€ **Valentino**. Extensive menu, including fish. Closed Wed. 7 Via Ronco Pisacane, T: 0931 881840.

Solarino

€€ **Arc en Ciel**. Quiet intimate atmosphere, well-prepared dishes, excellent wine list. Closed Wed. 22 Via Ruggero Settimo, T: 0931 921931.

Sortino

€ **Anaktoron**. Simple and homely, typical Hyblaean mountain food. Closed Tues. 42 Via Andrea Gurciullo, T: 0931 953676.

€ **Osteria da Vincenzo**. Simple and satisfying. Closed Mon. 35 Via Libertà, T: 0931 954545.

CAFÉS, PASTRY SHOPS & ICE CREAM

Syracuse

Bel Bon. For an incredible assortment of ice cream, also served in crêpes or waffles. 142 Viale Zecchino.

Bianca. Old-fashioned bakery for delicious bread, biscuits and snacks. 43 Via Roma

Caffè Minerva. Good coffee, snacks and great ice cream. 15 Via Minerva.

Corsino, at **Le Antiche Siracuse**. A famous name for the very best in Sicilian pastries, nougat, snacks, excellent arancini (fried rice balls). 2 Via Maestranza, T: 0931 465706, www.corsino.it

Il Gelatiere. Lots of different flavours of ice cream and granita. Closed Tues in winter. l66 Corso Matteotti and 166 Viale Tica.

Marciante. Excellent pastries and marzipan; suppliers of cassata di ricotta to the late Queen Mother, who was very partial to it. 9 Via Landolina.

Augusta

Cafè Principe. For coffee, aperitives, tea or hot chocolate, all perfectly served. 168 Via Principe Umberto.

Avola

Caffè Finocchiaro. Well-known throughout Italy for the excellent ice cream, granita, and almond nougat. Piazza Umberto.

Belvedere

Bar Ciccio. Astonishing array of cakes and pastries, memorable cannoli and tiramisu, also snacks and light lunches. 1 Via de Gasperi.

Floridia

Bar Centrale. In the central square, this is the oldest café in town, with a very good reputation. Try the *crèpe al gelato*, ice cream in a pancake, or the irresistible *gelato al torrone*; a good savoury snack is the *strudel salato*. 17 Piazza Umberto.

Noto

Corrado Costanzo. 7–9 Via Silvio Spaventa. Famous and old-fashioned.

Mandolfiore. For very good cakes, biscuits and ice cream; try tangerine sorbet or *dessert di carruba* made only with carobs. *Cubbaita nougat* (sesame seeds and honey) is available all year round. 2 Via Ducezio.

Caffè Sicilia. Has unusual home-made jams and ice cream; the owner, Corrado Assenza, is adept with the secrets of Sicilian confectionery. 2 Via Ducezio.

La Vecchia Fontana. Serves good coffee, and prickly-pear ice cream (when in season). 2 Via Ducezio.

Piero e Figlio. Under the cathedral, for tasty snacks, sandwiches and ice cream. Via Matteo Raeli.

Palazzolo Acreide

Corsino. Open since 1889 and is famous throughout Italy for excellent sweets, especially the nougat (*torrone*), but the fried rice balls (*arancini*), and other savoury snacks, are superb. 2 Via Nazionale (Piazza Pretura), T: 0931 875035, www.corsino.it

Caprice. For traditional *pignuccata* and *giuggiulena* made with local thyme honey. 1 Via Iudica.

LOCAL SPECIALITIES

Syracuse There are many places in this city where craftsmen make paper by hand, using papyrus which grows spontaneously in the Ciane river, then local artists paint or draw on the paper, turning each piece into a work of art. **Fish House**, 29–31 Via Cavour, T: 339 7771364, ceramics inspired by the sea. Useful, decorative and colourful articles. **Reoro**, 17 Via Landolina, T: 0931 465454, www.reoro.it; is where Massimo Sinatra creates stunning jewellery in gold and precious stones, including the rare amber from the River Simeto. **Bazar delle Cose Vecchie**, 7 via Carmera Regionale, sells interesting curios, antique jewellery and puppets. A daily **market** (not Sun) is held in the morning in Ortygia on the streets near the Temple of Apollo, around the former market building. Fresh fish, fruit and vegetables are sold here.

Avola

Sebastiano Munafò, 13 Via Monte Grappa, T: 0931 833552, for the famous local almonds.

Palazzolo Acreide

Cantine Colle Acre, Via Giuseppe Campailla (playing fields), T: 0931 883898 & 0931 881058, www.cantina-colleacre.it, a small winery offering DOC wines from grapes grown in the Val di Noto and the territory of Eloro.

Cose a Caso, 27 Corso Vittorio Emanuele, T: 0931 883684, open afternoons only, this is where you will find those beautiful bedspreads, tablecloths, curtains and cushions, inspired by the local Baroque and Art Nouveau.

Noto

Market day is Mon morning, there is a country fair on the first and third Tues of every month, and a flea market (public gardens) every third Sun of the month. **Andrea Alderuccio**, 2 Vicolo Pisacane, T: 329 0112365, www.terrecotteweb.it; the little shop of a young artist/geologist, inspired by the shards of pottery he picks up among

the ruins of Noto Antica. **Salvatore Campisi**, 103 Via Vittorio Emanuele, T: 0931 841166 f 0931 841835, www.specialitadelmediterraneo.it, for locally-prepared canned, bottled or smoked tuna, swordfish, macarel, sardines and anchovies; also vegetables from Pachino, olives, artichokes, etc.
Sortino
Associazione Apicoltori Ragioniere Pagliaro, 128 Via Raiti, T: 0931 953390, for the local honey.

FESTIVALS & EVENTS

Syracuse First and second Sunday in May: *Santa Lucia delle Quaglie*, commemorating a miracle of the saint which took place here in 1642, procession and fireworks. July: *Festival di Ortigia*, concerts, plays, music, cinema and exhibitions, info: www.ortigiafestival.it. 8 Dec: *Immacolata*, a procession for the Madonna. 13 Dec: *Santa Lucia*, procession from the cathedral to the church of Santa Lucia,
Avola Feb: Carnival, famous for the processions of sumptuous allegorical floats.
Marzamemi July: *Festival del Cinema di Frontiera*, open-air screenings of films dealing with adventure, explorations

and heroism—the 'frontier' can be geographical, mental or cultural.
Melilli 20 Jan & 3–11 May: Feast of St Sebastian, with a procession, a fair, and fireworks.
Noto 19 Feb, the last Sun in Aug, and the first Sun in Sept: Festivities in honour of San Corrado. The procession of the Holy Thorn takes place on Good Friday, and other religious ceremonies during Easter week. The *Infiorata*, when Via Nicolaci is carpeted with fresh flowers, is held on the 3rd Sun in May. *La Notte di Giufà* is a whole night dedicated to music and story-telling, from sunset till dawn; the musicians come from all over the world, at the end of July.
Noto Antica *Festa dell'Alveria*, when the inhabitants of Noto go for a stroll through the streets of the earthquake-destroyed town, accompanied by expert guides. Nostalgic and fun at the same time, fourth Sun in May.
Solarino Procession of tractors and other farm machinery to the church of Madonna delle Lacrime for a solemn Thanksgiving, 7 Nov.
Sortino Puppet Festival and a celebration of the area's famous thyme and orange-blossom honey, first weekend in Oct.

THE PROVINCE OF CATANIA

CATANIA

Catania is a lively city, the second largest on the island after Palermo. It has been destroyed nine times in the course of its history, variously by earthquakes, bombardments, and lava, yet has been rebuilt each time on exactly the same spot. The city enjoys a love–hate relationship with the volcano at whose foot it stands; the people never call Etna by its name, preferring instead to refer to it affectionately as '*a muntagna*, the mountain. The harmonious appearance of the centre, a World Heritage Site, with long straight streets of imposing Baroque churches and palaces, dates from the reconstruction which followed the earthquake of 1693. The colour scheme of the city centre buildings is black and dark grey, relieved with white limestone details around the doors and the windows. The dark colour is provided by the lava sand used in the plaster on the exterior walls. The effect is rarely sombre; Catania is one of the sunniest cities in Europe and can well afford to use the glittering black '*azzolu* on the house fronts. The result is extremely elegant. Blocks of basalt have also been used for paving the streets. The most prosperous city on the island, Catania was known in the 1960s as the Milan of the South, but the life of the city deteriorated drastically in the 1970s and 1980s due to chaotic local administration, when all enterprise was stifled. Things have been changing fast, however, in recent years. New factories have been opened for the manufacture of micro-electronic components and the University has opened a special school for micro-electronics, the first in Italy. Thousands are now employed in this sector. Large quantities of fruit, vegetables, wheat, wine and raw materials of many kinds are brought to Catania to be sorted, graded, packed and shipped. Noisy and untidy, it is also generous and fun; a city of enormous cultural fervour; of many theatres and occasions to listen to music.

EXPLORING CATANIA

Piazza del Duomo
The old centre of Catania is the well-proportioned Piazza del Duomo. In the middle of the piazza stands a fountain supporting an antique lava elephant, the symbol of Catania. On the elephant's back perches an Egyptian obelisk (once perhaps a turning-post in the Roman circus), erected here in 1736 by Giovanni Battista Vaccarini, who was responsible for much of the look of the square. The fountain is modelled on the monument by Bernini in Piazza Minerva in Rome. The people refer to the elephant as *Liotru*, after Heliodorus, a Byzantine necromancer who is supposed to have used it as a 'Jumbo Jet' to fly between Catania and Constantinople in the 6th century AD. The square is surrounded by 18th-century buildings, many by Vaccarini, and dominated by the superb cathedral on the east side.

To the right of the cathedral is the sumptuous Diocese Museum (*open 9–12.30; closed Mon; www.museodiocesicatania.it*), which displays the cathedral treasure, fine art works and objects relating to the cult of St Agatha. From the terrace there is an interesting view over the old city centre.

The Municipio (town hall), begun in 1695, was finished by Vaccarini in 1741. Two state carriages are on view in the courtyard. The vista on the south side of Piazza Duomo is closed by the fine Porta Uzeda (1696) which leads to the little public garden called Villa Pacini, often busy with old men playing cards and talking, and beyond to the harbour. The streets behind the striking 19th-century white marble Amenano Fountain (an underground river which emerges at this point), are lined with a colourful daily market, where fish, meat, cheese and vegetables are sold.

HISTORY OF CATANIA

Catania was perhaps a Sicel trading post when the first Greek colony (from Chalcis) established itself here in 729 BC, and, as *Katane*, it soon rose to importance. Hieron I of Syracuse took the city in 476 and exiled the inhabitants to *Leontinoi*, re-founding the town with celebrations for which Aeschylus wrote his *Women of Aetna*; the exiles returned and drove out his Doric colonists in 461. In 415 it was the base of the Athenian operations against Syracuse, but it fell to Dionysius in 403, when the citizens were sold as slaves. After the defeat of the Syracusan fleet by Magus the Carthaginian it was occupied by Himilco. Catania opened its gates to Timoleon in 339 and to Pyrrhus in 278, and was one of the first Sicilian towns to fall to the Romans (263). Its greatest prosperity dated from the time of Augustus who rewarded it for taking his part against Pompey.

In early Christian days Catania was the scene of the martyrdom of St Agatha (238–251), the patroness of the city (*see box on p. 406*). In the Middle Ages it was wrecked by an earthquake (1169), sacked by Henry VI (1194), and again by Frederick II (1232), who built the castle to hold his rebellious subjects in check. Constance of Aragon, his empress, died here on 23rd June 1222. The 17th century saw the calamities of 1669 and 1693, the former the most terrible eruption of Etna in history, the latter a violent earthquake. The lava flows which reached the town in 1669 can still be seen from the ring road. In 1943 Catania was bombarded from the air and from the sea, receiving more bomb attacks than Naples.

The duomo
Map p. 399, 11. *Open 7.30–12 & 4.30–7.*
Dedicated to St Agatha, the duomo was founded by Count Roger in 1094 and rebuilt after the earthquakes of 1169 and 1693. The granite columns on the lower storey of the Baroque façade (Vaccarini, 1736–58) come from the Roman theatre. The cupola, by Battaglia, dates from 1804. The north door, with three statuettes, is attributed to

Gian Domenico Mazzola (1577). The structure of the mighty 11th-century black lava apses can be seen from no. 159 Via Vittorio Emanuele.

The interior

During restoration work of the interior in the 1950s, the foundations of the 11th–12th-century basilica were revealed beneath the nave. The fine antique columns (of late Imperial and Byzantine date) in the transepts and three apses have also been uncovered. On the right, against the second pier is the tomb of the composer Vincenzo Bellini, by Giovanni Battista Tassara. All the gilded Baroque picture-frames in the cathedral are worthy of note. The second and third altarpieces are by Borremans. In the south transept, a doorway by Giovanni Battista Mazzola (1545) leads into the Norman **Cappella della Madonna** which preserves a Roman sarcophagus, with the figures (very worn) finely carved in the round, thought to come from Izmir. It contains the ashes of Frederick II (d. 1337), Louis (d. 1355), Frederick III (d. 1377) and other illustrious members of the House of Aragon. Opposite is the beautiful tomb of Queen Constance of Aragon (d. 1363), wife of Frederick III, with contemporary scenes of Catania. The sculptured fragment above the door dates from the 15th century. The other chapel in the south transept is the **Cappella di Sant'Agata**, seen through a magnificent wrought-iron gate, which prompted wry comments for being erected only once the body of the saint had been stolen. The chapel contains a marble altarpiece (*Coronation of the Saint*); the tomb (right) of the Viceroy Fernandez d'Acuña (d. 1494), a kneeling figure attended by a page, by Antonello Freri of Messina; and (left) the treasury, with the relics of St Agatha, including her reliquary bust by Giovanni di Bartolo (1376). These are displayed only for the saint's feast days (3rd–5th February, 17th August, and, in procession, on 4th and 5th February). The stalls in the choir, finely sculpted by Scipione di Guido (1588), represent the life of St Agatha and the adventures of her corpse.

In the north transept, the Norman Cappella del Crocifisso is approached through an arch designed by Gian Domenico Mazzola (1563). In the sacristy is a fresco painted in 1675 showing the destruction of Catania by the lava flow from Etna in 1669.

Piazza San Francesco, Via Crociferi and San Nicolò

From Piazza del Duomo the handsome, long, straight Via Vittorio Emanuele, which contains a number of Baroque church façades, leads west. In Piazza San Francesco a large votive deposit of 6th-century BC pottery came to light in 1959. Dominating the little square, which in the Middle Ages was the vegetable market, is the monument to the cardinal and archbishop Giovanni Benedetto Dusmet (1935), who died in 1894, already considered a saint by his flock. His body, uncorrupted, can be seen inside the cathedral, under the last altar in the south aisle. The church of **San Francesco** houses some of the *candelore*, the impressive candlesticks representing the city corporations used during the processions for St Agatha (*see p. 406*), so it is possible to take a close look at them, and appreciate the skill of the bearers. Each one weighs about a ton, and is borne by eight stalwarts chosen from the corporation represented.

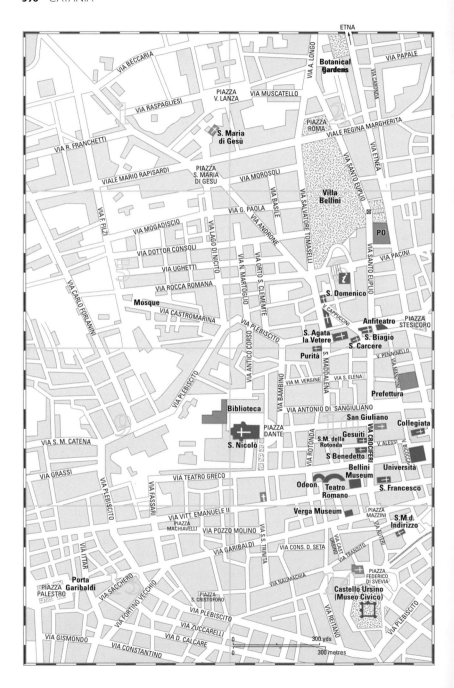

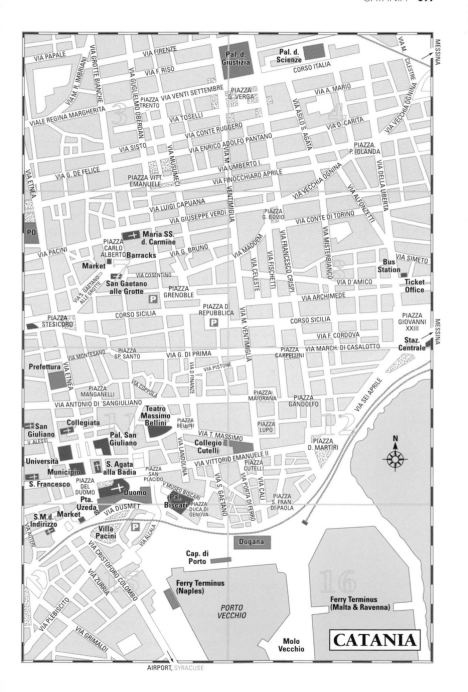

CATANIA

Facing the Baroque façade of San Francesco is a palace containing a small flat (across the courtyard to the left and up an old flight of steps) which houses the **Museo Bellini** (Map p. 398, 10. *Open 9–1; Tues and Thur also 3–6*). This delightful little museum has been recently restored and commemorates the great composer Vincenzo Bellini (1801–35), who was born here and lived here for 16 years. The charming rooms have retained their character and are crowded with mementoes, including his harpsichord (in the alcove where he is thought to have been born), several pianos and his death mask. The music library (open to students) preserves the original scores of *Adelson e Salvini, I Capuleti ed i Montecchi*, and *I Puritani*, besides fragments of all the remaining operas. On the opposite side of the same palace is the **Museo Emilio Greco** (*open 9–1; Tues and Thur also 3–6*), dedicated to the graphic works of the sculptor Emilio Greco, who was born in Catania.

From Piazza San Francesco, beyond the arch of San Benedetto (1704) begins **Via Crociferi**, the prettiest 18th-century street in Catania, lined with Baroque churches, convents and palaces, many of them approached by a short flight of steps. Recent excavations here have revealed remains of the Roman city. On the left, the church of **San Benedetto** (*open Thur 6.30–12 & 3.30–6; Sun and holidays 9–10 & 5–6*) has a graceful façade and vestibule of 1762. The softly-coloured interior, entrance in Via San Benedetto has an elaborate nuns' choir, a frescoed barrel vault by Giovanni Tuccari (1725), and a beautiful floor. Across Via Alessi, with its steps to the right a popular gathering place in the evenings, San Francesco Borgia or **Gesuiti** (*open 9–1 & 3-6.30; mornings only Sun and holidays*) is now an exhibition venue. On the north side is a statue of St Ignatius by Marabitti, and a wooden reliquary cross (1760) with skulls dimly visible behind glass. The dome was frescoed by Olivio Sozzi. Both the church and the large Jesuit college next door (with four courtyards) are the work of Angelo Italia (1754). Across the street, on the right, **San Giuliano** was begun in 1739 and continued by Vaccarini (who was responsible for the façade). In the fine elliptical interior is a 14th-century painted Crucifix. All these churches stand on pagan temples; this hill was the acropolis of the Greek and Roman city.

Via Antonio di Sangiuliano, a handsome street lined with oleanders, with views of the sea, then leads uphill, left, to the church of **San Nicolò l'Arena** (Map p. 398, 10. *Open 9–1, Tues and Thur also 3–6*). It faces a little crescent of houses designed by Stefano Ittar. This is the largest church in Sicily (105m long, transepts 42m wide), begun in 1687 by Giovanni Battista Contini, and rebuilt in 1735 by Francesco Battaglia, probably to the design of Antonino Amato. The dome was designed by Stefano Ittar. The striking façade, with its gigantic columns, was left incomplete in 1796.

The simplicity of the interior emphasizes its good proportions. The complex meridian line on the floor of the transept dates from 1841. The 18th-century choir-stalls were intricately carved by craftsmen from Naples. The huge organ (2,916 pipes), almost as big as a house, was intended to be played by three organists at once, and the monks also intended it to be the largest in Europe. Its builder, Donato Del Piano (d. 1775), lies buried beneath. It has been the subject of an 18-year restoration project, longer than it took Donato to build it. Goethe alluded to its wonderful sound

The church of San Nicolò l'Arena, left unfinished in 1796.

when he heard it in 1787, and it was played by Vincenzo Bellini when he was still a child—being so small, he got his friends to move the pedals for him while he was at one of the keyboards. The chapels at the east end have been made into war memorials. The roof is accessible and there is a breathtaking view.

Next door is the remarkable convent, the largest in Europe after that of Mafra in Portugal. When the traveller Patrick Brydone saw it in 1770 he thought it was a royal palace, only to discover it 'was nothing else than a convent of fat Benedictine monks, who wanted to assure themselves a paradise in this world, if not in the other'. It is now used by the university faculties of literature and philosophy (*sometimes shown on request by the porter, Mon–Fri mornings*). It was almost entirely rebuilt after 1693 to the design of Antonino Amato and his son Andrea; the rich detail of its Baroque ornamentation combines well with its simplicity of line.

The first court is overlooked by the splendid façade with delightful windows and balconies, completed in the early 18th century and decorated with an exuberant display of mascarons, cupids and varieties of fruit in a Mannerist style.

Excavations here have found prehistoric fragments as well as Greek and Roman remains, including a lava-stone road. In one of the cloisters there is a beautiful enclosed garden with palm trees and a majolica neo-Gothic tabernacle. Another cloister has a graceful arcade. The monumental Neoclassical staircase (1794) was designed by Antonio Battaglia. The impressive long corridors have fine vaults.

The remainder of the conventual complex (entered to the right of the church) is occupied by the **Ursino Recupero Library** (*open 9–1; Mon, Tues, Thur and Fri also 3.15–5.45; closed Sun and holidays*) and the monastic library, with its original bookcases and majolica floor of 1700 (the tiles are from Vietri). Outside the convent wall, to the left of the church façade (surrounded by railings), some remains of Roman baths can be seen, well below ground level.

The Archaeological Park and environs

Map p. 398, 10/14. *Open 9–1.30, Roman Theatre also 3–5. Tickets also allow entry to the Roman baths of Santa Maria della Rotonda and Terme dell'Indirizzo in Piazza Currò.*

Via Gesuiti, with herringbone paving in large blocks of basalt (typical of the side streets of the city), descends from San Nicolò and Piazza Dante back towards Via Crociferi past modest houses. Via Rotonda branches off to the right. Remains of Roman baths are visible here under the primitive domed church of **Santa Maria della Rotonda**. Many of the adjacent houses have been converted from another bath-house. Via Sant'Agostino continues back down to Via Vittorio Emanuele past the Odeon (*see below*). This old part of the city corresponds approximately to the area occupied by the Greek *Katane*, and is now an archaeological park , but a chronic shortage of custodians may mean that one or more of the monuments are closed.

At no. 266 Via Vittorio Emanuele is the inconspicuous entrance to the Roman Theatre, **Teatro Romano**, now overlooked by houses. This is a Roman building on the site of the theatre where Alcibiades harangued the men of Catania to win them to the cause of Athens (415 BC), in the final phase of the long war against Sparta. The building is of basalt, practically all of the marble facing having disappeared. The underground passageways which gave access to the cavea are very well preserved. The cavea has nine wedges of seats in two main tiers; the diameter was 86m, the depth of the orchestra 29m. The orchestra is sometimes flooded since the underground River Amenano tends to come to the surface here at certain times of the year. From the top of the cavea a path leads round to the small **Odeon**, a small semicircular building used for rehearsals and for competitions.

Not far from the cathedral, at 201 Via Vittorio Emanuele, is Catania's Toy Museum, the **Museo del Giocattolo** (*open 9.30–12.30; closed Mon*), housed in the lovely Baroque Palazzo Bruca, with a café and gift shop. A fascinating collection of toys has been carefully arranged here: old dolls and teddy bears, tea sets and dolls' prams, card games and puppets. One room provides space for temporary exhibits and impromptu creativity, with a little puppet theatre.

On the other side of Via Vittorio Emanuele, at no. 8 Via Sant'Anna, is **Casa Verga** (*open 8.30–1.30; Wed also 3–5.30; closed Mon*). On the second floor is the spartan apartment which belonged to the parents of the writer Giovanni Verga, who lived and died here. Some of the original furnishings have been preserved in his study, library and bedroom. The library is open to students and contains photocopies of the manuscripts of his most famous works (stored at the University for safe-keeping).

GIOVANNI VERGA (1840–1922)

Verga is famous for his naturalistic fiction, which gives a dramatic picture of the tragic social conditions of everyday Sicilian life using a simple and direct language and style. His first great success was *Storia di una Capinera* ('Story of a Black-cap', published in 1871) which was adapted for the screen by Franco Zeffirelli as *Sparrow* in 1993. His masterpieces include *Vita dei campi* (a collection of short stories, including *Cavalleria Rusticana*), *I Malavoglia* or *The House by the Medlar Tree*, and *Mastro-don Gesualdo*. Both these last were translated by D.H. Lawrence. By 1884 he was acclaimed as the greatest living Italian writer. He made contact with Emile Zola and remained a life-long friend of the writer Luigi Capuana, also born in the province of Catania. Both writers were fiercely proud of their roots in Sicily, in Verga's case being the town of Vizzini, and made frequent use of local dialect and idiom. Although his fame diminished towards the end of his life, his eightieth birthday was publicly celebrated in Catania with Luigi Pirandello as orator, and he was nominated senator in the same year. His influence remained strong on Italian novelists after the Second World War.

Around Castello Ursino

Map p. 398, 14. *Open 9–1 & 3–6; closed Mon; Sun and holidays 9–1.*
Via Sant'Anna leads on to the busy Via Garibaldi. The Baroque Porta Garibaldi (1768), or Porta Ferdinandea, can be seen at the west end, 1km away to the right. In the other direction is **Piazza Mazzini**, charmingly arcaded with 32 columns from the Roman basilica (beneath Sant'Agostino). Via Auteri, in a dilapidated poor district of the city, with a daily street market, leads south to Piazza Federico di Svevia, where low houses surround the Castello Ursino, built by Frederick II of Hohenstaufen. It was partly destroyed by the lava of 1669, which completely surrounded it.

The castle was restored after 1837 and for many years has housed the **Museo Civico**, but for over 40 years the museum has not been entirely open to the public. Material from the monastery of San Nicolò was augmented by the archaeological treasures collected by the Prince of Biscari in the 18th century. Although exhibitions are held here, and extensive repairs are now complete, the arrangement of the collections is still in progress at the time of writing. There are plans to house the archaeological collections in a new museum inside the old Bourbon Prison in Piazza Majorana. A fine courtyard contains sculptural fragments and sarcophagi. New archaeological excavations around the castle have revealed long sections of the Norman fortifications.

Near the submerged railway line just out of the Piazza is the simple little church of Santa Maria dell'Indirizzo. Behind it, in the courtyard of a school are the remains of Roman baths called **Terme dell'Indirizzo** and a tiny domed Greek-cross building in black lava. Via Zappalà Gemelli, with a Baroque palace, leads back through the market to Piazza Duomo.

Interior of the Teatro Massimo Bellini.

East of Piazza Duomo

Via Vittorio Emanuele leads east out of Piazza Duomo between the north side of the cathedral and the Baroque church of **Sant'Agata alla Badia** (*open 8–1*), another work by Vaccarini (1748–67; the Rococo interior was completed after his death). Beyond in a little Piazza on the right is the church of San Placido (usually closed) with a façade of 1769, attributed to Stefano Ittar, and a pretty interior; this church was built on top of a Roman temple dedicated to Hercules.

Via Museo Biscari is named after the **Palazzo Biscari**, the most impressive private palace in Catania. The best view of the magnificent exterior, by Antonino Amato, is from Via Dusmet. Here, in the 18th century, Ignazio Paternò Castello Prince of Biscari catalogued *objets d'art* for his famous collection, part of which is preserved in the Museo Civico (*see above*). Concerts are occasionally held in the lovely Rococo Salone della Musica.

On the other side of Via Vittorio Emanuele Via Landolina leads to the splendid opera house, **Teatro Massimo Bellini** (Map p. 399, 11. *T: 095 7306111 to request visit*), by Carlo Sada, 1873–90. The tenor Beniamino Gigli pronounced this theatre to have the finest acoustics in the world. The narrow streets in this area, once a run-down part of the city, are now full of life; many pubs and open-air cafés open in the evening, giving rise to the so-called *'movida'* of Catania: live music for all tastes, jazz, pop or classical, especially in the summer.

Via Vittorio Emanuele continues towards the sea passing on the right Via Bonaiuto, where the **Cappella Bonaiuto** (*open 9.30–1; closed Sun and Mon*), is a Byzantine chapel built between the 6th century and the 9th century. Further along is the Collegio Cutelli (left), with a remarkable round courtyard designed by Vaccarini (1779). Piazza dei Martiri has a statue of *St Agatha Trampling the Plague* on top of a column removed from the ancient theatre; the monument was erected by the city senate in 1743 when an epidemic of plague miraculously spared Catania. Here a wide terrace, popular in the 19th century for afternoon strolls, and often mentioned by Verga in his novels, overlooks the harbour.

Via Etnea to Piazza Stesicoro

On the north side of Piazza Duomo is the handsome Via Etnea, nearly 3km long, the main street of the city. It is lined with elegant shops (especially for clothes and books) and cafés, and its wide lava pavements are always crowded. It rises to a splendid view of the peak of Mount Etna in the distance.

Beyond the town hall is the distinguished **Piazza Università**, laid out by Vaccarini. The University, on the left, known as *Siculorum Gymnasium*, was founded in 1434 by Alfonso V of Aragon as the first in Sicily, and rebuilt after the earthquake of 1693; the courtyard was begun by Andrea Amato and finished in 1752 by Vaccarini.

Just beyond is the **Collegiata**, a royal chapel of c. 1768 by Stefano Ittar, with a dazzling Baroque interior, much in request for weddings. The paintings in the interior are by the little-known local artist Francesco Gramignani (1770), while the splendid canvas over the first south-aisle altar represents St Apollonia, by Olivio Sozzi. The main altarpiece is a copy made after the 1693 earthquake of a Russian icon, destroyed in the disaster.

Some way further on Via Etnea runs through **Piazza Stesicoro** (Map p. 398, 6), the heart of modern Catania, with a monument to Bellini by Giulio Monteverde (1882). Overlooking the piazza is the 18th-century church of San Biagio. In the centre are the scant ruins of the **Roman Amphitheatre** in black lava, thought to date from the 2nd century AD. The external circumference was 389m, and the arena was one of the largest after the Colosseum in Rome. There were 56 entrance arches. The visible remains include a corridor, part of the exterior wall, and fragments of the cavea supported on vaults. The rest of the structure still exists in part beneath the surrounding buildings. Its destruction had already begun under Theodoric when it was used as a quarry; Totila made use of the stone in building the city walls in 530, and Count Roger stole its decorative elements to embellish his cathedral in 1091. In 1693 the area was used as a dump for the rubble of the earthquake.

Nearby, in Piazza della Borsa, are remains of the 18th-century church of Sant'Euplio covering a 3rd-century Roman hypogeum. It was partially restored in 1978 after its destruction in 1943 (*for admission apply at the town hall*).

Via Manzoni, which leads out of the south side of the square parallel to Via Etnea, is interesting for its numerous well-stocked haberdashery shops and old-fashioned clothes shops for children.

Beyond the top west end of the square behind San Biagio is the church of the **Santo Carcere** (*open Thur and Sat 4–7; Sun and holidays 9.30–12*), flanked by a strong defence wall. Incorporated into the Baroque façade is a doorway, with grotesque animal heads, which dates from 1236, formerly in the façade of the duomo. In the interior is 'St Agatha's prison', with a Roman barrel vault, which is shown by the custodian on request.

Via Cappuccini continues uphill to Via Maddalena where the church of **Sant'Agata la Vetere**, probably built only a few years after the martyrdom of the saint in the 3rd century, stands opposite the church of the Purità (or the Visitazione), with a curving façade by Battaglia (1775) next to its handsome convent. Sant'Agata la Vetere was once Catania's cathedral; inside you can see the Roman marble sarcophagus that was the first tomb of St Agatha.

A little to the north is the church of **San Domenico** (*open before 9.30 and 5–6.30; ring at the convent next door*). It contains a beautiful *Madonna* by Antonello Gagini (1526), and a painting of *St Vincent Ferrer* by Olivio Sozzi (1757).

SAINT AGATHA

The Feast of St Agatha (Sant' Agata) galvanizes the whole population of the city during the first week of February, and again on 17th August. An early Christian martyr, Agatha was only thirteen years old when she was arrested for her religious beliefs. In spite of blandishments and then threats, she would not recant her faith. On 4th February 251 she underwent terrible tortures including the mutilation of her breasts. Miraculously recovering during the night, she also survived being burned the next day in the amphitheatre in front of the populace, on the orders of Quinziano, Roman governor of Catania. The flames would not touch her, and a sudden earthquake caused the Romans to flee the town leaving Agatha unscathed. She asked to be taken to her prison cell, where she died. Her body, still intact, was carried off to Constantinople by the Byzantine general George Maniakes as a gift for the emperor in 1040, but on 17th August 1126 she was brought back to Catania by two soldiers of the Imperial Guard, who had cut her body into pieces in order to smuggle her back home.

St Agatha is the patron saint both of women who have undergone mastectomy, and also of firemen. The processions in her honour are impressive and richly Baroque. The huge float, carrying boxes containing parts of her body and the 14th-century reliquary, glittering with jewels, which holds her torso and head, is dragged through the streets by thousands of *divoti* wearing traditional white robes and black caps, preceded by the *candelore*, enormous highly decorated candlesticks representing the corporations of the city. The celebrations are concluded with spectacular fireworks. The event is regularly attended by crowds of some 300,000 and has been declared a World Heritage Tradition.

North and east of Piazza Stesicoro

From Piazza Stesicoro on Via Etnea, with its monument to Vincenzo Bellini, Via San Gaetano alle Grotte with its daily market leads to the little church of **San Gaetano alle Grotte** which dates from 1700. The former church, built into a volcanic cavern beneath in 1262, is now usually closed but is sometimes open for Mass. The cave itself probably represents the oldest Christian place of worship in the city, and perhaps the first burial place of St. Agatha.

The main market for produce and textiles, known as 'a Fera d'o Luni, the Monday Fair, occupies Piazza Carlo Alberto. The piazza is overlooked by a fine palace occupied by the Lucchesi-Palli barracks, in the courtyard of which is an ancient tomb traditionally held to be that of Stesichorus, the poet Tisias of Himera (died c. 540 BC) next to the church of the Carmine.

Via Etnea continues north past the post office. Steps lead up to the charming **Villa Bellini** (Map p. 398, 2/6) a fine public garden laid out c. 1870. It contains busts of famous citizens (all without noses—local vandals) and a monument to Giovanni Pacini (1796–1867), another local composer. At the north end of the garden a gate leads out to Viale Regina Margherita, part of the modern east–west artery of the city, c. 5km long.

Further north is an important **Botanical Garden** (*open weekdays 9–1; www.dipbot.unict.it*). The main gate is on Via Etnea, but the usual entrance is on Via Longo. It is particularly famous for its cactus plants. Via Etnea ends at Parco Gioeni, on a lava flow, an attractive and unusual public park. About 500m west of the Botanical Garden, surrounded by tall, modern apartment blocks, is the church of **Santa Maria di Gesù**, founded in 1442 and built in 1465. On its north side is the pretty exterior of the Cappella Paternò which survived the earthquake of 1693. It is entered from the north aisle of the church through a doorway by Antonello Gagini (1519) with a *Pietà* in the lunette above. Inside is a fresco (transferred to wood) of the *Madonna with St Agatha and St Catherine* (signed 1525). Above the main altar of the church is a Crucifix by Fra' Umile da Petralia, and in the second north-aisle chapel, a *Madonna with Two Angels in Adoration* by Antonello Gagini.

Heading east from the north end of Villa Bellini, Viale Regina Margherita crosses Via Etnea and later continues as Viale XX Settembre into Piazza Giovanni Verga, a large square dominated by the Palazzo di Giustizia (1952; Map p. 399, 3/4) and the focus of a new and fashionable district. The fountain in the centre by local sculptor Carmelo Mendola (1975) is a monument to Giovanni Verga and represents the moment of tragedy in his masterpiece *The House by the Medlar Tree*, when the Malavoglia family lose their fishing boat, symbolically named *Provvidenza*.

Further east, in Corso Italia, the Palazzo delle Scienze (*open 9–1, closed Sun and holidays*), of 1942, houses the geological and volcanological collections of the university. The corso terminates at the sea in Piazza Europa, with a watchtower on top of a mound of lava, and a marble statue of a young girl by Francesco Messina. Viale Ruggero di Lauria leads from here to Ognina and the **Museo del Mare** or Museum of the Sea, at 14–17 Piazza Ognina and 18 Via dei Conzari, (*open 9–12.30 & 4.30–7, closed Mon*). Many of Catania's fishermen live in this part of town and the museum is a way of honouring the fishing community. Mementoes of fishing from the past, anchors and boats are on display, and traditional fishing methods are explained.

In the other direction Viale Africa leads south towards the main railway station past **Le Ciminiere** (*open Tues–Sun 9.30–12.30; Tues and Thur also 3–5; last tickets one hour before closing*) with its tall chimneys, which was built in the 19th century as a sulphur refinery. It has been restored as a cultural centre with exhibition halls and space for theatrical performances and concerts, and houses the Puppet Theatre and several museums: the Museo Storico Sbarco in Sicilia 1943 (the Museum of the 1943 Allied Landing in Sicily) being a collection of uniforms, weapons, photographs and films documenting the invasion codenamed *Operation Husky*; the Museo del Cinema and the Modern Art Gallery.

RISERVA NATURALE OASI DEL SIMETO

Open 9–6.

The Oasi del Simeto, at the mouth of the River Simeto a few kilometers south of Catania, is a nature reserve run by the provincial administration. Although numerous holiday villas were built here illegally from the 1960s onwards, it was first protected in 1975 and became a nature reserve in 1984, thanks mainly to the strenuous efforts of Wendy Hennessy Mazza, a British local resident and birdwatcher, a representative of Lega Italiana Protezione Uccelli (LIPU), the Italian society for bird protection. In 1989, 54 of the numerous houses erected within the area without building permission were demolished, but hundreds still remain. The marshes and brackish lakes offer protection to numerous birds, both nesting and migratory, including rare ducks, great white heron, flamingo, black-winged stilt, godwit, cattle egret, glossy ibis, avocet and spoonbill. The purple gallinule has recently been successfully reintroduced. Amber can sometimes be found on the shore here, the fossilized resin of almond trees which grew inland about 60 million years ago. The colour is rich chestnut brown, giving green or blue reflections in artificial light; sometimes there are insects or fragments of leaves trapped inside the jewel.

The entrance to the reserve is on the left bank of the river near Ponte Primosole on the main road (SS 114). On the left bank of the Simeto, close to the bridge, where you can see a low hill, stood the ancient Sicel town of *Symaethus*, whose necropolis survives on the Turrazza estate. The **Simeto**, 88km long, is the most important river in Sicily; it springs from Serra del Re in the Nebrodi mountains, and picks up some important tributaries on its way to the sea—the Salso, Troina, Dittaino and Gornalunga. In the course of time it has formed the immense alluvial Plain of Catania. The mouth was a marshy delta, drained in the 1930s under Mussolini, to create farmland and eliminate malaria, but this illness continued to be a problem for the local farmers until 1943, and the arrival of Allied troops, who eradicated the disease with DDT.

Mount Etna in winter.

MOUNT ETNA

Mount Etna, to the northwest of Catania, is the highest volcano (c. 3350m) in Europe and one of the largest and most active in the world. In 1987, the volcano was declared a regional park, protecting 59,000 hectares of unique geology, flora and fauna, the particular villages and farms, and traditional methods of forestry, bee-keeping, wine manufacture, stone work and carpentry. The ascent of Etna, although now easy and commonplace, is an experience which should not be missed, not only for its volcanic phenomena but also for the superb views. The extent of a visit is always subject to current volcanic activity, while the visibility is determined by cloud conditions (which tend to build up in the course of the day) and the direction of the smoke from the main craters. There are splendid views of the lava fields on the approach roads to Rifugio Sapienza and Piano Provenzana: the two starting points for the ascent to the top of Etna. Higher up it is often possible to see smoking and gaseous fissures, and explosions from the main craters, of which there are four—it is not permitted to approach these. There may be a strong smell of sulphur, and here and there the mountainside is covered by yellow sulphurous patches. The view, beyond the mountain's hundreds of subsidiary cones and craters, can extend across the whole of Sicily, the Aeolian Islands and Calabria. The spectacle is unique owing to the enormous difference in height between Etna and the surrounding hills.

HISTORY OF ETNA

Etna, called *Aetna* in ancient times and *Mongibello* (from *monte* and *jebel*, Arabic for mountain) by the Sicilians (often simply *'a muntagna*), probably originated from a submarine eruption which took place in the gulf which is now occupied by the plain of Catania. In ancient Greece the volcano was held to be the forge of Vulcan or of the Cyclopes, or the mountain from beneath which the Titan Enceladus, imprisoned by Zeus, forever struggled to free himself. Empedocles (*see p. 210*), the philosopher, scientist and statesman from Agrigento who lived in the 5th century BC, was said to have thrown himself into the crater to obtain complete knowledge. Among early eruptions that of 475 BC was described by Pindar and Aeschylus, while that of 396 BC, whose lava reached the sea, is said to have prevented the Carthaginian general Himilco from marching on Syracuse. Hadrian climbed Etna to see the sunrise and the conical shape of the mountain reflected on the island. The eruption of 140 BC covered the city of Catania and the surrounding countryside under a thick layer of sand, disastrous enough for the senate in Rome to exempt the inhabitants from tax for ten years. In 1169, 1329 and 1381 the lava again reached the sea, twice near Acireale, the third time at Catania. The largest eruption ever recorded took place in 1669 when an open cleft extended from the summit to Nicolosi and part of Catania was over-whelmed. The eruption's crater, which appears double, is called Monti Rossi.

Since 1800 there have been over 60 eruptions, the one in 1928 being the most destructive, obliterating the town of Mascali. In 1908 a huge pit of lava opened in the Valle del Bove. The eruption of 1947 threatened Passopisciaro, and that of 1950–51 menaced Rinazzo and Fornazzo before the lava halted. The 1971 eruption destroyed the observatory and the second stage of the cableway on the summit, as well as vineyards and some houses near Fornazzo. In 1978–79 four new cones erupted and the lava flowed into the Valle del Bove; the town of Fornazzo was again threatened. Nine British tourists were killed by an explosion on the rim of the main crater itself in 1979. In the spring of 1983 activity start-ed up on the opposite side of the mountain above Nicolosi and Belpasso, form-ing the southeast crater, which has since been the most active of the summit cones. In 1984 an earthquake damaged the town of Fleri. In 1991–2 eruptions took place over four months, threatening Zafferana Etnea. The eruption of sum-mer 2001 started just below the Montagnola at 2800m, on 18th July, but with-in a few days 18 temporary craters had opened up all over the top of the vol-cano, providing spectacular firework displays at night. The lava was successful-ly prevented from doing too much damage, by the use of bulldozers to form enormous dykes to contain and direct the flow. Another eruption, although less spectacular, occurred in 2004. The threat of serious eruptions continues, accept-ed by the local inhabitants with patience and fortitude.

EXPLORING MOUNT ETNA

The summit can be visited from either the southern or the northern side of the mountain. There are organized excursions from Rifugio Sapienza on the southern slopes (Etna sud) and from Piano Provenzana (under repair at time of writing) on the northern slopes (Etna nord). Both can be reached easily by car or bus. The upper part of the volcano can also be explored on foot from both these points, and there are some spectacular walks which are signposted on the lower slopes of the mountain. Near the top there is almost always a very strong wind and the temperature can be many degrees below freezing: a warm jacket, sturdy shoes and a hat are in order (shoes and jackets can be hired at the cableway station near Rifugio Sapienza). The four summit craters are strictly off limits. Signs warn visitors not to go beyond the bounds of prudence.

The southern approach: Etna Sud

The *Strada dell'Etna* was opened in 1934 by Vittorio Emanuele III. It is well signposted beyond **Nicolosi**, which is one of the best centres for visiting Etna. At no. 32 Via Cesare Battisti is the Museo Vulcanologico Etneo (*open 9–1 & 4–6; closed Thur*), an informative display about Etna and its phenomena, together with a collection of various types of lava and minerals. To the west of Nicolosi are the craters of the Monti Rossi (949m), which represent one of the most important subsidiary groups of craters (over 3km round), formed in 1669 by the biggest eruption ever recorded.

Beyond Nicolosi the road climbs through lava fields and some woods, crossing lava flows from 1886 and 1910; the names of the craters on either side of the road are indicated. Walks off this road are also signposted. The main road continues to the Casa Cantoniera at 1910m and ends at the 2001 lava stream beside the **Rifugio Sapienza**. Here there are souvenir shops, an information bureau, cafés and restaurants, and honey vendors. In the desert of hardened volcanic lava nearby several extinct craters can be explored easily on foot, and the 400 metre-wide 2001 lava flow is impressive, superimposed with the lava from 2002.

A cableway ascends from here up the slopes of the Montagnola (2507m), a crater of 1763, through a desert of lapilli with splendid views of the sea and port of Catania. It takes about 15mins to reach the site of the **Piccolo Rifugio**, destroyed during the 2001 eruption. Although at present you are not allowed any nearer to the main crater, from this distance you can usually see (and hear) volcanic activity. A road has been cut through the 2001 lava stream, making it possible to reach the Silvestri Craters, formed during the eruption of 1892, and continue down the thickly wooded eastern slopes of the mountain and across the 1892 lava to Zafferana Etnea.

Getting to the summit

Organised excursions to the summit leave from the Rifugio Sapienza and take about 2hrs. Tickets can be bought at the cableway station near the refuge. The cableway itself was severely damaged during the eruptions of July 2001 and November 2002, but has since been repaired. If weather conditions are adverse, 4WD vehicles are used to reach a height of about 2800m, where the guides take people on foot to the more interesting areas. From the Rifugio Sapienza guides also take people walking to the 2001 crater, close by. It is absolutely forbidden to approach the rim of the summit craters. Before undertaking the climb independently advice should be obtained about weather conditions at the SITAS offices at the cableway station, or at Nicolosi, where guides are available to accompany walkers. The easiest and most usual approach from Sapienza follows the track used by the 4WD vans. About 4hrs should be allowed for the return trip from the refuge. The most spectacular time for the ascent is before dawn.

The northern approach: Etna Nord

Linguaglossa is the best centre for excursions on the northern slopes of Etna. The peaceful little town has a number of late 19th- and early 20th-century houses. The doorways and windows of the 18th-century church are decorated with lava, and elaborate 19th-century lamps ornament the façade.

The mountain road, known as the *Mareneve*, which climbs towards the summit of Etna, begins here. It leads up through the Pineta Ragabo, ancient pinewoods of great interest to naturalists, to the ski-fields of **Piano Provenzana** (1800m), the main ski resort on Etna, with a refuge, and five ski-lifts (1800m and 2300m) completely destroyed by the earthquakes and lava during the 2002 eruption, and under repair at time of writing. From here excursions by 4WD vans are organized, arriving just below the summit. It is also possible to walk up the cone from here in c. 3hrs (the easiest way is to follow the track used by the excursion vans).

Another mountain road descends from Piano Provenzana following the eastern slope of the mountain passing beneath the **Rifugio Citelli** at 1741m, to Fornazzo.

THE FOOTHILLS SOUTH OF ETNA

ADRANO

Adrano was the ancient *Hadranon*, founded by Dionysius the Elder close to the site of a Sicel temple dedicated to the god Hadranon, said to have been guarded by hundreds of dogs called *cirnechi* (from Cyrenaica), originally purchased from Phoenician merchants, and still raised in the area today. Of medium size, with upright ears, a long, thin straight tail, ginger in colour with a pinkish nose, they are extremely intelligent.

Exploring Adrano

Overlooking the public gardens, Giardino della Vittoria (with superb trees), is the enormous former monastery of Santa Lucia, rebuilt in the 15th–16th centuries, and now a school, flanked by the towering façade (1775) of its church which has a pretty oval interior. The imposing black lava castle (*open 9–1 & 4–7; Sun 9–1; Mon closed*) was built in 1070 by Count Roger, on the site of much earlier Greek and Roman fortifications.

FLORA & FAUNA OF MOUNT ETNA

The soil at the foot of Etna is extraordinarily fertile because the volcanic ash is rich in nutrients. In the cultivated zone (*pedemontana*) oranges, lemons and tangerines are grown behind low black basalt dry-stone walls. The higher slopes of the mountain were forested up until the 19th century, but now they are planted with groves of olives, apples, pears, pistachios, hazelnuts and vineyards. The apparently delicate, willowy, pale green endemic Etna broom, *Genista aetnensis*, flourishes on many of the lava flows; it is one of the most important pioneer plants which help to break up the rock and turn it into soil, a process which takes about 400 years. At 1300m forest trees grow, especially oaks, chestnuts, pines and beeches. This is the southernmost point in Europe where the beech tree can be found, and this is also where it reaches its highest altitude, 2250m. It is also the extreme southern limit for the silver birch, which is found in its endemic form, *Betula aetnensis*. From 2000 to 3000m the black lava is colonized by tough little plants, most of them found only on this volcano, such as the Etna holy thorn (*Astragalus aetnensis*), or the Etna violet (*Viola aetnensis*), creating a wonderful carpet of flowers in the spring and early summer. Botanists should not miss the **Nuova Gussonea Alpine Garden** (*T: 095 502218 to request visit*), run by the University of Catania. It is not far from the Grande Albergo, and can be reached from the Nicolosi-Rifugio Sapienza road.

Since the creation of the park the golden eagle has returned after an absence of more than a hundred years, and nests regularly. Etna is the only place in Sicily where the long-eared owl can be found. Wolves and boars no longer roam through the forests, and there are no squirrels or badgers, but to compensate there are plenty of foxes and rabbits, hares, porcupines, wildcats, hedgehogs, the garden and the edible dormouse, many species of bats, five snakes (of which only the viper is venomous), tortoises and two kinds of toad. There are plans to reduce access to the area of maximum protection (*Zona A*) to allow nature to take over again, and to reintroduce some long-absent species, such as the roe deer and the griffon vulture. Local politicians, however, are pressing for the opening of a new ski centre on the northwest slope. Pot-holers or spelaeologists will find the numerous lava tunnels on Mount Etna fascinating, but exploration should not be attempted without expert help. Those interested should call the CUTGANA group at the University of Catania (*T: 095 317097, www.cutgana.it*), for these or other caves in Sicily.

The heat of the rocks and the hot vapours from the terminal cones cause the snow to melt partly even in winter, but in certain depressions with a northern aspect the snow used to be preserved for refrigeration purposes throughout the summer by covering it with volcanic ash. It was then transported as required on mule-back down to the towns.

The interior houses a delightful local museum. The archaeological section includes prehistoric material from Stentinello and Castelluccio (ground and first floors). On the second floor the later finds from Mendolito include a hanging *askos* and a 6th-century BC bronze figurine, *Il Banchettante*. In a little Norman chapel, with an apse fresco, is a collection of coins from ancient Adrano. On the third floor are paintings, many of them in very poor condition.

Next to the castle is the **Chiesa Madre**, of Norman origin. The interior incorporates 16 basalt columns, possibly from the ancient temple of *Hadranon*. High up above the west door is a fine polyptych by the 16th-century Messina school in its original frame. The painted 15th-century Crucifix was damaged by restoration work in 1924. In the transepts are four panels (*Two Saints* and the *Annunciation*) by Girolamo Alibrandi, the painter from Messina much influenced by Antonello da Messina. In the pretty sacristy is a fine painting of the *Last Supper* by Pier Paolo Vasta.

The opera house, **Teatro Bellini**, built in 1845 to replace an earlier theatre of 1742, has been restored and is now in regular use; its Art Nouveau façade was added in the early 20th century.

Off a byroad below the town (signposted *Strada per il Ponte dei Saraceni*) a poorly-surfaced road between low lava walls leads (in c. 1.5km) past citrus plantations and lovely old farmhouses to the Simeto river, spanned by the impressive 14th-century **Ponte dei Saraceni**, an extremely well-preserved bridge. It has four unequal arches decorated with black lava and the path over the top is still passable. In this beautiful peaceful spot there is a view of Etna and a waterfall on the rocky bed of the Simeto. Nearby (not signposted) are a few remains of the walls and south gate of the ancient Sicel town of *Mendolito*.

EAST FROM ADRANO

Southeast of Adrano is **Biancavilla**, where excellent oranges and clementines are grown; beside the extensive orange plantations are olive groves and hedges of prickly pear. At **Paternò**, another important centre for orange-growing, the town sprawls at the base of an 11th-century castle (*open 9.20–12.40 & 4.15–7.30; Sat 9.20–12.40; closed Sun and Mon*). The austere tower built of volcanic rock commands the wide Simeto valley. It was restored in 1900, with a fine hall and frescoed chapel. From the terrace there is a good view. Frederick II of Aragon died near Paternò while journeying to Enna. The churches of San Francesco and Santa Maria della Valle di Giosafat retain Gothic elements.

From Paternò the road continues to the town of **Motta Sant'Anastasia**, perched on an extremely interesting rock formation, a 'neck' of lava (visible close-up from Via Montalto and Via Vittorio Veneto), with a fine 12th-century Norman castle (*open 9.15–12.40; closed Sat and Sun*) which preserves its crenellations. The unusual name of **Misterbianco**, a town now swallowed up by Catania, with an industrial area, comes from a Benedictine monastery, the *monastero bianco*, which was destroyed along with the town, in the eruption of 1669.

A secondary road from Paternò leads up the volcano, to **Belpasso**. Once known as Malpasso, it was covered by lava in 1669 and rebuilt with the name Fenicia Moncada; destroyed once again by the 1693 earthquake, it was again rebuilt, this time with the more optimistic name, Beautiful Step, which it still holds. The bell in the tower of the Chiesa Madre, forged in 1815, is among the largest in Italy. The Art Nouveau opera house is dedicated to the popular local playwright Nino Martoglio.

The road continues to Nicolosi, Pedara, and **Trecastagni**, where the Chiesa Madre is perhaps the purest Renaissance building in Sicily, thought to be the work of Antonello Gagini. The Chiesa del Bianco has an elegant 15th-century campanile. The town is renowned for the production of wine, especially *Etna Rosso*.

Zafferana Etnea is the main town on the east side of Etna. It is one of the most important honey-producing areas of Italy, renowned for its *miele di zagara* or citrus-blossom honey (*see p. 320*). The area was damaged by an earthquake in 1984, and a lava flow in 1992 reached the outskirts of the town (this can now be visited, at the end of a signposted road, where a statue was set up as an offering to the Madonna). Climbs towards the Valle del Bove can be made from here.

THE FOOTHILLS NORTH OF ETNA

RANDAZZO

Above the Alcantara valley, Randazzo is a lava-built town of great antiquity, which has never in recorded history suffered volcanic destruction. Its medieval history resolves itself into a rivalry between the three churches of Santa Maria, San Nicolò, and San Martino, each of which served as the cathedral for alternate periods of three years. The parishioners of each church (of Greek, Latin and Lombard origin) spoke different dialects until the 16th century. The town was damaged during Allied bombing in August 1943, when the Germans made it the strong point of their last resistance on the island.

Exploring Randazzo

The present cathedral, **Santa Maria**, is a 13th-century church with fine black lava apses and a three-storeyed south portal (approached by two flights of steps) in the Catalan-Gothic style of the 15th century. The dome is attributed to Venanzio Marvuglia. The black and white tower was restored in 1863. The terrace, with another fine doorway and the sacristy with 16th-century portico, looks out over the Alcantara Valley.

The **interior** (1594) has fine black columns and capitals, one of which serves as an altar. Over the south door is a small painting with a view of the town attributed to Girolamo Alibrandi (15th century); over the north door is a fragment of a fresco of the *Madonna and Child* (13th century). The church contains six paintings by Giuseppe Velasquez (on the first north altar, the fourth and fifth altars in the north and south aisles, and on the south wall of the sanctuary). The Crucifix in the chapel to the right of the sanctuary is by Fra' Umile da Petralia. The second left-hand and second right-hand altarpieces are by Onofrio Gabrieli. The third south altarpiece is by Jean van Houbraken, of the 17th-century Messina school. Outside, the south side shows beautiful windows of the original structure and a magnificent Gothic-Catalan doorway with a tiny marble relief of the *Madonna* over it, probably from Pisa.

Via Umberto leads past the southern flank of Santa Maria past a little **natural history museum** (*open 10–1 & 4–7; summer until 10*), with an ornithological section and a collection of shells, to **Piazza Municipio** where the town hall occupies a 14th-century convent reconstructed in 1610. The lovely cloister has columns of lava.

From here the narrow, pretty Via degli Archi leads beneath four arches to the church of **San Nicoló** which dates mainly from the 16th–17th centuries (damaged in 1943). The apse, however, is original (13th century). In the north transept is a seated statue of St Nicholas (with two small reliefs below) by Antonello Gagini, signed and dated 1523. In the south transept is a 16th-century painted Crucifix and four delicately carved bas-reliefs of the *Passion* by Giacomo Gagini.

Outside, there is an 18th-century copy of a curious antique statue of a man, thought to symbolize the union of the three parishes (*see above*). Called Old Randazzo or *Piracmone* by the local people, the eagle represents the regality of the Latins, the snake the wisdom of the Greeks, and the lion the strength of the Lombards. Nearby is Palazzo Clarentano (1509) where a medieval arch tunnels beneath houses back towards the corso.

Via Umberto continues to the district of San Martino, with evidence of shell fire from the Second World War. At no. 197 is the information bureau (*open 9–1 & 3–7.30; Sun 9–1*). The damaged church of **San Martino** still has its fine 14th-century campanile. On the top is a charming old-fashioned iron weathervane, in the form of a cherub. The façade has 15th-century reliefs of saints and martyrs. In the interior are black lava columns and in the south transept a statue of the *Madonna and Child* by the Gagini school (which retains part of its polychrome decoration). In the north aisle is a triptych by a local painter influenced by Antonello da Messina. Here also is a papier-mâché crucifix, recently restored. The work of Giovannello Matinati, it is signed and dated 1540. It is known as the Crucifix of the Water, because when Matinati was transporting it from Messina, where he lived, to an unknown destination, he was waylaid by a deluge and took refuge in the church to protect his art work. Every time he tried to leave, it started raining again. In the end he left the Crucifix in the church where it apparently belonged. The marble font was made in 1447.

In front of the church is the 13th-century castle which was rebuilt in 1645 and used as a prison up until 1973. It has now been restored as the **Vagliasindi Museum** (*open 9–1 & 3–7, summer until 10*). The collection includes some fine vases from a neighbouring Greek necropolis (5th–2nd centuries BC), including a 5th-century red-figure oinochoe, as well as coins and jewellery. A collection of puppets is also displayed here. There is a lovely view of the church of San Martino from the uppermost tower. Just beyond is Porta San Martino (1753) in the walls.

BRONTE

Bronte is an important centre for the cultivation of pistachio trees (90 per cent of the pistachios produced in Italy are grown here). The fruit is harvested every two years at the end of August and beginning of September. Pistachios are used in local cuisine for pasta dishes, sweets and ice creams, and for flavouring mortadella sausage.

Abbazia di Maniace

Open 9–1 & 3–7; closed Mon.
In a little wooded valley to the north of Bronte, on the Saraceno, a tributary of the Simeto, is the Abbazia di Maniace or Castello Maniace. A convent was founded here in 1173 by Margaret of Navarre, mother of William II, on the spot where the Byzantine general George Maniakes defeated the Saracens in 1040, with the help of the Russian Varangian Guard and Norman mercenaries, among whom may have been the Scandinavian hero Harold Hardrada.

The house and estate were presented to Admiral Horatio Nelson in 1799 by Ferdinand IV (later King Ferdinand I of the Two Sicilies). Nelson was bestowed with the dukedom of Bronte in gratitude for his help the year before when the king had fled from Naples on Nelson's flagship during the Napoleonic invasion. Patrick Brunty from Ulster was a country parson in Yorkshire who was a great admirer of Nelson. In celebration of his hero's success he changed his name to Brontë and went on to father the Brontë sisters. Nelson himself apparently never managed to visit Maniace, but the title and estate passed, by the marriage of Nelson's niece, to the family of Viscount Bridport who sold the property in 1981 to the Bronte town council.

In the courtyard is a stone cross memorial to Nelson. The original 13th-century chapel, with the original portal, has a Byzantine *Madonna and Child*, two charming primitive reliefs of the *Annunciation*, and two 15th-century paintings. In the barn, where the roof has been restored, there are walkways above excavations of an older church. The house retains its appearance from the days when it was the residence of Alexander Hood who lived here from 1873 until just before the Second World War: it has lovely tiled floors and English wallpaper.

The delightful gardens, also designed by Hood (with palm trees, planted in 1912, magnolias, cypresses and box hedges), can also be visited. The Scottish writer William Sharp, who was once considered a father of the Celtic Renaissance and published under the pseudonym Fiona Macleod, died here in 1905 aged 55. He is buried beneath an Iona cross in the cemetery (*shown on request*).

Between Bronte and Randazzo the landscape is barren, with numerous volcanic deposits. The countryside, studded with little farmhouses built of black lava, is used for grazing and the cultivation of vineyards. There is a large lava stream of 1832 near Maletto, whose sandstone cliff called Pizzo Filicia (1140m) is the highest sedimentary rock on Etna (views). The vineyards in this region produce excellent red and white wines (*Etna rosso* and *Etna bianco*); the vines are grown close to the ground (known as the *alberello* method) for climatic reasons.

EAST OF RANDAZZO

To the east of Randazzo is the town of **Passopisciaro**. Beyond, near a massive lava flow (1981), oaks and chestnuts are now being replaced by vineyards and olive trees. Some of the prettiest scenery in the foothills of Etna can be seen here, with numerous handsome old russet-coloured houses (many of them now abandoned), excellent views of the volcano and, to the north, the wooded mountains beyond the Alcantara.

Castiglione di Sicilia is a quiet little town, in a stunning position perched on a crag. Founded by the survivors of the destruction of *Naxos*, wreaked by Dionysius of Syracuse in 396 BC, it was once a stronghold of Roger of Lauria, inveterate opponent of Frederick II of Aragon. Its many churches are all closed most of the time, a great pity because they contain remarkable works of art. The Chiesa Madre (San Pietro), however, whose magnificent 1105 apse is visible from outside, is usually open. Inside is an interesting meridian line traced by Temistocle Zona in 1882. Below it is the church of **Sant'Antonio** (key at wine shop in front), with an ingenious façade and campanile, in a charming little piazza. Inside it preserves delightful marble inlay work (1700) and four octagonal paintings by Giovanni Tuccari. In the sanctuary is an elaborate wooden confessional supporting a pulpit and a simple painted organ loft.

The **Rocca del Leone** (Castle of the Lion), which gives its name to the town, is worth the climb. Extremely interesting and of great antiquity, it is said to have been constructed in 750 BC by a Greek commander called Lion, even before the creation of the first colony at *Naxos*. The old stones are haunted by jackdaws and the views are peerless, over the rooftops to Mount Etna, the Alcantara Valley and the Peloritan Mountains. Castiglione is magical, especially on certain winter mornings when the air is crisp and clear, Etna is covered with snow, and the scent of woodsmoke lingers in the air; or on hot summer evenings, when the sky is like a bowl of deep blue Murano glass, and swifts screech and whirl untiringly among the steeples. Castiglione is twinned with Killarney in Ireland.

Below the town, off the Randazzo road (well signposted for the Cuba Bizantino), is another abandoned Byzantine-Arab building surrounded by vineyards, usually called the church of **Santa Domenica**. It is approached along a narrow country road beyond a railway line. Built of lava, probably in the late 8th century, it has an interesting plan and although very ruined the vault survives.

There are pinewoods and hazelnut groves near Linguaglossa, an important centre for excursions on Etna. **Piedimonte Etneo** is a village surrounded by fine citrus groves, with views of Taormina and Castelmola.

To the south is **Sant' Alfio**, near which is a famous giant chestnut tree, known as the *Castagno dei Cento Cavalli*, because its branches were reputed to be able to shelter 100 horses with their riders. It has a circumference of over 60m and is over 2,000 years old. The area was once a forest of chestnuts, nowadays largely coppiced for the valuable timber of the saplings. The numerous lovely old farmhouses in the district, built of lava, have almost all been abandoned. The fruit from the orchards in the district is sold on the streets in the autumn, together with chestnuts and wild fungi.

ACIREALE

Famous for exquisite almond confectionery, the sound of church bells, and the stubbornness of its people, Acireale is a beautiful and atmospheric little city, perched between Etna and the sea on a cliff of lava, verdant with lemon trees and Mediterranean maquis, called the Timpa. The maze of tiny jasmine-scented streets in the centre is often used as a film set. The surroundings are rich in mineral-water springs which have been exploited since Roman times for health cures. The city is particularly interesting for its Baroque buildings, erected after the earthquake of 1693. In 1642, Philip IV of Spain had decreed it to be a royal city; thanks to this status, Acireale gained considerable prestige. Acireale and eight other neighbouring towns and villages derive their name from the *Aci*, the mythical river which came into being on the death of Acis, the shepherd beloved by Galatea and killed by the Cyclops Polyphemus.

EXPLORING ACIREALE

The main Via Vittorio Emanuele leads up to Piazza Vigo. Here the church of **San Sebastiano** has a 17th-century façade in Spanish Baroque style with numerous statues and a delightful frieze of cherubs with garlands, considered by some to be the loveliest in Sicily. The balustrade and statues are by Giovanni Battista Marino (1754). Entered by the side door, the **Museo Basilica San Sebastiano** (*open 9–1; closed Mon*) houses (partly in the old crypt) a collection of paintings, wooden statues, and embroidered silk priests' robes.

On the other side of the Piazza Vigo, with fine palm trees and two charming little kiosks, is the large Neoclassical Palazzo Pennisi di Floristella, belonging to the foremost aristocratic family of the city, which now offers accommodation (*see below p. 433*). Beyond, the main streets of the town meet at the elegant **Piazza Duomo**. Here is the 17th-century Municipio with splendid balconies supported by grotesque figures, and the basilica of Santi Pietro e Paolo, with an asymmetric early 18th-century façade and just one bell-tower, instead of the two which were originally planned. The 17th-century **cattedrale** (Acireale has been a diocese since 1844) has a neo-Gothic façade which was added at the beginning of this century by Giovanni Battista Basile, and an interesting early 19th-century meridian line in the transept. It is dedicated both to the Madonna and the patron St Venera, a Roman martyr. At the east end are 18th-century frescoes by the painter Pier Paolo Vasta, although the best place to admire the work of this much-loved local artist is at the church of **Santa Maria del Suffragio** in Via Romeo, where a dazzling series of frescoes carried out in 1750 can be seen. There are more of his frescoes at the church of **San Camillo** in Via Galatea, called the 'church of the women' by the local people, because the theme chosen by Vasta for the frescoes was women of the Old Testament, such as Bathsheba, Judith, Abigail, and Rebekah. Vasta is noted for his soft pastel colours; his tender pinky-reds and mauves are unmistakable, as are the graceful dancing movements of his subjects.

Self portrait (c. 1763) by Vito D'Anna, in the collections of the Accademia Zelantea, Acireale.

Opposite the cathedral, Via Cavour leads to the church of **San Domenico**, which is both graceful and dramatic, close to the large 17th-century **Palazzo Musmeci** with an unusual curving façade and pretty windows. At no. 15 Via Marchese di San Giuliano is the **Accademia Zelantea** (*open Mon–Fri 10–1 & 3.30–6.30; Sat 10–1*) a handsome building of 1915. The Academy was founded in 1671, and the library in 1716. It now possesses a fine collection of artworks, a selection being displayed here, and some 150,000 volumes, one of the most important of its kind on the island.

A surprising and lovely walk follows Via Romeo from the cathedral, down to the perilous main road, which can be crossed, then down the many steps of the picturesque Strada delle Chiazzette through the Timpa nature reserve (run by the Azienda Forestale) to **Santa Maria la Scala**, a tiny fishing village. There are many springs of sweet water down here at sea level: the fishermen's wives were washerwomen, using the steps to carry their baskets of laundry up and down.

The **sulphur baths** of Santa Venera are at the south end of town in a park overlooking the Timpa; water and volcanic mud are used for treating various ailments. The spa building is of 1873, and was visited by Wagner. Just south of Acireale, in the district of Reitana, a Roman spa has been brought to light, and at Capomulini are the remains of a temple perhaps dedicated to Venus.

The coast south of Acireale

South of Acireale is **Acitrezza**, a fishing village which was described by Giovanni Verga in his masterpiece, *I Malavoglia (The House by the Medlar Tree)*. In the sea in front of the tiny harbour, with its boats in various stages of construction or repair, are seven lava-stone rocks called the Faraglioni del Ciclope, now protected as a marine nature reserve run by the University of Catania (*T: 095 7117322*). According to legend, the rocks are those thrown by the Cyclops Polyphemus at Ulysses, who had just blinded him. They are the result of an ancient eruption of Mt Etna, and represent the fragmentary rim of a crater. On one of the rocks, **Isola Lachea**, is a small house used by the University of Catania, which runs the reserve. The rocks have surprisingly varied fauna (as does the sea around them), including a tiny population of an endemic lizard, found only here, *Lacerta situla faraglionensis*.

    Aci Castello is a dormitory town on the coast close to Catania, but it still has a small quay with colourful fishing boats beneath the castle (*open summer 9–1.30 & 3.30–7; winter 9–2 & 3–5*) on a splendid basalt rock which rises sharply out of the sea, with interesting formations of 'pillow lava'. The town was covered with lava in the eruption of 1169. It was rebuilt (1297) by Roger of Lauria, the rebel admiral of Frederick II of Aragon. Frederick succeeded in capturing it by building a wooden siege tower of equal height alongside. A long flight of steps built in the lava leads up to the entrance to the small museum, with mineralogical, palaeontological and archaeological material, including underwater finds. According to Giovanni Verga, the castle is haunted by the ghost of an unfortunate lady, Donna Violante. From the terrace there is a fine view of the Faraglioni del Ciclope in front of Acitrezza. Further south, on a cove, is **Ognina**, now a suburb of Catania, perhaps the *Portus Ulixis* of Virgil's *Aeneid*, where Ulysses left his twelve ships on the fatal occasion when he met the Cyclops. The bay, originally much bigger, was half-filled with lava in the 14th century.

THE LEMON RIVIERA

To the north of Acireale the beautiful, fertile coastline is known as the **Riviera dei Limoni**; lemon groves are planted along the coast all the way to Taormina. The main road runs through **Giarre**, still paved in lava, where ceramics and Sicilian folk art are sold. The town has unexpectedly grand eclectic buildings and the huge church of Sant'Isidoro Agricolo (1794), the patron saint, with an impressive dome and two bell-towers. The ancient *Callipolis*, Giarre was a suburb of Mascali until 1815; the name derives from *giare*, the terracotta storage jars where the tenth part of the entire agricultural production of Mascali was stored, before being sent to the bishop of Catania, by ancient right also the baron of Mascali. This meant enormous quantities of wine, olive oil and wheat. Separated from Giarre by the railway line, on the sea, with an elegant yachting harbour and another imposing church, is **Riposto**, eternal rival of Giarre. The harbour was once used for shipping the baron of Mascali's wine to Catania; the local craftsmen are still able boat-builders.

    Mascali was completely rebuilt after being covered by the lava stream during the November 1928 eruption of Etna. **Fiumefreddo** takes its name (cold river) from the short river (only 1800m) close by, with abundant, but icy cold, waters, which enters the sea at **Marina di Cottone**. The area is a nature reserve (*WWF, 40 Via Diana, Fiumefreddo, T: 095 646277, www.riservewwfsicilia.it*), a protected area since 1984, because of the papyrus which grows along its course. This is one of only two rivers in Europe where the plant can be found growing spontaneously; the other is the River Ciane near Syracuse.

CALTAGIRONE

Caltagirone is one of the most important inland towns of the island. The old town, with dark, weathered Baroque and Art Nouveau buildings, is built on three hills, to which it owes its irregular plan and narrow streets, and its medieval name *Regina dei Monti*, or Queen of the Mountains. Traces of one or more Bronze Age and Iron Age settlements have been found in the area. During the Greek colonization, the town came under the influence of Gela. The present name is of Arabic origin (*kalat*, castle and *gerun*, caves). The town was conquered by Genoa in 1030 and destroyed by the 1693 earthquake. The old centre of Caltagirone, with its Baroque architecture, is a World Heritage Site. It has always also been renowned for ceramic ware thanks to a rich vein of high quality clay in the area. The Arabs opened many potteries here, introducing new techniques, colours and designs, and today there are numerous artisans' workshops here, and a prestigious School of Ceramics. The use of majolica tiles and terracotta finials is a characteristic of the local architecture.

EXPLORING CALTAGIRONE

Piazza Umberto

In the central Piazza Umberto a bank occupies the Neoclassical Monte delle Prestanze, erected by Natale Bonaiuto in 1783. The **duomo**, dedicated to St Julian, was completely transformed in 1920. In the south aisle are altarpieces by the Vaccaro, a 19th-century family of local painters, and in the south transept an unusual carved Crucifix attributed to Giovannello Matinati (1500). Beyond is the **Corte Capitaniale**, a delightful one-storey building decorated in the 16th–17th centuries by Antonuzzo and Gian Domenico Gagini. In Piazza del Municipio is the Neoclassical façade of the former opera house, which serves as an entrance to the **Galleria Luigi Sturzo**, a monumental building inaugurated in 1959. The town hall has a fine façade of 1895.

From Piazza del Municipio, Via Principe Amedeo returns to Piazza Umberto past (left) the **Chiesa del Collegio**, with a lovely façade decorated with statues, visible below the road. Built at the end of the 16th century, it contains a painting of the *Annunciation* by Antonio Catalano, and a *Pietà* by Filippo Paladini.

Adjacent to Piazza del Municipio rises the impressive long flight of 142 steps known as the **Scala Santa Maria del Monte**. It has colourful majolica risers, predominantly yellow, green and blue, on a white ground. They were designed and completed in 1606, and altered in the 19th century. It is a climb (past numerous little ceramic workshops) up to Santa Maria del Monte, once the Chiesa Madre. The Baroque façade is by Francesco Battaglia and Natale Bonaiuto. The campanile, by Venanzio Marvuglia, is one of the very few bell-towers which can be climbed in Sicily. A little spiral staircase, which gets narrower and lower as it reaches the top, leads to the bell-chamber, from which there is a fine view. The church owns a *Madonna* attributed to the workshop of Domenico Gagini. Further up the hill is the attractive former church of San Nicola, in a maze of medieval streets.

THE GAGINI FAMILY

A prominent family of Italian sculptors, metalworkers and architects, who managed their workshops along medieval lines, frequently collaborating on different tasks, the Gagini family was active in several parts of Italy from the 15th century until well into the 1800s. Examples of their work can be found in almost every town of any size in Sicily, as well as many villages. Domenico Gagini (c. 1420–92) was the most outstanding of the early artists, possibly a disciple of Brunelleschi. He was born in Bissone (Switzerland), worked for a time in Genoa, notably in the cathedral, and brought skills perfected in Lombardy to Palermo, where his son, Antonello Gagini (1478–1536) was born. Trained in his father's workshops, Antonello became the head of the family in Sicily. He was probably briefly an assistant to Michelangelo in Rome. His best-known works, carefully composed statues of the Madonna, also show the influence of Francesco Laurana. Less well documented is his work as an architect. Another talented member of the family, Antonello's near contemporary, was Antonio Gagini (fl. 1504–32) who also travelled originally from Genoa to Sicily, and whose finest work can be seen in Trapani. Antonello's son, Antonino (fl. 1537–81) continued to maintain the family's virtual monopoly on decorative religious art commissions on the island, although himself with less confident artistic talent. One of Antonello's younger brothers, Gian Domenico Gagini (c. 1503–c. 1567), was also a sculptor of note, and his son Antonuzzo (fl. 1576–c.1606) went on to collaborate with his own child, also named Gian Domenico, who was probably born in Caltagirone, where Antonuzzo died. Nibilio Gagini (fl. 1583–1607) was raised in Palermo, and became a much sought-after goldsmith and medal engraver, a craft also practised around the same time by Giuseppe Gagini (fl. 1575–1610).

Via Luigi Sturzo

From near the foot of the steps, Via Luigi Sturzo leads past the church of Santa Maria degli Angeli with a 19th-century façade, behind which the façade of **Santa Chiara** can be seen, by Rosario Gagliardi (1743–48), which contains majolica decorations. Further uphill is Palazzo della Magnolia (no. 76), an elaborate Art Nouveau house.

Just beyond, the 19th-century façade of **San Domenico** faces that of San Salvatore by Natale Bonaiuto (1794). It has a pretty white and gold octagonal interior with a Gaginesque *Madonna*. A modern chapel contains the tomb of Luigi Sturzo. The politician and priest Luigi Sturzo (1871–1959) is a much-honoured native of the town. He advocated local autonomy and he improved social conditions here while he was mayor. He was a founder of the national Partito Popolare in 1919, and remained secretary of the party until 1923. This was the first Catholic political party, a forerunner of the Christian Democrat Party which came into being in 1942, and was to remain at the centre of Italian political life for much of the 20th century. Via Sturzo continues uphill past the former Ospedale delle Donne, an attractive building, now the Galleria di Arte Moderna e Contemporanea. The road ends at **San Giorgio**, rebuilt in 1699, which contains a beautiful little *Trinity*, attributed to Rogier van der Weyden. From the terrace (left) there is a fine view of the countryside.

San Giacomo

From Piazza del Municipio the handsome Corso Vittorio Emanuele passes several fine palaces, and the Art Nouveau post office (still in use) on the way to the basilica of San Giacomo, rebuilt in 1708; at the side a pretty flight of steps ascends through the base of the campanile. In the interior, above the west door, the marble coat-of-arms of the city is by Gian Domenico Gagini. In the left aisle is a blue and brown portal (formerly belonging to the baptistery), and a blue and gold arch in the Cappella del Sacramento by Antonuzzo Gagini. In the left transept is the charming little Portale delle Reliquie, also by Antonuzzo, with bronze doors by Agostino Sarzana. In the chapel to the left of the sanctuary (behind glass doors) is a silver urn (illuminated on request), the masterpiece of Nibilio Gagini (signed 1604). In the sanctuary is a processional statue of *St James* by Vincenzo Archifel (1518) protected by a bronze canopy of 1964 (the original gilded throne is kept in the museum). This and the urn are carried through the streets of the town in a procession on 25th July.

The Museo Civico and Via Roma

To the south of Piazza Umberto is the Museo Civico (*open 9.30–1.30; Sun 9.30–12.30; Tues, Wed, Sat, Sun also 4–7; closed Mon*), housed in a massive building, originally a prison (Carcere Borbonico), built in 1782 by Natale Bonaiuto with an interior courtyard and double columns. On the stairs are architectural fragments and on the landing, four 19th-century terracotta vases by Bongiovanni Vaccaro. Beyond a room with modern local ceramics, another room contains the gilded Throne of St James (16th century, by Scipione di Guido; the statue is kept in the church of San Giacomo), a bishop's 19th-century sedan chair, and a Christmas crib. There is a room dedicated to the works (paintings and ceramics) by the local artists Giuseppe, Francesco and Mario Vaccaro. There are also some 16th–17th-century paintings (including *Christ in the Garden* by Epifano Rossi), and two cherubs by Bongiovanni Vaccaro. On the top floor are modern works. Beside the museum is the fine façade, also by Bonaiuto, of Sant'Agata (*closed*).

Via Roma continues south from Piazza Umberto to **Ponte San Francesco**, an 18th-century viaduct, which has pretty majolica decoration and a good view of Palazzo Sant'Elia below the bridge. The road continues past the piazza in front of the simple church of **San Francesco d'Assisi**, founded in 1226 but rebuilt after 1693. It contains paintings by Francesco and Giuseppe Vaccaro and a Gothic sacristy. Behind the church (reached by Via Sant'Antonio and Via Mure Antiche) is San Pietro with a 19th-century neo-Gothic majolica façade.

Via Roma continues past the **Tondo Vecchio**, an exedra built by Francesco Battaglia in 1766. Beside the church of San Francesco di Paola a road leads up past the Teatro

Politeama Ingrassia, with interesting Art Nouveau details, to the entrance gate of the delightful public gardens laid out in 1846 by Giovanni Battista Basile. The exotic trees include palms, cedars, ficus and huge pines. There is a long balustrade on Via Roma decorated with pretty ceramics from the workshop of Enrico Vella, and throughout the gardens are copies of terracotta vases and figures by Giuseppe Vaccaro and Giacomo Bongiovanni. There is also a 17th-century fountain by Camillo Camilliani and a decorative bandstand. The palace of Benedetto Ventimiglia, also on Via Roma, is preceded by a colourful ceramic terrace.

The Museo della Ceramica
Open 9–6.30.
The Museo della Ceramica is situated in the gardens, entered through the elaborate **Teatrino** (1792) by Natale Bonaiuto. From the top of the steps there is a good view beyond a war memorial and some palm trees to the hills (with the town on the left). The museum contains a fine collection of Sicilian ceramics from the prehistoric era to the 19th century. In the corridor to the right are 17th- and 19th-century ceramics from Caltagirone. Beyond a room with 18th- and 19th-century works, the archaeological material is displayed, including Hellenistic and Roman terracotta heads and figurines. Prehistoric pottery from San Mauro and Castelluccio is also exhibited. In case 26 is a krater depicting a potter at his wheel protected by Athena (5th century BC). Case 27 contains the Russo Perez collection, including 5th-century BC red- and black-figure vases.

In the courtyard, bases used in various potteries from the 11th–13th centuries are exhibited. In the large room on the left are Arab-Norman stuccoes from San Giuliano, 10th–12th-century Arab–Norman pottery, and medieval works.

On a lower level is a large hall with 17th–19th-century ceramics from Palermo, Trapani, Caltagirone and Sciacca, including blue enamelled vases and pharmacy jars. The fine collection of terracotta figures includes works by Giuseppe Bongiovanni (1809–89) and Giacomo Vaccaro (1847–1931). The hall is also used for exhibitions.

Via Santa Maria di Gesù leads south from the public gardens to (10mins) the church of Santa Maria di Gesù (1422), with a charming *Madonna* by Antonello Gagini.

AROUND CALTAGIRONE

Close to Caltagirone is an oak wood, the **Bosco di Santo Pietro**, now protected as a nature reserve run by the Azienda Forestale (*For information T: 0933 34191*). You may see (or hear) the great spotted woodpecker, and there are still many cork oaks.

North of Caltagirone is the clean and tidy **Mirabella Imbaccari**, famous for the lace and embroidery still made here. You can see their work at the Mostra del Ricamo e del Tombolo (*open 9–1 & 3.30–7.30; closed Mon*), in the central Via Alcide De Gasperi.

Grammichele, 15km east of Caltagirone, was founded by Carlo Maria Carafa Branciforte, Prince of Butera, to house the people of Occhiolà, and destroyed in 1693. The ruins of the old town, c. 2km away, are now a very interesting archaeological park (*open 9–5, until dusk in summer*). The new town was built to a concentric hexagonal plan, around the spacious central six-sided Piazza Carafa with an array of honey-coloured palaces between the six roads. Here the weather-worn, unfinished Chiesa Madre begun in 1723 by Andrea Amato and dedicated to St Michael Archangel, who protects against earthquakes, stands next to the elegant red and gold Palazzo Comunale (Carlo Sada, 1896). The **Museo Civico** (*open 9–1 & 4–6*) has a well-arranged, small collection of finds from excavations in the district, begun in 1891 by Paolo Orsi who identified a pre-Greek settlement at Terravecchia. Exhibits include prehistoric bronzes and Bronze Age ceramics, vases found in tombs (6th century BC), terracotta votive statuettes and 15th–16th-century majolica from Occhiolà. In front of the town hall is the Art Déco Teatro Intelisano (1940s), the balconies supported by ledges reproducing the faces of great personalities of the past, including Rossini and Leonardo da Vinci.

Vizzini

Further east, Vizzini nestles among the Hyblaean Mountains. On the summit of two hills, it occupies the site of ancient *Bidis*, recorded by Cicero. In the central **Piazza Umberto** is a stairway decorated with majolica tiles like the one in Caltagirone, leading up to the church of Sant'Agata (14th and 18th centuries). In the square is an unfinished 18th-century palace which used to be owned by Giovanni Verga's family: the great writer was born in Vizzini and most of his works are set here or in the vicinity, such as *Cavalleria Rusticana*, *La Lupa* (the she-wolf), and *Mastro-don Gesualdo* (*see p. 403*). Close by, in the 18th-century Palazzo Costa, no. 8 Via Vespucci, is the **Museo**

The abandoned homes of tannery workers near Vizzini.

Immaginario Verghiano (*T: 0933 966346 to request visit*), dedicated to the writer, with a collection of his photographs (he was a keen amateur photographer), and various memorabilia.

From Piazza Umberto, Via San Gregorio Magno winds its way up to the Chiesa Madre, dedicated to St Gregory the Great, who is the patron saint of Vizzini. His statue stands on a column by the side entrance into the church, which still shows some surviving pre-earthquake fragments, such as the splendid 15th-century Gothic-Catalan portal on the right side. The interior is decorated with Baroque stuccoes; in the south aisle are two paintings by Filippo Paladini: the *Martyrdom of St Laurence* (second altar), and the *Madonna of Mercy* (fourth altar). Vizzini is a prosperous farming community, renowned for its excellent sheep's milk cheese, olive oil, prickly pears and durum wheat. In the past leather was tanned at Vizzini, along the little River Dirillo just outside the town. Now the workshops and the vats, many carved out of the rock, and the homes of the workers, all long since abandoned (*pictured opposite*), are being repaired and transformed into a cultural centre called 'a Cunziria (the Tannery). The mountains around Vizzini are ancient volcanoes, now rich pastures or wheat fields, where flocks of ravens still fly.

Licodia Eubea

Situated on a crest overlooking to the south the River Dirillo, Licodia Eubea was probably founded in the 7th century BC as a sub-colony of *Leontinoi* (*Lentini*). In the Middle Ages it had a formidable castle, of which few traces remain today—it was destroyed by the 1693 earthquake. In the 15th century the town and castle became the property of the Catalan Santapau family. In recent years there has been considerable archaeological research in the area; the finds are displayed in the **Museo Civico Antonino Di Vita**, where besides the objects of Greek origin, there are interesting traces of the Sicel settlement which preceded their arrival.

Militello in Val di Catania

Thanks to the munificence of its prince, Don Francesco Branciforte, Militello in Val di Catania is a splendid little town with remarkable Baroque buildings designated a World Heritage Site. Don Francesco and his wife Donna Johanna of Austria, in the early 17th century, wanted their town to be the cultural centre of this part of Sicily, pouring money into public works, sponsoring religious communities, and inviting artists, architects and writers of fame to their court. The 22 lovely churches here contain paintings by Vito D'Anna, Olivio Sozzi, Pietro Ruzzolone and others.

The main square, Piazza Municipio, houses the great abbey and church of San Benedetto, now the town hall, modelled on the Benedictine Monastery of St Nicholas, Catania. Inside the church, the 18th-century carved walnut choir-stalls are of particular interest.

In Via Umberto, in the crypt of the Chiesa Madre, is the **Museo di San Nicolò** (*open 9–1 & 5–8; Tues closed; also guided tours of the town on request*) with 17th- and 18th-century works, including vestments, church silver, sculpture and paintings. In the treasury of the church of Santa Maria della Stella (*T: 095 655329 for opening hours*) there is an altarpiece in enamelled terracotta by Andrea Della Robbia (1487) with the *Nativity*, *Annunciation to the Shepherds*, and (in the predella) a *Pietà* and the *Twelve Apostles*. Another altarpiece, the **Retablo di San Pietro**, is thought to be the work of Antonello da Messina.

Another interesting museum has been opened in the ex-prison of Militello, near the Branciforte Castle at no. 21 Via Porta della Terra, the **Museo Civico Sebastiano Guzzone** (*open 9–1 & 3–7*), housing a collection of paintings, archaeological finds, medieval books, and the city archives. The half-ruined Santa Maria la Vetere, to the south of the historic centre, is a national monument. There is a porch supported on lions and a magnificent doorway of 1506.

Not far from Militello is **Scordia**, world-famous for its production of blood oranges. In the apse of the church of Sant'Antonio di Padova is an exceptional 18th-century floor of coloured tiles from Caltagirone, now rather fragmentary, showing a pelican shedding its own blood to feed its young, a symbolic rendering of the Church and the faithful.

Mineo

A small town on an ancient settlement founded by Doucetius, king of the Sicels, in the 5th century BC, Mineo was later occupied by the Greeks and Romans. High-quality olive oil is produced here. The church of the Collegio and Sant'Agrippina have 18th-century stuccoes. Behind the church of San Pietro at no. 40 Piazza Buglio, is the house where the writer Luigi Capuana (1835–1915) lived, now a museum: the **Biblioteca-museo Luigi Capuana** (*open 8–2*). A close friend of Giovanni Verga, Capuana wrote various works both in Italian and Sicilian, including tales for children. The museum holds his books, manuscripts, and photographs, and the library of the Capuchin monastery, with 16th- and 17th-century volumes. The medieval castle on the summit of one of the two hills of Mineo is now a romantically crumbling ruin. Near the town is a small group of caves called Grotte di Caratabia, where some Sicel graffiti of the 5th century BC have been found, representing a hunting scene with horses, hunters and their servants, and deer. The caves have now been acquired by the local council: the area will be restored and eventually opened to the public.

Palagonia

Palagonia is in a district well known for its oranges and tangerines. Outside the town is the 7th-century Byzantine church of **Santa Febronia**, with abundant traces of frescoes inside. Surrounded by orange groves is a national monument, the little basilica of **San Giovanni**, now believed to be a Cistercian structure. Palagonia was the ancient Sicel town of *Palica*, close to a sacred lake with two small geysers emitting gases (no longer visible since being exploited for industrial purposes), said to be the *Palikes*, twin gods who guaranteed justice; the spot became a sanctuary for runaway slaves. The town is on the edge of the fertile Plain of Catania, known to the Greeks as the Laestrygonian Fields, the home of the cannibal Laestrygones. Its vast groves are watered by the Simeto and its tributaries, the Dittaino and the Gornalunga.

PRACTICAL INFORMATION

GETTING AROUND

• **By train:** Catania railway station is at Piazza Papa Giovanni XXIII, T: 095 532719, www.trenitalia.com), for all services, on the line to Palermo via Enna and on the coastal line between Syracuse and Messina.

The Circumetnea, opened in 1898, provides a classic rail trip, but you need to take two trains to circumnavigate Etna. Circumetnea station (T: 095 541111, www.circumetnea.it) is at the top of Via Caronda, for the line which runs around the foot of Etna, to Linguaglossa.

From Catania (Borgo station) to Randazzo (in c. 2hrs), continuing less frequently to Giarre (in c. 1hr); from there the direct return (poor connections) may be made by the mainline train on the Messina–Syracuse line.

All trains stop at **Acireale**, which is on the main line.

Caltagirone (station in Piazza della Repubblica) is on the Catania–Caltanissetta line, it has services to Catania in c. 2hrs. Several towns around Caltagirone are served by the railway, but sometimes (**Vizzini**, **Mineo**, **Licodia**, **Militello**) the stations are a long way from the towns.

• **By bus:** In **Catania** an efficient network of yellow city buses is run by AMT (T: 095 7360111, www.amt.ct.it). Inter-city services: SAIS (T: 095 536168, www.saistrasporti.it) from 181 Via D'Amico run buses about every hour via the motorway to Palermo (2hrs 40mins) and Messina (1hr

30mins); less frequently via the motorway to Enna (1hr 30mins) and **Caltanissetta** (1hr 35mins); to Syracuse (c. 1hr); Taormina (45 mins–1hr); Agrigento (2hrs 30mins) and Noto (2hrs 30mins). Most of these also stop at the airport. Interbus (T: 095 532716) has services to Floridia, Solarino, Avola, Noto, Syracuse and Pachino.

AST (220 Via Sturzo, T: 095 7461096) run a bus from Piazza Giovanni XXIII outside the station to Gela, **Caltagirone**, and the province of Ragusa. AST also runs a daily bus (in c. 2 hrs) to the **Rifugio Sapienza**, departing early morning. An extra service runs in July and August, leaving Piazza Giovanni XXIII in the later morning for **Nicolosi** where a connecting bus continues to the **Rifugio Sapienza**. A bus returns to Catania in the afternoon.

There are frequent bus services from Catania to all the towns and villages on the slopes of **Etna**.

Buses run by Etna Trasporti (181 Via D'Amico, T: 095 532716) to Piazza Armerina (2hrs 30mins) and Aidone, Lentini, **Francofonte**, **Vizzini**, Giarratana, Ragusa, Giardini Naxos and Taormina.

AST T: 095 7461096, Buda T: 095 931905 and Etna Trasporti T: 095 532716) run services from **Catania** and **Giarre** and to the towns and villages in and around **Acireale**.

Caltagirone is the transport hub for the area; buses run by AST (T: 0933 54628) leave from the railway station to Catania and Piazza Armerina; to Palermo and Gela (SAIS), to Catania and to Ragusa and its province (Etna Trasporti, T: 095 532716).

Catania
APT, 10 Via Cimarosa, T: 095 7306211, www.apt.catania.it; for information on the whole province; 172 via Vittorio Emanuele, T: 095 7425573, www.turismo.catania.it
Cultural events: www.etnafest.it
Museums: www.turismo.catania.it/aptct-new/Musei/
Mount Etna
Funivia dell'Etna (cableway station), T: 095 914141 & 095 914142; Parco Regionale dell'Etna: Via Etnea 107, Nicolosi, T: 095 821111, www.parcoetna.ct.it: Parco Trekking (guided walking tours): 107/a, Via Etnea, T: 095 821111, www.parcoetna.ct.it: SITAS information offices: 45 Piazza Vittorio Emanuele, T: 095 911158; also at the cableway station, T: 095 916356: Guide Alpine (mountain guides), 49 Via Etnea, Nicolosi, T: 095 7914755; Guide Alpine (mountain guides), 24 Piazza Santa Caterina, Linguaglossa, T: 095 647833; Etna Trekking (guided walking tours), 15 Piazza Calì Poeta, Linguaglossa, T: 095 647592. From May–Oct excursions are organized in 4WD vehicles from Piano Provenzana (currently suspended for repairs) by STAR, 233 Via Roma, Linguaglossa, T: 095 643180.
Acireale 15 Via Oreste Scionti, T: 095 892129, www.comune.acireale.com
Adrano c/o Municipio, Via Spampinato, T: 095 7606111, www.comune.adrano.ct.it; Via Duca di Misterbianco, T: 095 7698849.

Bronte Pro Loco: 8 Via D'Annunzio, T: 095 691035, www.comune.bronte.ct.it
Caltagirone 3 Via Volta Libertini (off Via Emanuele Taranto), T: 0933 53809, www.comune.caltagirone.ct.it
Licodia Eubea c/o Municipio, Piazza Garibaldi, T: 0933 963000.
Linguaglossa Pro Loco: 5 Piazza Annunziata, T: 095 643094, www.prolocolinguaglossa.it
Maniace Pro Loco: 59/b Corso Margherita, T: 095 690823.
Militello Pro Loco: 17 Cortile Alemanna, T: 095 655155.
Mineo Pro Loco: 34 Via Umberto, T: 0933 980082.
Motta Sant'Anastasia Pro Loco: 42 Piazza Umberto, T: 095 308161, www.prolocomottasantanastasia.it
Nicolosi 63 Via Garibaldi, T: 095 911505, www.aast-nicolosi.it, www.comune.nicolosi.ct.it
Paternò Pro Loco: 11 Piazza Indipendenza, T: 095 623252.
Randazzo 51 Via Umberto, T: 095 444101, www.comune.randazzo.ct.it; Pro Loco: 17 Piazza Municipio, T: 095 799186.
Riposto Pro Loco: 56 Corso Italia, T: 095 934549, www.prolocoriposto.it
Sant'Alfio Pro Loco: 14 Piazza Duomo, T: 095 968772, www.prolocosantalfio.it
Scordia Pro Loco: 11 Via Vittorio Emanuele, T: 095 7936082.
Trecastagni Pro Loco: 173–145 Via Principe Umberto, T: 095 7936082, www.trecastagni.it
Vizzini Pro Loco, 47 Via Roma, T: 0933 965905, www.vizzinidascoprire.it
Zafferana Etnea Pro Loco: 1 Piazza Sturzo, T: 095 7082825.

HOTELS

Catania

€€€ **Romano Palace**. South of town at the Playa Beach, pool, comfortable rooms, good restaurant. Viale Kennedy, T: 095 5967111, www.romanopalace.it

€€€ **Excelsior Grand**. In the heart of the modern city, fitness centre. 39 Piazza Giovanni Verga, T: 0957 7476111, www.thi.it

€€€ **Una Hotel Palace**. Prestigious 19th-century hotel newly renovated, luxurious rooms, good restaurant, courteous staff. 218 Via Etnea, T: 095 2505111, www.unahotels.it

€€€ **Katane Palace**. Elegant 19th-century building, central, with a good restaurant and garage parking. 110 via Finocchiaro Aprile, T: 095 7470702, www.katanepalace.it

€€ **Villa del Bosco**. Turn-of-the-20th-century elegance, good restaurant called *Il Canile*—the Dog Kennel. 62 Via del Bosco, T: 095 7335100, www.hotelvilladelbosco.it

€€ **Del Duomo**. Delightful hotel tucked away between the cathedral and the University. 28 Via Etnea, T: 095 2503177, www.hoteldelduomo.it

€€ **Il Principe**. This new hotel, once a palazzo near Via Crociferi, the Baroque heart of Catania, has very comfortable rooms, and a fitness centre with Turkish bath. 24 Via Alessi, T: 095 2500345, www.ilprincipehotel.com

€€ **La Ville**. Small but luxurious, a hotel which also has self-catering apartments. 15 Via Monteverdi, T: 095 7465230, www.rhlaville.it

€€ **Liberty Hotel**. Beautifully restored in perfect Art Nouveau style, the bathrooms are gorgeous; the suites have frescoed ceilings. No restaurant. Car park. 40 Via San Vito, T: 095 311651.

€€ **Novecento**. Art Nouveau elegance, just behind the Opera House. No restaurant. 35 Via Ventimiglia, T: 095 310488, www.hotelnovecentocatania.it

€€ **Valentino**. Only 8 huge rooms with frescoed ceilings, in a run-down part of town. Picturesque. 39 Piazza Spirito Santo, T: 095 2503072, www.ilvalentino.net

€ **Gresi**. Family-run hotel, welcoming atmosphere. 28 Via Pacini, T: 095 322709.

€ **Rubens**. Large rooms with private bath, TV and air conditioning. Courteous management. 196 Via Etnea, T: 095 31707, www.rubenhotel.it

Acireale

€€ **Excelsior Palace Terme**. A converted pasta factory, comfortable and close to the centre, pool. 103 via delle Terme, T: 095 7688111

€€ **Aloha d'Oro**. Set in a park on the Timpa, dilapidated, but good restaurant. A steep path snakes its way down to the sea, for superb swimming; there are also 2 pools. 10 Viale Alcide De Gasperi, T: 095 7687001, www.hotel-aloha.com

€€ **Maugeri**. Very central. 27 Piazza Garibaldi, T: 095 608666, www.hotel-maugeri.it

€€ **Orizzonte**. Panoramic position, but out of town. Viale Cristoforo Colombo, T: 095 886006, www.hotelorizzonte.it

Aci Castello & Acitrezza

€€ **President Park**. On the hill overlooking Acitrezza; pool. 88 Via Litteri, T: 0957 116111, www.presidentparkhotel.com

€ **I Malavoglia**. In the heart of the village. 1 Via Provinciale, Acitrezza, T: 095

7117850, www.albergomalavoglia.it
€ **Park Hotel** Capomulini. On the sea, between Acitrezza and Acireale. Recently restored, pool, fitness centre and restaurant. 33 Via della Fiera Franca, T: 095 877511 f 095 877445, www.parkhotelcapomulini.it
€€ **Acitrezza Inn**. Simple but comfortable, all rooms have shower, TV and air conditioning; they also have apartments to rent. Via Livorno 97, T: 095 7117828, www.acitrezzainn.it

Caltagirone
€€€ **Villa Tasca**. Luxurious accommodation in this splendid old aristocratic villa, all rooms with private bath; pool, gardens, sauna, cycling track, horse-riding. Contrada Fontana Pietra, SP 37 km 11, T: 0933 22760, www.villatasca.it
€ **Villa San Mauro**. Modern hotel with good restaurant, breathtaking views of the city. 10 Via Porto Salvo, T: 0933 26500, www.framon-hotels.com

Ramacca
€ **Paradiso della Zagara**. Charming little Art Nouveau-style hotel, good restaurant. 4 Via Carducci, T: 095 653279.

Ragalna
€€ **Grande Albergo dell'Etna**. High up close to Rifugio Sapienza, this 1930s' hotel now belongs to the Etna Park organization and has been completely refurbished; good base for trekking. The astrophysical observatory is close by, phone to request visit (T: 095 7332111, www.ct.astro.it). Via Piano Vetore 1, Serra La Nave, T: 095 7971217.

Randazzo
€€€ **Parco Statella**. Gorgeous 18th-century villa surrounded by a park. The comfortable rooms were once the farm buildings. Very kind owners. 2–5 Via Montelaguardia, Località Montelaguardia, T: 095 924036, www.parcostatella.com
€€ **Monte Colla**. An out-of-the-way country house, which can only be reached by jeep (free transfer to/from Randazzo), good restaurant. Frazione Monte Colla, T: 348 1516352.
€ **Scrivano**. Very comfortable modern hotel, family-run, good restaurant. 121 Via Bonaventura, T: 095 921126, www.hotelscrivano.it

San Giovanni La Punta
€€ **Paradiso dell'Etna**. A beautiful little 1920s-style hotel, with garden, and excellent restaurant. 37 Via Viagrande, T: 095 7512409, www.paradisoetna.it

San Michele di Ganzaria
€ **Pomara**. An efficient, family-run hotel in an excellent position for touring central Sicily, pool. The restaurant serves marvellous local dishes, Sicilians come here from miles around, just for the food. 84 Via Vittorio Veneto, T: 0933 976976, www.hotelpomara.com

Zafferana Etnea
€ **Airone**. Out of town, on the fringe of the chestnut forest, pool.67 Via Cassone, T: 095 7081819.

BED & BREAKFAST

Catania
€ **Casa Conti**. In a central street. 78 Via Umberto, T: 095 2500058, www.casaconti.com
€ **Catania City Center**. In the old city. 103 Via Naumachia, T: 095 2246110, www.cataniacitycenter.com
€ **San Barnabà la Casa del Gelsomino**. Very central, beautiful rooms with en-suite baths, air condi-

tioning, nice breakfasts. 67 Via Santa Barbara, T: 095 311068.

€ **San Placido Inn**. Ideal position, have your breakfast on the terrace overlooking the sea. 3 Piazza San Placido, T: 095 315100, www.sanplacidoinn.com

€ **Stesicoro**. In a little alley where snow for the city was once stocked, near the Roman Amphitheatre. 7 Via Neve, T: 095 311178, www.bbstesicoro.it

€ **Like at Home**. A university professor's home, library, internet, English & German spoken. 66 Via Verdi, T: 095 7158576, www.bedandbreakfast.it/likeathome

€ **Teatro Bellini.** English spoken at this fashionable place in a happening part of town. 30 via Sant'Orsola, T: 392 7654144 or 347 0994545, www.bbteatrobellini.i.

Acireale

€ **Convento San Biagia.** Simple accommodation in a covent. 20 Piazza San Biagio, T: 095 601377, conventosbiagio@mail.gte.it

€ **Palazzo Pennisi di Floristella**. The palazzo of the local prince. 16 Piazza Vigo, T: 095 7633079.

€ **Villa Terra di Aci**. Very comfortable, lovely terrace and sumptuous Sicilian breakfasts, next to the famous Sanctuary. Longish walk into town. 2–6 Via del Santuario Loreto, T: 095 7633011, www.villaterradiaci.it

€ **Le Campane del Duomo**. In a lovely old district. 30 Via Santo Stefano, T: 095 7633026.

Castiglione di Sicilia

€ **Le Chevalier** (Vincenzo Fallone). In the main square, a café and pastry shop with lovely rooms. 12 Piazza Lauria, T: 0942 984679.

€ **La Dispensa dell'Etna**. Goodvalue. Comfortable rooms over a wine shop, delicious meals served on request. 2 Piazza Sant'Antonio, T: 0942 984258, www.ladispensadelletna.com

Pozzillo

€ **Pizzillo**. Charming village close to the sea, under the Timpa. 34 Via Ercole Patti, T: 095 7641414.

Scillichenti

€ **Casa Giulia**. Close to the sea; old winery surrounded by lemon groves, organic food. 39 Via D'Amico, T: 095 886733, www.annba.it/bb/casagiulia

Tremestieri Etneo

€ **Casa Vinciguerra**. In a small town on the lower slopes of Etna, the modern home of a university professor and a tour guide who also a wonderful cook. French and English spoken. 70 Via Guglielmino, T: 095 71251723.

Viagrande

€ **Cucina del Sole**. Eleonora Consoli is a well-known expert on Sicilian cuisine. In her beautiful home in the old town of Viagrande, she also offers cookery courses; French and English spoken. 9 Via Conte Mare, T: 095 7890116.

ROOMS & APARTMENTS TO RENT

Catania

€€ **Angiolucci**. Comfortable mini-apartments for short-term rental, in central 19th-century palace. 1 Via Pantano, T: 095 3529420, www.angiolucciresidence.com

€€ **Foresteria Palazzo Biscari**. 1 Comfortable apartments to sleep 4 if necessary, the best address in town. 6 Via Museo Biscari, T: 095 314595.

€ **Catania Centrale**. Nice rooms in a lovely street. 2/d Viale Regina

Margherita, T: 095 7164085.

€ **Stesicorea Palace**. Rooms in a central palace; air conditioning. 56 Piazza Stesicoro, T: 095 31520, www.stesicoro.com

Acireale

€ **Casa dei Mulini**. Mini-apartments in an old farmhouse close to town, lovely panoramic area.4 Via Scalazze, T: 095 877654.

Caltagirone

€€ **Gualtiero**. Rooms with view over old town; car park. 20 Piazza San Francesco d'Assisi, T: 0933 34222.

Vizzini

€ **'A Badia**. Rooms in a wing of the convent of Santa Maria de' Greci. 17 Via Etrusca, T: 0933 965398.

FARMHOUSE ACCOMMODATION

Catania

€ **Ruvitello**. Orange farm with pleasant atmosphere, all rooms with private bath, pool, delicious food. Open May–Oct. Contrada Cuba, Fondo Ruvitello, nr Misterbianco, T: 095 451405, www.ruvitello.it

Acireale

€ **Bioagriturismo La Timpa**. Peaceful and panoramic, this farm cultivates lemons organically; a short walk from the spa, or down the cliff to the sea. 68 Via Madonna delle Grazie, T: 095 608376, www.gte.it/agriturismolatimpa

Caltagirone

€€ **Il Casale delle Rose**. Hard to reach but worth it; marvellous food, 2 km from the centre. Contrada Santo Stefano, T: 0933 25064, casalerose@tiscali.it

€€ **Colle San Mauro**. Surrounded by vineyards, olive groves and peach orchards, the farm is close to the archaeological area of San Mauro; pool, archery, horse-riding. Contrada San Mauro Sotto, T: 0933 53890, www.collesanmauro.it

€ **La Riserva**. Simple little place in the Bosco Santo Pietro reserve. Contrada Vaccarizzo, Località San Pietro, T: 0933 20006.

Carruba di Riposto

€ **Giada**. Surrounded by lemon groves, close to the sea, lovely old building, no restaurant. 339 Via Provinciale IV, T: 095 964930, www.agriturismogiada.it

Castiglione di Sicilia

€ **San Marco**. Comfortable rooms in the old farmhouse in a wonderfully panoramic position, the owner, signora Rosaria, is a wonderful cook. Contrada Fossa San Marco, Rovittello, T: 335 7749337, www.agriturismosanmarco.com

Grammichele

€ **Valle dei Margi**. Beautiful old farm in a central position for touring this part of Sicily. Private bathrooms, air conditioning, very good food. Contrada Margi, T: 0933 940464, www.valledeimargi.it

Licodia Eubea

€€ **Dain**. Vineyards and olive groves, riding school, pony trekking, bowls, excursions. The food is very good, especially the breakfasts, with home-made bread. Contrada Alia, SS 194 km 52, T: 0933 965682, www.dain.it

Mascali

€ **Artale Marina di Patanè**. Small quiet farm close to the sea. Self-catering apartments, children welcome. 15 Via Torrente Vallonazzo, T: 095 7791754, artalemarina@tiscali.it

€ **Russo Rocca**. 200m from the sea,

this farm produces lemons, olive oil, cherries and honey; self-catering apartments. Contrada Artale Marina, T: 095 931259, www.agriturismorussorocca.it

Paternò

€€€ **Gianferrante**. Elegant and comfortable suites, lovely pool, tennis, good restaurant, free transfer to/from Catania airport.Contrada Gianferrante, T: 095 621721, www.gianferrante.it

€ **Il Casale dell'Etna**. Beautiful old farm surrounded by orange groves, organic farming methods, tennis, archery, horse-riding, good restaurant. Contrada Poggio Patellina, SP 56, km 11, T: 095 7977996, www.ilcasadelletna.it

Randazzo

€ **L'Antica Vigna**. Quiet farm not far from the town, producing olive oil and wine; tennis, horse-riding. Contrada Montelaguardia, T: 095 924003, www.anticavigna.it

Riposto

€ **Azienda Agrituristica dell'Etna**. Large farm in lovely position under the Timpa. 4 Via Strada, T: 095 964549, www.agrietna.com

San Michele di Ganzaria

€€ **Baglio Gigliotto**. A very beautiful large farm, with olive groves and vineyards, cereals and prickly pears. The farm buildings comprise the original 14th-century farmhouse and an ancient monastery. All the organic food and drink comes from the farm. SS 117 bis, Contrada Gigliotto, T: 0933 970898, www.gigliotto.com

Sant'Alfio

€€ **Case Perrotta**. This old farm, close to the village, is renowned for its excellent food. 2 Via Andronico, T: 095 968928, www.caseperrotta.com

€ **Ai Vecchi Crateri**. Hazelnut farm 1000m above sea level. Helpful owners and good food. 4 Contrada Rosella, T: 095 968151.

€ **La Cirasella**. Old winery in village within Etna Park, organic farming methods. Ancient Roman wine press and vats, home cooking, vegetarian meals on request, children very welcome. 13 Via Trisciala, T: 095 968000, www.cirasella.it

Santa Venerina

€€ **Tenuta San Michele**. Beautiful views of the volcano from this working wine farm producing the DOC Etna Rosso, Bianco and Rosato, offering very comfortable rooms with private bath and TV. English spoken, meals on request. 13 Via Zafferana, T: 095 950520, www.murgo.it

Vizzini

€€ **'A Cunziria**. In the old tannery and surrounding caves, with horse-riding, archery and bowls. Contrada Masera, T: 0933 965507.

RESTAURANTS

Catania

€€€ **Alioto** (ex Selene). A restaurant that has achieved legendary status for the people of Catania. Closed Mon. 24 Via Mollica, T: 095 494444.

€€€ **Il Cuciniere**. In the Katane Palace Hotel. This lovely restaurant is presided over by Carmelo Chiaramonte, TV personality, one of Italy's bright young chefs. 145 Via Capuana, T: 095 7470702.

€€€ **I Tre Bicchieri**. Superb food and good wine cellar. Closed midday Sun and Mon. 31 Via San Giuseppe al Duomo, T: 095 7153540.

€€€ **La Siciliana**. One of the *Buon Ricordo* restaurant chain. In the outskirts of town. Closed Mon, Sun and PH evenings. 52 Viale Marco Polo, T: 095 376400.

€€€ **Metrò**. Good traditional fare; very nice to eat out in the street on a hot summer night. Closed Sat & Sun. 76 Via Crociferi, T: 095 322098.

€€ **Cutilisci**. Innovative organic dishes and excellent pizza on the seafront, at San Giovanni Li Cuti. 67–69 Via San Giovanni Li Cuti, T: 095 372558.

€€ **Python Cafe**. Evenings only for wine, pizza and coffee in a welcoming atmosphere. 7 Via Terranova (Piazza Martiri), T: 095 7470004.

€€ **Il Carato**. Small intimate wine bar and restaurant, short menu, long wine list. 79–81 Via Vittorio Emanuele, T: 095 7159247.

€€ **Osteria Antica Marina**. Tiny restaurant tucked away inside the fish market. Booking is essential. *Alici marinati* (raw anchovy salad) or *spaghetti coi ricci* (spaghetti with sea urchins) are both very tasty dishes. Closed Wed. 29 Via Pardo, T: 095 348197.

€ **Taverna dei Conti**. Homely and friendly, famous for fish. 41 Via Oberdan, T: 095 310035.

€ **Trattoria Posillipo di Turi La Paglia**. Next door to the Osteria Antica Marina; also specializes in fish. 27 Via Pardo.

€ **Coppola**. Catania's favourite pizzeria, also famous for salads, carpaccio di pescespada (raw swordfish) and pannacotta for dessert. 51 Via Coppola, T: 095 317715.

Acireale
€€ **L'Oste Scuro**. Cook your own food on a hot stone. Lovely setting in front of St. Sebastian's. Closed Wed. 5 Piazza Vigo, T: 095 7634001.

€€ **Sotto il Convento**. Unusual and delightful restaurant situated in an old convent garden. The antipasti include excellent grilled vegetables; delicious pasta, many salads; good wine list. Closed Tues. 29 Via Vasta, T: 095 608243.

€€ **Al Ficodindia**. Excellent pizza, antipasto and pasta, in a beautiful setting. 1 Piazza San Domenico, T: 095 7637024.

€ **Il Tocco**. A pizzeria just off the busy main road between the city and the Timpa and a little hard to find, but it is worth the effort. Evenings only. 38 Viale dello Ionio, T: 095 7648819.

€ **La Taverna**. In the heart of the old fish market, a simple, friendly restaurant much favoured by the locals. 4 Via Ercole, T: 095 601261.

Acitrezza
€€ **Covo Marino**. 149 Lungomare Ciclopi, T: 095 7116649. Closed Mon.

€€ **da Federico**. 115 Piazza Verga, T: 095 276364. Closed Mon.

€€ **da Gaetano**. 119 Piazza Verga, T: 095 276342. Closed Wed.

€€ **Pellegrino**. 40 Via Nazionale, T: 095 274902. Closed Mon. These four restaurants are all renowned for excellent fish so they are crowded at weekends, booking necessary.

Bosco Santo Pietro
€ **La Quercia**. Outside the town. Home-made pasta and delicious grills. Closed Mon. Contrada Corvaccio, T: 0933 60381.

Bronte
€ **Don Ciccio**. A delightfully simple restaurant near Castello Maniace. T: 095 7722916.

€ **Fiorentino**. Another good restaurant not far from the castle. T: 095 691800.

Caltagirone

€€ **Floriano**. Good wine list. Try the *tagliolini al profumo di limone*, fresh egg noodles with lemon; also a pizzeria. Closed Mon. 29 Via Pirandello, T: 0933 54001.

€€ **La Piazzetta**, Besides pasta, meat, or pizza, wonderful vegetarian dishes. Closed Thur. 20/a Via Vespri, T: 0933 24178.

€ **La Scala**. Lots of atmosphere. Closed Tues. Also rooms to rent. 8 Scala Santa Maria del Monte, T: 0933 57781.

€ **Mamadina**. International award-winning pizzeria. 12 Via Galileo Galilei, T: 0933 25312.

€ **San Giorgio**. Self-service and pizzeria, local cheeses and pickled fungi. The spaghetti with basil and aubergines are good. Open midday only, Sat and Sun also evenings. 2 Via San Luigi Altobasso, T: 0933 55228.

€ **Trinacria**. Also a pizzeria 21 Via Sturzo, T: 330 591129.

Castiglione di Sicilia

€€ **La Dispensa dell'Etna**. Typical, simple local dishes, accompanied by all the best local wines. 2 Piazza Sant'Antonio, T: 0942 984258.

Militello

€€ **'U Trappito**. Delicious recipes typical of the interior of Sicily, served in a transformed oil press. Closed Mon. 125 Via Principe Branciforte, T: 095 811447.

Nicolosi

€€ **Antico Orto dei Limoni**. Old wine press, wonderful atmosphere, delicious food. 4 Via Grotte, T: 095 910808. Closed Tues.

Randazzo

€ **San Giorgio e il Drago**. Good value

for money; delicious local dishes. Closed Tues. 28 Piazza San Giorgio, T: 095 923972.

Riposto

€€ **Bistrò del Porto**. Renowned for fish dishes, they are very proud of their pistachio ice cream. Closed Tues. Porto Turistico (yachting harbour), T: 095 9700000.

€€ **Marricriu**. Near the yachting harbour, a great little trattoria run by competent and enthusiastic young people: superb seafood dishes, good local wines, simple Sicilian desserts. 160 via Gramsci (corner via Dogana), T: 340 9091513.

San Giovanni La Punta

€€ **Il Giardino di Bacco**. Good wine list. 3 Via Piave, T: 0957 512727.

Santa Maria La Scala

€€ **Al Molino**. Fish dishes in the tiny village of Santa Maria La Scala under the Timpa, prepared the moment the boats land. Closed Wed. 106 Via Molino, T: 095 7648116.

€€ **La Grotta**. This restaurant in a cave is legendary in Acireale, and they try to keep the secret to themselves. Fantastic fish; raw anchovy salad, fried shrimps, seafood antipasto, and lots more, always superb. 46 Via Scalo Grande, T: 095 7648153. Closed Tues.

Trecastagni

€€ **Villa Taverna**. Typical Catania fare. Closed Mon and Sun evening. 42 Via Cristoforo Colombo, T: 0957 806458.

€ **Osteria I Saponari**. Delicious Etna dishes and homemade yoghurt. Closed Mon. 201 Via Francesco Crispi, T: 0957 809907.

Vizzini

€€ **Tyndaris**. Out of town but worth searching for, this extraordinary restaurant is recommended by the Slow Food Association. Contrada Montealtore, T: 0933 965740.

Zafferana Etnea
€€ **Parco dei Principi**. Very elegant, member of the Buon Ricordo chain. Closed Tues. 1 Via delle Ginestre, T: 095 7082335.

CAFÉS, PASTRY SHOPS & ICE CREAM

Catania
Caprice. Also light lunches and snacks. 32 Via Etnea.
Comis. Very popular with local people for snacks, ice cream and light lunches. 7 Piazza Vittorio Emanuele.
Ernesto. Home-made ice cream. Closed Thur. 91 Viale Ruggero di Lauria.
Europa. Excellent pistachio sorbet. Closed Tues. 302 Corso Italia,
Lizzio. Delicious ice cream, try the Sachertorte flavour, or bitter chocolate with chilli pepper. Closed Mon morning. 54 Via Etnea (nr Piazza Università).
Mantegna. Cakes and pastries, Sicilian breakfast, opened more than 100 years ago. 350 Via Etnea.
Scardaci. About midnight the insomniacs and night-owls line up here for fresh breakfast pastries, the famous cornetti. 84 Via Santa Maddalena, also at 158 Via Etnea.

Acicastello
Viscuso. Excellent granita, especially the almond flavour sprinkled with espresso coffee, or gelsi (mulberry), available only when the fruit is in season. Via Re Martino.

Acireale
Bar Duomo. Authentic pistachio ice cream. 36 Piazza Duomo.
Castorina al Duomo. Famous open-air café for relaxing with a fantastic ice cream or granita, possibly with whipped cream. 21 Piazza Duomo.
Condorelli. The best granita, and home-made nougat; their unique breakfast pastry is called *senzanome alla ricotta* (nameless one with ricotta). 26 Via Scionti.
Gelato e Barocco. Very good ice cream. 34 Corso Umberto.

Acitrezza
Eden Bar. Excellent home-made ice cream in a beautiful setting. Closed Wed in winter. 91 Via Provinciale.

Bronte
Caffetteria Luca. For pistachio ice-cream and confectionery. 273 Via Messina.

Caltagirone
Caffè del Centro Storico. Local pastries, ice cream, light lunches. 3 Via Principe Amedeo, T: 0933 22433.

Militello
Snack Poker Bar. For Militello's celebrated pastries: the *cassatelline*, *infasciatelli*, *totò* and *inzulli*. Via Umberto.

Nicolosi
Café Esagonal. Right in front of the cableway station. Nunzio and Dominique serve delicious coffee, hot chocolate and snacks or pasta, and all the latest information on the volcano's activity. Gift shop too. T: 0957 807868.
La Capannina. By the Silvestri Craters, this little inn was almost swallowed up by lava in 2001. Honey and other souvenirs. T: 095 7808427.

Piedimonte Etneo
Caffè Calì. A bar famous throughout Sicily for the granita, but also for the superb pastries and cannoli. 19 Via Vittorio Emanuele,

Pozzillo Superiore
Bar Patané. About half way along the

main street of this little village at the foot of the Timpa, for award-winning ice cream. Try *fior di torrone* flavour.

Randazzo

Chiamatemi Pure Maestà (Alberto). Superb confectionery and snacks and a stunning Art Nouveau interior. 73 Via Umberto.

Musumeci. *Biscotti della nonna* (grandma's biscuits), *croccantini alla nocciola* (hazelnut crunchies), *paste di mandorla aromatizzate* (almond biscuits flavoured with lemon, orange or tangerine). Excellent pistachio cakes. 5 Piazza Santa Maria.

Sant'Alfio

Bar Papotto. Vittorio Papotto supplies the Italian prime minister with his exquisite confectionery. 12 Piazza Duomo.

Santa Maria la Scala

This tiny village at the bottom of the cliff is also a good place for granita: almond, fresh fig, or pistachio.

Santa Venerina

Russo. Excellent Sicilian breakfast: granita, *cornetti al miele* (honey pastries), and hot chocolate in winter. They make various biscuits which are packed in practical tins. 105 Via Vittorio Emanuele.

Trecastagni

Bar Sport. Delicious arancini, pastries and ice cream. 46 Piazza Marconi.

Zafferana Etnea

Ristorante Corsaro and **La Capannina** are both situated close to the Silvestri Craters and serve hot or cold drinks, snacks and lunches, and also sell souvenirs, honey and local liqueurs.

Salemi. Crunchy biscuits called *foglie da tè* (tea leaves), made with almonds and pistachios. 6 Piazza della Regione.

LOCAL SPECIALITIES

Catania

Markets are open mornings only, 7.30–1. A large daily food market is held in Piazza Carlo Alberto, called *'a Fera d'o Luni*, and a general market in the surrounding streets (including Via San Gaetano alle Grotte), now largely taken over by Chinese. In the streets to the south of Piazza Duomo and Via Garibaldi (including Via Gisira) there is another vast and colourful daily food market called *La Pescheria*, where fresh fish, meat and other foodstuffs are sold. **Gioielleria Fecarotta**, 162 Via Etnea, for jewellery made with amber from the Simeto. A wonderful pastry shop is **I Dolci di Nonna Vincenza**, at 7 Piazza San Placido,www.dolcinonnavincenza.it They also have an outlet at Catania Airport. Giovanna Tamburino paints delightful icons at **Le Icone Siciliane**, 11 via Medea. The *nocellara etnea* olive is grown on the slopes around Ragalna, and produces some of Sicily's finest olive oil, stone-ground, and processed on the day of harvesting.

Acireale

Pasticceria Bella, 66 Corso Umberto, is the place to buy candied and crystallized fruit, such as citron, orange, lemon, tangerine, pineapple and melon.

Belpasso

Bar Condorelli, at 536 Via Vittorio Emanuele, www.condorelli.it, for the world-famous nougat, *torroncini*.

Caltagirone

There are some 120 ceramic workshops in the town which sell their products. Many of them are around Piazza Umberto and on the Scala.

So.Gest, at 7 Via Vittorio Emanuele,

www.ceramicadicaltagirone.it, displays the work of about 60 different craftsmen, so you can compare and contrast.

Linguaglossa

Azienda Agricola Gambino, T: 349 8874223, www.agricolagambino.it, you can visit this high-altitude vineyard and taste the various wines in production; on-line shopping, too.

Passopisciaro

Antichi Vinai di Passopisciaro, at 49 Via Castiglione, for very good local wines, all the Etna DOCs, and their own *spumante*.

Ragalna

The **Barbagallo** farm uses no artificial fertilizers or pesticides; Azienda Agricola G. Barbagallo, visits by appointment c/o 5 Via Simili, Catania, T: 095 532817, studiobarbagallo@interfree.it

Vizzini

La Spiga D'Oro Terlato, at 6 Via Guzzardi (nr public gardens), is the best place in Vizzini for bread, biscuits, and snacks; always crowded.

FESTIVALS & EVENTS

Catania 3–5 Feb and 17 Aug: The Feast of St Agatha (Sant'Agata) is celebrated with traditional processions and magnificent fireworks. A music, dance and theatre festival is held in summer at *Le Ciminiere* (*Centro Culturale Fieristico*) near the station. In July, a popular outdoor music festival is held in the city.

Acireale 20 Jan: Colourful processions and fireworks for St Sebastian.
February: Carnival of Acireale is one of the most famous in Italy, T: 095 893134, www.carnevalediacireale.it
26 July: Feast of the patron St Venera,

including the procession of the candelore, Baroque candlesticks up to 5m high, one for each of the city corporations, and a magnificent firework display.

Acitrezza *'U Pisci a Mari*, on the feast day of their patron saint, John the Baptist, the fishermen enact a pantomime from their boats to ensure a good catch for the following year; one of them (the most agile) swims around the boats pretending to be a swordfish, until someone 'catches' him, and 'spears' him to death, 24 June.

Adrano The *Diavolata*, in the main square, a medieval-origin play celebrating the victory of Christianity over the Devils. Great fun, Easter Sun.

Bronte Pistachio festival, early Oct.

Calatabiano Feast of San Filippo Siriaco, when the statue of the saint is carried by the faithful down a steep path, and around the town; very exciting, because he has to run! Third weekend in May.

Caltagirone Feast of the Madonna of Conadomini with a procession of Sicilian carts and decorated tractors, to assure a good harvest, called *'a Russedda*. The Santa Maria del Monte stairway is completely decorated with vases of flowers, forming a design, last week of May; Procession of the Dead Christ, and other processions and events, including an exhibition of terracotta whistles (info: T: 0933 41363), Easter; the majolica-decorated stairway, the Scala Santa Maria del Monte, is illuminated with oil lamps, when there is a also a ceramics fair, and the procession of San Giacomo, 24–25 July; *'a Truvatura* (the treasure hunt), with puppet shows, concerts, and antique fairs,

every 3rd Sun of the month, throughout the winter.
Militello *Settimana del Barocco*, a celebration of Baroque art, last week in
Aug; prickly-pear festival, second Sun
in Oct.
Mineo *Natale nei Vicoli*, a series of displays in the little streets of the old centre, Christmas.
Motta Sant'Anastasia Feast of the
patron St Anastasia, with much flag-
tossing and fireworks, to celebrate the
victory of Count Roger over the
Saracens; also pageants in medieval costume to evoke the romantic story of
Queen Blanche of Navarre and her
would-be lover, Count Bernardo

Cabrera, 23–25 Aug.
Randazzo Festival of the Madonna, 15
Aug.
Sant'Alfio Feast of the patron saint, 10
May.
Trecastagni Feast for the three patron
saints—*i tre casti agni*—Alfio, Cirino
and Filadelfo, culminating on 10 May
with parades, Sicilian carts and fireworks, and Sicily's largest garlic market,
early May
Zafferana Etnea Autumn festival
known as the *Ottobrata*, with local specialities sold in the square, and craftsmen (carpenters, stonemasons and bee-
keepers) demonstrating their skills
along the main street, Sundays in Oct.

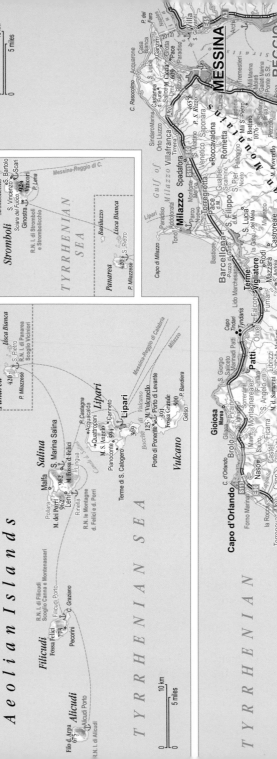

THE PROVINCE OF MESSINA

MESSINA

Messina, on the western shore of the Straits bearing its name, extends along the lowest slopes of the Peloritan Mountains above the splendid harbour, one of the deepest and safest in the Mediterranean. With its fine port and ideal position between Europe and Africa, the Straits of Gibraltar and the Bosphorus, Messina was long the centre of the world, an important trading post from the Bronze Age until the discovery of America, and for some time afterwards. Today the port is always busy with ferries and hydrofoils travelling to and from the mainland, although a controversial bridge is planned, which will also carry the railway. The third largest city in Sicily, Messina was completely wrecked by an earthquake followed by a tsunami in 1908, when 84,000 people died from a population of 120,000. It was soon rebuilt with broad streets planted with trees and low buildings to minimise the danger from future earthquakes. The centre of Messina now combines sea, sky and hills in a pleasant, open townscape. The prevailing wind is the *maestrale*, which blows from the northwest, making it one of the breeziest places in Sicily.

EXPLORING MESSINA

The Orion Fountain

In the centre of the city, Piazza Duomo was spaciously laid out in the 18th century. Beside the cathedral, the 1933 bell-tower stands next to the Orion Fountain (*pictured overleaf*), the masterpiece of Giovanni Angelo Montorsoli (1553), and thought by some to be the most beautiful Renaissance fountain in Italy. It was commissioned to celebrate the construction of an aqueduct from the nearby River Camaro, which made running water available to a large part of the city for the first time. Although the people had wanted Michelangelo to design the fountain, the commission went instead to his pupil, the Friar Montorsoli, who enjoyed his stay in Messina enough to delay his return to Tuscany for more than 10 years, and then only on the orders of the Pope. The male figures around the fountain represent the Nile, Tiber, Ebro and Camaro, and they are shown looking in the direction of their respective rivers. On the top is Orion, founder of the city, with his faithful dog Sirius.

The duomo

Open 8–7.

Despite successive reconstructions, the duomo retains much of the appearance of the original medieval church. Originally built by Count Roger, the cathedral was one of the greatest Norman churches in Sicily. It was consecrated in 1197 in the presence of Emperor Henry VI and was first destroyed in 1254 by a fire which broke out during

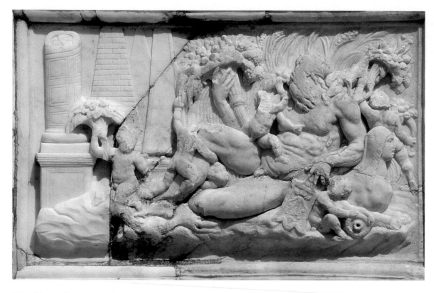

The River Nile on the Orion Fountain in Piazza Duomo.

a funeral service for Conrad IV, son of Frederick II, because the mourners had lit too many candles. The new building was shattered by earthquakes in 1783 and 1908 and in 1943 was hit by an incendiary bomb aimed at the port. The fire raged for three days, and many treasures were destroyed, including the mosaics and the frescoes, the royal tombs and choir-stalls. Everything that could be salvaged was carefully replaced in the reconstructed church. A surviving column can be seen outside the building on the north side, with a carved fragment from the church on top, erected as a monument in 1958 to record the 50th anniversary of the disaster. The lower part of the façade preserves much of the original sculpted decoration including panels in relief with delightful farming scenes, and three fine doorways, by 14th-, 15th- and 16th-century artists. The beautiful central doorway has a tympanum by Pietro da Bonitate (1468). On the south side is a doorway by Polidoro Caldara da Caravaggio and a wall, still intact, with fine Gothic-Catalan windows.

The interior
The majestic basilican interior, in pink and grey tones, was remarkably well restored after the fire. The side altars (copies of originals by Montorsoli), the columns (made of cement), the marble floor and the painted wooden roof were all replaced. In the south aisle on the first altar is a statue of *St John the Baptist* by Antonello Gagini (1525). At the end of the aisle is the so-called tomb of five archbishops (14th century), with five Gothic trilobed arches. On the nave pillar in the transept is the fragmented Byzantine-style tomb slab of Archbishop Palmer (d. 1195).

HISTORY OF MESSINA

Zancle, as Messina was called by the Greeks in allusion to the sickle-shaped peninsula enclosing its harbour, was probably a settlement of the Sicels before being occupied first by the Euboeans (from the island of Euboea east of Athens) and later by a colony from Chalcis. In 493 BC it was captured by Anaxilas, tyrant of *Rhegium*, and renamed *Messana*, in honour of his native country of *Messenia* in the Peloponnese. It took part in local wars against Syracuse and then against Athens, and was destroyed by the Carthaginian general Himilco. Rebuilt by Syracuse, it was occupied by the Campanian mercenaries of Agathocles, who called themselves Mamertines. These obtained the alliance of Rome against the Carthaginians and Messina prospered with the fortunes of Rome. Under Byzantium, and later under the Arabs, the surrounding hills were planted with groves of mulberry trees to support the burgeoning silk industry, which brought fame and fortune until the 19th century when the industry came to a standstill because of a minute parasite which attacked the silkworms.

Under the Normans the town was renowned for monastic learning and was important as a Crusader port. In September 1190 Richard Coeur de Lion and Philip Augustus of France arrived to spend the winter here before leaving for their Crusade in March 1191. Richard ensconced himself and his troops in the revered Basilian monastery of San Salvatore, and proceeded to ransack the city in redress for perceived offences to his sister Joanna, widow of William II. The Hohenstaufen emperor, Henry VI, died of dysentery at Messina in 1197. After a heroic and successful resistance to Charles of Anjou in 1282, the city flourished until losing privileges for rebelling against Spanish misrule in 1674.

It was from Messina that Cervantes sailed in the *Marquesa* to Lepanto (1571) and in the hospital of Messina that he recovered from the wound received in the battle. Shakespeare's *Much Ado About Nothing* is set in Messina.

Much of the city's history has been disastrous: plague in 1743, an earthquake in 1783, naval bombardment in 1848, cholera in 1854, another earthquake in 1894, culminating in the catastrophe of 1908, one of the most severe earthquakes on record. The first shock, at 5.20 in the morning of 28th December, lasted only some 20 seconds but destroyed almost the entire city, causing the shore to sink more than half a metre. The subsidence caused a violent tsunami which swept the coast, rising to a height of 8m, drowning many as they escaped from their ruined homes. A series of lesser shocks continued almost daily for two months. Reconstruction, though assisted by liberal contributions from all over the world, was by no means complete when the city was again devastated in 1943 by aerial bombardment. In 1955 a preliminary agreement was signed by 'the six' in Messina to found the European Union (EU).

From the south aisle is the entrance to the **treasury** (*open Apr–Oct Mon–Fri 9–1 & 4.30–7, Sat 9–1; Nov–Mar Mon–Sat 9–1*). Arranged in four rooms and on two floors, it is particularly rich in 17th- and 18th-century artefacts, including church silver made in Messina. Among the most important pieces are a 10th-century lamp in rock crystal, altered in 1250, and a very fine reliquary of the arm of San Marziano, commissioned by Richard Palmer (as the inscription states) when he was bishop of Syracuse. Brought with him when he became archbishop of Messina around 1182, it shows the influence of Islamic and Byzantine goldsmiths' art. The most precious piece in the treasury collection is the golden Manta, used only on important ceremonial occasions to cover the portrait of the *Madonna della Lettera*. It was made by a 17th-century Florentine goldsmith. Other works of particular interest include a 13th-century processional Cross, a large, brightly coloured 17th-century silk embroidery, and a pair of silver candlesticks made in 1701.

Outside the south apse chapel, elaborately decorated in marble, is the charming (though damaged) tomb of Archbishop De Tabiatis by Goro di Gregorio (1333). The sumptuous high altar bears a copy of the venerated Byzantine *Madonna della Lettera* which was destroyed in 1943. The canopy, the stalls, and the bishop's throne have all been reconstructed. In front of the high altar is a lower altar which encloses a silver frontal attributed to the local silversmith Francesco Juvarra (late 17th or early 18th century), depicting the Madonna in the act of consigning a letter to the ambassadors of Messina after hearing of the citizens conversion by St Paul. The dedication of the church dates back to 1638 and the foundation of the 'Congregation of the Slaves of the Madonna of the Letter' whose seat was the crypt of the church. The mosaic in the central apse has been recomposed. In the north apse chapel is the only original mosaic to have survived *in situ* from the 14th century. The monument to Bishop Angelo Paino (1870–1967), who rebuilt the cathedral after the last war, is to the left of the apse.

In the two transepts part of the organ can be seen, manufactured by Tamburini of Crema in 1948; with its 16,000 pipes and 127 registers it is the largest in Italy and one of the biggest in Europe. In the north transept the tomb effigy of Bishop Antonio La Lignamine is surrounded by 12 fine small panels of the Passion sculpted by the Gagini school. Nearby is a 17th-century bust of Archbishop Proto, and part of the tomb of Archbishop Bellorado by Giovanni Battista Mazzola (1513). In the north aisle, beside the doorway, is a 16th-century relief of *St Jerome* (the exterior of the 15th-century north doorway can be seen here).

The **campanile** (*open Mon–Sat, 9–1 & 4.30–7, Sun and holidays 10–1 & 4.30–7, last entry 30 mins before closing*) was designed by Francesco Valenti to house a remarkable astronomical clock, the largest of its kind in the world, built by the Strasbourg firm of Josef Ungerer in 1933. At noon the chimes herald an elaborate and very noisy movement of mechanical figures, representing episodes in the city's history, religious festivals, the phases of life and the days of the week, accompanied by the music of Ave Maria. On the right side of the tower are the quadrants showing the planetarium, the phases of the moon, and the perpetual calendar.

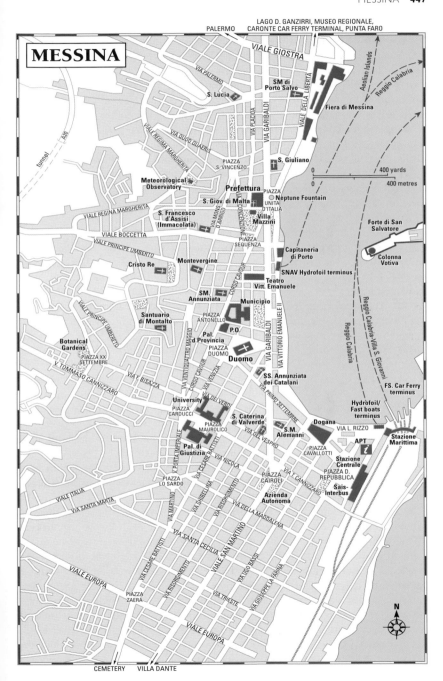

MESSINA

LAGO D. GANZIRRI, MUSEO REGIONALE,
CARONTE CAR FERRY TERMINAL, PUNTA FARO
PALERMO

VIALE GIOSTRA

VIA PALERMO

Aeolian Islands

Reggio Calabria

SM di
Porto Salvo

S. Lucia

VIA PLACIDA

VIALE DELLA LIBERTA

Fiera di Messina

VIALE REGINA MARGHERITA

VIA QUOD QUAERIS

VIA GARIBALDI

PIAZZA
S-VINCENZO

S. Giuliano

tunnel A20

Meteorological
Observatory

Prefettura

PIAZZA
UNITA
D'ITALIA

Neptune Fountain

0   400 yards
0   400 metres

VIALE REGINA MARGHERITA

S. Giov. di Malta

S. Francesco
d'Assisi
(Immacolata)

VIA MONS.
D'ARRIGO

Villa
Mazzini

Forte di San
Salvatore

VIALE BOCCETTA

VIALE PRINCIPE UMBERTO

PIAZZA
SEQUENZA

Capitaneria
di Porto

Colonna
Votiva

Cristo Re

Montevergine

CORSO CAVOUR

SNAV Hydrofoil terminus

VIALE PRINCIPE UMBERTO

SM.
Annunziata

Teatro
Vitt. Emanuele

Municipio

Reggio Calabria-Villa S. Giovanni

Santuario
di Montalto

PIAZZA
ANTONELLO

P.O.

VIA GARIBALDI

Botanical
Gardens

PIAZZA XX
SETTEMBRE

Pal.
d'Provincia

PIAZZA
DUOMO

VIA VITTORIO EMANUELE II

V. TOMMASO CANNIZZARO

VIA F. BISAZZA

VIA VENEZIA

Duomo

Reggio Calabria

VIA PRIMO SETTEMBRE

VIA XXIV MAGGIO

CORSO CAVOUR

University

PIAZZA
CARDUCCI

VIA DEI VERDI

SS. Annunziata
dei Catalani

FS. Car Ferry
terminus

VIA SANTA MARTA

PIAZZA
MAURICLIO

S. Caterina
di Valverde

VIA DEL VESPRO

S.M.
Alemanni

Dogana

Hydrofoil/
Fast boats
terminus

VIALE ITALIA

Pal. di
Giustizia

V. PORTA IMPERIALE

VIA CESARE BATTISTI

VIA NICOLA

PIAZZA
CAVALLOTTI

VIA L. RIZZO

APT

Stazione
Marittima

PIAZZA
LO SARDO

VIA GHIBELLINA

VIA RISORGIMENTO

PIAZZA
CAIROLI

VIA T. CANNIZZARO

Stazione
Centrale

PIAZZA D.
REPUBBLICA

Azienda
Autonoma

Sais-
Interbus

VIALE EUROPA

VIA CESARE BATTISTI

VIA SANTA CECILIA

VIA DELLA MADDALENA

VIA MARTINO

VIA SAN MARTINO

VIA SAN MARTINO

VIA UGO BASSI

VIA GIUSEPPE LA FARINA

VIA TRIESTE

PIAZZA
ZAERA

N

VIALE EUROPA

CEMETERY   VILLA DANTE

South from Piazza Duomo

South along Corso Cavour is the University (1927), whose library dates from the university's foundation in 1548, facing the Law Courts (1928), a monumental Neoclassical building in ochre stone, surmounted by a Roman chariot representing the victorious course of justice.

Via Primo Settembre (a stone on the corner records the outbreak of the Sicilian revolt against the Bourbons in 1847) leads southeast from Piazza Duomo towards the railway station. It passes two Baroque corner fountains, which survived the earthquake, near (left) the church of **Santissima Annunziata dei Catalani** (*open Mon–Sat 9–11*), a 12th-century Norman church, shortened under the Swabians. The exterior is remarkably fine. The apse, transepts and cupola, with beautiful arcading, date from the 12th century, while the three doors at the west end were added in the 13th century. The interior has a brick apse and dome in yellow and white stone, and tall dark grey columns with Corinthian capitals. The windows and nave arches are decorated with red and white stone. The large stoup is made up of two capitals. This church has always withstood the earthquakes remarkably well: perhaps because it was built on the site of the Greek temple dedicated to Poseidon, god of earthquakes. In the Piazza Catalani is a statue of Don John of Austria, by Andrea Calamech (1572), which was erected to celebrate Don John's victory over the Turks at Lepanto in 1571. On the morning after the battle, the General personally congratulated the wounded Miguel Cervantes on his devotion to duty.

Just off Via Garibaldi, the long broad thoroughfare which crosses Via Primo Settembre, are the ruins of **Santa Maria degli Alemanni** (c. 1220), founded by the Teutonic order of knights, damaged by the 1783 earthquake and recently restored, interesting as the one of the few Gothic churches in Sicily, and thought to have been built by German craftsmen, hence the name 'Alemanni'. On the opposite side of the street, the church of Santa Caterina di Valverde contains a beautiful 16th-century painting of the *Madonna dell' Itria between Sts Peter and Paul* by the local artist Antonello Riccio.

Via Garibaldi ends in **Piazza Cairoli**, the centre of the modern town and the most popular meeting place for those engaged in the *passeggiata*. Thanks to its fountains and magnificent ficus trees, it is always cool and shady.

Further south, **Viale San Martino**, one of the main shopping streets, with the tram running through the middle, traverses an area of attractive Art Nouveau-style houses. The avenue itself is now the most beautiful in Messina, with recently planted date palms (acquired fully grown from Egypt). It ends at the public gardens of **Villa Dante** beside the monumental cemetery, designed in 1872 by Leone Savoia. The luxuriant garden, built in terraces on the slopes of the hill, has a lovely view of Calabria. The Famedio, or Pantheon, was damaged by the 1908 earthquake, but almost all the smaller family tombs were left intact. In 1940 the British cemetery, founded during the Napoleonic wars, was transferred here (reached by a path on the extreme left side of the cemetery) by the Italian authorities, when its original site near the harbour was needed for defence works.

North from Piazza Duomo

A short way north of the cathedral is the circular **Piazza Antonello**, dedicated to the famous local painter Antonello da Messina, laid out in 1914–29 with a group of monumental buildings: the post office (1915), the seat of the Province (1918), the town hall (1924; its façade faces Via Garibaldi), and an arcade (1929) with a café, offices and shops.

In Via Ventiquattro Maggio, a street parallel to Corso Cavour, are the remains of the 18th-century **Monte di Pietà** (pawnshop), with a beautiful flight of steps, and the church of Montevergine with a lovely Baroque interior.

Via Garibaldi runs north-south, parallel to Corso Vittorio Emanuele and the waterfront, with a view of the busy harbour, and the sickle-shaped tongue of land protecting it that ends at the Forte di San Salvatore, erected by the Spanish in 1546. On the point of the sickle, at the entrance to the port, can be seen the golden statue of the Madonna, patron of Messina, on a white pillar 60m high.

The opera house, **Teatro Vittorio Emanuele** (*T: 090 5722111, www.teatrodimessina.it*), on Via Garibaldi, built in 1842, was re-opened in 1985 after repairs; strangely, the earthquake had spared the perimeter walls and only the interior was ruined.

The two parallel streets passing a statue of Ferdinand II, end in Piazza Unità d'Italia, with the **Neptune Fountain** by Montorsoli (1557; the figures of Neptune and Scylla are 19th-century copies, the originals being kept in the Museo Regionale). Behind is the huge 1920s Prefecture, and nearby the little church of **San Giovanni di Malta** (c. 1590; Camillo Camilliani). Here, in the Cappella Palatina, an exhibition of sacred art (*open Tues–Sat 9–1 & 3–7; Sun 9.30–12.30; closed Mon*) has been arranged, displaying vestments, church silvers and paintings. Also facing the piazza is Palazzo Carrozza built in the 1930s in an eclectic style. There is a garden with pines and ficus trees facing the waterfront, and, behind, the public gardens of **Villa Mazzini**, with beautiful trees and an aquarium with a collection of fish from the Straits (*open Tues, Wed, Thur 9.30–12.30; Fri 4–7; Sun 9.30–12.45*).

Viale Boccetta, which was a water-course before the earthquake, leads inland from Piazza Sequenza on Via Cavour to the church of **San Francesco d'Assisi**, better known by the inhabitants as the Immacolata. Built in 1252 with a large convent in Gothic-Sicilian style, it stood outside the city walls. The church can be identified in some of Antonello da Messina's works, as can the Straits of Messina, which often appear in the background.

Viale della Libertà, which follows the shore in full view of the Calabrian coastline, passes the *passeggiata a mare*, opposite which is the church of San Giuliano with red domes in eclectic style.

The road runs along the coast passing the church of **Gesù e Maria del Buonviaggio**, known as the church of Ringo, an old fishing village close by. Built in 1598 and dedicated to seamen, its façade is adorned with a fine portal, Corinthian capitals and two niches with statues of Christ and Mary: both statues have one hand pierced to hold oil lamps to guide passing boats. From here, Viale della Libertà leads to the regional museum (c. 3km from the Duomo).

Museo Regionale

Open Mon–Sat 9–13.30; Sun and holidays 9–12.30; Tues, Thur and Sat also 3–5.30.
Housed in an old silk mill since the 1908 earthquake, the important Museo Regionale holds a remarkable collection of local artworks, particularly strong in 15th- and early 16th-century paintings (many recently restored). The entrance to the museum is along a wide path lined by flower beds containing architectural fragments from the old city. The inner courtyard has more fragments, including capitals from the cathedral, three church doorways (from San Domenico, Santa Maria della Scala and Santa Maria di Basicò) and a 16th-century tomb.

Room 1: Byzantine and Norman. Exhibits include the sarcophagus of the archimandrite Luke, founder of the monastery of San Salvatore, for which he wrote the *Typikon*; an exquisite mosaic niche of the Madonna and Child, called *La Ciambretta* (13th century); and fragments of the medieval painted wooden ceiling salvaged from the cathedral. The marble bas-relief of the *Praying Virgin* (13th century) was made in Constantinople.

Room 2: Gothic period. A strangely twisted statue from the cathedral by Goro di Gregorio, known as the *Madonna degli Storpi* (1333), or the Madonna of the Cripples; and from the 14th–15th-century Venetian-Marche school, a polyptych of the *Madonna and Child with Four Saints*.

Room 3: Early 15th century. Dominated by an impressive painted wooden Crucifix, possibly the work of a Catalan artist, which was found on a donkey cart, abandoned by looters after the 1908 earthquake. The church from which it came remains a mystery. Here also are architectural fragments from the cathedral: a Della Robbia tondo of the *Madonna and Child*; bas-reliefs including *St George and the Dragon*

(attributed to Domenico Gagini); and a polyptych of the *Madonna and Child with Four Saints*, an example of florid Gothic.

Room 4: Late 15th century. Splendid works by Antonello da Messina, his school, and Flemish and Spanish artists. Displayed separately is the beautiful polyptych of the *Madonna with Sts Gregory and Benedict* (oil on panel), an ideal synthesis of Flemish and Italian Renaissance styles, painted by Antonello da Messina in 1473 and bearing his signature. Painted for the monastery of St Gregory and much damaged in the earthquake it has since been restored. Also here, among other works, are a polychrome marble statue of the *Madonna and Child* attributed to Francesco Laurana and a striking *Pietà and symbols of the Passion*, by an unknown Flemish painter.

Room 5: Girolamo Alibrandi and the early 16th century. A native artist who admired the work of Leonardo and Raphael whose influence can be seen in the two panel paintings of the *Circumcision* and the *Presentation in the Temple* (1519), this latter work is thought to be his finest. Recovered after the earthquake in more than 300 fragments, it has been extensively restored. Also here are a ciborium and a marble statue of the *Madonna and Child* by Antonello Gagini.

Rooms 6–7: Works of the 16th–17th centuries, in the Sicilian Mannerist style. But the *Adoration of the Shepherds* (1533) by Polidoro Caldara da Caravaggio, shows the influence of Raphael, with whom Polidoro studied. The statue of *Scylla* is by Montorsoli (the original from the Neptune fountain; *see p. 449*).

Detail from *The Adoration of the Shepherds* by Polidoro da Caravaggio (1533).

Room 8: Funerary monument of Francesca Lanza Cibo (1618, gilded copper), and a collection of majolica pharmacy vases (mostly from the Casteldurante and Venetian workshops).

Room 9: 17th-century paintings, including by Antonio Catalano il Vecchio, *Madonna Appearing to Sts Francis and Clare* (1604); Filippo Paladini, *St Francis Receiving the Stigmata*; Antonio Catalano il Giovane, *Madonna of the Letter* (1629).

Room 10: Two masterpieces by Caravaggio, both dramatic late works painted during his stay in Messina in 1608–09: *Nativity* (commissioned by the Senate of Messina for the Capuchin church) and *Raising of Lazarus* (*pictured opposite*), commissioned by the De Lazzari family for their private chapel in the church of St Camille. Sicilian works

of his school displayed here include: Alonzo Rodriquez *Meeting between Sts Peter and Paul*; Mario Minniti: *Miracle of the Widow of Naim*; and a beautiful painting by Carlo Sellito, *St Lucy.*

Room 11: 17th-century works such as inlaid marble panels, silverware, embroidery, two marble statues (*Faith* and *Hope*) from the church of the Annunziata dei Catalani, and paintings by Mattia Preti, who was a Calabrian disciple of Caravaggio, a tondo of the *Dead Christ*; and by Agostino Scilla (*see p. 240*).

Room 12: 18th-century paintings by Giovanni Tuccari, Filippo Tancredi; Sebastiano Conca among others.

Treasury. On the mezzanine floor, includes vestments, altar frontals, church silver (16th–18th century), and a 17th-century ivory and ebony cabinet.

Caravaggio (1573–1610)

Michelangelo Merisi was born in 1573 at Caravaggio, a village near Milan. When still very young, his genius was recognized, and he was soon much in demand in Rome. His vigorous, realistic style contrasted strongly with the Mannerism still popular at the time. Intemperate, and slovenly in his personal habits, he did not lead a quiet life. In 1606 he killed a man in a fight. Forced to leave Rome, he reached Malta, where he was awarded the Grand Cross. Involved in another fight, he was arrested and beaten, but escaped from prison and fled to Syracuse. Here he painted some of his finest works: the large dark canvases of his maturity in which rays of light allow the figures to emerge and the story to unfold. His attempted return to Rome after receiving his pardon failed due to a misunderstanding. He was arrested and imprisoned at Civitavecchia while his ship set sail with his painting materials and his pardon on board. Once released, he tried to catch up with the ship, walking all the way from Civitavecchia to Porto Ercole. The strain was too much, and he died, either from heat stroke or malaria.

Caravaggio: The Raising of Lazarus (1608–09).

ENVIRONS OF MESSINA

The outskirts and Punta Faro

On the slopes of the hillside above the town is the church of **Cristo Re** (Christ the King, 1939), which dominates the city with its huge dome, and was designed to be a collective memorial for the victims of the earthquake and for all those killed in war. To one side stands an old tower called the Torre Guelfonia (part of the old fortifications) with a great bell (diameter 3m) made from the melted-down enemy guns of the First World War. The interior of the church is richly decorated with fine marble and stuccoes; in the crypt is a sarcophagus on which lies the marble image of a soldier.

From here Viale Principe Umberto runs south, passing Torre Vittoria and the ruins of the 16th-century Spanish walls, and the striking sanctuary church of **Montalto** (rebuilt in 1930), with its twin bell-towers a landmark of the city, to the Botanical Gardens in Piazza XX Settembre (*open 9–12.30, closed Sun and holidays*).

Punta Faro (14km north), at the extreme northeastern tip of the island and the nearest point to Calabria, can be reached by the old road lined with a modest row of houses facing the sea front, which traverses the ambitiously named suburbs of Paradiso, Contemplazione, Pace, and Sant'Agata. It is at the mouth of the Straits of Messina, the *Fretum Siculum* of the Romans. This is the site of the legendary whirlpools called Scylla and Charybdis, greatly feared by sailors in ancient times. The name of Cape Peloro recalls Pelorus, Hannibal's navigator, who was unjustly condemned to be thrown into the sea for misleading the fleet. Further south the Calabrian coast is sometimes, in hot weather, strangely magnified and distorted by a mirage called *Fata Morgana*: what appears to be the city of King Arthur's half-sister, exiled here, floats on the water.

Just short of the cape is the fishing village of **Ganzirri**, on two little lagoons (the *Pantano Grande* and the *Pantano Piccolo*), separated from the sea by a dune barrier and fed by artesian water, famous for mussels and other shellfish.

The twin pylons, over 150m high, at Punta Faro are an impressive landmark, standing where the bridge between Sicily and the mainland is projected. The latest plan, proposed in 1986, and re-examined in 1997, involves a single-span suspension bridge for road and railway 3300m long carried on two pylons 376m high, the longest bridge of its kind in the world. Work on the bridge should begin in 2006, but locally it is strongly contested.

Swordfishing has taken place off the coast here since ancient times; it was for many years considered one of the sights of Messina. The traditional method of harpooning the fish from characteristic small boats (*luntri*) with tall look-out masts, is still carried out, but most fishermen nowadays use modern equipment and motor boats called *felucche*. Modern fishing methods, and above all, modern fishing fleets coming from the Far East, have decimated the quantity of fish found in this area.

West to the Badiazza and the Peloritan Mountains

The road is well signposted from the centre of Messina (Colle San Rizzo, Portella

Castanea, Santa Maria Dinnamare and Badiazza). Off the SS 113, a very poor road (almost impassable in places) leads right (signposted) past Sant'Andrea, a little church built in 1929, and poor houses to the head of the valley. Here, in a group of pine trees, is **La Badiazza** (also called Santa Maria della Scala or Santa Maria della Valle). This fine 13th-century church (abandoned) belonged to a ruined Cistercian convent and has an interesting exterior with lava decoration.

The main road continues uphill to enter all that remains of the forest which once covered the slopes of the Peloritan Mountains. Thick pinewoods survive here. The road sign indicating Palermo (250km) is a reminder that this was the main road to Palermo before the motorway was built. At **Colle San Rizzo** (460m) is a crossroads. From here a spectacular road (signposted *Santuario di Maria Santissima di Dinnamare*) leads for 9km along the crest of the Peloritan range to a height of 1130m. The first stretch is extremely narrow and dangerous but further on the road improves. The views on either side are breathtaking: on the right Milazzo can be seen and on the left the toe of Italy. The church of **Maria Santissima di Dinnamare**, built in the 18th century and restored in 1886, was rebuilt in 1899. The superb panorama, one of the most exceptional in Italy, takes in the whole of Calabria, the port of Messina and the tip of Punta Faro. On the other side the Aeolian Islands, including Stromboli (beyond Milazzo), and Mount Etna, can be seen.

From the Colle San Rizzo crossroads the road signposted to Castanea leads through fine pinewoods, with wide views down over the port of Messina to the right, and to the left of the Aeolian Islands, and the motorway snaking through the hills. In spring **Monte Ciccia** (609m) is on the migratory route from Africa to central Europe for thousands of birds, especially honey buzzards.

On the approach to the village of **Castanea delle Furie** is an unusual, castellated villa. Castanea, despite the menacing name, has a typical medieval town plan and some lovely old churches. The road continues down to Spartà past olives and pines. As the road nears the sea there is a wonderful view of Stromboli.

TAORMINA

Taormina is renowned for its magnificent position above the sea on a spur of Mount Taurus, covered with luxuriant vegetation, commanding a celebrated view of Etna. With a delightful winter climate, it became a fashionable international resort at the end of the 19th century, and during the 20th century was the most famous holiday place on the island. The small town, with the elegant *corso* off which lead intriguing little stepped streets, is now virtually given over to tourism and can be very crowded from Easter to September. Many of the villas and hotels, built in mock Gothic or eclectic styles at the beginning of the 20th century, are surrounded with beautiful luxuriant gardens. Too much building has been allowed on the hillsides of Taormina in recent years, although the medieval churches and palaces, the tiny streets and Roman remains, never subject to earthquakes, have lost none of their magic.

HISTORY OF TAORMINA

Tauromenium, probably founded by the Sicels, and then inhabited by the sur-vivors of the destruction of *Naxos* wreaked by Dionysius of Syracuse in 403 BC, was enlarged in 358 under Andromachus, father of the historian Timaeus.

It was favoured by Rome during the early days of occupation, and suffered in the Servile War (134–132) when the castle was held by slaves for several months, but forfeited its rights as an allied city by taking the part of Pompey against Caesar. In 902 it was taken by the Arabs, then again in 965 when the theatre was destroyed. Count Roger conquered the town in 1078. Here the Sicilian Parliament assembled in 1410 to choose a king on the extinction of the line of Peter of Aragon.

The town was visited and described by numerous travellers in the 18th and 19th century, and the famous view of Etna from the theatre was painted count-less times. John Dryden came here in 1701. John Henry (later Cardinal) Newman stayed in the town as a young man in 1833. In 1847 Edward Lear spent four or five days in what he described as 'Taormina the Magnificent'. Taormina was first connected to Messina by railway in 1866 and a year later the line to Catania was inaugurated. In 1864 the first hotel, the Timeo, was opened in the town, and it became internationally known as a winter resort soon after the first visit of the Kaiser (Wilhelm II) in 1896. The Kaiser returned in 1904 and 1905 with a large retinue, and set the fashion for royal visitors, many of whom came here in secret under false names. In 1906 Edward VII wintered at the San Domenico Hotel and George V made a private visit (incognito) in 1924. Before the First World War the town had a considerable Anglo-American, German, and Scandinavian colony, including the impoverished Baron Wilhelm von Gloeden (1896–1931), who took up photography here, specialising in child portraits, his studio becoming one of the sights of the town. The painter Robert Kitson built a villa for himself here where he lived from 1905 onwards. Kitson was also concerned with the poverty of the local inhabitants and encouraged Mabel Hill, another English resident, to set up a lacemaking school in the town. The writer Robert Hitchens arrived by car in Taormina in the winter of 1910, the first time a car had reached the town. D.H. Lawrence and his wife Frieda lived here from 1920–23.

The town attracted the attention of Allied aircraft in July 1943 when it tem-porarily became Field-Marshal Kesselring's headquarters. In the 1950s it also became known as a bathing resort and for its film festival. Famous visitors in this period include Truman Capote—who wrote *Breakfast at Tiffany's* and *In Cold Blood* while here—Cecil Beaton, Jean Cocteau, Osbert Sitwell, Salvador Dalí, Orson Welles, John Steinbeck, Tennessee Williams, Rita Hayworth, Greta Garbo and Cary Grant.

EXPLORING TAORMINA

The easiest route into town is from the motorway exit straight to Lumbi (where there is a large car park), with few hairpin bends. It is also still possible to use the old Via Pirandello which branches off from the main road (SS 114) at Cape Taormina and winds up the hill past lovely gardens. It passes the little 15th-century church of Santi Pietro e Paolo (*open only for services*), the ruins of the Kursaal and a series of Byzantine or Arab tomb-recesses in the wall below the former convent of Santa Caterina. Shortly after the junction with Via Bagnoli Croce it passes a little belvedere with a fine view of Isola Bella (*pictured on p. 463*) and Mazzarò. Beyond the bus terminal, on the right (no. 24), surrounded by a garden of date palms, is the Anglo-American church of St George's, built by the British community in 1922, with lava decoration on the exterior. It contains British and American funerary monuments, and memorials to the victims of the two World Wars. Beyond the cableway station Via Pirandello terminates outside Porta Messina, at the entrance to the town.

Piazza Vittorio Emanuele

Often called Piazza Badia, and the site of the ancient agora and the Roman forum, Piazza Vittorio Emanuele is now a favourite meeting place, with shady *Ficus benjamin* trees and a taxi stand. The two coffee bars are ideal for people-watching and good for a Sicilian breakfast, ice cream or hot chocolate. The Shaker Bar was the favourite of Tennessee Williams, who was in the habit of ordering a glass of whisky that he replenished from a hip flask, filled at a cheap wine store in the back streets, and sitting for hours here, reading or talking.

Opposite stands Palazzo Corvaja (15th century; the central tower is a 10th-century Arab structure), with mullioned windows and a 15th-century side-portal in Gothic-Catalan form. Inside the courtyard is a staircase with very worn reliefs of Adam and Eve. The limestone ornamentation with black and white lava inlay is characteristic of Taormina. The building houses the tourist information office. The great hall, meeting-place in 1410 of the Sicilian Parliament, and other rooms, now house the **Museo Siciliano di Arte e Tradizioni Popolari** (*open 9–1 & 4–8*), a collection donated by local antique dealer and antiquarian Giovanni Panarello, offering a synthesis of Sicilian handicrafts from the 16th–20th centuries. In the first room are pieces of decorated Sicilian carts, puppets, and puppet-show posters, along with a section dedicated to shepherding in the Peloritan Mountains and Calabria: items made of wood and horn (collars for cows and sheep, spoons, bowls, flasks, kegs, walking sticks and spindles). Engraved with geometric and fertility symbols, the decorations were also the proud stamp of property. The collars of animals never went with their sale. The spindles are usually decorated with a female figure. These, and decorated whalebones for corsets, were love-tokens from the shepherds to their women. There is also a good collection of anthropomorphic pottery from Caltagirone, Collesano, Patti and Seminara (Calabria), especially flowerpots representing human faces. In the second room is a collection of traditional Christmas cribs, made of ivory, coral, and mother-of-pearl.

The 17th-century church of **Santa Caterina** has three large white stucco Baroque altars and a panel painting on the high altar of the *Martyrdom of St Catherine* (16th century), by the native artist Jacopo Vignerio. In the floor of the nave, parts of a Hellenistic temple have been revealed. A 15th-century statue of St Catherine stands on a plinth with stories of her life. The macabre underground funerary chamber of 1662 is at present closed.

Behind the church are the scant remains of the **Odeon** or Teatrino Romano, incorporating part of the preceding Hellenistic temple. Built in the 1st century AD, it could hold 200 people. Excavations nearby have revealed public baths of the Imperial Roman period and traces of the forum. Outside Porta Messina, at the lower end of a large piazza busy with traffic, is the church of San Pancrazio (St Pancras is the patron saint of Taormina), built on the ruins of a 4th-century BC Greek temple to Isis, Zeus and Serapis, still partly visible.

South of the piazza, Via Teatro Greco leads past the congress hall and (on the right) the large Villa Papale (no. 41), once Palazzo Cacciola and the residence of Florence Trevelyan (*see p. 459 below*). The street ends at a group of cypresses covered with bougainvillea beside the delightful **Hotel Timeo**, with a pergola, the first hotel to be opened in the town in 1864, by Francesco Floresta. In 1850 W.H. Bartlett had complained that 'anywhere but in Sicily a place like Taormina would be a fortune to the innkeepers, but here is not a single place where a traveller can linger to explore the spot'. Illustrious guests of the hotel have included King George V, Winston Churchill, the writers Thomas Mann, Somerset Maugham, André Gide, and Tennessee Williams (who wrote *A Streetcar named Desire* and *Cat on a Hot Tin Roof* here).

Greek theatre

Open 9–1 hr before sunset.

Here is the entrance to the magnificent Greek theatre famous for its picturesque position. First erected in the Hellenistic period (4th century BC), it was almost entirely rebuilt under the Romans when it was considerably altered (1st–3rd centuries AD). This is the largest ancient theatre in Sicily after that of Syracuse (109m in diameter; orchestra 35m across). The cavea, as was usual, was dug out of the hillside; above the nine wedge-shaped blocks of seats, a portico (partially restored in 1955) ran around the top (a few stumps of the 45 columns in front survive). The scena is well preserved; it must have had a double order of columns, the four now visible were erected during restoration carried out in the 19th century. The outer brick wall is pierced by three arched gates; the inner wall was once cased with marble. The foundations of the proscenium, or stage, remain, together with the parascenia, or wings, and traces of porticoes at the back (perhaps shelters from the weather). The theatre was famous for its acoustics. The celebrated view from the top of the cavea inspired Gustav Klimt, Paul Klee and many other artists. Goethe, visiting in 1787, exclaimed: 'Never did any audience, in any theatre, have before it such a spectacle.' On a clear day Etna is seen at its most majestic. In the other direction the Aspromonte Mountains of Calabria extend to the northern horizon, and inland the hills stretch behind Castelmola.

The scena of the Greek theatre at Taormina.

Corso Umberto I

Corso Umberto is lined with shops selling elegant clothes, jewellery, local pottery, confectionery and antiques, with medieval doorways, flower-filled balconies and stepped alleyways. Only some 700m along Corso Umberto from Porta Messina to Porta Catania, at no. 42, is the pretty doorway and tiny rose window of the deconsecrated church of Santa Maria del Piliere. Beyond no. 100, steps (Via Naumachia) lead down to the so-called **Naumachia**, a long brick wall (122m) with niches (formerly decorated with statues) of late Roman date, now supporting a row of houses. Behind it is a huge cistern (*no admission*): it is thought to have been a monumental nymphaeum or a gymnasium. Between nos. 133 and 135 is **Vicolo Stretto**, only 52cm wide, one of the narrowest streets in Italy.

On the left steps lead down to Via Bagnoli Croce and the beautiful public gardens, **Parco Duca di Cesarò**. The gardens are a blaze of colour at all times of the year, with many different varieties of flowering plants and a vast array of Mediterranean and exotic trees. They were created in 1899 by Florence Trevelyan Cacciola (1852–1907), whose bust (a copy of her funerary monument) has been placed on the left of the main entrance on Via Bagnoli Croce. The daughter of Lord Edward Spencer Trevelyan (cousin of the historian), came to Taormina in 1881, married the local doctor Salvatore Cacciola in 1890 and dedicated herself to charitable works among the poor of the town. The most elaborate of the delightful Victorian follies here is the pagoda at the far end which was used by Lady Florence as a bird feeder, with a maze of wooden terraces, antique fragments and lava decoration. In Florence Trevelyan's day the gardens were known, after this construction, as 'The Beehives'.

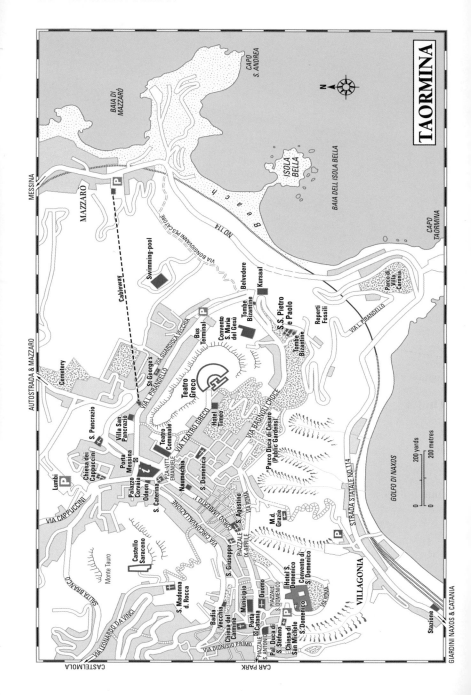

TAORMINA

Outside the gardens, a narrow road with steps descends past a plaque which records the work of Mabel Hill (1866–1940), who came to set up an embroidery school in the town to revive the traditional methods of making Taormina lace, and who, with the painter Robert Kitson, took an interest in local social conditions between the wars. Beyond a modern hotel (Monte Tauro) clinging incredibly to the steep hillside, a lane continues down to the coast at Villagonia near the railway station.

Corso Umberto opens into Piazza IX Aprile (often called Piazza Panoramica), where there is a superb view south across to the sea and Etna. The date refers to April 1860 when the people of Taormina rebelled against the authority of the Bourbons. House martins animate the rooftops. Several cafés here have tables outside, including the Mocambo, once one of the most celebrated cafés in the town, notorious for scandalous brawls and assignations among the rich and famous, now with a mildly decadent atmosphere.

On the left is the former church of Sant'Agostino (1448), now the public library, with a Gothic doorway, and to the right, approached by a pretty flight of steps, stands the 17th-century church of San Giuseppe, which has a heavily decorated Rococo stucco interior, much in demand for fashionable weddings, and often used as a film set. Beyond the Clock Tower (?12th century; restored 1679), is the so-called **Borgo Medioevale**. The corso is lined with small medieval palaces, with doors and windows where supposedly Arab influences linger among the 15th-century details of the Gothic-Catalan doorways and windows. The old hotel Metropol on the left (no. 154) has two columns from the Roman theatre. At no. 185 is the former church of San Giovanni (1533), which is now a club for war veterans and is full of trophies and photographs. Beyond no. 209 a wide flight of steps leads up to Palazzo Ciampoli (1412).

The duomo and environs

Opposite the town hall (18th century) is the duomo (St Nicholas of Bari), founded in the 13th century, with battlements, and two lovely side portals (15th and 16th century). The façade has a late rose window and portal of 1636. In the interior, with six monolithic antique pink marble columns, are a painting of the *Visitation* by Antonino Giuffrè (1463) and a polyptych by Antonello de Saliba (1504), from the former church of San Giovanni, both in the south aisle. In the chapel at the end of the aisle is a delicate tabernacle dated 1648, and an early 16th-century *Madonna and Child* in marble. In the north aisle, first altar, there is a 16th-century panel painting of the *Madonna Enthroned with Saints*, on the second altar, a 16th-century statue of St Agatha and on the third altar, *Adoration of the Magi*.

In the piazza is a charming fountain of 1635, the symbol of Taormina. The bizarre figure on the top would appear to be the bust of an angel on the body of a bull (adapted here as a pregnant female centaur with only two legs). Said to have been found in the ruins of the Greek theatre, it is probably a Baroque pastiche. Steps on the right of the fountain ascend past a small black-and-white Roman mosaic (right; within an enclosure) and (left) the rebuilt church of the Carmine with a pretty campanile. More steps lead up to (left) the Porta Cuseni (or Saraceni), the name given to the district just outside the walls. Outside the gate steps (the Salita Castelmola) continue up to Via Dionisio I which leads right to the Badia Vecchia, with its large crenellated tower with fine mullioned windows and black and white intarsias, now the Antiquarium or the **Museo Archeologico di Taormina** (*open Tues–Sun 9–12.45 & 4–7.45*). The museum has a collection of objects found during excavations around the theatre and nearby; some fragments of sculpture in marble, a list carved in stone of the magistrates of Taormina from the 2nd–1st centuries BC, the financial archives of *Tauromenium* inscribed on stone tablets, and a bronze Byzantine sword found on the sea bed close to Isola Bella.

From here Via Leonardo da Vinci leads past a wall in front of cypresses, bougainvillea and plumbago to **Casa Cuseni** (no. 7). The villa was built by Robert Kitson, a painter, in 1907. It later became a *pensione*, run by his niece, Daphne Phelps, author of *A House in Sicily*. In the opposite direction, above the town, from the Circonvallazione, a path (signposted) leads up through trees to the Madonna della Rocca and the Castello Saraceno (*closed*), from which there are wonderful views. The return can be made by the 738 steps that link the serpentine loops of the Castelmola road.

On the opposite side of Piazza Duomo, a street descends to the ex convent, Hotel San Domenico (first opened as a hotel in 1894), which has a late 16th-century cloister. Field-Marshal Kesselring set up his headquarters here in July 1943, and many of his staff were killed by an Allied air raid which destroyed the church.

Corso Umberto ends at Porta Catania or Porta del Tocco (1440), with the Aragon family emblem on the outside. By the walls here was the Jewish Ghetto (the Jews were forced to leave Sicily and all the Spanish possessions in 1492), with narrow alleys and the interesting old **Palazzo Duchi di Santo Stefano** (*open 9–1 & 3–8*). Built in the 14th–15th centuries, the palace formed part of the second ring of city walls, and with its decorative stone work in contrasting colours of black and white, is a masterpiece of Sicilian-Gothic architecture. The garden and upper floors have a permanent display of works by the sculptor Giuseppe Mazzullo, born in Graniti, a village near Taormina (d. 1988), while the lower floor (with four cross vaults) is used for exhibitions. The little 14th-century church of Sant'Antonio (Gothic portal) was damaged in an air raid in 1943. The church contains a crib made in 1953, which is modelled on the town. The Art Nouveau Hotel Excelsior, built in the 1920s, has a wonderful view from the terrace.

ENVIRONS OF TAORMINA

Mazzarò

A path descends from the Belvedere on Via Pirandello to Mazzarò opposite Capo Sant'Andrea, with fine views of Isola Bella. Another path, off the approach road from Mazzarò and the motorway, starts near the stadium and the cemetery (*open 8–12 & 2–4; Sun and holidays 9–12; closed Fri*), part of which is reserved for non-Catholics and the town's foreign community, to the lovely little Spisone beach. Mazzarò is a pretty bathing resort on Capo Sant'Andrea beneath the hill of Taormina, well supplied with hotels, and easily reached by the cablecar or by steep footpaths. Offshore is the **Isola Bella**, of great natural beauty, now run as a nature reserve by the WWF. In the 19th

Isola Bella from the Belvedere on Via Pirandello, Taormina.

century the Bourbon government sold the island to Florence Trevelyan for 5,000 liras. She built a house on it and later it came into the hands of the Bosurgi family, and was finally acquired by the Sicilian region in 1987. Off Capo Taormina 35 Roman columns lie submerged: they are unworked quarried stone, probably destined for a temple or the portico of a villa, which must have been lost in a shipwreck.

Castelmola

A small village with a dwindling population, Castelmola sits on top of a rock with a ruined Byzantine castle, high above Taormina; it forms part of the association of Italy's most beautiful villages. In the little square, with a view from the terrace of Etna and the bay of Naxos, the Caffè San Giorgio was founded in 1907 and has an interesting collection of autographs in the visitors' book. The village is well known for its almond wine, which was invented at the San Giorgio. Another picturesque café is in Piazza Duomo, the Caffè Turrisi. The façade of the parish church of San Giorgio, reconstructed in Gothic style, opens onto a balcony with another wonderful panorama. The view is still better from Monte Venere or Veneretta (884m), reached by a long footpath from the cemetery of Castelmola.

Giardini Naxos

Four kilometres south of Cape Taormina, Giardini Naxos was founded by a group of settlers led by Theocles of Naxos in 734 BC, and was the first Greek colony on Sicily, closely followed by Syracuse and Megara Hyblaea. It flourished, thanks to the strategic position at the bottom of the Straits, but in 402 BC Dionysius of Syracuse, while extending his power over the island, sent an army to destroy Naxos, possibly in fear of a revolt because of the inhabitants' good relations with the Sicels. Some of the survivors fled to join the Sicels in what is now Taormina, explaining the presence of a Greek theatre in that Sicel town, while the others settled at Francavilla di Sicilia. In the Middle Ages it became a town of fishermen and farmers (*giardini* means citrus groves in Sicilian). From this bay, Garibaldi, with two steamboats and 4,200 men, set out on his victorious campaign against the 30,000 Bourbon troops on the Aspromonte in Calabria (19th August 1860). This quiet place, with a long main street parallel to the sea, was developed in the 1960s into the largest holiday resort in Sicily. The wide bay is now lined with hotels, flats and restaurants from Capo Schisò as far as the railway station of Taormina-Giardini, and new buildings have been erected wherever possible. There are few signposts to Giardini Naxos from Taormina: the older city seems to want to ignore its existence. The point of the cape, Capo Schisò, was formed by an ancient lava flow which can still be clearly seen at the water's edge, by the little harbour. From the sea front there is a view of Monte Tauro, with Taormina and Castelmola above it to the left, and south, a splendid view of Mount Etna.

Museo Archeologico
Site and museum open daily 9–one hour before sunset.
By the modern harbour wall is the entrance to the excavations of Naxos and the Museo Archeologico. The entrance is through a pretty, beautifully tended little garden, in which an ancient lava stream is still visible. An old Bourbon fort here has been restored to house the museum, which has a collection displayed chronologically on two floors and is well labelled. Recent finds on the site include pottery of the 8th century BC coming from the island of Naxos in the Ionian Sea, the first tangible proof that at least some of the first settlers came from there, and gave the name to this first Greek colony on Sicily.

On the Ground Floor are Neolithic and Bronze Age finds from the Cape including Stentinello ware. A Neolithic village site near Syracuse, Stentinello has given its name to the type of Impressed Ware, which usually features round-based dishes with carefully stamped designs, and occasionally decorated to suggest human features, dating from c 5600–4400 BC. Also here are Iron Age finds from the necropolis of Mola including geometric-style pottery.

On the First Floor, the main part of the museum displays terracottas and architectural fragments from a sanctuary at Santa Venera (6th century BC) and finds from a tomb nearby of the 3rd century BC, including four pretty vases for perfume and a glass bowl; material found in the area of the ancient city including a fine antefix with polychrome decoration, and Attic pottery; a little altar dating from around 540 BC decorated with sphinxes in relief; a statuette of a goddess (late 5th century BC); a rare marble lamp from the Cyclades found in the sea (late 7th century BC); and some exceptionally fine Greek coins, dating from 410–360 BC, many of them bearing the head of

Silenus, the Satyr also known as Marsyas often associated with the god Dionysus. In the garden, beyond the lava flow, a collection of underwater finds has been arranged in a small fort. It includes anchors (7th–4th century BC) and amphorae dating from various periods.

The excavations

The fascinating excavations (well signposted) in the fields to the south are reached from the garden. A path, lined with bougainvillea, leads through the peaceful site of the ancient city. Excavations, which are on-going, were first carried out here in 1953.

On the right a path leads across a field planted with lemon trees to a stretch of Greek walls. The main area of excavation is about 15mins walk from the museum in a beautiful orchard planted with a wide variety of exotic trees, including lemon trees, palms, olives, orange trees, eucalyptus and medlar, above flowering bougainvillea, hibiscus and jasmine. Prickly pear, agave and oleander plants also flourish here.

There is an impressive stretch of city walls in black lava (c 500m) parallel to a line of eucalyptus trees. The West Gate is raised on two circular terraces. A path leads to the original entrance of the area sacra, and other remains from the 7th and 6th centuries, including part of the walls, an altar and a Temenos of Aphrodite. A simple temple, constructed towards the end of the 7th century, was built over with a larger temple at the end of the 6th century. Under cover, two kilns are preserved, a circular one for water jars, and a rectangular one for tiles; both were in use during the late 6th and 5th centuries BC. Beyond is the Sea Gate with a fine polygonal lava wall. The high wall, behind a row of cypresses, which blocks the view of the sea, was built during excavation work.

PARCO FLUVIALE DELL'ALCANTARA

From Giardini Naxos a road leads inland along the valley of the Alcantara (*el qantara*, meaning bridge in Arabic), which is verdant with lemon groves. The river, 50km long, springs from Mt Soro in the Nebrodi Mountains. Beside the car park is a lift which descends into the Alcantara Gorge (Gole dell'Alcantara), an unexpectedly deep gorge of basalt prisms, reminiscent of the organ-pipes of Fingal's Cave in the Hebrides or the Devil's Causeway in the Bay of Antrim. It was originally formed by a lava flow from nearby Mt Moio (a side crater), which was eroded by the river forming a narrow passage through the hard basalt. Waders can be hired to explore the gorge. A restaurant and coffee bar can be found by the lift, and a shop selling organic produce from the nearby farm. The whole river valley is now protected as a Regional Park (*www.parcoalcantara.it*). Along the river the vegetation is luxuriant, including willow, beech, oleander, birch, elm, and prickly pear. Mammals include the pine marten, porcupine, and wildcat; among the birds to be spotted are the golden eagle, red kite, dipper, kingfisher, bittern, and glossy ibis.

THE PELORITAN MOUNTAINS

The Peloritan Mountains, in northeastern Sicily, were once thickly forested. The highest peak is the Montagna Grande (1374m). The slopes are carpeted with wildflowers in the spring, and barren for the rest of the year. Conspicuous features of the countryside are the *fiumare*—wide, flat-bottomed torrent beds filled with gravel, similar to the wadis of the Middle East, and usually waterless. With the autumn rain storms the water descends these channels in spate, carrying a considerable quantity of alluvial matter.

SOUTHERN FOOTHILLS

Although the mountains are for the most part inaccessible, there are a number of remote little upland villages that can be reached by steep roads from the coast between Taormina and Messina.

Just to the north of Taormina, above the thriving holiday resort of Letojanni, with its sandy beach, bars and restaurants, are **Mongiuffi** and **Melia**, characteristic of the hill villages on the southern slopes of the Peloritans. Pilgrimages are organised in summer to several sanctuaries of the Madonna here.

Forza d'Agrò is a charming little medieval town, overlooking the privately owned Arab-Norman castle at Cape Sant'Alessio, from which the views extend along the straight coastline towards Messina, across the straits to Calabria and south to Taormina. Above the piazza a lane leads up to circular steps which ascend through a 15th-century Gothic-Catalan archway, Arco Durazzesco, in front of the church of the Santa Trinità, with a 15th-century façade and campanile. It stands next to the former 15th-century Augustinian convent, with a cloister. A fine view of the coast can be had from the terrace behind the church. From the other side of the piazza, a narrow road leads through the village past the Baroque Chiesa Madre, with a lovely 16th-century façade. Opposite is a charming abandoned old house with pretty balconies. The road continues past old houses covered with flowering plants to the castle which was strengthened at the end of the 16th century by a double circle of walls, and which was used for many years as the cemetery.

Savoca and Casalvecchio Siculo

From Santa Teresa Riva, the largest coastal town between Messina and Taormina, a byroad runs inland to Savoca, a village on a saddle between two hills. In the Middle Ages this was the most important town in the province, controlling more territory than Messina. In a private house at the entrance to the village is the Bar Vitelli, with a pretty terrace, a collection of local artisans' tools, and photographs taken when Francis Ford Coppola shot some scenes of *The Godfather* films here. It is easiest to park here and walk up through the old gate past the 15th-century church of San Michele with its two portals dating from the early 16th century. Near here is the **Museo Comunale Città di Savoca** (*open summer 9–12.30 & 4–8; winter 9–6*), displaying a collection of furniture, household equipment, and wise women's charms against illness and the Evil Eye. Beyond the church of San Nicolò, usually known as Santa Lucia (with a 16th-century bust of St Lucy above the portal), the road continues up to the Chiesa Madre, built in the 12th century and restored in the 15th century. By the church is a house with a Gothic-Catalan double window. From here the remains of the 17th-century church of the Immacolata and the ruins of the Norman castle can be seen. Outside the town in the church of the Cappuccini are catacombs (*open summer 10–1 & 4–7; winter 9.30–12.30*) which preserve the mummified bodies, fully dressed, of citizens who lived here in the 18th century.

The road continues over cultivated hills and valleys up to **Casalvecchio Siculo**, charmingly situated on the slopes of a hill. This was the Byzantine *Palachorion*, meaning 'ancient outpost'. Next to the 16th-century Chiesa Madre (which has a beautiful wooden Baroque ceiling), in the central Piazza Crisafulli, is an interesting little **Museo di Arte Sacra** (*T: 0942 761030 to book a visit*), with religious paintings and other works of art, dating from the 12th to the 20th centuries.

The narrow Via Sant'Onofrio continues through the village; beyond, after c. 700m a very narrow road (in places single track) leads left and descends through lovely countryside to one of the most complex and interesting Norman constructions in Sicily, the church of **Santissimi Pietro e Paolo d'Agrò** (*open 9–sunset*). On the site of a Basilian monastery built during the Byzantine domination in the 6th century, this imposing and elegant church occupies a beautiful and peaceful spot near the Agrò torrent. Begun in 1116, it is extremely well preserved both inside and out. An inscription over the door relates how Gerardo il Franco dedicated it to Sts Peter and Paul for the Basilian monks in 1172; having suffered intense damage from earthquakes and Arab incursions, it was probably also restored at this time. Built of brick and black lava, the exterior has splendid polychrome decoration. The Byzantine interior also shows Arab influence in the stalactite vaulting and the tiny domes in the apse and nave. The stucco was removed fom the walls in the 20th century to reveal the attractive brickwork. The columns made from Sardinian granite appear to be Roman in origin. It is possible to return to the coast road from here along a very rough road on the gravel bed of the wide torrent (*fiumara*).

Along the coast to Messina

Back on the coast road, a byroad leads inland to **Fiumedinisi**, where the duomo, probably of Norman origin, has an interesting interior with monolithic columns made of the local marble, and an unusual raised transept. Here, over the north altar, is a Byzantine-style fresco of the *Madonna with the Christ Child*. The Fiumedinisi torrent is one of the most important of these mountains; much of its water is channelled off to supply the needs of Messina. The bed of the torrent is rich in silver ore, exploited until the 18th century for minting coins.

Famous for its thermal baths and mineral-water springs, **Alì Terme** has been visited since the 18th century for the treatment of various ailments. From here the Calabrian coastline is in full view. A winding road leads up to the picturesque village of **Alì**, sadly suffering from depopulation. It is formed of two distinct parts, an Islamic settlement on the southern slopes of Mt Santa Lena, and a 16th-century enlargement on the eastern hill, where the Chiesa Madre (1582), dedicated to the patron St Agatha, is situated.

Itala is built on the side of a valley with lush vegetation. Above the village a road (very narrow in places) continues uphill and then left past ancient olive trees and lemon groves to the well-preserved church of San Pietro. It is preceded by a delightful little courtyard with a garden and palm trees. The priest who has the key lives in the house by the church. The church was built in 1093 by Count Roger in thanksgiving for the Norman victory over the Arabs and has a handsome exterior with blind arcading and a little dome; the interior also presents a raised transept, like that of the church of Fiumedinisi; among the works of art is a 16th-century painted Crucifix and a 16th-century panel painting of the *Madonna with Two Saints*.

Scaletta Zanclea has a long narrow main street (still the main coast road); fishing boats are kept in the alleyways which lead down to the sea under the railway line. The street is particularly busy in the mornings when fresh fish is sold from stalls here. In the upper town the remains of the 13th-century **Castello Ruffo** lie beneath Mt Poverello (1279m), one of the highest peaks of the Peloritans.

Mili San Pietro is in a pretty wooded valley with terraced vineyards and orange groves. On the outskirts of the village (by the school) is the primitive little Norman church of **Santa Maria di Mili** (*open 9–12 & 4–7*), dating from 1092 and founded together with a small convent of Basilian monks by Count Roger as a burial place for his son Jordain, killed in battle; it can be seen just below the road to the left. Steps descend to the ruins of a house, from which the church can be reached under the arch to the left. It has a very interesting vaulted interior.

THE NORTHERN PELORITANS

The northern coast road follows almost exactly the same route as the Roman consular route, *Via Valeria*, which once joined Messina to *Lilybaeum*. At sea off Venetico, Agrippa defeated the fleet of Pompeius at the Battle of Naulochos (36 BC). Inland from the attractive coastal town of **Spadafora**, famous for its bricks, a road climbs the mountains to **Roccavaldina**, with the imposing palace of its feudal Barone Valdina in the central Piazza Umberto. On the corner is the famous 16th-century **Farmacia** (*T: 090 9977741 to request a visit, weekdays only*). The Tuscan-style archway at the entrance to the pharmacy is very rare in Sicily. Inside are 256 pharmacy jars from Urbino, all made in the 16th century in decorated majolica, perfectly preserved on their original shelves.

Santa Lucia del Mela

A narrow road leads up to the fine cattedrale (if closed ring at no. 3 Via Cappuccini, the priest's house), which is of medieval origins with a 15th-century portal. In the south aisle, the first altarpiece of the *Martyrdom of St Sebastian* (in poor condition) is attributed to Zoppo di Gangi (*see p. 423*); on the second altar is a painting of *St Mark the Evangelist* by Deodato Guinaccia (1581) and a statuette of the *Ecce Homo* attributed to Ignazio Marabitti. In the south transept is a painting of *St Blaise* by Pietro Novelli. In the chapel to the right of the sanctuary there is a marble statue of *St Lucy* (1512). The high altarpiece of the *Assumption* is by Fra' Felice da Palermo (1771). In the chapel to the left of the sanctuary is an unusual little sculpted *Last Supper* in the frontal of the altar attributed to Valerio Villareale. The altarpiece in the north transept is by Filippo Iannelli (1676), and on the third north altar is an 18th-century Crucifix. The font dates from 1485.

Also in the piazza is the **Palazzo Vescovile** (Bishop's Palace, *T 090 935008 to request visit*), with a small collection of works of art. Other churches of interest (*open only for services*) include Santissima Annunziata with a campanile of 1461 and a painting of the *Madonna and Child* of c. 1400, and Santa Maria di Gesù (or Sacro Cuore) with a Crucifix by Fra' Umile da Petralia. The road leads up to the castle built by Frederick II of Aragon when he repopulated the town with a colony of Lombards in 1322. All that remains of the old structures is a triangular-plan tower and a round keep. Now it houses the seminary and the sanctuary of the Madonna della Neve (1673) with a *Madonna and Child* by Antonello Gagini.

A mountain road (surfaced as far as Calderado) leads into the Peloritan Mountains from Santa Lucia del Mela as far as Pizzo Croce (1214m). The beautiful **Scifo Forest** here, with chestnuts, oaks and ash trees, has recently been preserved with the help of the local division of the WWF.

Castroreale

An upland town, Castroreale was once the favourite residence of Frederick II of Aragon from whose castle (1324; now in ruins) it gets its name. Despite damage in the earthquake of 1978 the little town is unusually well preserved. The Chiesa Madre contains a *St Catherine* by Antonello Gagini (1534). From Piazza dell'Aquila there is a fine view of the fertile plain. The corso leads to the church of the Candelora, with a 17th-century carved wooden high altarpiece.

In Via Guglielmo Siracusa is the church of **Santa Maria degli Angeli** (*T: 090 9746444 to request a visit*) which contains a gallery with interesting paintings and two sculptures (*St John the Baptist* by Andrea Calamech, 1568; and a *Madonna* by Antonello Freri, 1510).

Further on at no. 31 is the fine **Museo Civico** (*open 9–1 & 4–8; winter 3–7; closed Wed pm*), housed in the restored former oratory of San Filippo Neri, with a charming balcony decorated with prancing horses and lions above the doorway. The collection of sculpture and paintings comes from local churches. On the ground floor are Crucifixes, including a painted one dating from the 14th–15th centuries, Antonello da Saliba's *Madonna and Child Enthroned with Angels*, and a sarcophagus with the effigy of Geronimo Rosso by Antonello Gagini (1507). On the first floor are displayed vestments, precious books, ceramic tiles, and 18th-century paintings, including works by Fra Felice da Sambuca. An 18th–19th-century silver Cross is from the Chiesa Matrice.

At the end of the street is the church of Sant'Agata, with a charming *Annunciation* by Antonello Gagini, dated 1519. At the top of the town a circular tower survives of the castle founded by Frederick II of Aragon in 1324.

Back on the coast road, just short of **Terme Vigliatore**, a thermal resort with a spring called *Fonte di Venere*, used for the treatment of gastrointestinal and liver ailments, at **San Biagio**, are the remains of a large Roman villa (*open Apr–Nov 9–1hr before sunset; Dec–Mar 9–1*). Dating from the 1st century AD, the remains of a large peristyle and part of the baths can be seen. Several rooms, protected by a plastic roof, have black and white mosaics, mostly geometric, and one floor is decorated with a lively fishing scene: dolphins, swordfish and other fish still found off the coast here can be made out. The main hall has a fine opus sectile pavement.

Inland near the long drawn-out settlement of **Rodì** and **Milici**, overlooking the Patti river valley, is the site of ancient *Longane*, a Sicel town of some importance, which was no longer inhabited by the 5th century BC. Traces of the walls survive and the foundations of a sacred building.

From Terme Vigliatore a road (SS 185) runs inland across the western side of the Peloritans (rising to a height of 1100m), connecting the Tyrrhenian coast with the Ionian Sea at Giardini Naxos. This quiet and exceptionally scenic road follows the wide Mazzarrà and Novara valleys, with their extensive citrus-fruit plantations.

Novara di Sicilia, the ancient *Noae*, refounded by the Normans who populated it with Lombards, is now a quiet little town below the main road; it forms part of the association of Italy's most beautiful villages. From Largo Bertolami, with a 19th-century bronze statue of David, Via Duomo leads down to the 16th-century duomo. In the south aisle is a wooden statue of the *Assumption* by Filippo Colicci. In Via Bellini there is a beautiful little 19th-century opera house.

The fantastic bare horn-shaped **Rocca Novara** (1340m) stands at the end of the Peloritan range. The pass of Sella Mandrazzi beyond is surrounded by thick woods of pine and fir. The view extends to the coastline and the sanctuary of Tindaris on its promontory. The scenery is particularly fine in this area. From here the mountain road descends through deserted pastureland and eventually left through orange groves to **Francavilla di Sicilia**. Above the cemetery on the outskirts is the well-signposted Convento dei Cappuccini (17th century) where the church has a beautiful 15th-century *Madonna and Child* attributed to the school of Antonello da Messina and the 17th-century funerary monument of the Ruffo family, among other works. A Greek sanctuary was excavated in the town in 1979–84 and the votive statues found here are now displayed in the Museo Archeologico of Syracuse. Among the objects discovered are *pinakes*, pictures made of terracotta relating to the cult of Persephone, which it was previously thought were unique to Locri in Calabria. It is believed that some of the survivors of Dionysius' destruction of *Naxos* in 402 BC took refuge here.

Another very winding minor road leads southwest from Terme Vigliatore to **Montalbano Elicona**, a little hill town in a fine position surrounded by woods, with a castle (1302–11), built by Frederick II of Aragon, open for exhibitions and concerts. Montalbano Elicona also forms part of the association of Italy's most beautiful villages.

MILAZZO

The main port for ferries and hydrofoils to the Aeolian Islands, Milazzo stands on the isthmus of a narrow peninsula on the northeast coast of the island. It is an old city with considerable charm, rather marred by an oil refinery and power station on the outskirts. Milazzo was the ancient *Mylai*, founded as a sub-colony by Greeks from *Zancle* (Messina) in 716 BC. Here Duilius defeated the Carthaginians in a sea battle (260 BC), and here in 1860 Garibaldi successfully assaulted the castle, garrisoned by Bourbon troops, promoting J.W. Peard, a Cornish volunteer, to the rank of colonel on the field. The castle, with its successive and extensive modifications, demonstrates the strategic importance of the town in the past.

EXPLORING MILAZZO

Borgo Piano

The town is divided into the older, higher district, Borgo Antico, and the lower-lying, more modern district, Borgo Piano, which is now the centre. The road for the centre passes the port where the boats and hydrofoils for the Aeolian Islands dock. In Via Crispi is the late 19th-century Neoclassical Municipio. On the other side of the building (reached through the courtyard) is Piazza Caio Duilio. Here is the harmonious red façade of the former convent of the Carmelitani (16th century; restored), with the tourist information bureau. Next to it is the Baroque façade of the Carmine (1574; rebuilt in 1726–52), and, on the other side of the square, Palazzo Proto, Garibaldi's headquarters for a time in 1860. In Via Pescheria, behind the post office, fresh fish is sold in the mornings from stalls in the street.

The marine parade (Lungomare Garibaldi), planted with trees, is a continuation of Via Crispi along the sea front. The 18th-century church of San Giacomo is well-sited at a fork in the road which leads to the **Duomo Nuovo** (1937–52), which contains paintings by Antonello de Saliba and Antonio Giuffrè, and sculptures attributed to the Gagini school. Further on, Via Colombo leads away from the sea past two little Art Nouveau villas, Villino Greco and Villa Vaccarino, now surrounded by unattractive buildings.

Borgo Antico

From Piazza Roma, Via Impallomeni leads up towards the castle past the Baroque 18th-century church of San Francesco di Paola, which contains six paintings of miracles of the saint by Letterio Paladino (1691–1743). The **Antiquarium Domenico Ryolo** (*open 9.30–1 & 3–6.30; closed Mon*) houses in six rooms a large collection of material found in the necropolis surrounding the city. The various burials shed interesting light on life and death in the area from the 8th to the 1st centuries BC, and show the evolution of Greek and Roman influence on the population. Terracotta vases were widely used for burying the dead, who were interred in the foetal position, or cremated. The presence of pottery from all over the Mediterranean demonstrates the role of ancient *Mylai*, an important harbour at the centre of the trade routes of the time. The old women's prison, built in 1816 and abandoned around 1960, has thus been put to good use.

From here the 17th-century church of the Immacolata and the church of San Rocco with its crenellated top can be seen above on the left. Just short of here, on the right, is the closed church of San Salvatore (18th century) by Giovan Battista Vaccarini. Picturesque low houses and open-air cafés (in the summer) surround the double walls of the castle (*for opening times T: 090 9221291; closed Mon*). Built by the Arabs in the 10th–11th centuries on the site of the Greek acropolis, enlarged by Frederick II in 1239, then by the Aragonese in the 14th century, by Charles V in the 16th century, and restored in the 17th century. The Spanish walls date from the 16th century and enclose a large area used for theatrical performances and concerts in the summer. Here are the remains of the Palazzo dei Giurati, used as a prison in the 19th century, and the **Duomo Antico**, an interesting late 17th-century building attributed to Camillo Camilliani or possibly Natale Masuccio. It was abandoned when the new cathedral was begun in 1937. In the same area a Gothic doorway leads to the oldest structures of the castle: the imposing Arab-Norman keep and a great hall known as the Sala del Parlamento.

From the castle, a flight of steps leads to the Church of the Rosary, built in the 16th century and restored in the 18th. The convent by the church housed the Inquisition.

Capo di Milazzo

The narrow peninsula of Capo di Milazzo is simply called *il capo* by the local people. The road threads its way through olive groves and prickly pears to a point where steps go down to the sanctuary of **St Anthony of Padua**, a little church (1575) built in a cave where the saint took refuge after a shipwreck in January 1221. A path continues to a lighthouse and down to a stony beach and the crystal-clear sea. It is a beautiful spot, but crowded on summer weekends with bathers. From the cape the view (on a clear day) encompasses all the Aeolian Islands, and also Mount Etna.

THE AEOLIAN ISLANDS

The name of the archipelago derives from *Aeolus*, the mythical guardian of the winds, who inhabited the largest island, Lipari, with his six sons and six daughters. This volcanic area marks the point where the African plate meets the European, folding over and forcing itself under the opposing plate. Two of the islands, Vulcano and Stromboli, are still active. All are protected as a nature reserve. On Stromboli the slopes on the opposite side to the lava flows are fertile and cultivated with vineyards. Vulcano smells strongly of sulphur and there is little cultivated land but it is a magical place where shepherds pasture their sheep and goats. In spring, when the yellow broom is in flower, it is breathtakingly beautiful. Alicudi and Filicudi still show signs of the the patient terracing carried out for many centuries to preserve the tiniest drop

The view from Punto Quattrocchi on Lipari towards the Faraglioni rocks and Vulcano.

of water. Salina, with its two extinct volcanic cones, is the greenest and the most fertile of the group, with extensive vineyards and forests where every effort is made to prevent summer wildfires. Lipari, the largest of the islands, has unfortunately suffered several in recent years, although the island's ancient tracks, ideal for gentle trekking, have been repaired. Panarea is a tiny island full of wild flowers, with pretty houses set in the vegetation. Capers grow everywhere on the islands, even on sheer rock faces. Flying fish can often be seen in the summer, and also groups of dolphins, close to shore. The whole archipelago is designated a World Heritage Site. Being small islands, Lipari, Panarea and Vulcano can become very crowded in July and August.

HISTORY OF THE AEOLIAN ISLANDS

The islands were important in ancient times because of the abundance of obsidian, a hard volcanic glass used for making tools and exported throughout the Mediterranean. The earliest traces of settlement found belong to the Stentinello culture of the Neolithic Age. In the Middle Bronze Age the islands were on the main trade routes between the Aegean Islands and the Western Mediterranean. The Greeks colonized Lipari in c. 600 BC, and in the following centuries the islands were attacked by the Athenians and the Carthaginians. They fell to Rome in 252 BC. The population dropped in later centuries, because of an increase in the activity of the volcanoes, especially on Lipari. In 836 the islands were raided by the Arabs, who destroyed the towns and burnt them, carrying off the inhabitants as slaves and scattering the remains of St Bartholomew. A stone sarcophagus containing the mummified body of a man who had been flayed alive, thought to be Bartholomew, had drifted onto a Lipari beach in the 5th century. From that time nobody returned to live on the islands until Count Roger sent a group of Benedictine monks there in 1083. In spite of the concession of various privileges, it was not easy to attract people to colonise the islands, because of the precarious security situation; an enterprising monk declared that he had miraculously traced all the remains of St Bartholomew, who would again protect the islands. But piracy, notwithstanding the good saint, was a constant threat; when the fearsome pirate Khaireddin the Redbeard attacked Lipari in 1544, burning the city and carrying off the entire population, there was pessimism about the islands ever being inhabited again. But the viceroy Pedro of Toledo immediately sent aid, rebuilt the fortifications, confirmed the old privileges and allowed so many new ones, that large groups of settlers came from Campania and Calabria. In the 19th century the citadel of Lipari was transformed into a prison, and in 1926 it became a place of isolation for the political opponents of the Fascist regime. Only in 1950 was the citadel opened again to visitors. A heavy blow to the economy came in the late 19th century, when thousands of people emigrated (mostly to Australia), because of a blight which destroyed the grape-vines.

LIPARI

The town

Lipari (37 square kilometres), ancient *Meligunis*, the chief island of the group and about 40km from Milazzo on the Sicilian mainland, has become a popular summer resort. About half of the island's 12,000 inhabitants are concentrated in the lively and attractive little town of Lipari with its low houses, their balconies decorated with plants, and maze of narrow streets. The citadel of deep red lava rock commands the shore above the town, and separates the two harbours. On the north side of the acropolis is the port used by hydrofoils and ferries, Marina Lunga or **Porto Sottomonastero**.

The main road of the town is Corso Vittorio Emanuele. On the far (west) side is Palazzo Vescovile, eventually to be restored as the seat of a Diocesan Museum. Beside it is the archaeological zone of Contrada Diana where two Roman hypogea were found, and where excavations revealed part of the Greek walls (5th–4th centuries BC) of the ancient city, and Roman houses. It is now very overgrown and no longer open regularly to the public.

Near Porto Sottomonastero is Piazza Mazzini, with a garden and some charming houses beside the neo-Gothic town hall. The 18th-century church of **San Francesco** has pretty marble altars. Steps lead down to the crypt which was the burial place for the islanders before the cemetery (which can be seen nearby) was opened. The route from Piazza Mazzini to the citadel or acropolis leads through impressive 16th-century Spanish fortifications, with double gates and an entrance tunnel which incorporate Classical fragments.

On the other side of the citadel, at **Marina Corta**, the fishing boats dock beside the picturesque church of the Anime del Purgatorio. Another attractive church close by is San Giuseppe, at the top of a ramp. Outside the church, fishermen are often at work mending their nets, their colourful boats pulled up on the quay beside a solitary palm tree, watched over by the statue of the patron St Bartholomew.

Via Garibaldi winds uphill through the town from Marina Corta. It passes a wide, scenic flight of steps constructed at the beginning of the 20th century up to the citadel, framing the façade of the Duomo at the top. The hill itself is a very peaceful spot, verdant with oleanders, prickly pear and ivy.

The **duomo** (*open 10–12*), dedicated to the patron saint Bartholomew, was first built on this site by Count Roger (c. 1084). The pretty interior, hung with chandeliers, has a vault frescoed in the 18th century. On the side altars are 18th-century reliquary busts in gilded wood. In the north transept is a *Madonna of the Rosary*, attributed to Girolamo Alibrandi, and a statue in silver of St Bartholomew which dates from 1728. The statue, together with an elaborate silver reliquary of a boat, is carried in procession through the streets on 24th August, 16th November, 13th February and 5th March. The Benedictine cloister has been restored. Dating from 1131, with later additions, it has vaulted walks, and columns of different shapes and sizes (some of them Doric, and some re-used from Roman buildings). Several primitive capitals are decorated with animals and birds.

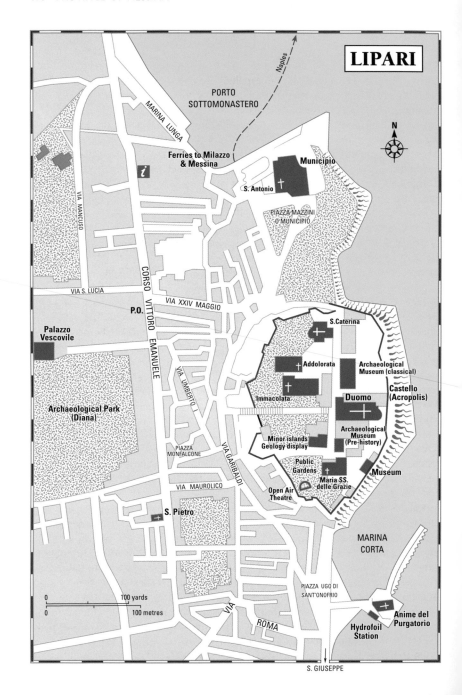

The last church on the hill is Maria Santissima delle Grazie, with a fine restored façade, reached down a few steps in a little garden. On the other side of the road are public gardens (with fine views) which have a large number of Greek and Roman sarcophagi. These were found in the necropolis of Contrada Diana (late 5th century and 4th century BC), at the foot of the acropolis (now covered by the modern town). There is also an open-air theatre here, built in 1978.

Museo Archeologico
Open 9–1.30 & 3–7; one or more of the buildings may be closed for want of custodians.
The Museo Archeologico Bernabò Brea is arranged in several separate buildings. The superb collections, beautifully displayed in chronological sequence (with labels also in English), contain finds from Lipari and other islands in the Aeolian group, as well as from Milazzo and southern Italy.

Beside the duomo is the former Palazzo Vescovile (early 18th century), with an attractive portal and balconies, which houses the first section dedicated to prehistory. A tour begins on the first floor here with Neolithic finds from Lipari, including painted vases, Serra d'Alto-style pottery (resembling southern Italian forms), and red pottery of the Diana style, so called because discovered nearby in the area known as Contrada Diana. Objects found here on the castle hill belonging to the Capo Graziano (1800–1400 BC) and Milazzese (c. 1400–1250 BC) cultures are displayed, showing Greek influences. Notable are the vessels on tall pedestals, thought to have been used from a sitting position on the floor.

The ground floor is dedicated to Ausonian culture (from southern Italy) and the finds made on the castle hill. Many show the influence of the Italian mainland: the vessels have a great variety of strangely shaped handles. There are also the remains of a small cooking device, and a large terracotta pot, the repository of almost 100kg of bronze objects from the 9th century BC. There are signs of a violent destruction of Lipari in the 9th century BC, and the island appears to have remained uninhabited for the next three centuries. The Greek and Roman period on Lipari is covered in Room 10. The large restored Attic vase, used for mixing water and wine, has an exquisite delicate black-figure decoration on the rim showing the *Labours of Hercules* and (inside) a frieze of ships. The couchant lion (c. 575 BC) carved from volcanic rock, probably guarded a votive deposit to the wind god Aeolus. Also here are a Roman statue of a girl of the 2nd century AD, found in the bishop's palace, and a statuette of Asclepius (4th century BC).

A door leads out to the garden which contains sarcophagi from Contrada Diana and the Epigraphic Pavilion (*not always open*) which contains funerary inscriptions of 5th–1st centuries BC. Opposite, a group of old houses display prehistoric finds from the minor islands: Panarea (from the Calcara and Milazzese sites), Filicudi and Salina. In the entrance are three huge pithoi from Portella on Salina. Next door is a building which houses a geological display on three floors with diagrams, maps, reliefs and models which illustrate volcanic activity and the formation of the Aeolian Islands. In the courtyard is a small collection of epigraphs.

On the other side of the cathedral is the pavilion devoted to the Classical period.

The displays in this building begin with finds from Milazzo displayed in chronological sequence from the Middle Bronze Age to the 3rd century BC. A reconstruction of a burial site shows the burial pots in the position in which they were found. Another reconstruction, of the Piazza Monfalcone necropolis (1125–1050 BC) in Lipari, is followed by the superb collection of terracotta and stone sarcophagi from Lipari, including the stone example found in Contrada Diana, which is perfectly preserved. It is thought to have been made by the sculptor in the 2nd or 1st centuries BC as his own tomb.

On the upper floors are Attic red-figure kraters of the 5th century BC and early Sicilian and Campanian red-figure vases (4th century BC) including a splendid krater by the 'Painter of Adrasto' with columns (c. 450 BC). Grave goods from a similar period, and Attic pottery on a white ground, are followed by a superb display of theatrical figurines in terracotta, statuettes (early 4th–mid-3rd centuries BC) found on Lipari. Especially striking are the statuettes of dancers, and Andromeda with her child. A fascinating and unique collection of tragic masks and theatrical terracottas can also be seen here along with some very fine gold jewellery. Further rooms contain brightly coloured vases by the Lipari Painter, a master who excelled in the representation of the female figure, and who enjoyed working with different colours, and southern Italian vases including a krater with Dionysus watching a nude acrobat and two actors, and a bronze hydra with a female bust (early 5th century BC). Hellenistic gold jewellery here includes a ring of the 4th century BC with a female nude. The top floor displays the latest finds from the hill showing evidence of the destruction of Lipari in 252 BC, and sporadic finds from the Roman and Norman periods, as well as medieval and Renaissance ceramics.

In the basement, underwater archaeology has provided finds dating from 2000 BC to the 5th century BC, discovered near Capistello (Lipari), and near Filicudi and Panarea, including a magnificent display of amphorae. There are also finds from the wreck of a 17th-century Spanish warship.

Outside, the extensive excavations begun in 1950 on the summit of the hill by Luigi Bernabò Brea, have revealed a sequence of levels of occupation, dating from the Neolithic Age when the islands were first inhabited. Because the prevailing winds have consistently brought volcanic dust to settle here, cuttings reveal the history of habitation in remarkable detail. The unique pottery strata (reaching a depth of 9m) make the acropolis the key dating-site for the central Mediterranean. The different levels are well labelled and explained by diagrams. The exterior of the church of Santa Caterina has been restored. Beyond the excavations, the small Baroque churches of the Addolorata and the Immacolata can be seen.

The island

A road (26.5km) encircles the island. It leads north from Lipari via the stony beach of **Canneto** to traverse magnificent white cliffs of pumice, with deep gallery quarries. The loading jetties protrude into the sea, a brilliant turquoise blue because of the pumice on the seabed. Beyond Porticello the road crosses remarkable red and black veins of obsidian, some of which reach the sea. The beaches are covered with pumice and obsidian, and some of the paths in the villages are cut out of obsidian. A road connects **Acquacalda** (where there are hot springs in the sea) with Quattropani. At **Piano Conte** lava battle-axes and Bronze Age weapons have been found. Near the coast (reached by a byroad) are the hot springs of **San Calogero** with remains of Roman baths. A tholos has come to light here. The road returns to Lipari past the viewpoint of **Quattrocchi**, literally 'four eyes', the number needed presumably to encompass the superb panorama (*pictured p. 473*). **Monte Sant'Angelo** (594m), in the centre of the island, is an extinct stratified volcano of unusual form (superb views).

PANAREA

Panarea (3.5 square kilometres; population 320) lies to the northeast (15km from Lipari), towards Stromboli. Its natural beauty and the style of the local architecture have been carefully preserved although the hotels and restaurants, popular with famous and wealthy Italians, are more expensive than those on the other islands. Electricity was only brought to the island in 1982. Near the fishing harbour hot spring water mixes with the sea.

A walk (c. 30 mins) leads to a naturally defended promontory on the southern tip of the island. On this superb site the Bronze Age village of the Milazzese culture (probably inhabited in the 14th century BC), with 23 huts, was excavated in 1948. Mycenaean ceramics and native vases showing Minoan influences were brought to light (now in the Museo Archeologico in Lipari, *see above*).

At the opposite end of the island, near the last houses on the coast, a path descends to the shore at Calcara where the fumaroles emit sulphurous gases. Nearby are traces of Neolithic pits made from boulders and volcanic clay, probably used for offerings. A Greek wreck was found offshore here in 1980, and from then until 1987 some 600 pieces of ceramics were recovered from its cargo of precious terracotta vases (5th–4th centuries BC), some of which are now exhibited in the Lipari Museum.

In the sea near the island the beautifully coloured rocks of **Lisca Bianca** and **Basiluzzo** (with many traces of Roman occupation) provide a foreground to the ever-changing view of Stromboli.

STROMBOLI

Stromboli (12.5 square kilometres; population 410), c. 28km from Lipari, is the best-known island of the archipelago because of its continual volcanic activity. It consists of a single cone (924m); the present active crater is 200m below the summit. It has been abandoned several times after severe eruptions, but is now again increasing in population, and is popular with tourists. Strong activity in December 2002 caused a tsunami, and considerable damage. The inhabitants were evacuated for several days.

The main village of Stromboli, **San Vincenzo**, is on the northeast side; ferries and hydrofoils dock at the harbour of **Scari**. The boats also call at **Ginostra**, an attractive small group of houses on a rocky headland on the southwest tip of the island, still using generators for electricity, and completely isolated from the rest of the island. A small dock for the ferries and hydrofoils has been built here at last, in spite of opposition, meaning that it is no longer necessary to use the tiny harbour of Pertuso, which has laid claim to being the smallest port in the world. Ginostra has about 30 permanent inhabitants, of whom ten are originally from Germany.

Eruptions occur on the northwest side of the volcano and are not visible from the villages. The cone should be ascended with a guide (c. 3hrs), because trekking on the volcano is dangerous, but an easy footpath from San Vincenzo ascends as far as the Semaforo (c. 1hr 30mins), from which point the explosions can usually be seen. Small eruptions normally occur at frequent intervals; on days of unusual violence the spectacle (best seen at night from the sea) of the volcanic matter rushing down the Sciara del Fuoco into the sea is particularly impressive. Climbs on the volcano (very strenuous, and particularly exhilarating at night) can be booked (well ahead, places are limited) with Magmatrek (*T: 090 9865768; www.magmatrek.it*).

Off the northeast coast is the striking rock of **Strombolicchio**, a steep block of basalt (43m).

SALINA

Salina (27 square kilometres; population 2,400), 4km northwest of Lipari, is the highest of the islands (962m), and is formed by two twin volcanic cones and the saddle between them. The shape of **Monte dei Porri** is one of the most perfect mountain cones in the world. It has been identified with *Anthemoessa*, Homer's island of the Sirens, and was anciently called *Didyme*. Its population lives in three municipalities, each formed of several picturesque villages: **Santa Marina**, **Malfa** and **Leni**.

On disembarking from the ferry or hydrofoil at Santa Marina, aim straight for the little square, where some of the best fresh fruit granita on the islands can be found at a small kiosk. But Salina is justly famous for its Malvasia wine (*see box opposite*). Capers are also grown here in abundance. The island is exceptionally green and very pleasant walks can be taken on the two mountains, the Monte dei Porri (mountain of leeks) and the Fossa delle Felci (glen of the ferns). The latter is partly covered in woods of chestnut. The attractive old houses and the fine scenery have been protected for many years, thanks to an enlightened local administration.

On the east coast, near the Santa Marina lighthouse, a Middle Bronze Age village has been excavated (*not open to the public*), and traces of Roman houses have been found on the island (those at the north end of the lungomare can be seen). After the Arab conquest of the Aeolian Islands in 838 the island remained virtually uninhabited until the 16th century. The island was the setting for the Oscar-winning film *Il Postino*, which describes an episode in the life of Pablo Neruda. Among the interesting varieties of bird life that can be spotted on a visit to Salina are flamingoes. They usually pause to rest during their migratory flights on the salt pan of Salina, at Lingua. The kestrel, sparrow hawk and buzzard are birds of prey present as nesting species, both here and on the other islands.

MALVASIA

This exquisite wine was once so much in demand that almost all the available land on the Aeolian Islands, including the tiny islet of Basiluzzo, was dedicated to its production. The industry supported a population (in 1880) of over 32,000 people, while today there are only 15,000 inhabitants in the archipelago. Most of the wine was exported, some of it to England where it was called Malmsey. In 1881 a terrible blight hit the islands and destroyed almost all the vines; at least 20,000 islanders emigrated, mostly to Australia.

New incentives for Malvasia came in the 1960s, when a young architect, Carlo Hauner, was invited to spend a few days painting on Salina, and he decided to take up the challenge of re-introducing the production of Malvasia to the island. Hauner is still the name to look for when buying this delectable drink; the winery is now run by his son. Made from white Malvasia grapes (95 per cent) and black Corinth (5 per cent), after harvesting the bunches are left to wither in the sun on wicker trays for 10 days before being pressed. Sweet but not cloying, it is best drunk chilled as an aperitif. It is thought that the Greeks first planted vines here in the 5th century BC.

FILICUDI

The remote and picturesque island of Filicudi (9.5 square kilometres; population 305) lies 19km west of Salina. Anciently called *Phoenicoesa*, it has comfortable accommodation and is a peaceful place to spend a holiday. Two prehistoric villages have been excavated on Capo Graziano; on the point (Montagnola) 12 huts were uncovered showing evidence of rebuilding before their destruction in the Milazzese period, while just inland, three oval huts yielded Bronze Age vases. Off the cape in 1975 a hoard of Bronze Age pottery was found on the site of a shipwreck. The picturesque little fishing harbour of **Pecorini** is very popular with the rich and famous in the summer. The offshore stacks are a haven for birds, especially Eleonora's falcon.

ALICUDI

The most westerly island is Alicudi, with a particularly far-away, lonely character, one-and-a-half hours' hydrofoil journey from Lipari. Here five square kilometres support a dwindling population of 102, several of whom are originally from Germany. It is a particularly beautiful island, with terraces and attractive local architecture. There are no roads, only steep tracks and steps over the hills, and no public illumination (it has only had electricity since 1990). Several houses can be rented, but it should be borne in mind that there is only one small shop selling basic necessities. Visitors should bring everything else with them, including a torch for getting around after dark, and camera films.

VULCANO

Vulcano (21 square kilometres; population 800) is the most southerly of the isles (separated from the southern tip of Lipari by a channel less than a kilometre wide) and easily reached from the Sicilian mainland or by frequent hydrofoil services from Lipari (and by local boat excursions). It is of outstanding interest because of its geological structure and the spectacular volcanic landscape with black lava rocks on the sea and black lava beaches. The last volcanic eruption took place from 1898 till 1890. It has simple houses mostly built in the 20th century in a disorderly way. Deserted out of season, it becomes very crowded in summer. Many northern Italians have their summer houses here. A characteristic of Vulcano is the strong smell of sulphur, especially in the area around the port. The easily accessible deposits of sulphur, alum, boric acid and other minerals, were first exploited industrially in the early 19th century; after 1860 the deposits were purchased for extraction by a certain Mr Stevenson, a Scot who had fallen in love with the island. He also planted vineyards and fruit orchards, dug wells, and tried to improve the lot of the islanders. The eruption of 1898 put a violent end to his dreams. His house, near the mud pools, can still be seen.

The boats dock at **Porto di Levante** near the makeshift quay used by the hydrofoils. A road with simple shops and a few cafés leads to **Porto di Ponente** with mud pools on the beach fed by hot springs. The fine black lava beach nearby, with a number of hotels, is crowded in summer. Caution is advised while swimming, because there are hot springs in the sea, quite close to the shore.

In the other direction from the port a straight road leads across the plain at the foot of the volcano. A narrow path (signposted; about 1km from the port) leads up across the fine volcanic soil and rocks to the top of the crater (391m), called **Fossa Grande**, in about 1hr. The route can be damaged and almost impassable after

Rock formation on Vulcano.

heavy rain, but is normally quite easy (although sturdy shoes are necessary). There is a remarkable view of the inside of the crater, and the rim steams constantly with sulphurous vapours. On a clear day all of the Aeolian Islands can be seen from here. The path can be followed right around the rim in about one hour.

Most of the islanders live in the upland plain of the island known as **Piano**, 7km from the port (reached by a few buses every day). Here there is one inn and bar, a shop, a church and a school: most of the fields have now been abandoned, and some of the houses are now only used in summer. The Piano road passes close to the volcano and at the top of the hill, by the first house on the corner, a byroad leads left. Another turn left leads to the edge of a cliff with a number of caves and a view of the coast. The road continues gently uphill past a road on the left for **Gelso**, with some restaurants open in summer and good sea bathing. Another byroad leads to **Capo Grillo** which has the best panorama on the island. The Piano road ends in front of the parish church destroyed by an earthquake in 1978 and rebuilt in 1988.

On the northern tip of the island is **Vulcanello**, a volcanic cone which rose out of the sea in 183 BC. Near the Faraglione della Fabbrica, a high rock with alum quarries, are the hot springs of Acqua Bollente and Acqua del Bagno. Between Vulcano and Lipari are some striking basalt stacks, including the Pietralunga, emerging from the sea, a 72-metre high obelisk of basalt.

THE COAST TO CAPO ORLANDO

The *Black Madonna*

On the headland of Capo Tindari stands a conspicuous church near the excavations of the ancient city of *Tyndaris* founded in the 4th century BC. The road leads to a car park below the church, a modern sanctuary built in 1957–79, to house a seated Byzantine-style statue of the *Black Madonna*, greatly venerated since the 10th century (pilgrimage on 8th September) when it was found in a wooden chest on the beach under the cliff, apparently abandoned by pirates. The statue, recently restored and divested of the white silk robe which covered her for centuries, is made of painted cedar wood from Lebanon and was probably made in the 7th or 8th century, although it is not known where. Life-size, the Madonna, her Child and her throne, are carved from one large block of wood. The well-preserved red and blue colours with which the group is painted symbolize divinity and humanity. Strongly reminiscent of Nefertiti, or of an Egyptian goddess, the statue may have been made for Egyptian Copts, deliberately similar to Isis and her son Horus. The structure of the new church encloses the old 16th-century sanctuary, on the seaward side, with a portal of 1598 (the custodian has the key) and an interesting reproduction of the Madonna, allowing a closer look. From the terrace in front of the church there are splendid views of the Aeolian Islands. The currents in the shallows at the foot of the cliffs produce beautiful formations of sand and gravel and areas of temporary marshland that are of great interest to naturalists.

Tyndaris

Open 9–1hr before sunset.
From the car park a path and steps lead up to the road which leads to the entrance to the impressive ruins of *Tyndaris*. The ancient city was founded by Dionysius of Syracuse in 396 BC after his victory over the Carthaginians, when he felt the need to have a permanent base on the north coast of the island. To achieve this aim, he forcibly transferred the entire population of *Leontinoi* there. Tyndaris remained an ally of Syracuse until taken by the Romans in 254. A large part of the city slipped into the sea during an earthquake caused by the eruption of Vesuvius in 79 AD, and then by another earthquake in 365 AD.

Excavations begun in the 19th century by Robert Fagan, then British Consul, were resumed from 1949–64, and are still in progress.

A path leads down through a little garden to the excavations in a grove of olives and pines planted with bougainvillea and prickly pear. The beautiful, peaceful site over-looks fields with olive trees on a cliff directly above the sea. To the right, along the *decumanus maximus* (main street), are the remains of Roman buildings, including a series of *tabernae* (shops), two private houses (with peristyle and mosaics), and a bath-house with black and white mosaics. At the end of the decumanus is the **Basilica**, once called the Gymnasium, but now thought to have been the Magistrates' Court, or a monumental entrance to the agora (the square in front of the church). The façade, which collapsed in Byzantine times, was restored in 1956. It is an unusual building with barrel vaulting across the main road of the city: formerly dated to the 1st century BC, it was actually built in the 1st century AD.

To the left of the entrance is the large **theatre**, a Greek building adapted by the Romans for use by gladiators. The Greek walls (3rd century BC), obscured by vegeta-tion on the seaward side, survive in a good state of preservation to the south (beside the approach road below the sanctuary), extending, with interval towers, for several hundred metres on either side of the main gate, a dipylon with a barbican.

The small **museum** has a reconstruction of the theatre's monumental stage and backdrop, and finds from the site, including two fragments of Hellenistic statues of winged victories, 4th century BC and 1st century BC statuettes, a colossal head of the emperor Augustus (1st century), vases, reliefs, a capital of the 1st century BC and a theatrical mask.

Patti

Some 7km west of Tindari, Patti is an important agricultural town on a hill. It was looted and burned by the pirate Khaireddin the Redbeard in 1554. More recently, in 1978 the town was severely damaged by an earthquake.

In the cathedral of Norman origin, dedicated to the patron St Bartholomew, is the Renaissance tomb of Adelaide (d. 1118), queen of Count Roger, the first king of Sicily. She died of leprosy. The 16th-century painting of the *Madonna enthroned with Child* is by Antonello de Saliba.

Close to the cathedral is the **Diocesan Museum** (*T: 0941 240800, www.diocesipatti.it*), with a rich collection of bishop's vestments, Missals, silverware, paintings and marble reliefs from the local churches, dating from 1534. Patti is renowned for its colourful and useful ceramics; as the proverb has it: 'If you want a tasty dish, cook it in a pot from Patti'.

During the construction of the motorway from Messina part of a large **Roman villa** (*open 9–1hr before sunset*) was uncovered here in 1973 (follow the signs for Marina di Patti and the motorway: the entrance to the site is beneath the motorway viaduct). This large villa (4th century AD; about 20,000 square metres) was made up of three main structures, with three different orientations. On the western side there are the remains of walls relating to rooms. The main structures centre on a large peristyle with the remains of a pillared portico; on the northeast side part of a thermae has been brought to light. The villa also contains a few polychrome mosaics with geometric and floral designs as well as hunting scenes.

Gioiosa Marea

A seaside resort, Gioiosa Marea was built in the 18th century after an earthquake destroyed the old town of Gioiosa Guardia (or Gioiosa Vecchia). The fascinating ruins of the old town survive high up (828m) on a hill beyond the motorway. A winding road leads up to them, from where there is a wonderful view of the coast and the Aeolian Islands. Vulcano is only 19km offshore.

Capo d'Orlando

Capo d'Orlando is another seaside resort with a rocky promontory and sandy beaches, off which Frederick II of Aragon was defeated in 1299 by Roger of Lauria, commanding the allied fleets of Catalonia and Anjou. The promontory, already occupied in the Greek era, is noted for its sudden storms. It is crowned by a 14th-century castle and the 16th-century sanctuary church of Maria Santissima.

Just outside the town of Capo d'Orlando, at 44 Contrada Vina, is the Fondazione Famiglia Piccolo di Calanovella (*open 9–12 & 4–6, summer also 3.30–7.30*), the house and garden of the Calanovella family, now protected as a foundation instituted by the last descendants. The beautifully well-kept rooms and gardens are a poignant testimony to the lives led by these artistic, withdrawn and proudly Sicilian aristocrats in the middle of the 20th century, and to an era that was drawing to a close. Baron Lucio Piccolo, a prize-winning poet, was a cousin of Giuseppe Tomasi di Lampedusa (*see p. 217*), and encouraged him to write his famous novel *The Leopard*, while his sister Agata Giovanna was a keen gardener and botanist, and their brother Casimiro a gifted photographer who also painted watercolours. Now and again they would all indulge in a séance. In the garden is the cemetery for their cats and dogs.

To the east, at **Lido di San Gregorio**, there is a beautiful sandy beach and a little fishing harbour. Nearby are the **Terme di Bagnoli** (*open 9–2*), surrounded by a little garden. These were Roman baths, part of a private villa built in the late 4th or 5th century AD. Eight rooms have been unearthed, some of which had been dislodged in an earthquake.

THE NEBRODI MOUNTAINS

The Parco dei Nebrodi is a protected area of great natural beauty, stretching from the Peloritans to the east, and the Madonie Mountains to the west. The mountains have an average height of 1200–1500m and are the largest forested area to survive on the island. The remarkable landscape changes constantly. The wide variety of trees includes oak, elm, beech, holm oak, cork, and yew, and is especially fine in the Caronia forest. The forests are home to the porcupine, the wildcat and the pine marten; the last wolves disappeared in the 1920s. At **Rocche del Crasto**, one of the highest peaks of the Park near Alcara Li Fusi, there are golden eagles and griffon vultures, besides the lanner and the peregrine falcons. These mountains have abundant water, with many streams, small lakes and springs. The upland plains provide pastureland for numerous farm animals which roam free, including cows, sheep, goats and black-and-white pigs. The San Fratello breed of horses (identified by their characteristic rounded noses) are now protected and allowed to run free in the forest. Renowned ricotta, cheeses and salted hams are made by the local farmers.

Monte Soro (1847m) is the highest peak of the Nebrodi. The **Biviere di Cesarò** (1200m) is a beautiful little natural lake with interesting birdlife (including herons, black-winged stilts and great white herons on migration), and a spectacular view of Etna. Nearby **Lago Maulazzo** is an artificial lake constructed in the 1980s for irrigation but never put into operation. In this area are numerous Turkey oaks, maple trees, beech woods, and wild mushrooms (especially the delicious *boletus*). In spring beautiful wild flowers bloom and the hillsides are covered with broom. The colours in autumn are also spectacular. The small towns and villages each have something particular to offer.

THE EASTERN NEBRODI

A road leads from Capo d'Orlando across the eastern Nebrodi Mountains to Randazzo below Etna. It passes picturesque **Naso**, which has 15th–17th-century tombs in the church of Santa Maria del Gesù. The church contains a monument to Artale Cardona (d. 1477) in Gothic-Renaissance style; the Cardona family were once lords of Naso. Other churches in Naso are the church of the Santissimo Salvatore, the Chiesa Madre and the church of San Cono which has a 17th-century chapel with inlaid marble walls, and the reliquary of San Cono, the patron saint of Naso. In the 19th century the town was prosperous enough to build an elegant theatre, the Teatro Alfieri.

Floresta, with its lovely pale grey stone houses, slow pace and women embroidering in front of their doors, is the highest town in Sicily, with winter-sports facilities. The road reaches a summit level of 1280m before descending in full view of Etna to Randazzo.

At **Frazzanò** Count Roger built the Basilian monastery and church of San Filippo di Fragalà (*open 9–1 & 3–7*), with three high apses, a large transept and a polychrome exterior of red bricks and local stone. A seat of learning, the monastery had an important library that was dispersed in 1866. Among the few remnants saved and now in

Palermo, is the oldest document yet found in Europe written on paper, an edict sent by Queen Adelaide to the abbot in 1099.

From here the road leads up to the ancient centres of **Longi** and **Galati Mamertino** which has some notable works of art, including two marble statues of the *Madonna* attributed to the Gagini school in the Chiesa Madre, and a Crucifix by Fra' Umile di Petralia, thought by some to be his finest, in the church of Santa Caterina.

San Marco d'Alunzio

At San Marco d'Alunzio, Robert Guiscard built the first Norman castle in Sicily in 1061 (it survives in ruins at the top of the hill). The interesting little hill town has 22 churches built of a distinctive local red marble (called *rosso di San Marco*). At the entrance to the town on a spectacular site overlooking the sea, is the **Temple of Heracles**, dating from the Hellenistic era: on the red marble basement a Norman church (now roofless) was built. Later a Baroque portal and windows were added. Above the road on the right is the church of the **Aracoeli**, with a Baroque portal. The interior, including the columns, has local red marble decorations. On the right side a marble altar has a gilded wooden statue of *St Michael Archangel*, and another chapel has a fine red marble altarpiece. Via Aluntia continues past (left) the deconsecrated 12th-century church of Santa Maria dei Poveri (used for exhibitions) and then descends past the town hall and a fountain. On the left is the **Chiesa Madre** (San Nicolò) built in 1584. It has a very unusual triumphal arch with large marble sculptures and an 18th-century organ. In the north aisle, the fourth chapel has a 16th-century painting of the *Madonna of the Rosary* in a fine frame, and the fifth chapel a wooden 16th-century processional statue of the Immaculate Virgin.

A road leads uphill to the left past the tiny church of San Giovanni and then down to the side of the hill where San Giuseppe has a lovely portal. There is a fine view of the sea from here. On the left of the façade is the entrance to the **Diocese Museum** (*T: 0941 797045 to request a visit*). In the vestibule are the original capitals from the portal of the church, as well as vestments and statues. The rest of the collection is arranged in the church which has a lovely red, grey and blue floor and decorative stuccoes. The collection of miscellaneous objects includes a sculpture of the *Madonna dell' Odigitria* by Giuseppe Li Volsi (1616), statues, reliquaries, and church furniture.

Higher up in the town is the tiny church of Maria Santissima delle Grazie with a delightful carved high altar with a statue of the *Madonna and Child with the young St John*, and, on either side, two imposing tombs of the Filangieri family, one with an effigy (1481) and the other in red marble (1600). Opposite, built on the rock, is the church of San Basilio.

A short distance south of San Marco d'Alunzio, by the church of San Teodoro, is the ex-Benedictine monastery or **Badia Nica** (no. 96 Via Ferrarolo), housing the Museo della Cultura e delle Arti Figurative Bizantine e Normanne (*open 9.15–12.45 & 3.30–7.30*) with a collection of frescoes removed from the many churches of the town, and displayed with admirable clarity. Beneath San Teodoro there is a Byzantine chapel with interesting remains of frescoes.

Sant'Agata di Militello and around

A seaside resort, from which climbing expeditions may be made in the Nebrodi Mountains Park, Sant'Agata also contains the **Palazzo Gentile** on Via Cosenz, on the sea front, which houses the **Museo Etnoantropologico dei Nebrodi** (*open Mon–Fri 9–12; Tues & Thur also 3–6; closed Sat, Sun and holidays*) with a collection devoted to mountain life, divided into three sections: the role of women and women's work; shepherds; and traditions and religious customs. In summer there is a boat service to the Aeolian Islands from Sant'Agata.

Alcara li Fusi is a little mountain village beneath the Rocche del Crasto (1315m). Excursions into the Nebrodi Park can easily be organised from here. The mountain, where golden eagles still nest, can be explored on foot to see the **Grotta del Lauro** (1060m), one of the most interesting caves in Sicily, with impressive stalagmites and stalagtites, an important bat population, and where traces of prehistoric habitation have been found. On one of the mountain peaks, **Rocca Traora**, is a flourishing colony of griffon vultures, successfully re-introduced after their accidental extermination in 1966.

A picturesque road leads south from Sant'Agata di Militello through the Nebrodi Mountains past **San Fratello**, a Lombard colony founded by Adelaide, wife of Count Roger; the people still use their ancient Gallic dialect. The old town is built of dark brown stone, with mellow, mossy roof-tiles. Recent archaeological surveys on nearby Mt San Fratello, called Monte Vecchio by the local people, show that the town is of prehistoric origin. It was the ancient *Apollonia*, and was moved to its present position by order of the queen. On Monte Vecchio is the 12th-century Norman sanctuary church of the three brothers, Sts Alfio, Cirino and Filadelfo, the three saints martyred in 253 AD. San Fratello is surrounded by forests; close by are two lakes: Maulazzo and Biviere, of great interest to bird-watchers and botanists.

Back on the coast, **Acquedolci** is a coastal resort whose name means sweet waters, a reference to the sugar industry founded here by the Arabs, which brought prosperity to the whole area. It also had a tuna fishery and a port for exporting wheat from the interior; now its fortunes are declining. A path leads south up the slopes of Mt Pizzo Castellano (c. 30mins) to the **Grotta di San Teodoro** (*T: 329 4756376*), where important Palaeolithic burials have been found including one of a woman, about 30 years old and 1.65m tall, who has been named *Thea* (*see p. 25*). Numerous fossils attest the presence of elephants and hippos here 150,000 years ago.

THE WESTERN NEBRODI

Caronia is in a beautiful forest of the same name. The town preserves a privately owned and still-inhabited Norman castle on the top of the hill, and traces of its 14th-century fortifications. On the outskirts, the site of ancient *Kalacte* has been identified, founded by Doucetius of the Sicels on his return from exile in the 5th century BC.

A mountain road leads across the Nebrodi from here to the hill town of **Capizzi**, one of the highest villages in Sicily. The road joins the beautiful SS 120 south of the

Nebrodi from Nicosia to Randazzo. East of Troina the road traverses rugged country with a superb view of Etna, passing below remote **Cesarò**, where the remains of its castle can be seen.

On the coast, at the western end of the Nebrodi, is **Santo Stefano di Camastra**, once situated further inland on a rise, and destroyed by a landslide in 1682. It is noted for fine ceramics, which are made and sold in potteries on the outskirts (most of which are east of the town on the road towards Messina), and for building materials. Local ware is also sold in numerous shops in the town. In the heart of the attractively designed town (the work of Giuseppe Lanza, Duke of Camastra, in 1693), at no. 2 Via Palazzo, is Palazzo Sergio-Trabia, seat of the **Museo della Ceramica** (*open summer 9–1 & 4–8; winter 9–1 & 3.30–7.30; closed Mon*), with a beautiful collection of the local pottery, with its bright colours and typical designs, including a section devoted to the famous floor-tiles.

A pretty road leads inland through the Nebrodi via **Mistretta**, an attractive old town with some beautiful Baroque and Rococo buildings, on the site of the ancient *Amestratus*. At the entrance to the town is the 16th-century church of **San Giovanni** with a fine flight of steps and a portal carved in 1534. The 17th-century Chiesa Madre (St Lucy), has some beautiful statues of the Gagini school and two interesting side portals carved in the 14th and 15th centuries respectively. The carved south portal of the church has been ascribed to Giorgio da Milano (1493). At Mistretta they make unique biscuits of white marzipan, which are baked until pale gold in colour.

At the northwestern corner of the province of Messina is **Castel di Tusa**. A road leads inland above the wide torrent bed of the Tusa river to the pretty little hill town of **Tusa**, which has interesting sculptures in the Chiesa Madre. Modern sculptures, works of well-known contemporary artists including Pietro Consagra, Tano Festa and Hidetoshi Nagasawa, which had been erected on the shore and in the riverbed in the 1980s, called **Fiumara d'Arte**, were ordered to be demolished by a court ruling in 1991, and again in 1993. Fortunately they are still here and now much appreciated; but some of them are in need of repair, and their sponsor, Antonio Presti, is drumming up public support. The same artists have designed 16 rooms of the Hotel Atelier sul Mare (*see p. 493*). The River Tusa, now usually dry, 21 km long, was the ancient *Halaesus*.

Off the road to Tusa is the site of **Halaesa** (*open 9–1hr before sunset*) on a hill. A road leads up from the gate on the byroad to the car park beside the restored convent and church and custodian's house. The attractive site, with ancient olives and almond trees, commands a fine view of the pretty Tusa valley, the little towns of Tusa and on a clear day, the Aeolian Islands. *Halaesa* was founded in 403 BC by Archonides, dynastic ruler of *Herbita*. The most conspicuous remains are those of the agora (partly protected by a roof), which preserves part of its marble wall panelling and brick paving on the west side, and the walls of the city (a stretch further uphill is strengthened by buttresses). On the hillside below, looking towards the sea, was the theatre, and there were two temples at the top of the hill. Excavations begun in 1952–56 were interrupted in 1972 and have never been resumed. A small antiquarium displays some of the objects found on the site.

PRACTICAL INFORMATION

GETTING AROUND

• **By bus** Inter-city bus services from **Messina** are run by SAIS-Interbus (terminal by the railway station, in Piazza della Repubblica, T: 090 771914, www.saisautolinee.it) to Catania (direct via the motorway) in 90 mins (continuing to Catania airport); to **Taormina** (via SS 114) in 90 mins, also to **Giardini, Forza D'Agrò, Santa Teresa di Riva, Alì Terme, Scaletta Zanclea, Barcellona** and **Terme Vigliatore**. There are local buses from Santa Teresa di Riva to **Savoca** and **Casalvecchio**.

Town buses are run by ATM (T: 090 2285262, www.atmmessina.it/orario. Useful services are no. 79 from the station—Via I Settembre—Duomo—Corso Cavour and via Garibaldi to the Regional Museum (continuing to Ganzirri and Punta Faro) and no. 28 (velocittà) from Piazza Cairoli and Via Garibaldi. No. 29 from Piazza Cairoli to the cemetery.

There are coach services by Giuntabus (T: 090 673782, www.giuntabus.it) from 8 Via Terranova (at the junction with Viale San Martino) to Milazzo in 50 mins (connecting with hydrofoils to the Aeolian Islands).

From **Taormina** there are buses to Mazzarò, Castelmola, the Alcantara Gorge and the towns on the foothills of Etna, as well as services to Catania (and Catania airport) and Messina.

From the port of **Milazzo**, Inter-city services run by Giuntabus (T: 090 673782, www.paginegialle.it/giuntabus) to Messina in 50mins, in connection with hydrofoils from the Aeolian

Islands, and to Catania airport (once a day, April–September only).

On **Lipari** buses run from Marina Lunga to Canneto and to the pumice quarries and Acquacalda; to Quattrocchi, Pianoconte, and Quattropani; also tours of the island in summer (info and tickets: Urso, 29 Via Cappuccini, T: 090 9811262). There are a few buses a day from the port on **Vulcano** to Piano.

In **Salina** buses run from Santa Marina Salina and Rinella to Leni, Pollara, Malfa and Lingua (Citis, T: 090 9844150).

• **By train:** Messina, **Giardini** and **Taormina** are on the main line which runs along the coast from Syracuse via Catania to Messina. Milazzo is on the Messina–Palermo line.

• **By road:** Cars are allowed (not July and August) on **Lipari, Vulcano, Filicudi** and **Salina**. However, visitors are not advised to take a car as distances are short and local transport good. It is a good idea to garage your car at Milazzo; the attendant will pick it up for you and then bring it back on your return. Some car-hire services operate on Lipari, Vulcano and Salina. On the other islands small motor vehicles are used to transport luggage, and on Alicudi and Stromboli, mules and donkeys. On Lipari and Vulcano, vespas and bicycles can also be hired.

• **By sea:** The most convenient starting-point for the **Aeolian Islands** is **Milazzo**. Throughout the year ferries, hydrofoils and catamarans run to the islands. For information on shipping lines, timetables, tariffs and buses to and from ports consult: www.bookingitalia.it

Hydrofoil and catamaran services run by Ustica Lines, 32 Via dei Mille (Cortina del Porto), T: 090/9287821, www.usticalines.it, and Siremar, Via dei Mille, T: 090 9283242, www.siremar.it take 45 mins to **Vulcano**, 1hr to **Lipari**. Car-ferries, run by Siremar and by NGI, 26 Via dei Mille, T: 090 9283415, leave several times a day for the islands (1hr 45mins to **Vulcano**, 2hrs to **Lipari**).

An overnight ferry run by Siremar (T: 090 9843004) calls at **Stromboli**, **Panarea**, **Salina**, **Lipari**, **Vulcano**; another (summer only) is run by Medmar (T: 081 5513352, www.medmagroup.it).

Ferry and hydrofoil ticket offices on the islands: Some ticket offices on the islands open only 30 minutes before sailing. All the islands are connected by ferry and hydrofoil services; the ferries are slower, cheaper, more reliable and often less direct than the hydrofoils. Fishing boats may be hired on all the islands, and the trip around the coast of the islands is strongly recommended.

Alicudi Siremar, T: 090 9889795.

Filicudi Siremar, Porto, T: 090 9889960; Ustica Lines, Porto, T: 340 9027986.

Lipari Siremar (hydrofoils), Marina Lunga Sottomonastero, T: 090 9812200; Siremar (ferries), Marina Lunga Sottomonastero, T: 090 9811312; NGI, Marina Lunga Sottomonastero, T: 090 9811955.

Panarea Siremar, Porto, T: 090 983007.

Salina Siremar, Porto, Santa Marina, T: 090 9843003; Siremar, Porto, Rinella, T: 090 9809170.

Stromboli Siremar, Porto di Scari, T: 090 986016; Siremar, Porto di Ginostra, T: 090 9812880.

Vulcano Siremar, Porto Levante, T: 090 9852149; NGI, Porto Levante, T: 090 9852401.

DIVING CENTRES

Filicudi
I Delfini, Pecorini, T: 090 9889077.
Marco Polo, Pecorini, T: 090 9889843.
Centro Nautico Filicudi, Via del Porto, T: 090 9889984.
Lipari
La Gorgonia, Salita San Giuseppe, Marina Corta, T: 090 9812060, www.lagorgoniadiving.it
Milazzo
FIPSAS, 6 Piazza Cesare Battisti, T: 090 9288540.

BOAT TRIPS & CHARTER

Lipari
Da Massimo, T: 090 9811714.
Massimo can be found at Marina Corta. Motor boat and dinghies for hire.
Regina, T:090 9822237, www.navigazioniregina.com. Excursions round the islands.
Salina
Onda Eoliana, Scalo Galera, Malfa, T: 339 7768098, for fishing- or motor-boats.
Stromboli
Antonio Caccetta, Vico Salina 10, T: 090 986023. Organizes boat trips round the island.

INFORMATION OFFICES

Messina APT Messina: 301 Via Calabria (corner of Via Capria), T: 090 640221, www.aapitme.it; for information on the whole province. Azienda

Autonoma Turismo: 45 Piazza Cairoli, T: 090 694780. Messina on line www.messinacitymap.com
Capo d'Orlando 67 Via Piave, T: 0941 912784, www.aastcapodorlando.it
Casalvecchio Siculo c/o Municipio, T: 0942 761008.
Castroreale Pro Loco Artemisia: 2 Via Trento, T: 090 9746673.
Giardini Naxos 54 Via Tisandro, T: 0942 51010, www.aastgiardininaxos.it
Filicudi www.filicudiresort.it is a website dedicated to private houses available to rent all over the island.
Lipari 202 Corso Vittorio Emanuele, T: 090 9880095, www.aasteolie.info, www.isolelipari.it
Milazzo 10 Piazza Duilio, T: 090 9222865, www.aastmilazzo.it, www.milazzo.me.it
Nebrodi Mountains Park Ente Parco dei Nebrodi, 126 Via Ruggero Orlando, Caronia, T: 0921 888211, www.parconebrodi.it; information offices also at **Alcara Li Fusi**, 1 Via Ugo Foscolo, T: 0941 793904; **Cesarò**, Strada Nazionale, T: 095 7732061; **Floresta**, c/o Biblioteca Comunale, T: 0941 662036; **Longi**, Portella Gazzana, T: 0941/485086; **Sant'Agata di Militello**, 155 via Cosenz, T: 0941/705934; **Santa Domenica Vittoria**, Piazza Moro, T: 095 925545; **Santo Stefano di Camastra**, Via Umberto, T: 0921/331199; and **Tortorici**, 57 Via Vittorio Emanuele, T: 0941 4231209.
San Marco d'Alunzio Pro Loco: T: 0941 797339, www.comune.sanmarcodalunzio.me.it
Sant'Alessio Siculo: Pro Loco: via Nazionale, T: 0942 751741.
Stromboli T: 090 986285 (summer only).

Taormina Palazzo Corvaja, T: 0942 23243, www.gate2taormina.com; for information on the summer arts festival, T: 0942 625197, www.taormina-arte.com
Tindari 15 Via Teatro Greco, T: 0941 369184, www.pattietindari.it
Tusa c/o Municipio, Piazza Municipio, T: 0921 330405.
Vulcano Via Porto Levante, T: 090 9852028 (summer only).

HOTELS

Messina
€€€ **Grand Hotel Liberty**. One of the oldest and most prestigious hotels, beautifully restored, central. 15 Via I Settembre, T: 090 6409436, www.framonhotels.com
€€ **Royal Palace Hotel**. Good location in the town centre. 224 Via Cannizzaro, T: 090 6503, reservation.rhp@framon.hotels.it
€ **Hotel Sant'Elia**. Small, friendly, central hotel, no restaurant. 67 Via I Settembre, T: 090 6010082, www.hotelsantelia.com
€ **Locanda Donato**. Charming hotel at Ganzirri, close to sea and lake, garden, vegetarian food on request. 8 Via Caratozzolo, T: 090 393150.
Alì Terme
€ **La Magnolia**. The roads in this area are a bit hectic but this little hotel is quite a find: family-run, with good food and Sicilian wine cellar. Just over the road is the wide beach (shale and sand). 18/A Via Lungomare, T: 0942 716377, hotellamagnolia@tiscalinet.it
Capo d'Orlando
€ **Il Mulino**. An excellent small hotel with a reputable restaurant. 46 Via

Andrea Doria, T: 0941 902431.

€ La Tartaruga. Comfortable hotel on sea front with a very good restaurant; part of the Buon Ricordo chain. 70 Lido San Gregorio, T: 0941 955012, info@hoteltartaruga.it

Capri Leone

€€ Antica Filanda. A lovely little inn with comfortable rooms, air conditioning, pool, and a fantastic restaurant. Contrada Raviola, T: 0941 919704, www.anticafilanda.it

Caronia

€€ Zà Maria. On the sea, quiet hotel, tennis, restaurant serving vegetarian meals on request; pool. 7 Via Nazionale, Canneto di Caronia, T: 0921 339661, www.zamaria.it

Castel di Tusa

€€ Atelier sul Mare. Close to the sea, many rooms have been 'created' by famous contemporary artists so you can 'sleep in a work of art'. 4 Via Cesare Battisti, T: 0921 334295

Castelmola

€€€ Villa Sonia. Superb position on top of the mountain. Pool, sauna, gymnasium, tennis. This hotel has an exceptionally good restaurant, worth a visit in its own right. 9 Via Porta Mola, T: 0942 28228, www.hotelvillasonia.com

Cesarò

€ Villa Miraglia. In the heart of the Nebrodi Mountains Park, at a height of 1500m, is this welcoming refuge with a good restaurant specializing in traditional mountain fare. Very cosy; horse-riding possible. Book early. SS 289, Portella Miraglia, T: 095 7732133, info@villamiraglia.it

Forza D'Agrò

€€ Baia Taormina. Modern hotel close to castle of Sant'Alessio, with

shuttle buses to the beach and Taormina. Via Nazionale km 39, T: 0942 756292, www.baiataormina.com

Giardini Naxos

€€ Castello San Marco. This medieval castle near the sea offers comfortable accommodation in a lemon grove; pool. 40 Via San Marco, Calatabiano, T: 095 641181, www.castellosanmarco.it

€€ Hellenia. Refined, good restaurant, tennis, beach and pool. 41 Via Jannuzzo, Località Recanati, T: 0942 51737, www.hotel-hellenia.it

€ Nike Hotel. Quiet position on lava-rock bay, clean and simple. 27 Via Calcide Eubea, Schisò, T: 0942 51207, www.tao.it/nike

€ Villa Taormina. Week-long stays only in this country inn. Mitoggio, nr Alcantara Gorge, T: 095 337996, villataormina@yahoo.it

Ginostra

€ Locanda Petrusa. Tiny inn run by Immacolata Petrusa, a famous cook. Via Sopra Pertuso, T: 090 9812305.

Letojanni

€€ Da Peppe. This is a simple hotel, but the restaurant is renowned; the fish soup (*zuppa di pesce*) is exceptional. 345 Via Vittorio Emanuele, T: 0942 36159,

Lipari

€€€ Arciduca. Luxurious modern hotel with pool, tennis. Via Franza, T: 090 9812136, info@arciduca.it

€€€ Meligunis. Right in the heart of the old city, beautiful rooms, atmosphere, and a rooftop terrace. Good restaurant serving vegetarian dishes on request, scuba-diving, water-skiing and sailing are organized. 7 Via Marte, T: 090 9812426, villameligunis@netnet.it

€€ Augustus. Just off the main street, with a garden. 16 Vico Ausonia, T: 090

9811232, info@villaaugustus.it
€€ **Carasco**. On the sea; pool. Porto delle Genti, T: 090 9811605, info@carasco.it.

€€ **Gattopardo**. A 19th-century villa in a beautiful sub-tropical garden, with little Aeolian cottages. 67 Via Diana, T: 090 9811035, www.gattopardoparkhotel.it

€€ **Giardino sul Mare**. Cottages in beautiful gardens going down to the sea; pool. 65 Via Maddalena, T: 090 9811004, giardino@netnet.it

€€ **Casajanca**. Interesting and comfortable little hotel in the village of Canneto, run by the daughter of a poet. 115 Marina Garibaldi, T: 090 9880222, www.casajanca.it

€€ **Oriente**. Very comfortable hotel, rather eccentric, with garden. 35 Via Marconi, T: 090 9811493, www.hotelorientelipari.com

€€ **Enzo il Negro**, Everyone knows Enzo! His rooms are spotlessly clean and there is a beautiful rooftop terrace for breakfasts; he can give you lots of help for finding boats or even apartments. 29 Via Garibaldi, T: 090 9813163, enzoilnegro@libero.it

Mazzarò
€€€ **Atlantis Bay**. First built for the Hollywood stars who came for the film festival, now completely refurbished, on the Bay of the Mermaids, good restaurant serving vegetarian meals on request. 161 Via Nazionale, T: 0942 618011, www.atlantisbay.it

€€€ **Mazzarò Sea Palace**. Delightful hotel, very comfortable, with its own private beach, close to cableway. 147 Via Nazionale, T: 0942 612111, www.mazzaroseapalace.it

€€€ **Capo Taormina**. The lovely pool has often been used as a film set. 105 Via Nazionale, T: 0942 572111, www.capotaorminahotel.com

€€€ **La Plage**. Little huts right on the beach in front of the beautiful island, good restaurant serving vegetarian meals on request. Via Nazionale a Isolabella, T: 0942 626095.

€€ **Villa Sant' Andrea**. Lovely position by the sea, conveniently close to the cable-car station, good restaurant. 137 Via Nazionale, T: 0942 23125, www.framonhotels.com

Milazzo
€€ **Esperia**. Delightful small hotel on Ponente beach, all rooms have a different style. 128 Via Tono, T: 090 9224951, www.albergo-esperia.it

€€ **Garibaldi**. Charming little hotel in the fishermen's quarter, with air conditioning. 160 Lungomare Garibaldi, T: 090 9240189, www.hotelgaribaldi.it

€€ **Riviera Lido**. On the cape with its own beach; restaurant, air conditioning. Via Panoramica, T: 090 9283456, www.milazzonline.it/rivieralido

Panarea
€€ **Cincotta**. Right on the brink of the cliff, home-made ice cream, disco, close to harbour. Via San Pietro, T: 090 983014, hotel.cincotta@exit.it

€€ **La Piazza**. Surrounded by vegetation; all rooms with view. Via San Pietro, T: 090 983154, www.hotelpiazza.it

€€ **Lisca Bianca**. Panoramic position in front of harbour; good restaurant. 1 Via Lani, T: 090 983004, liscabianca@liscabianca.it

€€ **Raya**. Perched on a hill dominating the port; exclusive clientele. Via San Pietro, Località Costa Galletta, T: 090 983029, info@hotelraya.it

Patti

€€ **Hotel Sacra Famiglia**. Old building recently restored, in the historic centre. 1 Via Dante Alighieri, T: 0941 241622, email: info@sacrafamiglia.it

€€ **La Playa**. On the beach, scuba-diving. 3 Via Playa, T: 0941 361398, info@laplaya-hotel.it

Salina

€€ **Bellavista**. Panoramic position in pretty village. 8 Via Risorgimento, Santa Marina T: 090 9843009.

€€ **Principe di Rinella**. In a charming fishing village.Via San Gaetano, Rinella, Leni, T: 090 9809308.

€€ **Santa Isabel**. Small hotel in a lovely position, accommodation in comfortable suites, restaurant. 12 Via Scalo, Malfa, T: 090 9844018, www.santaisabel.it

€€ **Signum**. Aeolian-style architecture, peaceful position surrounded by vineyards, pool. 15 Via Scalo, Malfa; T: 090 9844222, www.hotelsignum.it

€€ **L'Ariana**. Panoramic position, excellent restaurant. 11 Via Rotabile, Rinella, Leni, T: 090 9809075, www.hotelariana.it

San Fratello

€ **Monte Soro**. Simple inn with restaurant. 1 Via Latteri, T: 0941 794120.

Sant'Alessio Siculo

€ **La Scogliera**. 6km north of Cape Taormina, a simple inn, close to the sea (rocks). All rooms with bath but very basic; excellent home-made food, Sicilian breakfast with granita. 421 Via Nazionale, T: 0942 751390.

Stromboli

€€ **La Sirenetta**. One of the oldest hotels, recently restored. Scuba-diving centre, tennis, water-skiing, windsurfing, sailing. 33 Via Marina, T: 090 986025, lasirenetta@netnet.it

€€ **Hotel Villaggio Stromboli**. On the beach, pleasantly old fashioned. Via Regina Elena, T: 090 986018, villaggiostromboli@netnet.it

€€ **La Sciara**. Large garden and beautiful swimming pool. Via Soldato Cincotta, T: 090 986004, www.lasciara.it

Taormina

€€€ **Grand Hotel Timeo**. Luxurious old hotel; understated elegance; the very best in Sicily; good restaurant. 59 Via Teatro Greco, T: 0942 23801, www.framonhotels.com

€€€ **San Domenico**. An old convent; ambassadors, royalty and ageing film stars stay here. Piazza San Domenico, T: 0942 613111, www.thi.it

€€ **Miramare**. Just below town, with gorgeous views of the Straits. 27 Via Guardiola Vecchia, T: 0942 23401, ghmiramare@tiscali.it

€€ **Villa Angela**. This chic villa is the home of Jim Kerr (Simple Minds); way up above Taormina, on the road to Castelmola, stunning views, pool, tennis, great Scottish-style brunches. Via Leonardo da Vinci, T: 0942 27038, hotel@villaangela.it

€€ **Villa Diodoro**. Another famous old hotel, next to public gardens. 75 Via Bagnoli Croce, T: 0942 23312, diodoro@gaishotel.it

€€ **Villa Paradiso**. Small hotel, incomparable views. 2 Via Roma, T: 0942 23921, hotelparadiso@tao.it

€€ **Villa Schuler**. One of the nicest little hotels in town, attentive service. Also has apartments to rent. 16 Via Roma, T: 0942 23481, schuler@tao.it

€€ **Cableway**. Very convenient position at the bottom station of the cable-

way, rooms rather spartan but the restaurant is excellent. Piazzale Funivia, T: 0942 24739.
Terme Vigliatore
€€ **Grand Hotel delle Terme**. The hotel has a spa. 85 Viale delle Terme, T: 090 9781078.
Vulcano
€€ **Arcipelago**. This is in a quiet position on Vulcanello, with a breathtaking view embracing all seven islands. T: 090 9852002.
€€€ **Les Sables Noirs**. The most prestigious hotel on Vulcano. Porto Ponente, T: 090 9850, www.framon-hotels.com
€€ **Conti**. This pleasant hotel is on the beach of black sand. Porto Ponente, T: 090 9852012, conti@netnet.it
€€ **Orsa Maggiore**. Recently refurbished old hotel, with a good restaurant which serves vegetarian dishes on request. Also has scuba-diving centre and access to mud pools. Porto Ponente, T: 090 9852018, orsa-maggiore@usa.net

BED & BREAKFAST

Salina
€€ **Il Delfino**. This is also a very good restaurant for fish soup and grilled squid. 19 Via Garibaldi, Lingua, T: 090 9843024.
€€ **Villa Pittorino**. Beautiful house in central Leni. Piazza Pittorino, Leni, T: 080 5283327.
Stromboli
€€ **Giuseppe Acquaro**. Open year round. San Vincenzo, T: 090 986088.
Taormina
€€ **Casa Cinzia**. Charming rooms, central. 6 Via Verdi, T: 339 3774568.

FARMHOUSE ACCOMMODATION

€€ **Acquedolci**
Villa Nicetta. Very old fortified farmhouse with its own church. Many activities on offer, including horse-riding, trekking, organic food; it is possible to take part in harvesting, sheep-milking, etc. Contrada Nicetta, T: 0941 726142.
Castroreale
€€€ **Green Manors**. Olive farm, very comfortable accommodation; good restaurant. Lovely pool; horse-riding. Borgo Porticato, T: 090 9746515, www.greenmanors.it
Lipari
€€ **Tivoli**. The farm raises poultry, pigs and rabbits. There are vineyards and olive trees; bowls and volleyball. 17 Via Quartara, Quattropani, T: 090 9886031.
€€ **A Casa di Cerasella**. In Acquacalda. They also have a fast motor boat for visiting the other islands. Via Mazzini, T: 090 9821113.
Longi
€€ **Il Vignale**. In the heart of the Nebrodi Park, ideal for birdwatchers, close to the Rocche del Crasto (griffon vultures and golden eagles), but only for serious nature lovers; the building, an ancient silk mill which sleeps six, is on the wooded mountainside above the village of Longi, where the owners live, there is no telephone on the premises, self-catering only, the track is difficult after rain. Contrada Pado, T: 0941 485015, il.vignale@tiscalinet.it
Pettineo
€€ **Casa Migliaca**. At the far end of the province near Pettineo, a lovely old farmhouse where guests are encouraged to become part of the family. Meals are

served in the old farm kitchen and the farm produces olive oil. Contrada Migliaca, T: 0921 336722, www.casamigliaca.com

Reitano
€€ **Villa Mara**. A hazelnut farm and olive grove within the Park boundaries. Contrada Zucco, T: 0921 338286, roniceta@libero.it

Salina
€€ **Galletta**. Lovely farm producing capers and wine in the heart of the island, self-catering apartments, guests can help with harvesting. Valdichiesa-Ruvoli. T: 090 9809192, www.gallettasalina.com;

€€ **Al Cappero**. Caper farm in one of the loveliest spots on the island. Via Chiesa, Pollara, Malfa, T: 090 9844133.

San Piero Patti
€€€ **Il Daino**. Comfortable flatlets or rooms on this lovely old family-run farm, pool, guests can help, pricey. 5 Contrada Manganelli, T: 0941 660362, www.ildaino.com

San Salvatore di Fitalia
€€€ **Casali di Margello**. High standard accommodation in lovely restored oil mill and hamlet, spring water, superlative home-produced food and excellent Sicilian wine list, beautiful countryside for trekking and horseriding, swimming pools, also bowls, archery. Contrada Margello km 9, SP 155, T: 0941 486225, www.casalidimargello.it

Sant'Agata di Militello
€€ **Villa Luca**. Old country house close to the town, no restaurant. Contrada Luca, T: 0941 702394, www.aziendagrituristicavillaluca.it.

Sant'Angelo di Brolo
€€ **Antico Casale di Lisycon**. An old

farming village entirely restored, in the woods, with its own spring of pure water, home-made bread. Contrada Lisicò, T: 0941 533288, agrinatura@hotmail.com

ROOMS & APARTMENTS

Alicudi
€ **La Casa dell'Ibiscus**. Typical old Aeolian house to rent: sleeps four. www.alicudi.com

Lipari
€ **Diana Brown**. Nice rooms, very central. 3 Vico Himera, T: 090 9812584.

Panarea
€ **Casa del Postino**. This is the house where the film *Il Postino* was made. Very spartan accommodation, weekly stays only (4–6 people), linen not provided. Via Punta, Pollara, T: 335 6779733, www.pippocafarella.com

Taormina
€€ **Villa Giulia**. Apartments for short-term rental with garden and pool. 95 Via Pirandello, T: 0942 23312.

€€ **Villa Costanza**. Garden and pool. 40 Via Otto Geleng, T: 0942 24717.

RESTAURANTS

Messina
€€ **Il Gattopardo**. A favourite with local people; also serves pizza. Closed Mon. 184 Via Santa Cecilia, T: 090 673076.

€€ **Le Due Sorelle**. Vegetarian food, sushi, cous cous and other unusual dishes. Closed Sat and Sun midday. 4 Piazza Municipio, T: 090 44720.

€€ **Piero**. Marvellous fish. Closed Sun. 121 Via Ghibellina, T: 090 718365.

€ **Al Padrino**. Good pasta, simple

style. 54 Via Santa Cecilia, T: 090 2921000.

€ **Il Veliero**. Grungy seamen's bar, excellent local food, ice cream, and the best espresso in Messina. 301 Via Valori, close to maritime station, T: 090 771626.

Capri Leone

€€€ **Antica Filanda**. A long tradition for Nebrodi Mountains cuisine, making much use of local ham, lamb, kid, various cheeses, and wild fungi. Contrada Raviola, T: 0941 919704. Closed Mon.

Filicudi

€€ **Da Nino sul Mare**. A terrace overlooking the sea; good spaghetti with lobster. T: 090 9889984.

€€ **Villa La Rosa**. Aeolian dishes prepared by Adelaide, a great cook. 24 Via Rosa, T: 090 9889965.

Forza d'Agrò

€€ **L'Abbazia**. Very pleasant, especially if you can eat outside on the panoramic terrace. 2 Piazza Giovanni XXIII, T: 0942 721226.

Gallodoro

€€ **Noemi**. In a hilltop village above Letojanni, simple, superb Sicilian country food. Come here for an unforgettable gastronomic experience. Set menu—fixed price includes everything. 8 Via Manzoni, T: 0942 37338.

Giardini Naxos

€€ **Angelina**. By the docks. Superlative spaghetti with clams. T: 0942 51477.

Lipari

€€€ **Filippino**. One of the best-known restaurants in Italy, of the Buon Ricordo chain. Memorable *ravioli di cernia* (fish ravioli). Piazza Mazzini, T: 090 9811002.

€€€ **Al Pirata**. Fashionable and in a lovely setting. Salita San Giuseppe, T: 090 9811796.

€€ **Blue Moon**. Definitely a new rival for the best restaurants on the islands. 21 Piazza Mazzini, T: 090 9811756.

€€ **Le Macine**. Superb creative Aeolian cuisine at Pianoconte. T: 090 9822387.

€€ **La Nassa**. Friendly, family-run establishment. 36 Via G.Franza, T: 090 9811319.

€€ **La Piazzetta**. In a pretty square, ideal for people-watching; also pizzeria. 13–17 Piazza Luigi D'Austria, T: 090 9812522.

€ **Il Pescecane**. Good salads and pizza. 223 Via Vittorio Emanuele, T: 090 9812706.

€ **La Trattoria D'Oro**. There is an inexpensive set menu; they also make a delicious sauce for pasta using tattlers (a kind of squid), called *ragu di totani*. Service is slow. 28–32 Via Umberto, T: 090 9812591.

Mazzarò

€€ **Il Barcaiolo**. Tiny family-run restaurant for delicious fish; romantic dinner better than lunch. On the beach at Mazzarò opposite Hotel Villa Esperia. Don't forget the midge repellent. Open summer only. T: 0942 625633.

Milazzo

€€€ **Al Piccolo Casale**. Fashionable. Excellent fish; also pizzeria, nice desserts and amazing wine list. Closed Mon. 12 Via R. D'Amico, T: 090 9224479.

€€€ **Doppio Gusto**. Of course fish is the speciality in this new restaurant, with a terrace overlooking the sea; very nice hot and cold antipasti; home-made desserts. 44–45 Via Rizzo, T: 090 9240045.

€€€ **Salamone a Mare**. On the cape;

legendary fish dishes. Closed Mon. Via Panoramica, T: 090 9281233.

€€ **La Tavernetta**. Sicilian dishes. 19 Via Francesco Crispi (Marina Garibaldi), T: 090 9223217.

€€ **L'Ugghiularu**. Traditional Sicilian dishes. Closed Wed. 101 Via Acqueviole, T: 090 9284384.

€ **Don Ciccio**. Tasty pasta dishes. Via Nardi, corner Via Umberto.

€ **La Casalinga**. Homely cooking. Via D'Amico, T: 090 9222697.

Montalbano Elicona

€ **La Pineta**. Simple trattoria offering delicious food, home-grown fruit and vegetables, grilled lamb, home-made sausages, excellent house wine. Closed Mon. 159 Via Nazionale, T: 0941 650522.

Panarea

€€ **Cusiritati**. Friendly atmosphere; at the port. T: 090 983022.

€€ **Da Pina**. Pina is an institution, innovative and imaginative. Her *gnocchi di melanzane* (aubergine dumplings) are unique. Via San Pietro, T: 090 983030.

Patti

€€ **Mare e Monti**. Very fresh fish, creative cuisine, good service. 191 Via Colombo, Marina di Patti, T: 0941 362479.

Rodì-Milici

€€ **I Vicerè**. Farm restaurant which serves home-grown produce. Contrada Trappeto, T: 090 9741015.

Salina

€€€ **Portobello**. Famous for *spaghetti al fuoco* (fiery spaghetti) and a dessert made of fresh ricotta with honey, pine nuts and currants. Santa Marina, T: 090 9843125.

€€ **Franco**. Franco is very proud of his spaghetti with sea urchins. Via

Belvedere, T: 090 9843287.

€€ **Il Delfino**. At Lingua, perfect grilled squid or tattlers. 5 Via Marina Garibaldi, T: 090 9843024

€€ **Il Gambero**. For shrimps and grilled squid, or try the *pane cunzato* for lunch, at Lingua, T: 090 9843049.

€€ **Mamma Santina**. An unusual salad of fresh mint and capers is on the menu here. 40 Via Sanità, T: 090 9843054.

San Fratello

€ **Il Vecchio Carro**. Try the local sausage, salami or ham, prepared with meat from pigs living wild in the forest.100 Via Latteri, T: 0941 799096.

Savoca

€€ **La Pineta**. Country food. 3 Via Pineta, T: 0942 761094.

Stromboli

€€ **Ai Geki**. Open year round; a favourite with local people. 12 Via Salina, T: 090 986213.

€€ **Punta Lena**. On a panoramic terrace overlooking Strombolicchio; excellent grilled vegetables, fish is cooked on a hot slab of lava. 8 Via Marina, Ficogrande, T: 090 986204.

Taormina

€€€ **Casa Grugno**. Famous restaurant, near San Domenico, with a genial Austrian chef, Andreas Zangerl. Via Santa Maria de'Greci, T: 0942 21208.

€€€ **Duomo**. Very high standard; popular with celebrities. Closed Mon. 11 Vico Ebrei, T: 0942 625656.

€€€ **La Baronessa**. Refined and expensive, beautiful setting, exquisite dishes of fish and vegetables, good wines. 148 Corso Umberto, T: 0942 628191.

€€€ **La Giara**. Ava Gardner and friends really lived it up here in the 1950s, and it is still an excellent restau-

rant. 1 Via La Floresta, T: 0942 625083.
€€ Grotta di Ulisse. Live Sicilian
music. Closed Tues in winter. 3 Salita
Denti, T: 0942 625253.
€€ La Botte. Good Sicilian antipasti.
Piazzetta San Domenica, T: 0942
24198.
€€ La Griglia. The owner, Giorgio,
takes good care of his guests. 54 Corso
Umberto, T: 0942 23980. Closed Tues.
€€ La Piazzetta. Good food in a stun-
ning little square just off the main
street. Closed Mon in winter. 5 Via
Paladini, T: 0942 626317.
€ Licchio's. Close to Porta Messina,
has a garden where you can eat even in
winter; nice food, also pizza. 10 Via
Patricio, T: 0942 625327.
€ Vecchia Taormina. Exceptionally
good pizza. 3 Vico Ebrei, T: 0942
625589.

Vulcano
€€€ Da Maurizio. One of the best
restaurants of the archipelago. Via Porto
Levante, T: 090 9852426.
€€€ Vincenzino. Spaghetti with
shrimps and capers are excellent. Via
Porto Levante, T: 090 9852016.
€€ Don Piricuddu. Mixed grills and
salads. 33 Via Lentia, T: 090 9852424.
€€ Il Diavolo dei Polli. At Piano, in
the heart of the island, specializes in
grilled meat, such as chicken, kid, or
rabbit. T: 090 9853034.

CAFÉS, PASTRY SHOPS & ICE CREAM

Messina
Cardullo. Excellent ice cream and
snacks. 7 Via U. Bassi.
Irrera. One of the most famous historical pastry shops, especially renowned
for its *pignolata messinese* and *cassata*

siciliana. 12 Piazza Cairoli.
Furci Siculo
Mimmo. Absolutely fantastic *granita*,
especially with whipped cream! Closed
Mon in winter. 183 Via IV Novembre.
Giardini Naxos
Dolci Pensieri. Lovely home-made ice
cream, and all the traditional pastries. 6
Via Umberto (corner Via Roma), T:
0942 56296.
Letojanni
Niny Bar. Run by the same family for
three generations. Their speciality is
granita arcobaleno (rainbow), with alter-
nating layers of fresh fruit granita—
lemon, peach, mulberry, strawberry and
pineapple—in a glass. 214 Via Vittorio
Emanuele (corner Piazza Durante),
T: 0942 36104.
Lipari
Open-air cafés at Marina Corta for
Sicilian breakfast, aperitifs, ice cream
and *granita*.
Caffè Vela for rubbing elbows with the
jet set (the likes of Robert De Niro,
Dustin Hoffman, and Prince William,
and Caroline of Monaco have been seen
here). The owner, Carlo, has won prizes
for his superb Aeolian salads.
Mazzarò
La Frutteria. Bottom station of the
cableway, fresh fruit juices, milk shakes,
fruit salad.
Milazzo
L'Agora. Sandwich bar and snacks, deli-
cious food. Closed Tues in winter. Via
Duomo Antico, near the castle, T: 090
9283131.
Caffè Antico. Sandwich bar, in summer
only, near the castle. Piazzetta San
Gaetano.
Cream Caramel. One of the best pastry
shops. 16 Via Tenente La Rosa.

Gli Antenati. Pizza, sandwiches and snacks, in summer only. On the stairs leading up to the castle. Scalinata del Castello.

Nicotina. Almond biscuits. 113 Lungomare Garibaldi.

Puck Café. Bookshop-café. 62 Via Cumbo Borgia (Piazza Duomo)

Salina

At Lingua, **Da Alfredo** opposite the pier, for scrumptious fresh fruit *granita*: watermelon, peach or fig.

Taormina

Chemi, 112 and 102 Corso Umberto, are excellent pastry shops.

Vico dei Sapori. Good ice cream, and the best *cassata siciliana* and *cannoli di ricotta*. They have a shop offering fine olive oils and wines, spaghetti sauces and pasta. 13 Via Teatro Greco.

Gelatomania. For award-winning ice cream; try their delectable Ferrero Rocher, or in summer, mango flavour, prepared with locally grown fruit. 7 Corso Umberto.

Pigghia e Potta. A typical Sicilian snack bar, always crowded (a very good sign). 23 Via Di Giovanni (close to Palazzo Corvaja).

LOCAL SPECIALITIES

Lipari

Adriana Salvini, at 5 Via Marte, makes attractive jewellery from obsidian, the black glass-like volcanic stone.

Messina

Salumeria Francesco Doddis, at 317 Via Garibaldi, for cheese, salami and ham from the Nebrodi Mountains.

Mistretta

Antonino Testa, at 2 Via Libertà, for the local biscuits made of white marzi-pan, called pasta reale.

Novara di Sicilia

Coop Cucinotta, 3 Via Benigno Salvo, is a bakery where you will find the famous large, round, fragrant loaves of bread traditional here. The cafés in Novara serve *gelato di cedro*, made with large knobbly lemons with very thick peel and practically no flesh inside. The zest is particularly aromatic, the candied peel being used in many Sicilian confectionery recipes.

Salina

Carlo Hauner, at Via Umberto, Lingua, for some *malvasia* or *malvasia passito*.

Carpe Diem, at 28 & 156 Via Risorgimento, Santa Marina, for capers, among the finest in the world.

Taormina

Ricordi Siciliani, at 8 via Teatro Greco, for unusual souvenirs, including beautifully made replicas of Greek and Roman pottery and Etruscan jewellery, while **Blue Royal**, 236 Corso Umberto (nr Porta Catania), has exclusive Caltagirone pottery, blue designs on off-white, absolutely beautiful. **Liquirizia**, 30 Via Teatro Greco, for household linens, embroidered and trimmed with locally made lace. **Gladys Art**, at 6 corso Umberto (nr Porta Messina), sells work by a good local artist.

FESTIVALS & EVENTS

Messina *Le Varette*, traditional religious procession, Good Friday; Feast of the Madonna della Lettera, the patron saint, 3 June; *Corpus Domini* procession including a ship, the *Vascelluzzo*, June; *Fiera di Messina*, an international trade fair held during the first 15 days of August, coincides with the traditional processions of the *Giganti* (Giants) on 13 and 14 August and the *Vara* (float with tableau) for the feast of the Assumption, 15 August.

Alcara Li Fusi *Festa del Muzzuni*—the summer solstice (24 June) is celebrated in the village. The 'muzzuni' is a large glass bottle, or earthenware jar, one for each of the town quarters. On the evening of the 23rd the jars are richly decorated with silk scarves, gold jewellery and ears of wheat, and carried to roadside altars by young, unmarried girls. The altars are draped with brightly coloured 'pezzare', hand-woven rugs. The statue of St John the Baptist is carried in procession through the streets, blessing the muzzuni, thus guaranteeing prosperity and fertility to every part of the town.

Brolo *Medievalia*, a series of events on a variety of subjects, ranging from competitions for pastry-cooks, parades of hats, Frederick II of Hohenstaufen, castles and falconry, May–Sept.

Capo d'Orlando July: International Blues Festival, in the gardens of Villa Piccolo.

Lipari Our Lady of Portosalvo, a fishermen's celebration, 18 July; San Bartolomeo, the patron saint of the islands, 24 Aug; *Efesto D'Oro*, screening and prize-giving for films which have been inspired by, or made on, the islands, July–Aug.

Salina *Madonna del Terzito*, at Leni, very colourful and heartfelt, 23 July.

San Fratello The ancient *Festa dei Giudei* is celebrated; colourfully dressed 'Judaeans', wearing helmets, performing acrobatics and blowing trumpets, try to interrupt the solemn procession for the dead Christ, of course unsuccessfully, Good Friday; *Cavalcata*, a procession on horseback to the sanctuary-church (national monument) on the nearby mountain where the three patron saints, Alfio, Cirino and Filadelfo, stopped on their way to matyrdom at Trecastagni or Lentini (c. 350 AD), 10 May; *Mercato-Concorso del Cavallo di San Fratello*, traditional parade and market of the famous San Fratello horses, the only ones in Europe still living wild in their native habitat, 1st Sun in Sept. Feast of St Benedict the Moor, with a procession and fireworks, 17 Sept.

Taormina *Taormina Arte*, a series of events, starting with the Film Festival, including drama, concerts, and ballet, with top performers, June–Sept; info: www.taormina-arte.com

Tindari The old theatre is used for presenting concerts, plays and operas, May–July; info T: 0941 246318, www.teatrodeiduemari.it

Tortorici The annual feast of St Sebastian (here known as *Sammastianuzzu*) involves a dramatic procession of barefooted faithful who carry the heavy stone statue of the saint through the river in full flood, 20 Jan.

PRACTICAL INFORMATION

PLANNING YOUR TRIP

When to go

Travelling in Sicily is enjoyable year round. Travellers should bear in mind nonetheless that autumn rainstorms can be very heavy; that winters are mild, but there can be some very cold days; that it is usually very hot in July and August (sometimes 40°C or more); and that the dreaded *scirocco*, the hot, suffocating wind from Africa, can blow at any time of year. Springtime is ideal: February to March is the best time to see the wildflowers, and February is also Carnival time. Easter is celebrated with impressive traditional processions in many towns, but in March, April and May school groups descend on historical sites and museums. The best time to visit places such as the Roman villa at Piazza Armerina, or the Greek theatre in Taormina, for example, is at lunchtime, when they are likely to be quite peaceful. The *maestrale*, the prevailing wind around Messina and the Aeolian Islands, blows from the northwest, and is very strong in winter, often making it difficult for the hydrofoils to reach the offshore islands; sometimes even the ferryboats have problems, and the islands can be truly isolated for several days. Strong winds can sometimes also affect communications between Trapani and the Egadi Islands, and between Porto Empedocle and the Pelagian Islands. There are, however, distinct advantages to travelling in Sicily in winter: although the days are shorter, there are no crowds, the weather is usually mild with cloudless skies, and there' s the incomparable sight of Mount Etna covered in snow. At the end of October and early November there is much preparation for one of the island's most popular celebrations, the *Festa dei Morti*, literally Feast of the Dead (2nd November), when everyone takes sheaves of chrysanthemums to the cemeteries, and children receive toys, ostensibly from their dead ancestors. Special cakes and sweets are made for the occasion.

Maps

The best are published by the Touring Club Italiano (www.touringclubitaliano.com). They are constantly updated and indispensable to anyone travelling by car in Italy. Their *Grande Carta Stradale d'Italia*, on a scale of 1:200,000, is divided into 15 maps covering the regions of Italy, including Sicily (*foglio* 14). The road maps are also published in the handier form of a three-volume atlas called the *Atlante Stradale d'Italia*. The one entitled *Sud* covers Sicily.

Health and insurance

EU citizens have the right to health services in Italy with form E111 (available from Post Offices in the UK). Others are well advised to take out insurance before travelling. Remember to keep all receipts (*ricevute*) and medical report (*cartella clinica*) to give to your insurer if you need to make a claim. Thefts or damage to property must be reported immediately at the local police station; a copy of the *denuncia* will be needed to claim insurance.

Disabled travellers

Sicily is not good for disabled travellers, who will need all their resources of patience and adaptability in order to get around. Although legislation obliges public buildings to provide access for the disabled, and specially designed facilities within, it will be many years before Sicily catches up with mainland Italy or the rest of Europe in this field. Many churches have imposing flights of steps in front of the entrances as their only means of access, not to mention stepped streets and alleys. Toilets in coffee bars or restaurants are often on the first floor, and lifts are rare. In the annual accommodation list published by the local tourist offices, establishments which can offer hospitality to the disabled are indicated. Airports and railway stations now provide assistance and certain trains are equipped to transport wheelchairs. Access for cars with disabled people is allowed to town centres usually closed to traffic, where parking places are reserved for them. For more information, contact the local tourist offices.

ACCOMMODATION

A range of places to stay has been suggested, chosen for at least one of these qualities: character; historical interest; location; value for money; and comfort. They are classified as €€€ (200 euros or over), €€ (100–200 euros) or € (under 100 euros). Prices vary widely according to season and location.

Hotels

Hotels are officially classified into six categories according to the services they offer, denoted by stars, as in the rest of Europe, from one star (corresponding to the old definition *pensione*) to the luxuries of five stars plus S (*superiore*) or L (*lusso*). Not all hotels have restaurants but continental breakfast is usually included in the room price: by law it is an optional extra. Hotels are now also obliged (for tax purposes) to issue a receipt: in theory guests can be fined for leaving the premises without one.

Bed and breakfast

There is a wide choice of bed and breakfast accommodation in Sicily, both in the towns and in the countryside; legislation in Italy has been relaxed, making it much easier for those so inclined to offer rooms to paying guests, who are in turn likely to achieve a much better understanding of the places they visit. Sicilians are extremely hospitable, and their homes are comfortable. Most of the provinces classify this type of accommodation according to the star system: one star means you will have to share the bathroom with the family; three or more star establishments can be as good as luxurious small hotels.

Farm accommodation

Known as *agriturismo* in Italy, there are now hundreds of working farms in Sicily which offer accommodation, highly recommended for travellers with their own transport and families with young children. Terms vary from bed and breakfast to full board or self-contained flats; some farms require a stay of a minimum number of days. Cultural or recreational activities are sometimes provided, such as horse-riding, bowls, archery, trekking, arts and crafts; on some farms you can help with the work on a voluntary basis: milking sheep, gathering olives or fruit, harvesting wheat, and so forth. Again, most provinces use the star system to classify the standards.

Country houses

These are simply houses in the country without a working farm; some of them are aristocratic villas, others are quite basic. They can be recommended to independent travellers who enjoy the countryside.

Rooms and apartments to rent

A wide range of villas, farmhouses, beach bungalows, rooms and apartments is readily available for short-term rental. In some towns where the old centres are being abandoned, civic administrations are helping homeowners to restore their properties in order to provide accommodation for tourists in *paese albergo*. The owners usually live elsewhere. It is an adventurous (and inexpensive) solution for those who want to get a 'feel' for a town. The neighbours will probably be welcoming. Information from the town councils or from the Tourist Office.

Religious institutions

Many convents and monasteries have rooms available for visitors. These are very basic, but always with private bath or shower. Sometimes meals can be taken in the refectory. It is not required of guests to be a Catholic. It always represents very good value for money.

GETTING AROUND

By air

Both Palermo (Falcone Borsellino Airport, www.gesap.it) and Catania (Fontanarossa Airport, www.aeroporto.catania.it) are served by national and international flights. Trapani (Vincenzo Florio Airport, www.airgest.com) connects Rome and Milan to Pantelleria and Lampedusa. New airports are planned for Comiso to serve the Ragusa-Syracuse area, and Racalmuto for Agrigento-Sciacca. Air Europe (www.aireurope.it) offers direct flights from New York to Palermo, while Ryanair (www.ryanair.com) connects Palermo to Stansted, and Virgin Express (www.virgin-express.com) offers flights from Brussels to Palermo and Catania. Both British Airways (www.ba.com) and Air Malta (www.airmalta.com) offer flights from Gatwick to Catania. Direct charter flights in summer are organized to Palermo and Catania from many airports in the British Isles and Scandinavia. Apart from these, all international flights go via Rome or Milan. Most Italian mainland cities and Sardinia have frequent flights to Sicily.

By rail

Mainline trains from the north, via Milan, Turin, Rome or Naples, run to Villa San Giovanni and Reggio Calabria for the ferries to Sicily, with through carriages for Palermo, Catania and Syracuse. Overnight trains carry sleeping accommodation. Connecting car sleeper trains to Palermo and Catania are available from Turin, Milan, Bologna, Genoa and Rome. Beware: thefts from cars are not uncommon on these trains. Timetables and further information can be found on www.trenitaliaplus.com, www.trenitalia.com (Italian Railways).

Rail services in Sicily are lagging behind those provided on the mainland. Rolling stock is outdated while most lines are single track and in some cases are those laid in the 19th century. The journey from Catania to Palermo, c. 200kms, takes less than three hours by coach, but six hours by train.

The Italian Railway Company, Trenitalia, www.trenitalia.com, runs various categories of trains: ES (Eurostar), international express trains (with a special supplement, approximately 30% of the normal single fare) running between the main Italian and European cities (with obligatory seat reservation since no standing passengers are permitted), with first- and second-class carriages; EC and IC, international and national express trains, with a supplement (less than that for the Eurostar); *Espressi*, long-distance trains (both classes) not as fast as the Intercity trains; Diretti, although not stopping at every station, are slower than Espressi; and *Inter-regionali* and *Regionali*, local trains stopping at all stations, mostly with second-class carriages only. Many stations are now unmanned: tickets can be purchased in the nearest coffee bar, tobacconist or newsagent. Valid for two months after the day sold, they must be bought before the journey, and date-stamped in the machines you find on the platforms, otherwise the ticket-collector will exact a stiff fine. In Italy fares are still much lower than many other parts of Europe. Children under the age of four travel free, and between the ages of four and 12 travel half price. If you are planning a lengthy journey through Europe starting in Italy, then a Eurodomino pass (www.eurodomino.it) is useful, with a voucher for each country you intend to visit. Also for journeys starting in Italy, the Carta Verde and Carta Verde Railplus allow discounts on tickets.

By sea

Car ferries on the Straits of Messina operate from Villa San Giovanni (every 20mins 24hrs a day, no booking necessary), taking about 20mins to reach Messina. There are often long queues and frequent delays in the summer. Less frequent ferries to Messina, also hydrofoils, leave from Reggio Calabria, taking 40mins. Caronte (www.carontetourist.it) run a daytime car ferry service connecting Salerno to Messina in c. 9hrs. Overnight car ferries to Palermo operate from Naples, Cagliari and Tunis are run by Tirrenia (www.tirrenia.it), and from Livorno, Genoa, Malta and Tunis by Grandi Navi

Veloci (www.gnv.it). The London agent for these companies is Viamare Travel Ltd, Graphic House, 2 Sumatra Road, London NW6 1PU, T: 0871 4106040, www.viamare.com; book well in advance for a cabin and the space for your car. Ferries operate out of Catania for Malta, Venice, Ravenna, Livorno, Genoa, Salerno and Naples, run by various shipping companies. A good website giving up-to-date information on ferries to and from Italian ports is www.traghettionline.net. For a full list of the ferry services between Italian ports and Sicily, consult www.traghetti-sicilia.it.

By bus

Inter-city and inter-village services in Sicily are widespread, punctual (although perhaps infrequent) and fairly comfortable. Services tend to finish in the early evening. Detailed information on the bus companies and the routes they serve will be found in the chapter listings. Tickets can sometimes be purchased on board, sometimes at the nearest coffee bar or tobacconist.

By car

Stress and road rage are hardly known in Sicily; and the standard of the roads is quite good. In large towns, however, the traffic is chaotic, the streets congested and parking very difficult. Signposting has improved in recent years, but is still by no means complete; nobody minds if you stop to ask directions, even if you hold up the traffic. Tourist information offices are marked with an *i* symbol throughout Italy. Hotels and monuments of interest have yellow signs. Motorways (*autostrade*) are indicated by green signs, normal roads by blue signs. At the entrance to motorways, the two directions are indicated by the name of the town at the end of the road, not by that of the nearest town, which can be confusing. They are a fast and convenient way of travelling around, crossing difficult terrain by means of viaducts and tunnels, and in places they are spectacularly beautiful. Unfortunately the motorway system is not yet complete. Most stretches are toll free. Beware: always lock your car when parked, and never leave anything of value inside it. If purchasing fuel or oil at a motorway service station, always check that you have been given the right amount, that the seal on the oil can is intact, and that you have been given the correct change.

OPENING TIMES

The opening times of museums, churches and archaeological sites are given in the text as far as possible, though they are subject to change without warning. Churches (unless otherwise stated) open at 8am, sometimes closing as early as 11.45am, to reopen at 4.30pm, usually until 7.30pm. Visitors to churches are expected to dress suitably (no miniskirts, shorts, or bare shoulders), and to avoid eating, drinking, talking loudly or using mobile phones. Photography is always forbidden when Mass is in progress. In Holy Week most of the images are covered and are on no account shown. Many museums and archaeological sites are suffering from staff shortages and are unfortunately ever more likely to close in the afternoons and on public holidays (some will only be accessible three days a week). Local tourist offices are supposed to have up-to-date information, but this is often not the case.

ADDITIONAL INFORMATION

Crime and personal security

Pickpocketing is a widespread problem in towns all over Italy: it is always advisable not to carry valuables and to take special care of handbags or shoulder bags. Snatch thefts, especially by passing scooters, are common in Sicily. Crimes should be reported immediately to the police or local *carabinieri* office (found in every small town and village).

Emergency numbers

Police: 113 (*Polizia di Stato*) or 112 (*Carabinieri*).
Medical: 118

Telephone and postal services

For all calls in Italy, local and long distance, dial the city code (for instance, 091 for Palermo), then the phone number. For international and intercontinental calls, dial 00 plus the country code, then the city code (for numbers in the UK drop the initial zero) and number. When in Sicily, for local directory enquiries, dial 12 (for numbers in Italy) or 176 (for international numbers).

To call Sicily from abroad (not USA) dial 0039, then the city code and number. To call Sicily from the USA dial 00139, then the city code and number.

Stamps are sold at tobacconists (*tabacchi*, marked with a large white 'T') and post offices. *Posta ordinaria* is regular post; *posta prioritaria* receives priority handling, including transport by air mail, and is only slightly more expensive. Correspondence can be addressed to you in Italy c/o the post office by 'Fermo Posta' to the name of the locality.

Useful web sites

General: www.regione.sicilia.it/turismo • www.bestofsicily.com
www.sicilia.indettaglio.it • www.borghitalia.it • www.touringclub.it/bandierearancioni
www.si-sicily.it • www.sicilyguides.com • www.cookandsicily.com
www.sicilydeluxe.com
Museums and galleries: www.regione.sicilia.it/beniculturali
Food and drink: www.saporiegustidisicilia.it • www.slowfood.com
www.sicilytravel.net
Nature: www.siciliaparchi.com • www.parks.it • www.entefaunasiciliana.it
www.legambiente.sicilia.it • www.wwfitalia.it/sicilia • www.lipusicilia.it

FOOD & DRINK

A HISTORY OF SICILIAN CUISINE

by Nigel McGilchrist

Sicilian cuisine is perhaps the most complex regional cuisine of the Mediterranean basin. Historically, it is not one, but many cuisines. It reflects the fertility of the island, the antiquity and complexity of its history, as well as the deeply rooted ritualism of its culture. Often more poetic than practical, it makes the foods of mainland Italy seem sometimes prosaic by comparison. Ingredients and preparation techniques brought by settlers or invaders over 2,500 years of history have all been assimilated and transformed by the creativity of the Sicilian genius. Salt, sugar, rice, citrus fruits, pistachios, almonds, aubergines, sardines, tomatoes and tuna all find their most versatile (and sometimes their first) gastronomic expression in the food of Sicily. Technically, it is a cuisine of combination, rather than of synthesis. In this sense it lies at the opposite end of the gastronomic spectrum from traditional French cuisine. The emphasis, in other words, is on the often startling addition and combination of strong, individual flavours (as for example in the classic *caponata*), rather than the subordination of elements to a greater, unified whole. Visually, too, it is a courageous cuisine; not just because of the surprising combinations of colours and textures (for example *cassata*), or the intricate forms of its sweets, but for the sheer bravura of its foods for festivals, such as the famous and astonishing votive creations in bread for the saints' feasts.

Antiquity and the early Christian era

Accounts of Sicilian food in Antiquity abound. Already from Homer's vivid picture in the *Odyssey* of the fertility of the island as it appeared to 8th-century BC Greek eyes we have a valuable image of its basic agriculture, irrigation, fruits, vines, and cheese. But it is once the Greek colonies of Sicily are well established that we hear of gastronomy proper: of the school for professional cooks run by Labdacus in Syracuse; of the lost 5th-century BC text *The Art of Cooking* by Mithaecus of Syracuse; and of countless references to other lost works on food. The fame of Sicilian cuisine in Antiquity was so great that the extravagant *coquus siculus* became a familiar caricature figure in the works of later comedy writers. In one fragment of Alexis of Tarentum, for example, we find: 'I learnt to cook in Sicily so well that I will cause the banqueters to bite the dishes and plates for joy.' But this same hedonism was often viewed with distaste, by some of Sicily's more illustrious visitors, such as Plato.

Most illuminating of all are the poetic writings on food by Archestratos of Gela (mid-4th century BC). Archestratos is more a connoisseur of ingredients and of their flavours than a cook: he praises simplicity, quality and moderation, and is a man of refinement and encyclopaedic knowledge. For him, fish takes precedence over meat, and every product or ingredient has an ideal place of origin, where the quality is finest: swordfish from the straits of Messina, tuna from Tindari or Cefalù, lobster from Lipari, and so forth. With his eye on quality rather than artifice, he often recommends simple, minimal roasting, with herbs, good olive oil and salt to enhance the essential flavours of fresh foods. Although writing in a period of turmoil in Sicily, Archestratos gives us a unique vision of dining as a sophisticated, almost sacramental art, always to be performed with gratitude.

Where the Greeks may have moderated the luxury in food which Sicily's riches naturally invited, the Romans encouraged it. So many of the ingredients (pistachios, pine-nuts, artichokes, raisins, and fish sauce, for example) used by Apicius, Imperial Rome's collator and writer of recipes, originate in Sicily; and the elaborate combinations and preparations we find in his writings give us a glimpse of the excesses of sophistication to which Archestratos had been so opposed almost 600 years earlier. In Sicily it seems that pagan traditions rarely died, but were instead transformed; and with the advent of Christianity, ancient ritual foods were adopted by the new religion. The pagan *panspermia*, a ritual gruel prepared from boiled, unmilled seeds in honour of Apollo at the winter and summer solstices, reappears as the *cuccìa* or spelt pudding (often served with a reduced wine sauce, *vino cotto*, which was one of Apicius' most frequent condiments) at the feast of St Lucy, which likewise falls on the shortest day of the year. There were also sesame and honey cakes called *mylloi* which were moulded into the shape of the female pudenda as tokens of fertility during the pagan festivals in honour of Demeter and Persephone. Here we perhaps see the origins of the bizarre forms of later Sicilian pastries and breads: the *minni di virgini* (in the form of St. Agatha's breasts), and biscuits such as Palermo's *strunzi d'ancilu* (literally, 'angels' turds').

Arab and Norman occupations

The Arab invasions of the 9th century changed Sicilian food for ever, bringing rice, which was cultivated in paddies near Lentini; citrus fruits in plenty; the exotic aubergine; and sugar cane, which provided the first neutral sweetener in cooking and replaced honey and *vino cotto*, thereby radically transforming the confectioner's art. It is also possible that pasta was introduced into Italy through the Sicilian Arabs, who in turn may have brought it from further east in Persia. The making of *vermicelli* near to Palermo is described by the 12th-century Arab geographer, Al-Idrisi, a couple of generations before the journeys of the young Marco Polo. At first, pasta was a rich person's dish; it cost much more than bread. Eaten with broths, and with small fish, seasoned with wild fennel and raisins in these early times, pasta was to have to wait almost 500 years before its betrothal to the tomato.

The Arabs' more sophisticated techniques of irrigation transformed agriculture on the island, in particular the cultivation of fruit: different varieties of orange were combined in spiced salads with onions, with fish (in *sarde al becafico*), or with artichokes; and perhaps Sicily's most quintessential salad is that of fresh lemons, mint, garlic, salt and a very little *vino cotto*. Nonetheless, the Arab settlers are most famous for creating the cold sherbets and *granitas* which were based on these citrus fruits, and which built upon the Ancient Roman habit of using snow from Mount Etna which had been stored underground as ice until the summer came. Of these, the *granita di scurzunera*, made from the flower of the jasmine, evokes more directly than any the luxury of the orient and of the harem.

The harem (or women's quarters) is where the preparation of the exquisite sweet-meats—so important to Arab hospitality—traditionally took place. Once Sicily became Christian again under the Normans and Angevins, it was in the similar enclosure of the nunnery that those arts were perpetuated. The most famous example of this was the *frutta di Martorana* of Palermo's Martorana convent, where *pasta reale* (almond paste) was skilfully moulded and coloured by the nuns into the forms of fruits—to the delight and incredulity of visitors and natives—at the time of the feast of All Souls. Oriental in their delicacy, pagan in their memories of votive offerings, these fruits delighted both palate and eyes, and reminded the spirit of the triumph over death: they, unlike real fruit, did not decay.

Such sweets were not just the prerogative of the Martorana; the *cuscus dolce* of almonds and pistachios of the closed nuns of the Sacro Cuore in Agrigento, or the almond *paste dolci di riposto* of the nuns of Erice, as well as the creations of many other convents were equally renowned. Close in nature to these, and yet more Oriental in colour and appearance, is their extravagant 'lay' cousin, Sicily's famous *cassata*, named from the arabic word *quas'ah* for the terracotta bowl in which it is moulded, and which incorporates a core of sweetened *ricotta*, an element which might not have been unfamiliar to Odysseus, over two thousand years earlier.

From the Middle Ages to modernity

The characteristics of Sicilian food were laid down by this combination of ancient Greek and Arab ideas. Once the two strains are fully integrated by the 13th century, the fundaments of Sicilian cuisine are in place and subsequent centuries bring only modifications. The centuries of French and Spanish domination saw a decline in agricultural management, and were all too frequently punctuated by famines (to which Sicilian popular song bears testimony). As a consequence, bread—which to pagan Greeks, Christians, Jews and Muslims alike had a primary sacramental quality—was seen even more as an instrument of God's beneficence and punishment. Bread in Sicily was treated as an icon of divine grace, and it took an infinite variety of forms. The power and visuality of these Sicilian religious feasts (as expressed in particular by the *altari di San Giuseppe* or 'altars to Saint Joseph' of the Belice Valley) are renowned. In few other places in the world is bread used theatrically, architecturally, sculpturally and gastronomically at the same time. And almost every community in Sicily has its own individual forms and symbols in bread for its own particular festivals.

Bourbon Spanish domination in the 17th century brought with it new exotica: cocoa, the tomato, and the red chili-pepper (which had been first introduced into Spain from South East Asia by the Portuguese). Nevertheless, these elements only added to the variety of existing dishes rather than transforming methods of cooking. In Sicilian cuisine they remain afterthoughts, whereas in mainland Italian cooking they are often centre stage. At times they distracted Sicilian cooks from their ancient and great tradition. The tomato, on the other hand, enhances some of Sicily's most famous modern dishes: Catania's *pasta alla Norma*, named after Bellini's opera of that name, shows how those two ingredients, the tomato and the aubergine, one from far in the East and the other from far in the West, were united in a Sicilian marriage.

Bourbon links with Naples brought the fashion for things French: the theatrical, French (or French-trained) chef in a well-stocked kitchen became a status symbol for the well-to-do; and with the chef—or the *monzù* ('monsieur') as he came to be known in Sicily—came butter and cream, and a wholly different concept of food and its preparation. The banquets described by Lampedusa in *The Leopard* give a vivid picture of the *monzù's* art. Refined, essential and quintessential sauces, such as *essenza di cipolla* (a slowly cooked essence of onion which was henceforth to substitute the humbler garlic) and *velouté* sauces of aubergine, were the new fashion. The *monzù's* art was a combination of virtuosity and extreme delicacy, as for example in the preparation of *scuma*, a very fine pasta, boiled rapidly, then gilded with eggs and fine breadcrumbs, and fried in very hot lard; this could serve as a casing for some delicacy or it could be moulded into weightless baskets for some refined fish or mushroom filling. Short pastry also arrives with the *monzù*, and was used to encase oven-baked *timballi* of pasta or *pasticci di verdura* in a gilded crust.

Fortunately for all this diversity, Sicily is small enough for each area to have felt the influence of all the others; and it is this that has been the key to its gastronomic richness. In mainland Italy, the continuity with Antiquity had been broken by the repeated barbarian invasions; but not so in Sicily. In this way, both through the forced emigration of many Sicilian Jews in the late 15th century and through trade in primary ingredients with Genoa and Venice, Sicily was able to export its precious legacy in food back to the growing cultural centres of the Italian peninsula. Renaissance food in continental Italy owes a great debt to Sicily and, through her, to Antiquity. Without Sicily, it could even be argued, Italian food could never have become as splendid as it is.

FAVOURITE SICILIAN SPECIALITIES

Bread

It was the wheat-fields of Ramacca, in the province of Catania, that inspired Wagner's *Harvesters' Hymn*; the wheat-fields which were the gift of Demeter herself. Sicilian bread varies enormously in shape, size, colour and flavour. There are 72 different specialities. Each family eats an average of almost 100kg of bread a year, which is more than most other Italians (all great bread eaters), and they treat it with almost religious reverence. It is always placed face up on the table, and is kissed if it falls on the ground. Often made using the sourdough method, it is preferably cooked in stone ovens, which are heated by burning olive, almond, oak, lemon or orange wood, or even almond shells, depending on whatever fuel is more abundant. Some bakers can trace the origin of their sourdough back over 200 years. The basic ingredient is durum-wheat flour, usually a blend of different varieties. At Castelvetrano, for example, the coffee-coloured loaves owe their aroma and rich flavour to the use of *tumminia* flour, while in Lentini they add a little *timilia* wheat. Other localities renowned for the quality of the bread are Monreale, Favara, Novara di Sicilia and San Giuseppe Jato.

Olive oil

Sicilian olive oil is excellent. So many different soil types, and slight local variations in climate, mean that several different varieties of olive tree can be cultivated, some of which can be traced back thousands of years, and may be native to the island. Sicily provides only 10 per cent of the entire national production of oil, but by far the largest quantity of olives for salting and curing, both black and green. The finest groves are probably those of the province of Trapani, around Castelvetrano. Here the trees are pruned to stay very small, almost bonsai size, and the olives are picked by hand, resulting in perfect oil and sublime pickles. Oil to rhapsodise over is also produced at Caronia (Messina), Ragalna and Minco (Catania), Syracuse, and Chiaramonte Gulfi (Ragusa), where the precious liquid is the linchpin of the economy, and there is even an olive-oil museum. Nowadays the best oils are protected by the DOP seal (*denominazione d'origine di produzione*), a guarantee of quality similar to that offered to the finest wines.

Confectionery

Sweets and cakes in Sicily are a delightful riot of colours, aromas and flavours: there are the simple, fragrant breakfast pastries; crystallized and candied fruits; fruits made of marzipan; nougat; biscuits made with almonds, pistachios or hazelnuts; crunchy *cannoli* filled with *ricotta* cheese; and the elaborate Baroque complexities of the magnificent *cassata siciliana*, filled with ricotta. The light and delicate *paste di mandorla*, the almond pastries of Acireale, inspired emulation in Britain in the form of macaroons, though there is little real similarity between the two. Every town or village has its own speciality, and different sweets are prepared for the main feasts of the year.

Ice cream

Italians eat a lot of ice cream; apparently only Americans and Australians eat more. It is the Sicilians who push up the average national consumption; they like it so much, they even have it for breakfast. Alexander the Great has been improbably credited with discovering the method of storing snow underground, in the 4th century BC; his soldiers were able to dig it up when necessary, to offer the emperor cool fruit juices. It is quite possible that ice cream was invented in Sicily: we know that the Romans were bringing down snow from Mount Etna during the winter, using mule trains; they stored the snow in *neviere*, pits dug in cool cellars, covering it with a thick layer of straw or sawdust to keep it fresh until summer. It was then recovered and mixed with wine, honey and spices, and sold as a great luxury to those who could afford it. The Arabs in Sicily took the process one step further, by using sugar instead of honey, and fruit juice instead of wine; they called their confection *sciarbat* (hence sherbet; sorbet).

But the first confectioner to have the brainwave of adding cream to the mixture was a young late 17th-century Sicilian, Procopio de' Coltelli of Acitrezza. He took his discovery to Paris, to delight Louis XIV and the king gave him the exclusive rights of manufacture. He opened the Café Procope, still in existence, which claims to be the world's first coffee house, frequented by Voltaire, Benjamin Franklin and much of Parisian society.

In Sicily the manufacture of ice cream is still a point of honour, and there are plenty of pastry shops and coffee bars where you will find ice cream made on the premises. The coveted annual Procopio de' Coltelli award goes to the best ice cream maker on the island. A list of ingredients by the counter is a very good sign. *Gelato* is ice cream made with eggs and milk or cream. *Granita* is fruit juice (or coffee, or ground almonds or pistachios) and sugar, frozen together. The secret is to obtain a very fine-grained, thick but not too thick consistency. *Cremolata* and *sorbetto* are variations on the theme, sometimes with the addition of egg-whites.

In Sicilian towns from April until October the ice cream vendors take up their stands in the early morning, and blow a whistle or ring a bell to announce breakfast. People sometimes come down into the street in their pyjamas. Ice cream is usually served in a soft bun, like a sandwich. *Granita* comes in a plastic cup, into which pieces of bun are dunked. You can have several flavours at the same time, and even add a dollop of whipped cream. In city centres people will have their ice cream breakfast at the coffee bar. Wherever it takes place, it is the first moment of social aggregation of the day.

Soft drinks

The thirsty Sicilian asks for *latte di mandorla* (almond milk), made with crushed almonds and sugar diluted with water and chilled (the best will be found in Catania and Modica). Very sweet, it is surprisingly refreshing. In town centres, kiosks serve inexpensive thirst-quenchers: freshly squeezed lemon juice with soda water and a pinch of salt is one of the most popular (*selz, limone e sale*). Kiosk owners often make their own fluorescent fruit syrups, which are then diluted with soda water. Cheap and popular fizzy drinks, which have been around for generations, are *spuma*, *gazzosa*, and *chinotto*.

SPECIALITY FOOD BY PROVINCE

The geography of Sicily varies dramatically from area to area and it is only natural that different regions should have different specialities. The international Slow Food Foundation has a strong following here. This organization, present in over 100 nations, has indicated about 40 different Sicilian food products as *presidia*, or worthy of protection. Several risked disappearing altogether, due to the consequences of globalization, and tough EU laws on foodstuffs (the use of time-honoured equipment, and ancient farming methods, are not always compatible with strict modern hygiene standards). Special regional decrees have had to be issued for many of them, underlining their incalculable traditional value, to save them from oblivion.

Palermo

Pollina and Castelbuono in the Madonie mountains are the only places in the world where the manna ash trunks are incised (like maple trees) to collect the white syrupy sap, which is dried and used for making medicines and sweeteners. Also from the Madonie Mountains is *provola*, sweet-flavoured sheep's milk cheese, each weighing about 1kg with a little 'neck' to hang it from. On the island of Ustica, tiny, dark brown lentils are grown completely without herbicides or fertilizers; donkeys dragging stones are still used for threshing. They are soft, tender and quick to cook. Late-ripening tangerines can be found at Ciaculli, in the Conca d'Oro behind Palermo.

Trapani

The salt pans of Trapani, so jealously husbanded by the ancient Romans, and profitably used by the Florio family in the 19th century, meant that Trapani's tuna could be salted, preserved and exported widely; likewise the island's sardines and anchovies. Red garlic is grown in the salt marshes around Nubia. It has small corms, red skin, and an intense flavour. The island of Pantelleria is famous for its capers: very small and strong flavoured, they are the flower buds of the plant, gathered just before blossoming. Black bread is baked in stone ovens in Castelvetrano, using the sourdough method, and a mixture of two different kinds of durum wheat. Each loaf weighs 1kg. The crust is very dark brown, almost black, the crumb is golden, the flavour is sublime. *Vastedda* cheeses from the Belice Valley are the small round cheeses mentioned by Homer. Formed in a soup plate (the meaning of the name in Sicilian), they are made only from local sheep's milk, which is kneaded and pulled. Slightly elastic, it has a vague aroma of vanilla. The production is very small (only 15 people make it), and the cheese must be eaten fresh. Equally ancient are the winter melons from Trapani, quoted by Diodorus Siculus (4th century BC) as being among the fruits grown in Sicily. These bright yellow melons, very sweet, stay good until Christmas.

Agrigento

Girgentana goats from Agrigento are a highly prized breed. These attractive animals with their long horns are exploited for their milk and their skins. Wild strawberries from Ribera are derived from seedlings brought back to Sicily from the Alps, by soldiers who had fought in the First World War. The island of Lampedusa is famous for its *cernia* (sea-perch).

Caltanissetta and Enna

Inland, at Caltanisetta and Enna, we find the sheep's cheeses again first mentioned by Homer: *tuma*, *primosale* and *pecorino*, often with the addition of black peppercorns or coriander seeds, and even (in the province of Enna) of saffron. Here, too, are the finest beans and pulses, essential ingredients in dishes such as the *minestre di ceci* (chickpea potage) or *maccu di fave* (broad beans seasoned with wild fennel). Late peaches from Leonforte are protected: these strong-flavoured, yellow peaches ripen from September to November; each fruit is protected in its own little bag, from birds, insects and hail.

Ragusa and Siracusa

Modicana cattle from Ragusa and Modica graze in the open air, indifferent to the hot climate. The meat is tough but good; the excellent milk is used for making several different local cheeses, such as *caciocavallo*. It is pressed into long rectangular shapes, and then hung two by two over a beam to mature. Almond trees are grown everywhere in Sicily, and probably form part of the native flora, but those from Noto have the finest flavour of all.

Catania

Though the soil is good in central Sicily, no area can compare with the Catanian hinterland, whose rich volcanic soil and sunshine gives an intensity to the fruits and perfumes of its orchards. This lies behind the huge success of its ices and sorbets, and its citrus summer salads. In fact, a healthful simplicity informs the food of this area, so much of which is based upon the household bread-oven: *schiacciate*, richly filled *focacce*, vegetables roasted over charcoal, and fish and seafood wrapped in fig or citrus leaves and then roasted over the coals. Pistachios from Bronte were introduced by the Arabs and the nuts now grown on Mount Etna have a superb flavour. Snuff-box peaches from Mount Etna (*pesche tabacchiera*) are small, flat and intensely aromatic. Sicilian blood oranges are protected by the IGP seal (*indicazione geografica di provenienza*). There are several different varieties, all limited to the area of Mount Etna and the Plain of Catania, the only place in the world where the colour is so intense, almost purple. From the Gulf of Catania come anchovies, *masculini di magghia*, so good that they can be eaten raw; the *magghia* is the fine-meshed net with which they are caught, from small boats.

Messina

The tiny, offshore islands have based their dishes on the intense flavours of the capers (those from Salina are protected), oregano, and *nepitella* (calamint) which grow there; the currants and the Malvasia grapes which they produce; and the cactus fruits and miniature lentils which survive in their dry and rocky environment. The islands and the coastal cities have obviously always prized their abundance of fish: in Messina, particularly its *stocco* and sword-fish, intercepted in shoals at the yearly periods of migration. *Impanata di pesce spada* from here is a magnificent envelope of short-crust pastry containing the sword-fish and its accompaniments of olives, zucchini and capers. Salami and ham from the Nebrodi Mountains are protected. Black-and-white pigs, an ancient breed (seen in medieval paintings and probably introduced by the Normans), are allowed to live wild in the woods, eating acorns and beech-nuts. The result is excellent sausage, salami, ham and bacon. In Novara di Sicilia they make *maiorchino* cheese, the round, flat sheep's milk cheeses, with a dark brown rind, that are used at Carnival time for a race, rolling them down the main street. Unfortunately, they are becoming increasingly rare, as their manufacture is very time-consuming.

RESTAURANTS

A range of restaurants for all pockets is given at the end of each chapter. The choices reflect pleasant personal experience and an endeavour to introduce travellers to the very best local dishes and wines. They are categorised according to the approximate cost of a meal without drinks: €€€ means a fine-dining restaurant, over 35 euros per head (sometimes well over); €€ means a good restaurant, 20–30 euros per head; € means a simple trattoria where you will pay 10–25 euros per head.

Mealtimes
Service is always slow, the way Sicilians like it, and mealtimes are later than elsewhere in Italy: lunch usually about 1.30pm; dinner at 8.30pm or later. Service charges are included in the bill unless otherwise stated (some places also add a cover charge), so tipping is not an obligation, but always much appreciated. Meals can often be very long drawn-out affairs. The main meal of the day is lunch, almost invariably consisting of pasta; soup rarely appears on the menu. While eating, people like to relax and talk to their families or their friends. Restaurant meals are the occasion for dressing up, to look and be looked at, in the comfortable knowledge that each dish you have chosen will be specially prepared, and not warmed up in the microwave. Sicilians rarely ask for the menu, they prefer to accept the advice of the waiter, the cook, or the restaurant owner, who will describe the delicacies found at the market that morning, and how they will be prepared; eventually suggesting the best wine to accompany each course, or the whole meal.

WINE

Legend has it that the first grapevine sprang from under the foot of Dionysus, whirling in a frenzied dance on the foothills of Mount Etna. Archaeologists confirm the ancient origin of wine production on Sicily, where the first vines were certainly autochthonous. Bronze-age Phoenicians probably included wine (and perhaps saffron) from Sicily in the vast range of merchandise they traded, as far as the British Isles. New arrivals who had come to dominate, improved the production by imparting secrets of their expertise. The Greeks taught the trick of cultivating the vine *ad alberello*, close to the ground, increasing sugar-content and alcohol level; Romans introduced new varieties and new techniques of manufacture. The famous wine of ancient Sicily was Mamertino, said to have been the favourite of Julius Caesar. Even the Arabs, who as Muslims could not drink wine, carefully cultivated and improved the vines, in order to present the grapes as table fruit, and for drying as raisins and sultanas for use in the kitchen. In 1100 Roger de Hauteville founded the Abbazia Santa Anastasia winery near Cefalù, which is still going strong to this day. The heyday of Sicilian winemaking began in the 13th century and lasted some 200 years, a period when Sicilian wines were exported to Rome, Liguria, Venice and Tuscany, playing an important role in shaping the tastes of European palates. Real innovation began in the late 18th century, when the British wine merchant John Woodhouse introduced the Spanish and Portuguese methods of manufacture to Marsala, a great success. The late 19th-century phylloxera blight, which destroyed the vineyards, was a setback, followed after the Second World War by a total neglect of quality—the only thing that mattered at the time was quantity.

Thankfully those days are receding, and we are now seeing the dawn of some energetic and exciting new winemaking. In the last ten years local and foreign investors in Sicilian viticulture have begun drawing out the virtues of the island's *terroir*. Although traditional winemaking methods are giving way to modern vinification technology, the focus is firmly on getting the best out of indigenous grape varieties. An excellent example is the Avide cellar near Ragusa, one of the flagship wineries in terms of bringing back traditional grapes; or Calatrasi, in San Cipirello south of Palermo, whose best wines include Terre di Ginestra, Allora, Accademia del Sole and Terrale.

A new generation of producers, in the tradition of Vincenzo Florio's legendary Marsala and Duke Alliata di Salaparuta with his Corvo, are experimenting with new techniques, new varieties and new blends, while nurturing the native vines at the same time. The results are more than satisfactory: they are winning major international awards.

Nowadays the names to look for are Carlo Hauner (a producer of fine Malvasia wine on the island of Salina in the province of Messina; *see box on p. 481*); Rallo, from Donnafugata, producing robust Nero d'Avola reds and Ansonica white wines at their Contessa Entellina vineyards as well as the naturally sweet Moscato d' Alessandria made from Zibibbo grapes on Pantelleria; Di Gaetano from Firriato, with a range of whites and reds; Moncada Rudinì from Pachino (Province of Syracuse), an ancient family close to the original heartlands of Nero d'Avola; Planeta (in Noto they have a winery called Buonvini); Pellegrino, whose Marsala DOC Vergine Soleras, aged for five years, has won awards, still being made using the ancient Soleras method of percolation through a pyramid of oak barrels); Murgo, for wines from the volcanic slopes of Mt Etna; Montalto, where they make good white wine from the Catarratto grape; the superb dessert wines of Salvatore Murana of Pantelleria; and Palari of Messina with their wonderful red Faro. Good-quality whites from native grape varieties are made by Rapitalà. Regaleali, one of Sicily's most famous cellars, and one of the first to begin the Sicilian revival, has some splendid reds from the Nero d'Avola grape. Frappato is another red, light and bright and best drunk young. It can be very successfully blended with Nero d'Avola, as the noted Cerasuolo, from Vittoria, shows.

Noble grape varieties such as Chardonnay, Sauvignon Blanc, Cabernet Sauvignon, Syrah, Sangiovese and Merlot also flourish in the hot dry sulphurous soil, or in the richness of the black lava; even German varieties from the Rhine Valley are promising well. The grape harvest in Sicily begins earlier than anywhere else in the northern hemisphere; on some estates even in August. In one or two places the grapes are gathered in the time-honoured way, at night, when the fruit is cool, so that it doesn't start fermenting too soon. This technique probably goes back to the days of the Greeks.

There are at present 21 different high quality wines produced in Sicily and guaranteed by the DOC label (*denominazione d'origine controllata*), ranging from the Marsalas to the Moscatos, the Malvasias to the wines of Etna, the delicate white Alcamo to the full red Cerasuolo di Vittoria. Such a long and complete list means that the island is one of the most important wine-producing areas in Italy.

GLOSSARY

Abacus, flat stone in the upper part of a capital

Acroterion, an ornamental feature on the corner or highest point of a pediment

Aedicule, small opening framed by two columns and a pediment, originally used in classical architecture

Agora, public square or market-place

Ambo (pl. *ambones*) pulpit in a Christian basilica; two pulpits on opposite sides of a church, from which the gospel and epistle were read

Amphiprostyle, temple with colonnades at both ends

Amphora, antique vase, usually of large dimensions, for oil and other liquids

Antefix, ornament placed at the lower corner of the tiled roof of a temple to conceal the space between the tiles and the cornice

Antis, *in antis* describes the portico of a temple when the side-walls are prolonged to end in a pilaster flush with the columns of the portico

Architrave, lowest part of the entablature, horizontal frame above a door

Archivolt, moulded architrave carried round an arch

Atlantes (or telamones) male figures used as supporting columns

Atrium, forecourt, usually of a Byzantine church or a classical Roman house

Badia (*abbazia*), abbey

Baglio, from the medieval word *Ballium* meaning a large fortified building. It is now usually used to describe the warehouse of a wine distillery

Baldachin, canopy supported by columns, usually over an altar

Basilica, originally a Roman building used for public administration; in Christian architecture, an aisled church with a clerestory and apse, and no transepts

Borgo, a suburb; street leading away from the centre of a town

Bottega, the studio of an artist; the pupils who worked under his direction

Bouleuterion, council chamber

Bozzetto, sketch, often used to describe a small model for a piece of sculpture

Bucchero, Etruscan black terracotta ware

Caldarium or **calidarium**, room for hot or vapour baths in a Roman bath

Campanile, bell-tower, often detached from the building to which it belongs

Camposanto, cemetery

Capital, the top of a column

Cardo, the main street of a Roman town, at right-angles to the decumanus

Caryatid, female figure used as a supporting column

Cavea, the part of a theatre or amphitheatre occupied by the row of seats

Cella, sanctuary of a temple, usually in the centre of the building

Chiaroscuro, distribution of light and shade, apart from colour, in a painting

Chiesa Madre or **Chiesa Matrice**, parish church

Chryselephantine, overlaid with gold and ivory

Chthonic, dwelling in or under the ground

Ciborium, casket or tabernacle containing the Host

Cipollino, onion-marble; a greyish marble with streaks of white or green

Cippus, sepulchral monument in the form of an altar

Cista, casket, usually of bronze and cylindrical in shape, to hold jewels, toilet articles, etc., and decorated with mythological subjects

Console, ornamental bracket

Crenellations, battlements

Cuneus, wedge-shaped block of seats in an antique theatre

Cyclopean, the term applied to walls of unmortared masonry, older than the Etruscan civilisation, and attributed by the ancients to the giant Cyclopes

Decumanus, the main street of a Roman town running parallel to its longer axis

Diorite, a type of greenish coloured rock

Dioscuri, name given to Castor and Pollux, twin sons of Zeus

Dipteral, temple surrounded by a double peristyle

Diptych, painting or ivory tablet in two sections

Dipylon, a gateway such as that found on the west side of ancient Athens.

Dithyrambic, an ecstatic hymn of ancient Greece, especially one dedicated to Dionysus

Duomo, cathedral

Ekklesiasterion, council house for the assembly of the citizens of a town

Entablature, the part above the capital (consisting of architrave, frieze and cornice) of a classical building

Entasis, the difference in the diameter of a column at its top, middle and base.

Ephebos, Greek youth under training (military or university)

Epigraph, inscription, especially on coins or sculpture.

Exedra, semicircular recess

Ex-voto, tablet or small painting expressing gratitude to a saint

Fiumare, wide flat-bottomed torrent-bed filled with gravel, usually waterless

Forum, open space in a town serving as a market or meeting-place

Fresco (*affresco*), painting executed on wet plaster. On the wall beneath the sinopia is sketched, and the *cartone* is transferred onto the fresh plaster (*intonaco*) before the fresco is begun, either by pricking the outline with small holes over which a powder is dusted, or by means of a stylus which leaves an incised line on the wet plaster. In recent years many frescoes have been detached from the walls on which they were executed

Frigidarium, room for cold baths in a Roman bath

Fumarole, volcanic spurt of vapour (usually sulphurous) emerging from the ground

Gigantomachia, contest of Giants

Graffiti, design on a wall made with an iron tool on a prepared surface, the design showing in white. Also used loosely to describe scratched designs or words on walls

Greek cross, cross with arms of equal length

Hellenistic, the period from Alexander the Great to Augustus (c. 325–31 BC)

Herm (pl. *hermae*), quadrangular pillar decreasing in girth towards the ground, surmounted by a bust

Hexastyle, temple with a portico of six columns at the end

Hypogeum, subterranean excavation

for the interment of the dead (usually Etruscan)

Intarsia, inlay of wood, marble, or metal

Kore, maiden

Kouros, boy; Archaic male figure

Krater, antique mixing-bowl, conical in shape with rounded base

Kufic, early decorative, angular form of the Arabic alphabet

Kylix, wide shallow vase with two handles and short stem

Latomiae, the limestone quarries of Siracusa, later used as prisons, and now tropical gardens

Lekythos, container for storing oil, ointment or perfume

Loculus, one of many small cavities, especially in a catacomb or necropolis.

Loggia, covered gallery or balcony, usually preceding a larger building

Lunette, semicircular space in a vault or ceiling, often decorated with a painting or a relief

Mascaron, caricatured human face or mask used as architectural decoration

Marmi mischi, inlay decoration of various polychrome marbles and *pietre dure*, used in church interiors in the 17th and 18th century

Medallion, large medal, or a circular ornament

Megalith, a huge stone (often used as a monument)

Megaron, an oblong hall (usually in a Mycenaean palace)

Metope, panel between two triglyphs on the frieze of a temple

Monolith, single stone (usually a column)

Narthex, vestibule of a Christian basilica

Naumachia, mock naval combat for which the arena of an amphitheatre was flooded

Nymphaeum, a sort of summer-house in the gardens of baths, palaces, etc., originally a temple of the Nymphs, and decorated with statues of those goddesses

Octastyle, a portico with eight columns

Odeion, a concert hall, usually in the shape of a Greek theatre, but roofed

Ogee (arch.), arch shaped in a double curve, convex above and concave below

Oinochoe, wine-jug usually of elongated shape for dipping wine out of a krater

Opisthodomos, the enclosed rear part of a temple

Opus sectile, mosaic or paving of thin slabs of coloured marble cut in geometrical shapes

Ossuary, deposit of or receptacle for the bones of the dead

Palazzo, any dignified and important building

Pantocrator, the Almighty

Pax, sacred object used by a priest for the blessing of peace, and offered for the kiss of the faithful, usually circular, engraved, enamelled or painted in a rich gold or silver frame

Pediment, gable above the portico of a classical building

Pendentive, concave spandrel beneath a dome

Peripteral, temple surrounded by a colonnade

Peristyle, a columned portico surrounding a court or temple

Pietà, group of the Virgin mourning the dead Christ

Piscina, Roman tank; a basin for an officiating priest to wash his hands before Mass

Pithos, large pottery vessel

Podium, a continuous base or plinth supporting columns, and the lowest row of seats in the cavea of a theatre or amphitheatre

Polyptych, painting or tablet in more than three sections

Predella, small painting attached below a large altarpiece

Presepio, literally, crib or manger. A group of statuary of which the central subject is the Infant Jesus in the manger

Pronaos, porch in front of the cella of a temple

Propylon, propylaea. Entrance gate to a temenos; in plural form when there is more than one door

Prostyle, edifice with columns on the front only

Pulvin, cushion stone between the capital and the impost block

Putto, figure of a child sculpted or painted, usually nude

Quadriga, four-horsed chariot

Quadriporticus, courtyard surrounded on each side by a portico

Rhyton, drinking-horn usually ending in an animal's head

Sinopia, a reddish brown pigment used to mark the first outline of a fresco

Situla, water bucket

Squinch, arched space at the angle of a tower

Stamnos, big-bellied vase with two small handles at the sides, closed by a lid

Stele, upright stone bearing a monumental inscription

Stereobate, basement of a temple or other building

Stilted arch, round arch that rises vertically before it springs

Stoa, porch or portico not attached to a larger building

Stoup, vessel for Holy Water, usually near the west door of a church

Stucco, plasterwork

Stylobate, basement of a columned temple or other building

Tablinum, reception room in a Roman house with one side opening onto the central courtyard

Telamones, see Atlantes

Temenos, a sacred enclosure

Tepidarium, room for warm baths in a Roman bath

Tessera, a small cube of stone, terracotta, marble, glass, etc., used in mosaic work

Tetrastyle, having four columns at the end

Thermae, originally simply baths, later elaborate buildings fitted with libraries, assembly rooms, gymnasia, circuses, etc

Tholos, a circular building

Tondo, round painting or bas-relief

Transenna, open grille or screen, usually of marble, in an early Christian church

Triclinium, dining-room and reception room of a Roman house

Triglyph, blocks with vertical grooves on either side of a metope on the frieze of a temple

Trinacria, the ancient name for Sicily derived from its triangular shape

Triptych, painting or tablet in three sections

Tympanum, area above a doorway or the space enclosed by a pediment

Villa, country house with its garden

Xystus, an exercise court; in a Roman villa the open court preceding the triclinium

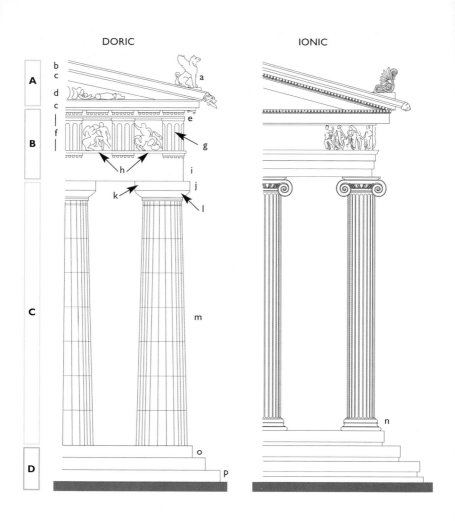

DORIC

IONIC

A Pediment	**B** Entablature	**C** Column	**D** Crepidoma
a Acroterion	e Mutules & Guttae	j Capital	o Stylobate
b Cyma	f Frieze	k Abacus	p Stereobate
c Cornice	g Triglyph	l Echinus	
d Tympanum	h Metopes	m Shaft with flutes	
	i Architrave	n Base	

ELEMENTS OF GREEK TEMPLE PLANS

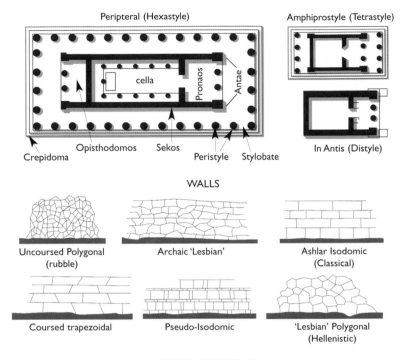

Peripteral (Hexastyle)

cella

Pronaos

Antae

Opisthodomos

Crepidoma

Sekos

Peristyle

Stylobate

Amphiprostyle (Tetrastyle)

In Antis (Distyle)

WALLS

Uncoursed Polygonal (rubble)

Archaic 'Lesbian'

Ashlar Isodomic (Classical)

Coursed trapezoidal

Pseudo-Isodomic

'Lesbian' Polygonal (Hellenistic)

GREEK THEATRE PLAN

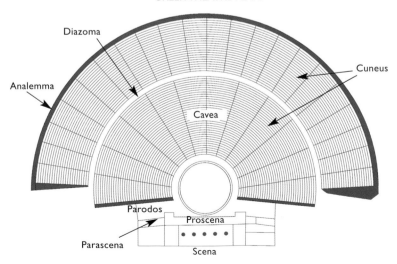

Diazoma

Analemma

Cuneus

Cavea

Parodos

Proscena

Parascena

Scena

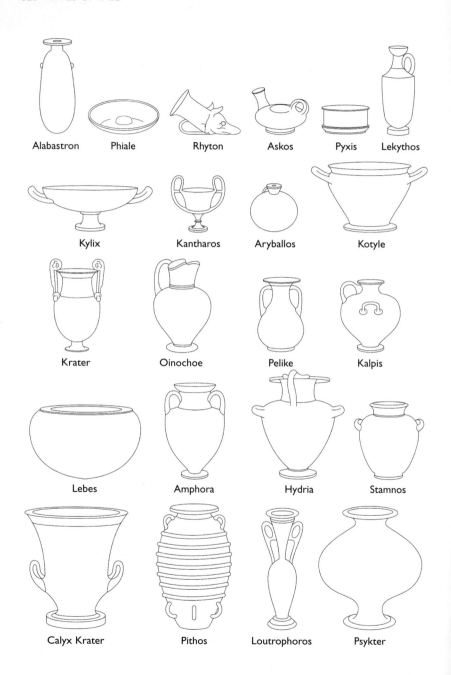

Alabastron   Phiale   Rhyton   Askos   Pyxis   Lekythos

Kylix   Kantharos   Aryballos   Kotyle

Krater   Oinochoe   Pelike   Kalpis

Lebes   Amphora   Hydria   Stamnos

Calyx Krater   Pithos   Loutrophoros   Psykter

INDEX

Explanatory or more detailed references (where there are many) are given in bold. Numbers in italics are picture references. Dates are given for all artists, architects and sculptors.

cont/d from p. 4

Editor-in-Chief: Annabel Barber
Editor: Charles Godfrey-Faussett
Assistant editor: Judy Tither
Contributing editors: Charles Freeman and Nigel McGilchrist

Early History: Charles Freeman. Charles Freeman is a freelance academic historian with a long-standing interest in Italy and the Mediterranean. His *Egypt, Greece and Rome, Civilizations of the Ancient Mediterranean* (second edition Oxford University Press, 2004) is widely used as an introductory text book to the ancient world. His most recent book, *The Horses of St Mark's* (Little Brown, 2004), is a study of the famous horses through their history from Constantinople and Venice. He leads study tours of Italy for the Historical Association and has recently been elected a fellow of the Royal Society of Arts.

Contributor (History of Sicilian Cuisine): Nigel McGilchrist
Contributor (to the wine sections): Joseph Kling

Design: Anikó Kuzmich
Regional maps by Dimap Bt
City maps, diagrams and floor plans © Blue Guides Limited
Architectural elevations: Michael Mansell RIBA & Gabriella Juhász
Floor plans: Imre Bába
The author would like to thank: all the tourist offices of Sicily; the Allegro family; Grazia Barbagallo; the Ente Teatro Massimo Bellini; Salvo Buffa; Fabio Bonnacorsi; Rosario Cassaro; Laura Cassataro; the town of Castelvetrano; Claudio Castiglione; Santi Correnti; Salvatore Cucuzza Silvestri; Franco d'Angelo; Michele Gallo; Alta Macadam; Giacomo Mazza; the Fratelli Napoli Puppet Theatre Company; Monsignor Giuseppe Pecoraro; Margherita Perricone; Emilia Poli Marchese; Franco Purpura; Carmelo Paci; Bruno Ragonese; Diana Mazza Rampf; Costanza Schacht; Aldo Scimé; Alfio Spartà of Fotoluce; Pamela Toti; the Touring Club Italiano; the Whitaker Foundation.

Photo Editor: Hadley Kincade
Photographs by Giacomo Mazza: pp. 29, 42, 57, 77, 80, 94, 98, 101, 102, 133, 138, 142, 144, 150, 168, 203, 210, 216, 223, 242, 253, 272, 273, 277, 301, 307, 310, 315, 316, 356, 366, 404, 409, 420, 426, 444, 459, 463, 473, 482;
Charles Godfrey-Faussett: pp. 25, 32, 161, 263, 401; Gábor Bodó: p. 200.
Other images are reproduced by kind permission of: Giuseppe Pecoraro (p. 55); Galleria Nazionale della Sicilia, Palermo © 1990 Photo Scala, Florence–courtesy of Ministero Beni e Att. Culturali (pp. 46, 48); © 1990, Photo Scala, Florence (p. 34)–courtesy of Miniestero Beni e. Att Culturali (Museo Archeologico Agrigento p. 207; Museo Archeologico Siracusa pp. 351, 352; Museo Regionale Messina p. 453); Maria Costanza Lentini (p. 249); Sebastiano Tusa (p. 173); Archivio Seat/Archivi Alinari (p. 288); Bridgeman Art Library (p. 451).
The publishers would also like to thank Richard Robinson for his assistance.

Statement of editorial independence: Blue Guides, their authors and editors, are prohibited from accepting any payment from any restaurant, hotel, gallery or other establishment for its inclusion in this guide, or for a more favourable mention than would otherwise have been made.

Every effort has been made to contact the copyright owners of material reproduced in this guide. We would be pleased to hear from any copyright owners we have been unable to reach.

Printed in China by Asianlink Enterprises Ltd

ISBN 1–905131–12–7